Lecture Notes of the Institute for Computer Sciences, Social Informatics and Telecommunications Engineering   66

Ioannis Tomkos   Christos J. Bouras
Georgios Ellinas   Panagiotis Demestichas
Prasun Sinha (Eds.)

Broadband Communications, Networks, and Systems

7th International ICST Conference
BROADNETS 2010
Athens, Greece, October 25–27, 2010
Revised Selected Papers

 Springer

Volume Editors

Ioannis Tomkos
Athens Information Technology
Peania 19002, Athens, Greece
E-mail: itom@ait.gr

Christos J. Bouras
University of Patras
Department of Computer Engineering and Informatics
26504 Rio, Patras, Greece
E-mail: bouras@ceid.upatras.gr

Georgios Ellinas
University of Cyprus
Department of Electrical and Computer Engineering
1678 Nicosia, Cyprus, Greece
E-mail: gellinas@ucy.ac.cy

Panagiotis Demestichas
University of Piraeus, 185 34 Piraeus, Athens, Greece
E-mail: pdemest@unipi.gr

Prasun Sinha
Ohio State University
Department of Computer Science and Engineering
Columbus, OH 43210-1277, USA
E-mail: prasun@cse.ohio-state.edu

ISSN 1867-8211   e-ISSN 1867-822X
ISBN 978-3-642-30375-3   e-ISBN 978-3-642-30376-0
DOI 10.1007/978-3-642-30376-0
Springer Heidelberg Dordrecht London New York

Library of Congress Control Number: 2012937588

CR Subject Classification (1998): C.2, H.4, H.3, D.2, J.1, K.4.4, K.6.5, D.4.6

Typesetting: Camera-ready by author, data conversion by Scientific Publishing Services, Chennai, India

Printed on acid-free paper

Springer is part of Springer Science+Business Media (www.springer.com)

Preface

This volume contains the proceedings of the 7th International ICST Conference on Broadband Communications, Networks, and Systems (Broadnets 2010), which was held in Athens, Greece, during October 18–20, 2010. The Broadnets conference is an international event focusing on broadband communications, networks, and systems and covers the entire gamut of next-generation networks, communications systems, applications, and services. This series of conferences has been held annually since 2004 in various US and European countries and covers the fields of optical, wireless, and Internet systems and networks and related areas.

In 2010, the Broadnets conference was organized by the Athens Information Technology and the University of Patras, Greece. The conference was held in Athens, Greece, where the participants had the opportunity to enjoy the technical program, as well as the rich cultural heritage of Greece. The conference venue location close to the historical center of Athens was perfect for allowing conference participants to discover the city and its history.

The Broadnets conference was divided into three tracks (Optical, Wireless, and Internet) and 29 papers were presented in these tracks (22 accepted papers and 7 invited papers authored by worldwide renowned scholars). The selection of the accepted papers was made after a thorough peer-review process, where each submission was evaluated by at least three reviewers. The submitted papers were authored by peer scholars coming from 20 different countries. In addition to the regular papers, the technical program featured a keynote lecture by Socrates Katsikas, the General Secretary of Telecommunications at the Greek Ministry of Infrastructures, Transportation, and Networks, and five plenary talks by distinguished members of the Greek academic community and telecommunications industry. Moreover, the first day of the conference was devoted to four workshops totalling 22 talks and spanning various up-to-date research areas. The workshop themes were as follows: "Cross-Layer Algorithms and Protocols for Optical Networks," "Multimode Wireless Access Networks," "Opportunities and Challenges in the Context of Next-Generation Optical Access Networks," and "Architecture, Protocols and Algorithms for a Sustainable Internet."

It is our pleasure to express our gratitude to everybody that contributed to the success of Broadnets 2010. In particular, we thank the members of the Broadnets Steering Committee for entrusting us with the organization of the conference. We would also like to express our sincere gratitude to the members of the Program Committee, all the reviewers, as well as the members of the

Organizing Committee, and the National Organizing Committee for their assistance in the organization of the conference. We would also like to thank the publisher, Springer, for cooperation in publishing the proceedings in the *Lecture Notes of the Institute for Computer Sciences, Social Informatics and Telecommunications Engineering (LNICST)* series. Finally, we thank all the authors who contributed to this volume for sharing their new ideas and results with the rest of the community.

Ioannis Tomkos
Christos Bouras
Georgios Ellinas
Panayiotis Demestichas
Prasun Sinha

Organization

General Co-chairs

Ioannis Tomkos — Athens Information Technology, Greece
Christos J. Bouras — University of Patras and RACTI, Greece

Technical Program Co-chairs

Georgios Ellinas — University of Cyprus, Cyprus
Panagiotis Demestichas — University of Piraeus, Athens, Greece
Prasun Sinha — Ohio State University, USA

Workshop/Tutorials Chair

Chava Vijaya Saradhi — CreateNet, Italy

Publicity Chair

Spyros Vassilaras — Athens Information Technology, Greece

Submission Chair

Daeyoung Choi — Ohio State University, USA

Local Organizing Committee Chair

Konstantinos Kanonakis — Athens Information Technology, Greece

Steering Committee

Imrich Chlamtac — CreateNet, Italy
Krishna Sivalingam — University of Maryland at Baltimore County, USA
Thomas Hou — Virginia Tech, USA
Ioannis Tomkos — Athens Information Technology, Greece

Technical Program Committee

Wireless Track

Novella Bartolini
Prithwish Basu
Mun-Choon Chan
Girish Chandranmenon
Mainak Chatterjee
Xiuzhen (Susan) Cheng
Yu Cheng
Kai-Wei Fan
Xiaohui Helen Gu

Ting He
Hung-Yun Hsieh
Sunggeun Jin
Bong-Jun Ko
Sung-Ju Lee
Thyagarajan Nandagopal
Xin Wang
Hongyi Wu
Fan Ye

Lei Ying
Joon Yoo
Hongwei Zhang
Wensheng Zhang
Dong Zheng
Zizhan Zheng
Hwangnam Kim

Optical Track

Fragkiskos Papadopoulos
Martin Maier
Galen Sasaki
Xavi Masip
Eric Bouillet
Zhensheng Jia
Antonis Hadjiantonis
Steve Lumetta

Ahmed Kamal
Mohan Gurusamy
Antonis M. Hadjiantonis
Suresh Subramaniam
Davide Careglio
Debasish Datta
Arunita Jaekel
Ken-ichi Kitayama

Vinod Vokkarane
Abdallah Shami
Marco Tacca
Mario Pickavet
Wojciech Kabacinski
Jason Jue
Kyriakos Vlachos
Salvatore Spadaro

Internet Track

Ciavaglia Laurent
Delahaye Philippe
Dousson Christophe
Feng Zhiyong
Gruber Markus
Holland Oliver
Manzalini Antonio

Matinmikko Marja
Merat Vincent
Moessner Klaus
Mueck Markus-Dominik
Peloso Pierre
Romero Jordi Perez
Sallent Oriol

Samir Ghamri-Doudane
Smirnov Mikhail
Stavroulaki Vera
Tiemann Jens
Tsagkaris Konstantinos
Vigoureux Martin

Table of Contents

Optical Track

MoWAN 2010 Workshop

Workshop on Cross-Layer Algorithms and Protocols for Optical Networks

Green Networking Workshop

Developing Information Networking Further: From PSIRP to PURSUIT

Nikos Fotiou[1], Pekka Nikander[2], Dirk Trossen[3], and George C. Polyzos[1]

[1] Athens University of Economics and Business, Athens, Greece
{fotiou,polyzos}@aueb.gr
[2] NomadicLab, Ericsson Research, Finland
pekka.nikander@ericsson.com
[3] Computer Laboratory, University of Cambridge
dirk.trossen@cl.cam.ac.uk

Abstract. PSIRP (Publish-Subscribe Internet Routing Paradigm) is an EU FP7 funded project that has developed a clean-slate architecture for the future Internet, based on the publish-subscribe primitives (rather than the send-receive ones), all the way down to the core networking functions. The PSIRP vision is a pure information-centric Internet architecture, possibly providing remedies to many of the current Internet problems. In PSIRP, all is information and everything is about information. Content-based identities, recursive application of ideas, cryptographic techniques, and the Trust-to-Trust principle are all extensively used to achieve the design goals. Furthermore, incentive compatibility and socio-economic considerations are guiding the design from the outset, to ground the project in reality and to provide credible and viable potential deployment paths. The project has developed, implemented, and preliminarily evaluated solutions for rendezvous, topology formation and routing, and information forwarding, with ongoing work currently focusing in experimenting.

A new (also EU FP7 funded) follow-on project, PURSUIT (Publish-Subscribe Internet Technologies), will refine and further explore and expand PSIRP's vision. We believe that this will eventually lead to a more complete architecture and protocol suite, thereby providing for more extensive performance evaluation and investigations on scalability. This paper provides an overview of the PSIRP concepts and the developed architecture, along with some key results, and outlines the research directions of the PURSUIT project, focusing on the project goals and its expected outcomes.

Keywords: PSIRP, PURSUIT.

1 Introduction

The current Internet architecture cannot effectively and efficiently handle various challenges, including security, mobility, scalability, quality of service, and economics, due to the focus and shortcomings in its original design [7]. The Internet, even though based on packet switching, a critical departure from circuit

I. Tomkos et al. (Eds.): BROADNETS 2010, LNICST 66, pp. 1–13, 2012.

switching used in the telephone network, still resembles significantly to the telephone network in many design choices — and since its inception this design has been hardly changed. A key goal of the Internet was to efficiently interconnect mainframes and minicomputers, and to provide efficient remote access to them. This end-to-end approach and especially its specific practical implementation, however, have been identified as a root cause of many limitations of the current Internet architecture. Various add-ons, such as NATs, Mobile IP, CDNs, p2p overlays, etc., all violate, in various ways, several aspects of the original Internet architecture in order to provide answers to features that were not part of the original design (or the original requirements). Moreover, the original Internet architecture and protocols were developed assuming a benign and cooperative environment, which is far from today's reality, where competition is widespread and lack of trust and security threats, such as malware, denial of service attacks, and phising, have become more and more prevalent.

More recently, it has been observed that information has become at the heart of almost all communication and, in particular, of Internet use [10]. This information-centric usage of the Internet raises various architectural challenges, many of which are not effectively handled by the current Internet architecture [29]. The challenges include medium-independent information access, tussle mediation through information governance, privacy and accountability through controlled information dissemination, and information scarcity.

It seems that it is time for a shift from the current Internet, which interconnects machines, towards a new Internet that interconnects information. PSIRP (Publish-Subscribe Internet Routing Paradigm), an EU FP7 funded research effort, has created, implemented, and initially evaluated a clean-slate, information oriented future Internet architecture, aiming at overcoming most limitations of the current Internet. Its goal is to bring out the role of information as the main building block of the (future) Internet. This new architecture is based on a paradigm completely different from the current one. PSIRP is based on pure, through-the-stack application of the Publish-Subscribe paradigm.

The Publish-Subscribe paradigm is an alternative to the commonly used Send-Receive paradigm. The communication architectures that are build based on this paradigm are composed of three basic elements: publishers, subscribers, and a network of brokers [6]. Publishers are information owners or disseminers that advertise information availability by issuing publication messages. Subscribers are information consumers, expressing their interest for specific information items by issuing subscriptions. Between the publishers and subscribers there exist a network of brokers that is responsible for routing publication and subscription messages, for matching publications with subscriptions, as well as for initiating the information forwarding process from publishers towards subscribers. The broker at which the publication-subscription matching takes place (for a particular publication) is known as the rendezvous point (RP) (of that publication). The existence of such rendezvous points allows for publisher-subscriber decoupling both in terms of location and time, location-identity split, multihoming and mobility, and anonymity.

The PSIRP project envisions a publish-subscribe-based, information-centric Future Internet architecture, in which the current Internet limitations will be removed through the design of a set of new core network mechanisms, rather than by add-on fixes. It envisions a robust, reliable, and extensible Internet. PSIRP has produced a specific internetworking architecture, with specific proposals in many key areas, such as rendezvous, topology formation and routing, and information forwarding. It includes integrated support for anycast and multicast, caching, multihoming and mobility, and security and privacy. A PSIRP prototype has been implemented and is available under open source license terms [24]. Moreover, a PSIRP testbed across Europe is already being established for testing native PSIRP applications.

The PURSUIT project can be considered as a continuation of the PSIRP work. Starting in fall 2010, PURSUIT is expected to revisit the PSIRP architecture, to develop missing or only partially developed components, and to produce and evaluate alternative designs, as well as to expand dissemination and exploitation. A significant challenge is to scale the practical experimental network from the current few nodes to hundreds or more. In this paper, we provide an overview of the PSIRP architecture and present its core elements and functions. The rationale and solutions that PSIRP has developed, in order to address the requirements of a Future Internet architecture, are being presented, along with our vision for their planned culmination in PURSUIT.

The remainder of this paper is organized as follows. Section II introduces PSIRP and its architecture, as well as its key contributions. In section III, the main goals of the PURSUIT project are highlighted, and, in Section IV, related work in other projects, worldwide, is presented. Finally, in Section V, our conclusions as well as thoughts for additional work are presented.

2   PSIRP

The PSIRP project investigates a clean-slate internetworking architecture focusing on the information itself, rather than on the location of the information. The system architecture is built around information from the viewpoints of 'semantics' (i.e. meaning) and 'scope' (i.e. breadth of coverage). Multicast, caching in the network, mobility of end-points and information are considered mainstream and not exceptional cases that should be handled with add-on mechanisms. Moreover, security is diffused throughout all the levels of the architecture.

The PSIRP architecture abides to the following principles [27]:

- PSIRP specific principles. Here, two concepts are fundamental: the recursive nature of *information semantics*, and the notion of *information scope* as a concept of reachability.
    - Information is organised in a *multi-hierarchical* manner.
    - *Scopes* act as a means of information organisation; there are mechanisms that allow for scoping information on different levels of semantics (e.g. via means of rendezvous, discovery, search, and others). This *limits the*

reachability of information to the parties having access to the particular mechanism (e.g. rendezvous) that implements the scoping.
- The architecture is *neutral* with regard to the semantics and structure of data.
- The architecture is *receiver-driven*; no entity shall be delivered data unless it has agreed to receive it beforehand through appropriate signalling methods (limitations to this principle can apply, for instance, at the physical level).

– General principles. These principles are shared with other architectural approaches, but are still fundamental to the PSIRP architecture.
- Trust-to-trust principle: Functions are implemented at points of the network that can be considered trustworthy from the user's (of the function) perspective.
- Market creation: The architecture supports potentially multi-dimensional metrics of compensation that will enable effective market creation.
- Multi-dimensionality: The effectiveness of any architectural solution is evaluated under a (multi-dimensional) metric along the dimensions of financial, social, environmental, and economical benefits.
- Evolvability: Any solution should enable proper evolution beyond itself.
- Minimality: No entities are introduced beyond the necessity to implement the design principles of the architecture.

2.1   Components and Functions

Information is the core component of the PSIRP architecture; in PSIRP everything is information [28], ranging from small ('meaningless') chunks of data to complex information items such as documents, images and videos. Information items are organized within *scopes*. Scopes may denote physical structures, e.g., a corporate network, or logical structures, e.g., my friends in *facebook*. This allows for information location and control over information dissemination. Every information item is uniquely identified by a pair of identifiers; a rendezvous identifier (RId) and a scope identifier (SId). The RId is information item specific and it has to be unique within a scope, whereas the SId denotes the scope in which an information item belongs. Scopes can be included within each other, creating a flexible structure. Both RIds and SIds are flat and endpoint independent. Flat and endpoint independent labels seem to be a natural choice for information oriented architectures as they clearly separate location from identity, allowing for properly incorporating mobility, multicasting, and multihoming into the architecture, as well as a more comprehensive notion of identity [2].

In order for a publisher to issue a publication in PISRP, it has to know the SId of a scope within which it wants the publication to be published, as well as to create a RId for the publication. The publication's RId is then forwarded to the rendezvous node of the SId rendezvous network, which manages the publication's RId. Figure 1 illustrates a publication example. A publisher creates a publication that she wants to publish in her blog scope. A publication message is created, carrying the publication's RId as well as the blog's SId. This publication message

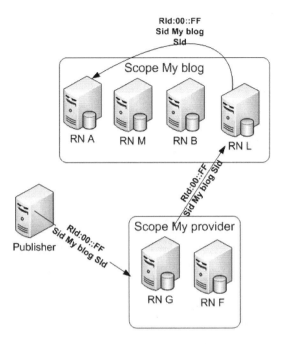

Fig. 1. Publication in a PSIRP network

is forwarded to the rendezvous node RN L, which is responsible for managing the blog's scope. In this case, the blog's scope consists of four rendezvous nodes, one of which (RN A) is the rendezvous point for this specific RId; therefore the publication message ends up at this node.

Subscriptions in PSIRP follow a similar process. A subscriber learns the RId and the SId of a desired piece of information and issues a subscription message towards the appropriate rendezvous point. When his subscription message reaches the rendezvous point, a forwarding path is created from the publisher towards the subscriber and the desired piece of information is sent through this path. The forwarding path creation process, as well as the forwarding procedure, follow an MPLS-like, label-based approach [28]. Each active publication is assigned a forwarding identifier (FId) that denotes the forwarding path that this item has to follow.

PSIRP's operation is based on three basic functions that are recursively executed in all layers of the architecture. These functions are the *rendezvous*, the *topology and routing*, and the *forwarding* functions [25]. The rendezvous function is responsible for matching subscribers' interests with publications. The topology function monitors the network topology and detects changes using various techniques, depending on the layer of the architecture within which it is implemented. Within the same module, the routing function is responsible for creating information delivery paths. Finally, the forwarding function implements information forwarding throughout the delivery paths.

2.2   Key Outcomes

PSIRP has studied the potential of having an Internet scale architecture where every information item is identified by flat, endpoint-independent identifiers. The notion of the organization of information items within scopes, introduced in this project, is expected to offer the desired scalability. Moreover, PSIRP has introduced the usage of algorithmically related information identifiers, allowing for information item grouping [28].

PSIRP has achieved line-speed label-based forwarding with the usage of an in-packet Bloom-filter (iBF) based mechanism [11]. An iBF is a data structure that encodes the data delivery path in a compact manner. Although constant in size, iBFs allow for Internet scale data delivery paths, enabling at the same time loop prevention, fast path recovery, and small-scale multicast. iBFs may be constructed in an information-flow-specific manner, with every delivery path being encoded in a flow-identifier dependent way. This makes it almost impossible for an attacker to create crafted iBFs that would lead to DoS attacks or to information leakage. As a backwards compatible option, iBFs formation is also possible through the usage of an MPLS-like approach, named MPSS [30]. MPSS is an approach designed to compute a delivery path or tree on the graph of the network, to compute an iBF for it, and to optionally allocate resources. Moreover, the NetFPGA implementation of the basic iBFs demonstrated the applicability of this technique over high-speed (1Gbps) links [17].

PSIRP has also studied the security requirements for a publish-subscribe based Internet architecture [21], as well as the possibilities for applying existing work on cryptographic protocol analysis in a pure publish-subscribe architecture [23]. Moreover, new security mechanisms have been developed. As an example, PLA [19] is a novel mechanism for protecting the networking architecture, based on the assumption that per-packet public key cryptographic operations are possible at wire speed in high speed networks, due to new cryptographic algorithms and advances in semiconductor technology. PLA can also be used to provide accountability, billing and Internet-wide roaming while maintaining privacy and reducing the burden on the access networks providers [20]. At the higher layers of the architecture, information-oriented solutions have also been investigated. For example, Information ranking [9] is a mechanism developed for ranking information items based on positive votes. This mechanism achieves better results, compared to the commonly used user's ranking-based mechanism, when it comes to polluted information pieces isolation, as well as to spam prevention in publish-subscribe architectures [8].

In order to evaluate PSIRP's efficacy as well as the applicability of PSIRP principles, an overlay architecture on top of access network routers was designed, supporting multicast, caching, and mobility. The goal of this architecture is to allow *proxy* participation of end-hosts into an inherently information-centric overlay architecture. In this way, operators are expected to gain control of the traffic in their network and benefit from the multicast data delivery mode, while improving the resulting data delivery structures by eliminating data forwarding from end-hosts. The information-centric character of the proposed architecture was further enhanced by a distributed caching scheme designed to operate in conjunction with the multicast delivery mechanism so that content is provisioned either via multicast or via unicast from a nearby cache location [16]. This overlay variant was evaluated through the simulation of large scale deployments and the results verified expectations. As far as the multicast tree creation is concerned, this overlay variant shows a significant improvement in the resulting tree properties, such as path stretch and link stress, as well as a reduction in the overlay network establishment and maintenance overhead, at the cost of increased forwarding overhead for the access routers [12]. Moreover, the caching mechanism achieves a high cache hit ratio, reaching values up to 98,5% when it comes to large cache sizes. Finally, it was found that when it comes to mobile nodes, our architecture achieves 50% less packet loss than Mobile IPv6 as well as almost zero resume time [14,15].

Taking a step further, since a synchronized Internet-wide deployment of any network architecture seems infeasible, particular attention was paid to the evaluation of this overlay architecture as it gradually gets deployed across the Internet. In this direction, the specifics of an *incremental deployment* process, in which the ISPs progressively add the overlay publish-subscribe functionality on top of their existing infrastructure, were investigated. This investigation included both the dimensions of *inter-ISP* and *intra-ISP* incremental deployment. The simulation results demonstrated that network operators have strong incentives to adopt the proposed architecture, such as significant gains in terms of transmission load in their network and end user satisfaction. Even after initial deployment, network operators supporting the proposed architecture have a consistent advantage over the remaining ones. The simulation results also show that sparse intra-domain deployments are sufficient, indicating that an operator can reap the benefits of the proposed architecture by deploying it at only 25% of its routers, regardless of what other operators do [13].

In order to perform experiments with native PSIRP applications, a multi-site PSIRP testbed is being created. Figure 2 shows the PSIRP testbed setup. The testbed spans across Europe – Athens, Sofia, Aachen, Essex, Cambridge, and Helsinki – and there are plans for expanding it to U.S., with M.I.T. participation. It includes VPN links, as well as two fibre links. Every node in the PSIRP testbed runs a PSIRP network prototype and applications, such as file transfer, real-time voice and video streaming, which will be tested and evaluated.

3   PURSUIT

PURSUIT aims at revisiting the PSIRP architecture, filling in missing components and improving the existing ones, by taking advantage of all the lessons learned and of all the experience that has been accumulated during PSIRP's span. All layers of the architecture, including the link and the physical layers, of both wireless and wireline technologies, will be considered with an *information-only* and *address-less* approach.

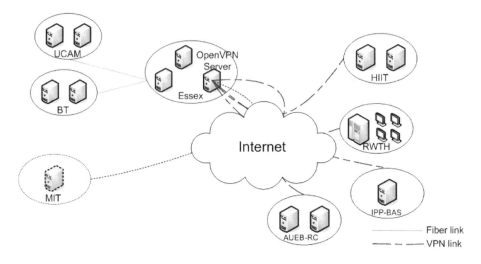

Fig. 2. PSIRP Testbed

The PURSUIT project will abide to the Design for Tussle approach [4], enabling flexibility when it comes to existing as well as to new tussles. The information-centric nature of this new architecture is expected to allow better resource utilization in both wireless and wireline environments. More specifically, in wireless environments, better spectrum allocation and effective mobility handling are anticipated, whereas in wireline environments, PURSUIT is expected to harvest the full potential of the future transparent optical networks. In particular, in-network caching will be further investigated and enhanced, leading to better and more effective information distribution, including completely new transport protocols. Throughout the project security will play crucial role, with trust, privacy, and information accountability being in the research spotlight.

3.1   Main Goals

The flat-label-based information identification introduced in PSIRP will be maintained in the PURSUIT architecture. Every information item in PURSUIT will be associated with – at least – one scope, and the information organization will follow the same principles as in the PSIRP architecture. One of the primary goals of PURSUIT is the development of solutions and mechanisms that will enable providers to take advantage of these new information structures and provide innovative services that will offer them competitive advantages. Moreover, these solutions and mechanisms should be able to resolve the tussles that will occur in this information oriented environment.

In PSIRP, the notion of the algorithmic identifiers was introduced. They provide a compact and convenient way to identify pieces of information collectively, but also to identify individual sub-pieces of information. In PURSUIT, it is expected that this notion will be further studied and ultimately it will be provided as a core service of the architecture. The possibility of correlating information items in an algorithmic manner opens the floor for new fragmentation techniques that will lead to the deployment of effective caching schemes. Information items will be intelligently distributed and cached. PURSUIT aims at providing caching as an in-network mechanism, in addition to the caching services that will be offered by various providers, achieving this way significant resource utilization improvement.

Caching is only one way to achieve the goal of better resource utilization, with multicast being another. In PURSUIT, we will also focus on the lower layers and on mechanisms that will enable better resource allocation and utilization at the link and physical layers, by taking advantage of the information structures that at the higher layers. We will try to show how wireless and wireline network access methods can benefit from a pure information oriented architecture.

The declared goal of PSIRP to consider mobility as a normal condition and to handle it with in-network mechanisms rather than with add-ons, remains in PURSUIT. Multicast and caching are expected to facilitate mobility support and enhance performance. Moreover, the recursive nature of the rendezvous, topology, routing, and forwarding functions is expected to allow for handling mobility as close to the mobile node as possible, meanwhile hiding it from the core network.

In PSIRP, PLA and information-centric security mechanisms were introduced. PURSUIT's goal is to enhance the notion of trust, to provide accountability mechanisms even at the physical layer, while maintaining privacy. In addition, to develop a framework that will enable the flexible definition of policies that will dictate topology formation, forwarding decisions and information dissemination, at all levels of the architecture.

In order for a publish-subscribe solution to be deployed, proper evaluation, understanding of the socio-economics forces as well as a realistic migration strategy are needed. PURSUIT anticipates achieving all of them. The PSIRP testbed, the large scale simulation tools whose development started during PSIRP, as well as the socio-economic work and the overlay variant of PSIRP are expected to be the driving forces that will lead to the achievement of this goal. Moreover, the PURSUIT team will seek collaborations with other projects developing similar architectures and technologies in order to join forces towards a realistic evaluation framework.

3.2   Expected Outcomes

One of the main outcomes of the PURSUIT project is expected to be a suite of information-centric protocols, solutions, and mechanisms that will handle all aspects of inter-networking, including mobility, caching, transport, flow and error control. PURSUIT's anticipation is that all these methods will have been properly tested and evaluated under realistic conditions, and, therefore, they will be relatively ready for deployment in the future Internet.

PURSUIT is expected to have a significant impact on the techniques used in order to build wireless and wireline networks. Applying an information-only approach to the physical as well as to the link layer will lead to a new form of network access. This new form of network access will cooperate with the higher layers of the architecture, which will also be organized around information (but for which this seems less of a dramatic departure from the status quo).

New models and tools regarding security and privacy will be created during the PURSUIT project. This new security architecture is going to consider new forms of threats and risks and their impact has to be modelled and evaluated. Furthermore, the novel security mechanisms that are expected to be created throughout the duration of this project will have to be tested and evaluated using new analytical techniques as well as new simulation frameworks.

A project such as PURSUIT is expected to have a significant socio-economic impact. An important outcome of this project will be estimation and evaluation of this impact. This estimation is planned to be achieved by identifying the tussles that will occur in this new form of inter-networking. PURSUIT will come with new socio-economic models as well as with solutions that aim towards enabling new market opportunities and a healthy socio-economic playground.

Finally, the PURSUIT project is expected to release various prototypes which, with the appropriate APIs, will allow researchers to develop new solutions that will take advantage of the PURSUIT architecture. The PURSUIT testbed, which will be deployed across all partners' sites, is hoped to play a significant role in achieving this objective.

4 Related Work

Significant, fundamental research has been undertaken in the last few years, investigating core issues of inter-networking and many of the known shortcomings of the current Internet technologies and practices.

The Internet Indirection Infrastructure (i3) [26] and the Host Identity Protocol (HIP) [22] introduced indirection as a solution to the problems that point-to-point communication poses to mobility, multicast, and multihoming. i3 implements an IP overlay network that replaces the point-to-point communication model with a rendezvous-based paradigm, where senders send packets to a specific rendezvous-point, while receivers issue triggers on specific packet identifiers. HIP introduces a new layer in the internetwork stack between the IP layer and the transport layer. This new layer decouples host identity from location identity. PSIRP uses similar concepts through the rendezvous and topology formation processes. The problem of routing based on flat information identifiers rather than on hierarchical location-based identifiers has also been studied in the Data-Oriented Network Architecture (DONA) [18] and in the Routing on Flat Labels (ROFL) [2] projects. PSIRP borrows the information identification concept of DONA, but chooses a separate inter-domain architecture with slow and fast paths. Moreover, PSIRP extends ROLF towards flat identifiers within hierarchical *scopes*, which are expected to offer faster information scoping, better scalability, and piecewise dissemination.

Various research projects are currently aiming at redesigning the Internet with an information-centric or content-centric perspective. CCNx [3] is a research effort that proposes routing based on hierarchical naming. In CCNx consumers ask for content by broadcasting 'Interest' packets that contain the name of the content requested. Any 'Data' packet whose content name is a suffix of the name in the 'Interest' packet is conspired that it satisfies this interest. PSIRP, on the other hand, introduces flat label identifiers organized into scopes, allowing for a variety of naming approaches to be layered on top of the internetworking architecture. Moreover, although overlaying PSIRP over the current Internet is possible, it is the declared goal of the PSIRP project to investigate a native solution that could replace the current inter-networking technology. This leads to a focus on inter-domain functions, which is not found in CCNx.

4WARD [1], another EU FP7 funded on-going research project, also advocates an information-centric Internet which will enable network diversity, allowing various types of networks to co-exist and cooperate in a smooth and cost-efficient manner. It envisions an Internet where networks will be self-manageable and network paths will be an active networking component that will be able to affect transport services. 4WARD borrows concepts from DONA in terms of labelling, and intends to shed light on business aspects, similarly to the socio-economic work in PSIRP. Finally, COMET [5] is a more recent (EU FP7 funded) research effort (launched in January 2010), aiming at creating a unified approach to content location, access, and distribution, irrespectively of the intermediary used. COMET, similarly to PURSUIT, plans on using some PSIRP, or similar, concepts. Nevertheless, COMET is more focused at the higher layers of the architecture.

5   Conclusion

The Publish-Subscribe Internet Routing Paradigm (PSIRP) project, concluding in the Fall of 2010, has developed a clean-slate information-centric architecture for the future Internet, based on publish-subscribe (rather than send-receive) primitives, all the way down to the core networking functions. Cryptographic techniques, layerless recursive design, and the Trust-to-Trust principle are extensively used to achieve the design goals. Incentive compatibility and socio-economic considerations are guiding the design, providing potential for a credible and viable deployment path. Solutions for rendezvous, topology formation and routing, information forwarding, including support for multicast, caching, mobility, and security, have been developed, preliminarily evaluated, implemented in prototypes, and are currently being experimented with within the PSIRP project. A new, follow-on project, PURSUIT (Publish-Subscribe Internet Technologies), will further refine and expand PSIRP's technologies, eventually leading to a more complete architecture and protocol suite and more extensive performance evaluation and investigation of scalability. In this paper, we have provided an overview of PSIRP concepts, the developed architecture, and briefly discussed key results. We have also outlined the research directions of PURSUIT, focusing on its goals and expected outcomes.

Acknowledgment. The work reported in this paper was supported in part by the ICT PSIRP project under contract ICT-2007-216173 and by the ICT PURSUIT project under contract ICT-2010-257217.

References

1. 4WARD. Web site (2010), http://www.4ward-project.eu
2. Caesar, M., Condie, T., Kannan, J., Lakshminarayanan, K., Stoica, I.: ROFL: routing on flat labels. ACM SIGCOMM Computer Communication Review 36(4), 374 (2006)
3. CCNx. Web site (2010), http://www.ccnx.org
4. Clark, D., Wroclawski, J., Sollins, K., Braden, R.: Tussle in cyberspace: defining tomorrow's internet. IEEE/ACM Transactions on Networking 13(3), 462–475 (2005)
5. COMET. Web site (2010), http://www.comet-project.org
6. Eugster, P.T., Felber, P.A., Guerraoui, R., Kermarrec, A.M.: The many faces of publish/subscribe. ACM Comput. Surv. 35(2), 114–131 (2003)
7. Feldmann, A.: Internet clean-slate design: what and why? SIGCOMM Computer Communication Review 37(3), 59–64 (2007)
8. Fotiou, N., Marias, G., Polyzos, G.C.: Fighting Spam in Publish/Subscribe Networks Using Information Ranking (2010)
9. Fotiou, N., Marias, G., Polyzos, G.C.: Information Ranking in Content-Centric Networks (2010)
10. Jacobson, V., Smetters, D.K., Thornton, J.D., Plass, M.F., Briggs, N.H., Braynard, R.L.: Networking named content. In: CoNEXT 2009: Proc. of the 5th International Conference on Emerging Networking Experiments and Technologies, pp. 1–12 (2009)
11. Jokela, P., Zahemszky, A., Esteve Rothenberg, C., Arianfar, S., Nikander, P.: LIPSIN: line speed publish/subscribe inter-networking. In: SIGCOMM 2009: Proc. of the ACM SIGCOMM 2009 Conference on Data Communication, pp. 195–206 (2009)
12. Katsaros, K., Bartsotas, N., Xylomenos, G.: Router assisted overlay multicast (2009)
13. Katsaros, K., Stais, C., Xylomenos, G., Polyzos, G.C.: On the incremental deployment of overlay information centric networks (2010)
14. Katsaros, K., Fotiou, N., Polyzos, G.C., Xylomenos, G.: Overlay multicast assisted mobility for future publish/subscribe networks (2009)
15. Katsaros, K., Fotiou, N., Polyzos, G.C., Xylomenos, G.: Supporting mobile streaming services in future publish/subscribe networks (2009)
16. Katsaros, K., Polyzos, G.C., Xylomenos, G.: A hybrid overlay multicast and caching scheme for information-centric networking (2010)
17. Keinänen, J., Jokela, P., Slavov, K.: Implementing zFilter based forwarding node on a NetFPGA. In: Proc. of NetFPGA Developers Workshop (2009)
18. Koponen, T., Chawla, M., Chun, B.G., Ermolinskiy, A., Kim, K.H., Shenker, S., Stoica, I.: A data-oriented (and beyond) network architecture. ACM SIGCOMM Computer Communication Review 37(4), 192 (2007)
19. Lagutin, D.: Redesigning internet-the packet level authentication architecture. Licentiate's Thesis in Computer Science, Helsinki University of Technology, Espoo, Finland (2008)

20. Lagutin, D., Tarkoma, S.: Cryptographic Signatures on the Network Layer - an Alternative to the ISP Data Retention. In: Proc. of IEEE Symposium on Computers and Communications, ISCC, Riccione, Italy (2010)
21. Lagutin, D., Visala, K., Zahemszky, A., Burbridge, T., Marias, G.: Roles and Security in a Publish/Subscribe Network Architecture (2010)
22. Moskowitz, R., Nikander, P.: Host identity protocol (HIP) architecture. Tech. rep., RFC 4423 (May 2006)
23. Nikander, P., Marias, G.: Towards Understanding Pure Publish/Subscribe Cryptographic Protocols. In: Sixteenth International Workshop on Security Protocols, Cambridge, England (2008)
24. PSIRP. Web site (2010), http://www.psirp.org
25. Särelä, M., Rinta-aho, T., Tarkoma, S.: RTFM: Publish/subscribe internetworking architecture. In: Proc. of the ICT Mobile Summit (2008)
26. Stoica, I., Adkins, D., Ratnasamy, S., Shenker, S., Surana, S., Zhuang, S.: Internet Indirection Infrastructure. In: Druschel, P., Kaashoek, M.F., Rowstron, A. (eds.) IPTPS 2002. LNCS, vol. 2429, pp. 191–202. Springer, Heidelberg (2002)
27. Tarkoma, S. (ed.): PSIRP deliverable 2.2, conceptual architecture of PSIRP including subcomponent descriptions, D2.2 (2008), http://www.psirp.org/
28. Tarkoma, S. (ed.): PSIRP deliverable 2.3, architecture definition, component descriptions, and requirements, D2.3 (2008), http://www.psirp.org/
29. Trossen, D., Sarela, M., Sollins, K.: Arguments for an information-centric internetworking architecture. SIGCOMM Comput. Commun. Rev. 40(2), 26–33 (2010)
30. Zahemszky, A., Jokela, P., Särelä, M., Ruponen, S., Kempf, J., Nikander, P.: MPSS: Multiprotocol Stateless Switching (2010)

Analysis of Block-Aware Peer Adaptations in Substream-Based P2P

Chamil Kulatunga[*], Dmitri Botvich,
Sasitharan Balasubramaniam, and William Donnelly

Telecommunications Software and Systems Group, Waterford Institute of Technology
Cork Road, Waterford, Ireland
{ckulatunga,dbotvich,sasib,wdonnelly}@tssg.org

Abstract. Peer-to-Peer (P2P) video delivery using substreams supports uplink heterogeneities of the peers and hence could optimise sharing capabilities with minimum free-riding peers. Therefore, substream-based applications such as PPLive and CoolStreaming have been well accepted after successful deployments in the public Internet. In this approach, a child peer can find a parent peer for a substream independent of the other parent peers that it receives the remaining substreams. In general, there can be more than one substream between a parent and a child. The block-aware adaptation algorithm in CoolStreaming changes the parent peer for all such substreams when a child peer experiences poor performance even on one of its substreams from the parent. However, lagging of one substream in such a scenario is likely while others are not affected, when the parent receives its substreams through multiple paths. We propose a fine-grained approach (changing substream by substream) in peer adaptations to improve overlay network performance. This approach will in turn, is designed also to minimise the diversity of parents at a child peer by attempting to join with a well-performing another parent, which is expected to curtail complexities in a network-assisted P2P framework.

Keywords: Video streaming, substream-based P2P, child-initiated block-aware peer adaptation.

1 Introduction

In recent years, Peer-to-Peer (P2P) multimedia streaming has gained increased popularity, due largely to its scalable solution for video streaming to a very large number of concurrent users. P2P file sharing was technically unbeaten mainly due to its flexibilities of distributing different amounts of data blocks (chunks) (i.e. due to its non-realtime application requirements) [1], where a peer can reliably collect the required set of blocks of a file from any number of peers within a reasonable time frame, disregarding the order of the blocks. However, this is not the case in P2P multimedia streaming, where playback delay and its continuity become vital Quality of Experience (QoE) factors. In the absence of the flexibilities available with file sharing, using the same approach for streaming video applications will face a number

---

[*] Corresponding author.

I. Tomkos et al. (Eds.): BROADNETS 2010, LNICST 66, pp. 14–27, 2012.

of serious challenges [2] [3]. A number of solutions have been developed to counter these challenges, such as applications like PPLive, CoolStreaming, SopCast, Babelgum, which are currently been deployed in the public Internet with a marginal streaming quality (i.e. bandwidth in a range of 300 to 500 kbps and playback delays of 10s to several minutes).

Many P2P streaming protocols use a hybrid push-pull approach to avoid instabilities of a tree-based push overlay structure owing to deep trees [4]. Pulling capability can be implemented replicating the same stream into multiple trees so that a peer can pull the stream from any tree which will improve its overall performance. However, this approach leads to unnecessary replication of data in the network and does not support uplink heterogeneities. A solution to this problem is to sub-divide the main stream into a set of substreams (known as substreamed P2P). In order to collect all the substreams (i.e. an essential requirement without SVC or MDC), a peer is required to join with multiple (but low-bandwidth) trees. This hybrid push-pull technique has become a victorious approach in deploying P2P video delivery over the public Internet especially with asymmetrical residential peers like ADSL to improve sharing capabilities minimising free-riding peers.

A prominent example of substreamed P2P is CoolStreaming. CoolStreaming [6] peer adaptations (i.e. the process that a peer selects a new parent during the session when a substream performance is degraded) are triggered by a child, which we categorise as a child-initiated process. The approach uses two inequalities (i.e. for testing the performance between the child and the parent and between the parent and the other partner peers). The only performance metric used by a child during the selection process is recording and comparing the latest received block at each substream. Therefore we categorise this also as a block-aware approach. Peer adaptations in non-substreamed P2P do not need to differentiate performances in source-to-parent or parent-to-child paths, since the entire session is received along a single path at a time. The only solution is to change the parent irrespective of the location of the degraded performance. It also has no flexibility of responding differently for peer dynamics (i.e. peer-churns) and network dynamics (i.e. congestion). However, in substreamed P2P, parent changes can be done independently from one parent to another or from one substream to another (one child may have multiple parents and one parent may deliver more than one substreams to a child) and can respond flexibly.

In this paper, we analyse and evaluate CoolStreaming peer adaptation algorithm, and propose a new algorithm that extends from CoolStreaming to capture the above mentioned criterions and flexibilities. The original CoolStreaming forces a child to change all the substreams from a parent even though only one substream is under-performing. However, in our proposed algorithm, we avoid changing all substreams where only the under-performing substream is required to find a new parent. We also propose removing one substream at a time by the child peer (i.e. a fine-grained conservative approach), if the identified congestion is in the uplink of the parent (expecting an improvement of congestion due to the granted space like in congestion control mechanisms).

The proposed solution also aims to minimise the diversity of parents (i.e. the number of parents that a child is required to acquire all the substreams) at a child peer without degrading the performance, which is expected to minimise overhead in a network-assisted P2P framework. This is achieved by joining with a well-performing another parent before seeking a new parent, when a substream needs to find a parent. We believe that since CoolStreaming will change all substreams when one of the substream is underperforming, this also could lead to instabilities of the P2P network.

The rest of the paper is organised as follows: Section 2 provides related works. Section 3 details the child-initiated block-aware peer adaptation algorithm and discusses the capabilities and complications. The proposed fine-grained algorithm is presented in Section 4. Section 5 provides the simulation results and Section 6 concludes the paper.

2   Related Works

P2P protocols like NICE [7] and ESM [8] use a tree-based approach for video streaming, which were first proposed as an alternative to solve infrastructure requirement of native IP multicast in group communications. This approach was initially thought to be the most suitable for streaming video when compared with mesh-based approaches [9], which was successfully used for file deliveries. The tree based approach supported low latency and low per-block overhead for long-lived streaming applications. However, many peers in a single tree topology were leaf-nodes, which did not contribute for data forwarding (only acted as data consumers). A peer-churn by an upper level node of the tree, in turn simultaneously affected a large number of nodes (i.e. especially when the tree depth is large) mounting instabilities of the overlay network. In order to minimise the above mentioned problems, the single tree-based streaming delivery approach has been extended to support multiple trees. AnySee [10] supports replication-based multi-tree approach. However, it does not support uplink heterogeneities. SplitStream [11], ChunckySpread [12] and mTreebone [13] principally introduced the substreaming approach without putting much attention on block-based video deliveries and the peer adaptation algorithm.

The substreamed approach has been practically deployed in the Internet by PPLive [14] and CoolStreaming [6]. It has been followed by recent works of P2P streaming as a solution to address the network heterogeneities and mutual contributions successfully [15]. CoolStreaming is the one which has published its peer adaptation algorithm. Zhenjiang Li et al. [18] has mathematically analysed the substream scheduling problem using max-flow model. Therefore it is important to further extend research works on performance optimisation of push-pull based substreaming algorithms for video delivery in the public Internet and in particular analyse more practical peer adaptation algorithms in detail.

3   Child-Initiated Block-Aware Peer Adaptations

In substreamed P2P, the source divides the main video stream into equal video blocks (e.g. with a one second play time) and delivers into N number of substreams. These blocks are assigned to substreams in revolving fashion. The receivers are required to collect all the substreams from at most N number of parent peers and reorder them according to the block number so that it can be played back with minimal disruption.

In the event that any block misses the playback point, the video is discontinued. A substream can lag due to a peer-churn or slow data-rate (due to congestion) in the last hop or above. In such a case the child peer can change the parent peer after exceeding a threshold specified in number of blocks.

In such a peer driven adaptation algorithm, a peer needs to know the block-maps (i.e. the list of latest received block number of each substream) of its own (C), its parent peers (P_i) and other partner peers (Q_i) those it can select to join. To maintain the scalability of the protocol, a peer will only exchange block-maps between a selected number of partner peers (among them at most N could become parents). They periodically exchange updated block-maps using a gossip algorithm [6]. There can also be other peers (besides P_is and Q_is) which are members (M_is) of the session without having any interaction with an identified child peer (peer C in Fig. 1).

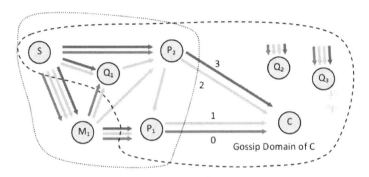

Fig. 1. An overlay network with 4 substreams

In Fig. 1, we assume that P_1, P_2, Q_1, Q_2 and Q_3 are the partners of child peer C and at present it receives the substreams 0 and 1 from parent P_1 and substreams 2 and 3 from parent P_2. If the current parent peer is needed to be changed, it will find a better parent (it will connect to Q_1, Q_2 or Q_3 to receive the substreams, if the received block-maps of them are better that of P_1 or P_2).

3.1 CoolStreaming Peer Adaptations

According to the peer adaptation approach used in CoolStreaming, a child peer will use two inequalities (given in the equations *1* and *2* [6]) to identify a requirement to change a parent for a substream j (j = 0 .. N-1). Satisfaction of either one of the inequalities will lead to a change in the parent.

$$\max\{|\,B_{i,C} - B_{j,P}\,| : i \leq N\} < TH_C \tag{1}$$

$$\max\{B_{i,Q} : i \leq N, Q \in Partners\} - B_{j,P} < TH_P \tag{2}$$

$B_{i,X}$ is the latest received block for substream i at node X, where X could be either a child node C, parents P or partners Q. TH_C is the threshold of the maximum deviation of latest received blocks allowed between the substream j at the parent and any substream at child node C. TH_p is the threshold of the maximum deviation of blocks allowed between the substream j at the parent and any substream at any partner.

These two tests are carried out periodically for all the parents at a child peer. The significant factor here is that if any substream (when receiving more than one substream from a parent) lags, CoolStreaming algorithm changes the parent for all the substreams originated from the same parent. This process will lead to find a new parent peer, which also satisfies the inequality (1).

3.2   Analysis of Triggering Events

In order to analyse the algorithm, we consider three distinguished generic substream lagging situations (Fig. 2), which could trigger a peer adaptation at a child peer. In the first case (a), both substreams from parent P_1 lag behind others. In the second case (b), only one substream (i.e. substream 1) from parent P_1 lags (this is possible when parent peer P_1 receives two substreams from two different routes; 0 through M_1 and 1 through P_2 in Fig. 1). In the third case (c), all the substreams are below the playback point.

Substreamed P2P is also a candidate transport mechanism that is compatible with recently accepted (by the IETF) multi-path TCP (MP-TCP) [5], which paves a path for resource pooling in the Future Internet. MP-TCP load balances a session in the transport layer through the available interfaces in a multi-home environment. Since the content layering is inherited in substreamed P2P, it can effectively be used over MP-TCP. In such a scenario a parent peer may have performance differences between substreams even thought they are received from the same upstream peer. Therefore decedent child peers need to identify this situation in the peer adaptation algorithm, which leads to case (b).

The factors that may affect the conditions in Fig. 2 may result from peer-churns or congestion in the core or access networks in the Internet. However, according to common analysis in P2P overlay networks, congestion is only considered in the uplink or downlink of a peer. We use the same assumptions in this analysis. We also assume that a peer-churn of an immediate parent can explicitly be identified by the child (may be using *ping*). Therefore peer-churn of such a parent (either P_1 or P_2 for child peer C in Fig. 1) has not been considered under the triggering events be discussed in the following paragraphs.

Each situation for peer adaptation (in Fig. 2) results in several events shown in Table 1, due to differing peer-churns or congestion in divided end-to-end overlay path; source-to-parent (multiple hops) and parent-to-child (last hop). In the table, L represents *Low* and H represents *High* in terms of the maximum available block at each substream. There can't be H at a child while having L at the parent since child can only acquire the data available at the parents. Theoretically, it is also not possible to have a situation where the parent's condition is H and child having L for one substream while another substream between the same pair of peers staying at H. We assume all the substreams between two peers follow the same path (if MP-TCP is used at a child, it is known to the peer and can remedy this situation) and experience the same congestion.

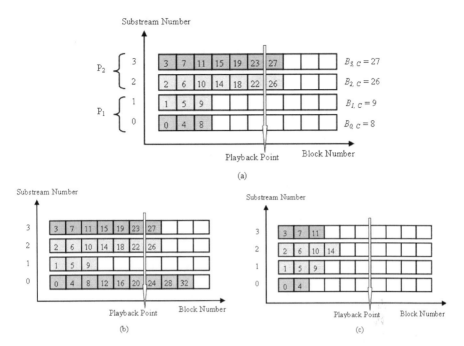

Fig. 2. Parent change triggering situations at a child peer

There can be two events between parent peer P_1 and the child peer C under the situation (a). The reason for case I to happen is when the parent P_1 receives delayed substreams from the source (i.e. due to either a peer-churn or congestion from source to parent). Solution for I is to change both substreams away from the current parent peer as quickly possible. The reason for case II could be due to congestion in the uplink at parent P_1. In our proposed solution, we would change one substream at a time rather than all practised in CoolStreaming. This would, therefore, allow space for other substreams to grow.

Table 1. Permutations for different triggering situations

Substream →		0		1		2		3		Congestion
Event ↓		C	P_1	C	P_1	C	P_2	C	P_2	
(a)	I	L	L	L	L					Source-Parent
	II	L	H	L	H					Parent-Child
(b)	III	H	H	L	L					Source-Parent
(c)	IV	L	H	L	H	H	L	H	L	Parent-Child
	V	L	L	L	L	L	L	L	L	Source-Parent

L-Low, H-High

The occurrence of case III is certainly due to poor performance above the parent P_1 since substream 0 does not show any performance degradation. According to Fig. 1, this can happen due to congestion between peers P_1 and P_2 or peer Q_1 leaving the overlay network. Therefore, only the lagged substream should be changed immediately. In CoolStreaming, the child unnecessarily changes the parent for both substreams due to the lagged substream 1.

The reason for case IV should be congestion in the downlink of child peer C or simultaneously in uplinks of both parents P_1 and P_2. We will follow the conservative approach by removing one substream from each parent. If this does not improve the performance, then the congestion in child peer's downlink maybe the factor resulting in poor performance. Case V arises when all substreams to the parents are delayed, in which case all substreams should be switched to new parents.

4   Fine-Grained Substream Change

This section describes the steps for the proposed fine-grained approach, which considers changing substreams more conservatively. Performance of each substream is tested independent of other substreams, even though they originated from the same parent.

4.1   Conservative Algorithm

The first step of the algorithm is to identify the most lagged substream (j) for a parent (l) among N_1 number of substreams received from the selected parent ($N_1 \leq N$). The algorithm will then test for inequality (3), and determines if the deviation from the most progressed substream (among all the N number of substreams of the session) has exceeded the defined threshed (TH_C).

If this condition is satisfied, then the child identifies the location of the problem (in source-parent or parent-child paths) using the bit-maps received. The maximum block of substream j at the child is compared with the maximum block of the substream at the current parent using inequality (4).

$$B_{j,P} - B_{j,C} > TH_C \tag{3}$$

$$\max\{|B_{j,P} - B_{j,Q}| : Q \in Partners\} > TH_P \tag{4}$$

If this condition (4) is satisfied, this means the parent's quality performance is good and the congestion is between the parent and the child. This will lead to a change of one substream, which has the least performance at the parent (if there is more than one substream from that parent). However, when selecting a new parent, the selection does not necessarily ensure that it is better parent than the existing one, where the selection will find a parent which satisfies the inequality (4). The sole objective is to change the path from the current parent. If the inequality (4) is not satisfied, this means there is no performance issue along the path from the existing parent to the child. The selected substream may have already received with a substantial delay at the parent. Therefore, it checks the comparative performance of the current parent with the other partners according to the inequality (5).

In contrast to the previous parent selection, in this case the substream changes the current parent only if a better partner is found. Otherwise it will continue with the current parent. Then the test (4) should be applied independently for all the remaining substreams of the selected parent and change the parent, if required.

Fine-grained Peer Adaptation Algorithm

```
for l = 0 … number of parents (L)
   |   find the most lagged substream (j) among N₁ ;
   |   if ( MAX | B_{i,c} - B_{j,c} | > TH_c : i = 0 … N-1)
   |   |   if ( B_{j,P} - B_{j,c} > TH_c )
   |   |   |   function-X ( );
   |   |   else
   |   |   |   if (MAX |B_{j,P} - B_{j,Q}| > TH_P : Q All Partners)
   |   |   |   |   function-Y ( );
   |   |   |   end
   |   |   end
   |   else
   |   |   if ( B_{j,c} - PLAYPOINT < TH_v )
   |   |   |   if ( B_{j,P} - B_{j,c} > TH_c )
   |   |   |   |   function-X ( );
   |   |   |   else
   |   |   |   |   if (MAX |B_{j,P} - B_{j,Q}| > TH_P : Q All Partners)
   |   |   |   |   |   function-Y ( );
   |   |   |   |   end
   |   |   |   end
   |   |   end
   |   end
end
function-X ( )
   |   remove 1 substream having least B_{m,P} : m = 0 … N₁ ;
   |   if (L > 1)
   |   |   find a parent with most number of substreams;
   |   |   check own substreams do not need a peer adapt;
   |   else
   |   |   find a parent satisfying inequality (4);
   |   end
end
function-Y ( )
   |   if (L > 1)
   |   |   find a parent with most number of substreams;
   |   |   check own substreams do not need a peer adapt;
   |   else
   |   |   change j to a new parent satisfy inequality (5);
   |   end
   |   test for other m values of the parent l
End
```

If test (*3*) is not satisfied, this means there is no much deviation between the best and the worst substreams. This can happen in two situations: all the substreams are good or all are bad. If all the substreams are much ahead of the playback point, we need to avoid any parent change. Therefore tests (*4*) and (*5*) will be applied only when the most lagged substream is less than a threshold (TH_V) of the playback point. Otherwise the same procedure is applied similarly for the other parents.

Downlink congestion: If all the substreams lag TH_V threshold, it could also be due to downlink congestion at the child. Therefore, the child memorises this peer adaptation. If the situation is not rectified after a certain number of attempts, the child will extend the cool-down time (the time duration that a child peer will not test for parent changes again) of peer adaptation to minimise unnecessary events (alternatively the child could also use multi-path transport).

If congestion is in the uplink of the parent peer, CoolStreaming child finds a new parent for all the substreams it receives from that parent. Also if there is more than one child at this parent, it will end up loosing all the child peers when triggering events come closely. This could add extra overhead to the parent. Therefore, one approach to minimise this is to synchronise triggering events under one parent and ensure they don't come too close to each other. However, synchronisation of triggering events may not be required in the fine-grained approach since it uses a conservative substream changing process.

4.2   Minimising the Diversity of Parents

It has been widely accepted that next generation P2P is an ISP-assisted network service. IETF is standardising a framework for this purpose called Application Layer Traffic Optimisations (ALTO) [16]. Here, a content provider needs to register with the ALTO service (owned by an ISP) to avoid throttling their P2P traffic. Through negotiations with the ALTO server, a peer can select its parent peers. Hence an ISP can enforce different policies like restricting traffic to its own network or local geography.

Although the standardisation through IETF is attractive and further increases the potential of P2P streaming, current approaches such as that used in CoolStreaming does not aim to minimise its complexities. For example, substreamed P2P may introduce an extra load on the ALTO server when requesting new parent peers for every single substream. Therefore, it could be desirable to minimise the diversity of parents at a child peer by reusing ALTO provided information. This will improve self-organising capability in an ALTO domain reducing cross traffic (that will cost ISPs compared with local traffic) and also overhead at an ALTO server.

The fine-grained approach that we have proposed in this paper will minimise this effect, where we introduce a seeking process for new parents for a substream among existing parents. Therefore, when a substream is required to find a new parent, it will first seek a parent, which already delivers a substream to the child (that substream should not look to change the parent). If there are more than one qualified parents, then it will select the one delivering most number of substreams. If no other qualified existing parent is found, it will seek a parent from the larger partner list. Algorithm 1 presents the pseudo-code of the fine-grained algorithm including the parent diversity minimisation process.

5   Performance Evaluations

We have simulated the CoolStreaming peer adaptation algorithm and the proposed fine-grained extension for two approaches; (A) seeking a new parent from the partner list, and (B) seeking a parent among the existing parents that the child is receiving other substreams, using OMNet++ simulator [17]. These algorithms were evaluated under a generic traffic model and a network topology. The time scale of a long-lived session has been contracted proportionately only to evaluate the peer adaptation process.

We used UDP implementation of OMNet++ in the transport layer for simplicity and implemented a basic congestion control algorithm over it. We did not explicitly implement a tracker service and the content server itself acted as the tracker for the peers. UDP was used for signalling messages too.

In all experiments, we used a traffic stream of 400kbps, which is appropriate for the public Internet, and it was divided into 4 substreams. The chunk size used for the substreams was 50 Kbytes, which is equivalent to a play time of 1s. The number of partners (those a peer was communicating) was limited to 5. Peer adaptation thresholds were chosen as; $TH_C = 20$, $TH_P = 16$ and $TH_V = 0$ in blocks. The cool-down time was 30s.

The uplink bandwidth at the server was 4 Mbps and at a peer it was randomly and uniformly distributed from 100 kbps to 1300 kbps in 100 kbps steps. This created a 400 kbps of average overlay uplink capacity on a participating peer (which has been changed in the second set of experiments). Traffic was not limited at any other location in the overlay network than the uplinks. Background traffic was changed at uplinks randomly in 20s intervals uniformly distributed between 0 to 600 kbps, and again in 100 kbps steps.

Peers joined randomly to a simple network topology (star). In order to simulate a heterogeneous substreaming scenario at a child peer, one third of the peers joined (i.e. at the start of their session) only with one parent for all the substreams. Then the subsequent one third of peers joined with totally different parents for each substream. The remaining peers joined with two parents with two substreams from each.

We measured QoE at a peer in terms of block continuity index (i.e. the number of blocks received at the playback point over total number of blocks it should receive). If one block misses the playback pointer, it backed-off 12 blocks rather continuing with the following block. This accounted a play-out event, which may have risen due to a peer-churn. We also monitored the diversity of parents at a child peer.

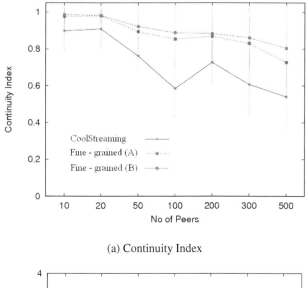

(a) Continuity Index

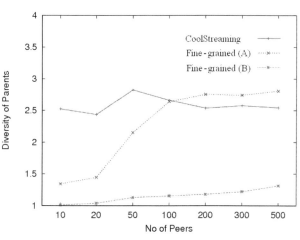

(b) Diversity of Parents

Fig. 3. Performance with different number of peers

We conducted all the experiments for a duration of 1000s. Half of all the peers continuously connected to the overlay network for the entire duration. Remaining half created peer-churns by leaving the overlay for a duration between 0 and 20s at a randomly selected time. We have monitored the performance matrices at a child peer in 10s intervals and the average values of all the peers are shown in the following graphs.

We have first simulated algorithms with different number of peers to investigate the consistency of the performance improvement of the new algorithm. According to Fig. 3 (a), a significant improvement of the continuity index can be seen with both proposed evolutionary approaches against the CoolStreaming peer adaptation algorithm (90% confidence intervals are shown in the graph). Fig. 3 (b) shows that the diversity of parents is lesser in the evolutionary algorithm (A) with a number of nodes less than 100. However, the diversity increases as the number of nodes increases. This is not a contradictory observation since we have not focused reducing the diversity of parents in algorithm (A). But the fine-grained algorithm (B) has notably reduced the diversity of parents.

We have then simulated three algorithms under different overlay network capacities to investigate the performance in over-provisioned and under-provisioned situations. The average network capacity of all the uplinks was selected as a proportion to the full stream bandwidth requirement (i.e. in Fig. 4, x-axis 2.00 indicates that the average uplink capacity is 800 kbps, which represents an over-provisioned network). The number of peers in these experiments was 100. According to Fig. 4 (a), there is a consistent improvement of the continuity index using the two evolutionary algorithms. The diversity of parents has also not been affected much in evolutionary algorithm (A) but drastically reduced in the evolutionary algorithm (B) as shown in Fig. 4 (b).

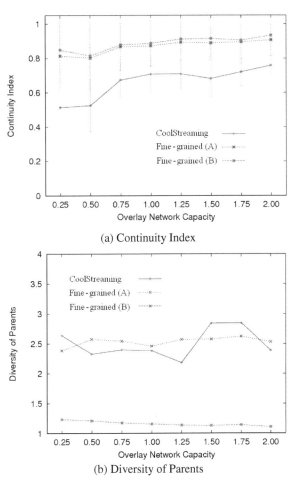

(a) Continuity Index

(b) Diversity of Parents

Fig. 4. Performance with different overlay network capacities

Fig. 5 shows the behaviour (from the start to the end of a session) of the continuity index at 20 randomly selected peers. According to the snapshot graphs and our observations, the continuity index approaches towards 1.0 and becomes steady during the entire session under the evolutionary approaches.

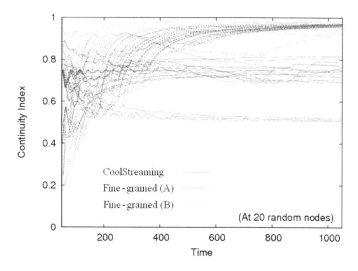

Fig. 5. Change of Continuity Index (at 20 selected peers)

6   Conclusions

P2P networking paradigm has been recognised by the IETF to outline as a non-aggressive and ISP-friendly network service in the Internet. Then P2P streaming will be used to solve future Internet bandwidth demands by federating core network resource requirements. Substreamed P2P is an important concept to support heterogeneous uplink bandwidths of residential peers and hence to improve co-operative resource sharing at the same time. Therefore, substreamed P2P concept needs to be developed while attempting to improve user's QoE. Especially peer adaptation algorithm has not been analysed to capture different network and peer dynamics in the end-to-end overlay path.

In this paper we have proposed a fine-grained approach for the child-initiated block-aware peer adaptation algorithm that extends from the CoolStreaming application. The proposed approach utilises inter-substream performance parameters to differentiate source-to-parent and parent-to-child congestion and hence conservatively respond to changes in substream performance. The proposed solution also aims to minimise the diversity of parents, which could be problematic with the new network-assisted P2P standardisation initiative proposed by the IETF. Simulation results have been evaluated to compare the proposed solution with CoolStreaming, and the results have shown considerable improvement in QoE. We also claim that the new approach has minimised the diversity of parents.

Acknowledgments. This work has received support from the Higher Education Authority (HEA) in Ireland under the PRTLI Cycle 4 programme, in the project FutureComm: Management of Future Communications Networks and Services, as well as Science Foundation Ireland under Grant Number 09/SIRG/I1643 ("A Biologically inspired framework supporting network management for the Future Internet").

References

1. Aggarwal, V., Feldmann, A., Scheideler, C.: Can ISPs and P2P users Cooperate for improved Performance? ACM CCR (July 2007)
2. Liu, J., Rao, S., Li, B., Zhang, H.: Opportunities and Challenges of Peer-to-Peer Internet Video Broadcast. Proceedings of the IEEE (January 2008)
3. Liu, H., Riley, G.: How Efficient Peer-to-Peer Video Streaming Could Be? In: IEEE CCNC (January 2009)
4. Hei, X., Liu, Y., Ross, K.W.: IPTV over P2P Streaming Networks: the Mesh-Pull Approach. IEEE Communications Magazine (February 2008)
5. Ford, A., Raiciu, C., Barre, S., Iyengar, J.: Architectural Guidelines for Multipath TCP Development. IETF Internet Draft (February 2010)
6. Zhang, X., Liu, J., Li, B., Yum, T.: CoolStreaming/DONet: A Data-driven Overlay Network for Efficient Live Media Streaming. In: IEEE INFOCOM (March 2005)
7. Banerjee, S., Bhattacharjee, B., Kommareddy, C.: Scalable Application Layer Multicast. In: ACM SIGCOMM (August 2002)
8. Chu, Y., Rao, S., Seshan, S., Zhang, H.: A Case for End System Multicast. IEEE Journal on Selected Areas in Communication (October 2002)
9. Stoica, I., Morris, R., Liben-Nowell, D., Karger, D., Kaashoek, F., Dabek, F., Balakrishnan, H.: Chord: A Scalable Peer-to-peer Lookup Protocol for Internet Applications. IEEE/ACM Transactions on Networking (February 2003)
10. Liao, X., Jin, H., Liu, Y., Ni, L.M., Deng, D.: AnySee: Peer-to-Peer Live Streaming. In: IEEE INFOCOM (April 2006)
11. Castro, M., Druschel, P., Kermarrec, A., Nandi, A., Rowstron, A., Singh, A.: SplitStream: High-bandwidth Multicast in Cooperative Environments. In: ACM Symposium on Operating Systems Principles (October 2003)
12. Venkataraman, V., Yoshida, K., Francis, P.: Chunkyspread: Heterogeneous Unstructured Tree-Based Peer-to-Peer Multicast. In: IEEE ICNP (November 2006)
13. Wang, F., Xiong, Y., Liu, J.: mTreebone: A Hybrid Tree/Mesh Overlay for Application-Layer Live Video Multicast. In: IEEE ICDCS (June 2007)
14. Hei, X., Liang, C., Liang, J., Liu, Y., Ross, K.: A Measurement Study of a Large-Scale P2P IPTV System. IEEE Transactions on Multimedia (December 2007)
15. Liu, Z., Shen, Y., Ross, K.W., Panwar, S.S., Wang, Y.: Substream Trading: Towards an open P2P live Streaming System. In: IEEE ICNP (October 2008)
16. Xie, H., Yang, R., Krishnamurthy, A., Liu, Y., Silberschatz, A.: P4P: Provider Portal for Applications. In: ACM CCR (October 2008)
17. OMNet++ Simulator, http://www.omnetpp.org
18. Li, Z., Tsang, D.H.K., Lee, W.C.: Understanding Sub-stream Scheduling in P2P Hybrid Live Streaming Systems. In: IEEE INFOCOM (March 2010)

Designing Repeatable Experiments on an Emulab Testbed

Andres Perez-Garcia, Christos Siaterlis, and Marcelo Masera

Institute for the Protection and Security of the Citizen
Joint Research Centre
Via E. Fermi 2749, 21027 Ispra (VA) Italy
{andres.perez-garcia,christos.siaterlis,marcelo.masera}@jrc.ec.europa.eu

Abstract. Emulation testbeds are increasingly used in an effort to promote repeatable experiments in the area of distributed systems and networking. In this paper we are studying how different design choices, e.g. use of specific tools, can affect the repeatability of experiments of an emulation testbed (e.g. based on the Emulab software).

Our study is based on multiple experiments that are checked for stability and consistency (e.g., repetition of the same experiment and measurement of the mean and standard deviation of our metrics). The results indicate that repeatability of quantitative results is possible, under a degree of expected statistical variation. The event scheduling mechanism of Emulab is proven to be accurate down to a sub-second granularity. On the other hand we demonstrate that there are significant differences between traffic generation tools in terms of consistent recreation of a predefined traffic pattern and therefore experiment repeatability.

The main contribution of this study is that based on experimental results we provide scientific proofs that Emulab as a platform can be used for scientifically rigorous experiments for networking research. New users of Emulab can benefit from this study by understanding that Emulab's scheduling mechanism, it's built-in packet generators and Iperf can sufficiently support repeatable experiments while TCPreplay cannot and therefore an alternative tool, i.e. TCPivo should be used.

Keywords: emulation, network test-bed, repeatability, traffic generators.

1   Introduction

Emulation testbeds are increasingly used in an effort to address the lack of scientific rigor [1] and realism as well as to promote repeatable experiments in the area of distributed systems and networking [2]. The study of complex systems or system of systems, e.g., the Internet, could be carried out by experimenting with real systems, software simulators or hardware emulators. Experimentation with real production systems suffers from the inability to control the experiment environment in order to reproduce results. Furthermore if the study intends

I. Tomkos et al. (Eds.): BROADNETS 2010, LNICST 66, pp. 28–39, 2012.

to test the resilience or security of a system, concerns about potential side-effects (faults and disruptions) to mission critical services rise. On the other hand the development of a dedicated experimentation infrastructure with real components is often economically prohibitive. Software based simulation would then appear as the best solution but due to the diversity and complexity of protocols, systems and architectures of the Internet hardware-based emulation is considered a flexible and powerful approach [3]. Indeed, emulation approaches and specifically those based on the Emulab software are becoming very popular [4]. Emulab is a network testbed, able to recreate a wide range of experimentation environments in which researchers can develop, debug and evaluate a complex system [5]. Emulation is particularly useful for security and resilience analysis [6],[7], because in order to study resilience a researcher has to expose the system-under-test to high load and extreme conditions.

In this paper we present a study of different parameters that might influence the repeatability of experiments on top of an Emulab-based testbed. We show that experimental results can be systematically reproduced (even in absolute numbers -quantitative- given a fixed hardware configuration). Furthermore we study the event scheduling system of Emulab as an important mechanism for repeating experiments as well as different traffic generating tools. To the best of our knowledge, previous studies compare different emulation/simulation approaches [8],[9] rather than systematically studying the repeatability of experiments by comparing different runs of the same experiment. In this paper, we take advantage of the automation functionality of Emulab in order to run multiple experiments (hundreds) and draw our conclusions after checking the experimental results for stability and consistency. Our contribution does not only lie on the presented experimental results but also in the transformation of our experience in terms of caveats, significant configuration parameters and limitations into a set of guidelines that researchers using Emulab could use as a reference. This would lower the barrier for new researchers trying to use Emulab and promote scientific rigorous experimentation.

The paper is structured as follows. We begin in Section 2 with a description of an Emulab-based testbed and its characteristics. Then we proceed in Section 3 with our study and experimental results. In Section 3.1 we present the experimental setup that is used in our experiments and in the following subsections we address how the repeatability of experiments can be influenced by the hardware allocation policy, Emulab's event scheduling mechanism and the use of various traffic generators. We conclude in Section 4 and summarize our findings.

2   The Emulab Platform and Its Features

One of the most promising approaches for experimentation with large and complex systems, e.g. those found in an industrial Supervisory Control and Data Acquisition (SCADA) network [10], is the use of emulation testbeds. Pure software simulation is often too simplistic to recreate complex environments and the use of an ad-hoc testbed is not recommended because it is very time-consuming

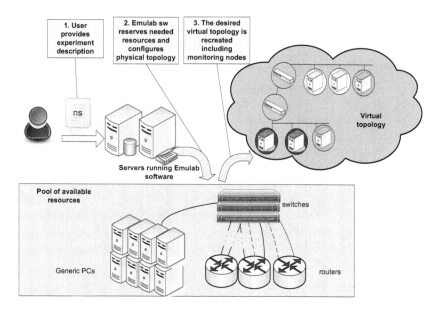

Fig. 1. Main steps for recreating a virtual network configuration within an Emulab-based testbed

and error-prone to setup, maintain and change. A trend, that is constantly becoming more popular, is the use of emulation testbeds like Emulab [5]. We have developed in our laboratory a testbed using the Emulab architecture and software, that allows us to automatically and dynamically map physical components (e.g. servers, switches) to a virtual topology. In other words the Emulab software configures the physical topology in way that it emulates the virtual topology as transparently as possible. This way we gain significant advantages in terms of repeatability, scalability, controllability and automation of our experiments.

Our emulation testbed consists mainly of two servers running the Emulab software and a pool of physical resources (e.g. generic PCs and network devices) that are free to be used as experimental nodes. The following steps (Figure 1) describe the re-creation of a virtual network configuration within our testbed:

1. First we need to create a detailed description of the virtual network configuration using an extension of the NS language [11] (the experiment script).
2. In our description we enumerate similar components as different instances of the same component type. This way pre-defined templates of different components (e.g a Linux server template) can be easily reused and automatically deployed and configured.
3. Whenever we want to run an experiment we instantiate it by using the Emulab software. The Emulab server automatically reserves and allocates the physical resources that are needed from the pool of available components.

This procedure is called *swap-in*, in contrast to the termination of the experiment which is called *swap-out*.
4. Furthermore the software configures network switches in order to recreate the virtual topology by connecting experimental nodes using multiple VLANs.
5. Finally, before the testbed is released for experimentation, the software configures packet capturing of predefined links for monitoring purposes.

At this point it is important to note that in step 4, the Emulab software uses two different strategies for network link emulation (e.g., delay, packet loss and bandwidth) according to the predefined instructions given in the experiment script. First, the *delay-node-shaping strategy* uses extra PCs to emulate network links. These PCs, called delay nodes, run Dummynet to simulate link level characteristics [12]. Second, the *end-node-shaping strategy* does not use extra resources and therefore runs Dummynet inside the end user nodes. In this paper we don't use the end-node-shaping strategy as it can lead to unstable and unrealistic results [13].

To achieve repeatable experiments on an Emulab testbed (i.e. the ability to repeat an experiment and obtain the same or statistically consistent results) a controlled environment is needed. In this paper we study how different tools and mechanisms can influence the repeatability of experiments and specifically:

1. *The hardware allocation strategy*, that matches physical resources, i.e., PC's and network links, to the virtual topology (at step 3). Emulab can use three different strategies:
   − the *fixed-hardware-allocation strategy* where all experimental nodes are matched with a specific hardware (e.g. a user node is always instantiated by PC10);
   − the *fixed-class-allocation strategy* where all experimental nodes are matched with a hardware of a specific class (e.g. a user node is always instantiated by a P4x2GHz);
   − the *free-hardware-allocation strategy* where experimental nodes are freely matched with any available hardware. We should note here that fixing the allocation of delay nodes is not possible.
2. *The event generation system*, that allows the researcher to schedule events. These events are an integral part of any experiment scenario. To reproduce a previously stored experiment scenario the researcher should be able to setup the experimental platform in the initial state and trigger all necessary events in the right order and time of occurrence.
3. *The traffic generating tools* and their ability to consistently reproduce the same background traffic environment. We consider two classes of tools: a) synthetic traffic generators (Iperf and emulab-buildin tools) b) tools that replay real traffic captures (Tcpreplay [14] and Tcpivo [15]).

3   Experimental Results

Based on a series of experiments, we study Emulab as a platform to conduct rigorous experiments in terms of repeatability. First we present our experimental

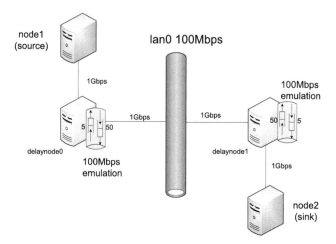

Fig. 2. The experimental setup that was used in our experiments

setup and then in the sections that follow, we present results demonstrating how different tools and mechanisms can influence repeatability.

3.1 Experimental Setup

We experiment with a topology that consists of a 100Mbps LAN with two user nodes. As we use the delay-node-shaping strategy, Emulab instantiates delay-nodes running Dummynet in order to model the network (Figure 2). Dummynet is configured with two pipes, inbound and outbound, to shape traffic entering and leaving a user node. In our experiments, inbound and outbound pipes have a queue size of 5 and 50 slots respectively. Physically, all interfaces in our testbed are configured at 1Gbps and it is left up to Dummynet to shape the traffic at the speed of our virtual topology, i.e. 100Mbps.

We have used two types of nodes in order to study the repeatability with different hardware. Experimental nodes are either Dell PC's with AMD 2GHz Athlon processor and 2GB RAM, or Fujitsu PC's with Intel PIV processor and 1GB RAM. As for the operating system, we have used both FreeBSD and Linux Fedora Core as user nodes, depending on the application, while only FreeBSD in delay-nodes.

The following tools have been used to launch the experiments and to collect and analyze experimental data:

- Iperf [16] is a tool to generate UDP traffic between a source node and a sink node. It also includes a build-in measurement functionality that provides statistics such as sustained bandwidth and packet loss, that we use to assess the network's performance.
- The CBR traffic generator that comes with Emulab works similar to Iperf. It does not provide statistics, but it is easier to use and schedule in the NS script.

- TCPReplay [14] uses a previously captured traffic file in libpcap format and replays it back onto the network, usually to test switches, routers and firewalls. It is a powerful tool that allows to classify traffic as client or server and rewrite Layer 2, 3 and 4 headers.
- TCPivo [15] is another, less known, free and open-source tool that supports high-speed packet replay from a trace file.

In order to run our experiments, we have made use of Emulab's potential to automatically launch scripts that configure and run the different experiments and store statistics in a repository for further analysis. This has allowed us to launch thousands of experiments in a short period of time without human interaction.

We have set up three sets of experiments to study how repeatability can be influenced by a) the hardware allocation strategy, b) the event generation system, and c) the use of different traffic generators. In the following sections we investigate these factors one by one.

3.2   Hardware Allocation Strategies

We have already demonstrated in [13] that the quantitative results of an Emulab-based experiment are hardware-dependent. On the other hand, the hardware allocation might change from one experiment to another due to (un)availability of resources, randomness in Emulab's swap-in algorithm or other testbed policies. For this reason, we have performed a set of experiments in order to study the influence of hardware allocation in the repeatability of an experiment. We measure the network performance, i.e. the traffic received by the sink node versus the traffic sent by the source node, along repetitive experiments of three distinct experiment sets corresponding to the three hardware-allocation-strategies:

1. the *fixed-hardware-allocation strategy*, where each experimental node is fixed to a specific PC;
2. the *fixed-class-allocation strategy* where experimental nodes are chosen from the class of Dell PCs;
3. the *free-hardware-allocation strategy* where experimental nodes are freely chosen from the two hardware classes, i.e., Dell and Fujitsu PCs.

In all experiments, we measured the sustained network performance using Iperf's built-in measurement functionality. We generated UDP traffic from node1 to node2 with 512 bytes of payload and bandwidth ranging from 0Mbps up to 100Mbps. In the first experiment set we did not swap in and out in order to preserve the exact hardware allocation (not even a change in delay nodes), while in the other two experiment sets we swapped in and out for each experiment, leaving Emulab to freely choose the hardware allocation according to the predefined strategy.

For each experiment set we run the same experiment 20 times and the results are depicted in Figures 3, while the statistics, average μ, standard deviation σ and coefficient of variation ($CV = \frac{\sigma}{\mu}$), are shown in Figure 3(d). From the figures

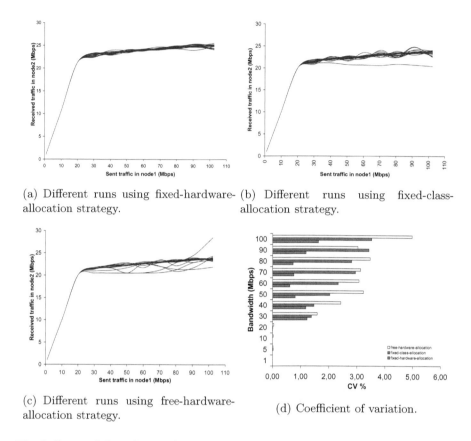

(a) Different runs using fixed-hardware-allocation strategy.

(b) Different runs using fixed-class-allocation strategy.

(c) Different runs using free-hardware-allocation strategy.

(d) Coefficient of variation.

Fig. 3. Repeatability of network's performance in three different strategies of hardware allocation

we can see that the 20 experiments in each case provide the same performance when traffic is under 20Mbps, i.e. when there are no packet losses. However, when Dummynet is not able to process all the packets and there are drops in the queues, we see that the hardware allocation introduces a higher variability in the results as we go from a fixed to a free allocation strategy.

In fact, if we look at the CV, which in general gets worse as the bandwidth grows, the best results in terms of repeatability are with the fixed-hardware-allocation strategy and the worst results with the free-hardware-allocation strategy. Another important observation is that even in the worst case the CV is under 5%, i.e., the maximum CV for the three allocation strategies is 1.63%, 3.52% an 4.98% respectively. This means that in experiments of moderate network load (where hardware dependence is not critical) even a free allocation strategy can result repeatable results.

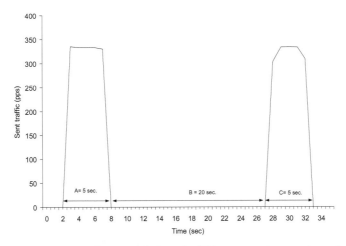

Fig. 4. CBR traffic scheduled in the NS script to be sent in node3

3.3 The Event Geeration System

In this section we study the accuracy of the event generation system in Emulab. In order to do that, we have run the same experiment 20 times (swapping in and out). In the experiment NS script we have scheduled four events to generate 2 pulses of CBR traffic from node1 to node2. Each pulse (events A and C) has a duration of 5 seconds, and the time between them (event B) is 20 seconds (Figure 4). The information registered by Emulab about event generation in each experiment is precise and consistent with the configuration.

We have captured the traffic with Tcpdump in delaynode0 and we have measured the time between the first and last packet of each pulse for the 20 experiments. Table 1 shows the statistics of the duration of events A, B and C along the 20 experiment runs. The standard deviation is always below 63 milliseconds, which should be precise enough for most experiments that schedule events in seconds or tens of seconds. In terms of CV, we see that the accuracy is better with longer periods.

This variation can be explained by looking at what happens after the events are scheduled by the system and before the traffic is captured. The events imply starting or stopping an application (CBR traffic generator) in a remote node, so there is a communication between the Emulab system and node1. Then, the traffic arriving to the delaynode0 has to pass through network cards, switch

Table 1. The average, standard deviation and coefficient of variation of the duration of events A, B, C

Event	Avg	Stdev	CV %
A	4.94	0.03	0.55%
B	20.08	0.05	0.25%
C	4.86	0.06	1.30%

and cables before it is captured. All these processes along with CPU scheduling inaccuracy result some time shifting. The conclusion is though that Emulab's event generation system is accurate and consistent.

3.4   Traffic Generators

In this part of the study, we have analyzed the repeatability of different traffic generators, namely Iperf, CBR, Tcpreplay and Tcpivo, by running each of them 10 times with the same configuration. For Iperf and CBR we generated pulses of 30 seconds with UDP packets of 512bytes of payload from node1 to node2 (synthetic traffic), while for Tcpreplay and Tcpivo, we reproduced a real trace of 30 seconds with TCP packets of random length (taken from the DATCAT repository [17]).

Figure 5 shows the traffic measured with Tcpdump in node2 for each of the traffic generators. At first sight, we see that tcpreplay is not able to reproduce a single trace with the same characteristics: each reproduction is different from the other. On the other hand the rest of the tools seem to generate traffic in a repeatable way. In fact, if we look at Table 2, the duration of traffic is practically the same for all the tools but Tcpreplay, where the CV is higher than 6% and the standard deviation is $\sigma = 3.27$ seconds. Furthermore we have subtracted the generated traffic signal that was produced by Tcpreplay and Tcpivo as measured in node2, i.e., $gen(t)$, from the original reference signal of the trace file we used as input to both tools i.e., $ref(t)$ and depicted the difference $ref(t) - gen(t)$ in Figure 6. We see that the differences are in the order of few Kbps in the case of Tcpivo, but it reaches up to 2Mbps with Tcpreplay. A small difference was expected due to the buffering mechanism in the network, but Tcpreplay wasn't able to provide repeatable results.

Table 2. Repeatability of traffic generators (traffic duration)

Tool	Avg	Stdev	CV %
Tcpreplay	48.45	3.27	6.74%
TCPivo	30.00	0.00	0.00%
CBR	30.07	0.02	0.05%
Iperf	30.00	0.00	0.00%

4   Conclusion

The study of complex systems and networks is a hard process. The limitations of software simulators and theoretic modeling as well as the required cost and effort to setup and maintain ad-hoc testbeds of real systems, make the use of emulation testbeds a promising approach. Emulation testbeds like Emulab are increasingly used in networking research in an effort to raise the level of scientific rigorousness and specifically by conducting repeatable experiments. In this paper we investigate how different mechanisms and tools of an Emulab testbed can influence the repeatability of experimental results.

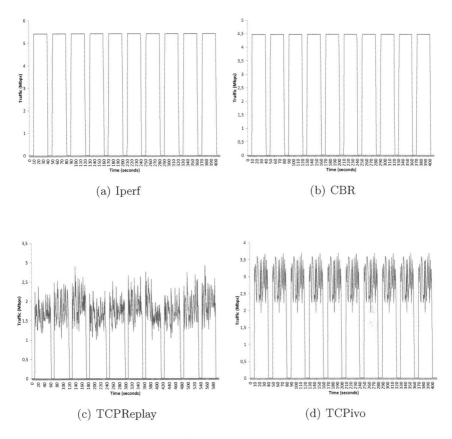

Fig. 5. Traffic generated by different tools and measured in the sink node

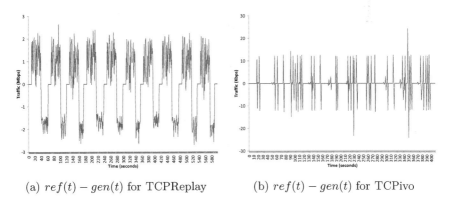

Fig. 6. Subtraction between traffic signals of the reference trace file $ref(t)$ and the generated traffic $gen(t)$ by TCPReplay and TCPivo

Our contribution can be summarized in the following points. We confirm that repeatability of quantitative experimental results on an Emulab testbed is possible, under a degree of expected statistical variation. If the *fixed-hardware-allocation strategy* is used the coefficient of variation (CV) of the results lies on average under 1%. Furthermore the event scheduling mechanism of Emulab is proven to be accurate down to a sub-second granularity, ensuring thus a reliable and accurate reproduction of an experiment script. Finally we demonstrate that there are significant differences between traffic generation tools in terms of consistent recreation of a predefined traffic pattern and therefore repeatability. For synthetic traffic Emulab's built-in packet generator as well as Iperf were proven as adequate. As for replaying real traffic traces, our results show that only the less known TCPivo tool can guarantee repeatability whereas the popular TCPreplay tool fails to do so. In general this work could be seen as an effort, part of a general trend of the networking research community, towards the execution of repeatable experiments, i.e., to results that can be reproduced and validated by other researchers.

References

1. Pawlikowski, K., Joshua Jeong, H.d., Ruth Lee, J.s.: On credibility of simulation studies of telecommunication networks. IEEE Communications Magazine 40, 132–139 (2002)
2. Benzel, T., Braden, R., Kim, D., Neuman, C., Joseph, A., Sklower, K., Ostrenga, R., Schwab, S.: Design, deployment, and use of the deter testbed. In: DETER: Proceedings of the DETER Community Workshop on Cyber Security Experimentation and Test on DETER Community Workshop on Cyber Security Experimentation and Test 2007, p. 1. USENIX Association, Berkeley (2007)
3. Neville, S.W., Li, K.F.: The rational for developing larger-scale 1000+ machine emulation-based research test beds. In: International Conference on Advanced Information Networking and Applications Workshops, pp. 1092–1099 (2009)
4. Emulab Bibliography, http://www.emulab.net/expubs.php/
5. White, B., Lepreau, J., Stoller, L., Ricci, R., Guruprasad, S., Newbold, M., Hibler, M., Barb, C., Joglekar, A.: An integrated experimental environment for distributed systems and networks. In: Proc. of the Fifth Symposium on Operating Systems Design and Implementation, pp. 255–270. USENIX Association, Boston (2002)
6. DETER. cyber-DEfense Technology Experimental Research laboratory Testbed, http://www.isi.edu/deter/
7. Mirkovic, J., Hussain, A., Fahmy, S., Reiher, P.L., Thomas, R.K.: Accurately measuring denial of service in simulation and testbed experiments. IEEE Trans. Dependable Sec. Comput. 6(2), 81–95 (2009)
8. Anderson, D.S., Hibler, M., Stoller, L., Stack, T., Lepreau, J.: Automatic online validation of network configuration in the emulab network testbed. In: ICAC 2006: Proceedings of the 2006 IEEE International Conference on Autonomic Computing, pp. 134–142. IEEE Computer Society, Washington, DC (2006)
9. Chertov, R., Fahmy, S., Shroff, N.B.: Fidelity of network simulation and emulation: A case study of tcp-targeted denial of service attacks. ACM Trans. Model. Comput. Simul. 19(1), 1–29 (2008)

10. Guglielmi, M., Fovino, I.N., Garcia, A.P., Siaterlis, C.: A preliminary study of a wireless process control network using emulation testbed. In: Proc. of the 2nd International Conference on Mobile Lightweight Wireless Systems. ICST, Barcelona (2010)
11. ISI, Network simulator ns-2, http://www.isi.edu/nsnam/ns/
12. Rizzo, L.: Dummynet: a simple approach to the evaluation of network protocols. SIGCOMM Comput. Commun. Rev. 27(1), 31–41 (1997)
13. Andres Perez Garcia, M.M., Siaterlis, C.: Testing the fidelity of an emulab testbed. In: Proc. of the 2nd workshop on Sharing Field Data and Experiment Measurements on Resilience of Distributed Computing Systems, Genova, Italy (June 2010)
14. Turner, A.: Tcpreplay tool, http://tcpreplay.synfin.net/trac/
15. Feng, W.-C., Goel, A., Bezzaz, A., Feng, W.-C., Walpole, J.: Tcpivo: a high-performance packet replay engine. In: MoMeTools 2003: Proceedings of the ACM SIGCOMM Workshop on Models, Methods and Tools for Reproducible Network Research, pp. 57–64. ACM, New York (2003)
16. NLANR/DAST, Iperf: The TCP/UDP bandwidth measurement tool, http://sourceforge.net/projects/iperf/
17. Cho, K.: WIDE-TRANSIT 150 Megabit Ethernet Trace 2008-03-18 (Anonymized) (collection),
http://imdc.datcat.org/collection/1-05L8-9=WIDE-TRANSIT+150+Megabit +Ethernet+Trace+2008-03-18+%28Anonymized%29

Hybrid Content Distribution Network with a P2P Based Streaming Protocol

Saumay Pushp[1] and Priya Ranjan[2]

[1] Dept. of Computer Science and Engineering, Kanpur Institute of Technology,
Kanpur, UP-208001, India
saumaypushp@gmail.com
[2] Dept. of Electrical Engineering, Indian Institute of Technology,
Kanpur, UP-208016, India
ranjanp@iitk.ac.in

Abstract. Multicast has been used as a one-to-many approach to deliver information; it is based on the idea that if one packet of data should be transmitted to several recipients, the information should be sent by the origin just one time. In this paper, we propose the use of IP based Pragmatic General Multicast (PGM) to distribute content and to make distribution more efficient; we combine it with a P2P approach. We focus on the problem of data redundancy (at each node), congestion and contention and show how severely it impacts the network economics and the experience of end-user and hence leads to low traffic load and redundancy.

Keywords: Multicast, Peer to Peer, Congestion, Contention.

1 Introduction

Since 20 years, internet has seen an exponential increase in its growth. With more and more people using it, efficient data delivery over the internet has become a key issue. Peer-to-peer (P2P)/efficient data sharing based networks have several desirable features for content distribution, such as low costs, scalability, and fault tolerance. While the invention of each of such specialized systems has improved the user experience, some fundamental shortcomings of these systems have often been neglected. These shortcomings of content distribution systems have become severe bottlenecks in scalability of the internet. The need to scale content delivery systems has been continuously felt and has led to development of thousand-node clusters, global-scale content delivery networks, and more recently, self-managing peer-to-peer structures. These content delivery mechanisms have changed the nature of Internet content delivery and traffic. Therefore, to exploit full potential of the modern Internet, there is a requirement for a detailed understanding of these new mechanisms and the data they serve. In this work, we focus on the problem of redundancy of data being transmitted using several state of the art content distribution systems and show how severely it impacts the network economics and the experience of end-user. We base our findings on real world large scale measurement studies conducted over Emulab, which is a network test bed hosted by the University of Utah.

I. Tomkos et al. (Eds.): BROADNETS 2010, LNICST 66, pp. 40–54, 2012.

1.1   The Problem of Data Redundancy

Consider the scenario shown in Figure 1. The network topology contains a file server which hosts a file to be downloaded by 9 clients. The file server is connected to a core router which is then connected to three other access routers. All the clients are connected to the access routers.

Each client establishes an independent TCP connection to the file server to fetch the file. If all the clients need to download the file at the same time, nine parallel TCP connections with file server as the source have to be started. This means that the server opens 9 different sockets to serve each TCP connection and essentially transmits the same data through each of these sockets. Thus, nine exact copies of the file available at server are sent across the link connecting the file server and the core router. The core router in turn sends 3 copies of the same data on each of the access links. Now imagine the scenario where the number of interested clients increases from nine to say around a few hundreds. This is common in case of new files (like movies) getting hosted on websites or critical security patches being made available by software companies. In that case, too much of server bandwidth and bandwidth of access routers is wasted. This leads to each client getting low download rates and bad user experience. We call this problem as the problem of data redundancy and work towards solving this by proposing a Hybrid content distribution network (CDN) which leverages the basic BitTorrent protocol.

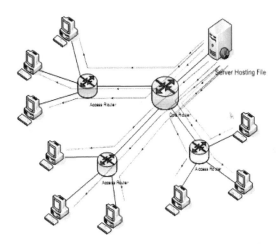

Fig. 1. Concurrent downloads cause heavy load on server bandwidth and network resources

1.2   BitTorrent Protocol

There are several systems that focus on file sharing; one widely deployed is BitTorrent [1]. BitTorrent is a "tit-for-tat" file sharing system whose operation is described in this section. The basic idea behind BitTorrent is to divide a file or set of files in several pieces also called fragments. BitTorrent distinguishes two kinds of peers, that is, down loaders and seeds. Down loaders are peers that have some fragments of the file, while seeds have a complete copy of the file. Down loaders and seeds that share a torrent form a swarm. A torrent file is usually published on the Internet as a text file, it contains the following information:

- Number of pieces, for each piece a checksum is created to guarantee its integrity, this checksum is created using the SHA1 hash function and included in this torrent file.
- The URL of a Tracker A tracker is responsible of keeping track of the down loaders and seeds that are in the swarm. When a peer needs to know which other peers or seeds are currently connected, it makes an HTTP request to the tracker asking for IP addresses and ports of other peers. In other words, the tracker is responsible to keep track of membership.

Since the file is broken into fragments, peers may share different fragments with other peers. As mentioned before, a peer is aware of other peers by querying the tracker; once it has their IP addresses, it can establish TCP connections with some of them to download or upload data. Each peer is responsible for keeping upload and downloads rates statistics of the connections it has established. This maximizes its download rate by downloading from whoever it can and make a decision of which peers to upload using a tit-for-tat approach. With this information, if one peer is not providing fragments, it may be choked, which is temporary refusal to upload to other peer.

1.3   Some Drawbacks of BitTorrent Protocol

BitTorrent protocol often sustains to following drawbacks:

- For Small files, BitTorrent tends to show higher latency and overhead.
- Even though several downloader's might be physically close to each other and downloading the same file (for example several clients on a LAN downloading a software patch) the tracker returns a random list of peers to which a new downloader should connect to. This leads to wastage of resources because of redundant downloads of same pieces by peers close to each other.

1.4   BitTorrent Location Aware Protocol

As mentioned above, the original BitTorrent protocol can lead to peers geographically distant from one another exchanging data when peers close by are also present, leading to suboptimal performance. A location-aware BitTorrent protocol has been proposed in [8]. However, the proposal is in a very lose form with no real world implementation or performance results. It requires each BitTorrent client to supply its approximate geographical location (longitude and latitude) when contacting the tracker to get the peer list. The tracker knows geographical locations of all down loaders and thus returns the list of peers to the original requesters which are closer to it, instead of returning a random list (as in case of the original Bit Torrent tracker).

Several issues arise here. Firstly, this protocol is not compatible with the original BitTorrent protocol and requires changes at the trackers. Secondly, assuming that the geographical location of a client would be known is not realistic. Thirdly, clients located close to each other geographically may not be having a fast network link between them and might be separated by several hops in terms of routing. Finally, absence of any implementation of this protocol makes one skeptical about the relative performance gain of it.

2   Performance Study of Content Distribution Models

Earlier, we talked about the content distribution models, including the Peer-to-Peer Systems model. With the help of an example scenario, we also illustrated the problem of same data being re-transmitted over internet links, leading to degraded performance and higher running costs. Now, we present the results of a large scale experimental study to understand the performance of each of the content distribution models. The study was conducted using the Emulab [9] emulation facility.

2.1   Experimental Setup

- **Network Topology:** The first step towards performing experiments on Emulab is to specify the network topology and the specification of hardware and software on each node of the network. This is done with the help of a topology specification script written in tcl programming language, in a format identical to that of NS-2 [10] (the program code is mentioned in 2.4). Internet can be assumed to be composed of following two entities.

Backbone Network: It consists of the high bandwidth, high delay, and long distance network links, which typically run across continents and countries. These backbone links are generally hosted by various Internet Service Providers (ISPs) and account for the main cost in running the internet.

High Speed LANs: Most organizations today have access to high speed local area networks (LANs) which in turn are connected to the backbone internet via particular nodes (routers). Such LANs are generally error-free and congestion free and are administered by the local organizations. Since the major cost in running Internet is in maintaining the backbone network, the ISPs are generally concerned about transferring the data across backbone links in the most cost-effective manner. The cost for a link is proportional to the amount of data (or the number of bytes) transferred across the link. In this study, we try to understand the typical amount of traffic which the ISPs need to transfer to support the different content distribution models. Also, as we show in this study, most of the current models end-up sending the same data again and again over the same links. We are interested in designing a hybrid CDN structure which restricts such retransmissions. Figure 2 illustrates the network topology used for this performance study on Emulab.

The internet backbone is made up of four core routers, named coreRouter0, coreRouter1, coreRouter2 and coreRouter3. Each of the core Routers run on the Red Hat Linux 9.0 Standard operating system. The four core routers are all connected to each other in a symmetrical manner and thus there are total six core links named corelink0 ... corelink5. Each of the core links is a 10Mb link with a 20 ms end-to-end delay and a Drop Tail queue. Three of the core routers (coreRouter0, coreRouter1 and coreRouter2) are each connected to a set of three high speed LANs via routers (router0, router1 and router2). Each of the three routers runs the Red Hat Linux 9.0 version of operating system. The link between a router and a core router is a 2Mb link with a 10 ms end-to-end delay and a Drop Tail queue. Each router is in turn connected to three 10 Mbps LANs (for example, router0 is connected to lan0, lan1 and lan2). Each LAN is composed of 4 end nodes and a switch. The nodes are named from node0 to node 35 (total 36 end-nodes/clients). A dedicated node (named seeder) is connected to coreRouter3 via a 2Mb link.

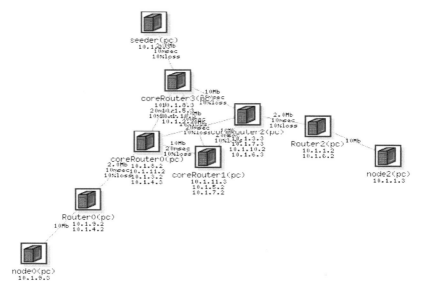

Fig. 2. The experimental setup used for the performance study

- **Performance Metrics:** In this study, we are concerned about quantifying the amount of data transmitted over backbone links in the various content distribution models. Thus, we measure two key metrics in each experiment run, for each link, in each direction:

  Number of Bytes: This represents the raw amount of data transferred over a link in a particular direction.

  Stress: This represents the ratio of number of total packets transmitted over a link and the number of unique packets transmitted over the link. For example, a stress of 2 represents a case where each packet is transferred twice over a link. As mentioned earlier, the running cost of a link for the ISP is proportional to the raw amount of data transferred over a link. A higher link stress refers to the case where higher redundant transmissions of the same data are happening over the link, thus wasting the bandwidth.

Emulab has simple support for tracing and monitoring links and LANs. For example, to trace a link:

set link0 [$ns duplex-link $nodeB $nodeA 30Mb 50ms DropTail]
$link0 trace

The default mode for tracing a link (or a LAN) is to capture just the packet headers (first 64 bytes of the packet) and store them to a tcpdump output file. In addition to capturing just the packet headers, one may also capture the entire packet:

$link0 trace packet

By default, all packets traversing the link are captured by the tracing agent. To narrow the scope of the packets that are captured, one may supply any valid tcpdump style expression:

$link0 trace monitor "icmp or tcp"

One may also set the **snaplen** for a link or LAN, which sets the number of bytes that, will be captured by each of the trace agents:

$link0 trace_snaplen 128

In our experiments, we set the snaplen to 1600 bytes. For each link (say link0, between nodeA and nodeB), 2 trace files of interest are generated by tcpdump: **trace nodeA-link0. recv** and **trace nodeB-link0.recv.** Here, the first trace file stores the packets sent by nodeA to nodeB over link0, while the second file stores the packets sent by nodeB to nodeA over link0. To analyze the tcpdump trace files, we modified a well-known tool tcptrace. We added a module in the tcptrace code to calculate the MD5 checksum of payload of each tcp packet and store the checksums of all payloads in a file. The number of checksums is equal to the total number of packets transmitted over a link. We then calculate the number of unique checksums in the file, which represents the number of unique packets transmitted. The ratio of these two gives the link stress. Also, the total number of bytes from payloads of all tcp packets on a link can be easily calculated from tcptrace.

In our experiment we designed a BitTorrent client which supports the following:

- Must support a console based interface to allow remote execution over Emulab nodes.
- We preferred it to be in java so that Datagram sockets could be used to extend it to support IP multicast [11].

2.2   Performance Evaluation

Performance evaluation of Peer to Peer and WWW model is illustrated below:

●   **Link Statistics for the File Download Using BitTorrent**

Link	Direction	No. of Bytes	Stress
coreLink0	coreRouter0 — > coreRouter1	4.1 MB	5.712
coreLink0	coreRouter1 — > coreRouter0	3.6 MB	6.078
coreLink1	coreRouter2 — > coreRouter1	3.9 MB	5.429
coreLink1	coreRouter1 — > coreRouter2	3.1 MB	5.896
coreLink2	coreRouter0 — > coreRouter2	2.8 MB	6.368
coreLink2	coreRouter2 — > coreRouter0	4.0 MB	5.221
coreLink3	coreRouter0 — > coreRouter3	15 KB	2.800
coreLink3	coreRouter3 — > coreRouter0	0.8 MB	1.544
coreLink4	coreRouter1 — > coreRouter3	16 KB	3.620
coreLink4	coreRouter3 — > coreRouter1	1.2 MB	1.855
coreLink5	coreRouter2 — > coreRouter3	15 KB	2.880
coreLink5	coreRouter3 — > coreRouter2	0.9 MB	1.366
link0	coreRouter0 — > router0	8.5 MB	6.630
link0	router0 — > coreRouter0	6.9 MB	7.013
link1	coreRouter1 — > router1	9.3 MB	7.155
link1	router1 — > coreRouter1	6.7 MB	7.300
link2	coreRouter2 — > router2	6.8 MB	6.516
link2	router2 — > coreRouter2	8.0 MB	6.933
link3	coreRouter3 — > seeder	47 KB	3.184
link3	seeder — > coreRouter3	3.0 MB	2.797

Fig. 3. The experimental setup used for the performance study

In the P2P model, clients download the file in a collaborative manner. Instead of depending only on the seeder for the file download, each client fetches data packets from other clients as well. Thus, in this case, clients have TCP connections between them, in addition to TCP connections with the seeder. In P2P model, since clients are also responsible for uploading packets to other clients, thus the uplink capacity is also used in P2P model as compared to the www model which is shown in figure 4 using Wget [12].

All the links see data transfers of the order of 4-6 MB, not like the case of WWW model, where several links had to transfer as much data as 14 MB. Data transfer happens in both directions (uplink and downlink). The other important observation is regarding the link stress. We observe that link stress values are smaller in case of the core links. This means that there is lesser number of duplicate packet transmissions happening over the internet links, thus avoiding the wastage of resources. This is due to the fact that each client observes the data pieces which are available with other clients and fetches them as well, instead of fetching pieces always from the seeder.

Link	Direction	No. of Bytes	Stress
coreLink0	coreRouter0 − > coreRouter1	0	0
coreLink0	coreRouter1 − > coreRouter0	0	0
coreLink1	coreRouter2 − > coreRouter1	0	0
coreLink1	coreRouter1 − > coreRouter2	0	0
coreLink2	coreRouter0 − > coreRouter2	0	0
coreLink2	coreRouter2 − > coreRouter0	0	0
coreLink3	coreRouter0 − > coreRouter3	1.3 KB	12.000
coreLink3	coreRouter3 − > coreRouter0	14.5 MB	11.585
coreLink4	coreRouter1 − > coreRouter3	1.3 KB	12.000
coreLink4	coreRouter3 − > coreRouter1	14.5 MB	4.573
coreLink5	coreRouter2 − > coreRouter3	1.3 KB	13.000
coreLink5	coreRouter3 − > coreRouter2	14.5 MB	4.485
link0	coreRouter0 − > router0	14.5 MB	11.585
link0	router0 − > coreRouter0	1.3 KB	12.000
link1	coreRouter1 − > router1	14.5 MB	4.573
link1	router1 − > coreRouter1	1.3 KB	12.000
link2	coreRouter2 − > router2	14.5 MB	4.485
link2	router2 − > coreRouter2	1.3 KB	13.000
link3	coreRouter3 − > seeder	3.9 KB	37.000
link3	seeder − > coreRouter3	43.6 MB	8.315

Fig. 4. Link Statistics for file download using Wget

2.3   IP-Multicast as Content Distribution Model

IP Multicast is a particularly attractive alternative for content distribution in such scenarios. All the clients can initially send IGMP request messages to join a multicast group and the source can multicast the data on this group. Since routers are aware of the physical topology and positions of clients, the data traverses the shortest path to reach each of the clients, guaranteeing optimal download time. Although such an approach is promising, it is not viable in today's Internet because of lack of support of IP Multicast on Internet. This means that two nodes on the Internet do not necessarily have a route between them which is IP Multicast enabled **There are several reasons why IP Multicast is not available on the Internet**. These include:

• Most routers on the Internet lack support for IP Multicast. Recollect that to support IP Multicast, a router needs to perform several additional operations like duplication of packets with PIM, IGMP support, Multicast forwarding etc. The routers available on Internet simply do not have resources or capabilities to perform all such operations. Upgrading such existing routers is clearly infeasible.
• Congestion control schemes are not well defined for multicast.
• Pricing policies in multicast are not clear. Hence, there are no incentives for the ISPs to be interested in deploying multicast support in the networks.

Therefore, it is almost clear that utilizing IP-level multicast for large scale content distribution in above mentioned scenarios is not feasible. The problem of IP Multicast as an unreliable protocol is that it works over UDP. This means that there is no guarantee that a packet multicast over UDP will be successfully received by other clients. Since IP Multicast does not have any mechanisms for rate control and checking packet losses (due to random errors etc.), it is not necessary that pieces shared by clients would be received by all other clients on the island. The clients which have low received buffer or which are busy with other operations often are unable to completely receive packets sent over multicast. We tackle the above problem in providing more efficient data sharing through the concept of 3-way Hand shake [13] and propose a method which co-exist with the standard BitTorrent protocol and leverage IP Multicast to distribute downloaded pieces to other BitTorrent clients on the same network.

2.4   Program Code

The NS-2 script used in the experiment is shown below:

```
#generated by Netbuild 1.03
set ns [new Simulator]
source tb_compat.tcl

set coreRouter0 [$ns node]
set coreRouter1 [$ns node]
set coreRouter2 [$ns node]
set coreRouter3 [$ns node]
set seeder [$ns node]
set Router0 [$ns node]
set node0 [$ns node]
set Router2 [$ns node]
set node2 [$ns node]

set link0 [$ns duplex-link $coreRouter0 $coreRouter3 10Mb
20ms DropTail]
tb-set-link-loss $link0 0.1
set link1 [$ns duplex-link $coreRouter0 $coreRouter1 10Mb
20ms DropTail]
tb-set-link-loss $link1 0.1
set link2 [$ns duplex-link $coreRouter0 $coreRouter2 10Mb
20ms DropTail]
tb-set-link-loss $link2 0.1
set link3 [$ns duplex-link $coreRouter1 $coreRouter3 10Mb
20ms DropTail]
tb-set-link-loss $link3 0.1
set link4 [$ns duplex-link $coreRouter1 $coreRouter2 10Mb
20ms DropTail]
tb-set-link-loss $link4 0.1
set link5 [$ns duplex-link $coreRouter2 $coreRouter3 10Mb
20ms DropTail]
tb-set-link-loss $link5 0.1
```

```
set link6 [$ns duplex-link $coreRouter3 $seeder 2Mb 10ms
DropTail]
tb-set-link-loss $link6 0.1
set link7 [$ns duplex-link $Router0 $coreRouter0 2Mb 10ms
DropTail]
tb-set-link-loss $link7 0.1
set link8 [$ns duplex-link $Router2 $coreRouter2 2Mb 10ms
DropTail]
tb-set-link-loss $link8 0.1


set lan0 [$ns make-lan "$Router0 $node0 " 10Mb 0ms]
set lan1 [$ns make-lan "$Router2 $node2 " 10Mb 0ms]


$ns rtproto Static
$ns run
#netbuild-generated ns file ends.
```

2.5   Our Approach

We used a highly modular approach to the problem. We figured out that there are basically 5 parts to the program:

1. **Database Manager:** This takes care of the list of chunks of different files available on the network.
2. **Chunk Maker/Assembler:** This creates chunks of a file and maintains a mechanism for testing the integrity of each chunk. It also assembles the chunks into a complete file when all the chunks of a file have been downloaded.
3. **Chunk Sender/Receiver:** This communicates on a single port with another host on a defined port and transfers file reliably. This throws back problems if encountered in the process or flags a success message if it is successful.
4. **User Interface:** This is where the user interacts with the program. We have 2 such interfaces, one is a GUI and another is a console one. Here the user can ask to share a file on the network and fetch a file from the network.
5. **The Head:** This interacts with every other part and decides what to do when. It basically deploys the work to other modules and also performs a 3-way handshake before a communication begins on a defined port using the Chunk Sender/Receiver.

Multicast packets on an island can be lost or delayed due to two things:

1. The clients and links on a LAN show abnormal behavior (due to load or miss-configuration) leading to random packet losses.
2. There is congestion on the LANs due to other heavy traffic being exchanged by clients, e.g., VoIP etc.

To overcome this problem we applied the method of 3-way handshake which is illustrated below:

The tracker when requested to fetch a file from the network, it does the following:

a. Asks the Managed Hash Table for the information of the locations of the chunks.
b. Now for each chunk, it contacts the Tracker of another host sending a Type1 packet requesting a chunk.
c. The peer host's tracker sends back a packet which can be:

• Type2 packet: This says that the peer host has accepted the request and it is designating a port for sending the chunk.
• Type3a packet: This says that the peer host does not have the chunk requested and thus is negating the connection.
• Type3b packet: This says that the peer host has the chunks but currently does not have any free ports to take the request.

d. If Type3a is received then the tracker tries to request the file from another source, if available.
e. If Type3b is received then the tracker would look for other sources and if it runs out of other sources it ask the same host after some time.
f. If Type2 packet is received, the Tracker sends a Type4 packet that carries the information about which port of this user would be listening for the packets and starts the Downloader.
g. On reception of Type4, the Up-loader is called.
h. If on any of these communications, a timeout is faced, it is gracefully handled
Thus we achieve a 3-way handshake similar to TCP for starting up the chunk transfer.

3   Results

For the sake of completeness, the topology is shown in Fig 2. There are two types of links in this topology:

Core links: which serve the traffic across the internet by connecting the **core routers**; and **Access links**; which are used to provide internet access to the islands consisting of various high-speed LAN's. Since the two types of links carry different type of traffic, we show the evaluation of both types separately.

Each island in our experimental topology consists of 3 high-speed (10 Mbps) LANs. All the LANs are connected to each other via the access router (i.e., router0, router1 or router2). Each of the access routers runs the Red Hat operating system. In order to allow IP Multicast across different LANs on the same island, we run mrouted [14] on each of the access routers. The mrouted utility is an implementation of the Distance-Vector Multicast Routing Protocol (DVMRP), an earlier version of which is specified in RFC-1075 [15].It maintains topological knowledge via a distance-vector routing protocol (like RIP, described in RFC-1058 [16]), upon which it implements a multicast datagram forwarding algorithm called Reverse Path Multicasting. The mrouted utility forwards a multicast datagram along a shortest (reverse) path tree rooted at the subnet on which the datagram originates. The multicast delivery tree may be thought of as a broadcast delivery tree that has been pruned back so that it does not extend beyond those sub networks that have members of the destination group. Hence, datagrams are not forwarded along those branches which have no listeners of the multicast group. The IP time-to-live of a multicast datagram can be used to limit the range of multicast datagrams. Thus, any multicast packet in one of the LANs reaches all other LANs on the same island, provided there are clients on the other LANs who have subscribed to the corresponding multicast group .Also, we set the TTL value of multicast packets to 3 to allow them to cross multiple levels of multicast enabled routers. Note that a TTL value of 1 means that packets are limited to the same subnet.

The seeder serves a file of size 1 MB. All the results reported in this section have been obtained after proper averaging over 5 to 10 runs of each experiment. Figure 5 below shows the comparison between the bandwidth utilization of BitTorrent client and the Hybrid CDN. Note that the steeper the plot is, the faster is the completion of download for all the clients. In the above figure 100 % of clients complete their download within 30 seconds while using Hybrid CDN. It takes about 60 seconds for all the nodes to complete their download using Bit-Torrent. Figure 6 show the effect of random link losses, a random packet loss module is installed in each of the LANs, whose packet loss rate can be configured. We varied the packet loss rate of each LAN from 0% to 5% and repeated the experiments for each case to measure the various performance metrics for both Hybrid CDN and BitTorrent. Experimental Client's download time increase after 4% packet loss, due to the fact that during multicasting maximum of the packets get lost and they are retransmitted using unicasting. However, random packet loss percentages as high as 4% are quite rare in most LANs today and thus represent an unnatural scenario. With the more common scenarios, Hybrid CDN is shown to have a better performance over BitTorrent.

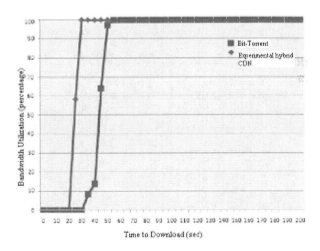

Fig. 5. Cumulative Distribution Function of time for download by each client

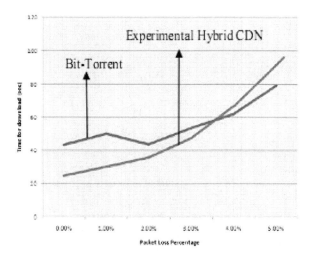

Fig. 6. Time for download with Packet Loss Percentage of each LAN

Finally, Figure 7 shows the variation of average link stress with packet loss percentage. Stress on the internet links increases with random packet loss due to the higher number of TCP retransmissions to deliver data across the LAN network. Note that more retransmission means same data packets traversing internet links again and again. To model the scenario of congestion in each island, we start a Constant-Bit Rate (CBR) traffic source on each of the LANs which send the traffic to one the clients on another LAN in the same island. Thus, each island has 3 CBR traffic sources. The rate of CBR traffic for each source is varied from 0 Mbps to 10 Mbps to model the severity of congestion. Figure 8 shows the variation of average time for download over all clients with increasing value of CBR traffic rates.

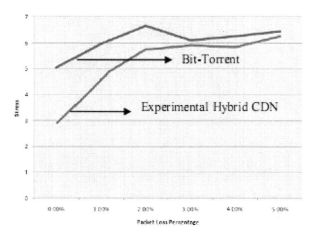

Fig. 7. Link stress with Packet Loss Percentage of each LAN

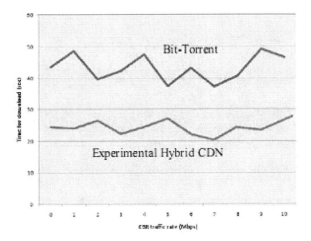

Fig. 8. Time for download with varying congestion level

4   Conclusion

We obtained the following three important results with the Hybrid CDN Model:

- Reduction in download time of each client using Hybrid CDN by 48% over Bit- Torrent and by 86% over WWW Protocol.
- Reduction in traffic load on Internet links and ISPs.
- Reduction in the wastage of resources like bandwidth due   to redundant packet.

Downloading time is the most critical performance metric for normal Internet users, whose experience with the system is largely determined by how fast they can Download   file   from the Internet. Also, recent applications of Peer-to-Peer systems like distributing the software updates and the images of operating systems, etc., over large networks spread across a geographically distributed area depend heavily on the download time for each computer. The delay in download in [7] can be overcome by the use of Hybrid CDN like model leveraging the IP-Multicast and Bit-torrent protocol applicability. Most ISPs today observe heavy traffic load on their Internet links due to increasing number of users using Peer-to-Peer file sharing systems.   Due to competition, ISPs are forced to reduce tariff continuously resulting in reduction in the margins of profit. However, with more users migrating to a system like Hybrid CDN, the load on ISP resources (Internet links) can be reduced by as much as 65%, for the comparable amount of downloads by end clients. Thus, the profit margins of ISPs can be increased heavily if they encourage more users to switch to such type of system. The load on access links is also reduced by similar proportions, the   island   owners have to pay for the Internet access links, on the basis of the usage of such links. With reduced usage of access links, the Internet consumption bills for island owners can be reduced considerably, which in turn will be a motivation for them to enable IP Multicast support on their networks requiring software (and in some cases hardware) upgrades. Thus, such models are economically sustainable.

Finally, our work is distinct from other similar research because of the following reasons:

Standard compliance: The proposed method is interoperable with BitTorrent protocol. It only requires changes at the end client level, unlike other solutions, which would need network wide support.

Actual Implementation: In place of theoretical results or Network simulations, we resorted to actually implementing a prototype system of our method and have evaluated it on a large scale real network.

References

1. Cohen, B.: Incentives build robustness in Bit-Torrent. In: Proc. of the First Workshop on the Economics of Peer-to-Peer Systems (2003)
2. Leibowitz, N., Bergman, A., Ben-Shaul, R., Havit, A.: Are file swapping networks cacheable? Characterizing p2p traffic. In: Proc. of the 7th Int. WWW Caching Workshop (2002)
3. Karagiannis, T., Rodriguez, P., Papagiannaki, K.: Should internet service providers fear peer-assisted content distribution. In: Proc. of IMC, pp. 63–76 (2005)
4. Wierzbicki, A., Leibowitz, N., Ripeanu, M., Wozniak, R.: Cache replacement policies revisited: the case of p2p traffic. In: Proc. of IEEE International Symposium on Cluster Computing and the Grid (CCGrid), pp. 182–189 (2004)
5. Saleh, O., Hefeeda, M.: Modeling and caching of peer-to-peer traffic. In: Proc. of IEEE International Conference on Network Protocols, pp. 249–258 (2006)
6. Vahdat, A., Yocum, K., Walsh, K., Mahadevan, P., Kostic, D., Chase, J., Becker, D.: Scalability and accuracy in a large-scale network emulator. In: Proc. of OSDI (2002)
7. BitTorrent used to update workstationsm,
   `http://torrentfreak.com/university-usesutorrent-080306`
8. BitTorrent location-aware protocol 1.0 specification,
   `http://wiki.theory.org/BitTorrentLocation-awareProtocol1.0Specification`
9. Emulab documentation, `http://www.emulab.net/doc.php3`
10. The network simulator - ns-2, `http://www.isi.edu/nsnam/ns`
11. IP-Multicast,
    `http://www.cisco.com/en/US/docs/internetworking/technology/handbook/IPMulti.html`
12. Gnu Wget, `http://www.gnu.org/software/wget`
13. 3-way Handshake,
    `http://www.inetdaemon.com/tutorials/internet/tcp/3-way_handshake.html`
14. How to set up Linux for multicast routing,
    `http://www.jukie.net/bart/multicast/Linux-MroutedMiniHOWTO.html`
15. Distance vector multicast routing protocol,
    `http://www.ietf.org/rfc/rfc1075.txt`
16. Routing information protocol, `http://www.ietf.org/rfc/rfc1058.txt`

Traffic Dynamics Online Estimation
Based on Measured Autocorrelation

Con Tran and Zbigniew Dziong

Department of Electrical Engineering,
Ecole de Technologie Superieure
Montreal, Canada
con.tran.1@ens.etsmtl.ca,
Zbigniew.Dziong@etsmtl.ca

Abstract. Estimation of traffic demand is a major requirement in telecommunication network operation and management. As traffic level typically varies with time, online applications such as dynamic routing and dynamic capacity allocation need to accurately estimate traffic in real time to optimize network operations. Traffic mean can be estimated using known filtering methods such as moving averages or exponential smoothing. In this paper, we analyze online traffic estimation based on exponential smoothing, with focus on response and stability. Novel approaches, based on traffic arrivals autocorrelation and cumulative distribution functions, are proposed to adapt estimation parameters to varying traffic trends. Performance of proposed approaches is compared to other adaptive exponential smoothing methods found in the literature. The results show that our approach based on autocorrelation function gives the best combined response-stability performance.

Keywords: Traffic measurement, estimation adaptation, trend detection, exponential smoothing; autocorrelation.

1 Introduction

An important need in network operation and management is the estimation of traffic demand. Depending on the network application, this demand is usually defined by the average arrival rate of data packets or user connections. Depending on the network management function performed, the network provider estimates this average rate using different techniques. Network planning targets a long timescale (months, years), and in this case, arrival rate is estimated in an offline manner based on past traffic statistics and marketing forecasts. Once the network is deployed, call routing and bandwidth allocation occur on a shorter timescale (minutes, hours) and can be classified as online management functions. At this timescale, typical network traffic show diurnal variation in average arrivals corresponding to user activity patterns [1], [2]: daily traffic is non stationary; rather it will go through stationary periods of quiet and busy traffic, joined by transition periods of trend traffic. Static bandwidth allocation based on peak demand would waste network resource in periods of low

I. Tomkos et al. (Eds.): BROADNETS 2010, LNICST 66, pp. 55–68, 2012.

traffic. Conversely, allocation based on the mean demand for the day will cause network congestion and service degradation in high traffic periods. For continued optimal performance, the online network functions must adapt to traffic diurnal variation. It is then crucial for network operators to have a traffic demand estimation method that is simple to be operated online, yet accurate to provide continuous efficient network optimization.

With the advent of adaptive state dependent [3] and revenue-maximizing [4], [5] traffic routing algorithms, traffic demand estimation algorithms such as [6] started to be proposed. Later on, with the possibility of adaptive bandwidth provisioning for network continued optimization (as in MPLS tunnels, virtual and overlay networks), several more online demand measurement and estimation approaches were proposed [7]-[12]. As arrival rate estimation is generally affected by measurement noise, several filtering techniques have been proposed to infer the average rate. In [8], an approach based on the Autoregressive Integrated Moving Average (ARIMA) is used to support bandwidth provisioning. In [9], approximate filtering algorithms based on general birth and death stochastic model were presented. In [10], Kalman filter theory is used in a traffic optimal estimation scheme to forecast link capacity requirements.

Simpler methods well fit for online computation, such as moving averages (MA) [11], weighted average (WA) [12] and exponential smoothing (ES) aka. EWMA (exponentially weighted moving average) [11], [13], [14], [15] have commonly been used to estimate and predict time series average. It was shown in [11] that one can obtain similar estimation accuracy from MA and ES by selecting appropriate controlling parameter values. In this paper, we focus on online estimation of network link traffic demand using modified exponential smoothing methods. We propose two new approaches for improving ES that are based on traffic trend estimation. In one, the trend is estimated based on the traffic arrival process autocorrelation function (acf); in the other, it is based on the process cumulative distribution function (cdf).

The algorithms presented in [16] address a similar problem and the proposed algorithms use an iterative procedure involving an ES scheme. The difference is that we estimate link traffic and use adaptive ES while [16] estimates path traffic and uses fixed ES. The drawback of the path approach is that for large networks the high paths cardinality can overwhelm online path demand estimation. In such networks, a decomposition of network into link processes [5], [11], reduces problem complexity, and link demand estimation can then be used to support online network optimization.

For the performance evaluation of online traffic demand estimation, we propose to use the following two criteria. When demand changes, *estimation responsiveness* criterion measures the lag of the estimated value in reaching the changed average arrival rate. A small lag allows faster reaction to traffic demand changes. Conversely, during periods of stationary demand, *estimation stability* criterion measures the deviation of estimated values from the invariant average arrival rate. In this case, stable estimations avoid unnecessary network operation changes, therefore limiting the volume of signaling messages and unnecessary actions in the network. We will define metrics for these criteria in this paper. Using these metrics, the proposed adaptive ES estimation approaches are compared to static as well as to other previously proposed adaptive ES estimations.

The rest of this paper is organized as follows. In Section 2, we present a traffic model considered in this work. Section 3 summarizes known estimation and forecasting methods that are based on exponential smoothing, and presents our new approaches. In Section 4, we define metrics and evaluate performance of our approaches, by comparing them to existing methods. Section 5 concludes and gives a direction of future research.

2   Model for Traffic Demand and Estimation

Internet traffic patterns and general characteristics were reported by Thompson in [1]. The majority of traffic graphs revealed that both the byte and flow volume follow clear 24-hour patterns that repeat daily over the week. In general, the patterns include two levels of traffic, high during day time and low during night time, showing a difference of as much as 300% - 500%. Transition periods between the levels can last a few hours. Fig. 1 reproduces (from existing literature) real one day traffic trace examples taken at different locations: a) flow volume monitored at a major U.S. East Coast city [1], b) link data traffic collected at University of Missouri-Kansas City [8], c) mean connection arrival rates for various network applications gathered at a Lawrence Berkeley Lab gateway [17]. These and more traces found at the WAND WITS web site [18] confirm the daily pattern.

In this paper, we will estimate traffic demand defined by the average connection arrival rate. Based on the above real traffic patterns, we build a connection arrivals model, shown in Fig. 1d, which we will use for evaluation of the demand estimation. The model presents two stationary periods where average traffic stays around a low and a high level, respectively, and two trend periods where traffic transitions between the mentioned levels. This model simulates the successive stationary and non-stationary periods characterizing the real traffic patterns. Below is the definition of parameters used in the model (expressed at time t):

- $\overline{\lambda}_t$: Average arrival rate (solid line in Fig. 1d). This denotes the theoretic average that should be estimated. This average is invariant in stationary periods, and it follows a linear trend in non-stationary periods.

- $\widetilde{\lambda}_t$: Measured arrival rate (dashed line in Fig. 1d).

- e_t : stochastic noise on arrival rates.

- λ'_t : Trend of arrival rate ($\lambda'_t = d\overline{\lambda}_t / dt$).

- λ_t : Estimated arrival rate

The following set of equations defines the model:

$$\overline{\lambda}_t = \overline{\lambda}_{t_i} + \lambda'_{t_i}(t - t_i) , \tag{1}$$

$$\widetilde{\lambda}_t = \overline{\lambda}_t + e_t , \tag{2}$$

$$\lambda_t = f_a(\widetilde{\lambda}) . \tag{3}$$

where trend λ'_{t_i} is nil in stationary periods and is assumed to be constant during a trend period; and arrival rate estimator f_a is a function of a vector of present and past values of measured arrival rate.

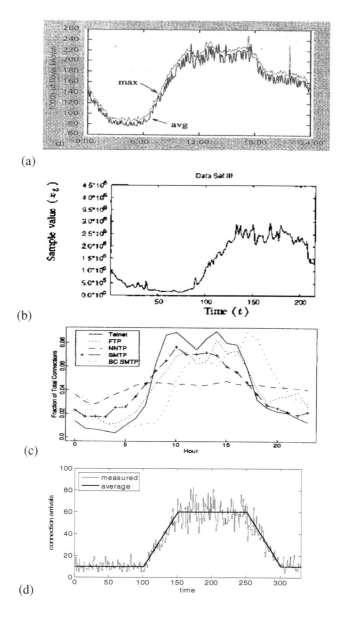

Fig. 1. One day traces of Internet traffic: a) link flow volume at U.S. East Coast [1],
b) link traffic at University of Missouri-Kansas City [8],
c) mean connection arrival rates at Lawrence Berkeley Lab gateway [17],
d) simulation model of demand (connection arrivals) pattern.

In this model, time and traffic demand are expressed in generic time units, and number of arrivals per time unit, respectively. Average traffic arrival rates $\overline{\lambda}_t$ show the low and high traffic levels with transition periods between them. Arrival rate trends λ'_t and trend period durations form the parameters of the pattern. Arrival rates $\tilde{\lambda}_t$ measured at regular time intervals follow a Poisson distribution with mean corresponding to $\overline{\lambda}_t$. $\overline{\lambda}_t$ and $\tilde{\lambda}_t$ can be generated to realize the patterned demand.

The estimation objective is to achieve values λ_t as close as possible to $\overline{\lambda}_t$. This translates into λ_t being stable (close to invariant $\overline{\lambda}_t$) in stationary demand periods, and responding quickly to changes of $\overline{\lambda}_t$ in transition periods.

3   Demand Estimation by Exponential Smoothing

Average arrival rate estimations are performed at regular time intervals as traffic demand evolves. Exponential smoothing is a well known technique that can be used to produce moving weighted averages of a time series. Different forms of ES have been documented in the literature. Applied to our estimation of average arrival rate, the *Simple ES* (SES) is formulated as follows:

$$\lambda_t = \alpha_t \tilde{\lambda}_t + (1-\alpha_t)\lambda_{t-1}. \tag{4}$$

where α_t is the level smoothing parameter, $0 < \alpha_t < 1$. The *Double ES* (DES) formulation introduces a second equation to account for the trend T_t in the time series, resulting in the set of equations:

$$\lambda_t = \alpha_t \tilde{\lambda}_t + (1-\alpha_t)(\lambda_{t-1} + T_{t-1}), \tag{5a}$$

$$T_t = \gamma_t(\lambda_t - \lambda_{t-1}) + (1-\gamma_t)T_{t-1}. \tag{5b}$$

where γ_t is the trend smoothing parameter, $0 < \gamma_t < 1$.

Performance of the online estimation, characterized by its stability and responsiveness, depends on the values of the smoothing parameters α_t and γ_t that can be fixed or adaptive. For example in SES, a low α_t will effectively dampen random $\tilde{\lambda}_t$ variations, giving better stability. On the other hand, a high α_t allows ES to better follow changes in traffic demand, improving estimation response [11]. In this section, we first summarize a selection of available methods for assigning α_t and γ_t. Then, we present our proposed approaches for adaptive ES based on the arrival process autocorrelation and cumulative distribution function. Each method will be identified with the convention *ES type-parameter type*, where *ES type* is *SES* or *DES* and *parameter type* denotes the smoothing parameters assignment strategy.

3.1   Literature Review of ES Methods

Currently available methods for choosing parameters α_t and γ_t include fixed and adaptive parameters [13]. A total of 24 ES techniques were reported in 1982 [19]. *Adaptive Extended ES* (AEES [14] and AEES-C [15]) were later developed which provide improved accuracy. For performance comparison with our proposed approaches, we selected two SES methods for its simplicity, and two AEES methods for its improved accuracy.

SES with fixed α_t **(SES-fix).** In this basic method, parameter α_t is fixed. α_t can be determined by model-fitting using the time series historical data. As mentioned earlier, a tradeoff between estimation stability and responsiveness is dependent on the value chosen for α_t.

SES with adapting α_t **(SES-err).** In this method, as in following adaptive methods, α_t is adapted at each estimation period as the time series evolves. For its improved accuracy provided, we chose to use the same adaptation formula, based on previous period error that was proposed for AEES:

$$\alpha_t = \left| (\lambda_{t-1} - \tilde{\lambda}_t) / \tilde{\lambda}_t \right|. \tag{6}$$

AEES (DES-err). This method as proposed by Mentzer applies to time series with level, trend and seasonal components [14]. Since seasonal variations are beyond the timescale of online estimation periods, we ignore that component and apply this technique to DES (5a), (5b). α_t is adapted by (6) and γ_t is fixed. Reported AEES tests in general showed better accuracy than previously available ES methods.

AEES-C (DES-derr). This method [15] extended AEES by also adapting trend smoothing parameter γ_t based on previous trend estimation error:

$$\gamma_t = \left| (T_{t-1} - T_{t-2}) / T_{t-2} \right|. \tag{7}$$

It was reported that accuracy performance comparisons between AEES-C and AEES were not consistent, but AEES-C was better in 10 of 14 cited test conditions. Given the double error based adaptations of both α_t and γ_t, this method is identified as *DES-derr*.

3.2   New Adaptive ES Approaches

As shown in Fig. 1, traffic demand will go through stationary and trend periods. In stationary periods, changes in arrival rate measurements $\tilde{\lambda}_t$ result solely from noise e_t (2), and use of *SES* with a low α_t as estimator function f_a (3) will provide better stability. In trend periods, the portion of change in $\tilde{\lambda}_t$ due to the trend λ'_t (1) increases with the trend amplitude. To better respond to that change, α_t in *SES* should be increased and therefore should be a function of the trend.

Trend Evaluation. As the trend is a key parameter influencing online estimation by adaptive ES, we need methods to detect and evaluate it. We propose to use the following two measures:

a) Process Autocorrelation Function (acf). The trend of the time series formed by the N successive arrival rate measurements to time t can be indicated by its autocorrelation coefficient at lag one r_t:

$$r_t = \frac{\sum_{n=t-(N-1)}^{t-1} (\tilde{\lambda}_n - \hat{\lambda}_t)(\tilde{\lambda}_{n+1} - \hat{\lambda}_t)/(N-1)}{\sum_{n=t-(N-1)}^{t} (\tilde{\lambda}_n - \hat{\lambda}_t)^2/N}. \tag{8}$$

where $\hat{\lambda}_t = \sum_{n=t-(N-1)}^{t} \tilde{\lambda}_n / N$ is the mean of the N measurements. With a large N, when the time series is completely random (nil trend), r_t is approximately $N(0, 1/N)$ and is then expected to be within $\pm 2/\sqrt{N}$ in 19 out of 20 instances [20]. When the series has a trend, it can be shown by experimentation that r_t is a function of trend amplitude $|\lambda_t'|$ and N. For given N, r_t increases with $|\lambda_t'|$.

b) Process Cumulative Distribution Function (cdf). In a time series of measurements of random Poisson distributed arrival rates, measured values $\tilde{\lambda}_t$ are concentrated near mean rate $\overline{\lambda}_t$. When a trend is present in the series, it will cause $\tilde{\lambda}_t$ to deviate further from the mean. The probability p_t that the arrival rate random variable x_t is at measured $\tilde{\lambda}_t$ or further from the mean can be obtained with the cdf (we assume that estimated λ_{t-1} approximates $\overline{\lambda}_t$). For the case of $\tilde{\lambda}_t > \lambda_{t-1}$:

$$p_t = \Pr(x_t > \tilde{\lambda}_t \mid \tilde{\lambda}_t > \lambda_{t-1}) = \frac{1 - \Pr(x_t \le \tilde{\lambda}_t)}{1 - \Pr(x_t \le \lambda_{t-1})} = \frac{1 - cdf(\tilde{\lambda}_t)}{1 - cdf(\lambda_{t-1})}. \tag{9}$$

and the case of $\tilde{\lambda}_t \le \lambda_{t-1}$:

$$p_t = \Pr(x_t \le \tilde{\lambda}_t \mid \tilde{\lambda}_t \le \lambda_{t-1}) = cdf(\tilde{\lambda}_t)/cdf(\lambda_{t-1}). \tag{10}$$

p_t is close to 1 when $\tilde{\lambda}_t$ is close to the mean λ_{t-1}, it decreases as $\tilde{\lambda}_t$ is further away. Therefore, the function p_t (of measured $\tilde{\lambda}_t$) can be used as a stationarity indicator, and its complement $1-p_t$ as a trend indicator.

The value range for both the *acf* and *cdf* trend indicators is [0..1]. Online measurements of the indicators, applied to our traffic model (Fig. 1d), are shown in Fig. 2. We can see that both indicators move to higher levels when traffic moves from stationary to trend periods.

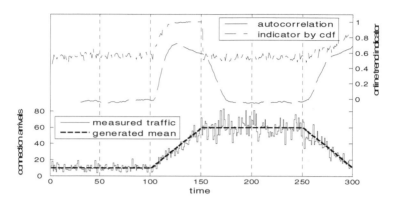

Fig. 2. Trend measurements based on autocorrelation and cdf

Trend Indicator Based Adaptive ES (SES-acf, SES-cdf). In this subsection, we propose two new ES adaptation approaches for dynamic traffic online estimation. The approaches are based on SES (4) and use a function of the trend indicator, r_t (acf approach) or $1-p_t$ (cdf approach), to adapt parameter α_t in (4). As mentioned, α_t should be low in nil trend traffic to provide stability, and increase when the trend increases to become more responsive to traffic demand changes.

a) Exponential Adaptation Function. Use of a simple exponential function of the trend indicator will limit α_t in stationary traffic and provide good stability. Let I_t denote the trend indicator, representing r_t (acf approach) or $1-p_t$ (cdf approach). The function can be expressed as:

$$\alpha_t = A_R^{1-I_t} .$$ (11)

where the base, $0 < A_R < 1$, is a constant chosen based on historical traffic data to provide estimation stability in stationary periods traffic. An example of this exponential function of I_t (case of $A_R=0.1$) is shown in Fig. 3.

b) Logistic Adaptation Function. In the trend indicator range, an exponential function (11) increases slowly with the indicator causing slow estimation response in trend traffic. Given the dual objectives of stability and responsiveness, a steeper change in α_t is needed when traffic transitions between stationary and trend periods. The logistic function fits well with this requirement, and in addition its parameters provide ease of control of the function inflexion point. We propose to use the following logistic based adaptation function:

$$\alpha_t = 0.05 + logistic(I_t) = 0.05 + [0.85/(1 + l_a e^{-l_b I_t})] .$$ (12)

where l_a and l_b are parameters determining the inflexion point $\left(\dfrac{\ln(l_a)}{l_b}, 0.05 + \dfrac{0.85}{2} \right)$.

Function (12) presents asymptotes at $\alpha_t = 0.05$ and $\alpha_t = 0.90$, and the inflexion point can be chosen based on historical trend indicator data. For example, logistic based functions used in the case of traffic and trend indicator of Fig. 2 are shown in Fig. 3. When compared to the exponential function, we can see that the logistic functions present distinct α_t levels for low and high trend indicator values, with a much steeper transition between them. Fig. 3 also shows distinct α_t increase start points (obtained by l_a and l_b choices) for the *acf* and the *cdf* indicator cases, corresponding to the respective indicator characteristics from Fig. 2.

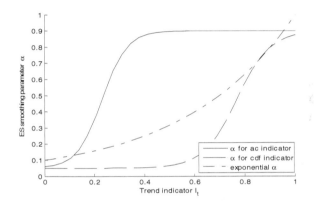

Fig. 3. SES parameter α as exponential and logistic functions of trend

4   Performance Analysis

In this section, performance of our proposed demand estimation methods based on logistic function of the trend indicator, under different traffic levels and trends, is evaluated by comparison with existing methods (Section 3.1). Poisson distributed traffic is generated following the model of Fig. 1d. The methods are compared under the previously mentioned stability and responsiveness criteria, whose metrics are defined below.

4.1   Performance Metrics

Estimation Stability in Stationary Traffic. In stationary traffic periods, a stable estimate of the average arrival rate is advantageous as it avoids unnecessary network routing and capacity allocation changes, therefore limiting the amount of control traffic in the network. We define estimation stability, denoted by σ_S, as the mean absolute deviation of the estimated arrival rate λ_t from the true (generated) average rate $\overline{\lambda}_t$, normalized by the standard deviation of measured arrival rates $\widetilde{\lambda}_t$:

$$\sigma_S = \sqrt{\frac{1}{n_s}\sum_{t=1}^{n_s}(\lambda_t - \overline{\lambda}_t)^2} \Bigg/ \sqrt{\frac{1}{n_s}\sum_{t=1}^{n_s}(\widetilde{\lambda}_t - \overline{\lambda}_t)^2} = \sqrt{\sum_{t=1}^{n_s}(\lambda_t - \overline{\lambda}_t)^2 \Bigg/ \sum_{t=1}^{n_s}(\widetilde{\lambda}_t - \overline{\lambda}_t)^2}. \tag{13}$$

where n_S is the number of samplings in the evaluated stationary traffic period. A smaller σ_S indicates a better stability.

Estimation Responsiveness in Trend Traffic. In trend traffic periods, arrival rate estimates should converge quickly to the true trending $\overline{\lambda}_t$. This is particularly important during increasing demand periods, as slow estimation response will delay network management reaction causing connection or packet losses. The measure of this responsiveness, denoted by σ_C, is defined by the average lag of estimated rates λ_t with respect to $\overline{\lambda}_t$ (a positive lag indicates that $\overline{\lambda}_t > \lambda_t$), normalized by $\overline{\lambda}_t$:

$$\sigma_C = \frac{1}{n_c}\sum_{t=1}^{n_c}(\overline{\lambda}_t - \lambda_t)/\overline{\lambda}_t. \tag{14}$$

where n_C is the number of samplings in the evaluated trend traffic period. Smaller amplitude of lag σ_C indicates a better responsiveness.

4.2   Performance Results

Proposed and existing estimation methods are evaluated under the traffic model shown in Fig. 1d. Arrival rate mean $\overline{\lambda}_t$ (1) are generated for successive periods of stationary and trend traffic. At regular time intervals, arrival rate samples $\widetilde{\lambda}_t$ are generated randomly (2) with a Poisson distribution having mean $\overline{\lambda}_t$. In our test traffic, 100 and 50 samplings are included in each stationary and trend period, respectively. Initial stationary rate is set to 10, and trend λ'_t cases of 0.5, 1.0 and 1.5, leading respectively to stationary period rates of 60, 85 and 110, are verified. Coefficients $r_i(8)$ needed in autocorrelation based methods are calculated using a time window of $N=30$ measurements. Parameters (l_a, l_b), realizing logistic based adaptation function(12), shown in Fig. 3, are (100, 20) for SES-acf and (100000, 15) for SES-cdf.

Stability and convergence metrics are computed for the arrival rate estimates produced by the different methods and compared. For responsiveness evaluation, we concentrate on the increasing trends as it is in these cases that response is a key in avoiding connection and packet losses. The results for stability and responsiveness are given in Tables 1 and 2, respectively.

Table 1. Demand Estimation Stability Performance

	Traffic estimation stability σ_S (90% confidence)			
Method	$\overline{\lambda} = 10$	$\overline{\lambda} = 35$	$\overline{\lambda} = 60$	$\overline{\lambda} = 85$
SES-fix, α=0.1	0.225 ± 0.009	0.218 ± 0.004	0.218 ± 0.006	0.217 ± 0.006
SES-fix, α=0.5	0.576 ± 0.004	0.570 ± 0.004	0.574 ± 0.006	0.572 ± 0.005
SES-err	0.713 ± 0.008	0.487 ± 0.014	0.399 ± 0.015	0.347 ± 0.013
SES-acf	**0.272 ± 0.010**	**0.261 ± 0.016**	**0.274 ± 0.013**	**0.269 ± 0.021**
SES-cdf	**0.495 ± 0.011**	**0.489 ± 0.012**	**0.494 ± 0.020**	**0.489 ± 0.009**
DES-err	0.753 ± 0.008	0.549 ± 0.015	0.470 ± 0.019	0.421 ± 0.017
DES-derr	1.026 ± 0.014	0.885 ± 0.024	0.832 ± 0.024	0.819 ± 0.027

Table 2. Demand Estimation Response Performance

	Traffic estimation response σ_C (90% confidence)		
Method	Trend λ'=0.5	Trend λ'=1.0	Trend λ'=1.5
SES-fix, α=0.1	0.161 ± 0.005	0.215 ± 0.004	0.247 ± 0.003
SES-fix, α=0.5	0.022 ± 0.006	0.030 ± 0.005	0.037 ± 0.004
SES-err	0.069 ± 0.007	0.083 ± 0.005	0.097 ± 0.004
SES-acf	**0.048 ± 0.007**	**0.031 ± 0.005**	**0.026 ± 0.005**
SES-cdf	**0.031 ± 0.006**	**0.041 ± 0.005**	**0.051 ± 0.006**
DES-err	0.037 ± 0.008	0.030 ± 0.007	0.029 ± 0.005
DES-derr	-0.034 ± 0.007	-0.034 ± 0.007	-0.025 ± 0.008

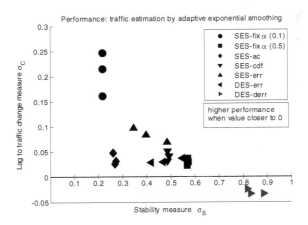

Fig. 4. Demand estimation combined stability-convergence performance.
SES-fix, SES-err, DES-err and DES-derr (section 3.1);
SES-acf and SES-cdf (section 3.2).

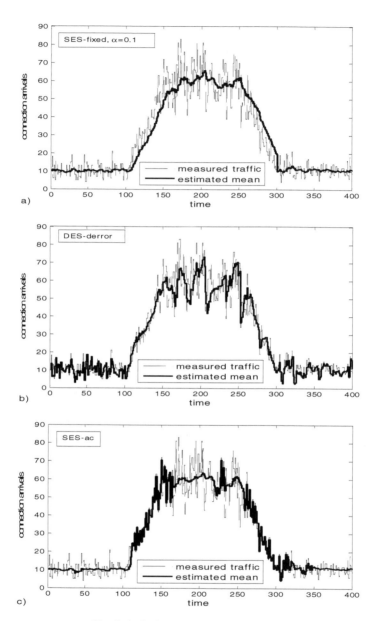

Fig. 5. Arrival rate estimation comparison :
a) *SES-fix with α=0.1*, b) *DES-derr*, c) *SES-acf*

Fig. 4 shows the methods combined stability-responsiveness performance. Each plotted point represents a dynamic traffic case, combining the responsiveness performance corresponding to a given trend λ' and the stability corresponding to the stationary level $\overline{\lambda}$ reached at the end of the trend period. Cases for (λ', $\overline{\lambda}$) values of (0.5, 35), (1.0, 60) and (1.5, 85) are represented in the figure. For most methods, a performance tradeoff is apparent, as a better stability is shown paired with a poorer responsiveness, and vice-versa. *SES-cdf* provides good responsiveness, although its stability is only average. The proposed *SES-acf* provides the best combined stability-responsiveness performance. For the case of $\lambda' = 0.5$, responsiveness for *SES-acf* is slightly slower. This can be explained by the imprecision of trend detection, caused by the limited number N of autocorrelation samples in an environment of low traffic trend to traffic noise ratio. For example, increasing N from 30 to 35 improves the method's responsiveness measure from 0.048 to 0.043, while stability performance is maintained (from 0.261 to 0.249).

To visualize online demand estimation performance, Fig. 5 compares estimation responses to real-time measured arrival rates for a) *SES-fix with $\alpha=0.1$*, b) *DES-derr*, c) *SES-acf*. a) shows good stability, however the lag in both increasing and decreasing trends is apparent. b) is very responsive to trends, but stability in stationary traffic is poor. Finally, c) our proposed *SES-acf* is capable of showing both trend responsiveness and reasonable stability.

5   Conclusion

In this paper, we proposed dynamic traffic demand estimation approaches that are simple to function online, yet accurate to allow for efficient network optimization and management. Exponential smoothing is adapted based on traffic trend that is estimated through the use of arrival process acf or cdf. When compared to known adaptive ES methods, proposed *SES-acf*, where adaptation is based on traffic trend evaluated by measured autocorrelation, provided the best combined stability-responsiveness performance. This feature makes it particularly fit for autonomic estimation of time-evolving traffic conditions.

In future research, we will investigate the possibility of online estimation using the Kalman filter, recognized as a general method for signal estimation in the presence of noise, and compare its performance to these proposed approaches.

References

1. Thompson, K., Miller, G.J., Wilder, R.: Wide-area Internet Traffic Patterns and Characteristics. IEEE Network 11(6), 10–23 (1997)
2. Roberts, J.W.: Internet Traffic, QoS, and Pricing. Proceedings of the IEEE 92(9), 1389–1399 (2004)
3. Krishnan, K.R.: Adaptive State-dependent Traffic Routing Using On-line Trunk-group Measurements. In: Proc. of the Thirteenth International Teletraffic Congress, Copenhagen, pp. 407–411 (1991)

4. Sultan, A., Girard, A.: Adaptive Implementation of the Revenue-maximization Optimal Routing Algorithm. In: Proc. of Telecommunication Systems, Modeling and Analysis Conference, Nashville, pp. 371–374 (1993)
5. Dziong, Z.: ATM Network Resource Management, ch. 5. McGraw-Hill, New York (1997)
6. Tu, M.: Estimation of Point-to-point Traffic Demand in the Public Switched Telephone Network. IEEE Transactions on Communications 42(2-4), 840–845 (1994)
7. Duan, Z., Zhang, Z.-L., Hou, Y.T.: Service Overlay Networks: SLAs, QoS, and Bandwidth Provisioning. IEEE/ACM Transactions on Networking 11(6), 870–883 (2003)
8. Krithikaivasan, B., Deka, K., Medhi, D.: Adaptive Bandwidth Provisioning Envelope Based on Discrete Temporal Network Measurements. In: Proc. of IEEE INFOCOM 2004 Conference on Computer Communications, Hong Kong, vol. 3, pp. 1786–1796 (2004)
9. Anjali, T., Bruni, C., Iacoviello, D., Koch, G., Scoglio, C.: Filtering and Forecasting Problems for Aggregate Traffic in Internet Links. Performance Evaluation 58(1), 25–42 (2004)
10. Anjali, T., Scoglio, C., Uhl, G.: A New Scheme for Traffic Estimation and Resource Allocation for Bandwidth Brokers. Computer Networks 41(6), 761–777 (2003)
11. Tran, C., Dziong, Z.: Service Overlay Network Capacity Adaptation for Profit Maximization. IEEE Transactions on Network and Service Management 7(2), 72–82 (2010)
12. Dasgupta, S., de Oliveira, J.C., Vasseur, J.-P.: Trend Based Bandwidth Provisioning: an Online Approach for Traffic Engineered Tunnels. In: Proc. of 4th EURO-NGI Conference on Next Generation Internet Networks, Krakow, pp. 53–60 (2008)
13. Gardner, E.S.: Exponential Smoothing: the State of the Art – Part II. International Journal of Forecasting 22(4), 637–666 (2006)
14. Mentzer, J.T.: Forecasting with Adaptive Extended Exponential Smoothing. Journal of the Academy of Marketing Science 16(3-4), 62–70 (1988)
15. Mentzer, J.T., Gomes, R.: Further Extensions of Adaptive Extended Exponential Smoothing and Comparison with the M-competition. Journal of the Academy of Marketing Science 22(4), 372–382 (1994)
16. Ching, W.-K., Scholtes, S., Zhang, S.-Q.: Numerical Algorithms for Dynamic Traffic Demand Estimation Between Zones in a Network. Engineering Optimization 36(3), 379–400 (2004)
17. Paxson, V., Floyd, S.: Wide Area Traffic: the Failure of Poisson Modeling. IEEE/ACM Transactions on Networking 3(3), 226–244 (1995)
18. WAND Network Research Group, WITS: Waikato Internet Traffic Storage, http://www.wand.net.nz/wits/
19. Makridakis, S., et al.: The Accuracy of Extrapolation (Time Series) Methods: Results of a Forecasting Competition. Journal of Forecasting 1(2), 111–153 (1982)
20. Chatfield, C.: The Analysis of Time Series: An Introduction, 6th edn., section 2. Chapman & Hall/CRC, Boca Raton (2003)

Ethernet Services Transport Protocol
with Configurable-QoS Attributes for Carrier Ethernet

Claudio Estevez[1], Georgios Ellinas[2], and Gee-Kung Chang[1]

[1] School of Electrical and Computer Engineering,
Georgia Institute of Technology, Atlanta, USA
{estevez,geekung.chang}@ece.gatech.edu
[2] Department of Electrical and Computer Engineering,
University of Cyprus, Nicosia, Cyprus
gellinas@ucy.ac.cy

Abstract. Carrier-grade Ethernet has evolved greatly since its creation. Its simplicity, scalability, and inexpensiveness have made it an attractive technology for enterprises to interconnect their metro area networks (MANs). Today, Carrier Ethernet can span over 10,000 km. Ethernet Services were created to enable companies to distribute their own services through the carrier-grade network. All the data that enters the Carrier Ethernet network (CEN) is policed by the CEN provider based on the service level agreement (SLA). Among the QoS attributes that are agreed upon is the packet loss rate (PLR) guarantee, committed information rate (CIR) and excess information rate (EIR). In this work we study the relation between PLR and throughput performance. This relationship can then be used to increase the throughput performance of the Ethernet Services transport protocol (ESTP). It achieves this by configuring an ESTP parameter that allows the CEN provider to increase the user's throughput at the cost of PLR or vice versa. This increase is done while main maintaining the throughput above the CIR and below the EIR using only transport-layer algorithms.

Keywords: Carrier Ethernet, Ethernet Services, packet loss, QoS, throughput performance.

1   Introduction

Ethernet networks started as a means to interconnect multiple devices, and it began covering only a small office area. Since then they have transitioned to much larger areas like building, campus, and metropolitan areas. This interconnection of nodes is expected to keep growing. Metropolitan Ethernet networks integrated network-to-network interfaces that connected multiple MEN domains through high capacity lines such as fiber optic links. With the increasing size of the networks the need for privacy measures increased as well. The Ethernet virtual connection (EVC) was created to resolve these issues. EVCs were designed to engage connections between end-users while isolating them from other user's connections using the same physical lines.

I. Tomkos et al. (Eds.): BROADNETS 2010, LNICST 66, pp. 69–83, 2012.
© Institute for Computer Sciences, Social Informatics and Telecommunications Engineering 2012

The combination of multi-domain interconnections and EVCs enabled the launch of carrier-grade Ethernet networks, and along with this Ethernet Services.

The metro Ethernet forum (MEF) is an organization that has been designing the standards for carrier Ethernet networks, releasing the first publications in 2004 and kept adding and updating them since. Among the services provided are point-to-point connections called Ethernet virtual private lines (EVPLs), which is the most prevalent service that CEN providers offer. The details of the EVPL service for specific customers is agreed upon and documented in an SLA. Some common parameters that are included in this agreement are the committed information rate, excess information rate, and the packet loss rate guarantee. These QoS parameters are controlled by a traffic policer at the network edge.

One of the main limitations of CENs is that they are high-bandwidth-delay-product networks. This creates a bottleneck at the transport layer, which is dominated by TCP and its variants. TCP relies on the acknowledgement of datagrams to successfully confirm arrival and order of the data and preserve the integrity of the original information. Because the server waits for acknowledgement (ACK) datagrams, long delays will severely degrade the overall throughput performance. For this reason a protocol called Ethernet Services transport protocol or ESTP was designed [1]. This protocol was designed to not only deal with throughput issues of high-bandwidth-delay-product networks but to also provide QoS at the transport layer, which aids the performance of CENs by relieving the transport layer from TCP's limitations and shaping the traffic such that it is compliant with the SLA requirements and therefore little information will be lost due to traffic policing.

This work is organized in the following way. The limitations of Traditional TCP and other transport layer protocols are presented in section 2. The details of ESTP are presented in section 3. In section 4, the relationship between throughput and PLR is presented followed by (section 5) the congestion avoidance algorithm derived from this relationship. The channel model described in section 6 is the basis for the simulation scenario shown in section 7. The results are found in Section 8 and the concluding remarks in section 9.

2   Limitations of Traditional TCP and Other Prominent Transport Protocols Paper Preparation

Transport Control Protocol (TCP) started as a request for comment (RFC) memorandum in 1974, with several additions in subsequent years. TCP provides congestion avoidance, delivery guarantee, and data sequence organization, making the Internet Protocol (IP) best-effort network a reliable one. The trade-off for reliability is delay. TCP is not well-suited for time-sensitive applications, such as voice over IP (VoIP). With a new generation of networks arising, the link capacity is increased and the networks extend to cover greater distances (i.e., increasing delay). These large bandwidth-delay product (BDP) networks will pose a problem to TCP. The BDP is a measure of how much data is in-flight at one point in time. The in-flight data in TCP is controlled by the congestion window (cwnd) size. The cwnd size is determined by the additive-increase multiplicative-decrease (AIMD) algorithm of TCP. This algorithm decreases the cwnd aggressively in the event of a packet loss and increases the cwnd very conservatively, making it difficult to reach the full available bandwidth. It is necessary to make modifications to the standard type to be able to fully utilize the provided bandwidth in newer versions of the transport protocol. TCP is composed of four intertwined congestion-control algorithms: slow-start, congestion avoidance, fast retransmit, and fast recovery [9]. TCP went through several versions like Tahoe, Reno, New Reno, and Sack. A simulation-based comparison of the performance of these different versions is compared in earlier work [10]. TCP Tahoe, the most native of these four versions, had the slow-start, congestion avoidance and fast retransmission algorithms. In TCP Reno, fast recovery was integrated to the TCP Tahoe congestion-control algorithms. TCP New Reno is very similar to Reno, with the exception that the retransmit wait time, after multiple consecutive packet losses, was eliminated. TCP Sack is built on top of TCP New Reno with an added feature called selective acknowledgement, hence the name Sack. In previous implementations of TCP, the receiver acknowledges the last successful segment received. However, other non-contiguous segments could have been received but not notified to the sender. If segments time out, this forces the sender to retransmit all segments after the last successful segment. With selective acknowledgement the sender acknowledges multiple non-contiguous segments such that the receiver only has to retransmit the lost segments. The analytical expression for TCP-Sack throughput is as derived in [4].

$$B = \frac{MSS \sqrt{3}}{RTT \sqrt{2b\,p}} \tag{1}$$

MSS corresponds to the maximum segment size, RTT is round trip time, b is the number of packets acknowledged per ACK and p is the packet loss rate. Note that MSS is usually specified in bytes and throughput in bits (per second) so a trivial unit conversion is needed.

TCP Sack became the root from which many other protocols branched out, including HighSpeed TCP [8], Scalable TCP [6], Explicit Control TCP (XCP) [7], and SLA-aware Transport Protocol [3]. The proposed protocol is built on top of the SLA-aware Transport Protocol, which is a shifted-lower-bound version of TCP Sack. Like the proposed work, the SLA-aware Transport Protocol assumes a reserved bandwidth so it shifts the lower bound of TCP Sack to match the data rate of the reserved bandwidth. HighSpeed TCP tweaks the AIMD parameters of TCP to perform better in high-bandwidth-delay networks; the parameters are obtained empirically. Scalable TCP runs a multiplicative-increase multiplicative-decrease algorithm to compute the cwnd size. The main problem with this technique is that it is very aggressive in both directions (increase and decrease), and for networks with long delays this protocol could be unstable. In XCP a congestion header is added to the packet format. Routers communicate with the transport protocol through this header field to obtain congestion feedback. The problem with this protocol is that this capability is not available in TCP so current networks are not designed to have this feature; and replacing or reprogramming all the routers in the network to support this feature might not be a feasible solution. Another problem is that routers are designed to route by reading layer 2 or 3 information, and for the router to write congestion feedback in the layer 4 packet format requires further decapsulation of the packet and adds more delay, which defeats the purpose.

3   Ethernet Service Transport Protocol

In Ethernet Services the QoS parameters specified by the SLA offer valuable information. One of the goals of ESTP is to incorporate this information into the transport protocol to have better control of the data flow over a network that employs Ethernet Services, and therefore this protocol is referred to as the Ethernet Services Transport Protocol.

ESTP can be summarized in three parts: network congestion detection mechanism, mapping function, and the congestion avoidance control algorithm. These are explained below.

3.1   Network Congestion Detection Mechanism

The principle of this method is based on the estimation of the congestion level of the network. The level of congestion is related to the amount of packets successfully delivered between two packet losses. The instantaneous amount of packets delivered between two packet losses is defined here with the parameter α. The value of α is mapped into an exponential profile to determine a less strenuous multiplicative-decrease factor defined as $map(\alpha)$. The purpose of choosing an exponential profile is to match the exponential probability distribution exhibited by the variable of the distance between two packet losses. By having the congestion window dependent on the network congestion level, the size of the congestion window can be controlled more efficiently.

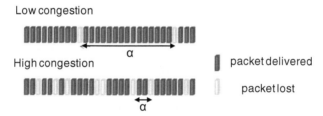

Fig. 1. Value of α is the amount of successfully transmitted packets in-between two packet losses plus one

The exact definition of α is the amount of successfully delivered packets found between two packets losses plus one. This can be easily seen by considering the metric distance to be one packet. Then, the distance between two lost packets is the amount of successfully delivered packets found in-between these two losses plus one (the lost packet). The value of α will range from 1 to ∞, which implies that the extreme cases are two consecutive losses and a lossless transmission. The value of α is mapped to the value of $map(\alpha)$, which ranges from 2 to 1. This means that the proposed protocol can decrease the congestion window size by a factor no greater than two (inclusive), and no smaller than one (exclusive). Since a factor of 1 is selected for $\alpha = \infty$ (lossless transmission), it is obvious that the protocol will never choose the exact factor of $map(\alpha) = 1$. This mapping scheme is desirable because if α takes a small value, it is assumed to be the result of a highly congested network and therefore the congestion window size is reduced more aggressively. Inversely, if the value of α is large, it is assumed that the network is not experiencing high levels of congestion (Fig. 1) and the congestion window is only slightly reduced in size. To achieve this mapping and at the same time match the traffic loss probability distribution, an exponential function is chosen. The details of how to obtain the mapping function are found in the next section.

3.2   Mapping Function

To obtain the mapping function of ESTP it is necessary to become familiar with the probability density functions (pdf) of the period of time between two packet losses. The probability of a packet loss has a Bernoulli distribution. If we assume that a packet loss is a successful event, then the number of successful events in a fixed period of time has a Poisson distribution, i.e., the packet loss rate can be modeled as a Poisson distribution. The time between two Poisson distributed events can then be modeled as an exponential distributed process.

The pdf of an exponential distribution is:

$$f(\alpha;\tau) = \begin{cases} \dfrac{1}{\tau}e^{-\alpha/\tau} & \alpha \geq 0 \\ 0 & \alpha < 0 \end{cases} \tag{2}$$

were τ is the $E[\alpha]$.

Since the main objective is to have effective congestion control, while increasing performance, the mapping function is chosen to match the pdf of the metric distance between two packets. The multiplicative decrease factor of Traditional TCP is 1/2. The metric distance unit is defined as a single packet independent of its length in bytes as this work focuses on the transport layer. Under this definition the minimum distance between two packets is one, since the measurement is taken from the start of one packet to the start of the subsequent packet. In this work the mapping function is placed in the denominator of the multiplicative decrease factor, so for the proposed protocol to be lower-bounded by the performance of Traditional TCP one of the boundary conditions has to map one metric distance to a value of 2, rather than 1/2. This will cause two consecutive packet losses to reduce the cwnd by a factor of 1/2, which is the behavior of Traditional TCP. If we never had a loss, such that the distance is infinite, the desired mapping factor is then 1. In summary, our boundary conditions are: $map(1) = 2$ and $map(\infty) = 1$.

As discussed previously, we want to match the mapping function to the pdf of the distance between two events. Thus, since $\exp(\infty) = 0$ then one has to be added to the exponential term. This yields $map(\alpha) = \exp(-\alpha/\tau) + 1$. To satisfy $map(1) = 2$ we need to shift the expression by 1 (see Fig. 2), which yields:

$$map(\alpha) = e^{\frac{\alpha-1}{\tau_\alpha}} + 1 \tag{3}$$

The *cwnd* expression is then:

$$cwnd_{n+1} = cwnd_n \left(e^{\frac{\alpha-1}{\tau_\alpha}} + 1 \right)^{-1} \tag{4}$$

This excludes the effects of $cwnd_{MIN}$, which is explained in Section 3.3.

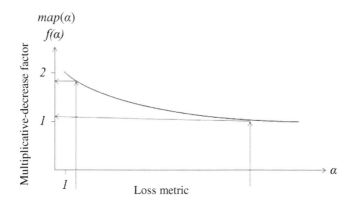

Fig. 2. Proposed protocol mapping of the distance between two packet losses to the multiplicative decrease factor mapping

Notice that for the extreme case of two consecutive packet losses ($\alpha = 1$), the proposed protocol behaves like the SLA-aware protocol [3], which means that the proposed protocol is lower-bounded by the SLA-aware throughput performance. If the SLA information is not taken into account, such that $cwnd_{MIN} = 0$, then for $\alpha = 1$ the proposed protocol behaves like Traditional TCP.

3.3   Congestion Avoidance Control

By incorporating Ethernet Services information, in addition to the dynamic multiplicative-decrease factor mapping, ESTP can further show improvement in terms of throughput performance, since these techniques are independent of each other. Combining the congestion control mechanisms discussed in the previous subsection with the SLA-aware mechanisms, the following multiplicative decrease expression can be derived for congestion control:

$$cwnd_{n+1} = \frac{cwnd_n - cwnd_{MIN}}{map(\alpha)} + cwnd_{MIN} \tag{5}$$

$$cwnd_{n+1} = \left(cwnd_n - cwnd_{MIN}\right)\left(e^{-\frac{\alpha-1}{\tau_\alpha}} + 1\right)^{-1} + cwnd_{MIN} \qquad (6)$$

This technique takes full advantage of the bandwidth provided to the subscriber by maintaining the throughput above the CIR (see Fig. 3a). The $cwnd_{MIN}$ is computed in the following way: $cwnd_{MIN} = RTT\cdot CIR$. The throughput can be further improved by utilizing the EIR information. $cwnd_{MAX}$ can be obtained similarly to $cwnd_{MIN}$ but using EIR rather than CIR: $cwnd_{MAX} = RTT\cdot EIR$. With this value, the upper bound of the congestion window can be controlled. An upper bound is set because once the $cwnd$ exceeds $cwnd_{MAX}$, the throughput will exceed EIR and the traffic policing enforced at the lower layers will discard packets exceeding this rate. Once that happens, the protocol at layer 4 will initiate its congestion control mechanism and decrease the congestion window. This is unnecessary since there is no congestion in the network. By maintaining the $cwnd$ at its maximum value, the throughput will not be reduced by the protocol's congestion control and the subscriber will get maximum throughput until a random loss (e.g. link loss) or congestion loss occurs.

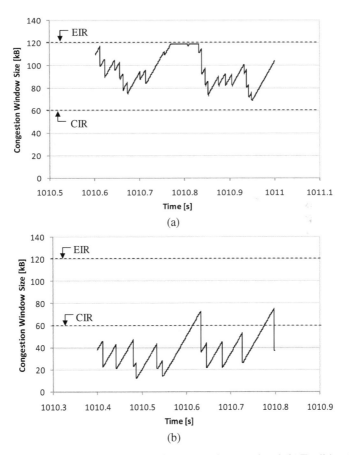

Fig. 3. Congestion window behavior of *(a)* the proposed protocol and *(b)* Traditional TCP

The additive increase properties of AIMD of the proposed protocol will then be expressed as:

$$cwnd_{n+1} = \min(cwnd_{MAX}, cwnd_n + 1/cwnd_n) \qquad (7)$$

Traditional TCP is then a special case when $cwnd_{MAX} = \infty$. The traffic-loss profile matching and the *cwnd* boundary mechanism implemented by the additive-increase multiplicative-decrease techniques distinguishes ESTP from other transport protocols and makes its implementation desirable for Ethernet Services. In Fig. 3a it can be seen how ESTP successfully maintains the congestion window within the designed limits, and the contrasting behavior of Traditional TCP can be observed in Fig. 3b.

4   Throughput and Packet Loss Rate Relationship

For connection-oriented transport protocols, such as TCP, the throughput is greatly affected by the packet loss rate. As seen in (1), the throughput of Traditional TCP decreases as the packet loss rate increases by a factor of its square root. One method to improve the throughput is to study the loss pattern of data traffic and use this information to design a more efficient congestion avoidance algorithm.

In section 3.1, a parameter α is defined as the distance between two packet losses. This parameter is the key to determine the congestion level of the network, but it is also the link between the PLR and the throughput. It is clear that the α term is related to the packet loss rate, since both can be computed from packet losses. What is less intuitive is that the average α can be used to estimate the throughput of ESTP, since ESTP uses this parameter to adjust the congestion window size, and hence the throughput. By linking the throughput to the PLR, we can adjust the congestion window size such that we provide higher throughputs without increasing significantly the PLR. The details of this principle follow below.

Packet loss can be categorized into two types: intrinsic and extrinsic. Intrinsic losses are the losses that cannot be avoided (by the transport layer protocol) because they are embedded in the system. An example of intrinsic loss is those caused by

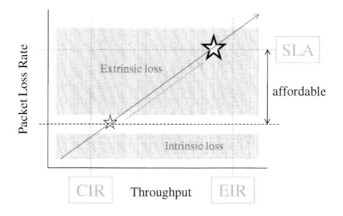

Fig. 4. Illustration of the throughput limited by PLR guarantee principle

faulty transmission lines. In contrast, extrinsic losses are the losses caused by external reasons such as congestion discarding or traffic policing, which can be avoided with appropriate control mechanisms. If the throughput were to increase the intrinsic packet loss rate will not change, because it is a fixed loss rate embedded in the system, but the extrinsic packet loss rate would increase because the risk of congestion and losses due to traffic policing will increase as the data rate increases. In CEN, the customer is allowed to customize the QoS parameters to suit the needs of their networks. As discussed in the introductory section, one the QoS services users can purchase is a PLR guarantee. This loss rate is chosen according the amount of loss that the applications running on the network can tolerate. The main idea (depicted on Fig. 4) is to increase the throughput to the highest possible value in which the PLR specification is not exceeded, and doing this in an innate manner (naturally embedded in the algorithm) so that no additional policing is required at the transport layer.

5   Congestion Avoidance Control with Configurable-QoS

The congestion avoidance control with configurable-QoS is a closed-loop feedback control system, were the input parameter is α and the output parameter is the congestion window size. To provide a PLR boundary, we compute what the average α (i.e. $E[\alpha]$) needs to be for this specific PLR and make sure the average does not exceed a predefined threshold. To do this we use the assumptions used to find the mapping function described in section 3.2. These assumptions are: the packet loss event has Bernoulli distribution and the distance between two Bernoulli distributed events has exponential distribution with average $E[\alpha] = \tau_\alpha$. The PLR is translated to the $E[\alpha]$ using the following equation (see Fig. 5):

$$\tau_\alpha = \frac{average\ packet\ transmission\ period}{PLR} \tag{8}$$

and the resulting value of τ_α is used in (6).

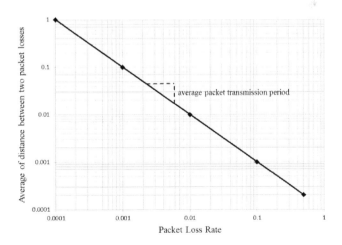

Fig. 5. Relationship between $E[\alpha]$ and *PLR*

It should be emphasized that this is only true under the assumption that the PLR increases if the throughput is increased. This is a fair assumption and is true for most, if not all, networks. To visualize the mechanics of this algorithm assume the system has encountered two losses, and the transport protocol has computed its respective α and this value is much smaller than $E[\alpha]$. The protocol assumes the network is congested and will reduce the congestion window size aggressively (see section 3 for details). This will cause the throughput to reduce drastically, hence reducing the congestion in the network and consequently next value of α will probably be higher than $E[\alpha]$. This iterative process will generate values of α that surround $E[\alpha]$ and therefore maintaining a relatively constant PLR. So the guarantee is an indirect effect of the congestion avoidance mechanism. Since the average packet transmission period is inversely proportional to throughput from (8) is it clear that increasing τ_α will lower the throughput but advantageously will also decrease the PLR; inversely, increasing the τ_α value will increase the throughput but at the cost of increasing the PLR. So τ_α is a design parameter of ESTP and the main focus of this work.

6   Channel Model

According to information theory, the capacity of a channel, which is defined as the amount of information transmitted between sender and receiver, is the upper bound of the data rate that can be delivered through the channel without error. Since Internet is known to be composed mainly by TCP transmissions and In order to evaluate the channel capacity of a CEN line, an erasure channel model is proposed. As shown in Fig. 6, the traffic from the sender is policed according to the SLA at the egress point. The packet that falls into the CIR profile will be marked with high priority and delivered with guaranteed QoS. A packet that falls out of the CIR profile, but still in the EIR profile, will be marked with low priority and delivered in a best effort manner. A packet that falls out of the EIR profile will be discarded immediately. Within the transport network, a high priority packet suffers a loss probability of p_1, which is defined in the SLA. A best-effort packet suffers a loss probability of p_2, which depends on background traffic, and can be any value between 0 and 1. For a prioritized channel as shown in Fig. 6, the capacity can be expressed as:

$$C = CIR \cdot (1 - p_1) + EIR \cdot (1 - p_2)$$ (9)

Given that $0 \leq p_2 \leq 1$, the lower bound of the channel capacity can be derived as

$$C = CIR \cdot (1 - p_1)$$ (10)

which is the minimum capacity of a CEN channel.

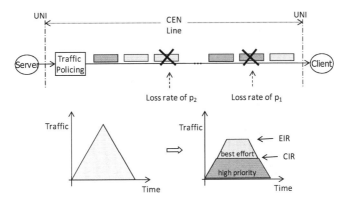

Fig. 6. Channel model for a Carrier Ethernet Network Line

7   Simulation Scenario

The simulations were realized in OPNET Modeler 16.0 based on the channel model described in the previous section. A server transmits a 2 GB file to the client using the QoS and ESTP parameters specified in Table 1. The channel has an extrinsic loss rate that is dependent on the throughput, and modeled by the empirical formula described by (11).

$$p_{chLoss} = p_1 \left(\frac{p_2}{p_1} \right)^{\left(\frac{Throughput-CIR}{EIR-CIR} \right)} \tag{11}$$

This only applies to the best-effort traffic; the CIR traffic is only subjected to the intrinsic loss rate. The first simulation is to prove the concept of throughput increase by sacrificing PLR. To prove concept it is necessary to accurately know the packet loss model of the CEN line, which is the reason for inducing a controlled loss. The realness or practicality of the CEN line loss model is a secondary issue, but as long as the loss is monotonically increasing with increasing throughput the proof of concept can be realized with any CEN line model. The simulation parameters used for Simulation I are found below (Table 1).

Table 1. Simulation I Parameters

Parameter description	Value
CIR	0 Mbps (no CIR)
EIR	500 Mbps
p_1	0.0000001
p_2	0.01
τ_α	[0.01, 0.0001]
Round-trip propagation delay	1 ms
Receiver buffer size	1 MB
Maximum segment size	1460 bytes
Max ACKed packets (b value)	2

The value of τ_α is varied to see the throughput improvement, while keeping a log of successfully delivered packets and packet losses. The throughput versus the PLR is found and analyzed in the following section.

The second simulation consists on showing the CIR and EIR functionalities of the protocol. In this case the RTT is varied from 1 to 10ms and the throughput is recorded for each event. The τ_α is left constant. The throughput versus RTT is analyzed. The simulation parameters for this case are found in Table 2.

Table 2. Simulation II Parameters

Parameter description	Value
CIR	200 Mbps
EIR	400 Mbps
p_1	0.0000001
p_2	0.01
τ_α	0.01
Round-trip propagation delay	[1, 10] ms
Receiver buffer size	1 MB
Maximum segment size	1460 bytes
Max ACKed packets (b value)	2

Also the pdf of the distribution of α in the simulation is provided to show the similitude to the theoretical case, the plot is provided in the results section.

8   Results

The PLR versus throughput is plotted in Fig. 7. It can be seen that for the same RTT the throughput can be further increased by varying the value of τ_α. The throughput is

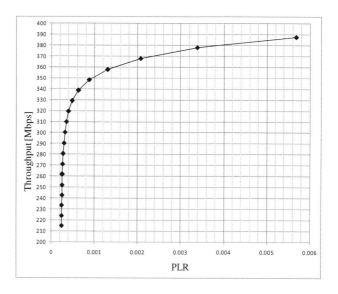

Fig. 7. Throughput versus *PLR*

more sensitive to this change at the lower PLR, as the PLR increases the throughput becomes less sensitive to this change.

This plot shows the ability of the protocol to reconfigure its parameters to satisfy the changing needs of the customer. If the applications that are been ran in the network need to prioritize throughput or PLR this can easy be achieved by changing the ESTP's parameters accordingly.

For the second simulation case the main interest is to show the CIR and EIR boundaries. Fig. 8 shows the results of the throughput versus RTT.

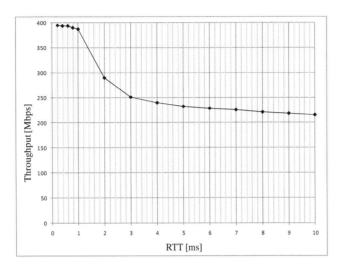

Fig. 8. Throughput versus *RTT*. Shows CIR advantage and EIR enforcement

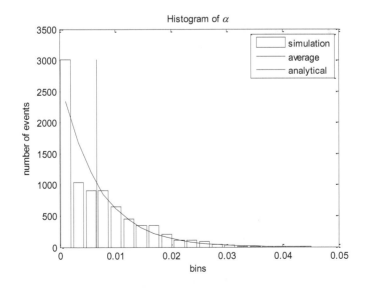

Fig. 9. Simulation histogram of the probability distribution of α

It can be seen that all the best-effort traffic is found between these boundaries. Because the CIR is bandwidth that is guaranteed to the customer ESTP can lower bound the congestion window size, which will maintain the throughput above the CIR. If the customer required more or less bandwidth the provider can reserve the adjusted bandwidth for the customer and change the ESTP's parameters accordingly so that the transport layer performs more efficiently based on the available resources and customer's needs.

The pdf of α is provided for work completeness. It is interesting to see the behavior of the loss pattern. Our initial assumption was that the behavior is exponential and Fig. 9 shows that the simulation behavior is in agreement with the hypothesis.

9   Summary

A summary of all the QoS-configurable parameters in ESTP follows (Table 3). These parameters can be computed from the specifications established in the SLA and legacy parameters of Traditional TCP, available at the transport layer.

Table 3. Configurable QoS Parameters of ESTP

Parameter	Parameter description
$cwnd_{MAX}$	Upper bounds the congestion window. It prevents the throughput from exceeding the EIR and therefore will prevent packet loss due to policing, and therefore congestion window will not be penalized and the throughput will remain closer to the EIR. $$cwnd_{MAX} = RTT \cdot EIR$$
$cwnd_{MIN}$	Lower bounds the congestion window. It allows the throughput to remain at or higher than the CIR. This will allow the protocol to fully utilize the available bandwidth even in the event of a packet loss. $$cwnd_{MIN} = RTT \cdot CIR$$
τ_α	Establishes a packet loss rate guarantee. A high value will lower the PLR, but at the cost of lowering the throughput. It should be calculated based on the packet loss rate that the applications of the network can tolerate.

10   Conclusions

A broadband data transport protocol was designed for Carrier Ethernet Networks. The protocol has a unique congestion avoidance algorithm and has many configurable parameters to suit the reconfiguration needs of CEN providers and can fulfill the throughput needs of the CEN customers. ESTP can fully utilize the reserved bandwidth provided to the customer by lower bounding the congestion window size, the end result of this bounding technique is that the throughput will be lower bounded to the CIR value, as agreed on the SLA. The ability to reconfigure is attractive to CEN providers and this protocol can support these QoS attributes using only resources available at the transport layer. Its compatibility with CEN traffic policing makes it highly suitable for carrier-grade applications running on Carrier Ethernet networks.

References

1. Estevez, C., Ellinas, G., Chang, G.-K.: Broadband Data Transport Protocol Designed for Ethernet Services in Metro Ethernet Networks. In: IEEE GLOBECOM 2008, New Orleans, LA (November 2008)
2. Xiao, C., Estevez, C., Ellinas, G., Chang, G.-K.: A Resilient Transport Control Scheme for Metro Ethernet Services Based on Hypothesis Test. In: Proc. IEEE GLOBECOM 2007, Washington, DC (November 2007)
3. Xiao, C., Chang, G.-K., Bing, B.: An SLA-aware Transport Protocol for High Throughput Wide Area Ethernet Services. In: Proc. IEEE GLOBECOM 2006, San Francisco, CA (November 2006)
4. Padhye, J., Firoiu, V., Towsley, D., Kurose., J.: Modeling TCP Throughput: A Simple Model and its Empirical Validation. In: Proceedings of ACM SIGCOMM 1998, Vancouver, B.C. (September 1998)
5. Yang, Y.R., Lam, S.S.: General AIMD Congestion Control. Technical Report TR-2000-09, The University of Texas at Austin (May 2000)
6. Kelly, T.: Scalable TCP: Improving Performance in Highspeed Wide Area Networks. Computer Communication Review 33(2), 83–91 (2003)
7. Zhang, Y., Henderson, T.R.: An Implementation and Experimental Study of the eXplicit Control Protocol (XCP). In: Proc. IEEE Infocom 2005, Miami, FL (March 2005)
8. Floyd, S.: HighSpeed TCP for Large Congestion Windows. IETF RFC 3649 (December 2003)
9. Allman, M., Paxson, V., Stevens, W.: TCP congestion control. IEFT RFC 2581 (April 1999)
10. Fall, K., Floyd, S.: Simulation-based comparisons of Tahoe, Reno and Sack TCP. Computer Communication Review (July 1996)
11. Vertical Systems Group: Business Ethernet Expands 43% in 2008. Vertical Systems News (February 2009)
12. Vertical Systems Group: Worldwide Business Ethernet Services Market Rises to $38.9 Billion by 2013. Vertical Systems News (March 2009),
   http://www.verticalsystems.com/news.html
13. Rejaie, R., Handley, M., Estrin, D.: RAP: An End-to-end Rate-based Congestion Control Mechanism for Realtime Streams in the Internet. In: Proceedings of IEEE INFOCOM 1999, vol. 3 (March 1999)
14. Sisalem, D., Schulzrinne, H.: The Loss-delay based Adjustment Algorithm: A TCP-friendly Adaptation Scheme. In: Proceedings of NOSSDAV 1998, Cambridge, UK (July 1998)
15. Kurose, J., Ross, K.: Computer Networking: A Top-Down Approach Featuring the Internet, 3rd edn. Pearson Addison-Wesley (2005)

Hybrid Demand Oblivious Routing: Hyper-cubic Partitions and Theoretical Upper Bounds

Gábor Németh and Gábor Rétvári[*]

Dept. of Telecommunications and Media Informatics
Budapest University of Technology and Economics
Magyar tudósok körútja 2., Budapest, Hungary, H-1117
{nemethgab,retvari}@tmit.bme.hu

Summary. Traditionally, network routing was optimized with respect to an expected traffic matrix, which left the network in a suboptimal state if user traffic did not match expectations. A demand-oblivious routing is, contrarily, optimized with respect to all possible traffic matrices, obviating the need for traffic matrix estimation. Oblivious routing is a fundamentally distributed scheme, so it can be implemented easily. Unfortunately, in certain cases it may cause unwanted link over-utilization. Recently, we have introduced a hybrid centralized-distributed method to mitigate this shortcoming. However, our scheme did not provide a theoretical upper bound for the link over-utilization. In this paper, we tackle the problem again from a different perspective. Based on a novel hyper-cubic partition of the demand space, we construct a new algorithm that readily delivers the theoretical bounds. Simulation results show the theoretical and practical significance of our algorithm.

Keywords: oblivious ratio, demand-oblivious routing, hyper-cubic region.

1 Introduction

Traffic Engineering (TE) [1] has become the key tool used in the majority of autonomous systems, whose task is to map user traffic to the physical network efficiently. This is important given the high cost of the elemental network infrastructure and the highly competitive nature of the ISP market. Most of the TE methods are offline methods: forwarding paths are optimized with respect to some measured and/or expected traffic matrices over some period of time, and over-provisioning of network capacity ensures that unpredictable traffic spikes do not cause violation of link capacities [2, 3]. In a more dynamically changing environment, this routing strategy has become more and more inadequate. Thus, several proposals have surfaced to reduce the significance of traffic matrices (e.g., [4–7]) or even eliminate them (e.g., [8–13]) in intra-domain traffic engineering.

---

[*] The second author was supported by the Janos Bolyai Fellowship of the Hungarian Academy of Sciences.

I. Tomkos et al. (Eds.): BROADNETS 2010, LNICST 66, pp. 84–100, 2012.

A practical method to deal with unpredictable traffic matrices is called *(demand) oblivious routing* [14–22]. Here, the basic idea is to handle *all* legitimate traffic matrices simultaneously. Demand-oblivious routing is a fundamentally distributed scheme, meaning that the amount of traffic sent to a forwarding path by a router only depends on information available locally at that router. This ensures simplicity and scalability. Unfortunately, not all traffic matrices can be routed equally efficiently in oblivious routing, therefore, the routing might underperform for the everyday traffic scenario and consequently the network will operate in a suboptimal state in the majority of the time. Moreover, there is no theoretical upper bound on the capacity oversubscription, and hence, congestion demand-oblivious routing might cause [16].

Based on this insight, hybrid methods, combining the advantages of oblivious routing with some minimal central knowledge, have drawn the attention of the research community lately. The first hybrid algorithm was introduced in [23]. The main idea is to split the set of all legitimate traffic matrices (the so-called throughput polytope [24]) into multiple hyper-cubic regions, and assign a separate routing function to all of these regions. The individual routing functions are distributed, because the amount of traffic sent to a path at a source node only depends on the actual demand at that node, and it is independent of the demands at other nodes. A central controller, meanwhile, periodically observes the traffic matrix, decides in which operating region the network is, and installs the corresponding traffic splitting rations at the routers. This is exactly why hyper-cubic regions are a key concept in the algorithm: a hyper-cubic region provides the easiest way to decide whether the actual throughput is part of it. Thus, this architecture only needs a limited amount of central control. Although it has been shown that using the algorithm in [23] a significant improvement in the link over-subscription can be achieved by only a few cuts, it is still unclear whether the maximal link over-utilization converges to a minimum value.

In this paper, we analyze the properties of the maximal link over-utilization over hyper-cubic regions. In particular, we answer the questions

- how to create a finite hyper-cubic partition of the throughput region and
- what is the maximum size of each hyper-cubic region when fixing the maximal link over-utilization at a previously given value.

The rest of the paper is organized as follows. In Section 2, notations and definitions are introduced. In Section III, we introduce the mathematical backgrounds of our new algorithm. Simulation results are discussed in Section 4, related work is assessed in Section 5 and finally, Section 6 concludes the paper.

2   Notations and Definitions

Before introducing our main theorem, we need to summarize the main ideas of the geometric framework described in [23]. We need some basic terms and definitions from convex geometry also, thus we refer the reader to the introductory material in [25] and [26].

Suppose that we are given the network topology as usual, in the form of a directed graph $G(V, E)$ and a vector of positive, finite link capacities $c = [c_e > 0 : e \in E]$ (see Table 1 for a summary on notations). Each user is associated with a unique source-destination pair $(s_k, d_k) : k \in \mathcal{K}$ and a set of static paths $\mathcal{P}_k$. Additionally, each user k independently presents its demand θ_k at the source node s_k. The task of the routing algorithm is to distribute the demands θ_k between the paths $\mathcal{P}_k$, $\forall k \in \mathcal{K}$ in a way as to avoid or minimize link oversubscription.

Table 1. Notations

$G(V, E)$	a directed graph, with the set of nodes V ($|V| = n$) and the set of directed edges E ($|E| = m$)
c	the column m-vector of edge capacities
ξ_e	the number of paths sharing the edge $e \in E$
(s_k, d_k)	the set of source-destination pairs (or users) for $k \in \mathcal{K} = \{1, \ldots, K\}$
$\mathcal{P}_k$	the set of $s_k \to d_k$ paths assigned to some $k \in \mathcal{K}$
p_k	the number of paths for user k, $p_k = |\mathcal{P}_k|$
p	number of all paths, $p = \sum_{k \in \mathcal{K}} p_k$
P_k	an $m \times p_k$ matrix. The column corresponding to path $P \in \mathcal{P}_k$ holds the path-arc incidence vector of P
u_P	scalar, describing the traffic routed at path P
u_k	a column-vector, whose components are $u_P : P \in \mathcal{P}_k$ for some $k \in \mathcal{K}$ (whether we mean u_k or u_p will always be clear from the context)
u	a column vector representing a particular choice of u_{PS} (a "routing")
θ_k	the demand/throughput of some user $k \in \mathcal{K}$
θ	a column K-vector representing a particular combination of throughputs (a "traffic matrix")
M	flow polytope, the set of path flows corresponding to $\mathcal{P}$ subject to non-negativity and capacity constraints
T	throughput polytope, i.e., the set of throughputs realizable over $\mathcal{P}$ subject to capacity constraints
$\mathcal{S}, \mathcal{S}_k$	a routing function, $\mathcal{S} : \mathbb{R}^K \mapsto \mathbb{R}^p$ and the routing function corresponding to $k \in \mathcal{K}$, $\mathcal{S}_k : \mathbb{R}^K \mapsto \mathbb{R}^{p_k}$, respectively
$\mathcal{S}_R, \mathcal{S}_b$	the optimal routing function over the region $R \in \mathbb{R}^K$, or for the throughput $b \in \mathbb{R}^K$

A routing is, consequently, represented by a vector of path flows: $u = [u_k : k \in \mathcal{K}] \in \mathbb{R}^{p_1} \times \mathbb{R}^{p_2} \times \ldots \times \mathbb{R}^{p_K} = \mathbb{R}^p$, where p_k is the number of paths for k and p is the number of all paths.

Definition 1. *The polytope $M = \{u : \sum_{k \in K} P_k u_k \leq c, u \geq 0\} \subset \mathbb{R}^p$ is called* flow polytope. *M contains all admissible routings, subject to link capacities and non-negativity constraints.*

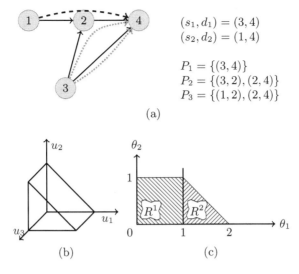

Fig. 1. The *(a)* sample network with unit edge capacities, source-destination pairs, the set of paths for each user and the corresponding *(b)* flow and *(c)* throughput polytopes

Consider the affine transformation (the so called *throughput mapping*) $\mathcal{T}$: $\mathbb{R}^p \to \mathbb{R}^K$ that from a routing u generates the corresponding traffic matrix θ by summing up the path flows for each particular path of a user:

$$\theta = \mathcal{T}(u) = [\theta_k = \sum_{P \in \mathcal{P}_k} u_P : k \in \mathcal{K}] .$$

Definition 2. *Mapping the flow polytope M through $\mathcal{T}$ gives the* throughput *polytope T [24]:*

$$\mathbb{R}^p \supset M \xrightarrow{\mathcal{T}} T \subset \mathbb{R}^K .$$

The throughput polytope contains all the traffic matrices realizable in the network by some properly chosen static routing without violating link capacities:

$$T = \{\theta : \exists u \in M \text{ so that } \mathcal{T}(u) = \theta\} .$$

Consequently, we call $\theta \in T$ admissible.

A sample network and the corresponding polytopes are depicted in Fig. 1.

The other central object in the framework is the *routing function* $\mathcal{S}$, which determines the way a traffic matrix θ is mapped to the paths: $u = \mathcal{S}(\theta)$. The routing function $\mathcal{S}$ must always satisfy the *throughput invariance* rules, i.e., $\mathcal{S}(\theta)$ must realize precisely θ: $\forall \theta \in \mathbb{R}^K : \mathcal{T}(\mathcal{S}(\theta)) \equiv \theta$. Throughout this paper, we only consider affine routing functions of the form $\mathcal{S} : \mathbb{R}^K \to \mathbb{R}^p; \; \theta \mapsto F\theta + g$ (component-wise we have $\mathcal{S}_k : \theta \mapsto F_k\theta + g_k$), where F (F_k) is a $p \times K$ $(p_k \times K)$ matrix and g (g_k) is a column vector of size p (p_k). Throughput invariance implies:

$$1^T F_{kl} = \delta_{kl} = \begin{cases} 1 & \text{if } k = l \\ 0 & \text{otherwise} \end{cases}, \qquad 1^T g_k = 0 ,$$

where F_{kl} denotes the lth column of F_k. We call a routing function *distributed*, if

$$\frac{\partial \mathcal{S}_k}{\partial \theta_l} = 0 \text{ if } k \neq l$$

wherever the derivative is defined. The main advantage of distributed routing functions is that the amount of traffic sent to a path at a source node only depends on the actual demand at that node, and it is independent of the demands at other nodes.

Note that distributed routing functions can be treated as affine routing functions by restricting F to block-diagonal matrices. Another restriction can be made by fixing g at zero. In the latter case the routing function is a simple block diagonal linear transformation, i.e., it only specifies the splitting ratios based on which demands are distributed among the paths with the same ingress/egress nodes. Letting g be different from zero allows more freedom in assigning path-flows, though, this option might raise implementation issues as traffic splitting ratios need to vary in small steps in this case.

So far we have dealt with *simple routing functions*, in the sense that we tried to route all the admissible traffic matrices, that is, cover the whole throughput polytope, with one routing function. It is tempting to combine several routing functions into a single one. Such a *compound routing function* would be able to accommodate any admissible traffic matrix $\theta \in T$ with causing less link overload. To do this, we associate different routing functions with different regions of the throughput space, so $\mathcal{S}$ takes the form $\mathcal{S} = \{(R^i, \mathcal{S}^i) : i \in \mathcal{I}\}$ where R^is give a disjunct partition of the throughput space (e.g., see Fig. 1c, where two such a regions are depicted), and we use the mapping $\theta \mapsto \mathcal{S}^i(\theta)$ whenever $\theta \in R^i$.

Now, we are in a position to formulate the demand-oblivious routing problem in geometric terms.

Definition 3. *The minimal scalar α solving the optimization problem*

$$\min_{\mathcal{S}} \alpha : \mathcal{S}(T) \subseteq \alpha M \tag{1}$$

is called the oblivious ratio *and the corresponding routing function is called* demand-oblivious routing.

The interpretation of the optimization problem (1) is as follows. The set $\mathcal{S}(T)$ represents all the routings one can get when applying $\mathcal{S}$ to the set of admissible traffic matrices T. The objective is to up-scale the capacities of the network, and so the flow polytope of the network, to make all the routings in the set $\mathcal{S}(T)$ feasible. Hence, α signifies the maximal link over-utilization caused when routing *any* admissible traffic matrix over $\mathcal{S}$. This also implies that $\alpha \geq 1$.

So far, the oblivious ratio was defined with respect to the throughput set T. We need to find the oblivious ratio with respect to arbitrary regions and sometimes to arbitrary routing function. Thus, we need to introduce the following generalization.

Definition 4. *Given an arbitrary set of traffic matrices $\mathbb{R}^K \supset X \neq \emptyset$ and a routing function $\mathcal{S}$, the oblivious ratio $\alpha(X, S)$ with respect to X and $\mathcal{S}$ is the optimal solution of the optimization problem:*

$$\alpha(X, S) = \underset{\alpha}{\operatorname{argmin}}\{\mathcal{S}(X) \subseteq \alpha M\} . \tag{2}$$

Definition 5. *Given an arbitrary set of traffic matrices $\mathbb{R}^K \supset X \neq \emptyset$, the oblivious ratio $\alpha(X)$ with respect to X is the optimal solution of the optimization problem:*

$$\alpha(X) = \min_{\mathcal{S}} \alpha : \alpha(X, \mathcal{S}) \equiv \min_{\mathcal{S}} \alpha : \mathcal{S}(X) \subseteq \alpha M . \tag{3}$$

Remark 1. Note that $\alpha(X)$ is equivalent to the conventional notion of oblivious ratio when $X = T$. In other cases, it depends on X and it may even be smaller than 1 when $X \subset T$.

Remark 2. The routing function S minimizing the optimization problem 3 is called *optimal routing function* over the set of traffic matrices X.

Definition 6. *Given a throughput polytope T and a compound routing function $\mathcal{S} = \{(R^i, \mathcal{S}^i) : i \in \mathcal{I}\}$ the cumulative oblivious ratio of the system is defined as follows.*

$$s_\alpha(\{R^i\}_{i\in\mathcal{I}}) = \max_{i\in\mathcal{I}}\{\alpha(R^i)\} . \tag{4}$$

Note that the previous definition of cumulative oblivious ratio is the natural generalization of the oblivious ratio for compound routing functions, recalling that the oblivious ratio can be interpeted as the maximal link over-utilization.

3   Cumulative Oblivious Ratio over Hyper-cubic Regions and a Partitioning Algorithm

In this section, we analyze the cumulative oblivious ratio, when dividing the throughput polytope T into finite hyper-cubic partitions. First, we prove some theoretical properties of these partitions. Then, we introduce a novel algorithm, which, in contrast to the algorithm given in [23], provides provable guarantees on the cumulative oblivious ratio.

3.1   The Theoretical Upper Bound

The proof of our main theorem is based on some basic properties of hyper-cubic throughput regions. Thus, we first introduce an auxiliary theorem summarizing these observations.

Theorem 1. *Let $a_i, b_i \in \mathbb{R}_+, \forall i \in \{1, \cdots, K\}, a_i \leq b_i$ and $H = \underset{i=1}{\overset{K}{\times}} [a_i, b_i] \subset \mathbb{R}^K$ a hyper rectangle in the K dimensional throughput space. The optimal routing function $\mathcal{S}_H$ for the throughput region H is block diagonal and $\mathcal{S}_H = \mathcal{S}_b$, where $b = (b_1, \cdots, b_K)$ and $\mathcal{S}_b$ is the optimal routing function for the (singleton) throughput set $\{b\}$.*

Proof. Obviously, the routing function $\mathcal{S}_b$ can be written in block diagonal matrix form, viz., the routing function for a single throughput simply defines the distribution of demand between the routes being used.

Moreover, $\forall \theta \in H : \theta \leq b$ results that $\mathcal{S}_b$ is routing function for θ and $\mathcal{S}_b(b) \geq \mathcal{S}_b(\theta)$. The lowest possible oblivious ratio for b is achieved using the $\mathcal{S}_b$ routing function (because of the optimality of $\mathcal{S}_b$), thus $\mathcal{S}_H = \mathcal{S}_b$ is the optimal routing function over the whole region H.

Remark 3. $\underset{i=1}{\overset{K}{\times}} [a_i, b_i] \subset T \Rightarrow \alpha(\underset{i=1}{\overset{K}{\times}} [a_i, b_i]) \leq 1.$

Remark 4. The routing function $\mathcal{S}_b$ is distributed linear, i.e.,

$$0 \leq \{\mathcal{S}_b\}_{ij} \leq \begin{cases} 1 & \text{if } ij \text{ is a block diagonal element} \\ 0 & \text{otherwise} \end{cases} .$$

Let us take a closer look on the network configuration depicted in Fig. 1. We derive the routing function of the hyper-cubic region R^1. The maximum point of this region is the point $(1,1) \in \mathbb{R}^2$, which can be routed using the routing function

$$\mathcal{S}_{(1,1)} : \theta \longmapsto \begin{pmatrix} 1 & 0 \\ 0 & 0 \\ 0 & 1 \end{pmatrix} \theta; \quad \theta \in R^1 .$$

Observe that $\mathcal{S}_{(1,1)}$ is a distributed linear routing function. Additionally, $\mathcal{S}_{(1,1)}$ routes any demand in R^1 without causing link over-utilization, as the first demand is routed using path P_1, while the second demand uses only P_3. Moreover, all other demands in the region R^1 can be routed using this routing function, too.

Now, we are ready to state the main theorem that gives an easy-to-compute upper bound for the cumulative oblivious ratio over finite hyper-cubic partitions.

Theorem 2. *Let $\{H_i^\epsilon\}_{i \in \mathcal{I}}$, $H_i^\epsilon \subset \mathbb{R}_+^K$ be finite partition of any finite hypercube containing the throughput polytope T. Suppose, that H_i^ϵ are mutually exclusive and collectively exhaustive hypercubes with side length ϵ. Moreover, let $a_i = \min\{x : x \in H_i^\epsilon\}$ and let $\mathcal{S}_{a_i}$ be the optimal routing function for the point a_i. For any such partition of T, the cumulative oblivious ratio is given by:*

$$s_\alpha^\epsilon \leq 1 + \max_{e \in E} \left\{ \frac{\xi_e}{c_e} \right\} \epsilon ,$$

where c_e and ξ_e denotes the capacity and number of paths sharing the edge $e \in E$, respectively.

Proof. Introducing the notation $\overline{T} = \mathbb{R}_+^K \setminus T$ we have:

$$s_\alpha^\epsilon = s_\alpha(\{H_i^\epsilon \cap T\}_{i \in \mathcal{I}}) = \max_{i \in \mathcal{I}} \{\alpha(H_i^\epsilon \cap T)\} =$$

$$= \max_{\substack{i \in \mathcal{I} \\ H_i^\epsilon \cap T \neq 0}} \{\alpha(H_i^\epsilon \cap T)\} = \max_{\substack{i \in \mathcal{I} \\ H_i^\epsilon \cap T \neq 0 \\ H_i^\epsilon \cap \overline{T} \neq 0}} \{\alpha(H_i^\epsilon \cap T)\},$$

where the last equality is valid, because all the boundary points of T have at least oblivious ratio equal to 1 (note that each boundary point of T fills the capacities along at least one edge of the network). Simply put, when calculating the oblivious ratio only hypercubes (hypercube splits) containing at least one boundary point from T count.

Let P_k^e denote the row of the arc-path incidence matrix of k corresponding to link e. Now, we have

$$s_\alpha^\epsilon \overset{\boxed{1}}{\leq} \max_{e \in E} \max_{\substack{i \in \mathcal{I} \\ H_i^\epsilon \cap T \neq 0 \\ H_i^\epsilon \cap \overline{T} \neq 0}} \frac{\sum_{k=1}^{K} P_k^e \mathcal{S}_{a_i}(H_i^\epsilon \cap T)}{c_e} \leq \max_{e \in E} \max_{\substack{i \mathcal{I} \\ H_i^\epsilon \cap T \neq 0 \\ H_i^\epsilon \cap \overline{T} \neq 0}} \frac{\sum_{k=1}^{K} P_k^e \mathcal{S}_{a_i}(H_i^\epsilon)}{c_e}$$

$$\overset{\boxed{2}}{\leq} \max_{e \in E} \max_{\substack{i \in \mathcal{I} \\ H_i^\epsilon \cap T \neq 0 \\ H_i^\epsilon \cap \overline{T} \neq 0}} \frac{\sum_{k=1}^{K} P_k^e \mathcal{S}_{a_i}(a_i + \underline{1}\epsilon)}{c_e}$$

$$\overset{\boxed{3}}{=} \max_{e \in E} \max_{\substack{i \in \mathcal{I} \\ H_i^\epsilon \cap T \neq 0 \\ H_i^\epsilon \cap \overline{T} \neq 0}} \left\{ \frac{\sum_{k=1}^{K} P_k^e \mathcal{S}_{a_i}(a_i)}{c_e} + \frac{\sum_{k=1}^{K} P_k^e \mathcal{S}_{a_i}(\underline{1}\epsilon)}{c_e} \right\}$$

$$\overset{\boxed{4}}{\leq} 1 + \max_{e \in E} \max_{\substack{i \in \mathcal{I} \\ H_i^\epsilon \cap T \neq 0 \\ H_i^\epsilon \cap \overline{T} \neq 0}} \frac{\sum_{k=1}^{K} P_k^e \mathcal{S}_{a_i}(\underline{1}\epsilon)}{c_e} \overset{\boxed{5}}{\leq} 1 + \max_{e \in E} \left\{ \frac{\xi_e}{c_e} \right\} \epsilon,$$

where $\boxed{1}$ is valid, because instead of the optimal routing function we introduced a special (maybe not optimal) one in the formulae; $\boxed{2}$ is valid because of Theorem 1; $\boxed{3}$ is valid because of the linearity of $\mathcal{S}_{a_i}$ (see Remark 4); $\boxed{4}$ is valid because $a_i \in T$; $\boxed{5}$ is valid because of Remark 4.

Remark 5. During the proof we used the routing function $\mathcal{S}_{a_i}$, which belongs to the strictest class of possible routing functions covered in this paper ($\mathcal{S}_{a_i}$ is a distributed linear routing function; recall Remark 4). Thus, the derived formula is valid for more general affine functions, too (that is, when we let $g \neq 0$).

The results of Theorem 2 empowers us to analyze the behaviour of the *cumulative oblivious ratio over infinitesimally small hyper-cubic regions.*

Corollary 1. $\lim_{\epsilon \to 0} s_\alpha^\epsilon = \lim_{\epsilon \to 0} \left(1 + \max_{e \in E} \left\{ \frac{\xi_e}{c_e} \right\} \epsilon \right) = 1$

Simply put, Corollary 1 states that using smaller and smaller hyper-cubic regions as partitions the cumulative oblivious ratio converges to its minimum. In other words, link over-utilization can be eliminated be using sufficiently small regions.

3.2   The Partitioning Algorithm

After the theoretical considerations, we introduce a novel algorithm to compute a hybrid demand-oblivious routing function that guarantees that link over-utilization does exceed a given parameter. The input to the algorithm is, consequently, the desirable oblivious ratio δ. This parameter then, according to Theorem 2, determines an upper bound ϵ on the size of hypercubes we need to cover the throughput polytope as follows:

$$\epsilon \leq \frac{\delta-1}{\max_{e \in E}\{\xi_e/c_e\}} . \tag{5}$$

Calculating the optimal routing functions over these hypercubes (i.e., solving Equation (3) for each hypercube R^i, $i \in \mathcal{I}$, separately), a compound routing function $\mathcal{S} = \{(R^i, \mathcal{S}^i) : i \in \mathcal{I}\}$ can be constructed with guaranteed oblivious ratio δ (see Algorithm 1).

Algorithm 1. Partitioning algorithm

---

function PARTITIONING_OBLIVIOUS_ROUTING(δ)

$\quad \epsilon \leftarrow \frac{\delta-1}{\max_{e \in E}\{\xi_e/c_e\}}$

$\quad \{H_i^\epsilon\}_{i \in \mathcal{I}} \leftarrow \cup_{i \in \mathcal{I}} H_i^\epsilon$ so that $T \subseteq \{H_i^\epsilon\}_{i \in \mathcal{I}}$

$\quad$**for** $i \in \mathcal{I}$

$\quad\quad R^i = H_i^\epsilon \cap T$

$\quad\quad (\alpha^i, \mathcal{S}^i) \leftarrow \min_{\mathcal{S}} \alpha : \mathcal{S}(R^i) \subset \alpha M$

$\quad\quad$store $(\alpha^i, \mathcal{S}^i, R^i)$

$\quad$**end for**

end function

Hitherto, we have not specified the type of the routing functions used in the partitioning algorithm. According to Theorem 2, it is possible to use any kind of routing functions, however, it is a good decision to restrict the routing functions to affine distributed functions. The main advantage of the distributed routing functions is that the actual splitting ratio for a given demand depends only upon that demand, and it is not dependent upon other demands.

Hence, our scheme will require minimal central control, only to lookup the right routing region based on the actual demands. For this, the central controller periodically determines the actual traffic matrix and checks whether the current demand θ still resides in the current routing region R^i. If yes, no action is taken as the current routing function is correct. Otherwise, the controller searches for a new region. Organizing the regions into a decision tree improves the online complexity to $\mathcal{O}(\log|\mathcal{I}|)$, where $|\mathcal{I}|$ denotes the number of routing regions.

Recall the sample network depicted in Fig. 1. For this configuration, due to the edge between the nodes labelled by 2 and 4, and due to the unit capacity of the edges, $\max_{e \in E} \xi_e = 2$. Suppose that we need to fulfill a given constraint, say, the cumulative oblivious ratio should be less than $\delta = 3$. According to expression (5), we get $\epsilon = 1$ as the size of the hypercubes needed to cover the throughput polytope to attain this δ as the oblivious ratio. A possible partitioning is depicted in Fig. 1c. Then, running Algorithm 1 over this partitioning (that is, solving (3) for each hyper-cubic region in Fig. 1c) over the class of distributed affine functions, we obtain the following routing functions:

$$\mathcal{S}^1 : \theta \mapsto \begin{pmatrix} 1 & 0 \\ 0 & 0 \\ 0 & 1 \end{pmatrix} \theta; \quad \theta \in R^1$$

$$\mathcal{S}^2 : \theta \mapsto \begin{pmatrix} 0 & 0 \\ 1 & 0 \\ 0 & 1 \end{pmatrix} \theta + \begin{pmatrix} 1 \\ -1 \\ 0 \end{pmatrix}; \quad \theta \in R^2$$

Note that for this compound routing function the cumulative oblivious ratio is not only less than the desired one, but it is equal to 1. This suggests that our theoretical bound on the oblivious ratio is somewhat pessimistic.

4 Evaluation

Algorithm. During the simulations, we used a bit different version of the previously introduced partitioning algorithm. Instead of the desired oblivious ratio, the parameter of the modified algorithm is rather the iteration depth, that is, the number of cutting planes in each dimension of the throughput space (cutting planes are equally distanced in each dimension). Note that there is a direct connection between the cube-size value ϵ and the iteration depth j, namely, $\epsilon^j = \max_{k \in \mathcal{K}} \frac{m_k}{j}$, where m_k is the (single-commodity) maximum flow for the k-th source-destination pair. We chose this modification of the algorithm because it fits better the purposes of our simulation studies: we can increase the iteration depth and observe the change in the cumulative oblivious ratio, instead of having to guess the latter value and calculating the size of hypercubes used by partitioning. Moreover, in this way it can be guaranteed that for different iteration depth the number of control regions is different, too. However, we cannot warrant anymore that the oblivious ratio decreases when increasing the iteration depth.

Performance Metrics. We used the following three performance metrics to characterize the efficiency of our algorithm: *(i)* the oblivious ratio as defined in the optimization problem (1); *(ii)* the cumulative oblivious ratio as defined in Equation (4); and *(iii)* the number of control regions denoted by $|\mathcal{I}|$. Note that the number of control regions is directly related to the complexity of the routing function: the more regions, the more routing functions must be calculated and stored, and hence the more lookups are needed during the operation of the network.

Simulation Instances. We ran our evaluations on ISP data maps from the Rocketfuel dataset [27]. We used the same method as in [14] to obtain approximate POP-level topologies: we collapsed the topologies so that nodes correspond to cities, we eliminated leaf-nodes and we set link capacities inversely proportional to the link weights. The number of users was increased from 2 to 8, source-destination pairs were chosen according to the bimodal distribution and paths were provisioned maximally node-disjoint. The number of cutting planes (the iteration depth) was increased from 1 to 4. Fifteen evaluation runs, using distributed affine (denoted by 1 in the superscript) and distributed linear (denoted by 2 in the superscript) routing functions, respectively, were conducted on different randomly chosen network samples and the results were averaged. The results are depicted in Table 2.

Apart from the realistic network topologies supplied by the Rocketfuel data set, we also conducted simulations on artificial networks in order to assess the worst case performance of our algorithm. The networks marked by OK-x (for $x = 3, 4, 5$ and 6, resp.) were originally constructed in [16] to derive the worst-case value of the oblivious ratio in specially crafted networks. For a given value x, the OK-x network is constructed as follows. It has $N = \binom{x}{2} + x + 1$ vertices denoted by $a_{i,j}$ for all $1 \leq i \leq j \leq x$, b_i for all $1 \leq i \leq x$ and a vertex denoted by t. The edges of the network are all of unit capacity and are as follows: $(a_{i,j}, b_i)$ and $(a_{i,j}, b_j)$ for all $1 \leq i \leq j \leq x$, and (b_i, t) for $1 \leq i \leq x$. The source-destination pairs are $(a_{j,y}, t)$ for all $1 \leq j \leq y - 1$, and $(a_{y,j}, t)$ for all $y + 1 \leq j \leq x$. The simulation results for these networks are depicted in Fig. 2.

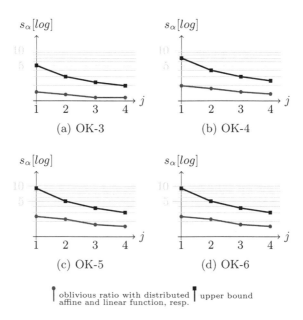

(a) OK-3   (b) OK-4

(c) OK-5   (d) OK-6

oblivious ratio with distributed affine and linear function, resp.   upper bound

Fig. 2. Measured oblivious ratio for the selected artificial networks and iteration depths

Table 2. Measured cumulative oblivious ratios for the selected rocketfuel topologies. α^2 and α^1 denotes the cumulative oblivious ratio using distributed linear and distributed affine routing functions, resprectively. α_j^2, α_j^1 and β_j denote the average normed cumulative oblivious ratio (i.e, α_j^2 is the average of the normed values $s_{\alpha_j^2}/\alpha^2$) and the calculated average normed upper bound for the j-th iteration, respectively.

K	oblivious ratio		2				3				4			
	α^2	α^1	α_2^2	α_2^1	β_2	$|\mathcal{I}_2|$	α_3^2	α_3^1	β_3	$|\mathcal{I}_3|$	α_4^2	α_4^1	β_4	$|\mathcal{I}_4|$
2	1.012	1.012	0.997	0.990	2.687	4.0	0.998	0.989	2.121	9.0	0.996	0.989	1.838	15.9
3	1.095	1.095	0.989	0.937	2.734	8.0	0.963	0.940	2.129	26.8	0.960	0.932	1.826	62.7
4	1.139	1.139	0.978	0.929	3.228	15.9	0.947	0.919	2.446	76.2	0.945	0.908	2.055	228.0
5	1.119	1.119	0.983	0.940	2.721	31.7	0.960	0.936	2.114	231.6	0.955	0.926	1.810	930.1
6	1.229	1.229	0.981	0.911	3.440	60.8	0.929	0.895	2.566	618.9	0.919	0.878	2.128	3090.4
7	1.231	1.231	0.976	0.924	4.213	114.7	0.933	0.897	3.081	1652.4	0.919	0.878	2.515	10674.7
8	1.269	1.269	0.968	0.914	3.452	244.3	0.923	0.888	2.565	5217.6	0.905	0.867	2.121	45566.7

(a) AS 1239

K	oblivious ratio		2				3				4			
	α^2	α^1	α_2^2	α_2^1	β_2	$|\mathcal{I}_2|$	α_3^2	α_3^1	β_3	$|\mathcal{I}_3|$	α_4^2	α_4^1	β_4	$|\mathcal{I}_4|$
2	1.025	1.025	0.998	0.987	3.414	4.0	0.994	0.982	2.602	8.9	0.991	0.982	2.196	15.5
3	1.062	1.062	0.987	0.972	4.138	8.0	0.980	0.960	3.075	26.4	0.971	0.961	2.543	61.4
4	1.163	1.163	0.986	0.938	5.156	15.6	0.956	0.912	3.725	75.4	0.939	0.904	3.010	220.7
5	1.188	1.188	0.983	0.939	3.836	31.5	0.956	0.905	2.839	211.9	0.931	0.898	2.340	829.3
6	1.208	1.208	0.978	0.942	5.261	62.4	0.959	0.914	3.783	617.3	0.933	0.898	3.045	3231.2
7	1.235	1.235	0.969	0.929	5.997	120.0	0.946	0.906	4.268	1616.7	0.918	0.885	3.404	10077.9
8	1.273	1.273	0.964	0.932	6.893	228.3	0.933	0.900	4.858	4154.8	0.909	0.876	3.840	33333.1

(b) AS 1755

K	oblivious ratio		2				3				4			
	α^2	α^1	α_2^2	α_2^1	β_2	$|\mathcal{I}_2|$	α_3^2	α_3^1	β_3	$|\mathcal{I}_3|$	α_4^2	α_4^1	β_4	$|\mathcal{I}_4|$
2	2.000	1.000	1.000	1.000	3.764	4.0	1.000	1.000	2.843	9.0	1.000	1.000	2.382	16.0
3	2.061	1.096	0.996	0.939	3.822	8.0	0.989	0.930	2.872	27.0	0.987	0.930	2.397	64.0
4	2.196	1.143	0.985	0.942	5.994	16.0	0.965	0.912	4.301	79.2	0.953	0.907	3.454	246.4
5	2.248	1.210	0.989	0.924	3.973	32.0	0.964	0.890	2.947	237.6	0.949	0.875	2.434	985.6
6	2.289	1.175	0.989	0.929	4.626	64.0	0.961	0.902	3.377	712.8	0.946	0.895	2.752	3942.4
7	2.357	1.228	0.991	0.931	5.657	128.0	0.959	0.898	4.054	2138.4	0.933	0.882	3.253	15769.6
8	2.406	1.281	0.983	0.902	6.175	256.0	0.940	0.871	4.394	6269.4	0.923	0.850	3.504	60620.8

(c) AS 3257

K	oblivious ratio		2				3				4			
	α^2	α^1	α_2^2	α_2^1	β_2	$|\mathcal{I}_2|$	α_3^2	α_3^1	β_3	$|\mathcal{I}_3|$	α_4^2	α_4^1	β_4	$|\mathcal{I}_4|$
2	1.044	1.044	0.993	0.971	3.626	4.0	0.983	0.969	2.738	8.9	0.979	0.967	2.294	15.7
3	1.108	1.108	0.980	0.944	4.185	8.0	0.962	0.930	3.092	26.6	0.953	0.924	2.546	62.1
4	1.176	1.176	0.986	0.940	6.610	16.0	0.954	0.907	4.692	78.0	0.933	0.898	3.733	236.8
5	1.190	1.190	0.983	0.932	6.645	31.5	0.956	0.911	4.713	222.8	0.938	0.895	3.746	888.0
6	1.232	1.232	0.977	0.926	5.286	62.7	0.939	0.905	3.797	654.6	0.921	0.884	3.053	3304.5
7	1.314	1.314	0.951	0.911	6.042	124.5	0.906	0.869	4.284	1893.9	0.881	0.847	3.405	12333.0
8	1.334	1.334	0.953	0.912	7.420	235.5	0.910	0.874	5.198	5139.5	0.884	0.850	4.087	43033.1

(d) AS 3967

Evaluation results. The main observations are as follows. First, as the theoretical results suggest the measured oblivious ratio is always less than the predicted one. However, the difference between the two values can become significant. This is the cost we must pay for using rough approximations in order to be able to derive a simple theoretical upper bound. Second, we can clearly see that using the more general distributed affine functions (recall, the ones marked with 1 in superscript) better cumulative oblivious ratio can be obtained. Thus, it might be tempting to use affine routing functions for real life networks. However, the simulation results also show that the benefit is highly network dependent. For example, in case of the network topology AS3257 this difference is quite straightforward, but for the other ones the benefits of the general routing function is not that significant. Third, the benefit caused by increasing the iteration depth is also dependent on the type of the routing function. Using the more general distributed affine function, naturally, yields better results than distributed linear functions.

Lastly, we consider the complexity of the routing (functions) expressed in terms of the depends on the number of routing regions. As it is clearly observable, the number of routing regions increases rapidly with the iteration depth increasing the complexity of the routing function, making the proposed algorithm somewhat inefficient. Contrasting these results to the ones in [23], we see that the algorithm in [23] is more efficient and less complex. The algorithm in this paper, though, is still extremely important, because it provides a firm theoretical worst-case bound on the oblivious ratio, and hence, link over-utilization experienced by the network in case of *any* admissible traffic matrix. This was impossible with previous algorithms.

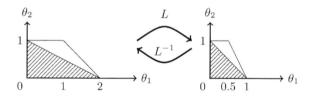

Fig. 3. Due to the down-monotonicity of the throughput polytope, after the linear transformation L the K-simplex is going to be the part of the transformed throughput polytope. Thus, the number of hypercubes covering the standard K-simplex is less than the number of the routing regions.

It is tempting to investigate, whether a hyper-cubic partitioning algorithm exists that is both efficient and simple (i.e., contains at most a polynomial number of hyper-cubic regions) at the same time. Unfortunately, this does not seem to be the case, as the following lower bound on the number of routing regions suggests:

$$|\mathcal{I}| \geq \lceil \frac{v(K)}{(1/j)^K} \rceil .$$

In this expression, $v(K)$ denotes the volume of the standard K-simplex and j, as before, is the iteration depth. The expression compares the volume of the standard K-simplex and the hypercubes with side length $\frac{1}{j}$. We used the observation that the standard K-simplex can be naturally transformed, using a linear transformation, into the interior of the throughput polytope, and vice versa (for more details, consult Fig. 3). What the expression states is that halving the permitted link over-utilization (i.e., halving the value of ϵ) needs about $\mathcal{O}(2^K)$ times more regions.

5   Related Work

Demand-oblivious routing has rich literature [14, 16–19, 21]. There are various results regarding the worst-case performance: Räcke gives a method with poly-logarithmic oblivious ratio in undirected graphs [15], while Azar *et al.* proves that no such bound exists for directed graphs: they give a directed graph of $\binom{k}{2} + k + 1$ nodes, $\binom{k}{2}$ source-destination pairs where the oblivious ratio is at least $\binom{k}{2}$ [16].

Recently, in [28] it was shown that for every network the link over-utilization can be eliminated introducing compound affine routing functions. Here, the routing functions are calculated using multi-parametric linear programs. However, in contrast to the algorithm presented in this paper, the optimal algorithm uses extensive central control, both for setting the traffic splitting ratios and for the selection of the actual routing region.

The idea of compound routing functions inspired the development of a hybrid algorithm [23]. This algorithm simplifies the type of the routing regions, as it generates only hyper-cubic regions. The algorithm uses heuristics when creating the routing regions: in each step the algorithm tries to minimize the cumulative oblivious ratio by slicing each (previously created) routing region into two new hyper-cubic regions. The algorithm is a conquer-and-divide fashion algorithm, i.e., for each region the cutting plane is selected, which minimizes the oblivious ratio. According to [23], by only a few cuts the oblivious ratio can be drastically decreased, however, no convergence results exist.

Our recent algorithm can be viewed as the successor of the previous algorithm. It keeps all of its advantages, but tries to solve the problem from the bottom-up perspective, instead of the top-down one. As a result, it can give a theoretical upper bound for the cumulative oblivious ratio, and it can be used to design routings satisfying any given maximal link over-utilization. Unfortunately, the comparison of the simulation results of the two methods show that our recent method needs more routing regions to achieve the prescribed oblivious ratio than the one in [23].

There are several methods combining basic oblivious routing with some real life measurements to predict future state. These prediction based algorithms work on traffic matrix samples collected during some time interval. Instead of optimizing oblivious ratio over the full throughput polytope, as it is done in demand-oblivious routing, here the optimization is performed – and the routing function is calculated – only over the convex hull of the collected traffic matrices. Thus, these algorithms are effective when the future demands fall into the computed convex hull. Unfortunately, fulfillment of this condition cannot be guaranteed. One method solving this problem is called COPE [7]. In COPE, a penalty envelope is introduced, thus, not only the oblivious ratio is optimized over the convex hull of the collected traffic matrices, but also some penalty function of the routing function over the whole throughput polytope is bounded. Simulation results in [7] show that COPE can achieve efficient resource utilization under a variety of real topologies and scenarios.

There are also several on-line TE methods, which, in contrast to our algorithm, use feedback from the network. For example, REPLEX [13] and DATE [10] are both such methods. They both solve the routing problem in a distributed manner, i.e., there is a given convergence time to calculate the appropriate routing function. In contrast, in our algorithm a central controller is needed to periodically determine the actual traffic matrix and select the right routing region and the (previously, offline calculated) routing function.

6   Conclusion

In this paper, we analyzed the properties of demand-oblivious routing over hyper-cubic regions. We determined an easy to computable worst case bound for the cumulative oblivious ratio, which empowered us to design a hybrid centralized-distributed partitioning algorithm for calculating a compound routing function with upper bounded oblivious ratio (and hence link over-utilization). To the best of our knowledge, this is the first time that a demand-oblivious routing algorithm with provable worst-case performance in directed graphs is presented.

Simulation studies using several real-life network topologies showed that our algorithm indeed admits the theoretical worst-case behavior. In addition, the algorithm successfully decreases the cumulative oblivious ratio in only a few iterations. Though, a closer investigation of the compound routing functions generated unearthed complexity problems: halving the link over-utilization needs about $\mathcal{O}(2^K)$ times as many regions, where K is the dimension of the throughput space.

We were able to prove that link over-utilization can be fully eliminated when decreasing the size of the hyper-cubic regions to infinitesimally small, (i.e., using infinity number of routing regions) regardless of the type of the routing function. The question arises, whether there are networks for which the link over-utilization can be eliminated with using only a finite number of hyper-cubic routing regions. Our future work will focus on finding the class of networks having this property.

References

1. Awduche, D., Chiu, A., Elwalid, A., Widjaja, I., Xiao, X.: Overview and principles of Internet traffic engineering. RFC 3272 (May 2002)
2. Cantor, D.G., Gerla, M.: Optimal routing in a packet-switched computer network. IEEE Transactions on Computer 23(10), 1062–1069 (1974)
3. Fortz, B., Rexford, J., Thorup, M.: Traffic engineering with traditional IP routing protocols. IEEE Communications Magazine 40(10), 118–124 (2002)
4. Roughan, M., Thorup, M., Zhang, Y.: Traffic engineering with estimated traffic matrices. In: IMC 2003: Proceedings of the 3rd ACM SIGCOMM Conference on Internet Measurement, pp. 248–258 (2003)
5. Zhang, C., Liu, Y., Gong, W., Moll, J., Towsley, R.D.: On optimal routing with multiple traffic matrices. In: INFOCOM 2005, vol. 1, pp. 607–618 (2005)
6. Medhi, D.: Multi-hour, multi-traffic class network design for virtual path-based dynamically reconfigurable wide-area ATM networks. IEEE/ACM Transactions on Networking 3(6), 809–818 (1995)
7. Wang, H., Xie, H., Qiu, L., Yang, Y.R., Zhang, Y., Greenberg, A.: COPE: traffic engineering in dynamic networks. SIGCOMM Comput. Commun. Rev. 36(4), 99–110 (2006)
8. Bertsekas, D.P.: Dynamic behavior of shortest path routing algorithms for communication networks. IEEE Trans. on Automatic Control 27, 60–74 (1982)
9. Chiang, M., Low, S.H., Calderbank, A.R., Doyle, J.C.: Layering as optimization decomposition: A mathematical theory of network architectures. Proceedings of the IEEE 95(1), 255–312 (2007)
10. He, J., Bresler, M., Chiang, M., Rexford, J.: Towards robust multi-layer traffic engineering: Optimization of congestion control and routing. IEEE Journal on Selected Areas in Communications 25(5), 868–880 (2007)
11. Lagoa, C.M., Che, H., Movsichoff, B.A.: Adaptive control algorithms for decentralized optimal traffic engineering in the internet. IEEE/ACM Trans. Netw. 12(3), 415–428 (2004)
12. Kandula, S., Katabi, D., Davie, B., Charny, A.: Walking the Tightrope: Responsive Yet Stable Traffic Engineering. In: ACM SIGCOMM 2005 (August 2005)
13. Fischer, S., Kammenhuber, N., Feldmann, A.: REPLEX: dynamic traffic engineering based on wardrop routing policies. In: Proceedings of CoNEXT 2006, pp. 1–12 (2006)
14. Applegate, D., Cohen, E.: Making intra-domain routing robust to changing and uncertain traffic demands: understanding fundamental tradeoffs. In: Proceedings of SIGCOMM 2003, pp. 313–324 (2003)
15. Räcke, H.: Minimizing congestion in general networks. In: FOCS 2002, pp. 43–52 (2002)
16. Azar, Y., Cohen, E., Fiat, A., Kaplan, H., Räcke, H.: Optimal oblivious routing in polynomial time. J. Comput. Syst. Sci. 69(3), 383–394 (2004)
17. Wellons, J., Xue, Y.: Oblivious routing for wireless mesh networks. In: ICC 2008, pp. 2969–2973 (May 2008)
18. Li, Y., Bai, B., Harms, J.J., Holte, R.C.: Stable and Robust Multipath Oblivious Routing for Traffic Engineering. In: Mason, L.G., Drwiega, T., Yan, J. (eds.) ITC 2007. LNCS, vol. 4516, pp. 129–140. Springer, Heidelberg (2007)
19. Applegate, D., Breslau, L., Cohen, E.: Coping with network failures: routing strategies for optimal demand oblivious restoration. SIGMETRICS Perform. Eval. Rev. 32(1), 270–281 (2004)

20. Hajiaghayi, M., Kim, J., Leighton, T., Räcke, H.: Oblivious routing in directed graphs with random demands. In: STOC 2005, pp. 193–201 (2005)
21. Bansal, N., Blum, A., Chawla, S., Meyerson, A.: Online oblivious routing. In: SPAA 2003, pp. 44–49 (2003)
22. Towles, B., Dally, W.: Worst-case traffic for oblivious routing functions. In: SPAA 2002, pp. 1–8 (2002)
23. Rétvári, G., Németh, G.: Demand-oblivious routing: distributed vs. centralized approaches. In: INFOCOM 2010 (March 2010)
24. Rétvári, G., Bíró, J.J., Cinkler, T.: Fairness in capacitated networks: A polyhedral approach. In: INFOCOM 2007, vol. 1, pp. 1604–1612 (May 2007)
25. Ziegler, G.M.: Lectures on Polytopes. Graduate Texts in Mathematics, vol. 152. Springer, Heidelberg (1998)
26. Grünbaum, B.: Convex Polytopes. John Wiley & Sons (1967)
27. Mahajan, R., Spring, N., Wetherall, D., Anderson, T.: Inferring link weights using end-to-end measurements. In: IMW 2002: Proceedings of the 2nd ACM SIGCOMM Workshop on Internet Measurment, pp. 231–236 (2002)
28. Rétvári, G., Németh, G.: On optimal rate-adaptive routing. In: ISCC 2010, pp. 605–610 (2010)

Optimizing the Update Packet Stream
for Web Applications

Muthuprasanna Muthusrinivasan[1] and Manimaran Govindarasu[2]

[1] Google Inc., Mountain View CA 94043, USA
`muthup@google.com`
[2] Iowa State University, Ames IA 50011, USA
`gmani@iastate.edu`

Abstract. The Internet has evolved to an extent where users now expect any-where any-time and any-form access to their personalized data and applications of choice. However providing a coherent (seamless) user experience across multiple devices has been relatively hard to achieve. While the *how to sync* problem has been well studied in literature, the complementary *when to sync* problem has remained relatively unexplored. While frequent updates providing higher user satisfaction/ retention are naturally more desirable than sparse updates, the steadily escalating resource costs are a significant bottleneck. We thus propose extensions to the traditional periodic refresh model based on an adaptive *smart sync approach* that enables variable rate updates closely modeling expected user behavior over time. An experimental evaluation on a size-able subset of users of the GMAIL web interface further indicates that the proposed refresh policy can achieve the best of both worlds - limited resource provisioning and minimal user-perceived delays.

Keywords: data synchronization, web applications, cloud computing.

1 Introduction

The World Wide Web has seen tremendous growth since its early days at CERN [1], and in the past few years has witnessed a steady shift away from the traditional desktop computing paradigm. The rapid emergence of cloud computing [2] has given rise to - *service providers* who build/manage universally accessible, massively scalable, highly reliable compute infrastructure as an utility/commodity, *software vendors* who host their applications in this cloud avoiding capital expenditure and instead paying only for their resource utilization, and *end users* who can now access technology-enabled applications easily without knowledge of the underlying infrastructure. While cloud/service providers [3] benefit from multi-tenancy and economies of scale, the software vendors benefit from *on-demand* access to resources for their SaaS [4] deployments worldwide.

The greatest beneficiaries though have been the end users - the use of open standards, technological convergence [5] and pervasive computing [6] have enabled users to access information through a multitude of devices - instant

I. Tomkos et al. (Eds.): BROADNETS 2010, LNICST 66, pp. 101–118, 2012.

messaging through desktop clients, web browsers, mobile phones, interactive TV etc. is now possible. Users can thus access their data in the cloud using any device, at any time, anywhere in the world, and in any desired form, with no restrictions whatsoever. The widespread adoption of these ubiquitous applications is now primarily governed by natural expectations of a *coherent user experience*. In applications where data reconciliation can be quick and easy, seamless on-access device sync would suffice. However, it is untenable for applications requiring longer synchronization cycles or needing a complex update mechanism, due to undesirable user-perceived delays and slow application response times.

The traditional approach towards data reconciliation has been to execute mutually agreed update protocols at regular intervals. However, high frequency updates for devices having low user activity leads to a large number of redundant *null* updates. Such a non-optimal use of resources does not scale well for the cloud managing millions of users each possibly using tens of remote devices. Hence we propose a *smart sync approach* that exploits user behavior (past access patterns) to determine the likelihood of an impending user access to trigger a pro-active update. This would not only consume far fewer resources due to throttling of updates during periods of expected user inactivity, but also provide maximal data coherence across devices due to pro-active data synchronization. In this paper, we analyze a sizeable subset of GMAIL user interactions with the cloud, to determine optimal user behavior models for likelihood estimation (update interval adaptation) and to also study the resulting benefits for the users and the application in the cloud.

2   Related Work

Continuous harmonization of data over time across multiple remote sources, or *data synchronization* [7], has been a well studied topic [8], and has been explored in multiple contexts such as database design [9], secure communications [10], memory architectures [11], distributed computing [12], etc.

The research on data synchronization for ubiquitous computing has proceeded mainly along two lines, namely the *how to sync* and *when to sync* paradigms. The 'how to sync' issue deals with designing optimal data sync protocols that are scalable with network size and the resulting bandwidth/storage considerations. The traditional approach has relied on the use of timestamps [13] for version control, and delta compression [14] for minimal data transmission. Recent approaches relying on robust mathematical [15], information-theoretic [16], and probabilistic [17] techniques have provided greater flexibility.

Also, commercial solutions including Palm's HotSync [18], Microsoft's ActiveSync [19], Nokia's IntelliSync [20], etc. are in wide use today. This proliferation of proprietary sync protocols and their mutual incompatibilities led to the

Open Mobile Alliance [21] and the emergence of a platform-independent open standard known as SyncML [22].

The complementary 'when to sync' issue deals with the formulation of an optimal update policy - good data coherence while consuming fewer resources in the device, the cloud, and the network. The classic 'push vs pull' debate arises in this context [23]. In a *push* model the server (cloud) keeps track of all the connected clients (devices) and triggers updates as soon as they are generated. While it guarantees maximal data coherence and least resource consumption, scalability has been a minor concern due to expensive state maintenance for the dynamically-changing heterogeneous network topology.

In a *pull* model, the different clients (devices) fetch data from the server (cloud) at some pre-defined intervals. While a lower pull frequency leads to delayed data coherence, a higher pull frequency leads to increased resource consumption. Although achieving an optimal threshold has proven to be difficult, most web applications today use periodic polling for updates as it is both lightweight and easily deployed. Recently hybrid push-pull mechanisms [24] exploiting persistent (keep-alive) HTTP connections and reverse-AJAX style asynchronous polling such as COMET [25] and the Bayeux protocol [26] have been proposed. In parallel, tool-kits such as Google Gears [27], Microsoft Sync Framework [28] and others provide the ability to use applications off-line, yet seamlessly synchronizing with the cloud whenever possible.

Our focus here is on continual adaptation of the popular periodic polling technique based on past access patterns to both improve user satisfaction and network/cloud performance. The rest of the paper is organized as follows. Sections 3 and 4 present the system architecture used for analysis and a few key preliminary observations respectively. Sections 5 and 6 then present the proposed adaptive sync techniques and the results of their experimental evaluation respectively.

3   Analysis Framework

GMAIL [29] is a popular cloud-based email solution used by a large number of people world-wide on multiple platforms/devices. As a means of evaluating our proposed smart sync approach, we analyze a sizeable subset of GMAIL user interactions for a five-week duration (25 week-days). In this context, we wish to categorically state that the web access logs used in this experiment were fully anonymized to mask all user and location identifying information with due concern for privacy. Fig. 1 represents the analysis framework used for our experimental evaluation here. All user queries served by the many GMAIL frontend servers have historically been anonymized and per query statistics archived in the Google File System [30]. We mine these per query logs to construct aggregate per user logs, and run them through a Sawzall/Map-Reduce [31] [32] based pattern extraction engine that generates session signatures in Bigtable [33].

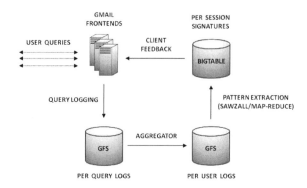

Fig. 1. Analysis Framework

Lastly we design a query replay mechanism that can gather/compute per user statistics based on continual adaptation of the individual session signatures.

For privacy and confidentiality reasons, our results here primarily focus on frequency distributions and behavioral trends, not absolute statistics and raw numbers. Additionally, the results are expected to have a minor loss of fidelity induced by the anonymization process used to strip sensitive user/location information from the user access logs.

4   Preliminary Study

We now present our initial observations along with a formal definition of a few terms loosely used thus far.

4.1   Terminology

While we expect the terms *user*, *device* and *location* to refer to a person, physical gadget, and some geo-coordinate respectively, their usage in the world of web applications is slightly skewed - every HTTP request is instead represented by a triplet *(user_id, location_id, cookie_id)*.

While *user_id* directly maps a digital identity to a physical person, it is not guaranteed to be unique due to the use of multiple accounts by a single person or sharing of a single account by a group of users. Similarly *location_id* cannot guarantee a unique mapping from a network address to the Internet host that issued that particular request due to the use of network address translation, proxy servers etc. The other means of tracking distinct devices using browser cookies (*cookie_id*) also cannot guarantee unique device identification due to browser state synchronization across devices by various applications [34] and proactive user deletion of cookies due to privacy/anonymity concerns or otherwise.

Fortunately these anomalies are relatively fewer and hence *we unify the terms cookie, location and device and use them interchangeably henceforth.* We thus restrict our analysis here to appropriate (user_id, cookie_id) tuples as representative of true user migration patterns on the Internet as a whole.

4.2   Initial Observations

As previously stated, data sync techniques relying on a client pull design require server polling at regular intervals. However the ever-increasing bandwidth needs coupled with higher demand for cpu, memory and disk resources mandate the design and use of a more efficient sync mechanism. Our key observation in this regard has been that most users display fairly stereotypical intra-day access patterns in addition to regular everyday usage, making them fairly repetitive and their access patterns relatively easy to predict.

User Persistence: A critical requirement of any adaptive technique is the availability of sufficient per-user data over extended durations of time to make reasonably accurate predictions. Fig. 2 shows the user persistence histogram for the 25-day window. The x-axis represents the total duration (in days) an user accessed the GMAIL web interface, while the (log-scale) y-axis tracks the total number of users in each of those intervals. Herein we notice the large number of highly persistent (heavy) users (long-tail) which provides sufficient scope for reliable data gathering and analysis, for accurate user behavior predictions.

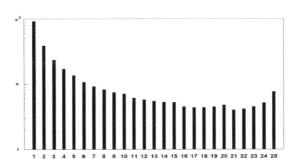

Fig. 2. User Persistence

Device Spread: The user persistence metric measures the time spread, but not the location/device spread for any user. The device spread histogram in Fig. 3 plots the maximum/average/minimum number of cookies accessed by the user during the 25-day observation window. The x-axis represents the total number of distinct cookies, while the (log-scale) y-axis tracks the number of users accessing the corresponding number of cookies. Herein we notice a large number of users who interact with multiple cookies/devices on a regular basis. The seemingly large number of cookies for certain users is probably due to extensive account sharing or incorrect query to device attribution as explained previously.

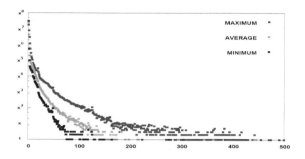

Fig. 3. Device Spread

Time Persistence: Varying the data sync update interval yields higher resource savings for mostly idle users than always-on users, and hence the practical feasibility of any adaptive sync technique is impacted by the cumulative time duration an user accesses a particular session. Fig. 4 represents the time persistence histogram where the x-axis represents the time persistence intervals (in minutes/day), while the (log-scale) y-axis tracks the number of users in each of those intervals. We notice that a majority of users show activity for less than a few hours a day, and hence a periodic polling strategy would perform poorly. The presence of user accounts having extremely high time persistence can be attributed to coarse-grained time data available and mismatched query to user attribution, both induced by content stripping for logs anonymization.

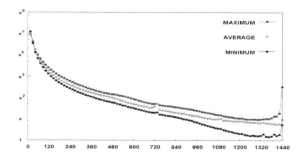

Fig. 4. Time Persistence

Thus high user persistence and device spread combined with low time persistence for a large majority of GMAIL users indicates that an adaptive sync approach can easily outperform the periodic polling mechanism. We now seek to analyze in greater detail these stereotypical trends in daily user access patterns to design an optimal data refresh policy.

5   Smart Sync Approach

We have thus far focused on the basic *can we adapt* issue, while we now try to address the more critical *how to adapt* issue by analyzing a few user behavior models for simplicity, scalability, and impact on overall user satisfaction.

5.1   Basic Representation

As stated previously, we use a *(user_id, cookie_id)* tuple as the basic unit of data measurement, analysis and subsequent optimization - henceforth simply referred to as a *session*. A steady increase in the number of users and their personal devices can quickly lead to scalability issues with respect to storage and computational needs, and hence we need small light-weight *session signatures* that lend well to easier generation and real-time adaption. Thus complex pattern analysis or correlation techniques need to be discarded in favor of simple resource-efficient approximate solutions.

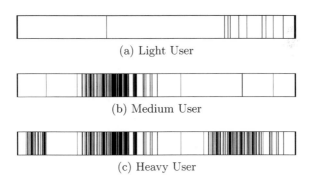

(a) Light User

(b) Medium User

(c) Heavy User

Fig. 5. User Session Activity (1 day)

Click Tracking: A simple means of characterizing session activity would be to analyze user-generated clicks in any browser session - while a single click indicates user presence, a corresponding absence may not accurately differentiate an inactive session from an idle user processing related/other information. However, if we presume higher likelihood of an user click in the close neighborhood of a previous click than farther away from it, it provides an indirect means of session state inference - the terms *idle* and *inactive* now assume a more continuous interpretation, lower (higher) deviations indicate idle (inactive) behavior respectively.

In Fig. 5, we partition user session activity patterns into three categories. While Fig. 5a and Fig. 5c represent the two extremes of daily user click activity, Fig. 5b better represents a typical user behavior over a 24-hour period. In Fig. 6, we plot corresponding user activity patterns across multiple days, each day with a different color. While Fig. 6a shows an user having a very high correlation across days, Fig. 6b indicates a moderate level of correlation having a few outliers.

On the other hand, Fig. 6c represents an user showing practically no correlation across days. The higher the correlation measured, the more reliable are the resulting user behavior models, and hence better the user click predictions.

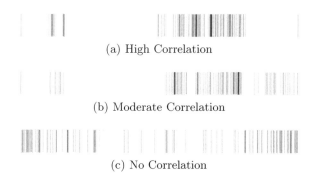

(a) High Correlation

(b) Moderate Correlation

(c) No Correlation

Fig. 6. User Session Activity (multiple days)

Click Probability Tracking: Representing a session signature as the union of multiple user click instances on a daily basis leads to variable-sized session signatures. Thus we not only require multiple session signatures for high-activity users, but also larger session signatures due to the higher number of clicks generated. An alternate fixed-size representation that tracks the probability of an user click across multiple contiguous yet disjoint time intervals can alleviate this problem. The session signature size is now determined by the granularity of the individual time intervals and also the precision of the click probabilities in each time interval, and can thus be easily provisioned for better scalability.

Finally, we propose a simple *exponentially weighted moving average* technique to succinctly capture user access patterns across multiple days. Eqn. 1 now represents the session signature (S_n) as the union of multiple user click probabilities (P_n^t) for the different time instances - where α is the weight assigned to any new entry p^t with respect to the previously measured user click probability (P_{n-1}^t) in that time interval (t) but in the older session signature (S_{n-1}).

$$S_i = \bigcup_{\forall t} P_i^t = \bigcup_{\forall t} (\alpha * p^t + (1 - \alpha) * P_{i-1}^t) \qquad (1)$$

We now extend this basic representation to formulate precise/imprecise models based on individual click probabilities for optimal update interval adaptation.

5.2   Click Tracking: Precise Models

We now propose three simple adaptive sync models each displaying a different update interval adaptation around any *single user click*. We then discuss how

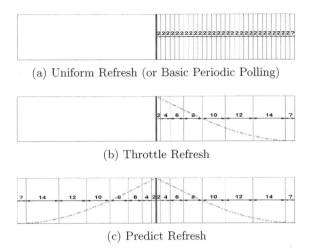

(a) Uniform Refresh (or Basic Periodic Polling)

(b) Throttle Refresh

(c) Predict Refresh

Fig. 7. Per-Click Sync Models

these per-click models can be easily combined across multiple user clicks both intra-day and inter-day, thereby achieving better resource utilization.

Uniform Refresh: This model assumes an uniform access probability distribution around any user click, and represents the basic periodic polling technique. Fig. 7a thus represents the uniform refresh (periodic polling) at some user click, while Eqn. 2 depicts the individual time instances of subsequent updates, where U_0 represents the registered user click, and Δ is a constant (say, 2 time units).

$$U_n = U_{n-1} + \Delta = U_0 + n * \Delta, \quad \forall \, n > 0 \tag{2}$$

Throttle Refresh: This model assumes a monotonically decreasing access probability distribution around any user click, and hence the refresh interval also steadily increases. Our experimental evaluation of refresh interval adaptation indicates that an arithmetic growth models user access trends more closely than a geometric/exponential growth. Fig. 7b thus represents the throttle refresh at some user click and the decaying access probability, while Eqn. 3 depicts their individual time instances following an additive growth model.

$$U_n = U_{n-1} + n * \Delta = U_0 + \frac{n * (n + 1)}{2} * \Delta, \quad \forall \, n > 0 \tag{3}$$

Predict Refresh: This model accounts for refresh interval adaptation not only leading away from the user click, but also leading towards that user click. Thus it supports pro-active updates for better data coherence, and represents an axial reflection of throttle refresh about the user click. Fig. 7c thus shows the access probability ramp up leading towards and ramp down leading away from some user click, while Eqn. 4 represents the (additive) modulation of the corresponding refresh time instances around the user click.

$$U_n = \begin{cases} U_{n+1} + n * \Delta = U_0 - \frac{n*(n-1)}{2} * \Delta \text{ if } n < 0 \\ U_{n-1} + n * \Delta = U_0 + \frac{n*(n+1)}{2} * \Delta \text{ if } n > 0 \end{cases} \quad (4)$$

The global sync schedule for any session can now be viewed as the interference pattern of the individual sync schedules at each user click, smoothed across multiple days using a simple exponentially weighted moving average technique. It is important to note that we can obtain these precise adaptive sync models only for users having a high click-behavior correlation across multiple days. For users having lower click-behavior correlation, and deployments with limited storage capacity or requiring greater privacy, these models tend to be insufficient.

5.3   Click Probability Tracking: Practical Models

To alleviate privacy concerns surrounding explicit click tracking, we now propose imprecise yet more practical models based on aggregate click probability tracking across multiple contiguous yet disjoint time intervals. In any session, predicting the exact time instant of any user click is infeasible and dependent on myriad factors including the number of emails received, their relative priorities, average user response times etc. Not so surprisingly, it is not infeasible to determine the user click probabilities over longer time intervals - longer the time interval, more precise the click predictions can be. However these longer time intervals render click predictions virtually useless as they cannot guarantee better data coherence (by update pre-fetching) due to the very size of the intervals themselves. Thus we need appropriately-sized time intervals that provide good click predictions (better data coherence), while limiting the session signature storage overhead.

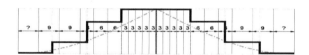

Fig. 8. Slotted Refresh Sync Model

Slotted Refresh: This model is similar to the *predict refresh* model discussed previously, but assumes a discrete probability distribution across the many time interval boundaries. This results in a non-continuous (step-like) growth in refresh intervals, increasing as we traverse time interval boundaries away from an user click. Fig. 8 now represents this slotted refresh model with an additive growth rate (3 time units) across the different static time intervals (15 time units).

Idle Behavior: We introduce another critical parameter here known as the *window/probability spread factor* that accounts for expected idle time between user clicks. User activity typically spans multiple neighboring time intervals wherein not all of them register an user click everyday - these sandwiched zero-activity time intervals thus represent idle user behavior. We now propose a few probability smoothing functions each differently scaling user access probabilities across multiple neighboring time intervals to accurately model these *passively active* idle time intervals. Fig. 9a represents a session signature with distinct click probabilities for each of the user clicks. In Fig. 9b (Fig. 9c) we assume that the idle behavior extends to one (two) time intervals on either side of the user click (scaled probability value). It is critical to note that while a low probability spread results in increased sync lag during idle times, a higher spread leads to gradual probability homogenization and uniform click probabilities across the entire time spectrum, and an appropriate window size is hence critical.

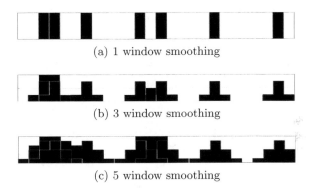

(a) 1 window smoothing

(b) 3 window smoothing

(c) 5 window smoothing

Fig. 9. Probability Smoothing: Window Spread Factor

Finally, the *global sync schedule* can again be viewed as the interference pattern of the individual sync schedules wherein the click probability in any time interval is the sum of the individual (scaled) click probabilities as determined by the window spread factor of its neighboring user click regions. As discussed above, a simple exponentially weighted moving average technique can once again be used to smooth the effect of variations in user behavior across multiple days.

To summarize, we have thus far modeled session signatures as a collection of contiguous yet disjoint time intervals, wherein each unit represents the user access probability (and hence the associated sync lag) for that time interval. We have also sought to detect idle user behavior and subsequently employed a smoothing function to guarantee better data coherence and thus higher user satisfaction. We now seek to individually evaluate both the precise and the imprecise adaptive sync models against a large number of GMAIL user activity streams to study their relative benefits and performance characteristics.

6   Experimental Evaluation

We now analyze both the per-click adaptive sync models and the more practical slotted refresh model by experimental evaluation on a large sample of GMAIL user activity streams. We mainly focus on two critical metrics, resource utilization with respect to the total number of refresh queries issued by any client device/session, and user satisfaction based on the instantaneous data sync lag experienced by the users. In this context, we assume that every refresh query consumes a fixed amount of resources in the client (device), the network, and the server (cloud), to simplify the amortized cost calculations.

6.1   Click Tracking: Precise Models

The per-click models capture the total automated refresh query overhead associated with any user click - we compare the traditional periodic polling (uniform refresh) model against the proposed throttle/predict refresh models here. For sparse user click distributions (Fig. 5a) the growth rate is roughly linear in the total number of uncorrelated user clicks, while it is largely sub-linear for a denser distribution (Fig. 5b), as explained previously.

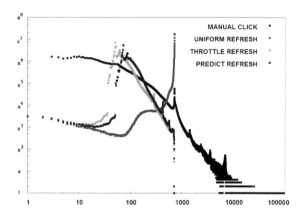

Fig. 10. Query Histogram: Manual vs Refresh Queries (2 minute intervals)

Resource Utilization: Fig. 10 shows the query histogram for all GMAIL users measured over a 24-hour period. The (log-scale) x-axis represents the total number of queries, while the (log-scale) y-axis represents the number of users that generated the corresponding number of queries. We notice that the manual clicks closely follow a *power law* distribution with very few users showing very high user activity (Fig. 5c). Figs. 11a, 11b now depict the same background refresh query trends for the three per-click models with a linear scale x-axis and different minimum refresh intervals. The uniform refresh curve with a positive slope provides a non-scalable model to support an ever-expanding user base and emerging trends in higher device spread (Fig. 3) and lower time persistence (Fig. 4). On the other hand, the throttle and predict refresh curves with a negative slope provide a more scalable model, with fewer users requiring a high number of background queries. While the predict refresh curve closely tracks the throttle refresh curve for the longer interval here, it shows a greater divergence for the shorter interval - this strange behavior can only be attributed to the specific user click distributions and the refresh interval durations analyzed, and displays high variance across days to postulate any reasonable generalization of this trend.

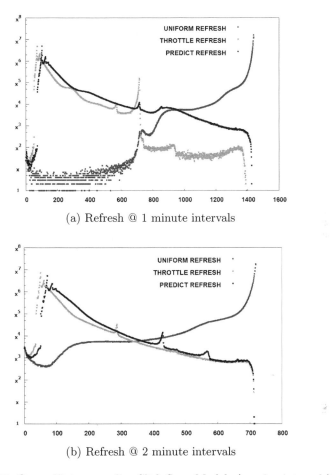

(a) Refresh @ 1 minute intervals

(b) Refresh @ 2 minute intervals

Fig. 11. Query Histogram: Per-Click Sync Models (varying intervals)

User Satisfaction: We now measure content sync lag at any user click instance as a means of measuring user satisfaction or data coherence. A lower data sync lag provides greater data coherence, and hence better user satisfaction. While the uniform and predict refresh models consume more resources, they bound the maximum (user-perceived) sync lag to pre-determined values, and hence provide greater control over data coherence. On the other hand, the throttle refresh model provides greater resource savings at the cost of potentially unbounded sync lag - not only across different sessions, but also across user clicks within a single session. Fig. 12 now shows the (throttle refresh) delay histogram for all user sessions, the x-axis representing the sync lag (in minutes) and the (log-scale) y-axis representing the number of users experiencing the corresponding sync lag. We see that the shorter interval refreshes naturally provide a better data coherence, and also that very few users experience a large sync lag. While the mean and standard deviation of sync lags display a wide spread, their average values across all user sessions is of the order of 2-4 minutes at best, and thus provides maximal user satisfaction.

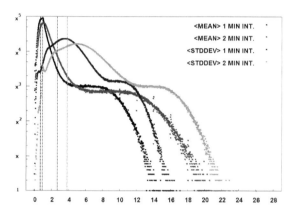

Fig. 12. Throttle Refresh: User-Perceived Sync Lag

Thus the throttle refresh model providing no guarantees on maximum sync lag does a reasonably good job of maintaining good data coherence. To summarize, while the uniform and predict refresh models provide fine-grained control over user-perceived data sync lag, the throttle refresh model behaves more like a best effort model with a few outliers. In short while throttle refresh would suffice for casual users, it might be prudent to employ the predict refresh model for the business or power users - the extra incentive of a relatively smaller data sync lag being delivered at slightly higher resource costs for the service provider.

6.2   Click Probability Tracking: Practical Models

For our analysis here, we aggregate daily user click activity into 15-minute time intervals - each session signature thus tracks 96 independent user access probability values. In order to quickly discard spurious one-off user sessions and to efficiently manage the storage requirements for caching multiple user session signatures, we propose limits on the number of session signatures being tracked on a per-user basis using an *adaptive replacement cache (ARC)* [35] policy.

Resource Utilization: Fig. 13a shows the query histogram for all GMAIL users for the different window spread factor sizes, where the (log-scale) x-axis and (log-scale) y-axis represent the number of queries and the number of users that generated the corresponding number of queries respectively. We notice that the background refresh queries here show a similar negative-slope as the per-click models discussed previously. In Fig. 13b we notice the slight shift in the waveform shape as the window spread factor size increases. This result can be interpreted as follows - while the higher window spread factor size does increase the click probability in neighboring time intervals, it also scales down the relative click probability in the current time interval. The net effect of the inter-day exponentially weighted moving average smoothing and that of the intra-day probability scaling (window spreading) in this case yields lower update prefetches as the window spread factor increases.

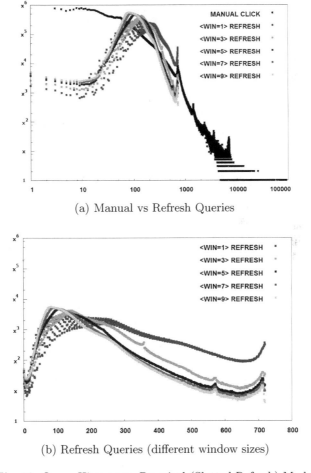

(a) Manual vs Refresh Queries

(b) Refresh Queries (different window sizes)

Fig. 13. Query Histogram: Practical (Slotted Refresh) Model

In order to determine the optimal window spread factor for any user given its many indirect dependencies as listed above, we adopt the *periodic window spread tightening* concept here. We bootstrap with a high probability spread, and then relatively tighten the adapted click probability distribution every few weeks - the lower the session signature correlation across multiple days, the lesser is the window spread tightening provided and vice versa (Fig. 14). While this issue merits an in-depth discussion in itself, we do not delve into greater details here due to space constraints. We suffice it to mention that while this optimization is optional, it does provide incrementally higher benefits.

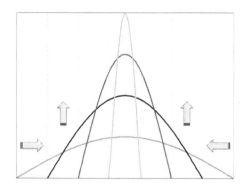

Fig. 14. Probability (Window) Spread Tightening Concept

User Satisfaction: We now measure the effect of the different window spread factor sizes on user-perceived data sync lag. Fig. 15 shows the delay histogram for all user sessions, the x-axis representing the sync lag (in minutes) and the (log-scale) y-axis representing the number of users experiencing the corresponding sync lag. We see that better data coherence is achieved for smaller window spread factor sizes, and this can similarly be explained on the basis of relative probability scaling as discussed above. While the mean and standard deviation of sync lag displays a wide spread, their average values across all user sessions is less than a minute - thereby achieving maximal user satisfaction levels.

To summarize, the proposed data sync models vastly outperform the naive periodic polling mechanism - amongst the many adaptive sync models proposed, the slotted refresh model provides the most practical means of achieving better resources utilization and higher user satisfaction. We also wish to state that the *one-size fits all approach* may not work here - different cloud-based applications might benefit from vastly different models and appropriate choices can only be made by analysis of the individual application requirements and their corresponding user traffic patterns. In this context, we wish to again state that a vastly superior but complex (not cheap) model may not be the most prudent choice with respect to scalability concerns and the resulting computation costs.

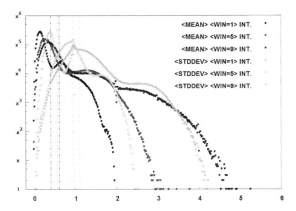

Fig. 15. Slotted Refresh: User-Perceived Sync Lag

7   Conclusions

Web applications today have greatly evolved to provide users instantaneous access to their personalized data from any device/location and in any form with extreme ease. While users today have come to expect seamless data migration across their many devices, various technological constraints with respect to high data coherence and better data synchronization do impose certain barriers. The traditional approach of periodic data fetch by the clients from the different servers in the cloud faces critical limitations with respect to scalability and prohibitively high costs. We thus seek to address the dual-fold problem here - increased user satisfaction and resource savings - by proposing novel extensions to the popular periodic polling technique.

The focus of this work is on addressing the classic trade-off between resource utilization and user satisfaction. Higher the data refresh rate, higher the costs, but also higher the user satisfaction. Conversely, lower the data refresh rate, lower the costs, and correspondingly lower the user satisfaction. The opportunity thus lies in identifying the sweet spot along the entire spectrum that achieves the right balance between the two metrics. Our approach here has been to understand individual user behavior based on past access patterns and thereby derive future predictions for user access with high confidence, so that preemptive/throttled data sync can be easily achieved. An experimental evaluation of a large sample of GMAIL user activity streams successfully validates our approach, and we now plan to perform limited user trials hopefully leading to wide-spread deployment.

References

1. Website of the world's first-ever web server, http://info.cern.ch
2. Cloud Computing, http://en.wikipedia.org/wiki/Cloud_computing
3. A guided tour of Amazon, Google, AppNexus,
   http://www.infoworld.com/article/08/07/21/30TC-cloud-reviews_1.html

4. SaaS, http://en.wikipedia.org/wiki/Software_as_a_service
5. Convergence, http://en.wikipedia.org/wiki/Media_convergence
6. Pervasive Computing, http://en.wikipedia.org/wiki/Pervasive_computing
7. Pikovsky, A., Rosenblum, M., Kurths, J.: Synchronization: A Universal Concept in Nonlinear Sciences. Cambridge University Press (2001)
8. Kautz, W.: Fibonacci codes for synchronization control. IEEE Trans. on Information Theory 11(2), 284–292 (1965)
9. Kistler, J.J., Satyanarayanan, M.: Disconnected Operation in the Coda File System. ACM TOCS 10(1), 3–25 (1992)
10. Liao, T.L., Tsai, S.H.: Adaptive synchronization of chaotic systems and its application to secure communications. Chaos, Solitons, Fractals 11(9), 1387–1396 (2000)
11. Mellor-Crummey, J., Scott, M.: Algorithms for scalable synchronization on shared-memory multiprocessors. ACM TOCS 9(1), 21–65 (1991)
12. Kopetz, H., Ochsenreiter, W.: Clock synchronization in distributed real-time systems. IEEE Trans. on Computers 36(8), 933–940 (1987)
13. Bernstein, P., Goodman, N.: Timestamp-based algorithms for concurrency control in distributed database systems. In: VLDB, pp. 285–300 (1980)
14. RSync, http://en.wikipedia.org/wiki/Rsync
15. Minsky, Y., Trachtenberg, A., Zippel, R.: Set reconciliation with nearly optimal communication complexity. IEEE Trans. on Info. Theory 49(9), 2213–2218 (2003)
16. Starobinski, D., Trachtenberg, A., Agarwal, S.: Efficient PDA synchronization. IEEE Trans. on Mobile Computing 2(1), 40–51 (2003)
17. Fan, L., et al.: Summary Cache: A Scalable Wide-Area Web Cache Sharing Protocol. IEEE/ACM ToN 8(3), 281–293 (2000)
18. Palm HotSync, http://www.palm.com/us/support/hotsync.html
19. Using ActiveSync,
    http://www.microsoft.com/windowsmobile/en-us/help/synchronize/default.mspx
20. Nokia IntelliSync, http://europe.nokia.com/A4164024
21. Open Mobile Alliance, http://www.openmobilealliance.org
22. SyncML, http://www.syncml.org
23. Bozdag, E., Mesbah, A., Duersen, A.V.: A Comparison of Push and Pull Techniques for Ajax, CoRR (2007), http://arxiv.org/abs/0706.3984
24. Bozdag, E., Duersen, A.V.: An Adaptive Push/Pull Algorithm for AJAX Applications. In: AEWSE, pp. 95–100 (2008)
25. Low Latency Data for the Browser, http://alex.dojotoolkit.org/?p=545
26. Bayeux Protocol, http://svn.xantus.org/shortbus/trunk/bayeux
27. Google Gears, http://gears.google.com/support
28. Sync Framework, http://msdn.microsoft.com/en-us/sync
29. The official GMAIL Blog, http://gmailblog.blogspot.com
30. Ghemawat, S., Gobioff, H., Leung, S.: The Google File System. In: ACM SOSP (2003)
31. Pike, R., Dorward, S., Griesemer, R., Quinlan, S.: Interpreting the Data: Parallel Analysis with Sawzall. Scientific Programming Journal 13(4), 277–298 (2005)
32. Dean, J., Ghemawat, S.: MapReduce: Simplified Data Processing on Large Clusters. In: OSDI, pp. 137–150 (2004)
33. Chang, F., Dean, J., Ghemawat, S., Hsieh, W., Wallach, D., Burrows, M., Chandra, T., Fikes, A., Gruber, R.: Bigtable: A Distributed Storage System for Structured Data. In: OSDI, pp. 205–218 (2006)
34. Mozilla Weave, http://labs.mozilla.com/projects/weave
35. Cache Algorithms, http://en.wikipedia.org/wiki/Cache_algorithms

Hi-sap: Secure and Scalable Web Server System for Shared Hosting Services

Daisuke Hara, Ryohei Fukuda, Kazuki Hyoudou,
Ryota Ozaki, and Yasuichi Nakayama

Department of Computer Science,
The University of Electro-Communications
Chofu, Tokyo 182–8585 Japan
`hara-d@igo.cs.uec.ac.jp`

Abstract. We propose *Hi-sap*, a Web server system that solves internal security problems in a server used for shared hosting services and that achieves high site-number scalability with little performance degradation. Customers are often exposed to internal attacks, i.e., malicious customers illegally access other customers' files. Existing approaches solve a portion of this problem, but they are not enough from the view point of performance, site-number scalability, or generality. The proposed system protects customers' files by isolating them in separate security domains, "partitions" that are unit of protection, using a secure OS facility. A default partition is a Web site, and each partition has a Web server instance that runs under the privilege of an individual user and serves files in the partition. Since the Web servers reuse server processes and can run without the burden of a security mechanism themselves, there is little performance degradation. In addition, since Hi-sap dynamically controls the number of Web servers, the number of partitions in a server is scalable. We implemented Hi-sap on a Linux OS and evaluated its effectiveness. Experimental results show that Hi-sap has up to 14.3 times the performance of suEXEC and achieves high scalability of 1000 sites per server.

Keywords: Security in a Server, Shared Hosting Service, Web Server Architecture, Site-number Scalability.

1 Introduction

More people are creating their own contents and publishing them on the Web as the Internet grows in popularity. Although there are various types of services for creating Web contents, many powerful Web publishers tend to use shared hosting services. In the services, service providers typically lease server resources for a monthly/yearly fee for use in building Web sites. Customers login to an assigned server with a given account and install favorite weblogs, wikis [1], and content management systems (CMSs) [2], etc. A customer can thereby publish

I. Tomkos et al. (Eds.): BROADNETS 2010, LNICST 66, pp. 119–137, 2012.

its contents more flexibly and powerfully. The shared hosting service's requirements for a Web server are security in the server, site-number scalability[1], and performance.

Security is one of the most important concerns on the Web. Vulnerabilities in Web browsers and Web servers are daily found, and both site administrators and site audiences face security risks. Common attacks on the Web, such as cross site scripting and cross site request forgeries, are conducted by external attackers. In addition, the customers are exposed to internal attacks by malicious customers in a shared server. Malicious customers who share a server can illegally access other customers' files on traditional Web servers and OSes. In the server configuration, the customers have to set access permissions[2] on their files so that Web servers can access them. This means that the files can be accessed illegally by malicious customers using command-line tools or through a Web server.

Scalability is also one of the most important concerns on the Web. As the number of Web sites grows, many server machines are required to house them. There are some hardware approaches to improve performance per unit area. For example, blade servers are optimized to minimize physical space and can reduce the server footprints at the data center. However, much more sites must be housed in a machine at shared hosting services. To achieve it, software approaches are also required. That means an innovative server software is desired.

Additionally, we take into consideration *generality*. Generality means a kernel modification is unnecessary and any programming language are supported. If a kernel is modified, it is difficult to keep OS version up to date because of the porting cost. If customers cannot use various programming language, it is inconvenient and does not attract many customers.

It is thought that there was no approach that took into account these requirements. Although existing approaches solve a portion of the security problem, they are not enough from the view point of performance, site-number scalability, or generality. An approach that uses suEXEC [3,4,5] and POSIX ACL [6] (suEXEC & POSIX ACL) has poor performance because they cannot be applied to server-embedded interpreters [7,8,9,10] that process requests for dynamic contents at high speed. Harache [11] performs poorly for server-embedded interpreters. In addition, virtual machines (VMs) or containers which have advanced due to increase hardware performance and the number of CPU cores are problematic for shared hosting services because they have low scalability or low generality; i.e., they typically require modifying the kernel.

To satisfy the requirements of shared hosting service, we propose a secure and scalable Web server system called "Hi-sap" [12] that solves the problems. Customer files are isolated in separate security domains, "partitions" that are unit of protection, using a secure OS [13] facility. A default partition is a Web

---

[1] Scalability of the number of sites in a server.

[2] To publish static files, for example HTML and image files, read permission must be granted to "other", which is defined by the UNIX permission model "owner/group/other". To publish CGI scripts, execution permission must also be granted.

site, and each partition has a Web server instance that runs under the privilege of an individual user and serves files in the partition. Since the Web servers reuse server processes and can run without the burden of a security mechanism themselves, there is little performance degradation. In addition, Hi-sap implements a Web-server-level scheduler called "content access scheduler", which dynamically controls the number of Web servers. The scheduler reduces memory consumption by partitions for which the Web server is not accessed by clients, so the number of partitions in each server is scalable.

The target of our system is shared Web hosting services in which a server houses from several hundred to one thousand sites. In contrast, VMs and containers target a server machine consolidation or virtual private server in which a server houses from several to dozen OSes or server software programs.

We implemented Hi-sap on a Linux OS and evaluated its effectiveness. Experimental results show that Hi-sap has up to 14.3 times the performance of suEXEC and achieves high scalability of 1000 sites per server.

The remainder of this paper is structured as follows. In section 2, we describe the background. In section 3, we describe the key aspects of our design. In section 4, we describe the implementation of Hi-sap on a Linux OS. In section 5, we describe our evaluation of the system. In section 6, we discuss benefit and limitation of the system. Finally, in section 7, we summarize this work and discuss future work.

2   Background

In this section, we describe shared hosting services, security threats in a shared server, and existing approaches.

2.1   Shared Hosting Services

Providers of shared hosting services lease server resources, such as computing power, network bandwidth, and data storage, to customers for a monthly/yearly fee. The customers login to an assigned server with a given account and build their Web sites on the server, which is usually shared with many other customers. The customers share the same OS image. The number of customers housed on a commodity server is generally from several hundred to one thousand.

The biggest concern of the service providers is the server footprints at the data center. To reduce operating expense, it is important to reduce the footprints. Recent virtualization technologies described later in section 2.3 and blade servers aim at doing this. The service providers therefore want to maximize the number of customers housed on a server. Their servers thus need to process requests for contents at high speed and use computation resources, for example CPU, memory, and disk, effectively.

An effective common approach to processing requests for contents at high speed is to use server-embedded interpreters for dynamic contents, which consume more computing resources than static contents. Dynamic contents are essential for a rich user experience on the Web. A common gateway interface (CGI) has traditionally been used to generate dynamic contents. However, it is difficult for CGI to process dynamic contents at high speed because it requires a process termination, i.e., invoking fork() and execve() system calls, for each request. Therefore, server-embedded interpreters, such as mod_ruby [8], mod_perl [9], and mod_python [10], have been used as an alternative to CGI. The interpreters are contained in a server process and run as a part of the process. Although server-embedded interpreters are commonly used on the Web, it is difficult to use them for shared hosting services because of a security problem described later in section 2.2. Therefore, suEXEC and the PHP: Hypertext Preprocessor (PHP) safe mode [7] described later in section 2.3, 2.3 are still used in the service.

One way to use computation resources effectively is to assign resources to sites in proportion to the volume of access traffic at each site to reduce resource consumption by each site. The traffic distribution on the Web is known to follow Zipf's law [14]; i.e., while a few sites get a large amount of traffic, most sites get little traffic. Resource allocation for sites that are not accessed at all should be avoided.

The service providers additionally want to use general technologies to do maintenance easily. For example, they want to avoid modifications of kernel or server software.

2.2   Security Threats in a Shared Server

The sharing of a server by many customers has caused new security threats. The seed of them is the roughness of traditional OS access control; i.e., the file permissions are managed for only three classes, owner, group, and other.

The customer is given an account and assigned a user ID by the service provider for use in logging in to the assigned server. The "owner" of the customer's files is set to the user ID, and the files can be accessed only by the customer. Thus, permissions must be granted for the files to "group" or "other" so that the Web server, which is assigned a dedicated user ID[3], can access them (Figure 1 (0)). In this situation, the files can be illegally stolen, deleted, or tampered with by malicious customers that share the server by using command-line tools, for example *cp* and *rm* (Figure 1 (1)). They can additionally attack through the Web server (Figure 1 (2)). For example, a malicious CGI script that deletes an other customer's writable files[4] can run because the script runs under the privilege of the dedicated user, which can write the file.

We identified the factors in the security scenario for a server:

- Worth protecting: customer files
- Threat: stealing, deletion, or tampering with files by malicious customers that share a server
- Vulnerability: coarse-grained isolation of files in traditional OSes.

The *one-to-one* approach can be used to solve this security problem. In this approach, customer files are isolated in separate domains. Each domain has a

---

[3] e.g., *apache, www-data, www*.
[4] e.g., a log file, wiki's data file.

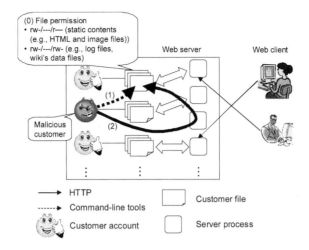

Fig. 1. Internal security treats at a shared hosting service

Web server instance that serves only files in the domain. There is also a reverse proxy server that dispatches requests from Web clients to the instance. However, this approach is unsuitable for shared hosting services because of its poor site-number scalability. This is because all instances run all the time though most sites get little traffic, as mentioned in section 2.1.

2.3 Existing Approaches and Their Limitations

Although there are approaches that solve the security problem, they have limitations.

Container and Virtual Machine. Containers [15,16,17,18,19] are OS-level virtualization methods. Multiple containers with server software programs can run concurrently in an OS (Figure 2 (1)). Each container has a different namespace. Assigning a container to every site creates high security in the server. However, using containers at shared hosting services is difficult because of their low scalability for the number of sites in a server. Although this mechanism can scale up to a few hundred sites, service providers require up to about 1000 sites. In addition, some containers, for example Linux-VServer [17], need to modify the kernel. Kernel modifications are dependent on the kernel version, so keeping them up to date generally requires significant porting [19]. If the porting is not done, the kernel's latest features and devices cannot be used.

In VMs [20,21,22,23,24,25], a hypervisor can run multiple OSes concurrently on the same server machine (Figure 2 (2)). Assigning an OS to every site also creates high security in the server. However, using VMs at shared hosting services is difficult because of the overhead involved. The utilization of computation resources for each site dramatically increases when this mechanism is used. This strongly affects the scalability of the number of sites in a server. For example,

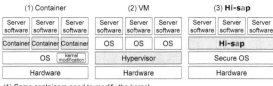

Fig. 2. Software stack of container, VM, Hi-sap

an OS that runs server programs on VMware ESX Server reportedly uses about 200 MB of memory [21]. That means about 200 GB of memory is required to provide 1000 sites. Although some mechanisms of memory sharing between VMs are proposed recently [22,23,24], no reports show that the number of sites in a server reaches up to 1000. Vrable *et al.* described that Xen could not run concurrently more than 116 VMs because of Xen's limitation [22]. Gupta *et al.* [23] described that their evaluations only used up to 6 VMs. In addition, paravirtualization [25] needs to modify the kernel, and it has low generality.

In Hi-sap, server software programs share a single namespace in an OS (Figure 2 (3)). Therefore, our system can control each server software program by using content access scheduler and achieves high scalability of the number of sites. It also achieves high generality because it does not need to modify the kernel, and it can use any secure OS, which is described later in section 3.1.

PHP Safe Mode. PHP [7] has a *safe mode*. This mechanism maintains a high level of security in a server by restricting the operations of PHP scripts.

 − File handling is permitted only when the owner of the script is the same as the owner of the file that the script is about to handle.
 − File handling is permitted only below specific directories.
 − Environment variables that can be changed are restricted.
 − Specific functions and classes are disabled.

However, this mechanism depends on the language processor and is not commonly used. There are also many cases when using this mechanism is difficult because of its restrictions.

Hi-sap supports any programming language because it provides a security mechanism outside the language processor.

suEXEC & POSIX ACL. The suEXEC program uses "setuid bit" to run CGI scripts under the privilege of an individual user different from a dedicated user. POSIX ACL provides access control for each user, unlike traditional access control, i.e., owner/group/other.

In this approach, first, read and execution permission for public access files is granted only to a dedicated user by using POSIX ACL. Files can therefore be

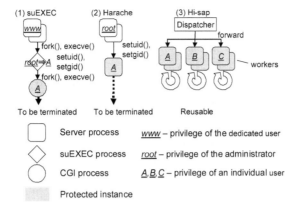

Fig. 3. Process composition of Web server systems

published without granting permission to "other". Second, CGI scripts run under the privilege of the site owner by using suEXEC. This approach can therefore prevent execution of cp and rm commands and prevent malicious customers that share the server from using CGI scripts to steal, delete, or tamper with files.

However, suEXEC cannot achieve the speed of server-embedded interpreters since it needs a process termination after each request (Figure 3 (1)). In addition, because server-embedded scripts that are executed by using server-embedded interpreters run under the privilege of the dedicated user, they cannot ensure the security in a server. suEXEC is therefore applied only to a CGI.

Harache. Our previously proposed Web server system, Harache [11], enables safe and convenient use of server-embedded programs. With Harache, each process of a Web server runs under the privilege of an individual user for every site. Harache therefore requires that permission be granted to only "owner" for any contents that include server-embedded scripts. Although Harache has up to 1.7 times the performance of suEXEC, it cannot achieve the speed of server-embedded interpreters since it needs a process termination after each HTTP session (Figure 3 (2)).

3   Design

We designed our proposed server system, Hi-sap, which can be used with UNIX-like OSes, with two goals in mind.

– High security with little performance degradation
– High site-number scalability in a shared server.

3.1 Security with Little Performance Degradation

Performance Degradation in Existing Systems. In general, a fundamental requirement for protecting files completely in a server is that the files are accessible only by the owner. This requires that processes that access the files have to be an owner of the files. In a shared server, Web servers have to run under the privilege of an individual user. However, changing the server privilege is problematic. Popular types of Web servers, such as Apache [3], consist of several server processes. Since the processes share the listen port (usually port 80) to accept requests from Web clients, the Web server system cannot control which of the requests a process grabs. Therefore, changing the privilege of a process, i.e., invoking setuid() system call, has to be done after a request is grabbed because the Web site (and in turn the customer files) about to be accessed by the request is not known until the request arrives. However, changing the privilege of a process is noninvertible because setuid() requires the administrator privilege. Consequently, the approaches that use an ordinary Web server system have a problem: the processes have to be terminated after finishing a request or an HTTP session (Figure 3 (1)(2)). For example, the CGI processes in the suEXEC & POSIX ACL approach and the server processes in Harache have to be terminated. Unsurprisingly, this degrades performance due to the increase in process terminations and activations. This means that improving security with little performance degradation requires a proactive privilege change ability.

The Hi-sap Approach. In the Hi-sap approach, the privilege of processes is changed in advance to avoid performance degradation (Figure 3 (3)). A "dispatcher" distributes requests to "workers" that run under the privilege of an individual user. The system protects customer files by isolating them in separate security domains, called partitions that are unit of protection, using a secure OS facility.

Partition: A partition in our system is a site or content. A default partition is a site. Each partition has a Web server instance (worker) that serves files in the partition. File permissions are granted for any files in a partition to only owner. A worker can therefore access only a specific dedicated partition (cannot access any other partitions) because workers run under the privilege of an individual user.

In the example shown in Figure 4, there are two sites (site X and Y). Site Y contains two contents (content $Y1$ and $Y2$). A partition is assigned to site X, content Y1, and content Y2. The worker dedicated to processing requests for content Y1 (worker (B)) cannot access files on site X (Figure 4 (a)). Even if the files are on the same site, the worker cannot access them if they are in an other partition (Figure 4 (b)).

Since the Web servers reuse server processes and do not bear any overhead for security, there is little performance degradation.

Combination with Secure OS: If the privilege of the administrator account is appropriated due to a security hole or mis-configuration, there is no effect on the access control of Hi-sap, which uses individual user privileges.

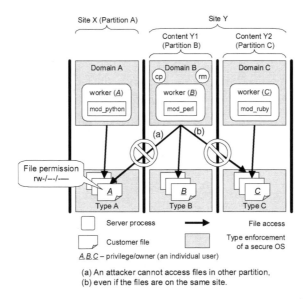

(a) An attacker cannot access files in other partition,
(b) even if the files are on the same site.

Fig. 4. Partitions

The Hi-sap enables access control in combination with a secure OS [13]. A secure OS enhances security features, e.g., mandatory access control (MAC) [26] and least privilege [27] security. The MAC mechanism enforces access control for all users and processes without exception. In the least privilege security model, a higher-than-needed privilege level is not granted to users and processes. These mechanisms isolate server software programs from the other server software programs in the same OS; i.e., cracking one server software program does not affect the other programs.

To prevent files from being stolen, deleted, or tampered with when the administrator account is appropriated, our system assigns "domain" of a secure OS to every worker and assigns "type" to every partition. In Figure 4, domain A, B and C are assigned to worker (A, B and C), and type A, B and C are assigned to files of partition A, B and C. If worker (B) is cracked and the privilege of the administrator account is appropriated, the attacker can access only partition B (content Y). Therefore, the system ensures the security for each partition by using a secure OS.

The system requires MAC and the least privilege security model; i.e., it can use any secure OS.

3.2 Scaling Number of Customers

Our content access scheduler is a Web-server-level scheduler that enhances the scalability of the number of partitions in a server. It controls the creation and termination of workers.

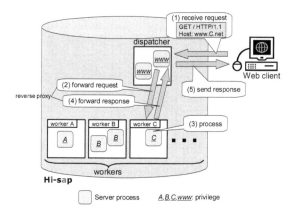

Fig. 5. Overview of Hi-sap architecture

In a Web server, memory utilization strongly affects scalability. Thrashing decreases the performance of Web servers dramatically [11]. Therefore, the system dynamically terminates workers not required to save memory resources. This means the system keeps only necessary workers. This scheduler works well because of Zipf's law described in section 2.1; i.e., while workers for a few sites that get a large amount of traffic are always active, workers for most sites that get little traffic are usually inactive.

The scheduler enables high scalability, in particular, by optimizing the algorithm used to create and terminate workers in accordance with the characteristics of the contents.

3.3 Hi-sap Architecture

An overview of the system architecture is shown in Figure 5. The system consists of a dispatcher and many workers. Each worker runs under the privilege of an individual user and processes requests for a specific dedicated partition. The dispatcher is a reverse proxy server and distributes requests to workers.

Secure OSes have trouble when transferring user privileges. If the policy of a secure OS permits workers that run under the privilege of the administrator account to transfer privileges to ordinary users, problems may occur if workers are appropriated. That means secure OSes are ineffective because a worker that is appropriated can transfer privileges to any ordinary user. Therefore, in our system, workers initially run under the privilege of ordinary users.

4   Implementation

We implemented Hi-sap on a Linux OS with SELinux [13]. The dispatcher was implemented as an Apache module, *mod_hisap*, on an Apache HTTP server (ver. 2.0.55) [3]. One thousand Apache HTTP servers (ver. 2.0.55) were used

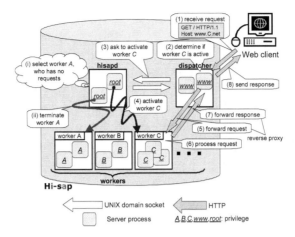

Fig. 6. Overview of Hi-sap request processing

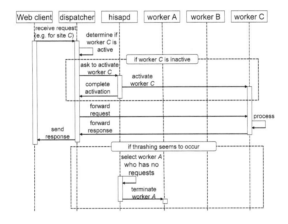

Fig. 7. Sequence of Hi-sap request processing

as workers. Each worker waited for requests at a unique port. The content access scheduler and other management facilities of the workers were implemented as a daemon, *hisapd*. An overview and sequence of request processing for the system is shown in Figure 6, Figure 7.

Our system has a simple and user-level implementation and does not need to modify the kernel, and it can use any secure OS. Therefore, our system can be easily ported to any UNIX-like OSes. In addition, our system can easily scale out because workers can be distributed to many server machines.

The details of the dispatcher and hisapd are as follows.

4.1   Dispatcher

If the dispatcher receives a request, e.g., for partition C in Figure 6, from a Web client (Figure 6 (1)), the dispatcher determines whether the dedicated worker for partition C is active (Figure 6 (2)). If the worker (worker C) is inactive, the dispatcher asks hisapd to activate it (Figure 6 (3)). The communication between the dispatcher and hisapd uses a UNIX domain socket. "Worker ID", the identifier of the requested worker, is then recorded in a dedicated log file, "worker request log". After hisapd activates the worker (Figure 6 (4)), the dispatcher forwards the request to the worker (Figure 6 (5)). The worker processes the request (Figure 6 (6)) and forwards the response to the dispatcher (Figure 6 (7)). The dispatcher sends the response to the Web client (Figure 6 (8)).

4.2   hisapd

As described in section 4.1, hisapd dynamically activates workers after receiving requests from the dispatcher.

There is also a procedure for worker termination. When thrashing seems to occur, hisapd terminates workers that have not been requested recently. The conditions under which hisapd judges thrashing seems to occur are as follows.

- A swap-in occurs.
- A swap-out occurs.
- Memory utilization is equal to or greater than 99%[5].

It checks for these conditions every five seconds[5]. When all conditions are met, hisapd starts terminating workers. It selects which workers to terminate on the basis of two conditions.

- The worker is active.
- The worker is not recorded in the most recent 10,000[5] requests in the worker request log.

The pseudo least recently algorithm is used to reduce the time for searching the worker request log. As illustrated in Figure 6, when thrashing seems to occur, hisapd selects worker A because it has not been requested recently (Figure 6 (i)) and terminates it (Figure 6 (ii)).

4.3   SELinux Configuration

The SELinux file context (FC) file defines the relationship between a file and the security context of SELinux. Each worker is installed at /vhosts/"Worker ID"/. The /vhosts/"Worker ID"/bin/apachectl scripts for starting and stopping workers are assigned the same security context. Other files are assigned a different security context in every partition because they are used while a worker is running.

---

[5] This value is adjustable.

5   Evaluation

We evaluated Hi-sap using the hardware configuration listed in Table 1.

Table 1. Hardware configuration of experimental environment

Network	
Switching Hub	Dell PowerConnect 2724
	1000 BASE-T × 24

Client	
CPU	Intel Pentium III Xeon 500 MHz × 4
Memory	256 MB (swap 512 MB)
OS	Fedora Core 4 (Linux 2.6.14)
NIC	Intel PRO/1000XT (1 Gbps)

Server	
CPU	AMD Opteron 240EE 1.4 GHz × 2
Memory	4 GB (swap 8 GB)
OS	Fedora Core 4 (Linux 2.6.14)
NIC	Broadcom BCM5704C (1 Gbps)

5.1   Basic Performance

We evaluated the basic performance of Hi-sap when processing dynamic contents to determine its effectiveness. An Apache HTTP server ver. 2.0.55 (Apache), an Apache enabling suEXEC (suEXEC), and a one-to-one approach that described in section 2.2 were used for comparison. A one-to-one system enables access control in combination with a SELinux to isolate each worker. Although a one-to-one system is similar to our system, mod_hisap and hisapd were not installed. Therefore, all workers ran from beginning to end. Apache and suEXEC did not enable a SELinux. In our system, Apache, and one-to-one, a PHP script was executed by the server-embedded interpreter. In suEXEC, a PHP script was executed as a CGI. Our system, Apache, suEXEC, and one-to-one used the default configuration files. We used httperf benchmark ver. 0.8 [28] to measure performance.

We sent requests to the PHP script and measured the response throughput. The script calls *phpinfo()*, which displays the system information of the PHP language processor. The traffic generated by the script is 40 KB per request. As shown in Figure 8, the throughput with our system was, on average, 28.0% lower than with Apache and was a maximum of 56.5% lower. This was due to the overhead of the reverse proxy operation. However, the throughput was, on average, 10.2 times that with suEXEC and was a maximum of 14.3 times the throughput. It was, on average, 1.0% lower than with one-to-one and was a maximum of 2.6% lower. This was due to the overhead of mod_hisap and hisapd operation. Since this overhead is very low, this implementation is effective.

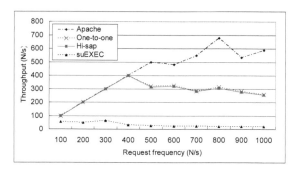

Fig. 8. Basic performance evaluation

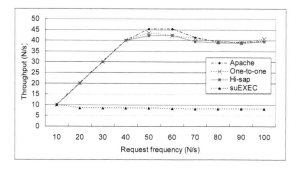

Fig. 9. Basic performance evaluation: Weblog

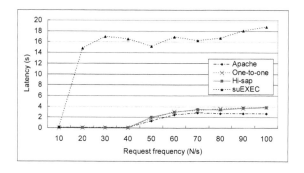

Fig. 10. Basic performance evaluation: latency

In addition, we performed the same experiment for a real application (Weblog). We used tDiary[6] ver. 2.0.2 written in Ruby. As shown in Figure 9, the throughput with our system was, on average, 2.0% lower than with Apache and

---

[6] http://www.tdiary.org/

was a maximum of 6.9% lower. It was, on average, 1.1% lower than with one-to-one and was a maximum of 3.7% lower. The reason for reducing performance difference between Apache and our system compared to the experiment using the PHP script is that the processing time for communication increased. As shown in Figure 10, the latencies of Apache, one-to-one, and our system were small. In contrast, the latency of suEXEC was very large, so suEXEC is not suitable.

This evaluation demonstrates the system has sufficiently high performance while ensuring security in a server.

5.2   Scalability

We evaluated the site-number scalability of Hi-sap when processing dynamic contents. The one-to-one approach was used for comparison. This experiment was designed to determine the effectiveness of the content access scheduler.

We sent 100 requests to a PHP script in each partition sequentially and measured the response throughput. The script was the same as that described in section 5.1. We used the Apache HTTP server benchmarking tool (ver. 2.0.41-dev). As shown in Figure 11, our system had substantially higher throughput

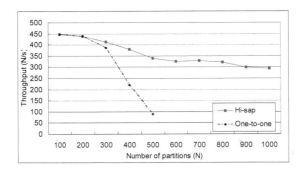

Fig. 11. Scalability evaluation

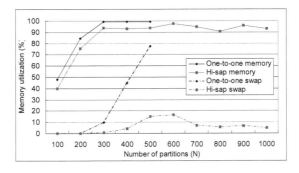

Fig. 12. Scalability evaluation: memory utilization

Table 2. Comparison of approaches (overall evaluation)

	Security in Server	Basic Performance	Site-number Scalability
Apache	poor	excellent	excellent
suEXEC & POSIX ACL	good	poor	excellent
One-to-one	good	excellent	poor
Hi-sap	**excellent**	**excellent**	**excellent**

than one-to-one from beginning to end. The reduction in throughput with our system as the number of partitions increased was lower than with one-to-one. With one-to-one, the OS crashed due to a memory shortage when the number of partitions reached about 600.

The change in memory utilization is plotted in Figure 12. The swap utilization of one-to-one increased dramatically as the number of partitions increased, which is the reason for the OS crashing. In contrast, our system does not use swap space as much because of the content access scheduler. In addition, although our system could avoid swapping by advancing the scheduling algorithms, it gave priority to immediate evaluation of the entire system.

This experiment demonstrates that the system has high site-number scalability.

5.3   Comparison of Approaches

As shown in Table 2, suEXEC & POSIX ACL had poor performance, and scalability of one-to-one was lower than that of others. Our system ranked high for all items and did not have any weak points. It is therefore the most effective.

6   Discussion

In this section, we discuss benefit, limitation, and target of the system.

6.1   Benefit of a User-Level Approach

In our system, server software programs of all sites share a single namespace in an OS. Computation-resource utilization of our system is much less than that of VMs and containers because all sites share computation resource except Web server processes. Therefore, it achieves high site-number scalability.

It also achieves high generality because it does not need to modify the kernel, and it can use any secure OS. As described in section 2.3, kernel modifications require significant porting effort. Our user-level approach enables compatible between different kernel versions for binary compatibility, and also compatible with other UNIX-like OSes for source compatibility.

6.2   Limitations

Network Isolation: VMs and containers provide a network isolation mechanism. A server software program on them is isolated at layer 2 or 3 from the others.

In our system, workers share a single IP address and use a unique port. SELinux can restrict access to each port. A worker therefore cannot sniff packets of the others.

Administrative Cost: Our system has many workers. Installation and maintenance costs increase in proportion to the number of workers that include a Web server instance and contents. To add or remove a worker, configuration of a dispatcher and SELinux is also required.

Because VMs and containers require installation of an OS or a container in addition to setup Web server instance and contents, administrative cost of our system is believed to be lower than that of VMs and containers.

Response Time for Request to Inactive Workers: Our system control the creation and termination of workers by using content access scheduler to achieve high site-number scalability. A response for a request to inactive workers thus takes a longer time than that to active ones because worker activation is required. However, this latency does not matter because running a server software program is very fast.

On the other hand, VMs and containers require to boot an OS (VM) or a container in addition to run a server software program. This takes a lot of time.

6.3   Target of Hi-sap

Our system is applicable to Web hosting services with following conditions.

- A dedicated OS for each Web site is unnecessary.
- The demand of communication confidentiality is not severe.
- The demand of real-time processing is not severe.

The target of our system is therefore shared Web hosting services in which a server houses from several hundred to one thousand Web sites.

If the demands are much severe, a dedicated server or a virtual private server is available.

7   Conclusion

This paper has three contributions. First, we have clarified security problems and requirements of shared hosting services. The requirements are security in the server, performance, and site-number scalability. Second, we have clarified that existing approaches and their limitations. It is thought that there was no approach that took into account these requirements. At last, we have designed a secure and scalable Web server system for shared hosting services, and implemented it on a Linux OS with SELinux. Our evaluation results demonstrate our system qualitatively and quantitatively satisfies the requirements.

We plan to optimize the content access scheduler algorithm to avoid swapping and to enable more than 1000 sites to be housed. In addition, the concept of Hi-sap can be applied other daemons, for example mail servers and network file systems, which provide the service to many users in a server.

Acknowledgments. This work was supported in part by the Exploratory Software Project of the Information-technology Promotion Agency, Japan.

References

1. WikiWikiWeb, http://c2.com/cgi/wiki?WikiWikiWeb
2. Goodwin, S., Vidgen, R.: Content, content, everywhere...time to stop and think? The process of Web content management. IEE Computing & Control Engineering Journal 13(2), 66–70 (2002)
3. Apache HTTP Server, http://httpd.apache.org/
4. Neulinger, N.: CGIWrap: User CGI Access, http://cgiwrap.sourceforge.net/
5. Marsching, S.: suPHP, http://www.suphp.org/
6. Grunbacher, A.: POSIX Access Control Lists on Linux. In: Proc. FREENIX Track: 2003 USENIX Annual Technical Conference, pp. 259–272 (2003)
7. PHP: Hypertext Preprocessor, http://www.php.net/
8. mod_ruby, http://modruby.net/
9. mod_perl, http://perl.apache.org/
10. mod_python, http://www.modpython.org/
11. Hara, D., Ozaki, R., Hyoudou, K., Nakayama, Y.: Harache: A WWW Server Running with the Authority of the File Owner. J. IPS Japan 46(12), 3127–3137 (2005) (in Japanese)
12. Hara, D., Nakayama, Y.: Secure and High-performance Web Server System for Shared Hosting Service. In: Proc. the 12th International Conference on Parallel and Distributed Systems (ICPADS 2006), pp. 161–168 (2006)
13. Loscocco, P., Smalley, S.: Integrating Flexible Support for Security Policies into the Linux Operating System. In: Proc. FREENIX Track: 2001 USENIX Annual Technical Conference, pp. 29–40 (2001)
14. Classman, S.: A Caching Relay for the World Wide Web. In: Proc. the 1st International World-Wide Web Conference, pp. 69–76 (1994)
15. Kamp, P., Watson, R.: Jails: Confining the omnipotent root. In: Proc. the 2nd International System Administration and Networking Conference (2000)
16. Dike, J.: A user-mode port of the linux kernel. In: Proc. the USENIX Annual Linux Showcase and Conference (2000)
17. Linux-VServer, http://linux-vserver.org/
18. Linux containers, http://lxc.sourceforge.net/
19. Suranyi, P., Abe, H., Hirotsu, T., Shinjo, Y., Kato, K.: General Virtual Hosting via Lightweight User-level Virtualization. In: Proc. the 2005 International Symposium on Applications and the Internet (SAINT 2005), pp. 229–236 (2005)
20. Barham, P., Dragovic, B., Fraser, K., Hand, S., Harris, T., Ho, A., Neugebauer, R., Pratt, I., Warfield, A.: Xen and the Art of Virtualization. In: Proc. the 19th ACM Symposium on Operating Systems Principles (SOSP 2003), pp. 164–177 (2003)

21. Waldspurger, C.A.: Memory Resource Management in VMware ESX Server. In: Proc. the 5th Symposium on Operating Systems Design and Implementation (OSDI 2002), pp. 181–194 (2002)
22. Vrable, M., Ma, J., Chen, J., Moore, D., Vandekieft, E., Snoeren, A., Voelker, G., Savage, S.: Scalability, Fidelity and Containment in the Potemkin Virtual Honeyfarm. In: Proc. the 20th ACM Symposium on Operating Systems Principles (SOSP 2005), pp. 148–162 (2005)
23. Gupta, D., Lee, S., Vrable, M., Savage, S., Snoeren, A.C., Vahdat, A., Varghese, G., Voelker, G.M.: Difference engine: Harnessing memory redundancy in virtual machines. In: Proc. the 8th Symposium on Operating Systems Design and Implementation (OSDI 2008), pp. 309–322 (2008)
24. Milos, G., Murray, D.G., Hand, S., Fetterman, M.A.: Satori: Enlightened page sharing. In: Proc. the 2009 USENIX Annual Technical Conference (USENIX 2009), pp. 1–14 (2009)
25. Whitaker, A., Shaw, M., Gribble, S.: Denali: Lightweight Virtual Machines for Distributed and Networked Applications, University of Washington Technical Report, 02-02-01
26. McLean, J.: The algebra of security. In: Proc. 1988 IEEE Symposium on Security and Privacy, pp. 2–7 (1988)
27. Saltzer, J.H., Schroeder, M.D.: The protection of information in computer systems. Proc. the IEEE 63(9), 1278–1308 (1975)
28. Mosberger, D., Jin, T.: httperf—A Tool for Measuring Web Server Performance. In: Proc. the 1st Workshop on Internet Server Performance, pp. 59–67 (1998)

Chameleon: On the Energy Efficiency of Exploiting Multiple Frequencies in Wireless Sensor Networks

Jing Li, Wenjie Zeng, and Anish Arora

Department of Computer Science & Engineering
The Ohio State University
{ljing,zengw,anish}@cse.ohio-state.edu

Abstract. We consider the energy efficiency of medium access control (MAC) in low power wireless communication where multiple channels are available and the duty cycle of (send, receive, and idle) channel access is controllable. We show that in this setting maximization of MAC energy efficiency reduces to maximizing the aggregate channel utilization and minimizing the aggregate duty cycle channel access. Based on the reduction, we show the theoretical existence of centralized, global information protocols which achieve optimal energy efficiency in terms of channel assignment and duty cycle scheduling. Then, towards practically realizing these protocols in a distributed fashion with local information only, we present Chameleon, which assigns channels based on lightweight estimation of channel utilization and adapts the duty cycle of node reception relative to the incoming traffic. Chameleon improves energy efficiency and channel utilization not only among users internal to the network, but also in the presence of external users that share the spectrum. We compare Chameleon with state-of-the-art single-channel and multi-channel protocols. Our experimental results show substantial energy efficiency gains over these protocols, which range from an average of 24% to 66%.

Keywords: Energy Efficiency, Multichannel, Duty Cycling, Wireless Sensor Network, TinyOS.

1   Introduction

Energy constraints in wireless sensor networks mandate efficiency of energy spent on communication, sensing, as well as computing. While a good rule of thumb is to design applications whose energy consumption is equal across these three categories, communication energy has dominated in early network deployments. The motivation to particularly improve communication energy efficiency has only increased as the growth in application complexity to date has by far outstripped the growth in available energy.

At the MAC layer, which is a critical component of communication energy efficiency, many protocols have relied on almost-always-off communication. Duty

I. Tomkos et al. (Eds.): BROADNETS 2010, LNICST 66, pp. 138–157, 2012.
© Institute for Computer Sciences, Social Informatics and Telecommunications Engineering 2012

cycling is the norm in state-of-the-art MAC protocols. Ideally the duty cycle should be at a rate that is just sufficient to accommodate the traffic. The choice of the MAC protocol and the duty cycle determine the resulting communication energy efficiency at the MAC layer. In this paper, we consider achievable energy efficiency of duty-cycled MAC operation in networks where multiple channels (equivalently, frequencies) can be exploited.

The few multi-channel protocols that have been proposed in recent years are essentially categorized into four approaches: 1) Statically partition network nodes across multiple channels so that the density of nodes on a given channel is reduced, e.g., MMSN [18] and TMCP [16]; 2) Explicitly negotiate channels to exchange data for collision avoidance based on current usage information of each channel, e.g., MMAC [14] and TMMAC [17]; 3) Migrate network nodes probabilistically at runtime from one channel to another so as to balance traffic load, using control theoretic techniques, e.g., [11] and [10]; and 4) Balance traffic load (deterministically or randomly) across multiple channels evenly so as to reduce potential interference, e.g., Y-MAC [9] for sensor networks and SSCH [3] for more general wireless networks.

All of these approaches significantly improve network goodput and, in turn, energy efficiency, in comparison with MACs that use only one single channel. Several extant protocols do not per se consider duty cycling, but we find that even if one were to include duty cycling along with these approaches, there is room for substantial improvement in goodput and energy efficiency. In the first approach, different channels are assigned to two-hop neighbors to avoid the possibility of interference; since the actual traffic is not considered, it is possible that some channels are lightly loaded and the node partitioning is thus too conservative. This approach also incurs the overhead of distributed distance-2 coloring. For the second approach, although traffic load is considered when assigning frequencies, the explicit channel negotiation for each data communication involves nonnegligible overhead. In addition, the channel usage information has to be updated online within the distance-2 neighborhood. The third approach starts off by utilizing one channel and alleviates unfairness by probabilistically allocating a fraction of nodes into the next channel. In other words, channel utilization is expanded gradually when the goodput drops to a certain empirical threshold as measured in terms of Packet Reception Ratio or percentage of successful channel accesses. Nevertheless the goodput over the available channels is not optimized, nor is the instantaneous condition of every channel taken into account when nodes perform channel switching. As for the fourth approach, although splitting traffic loads evenly over multiple channels achieves fairness, the aggregate goodput of the network is again not necessarily maximized.

None of these approaches choose channels based on a comprehensive (albeit local) view of the current condition of all channels. Thus, the channels to which nodes are switched into may not represent the best choice. This is especially true if we take into account interference that results from the concurrent operation of external networks. Selecting channels based on a locally comprehensive yet lightweight estimator of channel utilization efficiently is the starting point for our design of a multi-channel MAC protocol, Chameleon [1].

Chameleon has two main components for maximizing energy efficiency. One, its multi-channel scheduler, uses the lightweight estimator to select channels in accordance with an optimality analysis presented in the following section. And second, its radio scheduler, uses a receiver centric approach to coordinate senders and receivers with approximately optimal efficiency; receiver centric MACs were independently introduced in OMAC [5] and Crankshaft [7] and shown analytically to have higher energy efficiency than sender-centric MACs [5]; more recently, the RI-MAC receiver centric protocol was experimentally shown to have energy gains over state-of-the-art sender-centric MACs [13,4]. This component also realizes locally adaptive duty cycling, which staggers data communication periods so that the resulting energy efficiency is highest at the chosen duty cycle.

The main contributions of the paper are as follows.

- We formalize the optimization of MAC energy efficiency in a setting where duty cycling and multiple channel utilization is possible. We show that the optimization reduces to maximizing the spectrum utilization over all available channels while minimizing the duty cycle.
- We provide a protocol that optimizes MAC energy efficiency, assuming the existence of two components, one for precisely quantifying node utilization on each channel and the other for minimizing the send-receive-idle duty cycle for a given node traffic.
- We give lightweight implementations that approximately satisfy these two components, and thus obtain the Chameleon protocol that approximates the optimal protocol. Our implementation of the first component uses a lightweight metric w which is passively computed at each receiver node. Our implementation of the second component uses a receiver centric pseudo-random scheduling of wakeup times, so that receivers within each other interference range are unlikely to be up simultaneously; it also chooses the receiver duty cycle to be just enough such that the receiver experiences low sender collision rate. A side-effect of this approach is that Chameleon intrinsically accommodates external interference.
- We validate, using experiments on the TelosB mote platform, that Chameleon is capable of maintaining substantially higher energy efficiency than both representative single-channel and multi-channel MAC protocols, including MMSN, Y-MAC, BoX-MAC, and O-MAC.

The rest of this paper is organized as follows. We present, in Section 2, the system model as well as an analysis of energy efficiency optimization. We discuss

---

[1] Recent research shows that chameleons change color not to camouflage themselves but to communicate. Their "bandwidth" of communication (aka signalling) is related to the number of colors that they use. Cf.: D. Stuart-Fox and A. Moussalli, "Selection for social signalling drives the evolution of chameleon colour change", *PLoS Biol* 6(1): e25, 2008.

a solution approach for implementing an optimal protocol and design our multi-channel protocol, Chameleon, in Section 3. In Section 4, we present experimental evaluations of relevant aspects. We discuss related work in Section 5 and our conclusions in Section 6.

2   Energy Efficiency Analysis

In this section, we first define channel utilization, spectrum utilization, and energy efficiency. We then discuss maximization of energy efficiency for a receiver given network traffic load, in terms of expected spectrum utilization and duty cycling.

2.1   System Model

The network consists of N energy-constrained half-duplex wireless sensor nodes. Radio operation of each node is represented by a contiguous sequence of frames. Each frame consists of a number of time slots; for ease of exposition, we let this number be a global constant. We define a node's *duty cycle*, implicitly over some number of frames, to be the percentage of the time slots, ψ, when its radio is active; $\psi \in [0, 1]$. A node's duty cycle is further decomposed into its transmit duty cycle, the percentage of the slots when its radio is transmitting, and its receive duty cycle, the percentage of the slots when its radio is in receive or listen mode.

For a given node i, we refer to the packets that are sent to i as its "in-traffic", while packets that are not sent to i but are overheard by i or whose collision is overheard by i are its "interference traffic".

The cumulative wireless bandwidth that can be utilized by nodes denotes the network "spectrum". Spectrum is divided into several orthogonal "channels" (or "frequencies") such that communications on different channels either never or only barely interfere with each other (in practice, adjacent channels are typically not completely interference free from each other [2]). Within each channel, collisions may occur if wireless devices attempt to transmit simultaneously.

The wireless network is viewed as formed by overlapping broadcast domains. Accordingly, we define a receiver's interference set as the set of nodes whose broadcast domain covers the receiver.[2] We let η denote the average size of the interference set for a given node. Let i, j, h range over nodes in the network and k range over channels of the spectrum.

With respect to a given receiver and its interference set, we define the **channel utilization** for a given channel, k, as the ratio, $E(k)$, of the number of time slots where a packet is successfully received to the total number of time slots. (The definition may be relativized to the number of frames considered in the definition of duty cycle.)

---

[2] We note that several of our definitions are receiver-centric rather than sender-centric, as this significantly simplifies our exposition.

Consequently, **spectrum utilization** with respect to a receiver and its inter-ference set denotes the overall successful transmissions among all channels over the total number of time slots normalized by the number of channels, M. Hence, spectrum utilization is defined as:

$$E_S = \frac{\sum_{k=1}^{M} E(k)}{M}. \tag{1}$$

Our primary interest is in the metric of **energy efficiency**, which refers to the goodput for a given energy budget [5]. Basically, this metric refers to the ratio of the number of time slots with successful receptions to the number of slots in which radios are active, albeit they are transmitting, idle, or active. Eq. (2) defines energy efficiency for a unicast scenario. Notation T in the formula is the total number of slots considered. Compared to channel and spectrum utilization, duty cycling of a node is taken into consideration in the metric.

$$E_E = \frac{\sum_{l=1}^{T} \sum_{j=1}^{N} Z_j^l}{\sum_{l=1}^{T} \sum_{j=1}^{N} (S_j^l + R_j^l)} \tag{2}$$

where

$$S_j^l = \begin{cases} 1, \text{ when node } j \text{ transmits in slot } l \\ 0, \text{ when node } j \text{ sleeps in slot } l \end{cases}$$

$$R_j^l = \begin{cases} 1, \text{ when node } j \text{ listens in slot } l \\ 0, \text{ when node } j \text{ sleeps in slot } l \end{cases}$$

$$Z_j^l = \begin{cases} 2, \text{ node } j \text{ succeeds receiving its packets in slot } l \\ 0, \text{ otherwise} \end{cases}$$

In the following analysis, we focus on exploring how to maximize energy efficiency at the receiver for the case of unicast traffic.

2.2 Energy Efficiency Optimization

Problem Statement. Given a node i, whose interference set is of size η, our goal is to schedule its in-traffic—i.e., choose channels and wakeup times for the i and nodes sending packets to i— such that the resulting energy efficiency E_E of i is maximized.

We approach this problem by first simplifying Eq. (2) for the given node i. First, spectrum utilization reflects the goodput resulting from communications of the nodes in the interference range of node i, which is $\sum \sum Z_j^l$. It follows that $\sum \sum Z_j^l = 2TM E_S$, where $2M E_S$ equals the aggregate spectrum utilization and the factor of 2 reflects the benefit to both parties in a communication. The energy consumption of node i, which is determined by the duty cycle control scheme, is $\sum \sum (S_j^l + R_j^l) = T \sum_{j=1}^{\eta} \psi_j$. Thus, the formula below is an equivalent representation of energy efficiency.

$$E_E = \frac{2ME_S}{\sum_{j=1}^{\eta} \psi_j} \qquad (3)$$

In order to optimize E_E via maximizing E_S as well as minimizing $\sum_{j=1}^{\eta} \psi_j$, the scheduler has to choose channels and wakeup times. We will first consider channel selection that maximizes the expected spectrum utilization $\hat{E}_S$, then we will discuss how to schedule the wakeup times of nodes to minimize $\sum_{j=1}^{\eta} \psi_j$.

Maximizing $\hat{E}_S$. Recall that $E(k)$ is the successful reception probability in the interference set of the given node. For the purpose of analysis, in this subsection, we make two assumptions. One is that the in-traffic of nodes follows a stationary process with uniform distribution of arrival times; let the in-traffic load at node i, denoted by p_i, be the probability that on average a packet is sent to i. And two, that the node and its interference set form a clique, i.e., each of these nodes can overhear each packet sent by another of these nodes; thus if packets are concurrently sent to different nodes, collisions will result at each receiver. It follows that all nodes in the network hold the same $E(k)$, which is defined by Eq. (4).

$$E(k) = \sum_j p_j \prod_{h \neq j} (1 - p_h) \qquad (4)$$

where j and h range over these nodes. Initially, $E(k)$ increases as traffic loads increase. However, utilization decreases when the channel becomes overloaded, in which case collisions (or, in a contention based scheme, backoff procedures) dominate the communication.

Lemma 1. *The expected channel utilization with respect to node i, $\hat{E}(k)$, is maximized when the aggregate traffic load in the interference set of i, $\sum_{j=1}^{\eta} p_j(k)$, increases to 1.*

Proof. The average traffic load on channel k is $\bar{p}(k) = \sum_{j=1}^{\eta} p_j(k)/\eta$. Hence, by Eq. (4), the expected channel utilization $\hat{E}(k) = \eta \bar{p}(k) (1 - \bar{p}(k))^{\eta-1}$. Fig. 1(a) plots how $\hat{E}(k)$ changes as $\bar{p}(k)$ changes with interference size η. The expected channel utilization is maximized when $\bar{p}(k) = 1/\eta$. Since $\bar{p}(k) = 1/\eta$ implies $\sum_{j=1}^{\eta} p_j(k) = 1$, it follows that maximal utilization is achieved when the aggregate load, $\sum_{j=1}^{\eta} p_j(k)$, equals 1. Alternatively speaking, $\hat{E}(k)$ increases as the aggregate load increases up to 1; after reaching 1, $\hat{E}(k)$ decreases as the aggregate load increases. Hence, the total traffic load should be 1 to achieve maximal channel utilization $\hat{E}(k)$.

Lemma 1 corroborates two facts: 1) the aggregate traffic load, $\sum_{j=1}^{\eta} p_j(k)$, is a judicious estimator of the expected channel utilization; and 2) when the estimator equals 1, channel utilization is expected to be optimum.

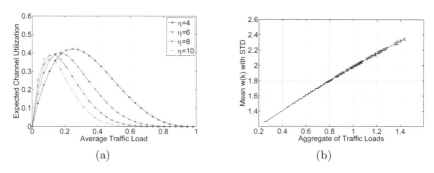

Fig. 1. (a) $\hat{E}(k)$ vs $\bar{p}(k)$ and (b)Mean $w(k)$ with std vs Metric $\sum p_j(k)$

Now, let us consider channel selection for in-traffic p_i at receiver i. Theorem 1 states a sufficient condition for selecting channels for load p_i that maximize $\hat{E}_S$.

Let $\bar{p}_I(k)$ be the average interference load over η on each channel k. Define $q(k)$ as 1 minus the current total load on channel k, i.e., $q(k) = 1 - \eta\bar{p}_I(k)$. Let $\boldsymbol{q}$ be the vector of qs for all channels that is sorted in a nonincreasing order. Thus, q_s represents the s-th greatest element in $\boldsymbol{q}$, corresponding to channel of index $C(q_s)$. Let vector $\boldsymbol{\alpha} = \{\alpha(k) : k = 1, ..., M\}$ denote the percentages of in-traffic allocated to each channel, i.e., $\alpha(k) \cdot p_i$ is loaded on channel k.

Theorem 1. $\hat{E}_S$ *is optimized if we allocate traffic load p_i to channels according to fractions $\boldsymbol{\alpha}$ computed in Eq. (5).*

$$\alpha(C(q_s)) = \begin{cases} \frac{q_s}{p_i}, & p_i - \sum_{t=1}^{s-1} q_t \geq q_s \\ \frac{p_i - \sum_{t=1}^{s-1} q_t}{p_i}, & 0 < p_i - \sum_{t=1}^{s-1} q_t < q_s \\ 0, & p_i - \sum_{t=1}^{s-1} q_t \leq 0 \end{cases} \tag{5}$$

Proof. $\boldsymbol{q}$ represents residual quota of load on each channel for maximizing channel utilization according to Lemma 1. The essential idea here is to prioritize filling up channels based on $\boldsymbol{q}$, i.e., giving preference to those which have more residual capacity, until load p_i has been assigned completely or all qs in $\boldsymbol{q}$ have been consumed.

Define Δp to be the smallest unit of load that can be assigned on a channel. Hence, load p_i consists of $\lceil p_i/\Delta p \rceil$ units. Before adding a unit Δp into channel k, the expected utilization on channel k is $\hat{E}(k) = \eta\bar{p}_I(k)(1 - \bar{p}_I(k))^{\eta-1}$. After adding Δp, by Eq. (4), the expected utilization becomes $\hat{E}'(k) = \eta\bar{p}_I(k)(1 - \Delta p)(1 - \bar{p}_I(k))^{\eta-1} + \Delta p(1 - \bar{p}_I(k))^\eta$. Thus, the utilization gain, $\Delta\hat{E}(k)$, on channel k after appending each Δp would be

$$\Delta\hat{E}(k) = \Delta p(1 - (\eta+1)\bar{p}_I(k))(1 - \bar{p}_I(k))^{\eta-1}, \tag{6}$$

which is a monotone decreasing function of $\bar{p}_I(k)$. The smaller the $\bar{p}_I(k)$, the higher the utilization gain will be. Since Δp is an atomic unit, assigning the channel with lowest $\bar{p}_I(k)$ will provide the highest $\Delta \hat{E}_S$, where $\Delta \hat{E}_S = \Delta \hat{E}(k)$ and k is the channel assigned to the Δp load.

Ideally, all $\lceil p_i/\Delta p \rceil$ units would be added into the channel with the lowest $\bar{p}_I(k)$ to maximize total utilization gain. According to Lemma 1, however, the total load on each channel k should not exceed 1 to achieve maximal utilization. $C(q_s)$ denotes the channel which has s-th smallest $\bar{p}_I(k)$ and $q_s/\Delta p$ is the number of units that can be added to a given channel before exceeding the maximum. Therefore, sequentially filling up each channel according to the order in q will maximize total $\hat{E}_S$.

Consider the assignment of load to channel $C(q_s)$. The number of load units of p_i that are yet to be assigned is $(p_i - \sum_{t=1}^{s-1} q_t)/\Delta p$. If this number is non-positive, indicating that all units of p_i have been assigned to channels earlier in the order of q, the fraction assigned to channel $\alpha(C(q_s))$ is 0. Otherwise, if the number of unassigned load units is less than q_s, we can assign all of $(p_i - \sum_{t=1}^{s-1} q_t)/\Delta p$ units to channel $C(q_s)$. $\alpha(C(q_s)) = (p_i - \sum_{t=1}^{s-1} q_t)/p_i$ in this case. If the number of unassigned units is not less than q_s, we can fill up this channel with $\alpha(C(q_s)) = q_s/p_i$.

In essence, Theorem 1 yields one approach for optimizing the spectrum utilization by choosing channels for the in-traffic at a node.

Minimizing ψ. We now consider scheduling for duty cycle minimization. It is straightforward to show a "centralized TDMA and duty cycling" scheduler that has full information of the arrival times of all packets would suffice to this end. This scheduler (having scheduled the existing traffic in the network) can schedule packet communication time so that no collisions happen, as well as senders and receivers are scheduled to wakeup exactly at these times. Lemma 2 states that nodes running the duty-cycled TDMA will minimize gross duty cycle $\sum_{j=1}^{\eta} \psi_j$.

Lemma 2. *Given traffic load p_i and the arrival time of the in-traffic of i, the centralized TDMA and duty cycling scheduler minimizes the total duty cycle $\sum_{j=1}^{\eta} \psi_j$.*

Proof. Duty cycles of nodes that are neither senders nor receivers of packets in the in-traffic of i will remain unchanged. As for nodes involved in the traffic, the scheduler trivially minimizes the wakeup times, since there are no superfluous sends or receives or idle slots. The total duty cycle consumed by the load p_i is minimized to be twice of the load, i.e., $2p_i$.

3   Energy Efficient Multi-channel Protocol Design

In this section, we present our energy efficient multi-channel access protocol, Chameleon. First, guided by Theorem 1 and Lemma 1, we present the component that (re)assigns channels to load units. Then, we design a light-weight, local, receiver-centric scheduler that approximates the heavy-weight centralized scheduler indicated in Lemma 2. We conclude with an overview of our TinyOS implementation of Chameleon.

3.1   Channel to Load Assignment

In Lemma 1, channel utilization is estimated via the sum of traffic loads, including in-traffic load and interference load. These two loads also determine channel assignment according to Theorem 1. Basically, each node, say i, continually performs three tasks: (i) determines the in-traffic for i, (ii) determines the interference traffic to i, and (iii) chooses channels for the in-traffic according to Eq. (5).

For task (i), the in-traffic load at node i (i.e., the exact instantaneous p_i value) can be computed either by appending rate information to data packets sent to receiver i or by locally calculating the rate of incoming load at i; we chose the former.

Task (ii) involves collecting information about the interference load at node i, $\eta \bar{p}_I(k)$ for each channel k. Rather than let i actively coordinate with all nodes in its interference set to compute the value, we introduce a local interference estimator for $\eta \bar{p}_I(k)$ in the next subsection.

Local Interference Estimator. Let interference estimator $I(k)$, defined in Eq. (7), refer to the probability that some interferers of node i transmit on channel k.

$$I(k) = 1 - (1 - \bar{p}_I(k))^{\eta} \tag{7}$$

It follows that $\eta \bar{p}_I(k)$ is estimated by the exponential function of $I(k)$, i.e., $e^{I(k)}$. We leverage the similarity between the sum of traffic loads, notated by $\sum_{j=1}^{\eta} p_j(k)$, and $p_i(k) + e^{I(k)}$, denoted by $w(k)$. Hence, $w(k)$ is employed to compute channel utilization.

Fig. 1(b) shows an instance of the relation between $\sum p_j(k)$ and $w(k)$. We consider a clique network wherein six pairs of nodes communicate independently on the same channel, each with an arbitrarily chosen traffic load in the range [0,1]. Each receiver locally computes the metric $w(k)$, where k is fixed. Fig. 1(b) plots the mean value $w(k)$ and the standard deviation of the six receivers versus the aggregate traffic load $\sum p_j(k)$. Here, the same value of the aggregate load corresponds to a few different sequences of traffic loads $\boldsymbol{p}$. We observe in the figure that $w(k)$ is approximately linear with $\sum p_j(k)$, which verifies that $e^{I(k)}$ is a feasible estimator for interference load, in lieu of the metric $\eta \bar{p}_I(k)$. Additionally, the locally computed deviation of the $w(k)$s is very small, i.e., the average standard deviation shown in the figure is around 0.005. Another relevant observation from our analysis is that when $\sum p_j(k)$ equals 1, $w(k)$ is equal to 2 (see the figure). This is the state where $\hat{E}(k)$ is optimized, and we refer to it as w^*. Moreover, when parameter $\eta > 2$ and $e^{I(k)} \leq w^*$, the linear relation between

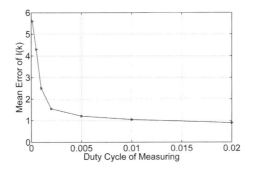

Fig. 2. Mean Error of Measured I(k) versus the Duty Cycle of Measurement

$\sum p_j(k)$ and $w(k)$ is preserved for different configurations of η. It follows that metric $q(k)$ in Theorem 1 may be substituted by the local metric $w^* - e^{I(k)}$ as we perform task (iii).

In particular, the computation of $I(k)$ does not involve sending any specific information, in contrast with the Channel Access Ratio message used in many multi-channel protocols, such as [11]. We explain how interference level $I(k)$ is measured in the next subsection, and how the local metric is used in task (iii) in the following subsection.

Estimator Implementation. The value of $I(k)$ is measured passively at node i by randomly listening to channel k when i is not performing data reception or data transmission. Measurement is performed periodically (at a low duty cycle). For each period, the ratio of the number of busy slots to the total number of checked slots yields the value for $I(k)$.

In terms of implementation, we let nodes perform a continuous Clear Channel Assessment (CCA) check on a given channel during each check slot to determine whether that slot has interference traffic or not. (For the TelosB platform, we empirically chose the channel monitor slot length to be 3ms.) Due to the inefficiency of float operation in the mainstream sensor platforms, we normalize and quantize load into integer "levels". We let the unit of load, δp, be 0.01; 0.01 thus corresponds to the integer level 1. Traffic p_i and interference $I(k)$ are normalized to $\lceil p_i/\delta p \rceil$ and $\lceil I(k)/\delta p \rceil$, respectively. Furthermore, we pre-compute the corresponding value of $e^{I(k)}$ for each level of $I(k)$, thus every receiver maintains a vector $\exp I = \{e^{I(k)} : k = 1, 2, ..., M\}$, representing the interference traffic load on each channel.

The choice of measurement period involves a tradeoff between accuracy and energy consumption. To understand this tradeoff, we conducted experiments in which all 5 nodes transmit independently at a specified rate. Each experiment was repeated for traffic loads of 0.01 (approximately 1 packet per second), 0.05, and 0.1, respectively, and also with the nodes performing channel measurement at different duty cycles. We let channel monitoring be triggered by a randomized timer that fires between $0.5T$ and $1.5T$, where $T = 15s$. When the timer fires, the node monitors the channel for several slots if the radio is not being occupied; otherwise, it waits to measure until the radio is released by other processes. The cumulatively measured value of $I(k)$ is reported at a fixed interval of every 5 minutes. To further reduce error, a weighted moving average to consecutive measurements is computed. Hence, $I(k) = \alpha I(k) + (1 - \alpha)I'(k)$, where $I'(k)$ is the value of last measurement. We let α be 0.6 in our experiments. After each report, the counter of $I(k)$ is cleared to zero and another period of monitoring started.

Fig. 2 plots the mean error between the measured level and the expected value with the monitoring channel at different duty cycles ranging from 0.01% to 2%. The x axis represents the duty cycle of passive channel monitoring. Initially, as the monitoring duty cycle increases, the precision of measure increases significantly; however, the improvement reduces when duty cycle is greater than 0.2%. The corresponding average error is at a level of 1 to 2. Thus, to update channel interference level $I(k)$ at an interval of 5 minutes, a duty cycle of 0.1% to 0.2% for channel measurement seems adequate. Alternatively, checking randomly every 200 slots would provide an acceptable measurement for a channel (recall that each slot is 3 ms).

Chameleon offers upper layers the option to adapt channel update interval from time to time to deal with dynamic environments. In the following experiments, we use a 0.2% duty cycle for interference monitoring, unless stated otherwise.

Algorithm for Channel to Load Assignment. Having obtained in-traffic and interference load, task (iii) is implemented by Algorithm 1. Given normalized levels of p_i and **exp** I, we first compute the number of acceptable units on each channel, in q (lines 1 to 7). Lines 17 to 26 assign units to each channel according to Theorem 1, which results in a vector V of size M, e.g., $V = (3, 7, 1, 0, ..., 0)$, where each element represents the units allocated to the channel. Thus, p_i is split across the channels in proportion to V. (Which channels to use in which frame is discussed later in this section.) If the sum of the available capacity, $\sum_{k=1}^{M} q(k)$, is less than the total p_i, cf. line 9, senders are notified to reduce their outgoing traffic if possible.

Each node starts with conducting a cumulative measurement for every available channel, followed by independently allocating its load to the corresponding channels. As network load varies, the channel monitoring daemon updates channel assignment (in vector V) at each receiver. To alleviate fluctuations caused by simultaneously channel switching, every receiver carries out its channel reassignment with a random interval.

3.2   Receiver-Centric Wakeup and Channel Scheduler

Lemma 2 indicates that there exists in theory a centralized, global information scheduler for maximizing energy efficiency. The scheduler continually performs for each node, say i, the following task: it computes the time at which each in-packet at i is sent without interfering with any of the packets scheduled thus

Algorithm 1. *Channel to Load Assignment*

Require: $p_i, \exp I$

1: **for** $k = 1$ *to* M **do**
2:    **if** $w^* - e^{I(k)} \leq 0$ **then**
3:       $q(k) \leftarrow 0$;
4:    **else**
5:       $q(k) \leftarrow w^* - e^{I(k)}$;
6:    **end if**
7: **end for**
8:
9: **if** $\sum_{k=1}^{M} q(k) < p_i$ **then**
10:    *Inform senders (optional)*;
11: **end if**
12:
13:

14: *Sort* q *in non−increasing order*
15: $q = (q_1, q_2, ..., q_M)$
16: *the channel index of* q_s *is* $C(q_s)$;
17: **for** $s = 1$ *to* M **do**
18:    **if** $p_i - \sum_{t=1}^{s-1} q_t \geq q_s$ **then**
       $V(C(q_s)) \leftarrow q_s$;
19:    **else**
20:       **if** $p_i - \sum_{t=1}^{s-1} q_t < q_s$ **then**
21:          $V(C(q_s)) \leftarrow p_i - \sum_{t=1}^{s-1} q_t$;
22:       **else**
23:          $V(C(q_s)) \leftarrow 0$;
24:       **end if**
25:    **end if**
26: **end for**

---

far; it also updates the sleep-wakeup schedule of the nodes so that they wake up only when they are involved in transmitting or receiving each in-packet to i. Note that the packet transmission time scheduling yields an in-traffic whose arrival time may no longer satisfy a uniform distribution, which we assumed in the analysis shown in Section 2, but since this scheduler enforces collision freedom, the expected E_S and E_E are not negatively affected. However, this centralized scheduler is of high complexity.

Wakeup Scheduler. We now discuss a distributed, light-weight component that efficiently approximates the centralized scheduler. Specifically, we adopt a synchronous, receiver-centric scheduling approach that locally avoid collision and schedules sleep-wakeup. This approach is exemplified by O-MAC [5] and Crankshaft [7]; the approach is in contrast to RI-MAC [15], which is also receiver-centric but is asynchronous.

The basic idea that we borrow from synchronous receiver-centric MACs is this: Each receiver has a pseudo-random scheduler which determines its wakeup slots. The wakeup schedule is advertised to neighbors, compactly since essentially the pseudo-random seed needs to be shared, via a neighbor discovery process. When a node discovers this receiver, it also obtains this receiver's state (of pseudorandom generation), and thus the node can generate the receiver's wakeup schedule. When the node wishes to send to the receiver, it wakes up at the next slot at which the receiver will be awake and attempts to communicate. Two basic modules, neighbor discovery and time synchronization, are used and in turn the module offers Send and Receive interfaces.

Chameleon adopts these basic interfaces from those in O-MAC. This decentralized pseudo-random scheduling staggers nodes' wakeup times with high probability, and has been proven [5] to utilize less duty cycle (i.e., to have higher energy efficiency) under the same traffic load in network than other sender-centric protocols, such as B-MAC, BoX-MAC [13], X-MAC [4] and others. As

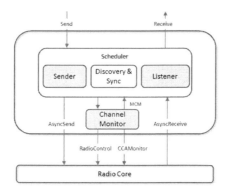

Fig. 3. Composition of the Chameleon Protocol

compared to asynchronous receiver-centric protocols, such as RI-MAC, a sender in O-MAC will not wakeup for an average of half a frame waiting for beacon from its receiver, thus the duty cycle at sender side of O-MAC is obviously less than that of RI-MAC although the receiver's duty cycles are comparable in two protocols.

In other words, in Chameleon's receiver-centric scheme, the senders' wakeup times are implicitly scheduled. Since receivers wakeup at random times in each frame, the likelihood that two interfering receivers will simultaneously receive is low. In O-MAC, a short beacon is broadcast by the receiver as it wakes up to compensate for slot misalignment with potential senders. The beacon contains an adaptive contention window size determined by the receiver side for collision avoidance, based on the expected number of concurrent senders for that receiver. O-MAC is also flexible in adapting duty cycle to incoming traffic load. A sender is allowed to continuously send queued packets to a receiver as long as the sender grabs the channel for the first packet. When a node fails in competition, it continues to compete for the next frame.

Channel Scheduler. We extend the basic O-MAC scheduler in two ways: 1) channel association with frames; 2) channel notification from receivers to senders.

First, the scheduler associates a channel with each frame. This channel is used by the receiver in all slots in which it wakesup during that frame. We implement this association using a vector of units assigned to each channel, V, which has size M. Given an assignment V, the receiver maintains a shadow copy V', which is initially set to V. In each frame, it checks the next k in V'. If the value of $V(k) > 0$, then channel k is used in the next frame and the current value in V' is decremented; otherwise, the next channel is checked until all values become 0. Then, V is copied to V' again and the above procedure repeated. In this way, nodes uses multiple channels in proportion to V. Equivalently speaking, the incoming traffic to the node is split over multiple channels.

Second, there are two ways in which the receiver shares its updated channel assignment with senders in the receiver-centric approach: asynchronously, through the neighbor discovery process and, synchronously, through beaconing in the first wakeup slot at the beginning of each frame. In the former case, nodes independently compute each other's wakeup slot and channel. The updated channel-wakeup schedule V has to be notified to neighbors via the discovery module within certain amount of time. Each sender keeps its own updated V' and the current index of the receiver, generating future wakeup slots and channels independently. This scheme is realized by leveraging the asynchronous neighbor discovery protocol, Disco [6], which schedules radio wake times at multiples of prime numbers, ensuring deterministic pairwise discovery and rendezvous latency. Disco operates on a wellknown channel, called the home channel. We add several small pieces of information to the packets sent out by Disco, related to time synchronization, channel assignment, and wakeup schedule. When a receiver starts to change its channel assignment schedule, it may accelerate propagating a channel update, by increasing the duty cycle of Disco. After exceeding the deterministic rendezvous period, Disco goes back to previous low duty cycle. The energy cost of updating schedules through Disco is nontrivial, especially when frequent updates exist. Moreover, the discovery schedule may interrupt with node's listen schedule more frequently in this case.

In the latter case, status is updated by advertising the receiver's current channel at the beginning of each frame, using the home channel. Senders do not maintain any channel information, instead they listen to the home channel during the wakeup slot of receiver. The receiver broadcasts the channel it is going to use for current frame in a short beacon on the home channel. Note that the beaconing is part of O-MAC protocol. Following this beacon, potential senders and receiver all switch to the chosen channel for the rest of communication. Specifically, receiver switches to the chosen channel after sending out beacon and senders change to the channel after receiving the beacon. The total beaconing and channel switch time is approximately 5 ms on the TelosB platform.

3.3   Implementation

We implemented Chameleon in TinyOS 2.x for the CC2420 radio platform, which is a packetizing radio used in popular TelosB and MicaZ motes; the code is readily ported to motes with streaming radios such as the CC1000. The composition of Chameleon is shown in Fig. 3.

The Scheduler module in Fig. 3 includes three basic modules provided by O-MAC: listener, sender, and discovery & synchronization. The Listener module decides node wakeup times and durations, while Sender determines when to transmit application packets given the state maintained in the neighborhood table. The Discovery & Sync module performs relative slot synchronization (with a modified FTSP protocol) on the basis of asynchronous discovery (with Disco); these processes have rather low overhead.

The ChannelMonitor module realizes the bulk of the functionality of Chameleon, including the periodic measurment of $I(k)$ and the channel selection. It implements and provides the interface RadioControl for the purpose of transparently performing channel monitoring task, giving higher priority to O-MAC tasks with the radio resource. Chameleon only uses the radio when O-MAC is not occupy-ing the resource. Whenever O-MAC attempts to start the radio, Chameleon im-mediately stops its monitoring task and returns the control of radio to O-MAC. ChannelMonitor also generates the channel schedule, which is input to the Listener module which implements the desired channel switching upon wakeup. In the di-agram, colored components represent Chameleon modules which are modified or new with respect to the original O-MAC protocol. The Sender module is also mod-ified to incorporate multichannel feature when transmission. The interfaces pro-vided by Chameleon are MCM (Multi-Channel Monitoring) as follows.

```
interface MCM {
command   error_t   start ();
command   error_t   stop ();
command   uint8_t   getCh ();
command   void      setCh (k);
event     void      setChDone (error);
command   ch_arr    chVector ();
command   void      setUpdateInterval (t); }
```

Command getCh returns the index of the channel to use for communication based on recent channel monitoring result. The returned value of this command is included in the beacon sent out when the receiver wakes up. Command setCh is called to switch the channel for data transmission and the setChDone event is sig-naled after radio has stabilized on the new channel. chVector returns the current channel allocation in an array as V, while command setUpdateInterval provides a way for the application to adjust the update interval of channel assignment.

4   Protocol Evaluation

We evaluated Chameleon via both simulations, in Matlab, and experiments, based on an implementation in TinyOS 2.x for the TelosB platform[1]. We show, using simulation[12], that the performance of not only the metric w but also Chameleon compares favorably with other multi-channel MAC protocols under various traffic scenarios and network topologies. To validate Chameleon's perfor-mance in the presence of a realistic environment and (TelosB) platform effects, we experimentally evaluated three main metrics, namely, the end-to-end delivery ratio, the average receive duty cycle, and energy efficiency, of Chameleon with other benchmark protocols under various circumstances.

Delivery ratio is computed periodically, i.e., the number of successfully re-ceived packets at destinations divided by the number of packets attempted to be sent from sources. Due to the receiver-centric nature of these multi-channel protocols, we only consider the receive duty cycle at a node, which is represented by the fraction of active periods for listen or receive to the total period of time. The transmit duty cycle is approximately equal to the receive duty cycle because both Y-MAC and Chameleon are synchronous protocols. Given that data period of each slot takes t time, the energy efficiency is t multiplied by the number of slots that received packets successfully divided by the total active time for listening or receiving. We likewise corroborated its ability to tolerate external traffic and its relative improvements over both single channel (specifically, BoX-MAC and O-MAC) and multi-channel protocols (MMSN and Y-MAC).

Towards comparing with the other two multi-channel protocols in a fair manner, we made several necessary modifications to MMSN [18]. The frequency assignment of MMSN evenly allocates the available channels to neighbors. For media access, MMSN as specified does not consider duty cycling. As in Chameleon, however, we let each receiver listen at its own slot, and thus avoid the more expensive frequency toggle preamble incurred in the original specification of MMSN, given that senders are aware of receiver schedule. In other words, the modified version of MMSN that implemented has reduced protocol overhead. We implemented the modified MMSN and Y-MAC on TelosB platform. Based on current implementation of O-MAC, the average slot length of Chameleon is 16ms (same as O-MAC) and of Y-MAC is 20ms; the latter is larger since channel switching (and synchronization) is performed in every slot. MMSN operates at full duty cycle as in its original specification. The data packet size is fixed at 60 bytes. All data communications are performed in unicast mode. The size of the backoff window in each slot is 4ms. Neighbor discovery and time synchronization services are provided by O-MAC. In the comparison, we did not let Chameleon enforce restrictions on incoming traffic even if all channel capacities had been exceeded. (Such policing would, however, help the performance of Chameleon.) The monitoring overhead is zero for both MMSN and Y-MAC since channel assignment is done either a priori or deterministically; and around 0.6% duty cycle for Chameleon under three channels.

As for the single channel protocols, we used existing implementation of BoX-MAC, which is representative of duty-cycled asynchronous protocols, and O-MAC, which is representative of duty-cycled synchronous protocols. BoX-MAC [13] is the default low power listening protocol implemented in TinyOS-2.x. We let its receive check interval be set to 100ms.

Metrics for a Clique Network. Our first experiment was repeated for the five protocols in a clique network whose traffic load increases over time. The load increases adding independent flows to the network, with no flow sharing a source or a destination node with any other flow. Flows have one of three rates, with 1 packet every 100 milliseconds or 50 milliseconds, or 25 milliseconds, resulting in a load of approximately 10%, 20%, or 40% duty cycle, respectively. 6 independent flows are successively added in the network, with loads of 10%, 20%, 40%, 40%, 10%, and 20% respectively.

To avoid experimental error due to external interference from the environment, we collected measurements on the noise level for every available channel in our testbed. This gave us three relatively free channels in our testbed for this experiment, i.e., channels 22, 24, and 18. (Note that although there are 16 channels available on TelosB platform, it has been shown that adjacent channels actually interfere with each other [8]. Therefore, we avoided using adjacent channels in all our experiments.)

Fig. 4 (a)(b)(c) plot the metrics for these five protocols. We see that single channel protocols are much more negatively affected by the augmentation of traffic load than are multi-channel protocols. The packet delivery ratio of O-MAC is only slightly higher than that of BoX-MAC, but the duty cycle of BoX-MAC is 2 to 4 fold of O-MAC, suggesting that synchronous receiver-centric MAC protocol may be substantially more energy-efficient than asynchronous sender-centric protocols. The efficiency of both protocols decreases significantly as the traffic load increases. We also see that the overhead involved in Chameleon over O-MAC is within a 1% duty cycle.

Chameleon maintains the highest delivery ratio of the three multichannel protocols as the traffic loads increases. In comparison with Y-MAC, MMSN has a worse delivery ratio because channel 22 is overloaded with flows (3 receivers are statically assigned to the same channel). Fig. 4(b) shows the average duty cycle of the receiver, which is proportional to the average traffic load. Y-MAC incurs about 10% higher overhead than Chameleon due to its continuous channel switching scheme. On the other hand, the primary overhead of Chameleon—channel monitoring—involves insignificant energy consumption. Fig. 4(c) illustrates the overall energy efficiency of each protocol. Chameleon has 62% to 55% efficiency as internal network load grows, which is on average 40% and 20% more efficient than modified MMSN and Y-MAC, respectively.

Metrics for a Clique Network with External Interference. Static assignment of load to channels, as in Y-MAC and MMSN, is inherently inefficient if the utilization of the shared spectrum by external systems is not monitored. Since Chameleon monitors channels comprehensively, it is intrinsically adaptable to dynamic and unknown wireless environments. Our next experiment introduced an external interferer to the network. In this experiment, 3 flows with duty cycles of 10%, 20%, and 40% exist in the network, and they use 3 of available channels. Time is divided into 8 periods. In period 1, there is no external interferer. During times 2 to 4, the interferer transmits on channel 18 with loads of 20%, 40%, and 60% sequentially. Later, interferers switch to channel 22 at time 5 and repeat the same increasing load pattern on channel 22.

Fig. 4(d)(e)(f) shows the resulting delivery ratio, mean receive duty cycle, and energy efficiency. Initially, Chameleon and MMSN both distribute three flows into the three channels while Y-MAC evenly allocates traffic onto every channel. When the interferer on channel 18 increases its load, both MMSN and Y-MAC retain their current channel usage resulting in a reduced delivery ratio. In constrast, Chameleon detects the interference level increase on channel 18 and moves its traffic to other better channels. Thus, a high packet reception ratio as well as high energy efficiency is maintained by Chameleon's channel allocation scheme.

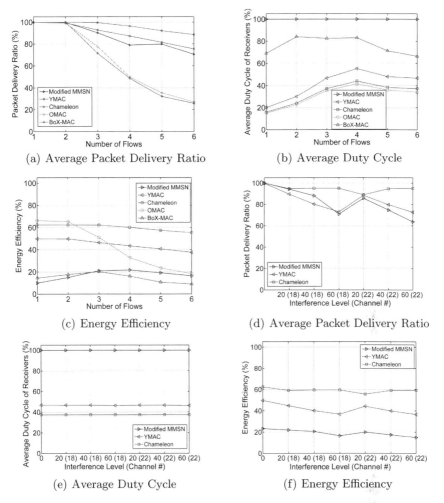

Fig. 4. (a)(b)(c) The Number of Internal Network Flows Increases in an Experimental Clique Network, and (d)(e)(f) External Interference Load Changes in an Experimental Clique Network

5   Related Work

The state-of-the-art in research includes a significant number of multi-channel MAC protocols for sensor networks. Per our earlier classification, the first category statically assigns multiple frequencies to nodes in the network as a way of topology control, in order to reduce potential interferences. Channel allocation is carried out beforehand, and is independent of real traffic conditions, such as in [18][16]. In [18], every node is assigned a channel for data reception such that most of two-hop neighbors do not communicate on the same channel. The TMCP protocol [16] divides nodes into several subsets of different channels, wherein nodes only communicate within their subset for simplicity of implementation. These schemes require a centralized channel assignment algorithm to execute in the beginning and the channel utilization is not adjusted according to communication load or interference on each channel.

Another approach expands the set of channels being used when the contention on the current channel become higher than an empirically chosen threshold. A distributed protocol in [11] lets all nodes in the network start in their home channel. When the channel becomes overloaded, a fraction of the nodes migrate to the next one. Channel switching is performed with a probability such that while alleviating congestion, it avoids having all nodes jump to the new channel. However, this protocol does not have a global view of the quality of each channel, thus, channel switching need not result in higher efficiency. Another work [10] presents a centralized protocol for load balancing across channels for throughput maximization. Each node periodically decides which channel to use based on measurements from the base station. The authors assume that network throughput is optimized as long as loads are distributed equally on each channel. There are also schemes based on frequency hopping [3] which are designed mainly for wireless ad hoc networks, which involve continuous switching of channel from slot to slot even when there is no need for transmission.

Few MAC protocols explicitly design multichannel scheduling with duty cycling to achieve high energy efficiency, which is the focus of this paper. A relatively recent multi-channel protocol, Y-MAC [9], exploits both duty cycling and multi-channel utilization. Every receiver wakes up at its non-overlap slot within each frame on home channel. If more packets need to be received, the receiver will stay awake but hop to the next channel for reception. The merit of this scheme lies in its staggered non-overlapping channel utilization over the extended M slots, while its weakness is that contiguous channel switching is expensive and the non-overlapping is guaranteed only within the M slots.

6   Concluding Remarks

This paper presented a new multi-channel MAC protocol, Chameleon, for duty-cycled wireless sensor networks. Chameleon betters the energy efficiency of existing protocols by adapting both the duty cycle and the channels that are being used. On one hand, it attempts to maximize spectrum utilization, via a light-weight channel utilization metric w that lets it split loads across channels effectively. On the other hand, it uses a receiver-centric approach to minimize on-duty time at the receiver, while letting senders wakeup only when they need to send and know the receiver is awake.

Experimental results confirm that Chameleon enhances energy efficiency substantially as compared to other multi-channel protocols under various internal traffic scenarios. Related experiments have shown us that external interference in long-lived WSNs is nontrivial, and is also typically unpredictable. Chameleon naturally coexists with dynamic conditions in spectrum and improves energy efficiency to a large extent.

The current design of Chameleon has not involved the broadcast scenario, which will be extended in the future. Future work will also examine the dynamics of Chameleon under different network topologies. We seek to address potential stabilization issues in channel selection via lightweight coordination among receivers.

References

1. CC2420 Datasheet, http://www.ti.com
2. Ahmed, N., Kanhere, S., Jha, S.: Multi-channel interference measurements for wireless sensor networks (poster). In: IPSN
3. Bahl, P., Chandra, R.: SSCH: Slotted seeded channel hopping for capacity improvement in ieee 802.11 ad-hoc wireless networks. In: MobiCom, pp. 216–230 (2004)
4. Buettner, M., Yee, G., Anderson, E., Han, R.: X-MAC: A short preamble mac protocol for duty-cycled wireless sensor network
5. Cao, H., Parker, K.W., Arora, A.: O-MAC: A receiver centric power management protocol. In: The 14th IEEE International Conference on Network Protocols, ICNP (2006)
6. Dutta, P., Culler, D.: Practical asynchronous neighbor discovery and rendezvous for mobile sensing applications. In: SenSys, pp. 71–84 (2008)
7. Halkes, G.P., Langendoen, K.G.: Crankshaft: An Energy-Efficient MAC-Protocol for Dense Wireless Sensor Networks. In: Langendoen, K.G., Voigt, T. (eds.) EWSN 2007. LNCS, vol. 4373, pp. 228–244. Springer, Heidelberg (2007)
8. Jain, N., Das, S.R., Nasipuri, A.: A multichannel csma mac protocol with receiver-based channel selection for multihop wireless networks. In: Proceedings of IEEE, IC3N (2001)
9. Kim, Y., Shin, H., Cha, H.: Y-MAC: An energy-efficient multi-channel mac protocol for dense wireless sensor networks. In: IPSN, pp. 53–63 (2008)
10. Le, H.K., Henriksson, D., Abdelzaher, T.: A control theory approach to throughput optimization in multi-channel collection sensor networks. In: The 6th International Conference on Information Processing in Sensor Networks, IPSN (2007)
11. Le, H.K., Henriksson, D., Abdelzaher, T.: A practical multi-channel media access control protocol for wireless sensor networks. In: IPSN, pp. 70–81 (2008)
12. Li, J., Arora, A.: Chameleon. Technical Report OSU-CISRC-11/09-TR52, The Ohio State University, CSE (2009)
13. Moss, D., Levis, P.: BoX-MACs: Exploiting physical and link layer boundaries in low-power networking. In: Technical Report SING-08-00
14. So, J., Vaidya, N.: Multi-channel mac for ad hoc networks: Handling multi-channel hidden terminals using a single transceiver. In: ACM MobiHoc (2004)
15. Sun, Y., Gurewitz, O., Johnson, D.B.: RI-MAC: A receiver-initiated asynchronous duty cycle mac protocol for dynamic traffic loads in wireless sensor networks. In: SenSys, pp. 1–14 (2008)
16. Wu, Y., Stankovic, J.A., He, T., Lin, S.: Realistic and efficient multi-channel communications in wireless sensor networks. In: Infocom, pp. 1193–1201 (2008)
17. Zhang, J., Zhou, G., Huang, C., Son, S.H., Stankovic, J.A.: TMMAC: An energy efficient multi-channel mac protocol for ad hoc networks. In: IEEE ICC (2007)
18. Zhou, G., Huang, C., Yan, T., He, T., Stankovic, J., Abdelzaher, T.: MMSN: Multi-frequency media access control for wireless sensor networks. In: The 25th IEEE International Conference on Computer Communication, Infocom (2006)

Practical Multi-antenna Spatial Reuse
in WLANs

Sriram Lakshmanan[1], Karthik Sundaresan[2],
Mohammad Khojastepour[2], and Sampath Rangarajan[2]

[1] School of ECE, Georgia Institute of Technology, Atlanta, GA
[2] NEC Laboratories America Inc., Princeton, NJ

Abstract. Smart antennas can improve spatial reuse in a wireless network through interference suppression. However, interference suppression requires support from clients in the form of channel estimation, which existing clients do not support. In this work, we explore practical solutions to obtain spatial reuse with smart antennas without requiring hardware changes to clients. To this end, we design a novel solution for improving spatial reuse in indoor WLANs which uses 'approximate' channel estimates and still yields close to ideal performance. Our solution called Light-weight Multi-Antenna Spatial Reuse (*LSR*) consists of (i) a multi-link channel estimation scheme that can be realized with simple *Received Signal Strength (RSSI)* measurements that existing WLAN clients provide readily, (ii) a low-complexity scheduler to decide the subset of beamformed links that must be active concurrently. We demonstrate that the estimates obtained using this scheme when used with a multi-link beamforming technique such as Zero Forcing yields significant interference suppression benefits. We implement the channel estimation scheme on a testbed of software radio clients to demonstrate its practical feasibility. Further, we evaluate the performance of *LSR* using extensive signal strength traces from 802.11g Access Points equipped with eight element antenna arrays in an indoor office environment. The results indicate that *LSR* achieves close to the performance obtained with an optimal scheme that uses accurate channel estimates and also improves the median sum rate of indoor users by up to 2.7x over competing approaches.

Keywords: smart antennas, spatial reuse, interference suppression.

1 Introduction

The growing density of wireless networks and limited spectrum availability are posing severe challenges to achieving high performance in wireless networks. Consequently, significant attention is being devoted to improving the number of successful concurrent transmissions in a given network area (also called spatial reuse). Due to their ability to control signal transmissions spatially, smart antennas have emerged as promising candidates to achieve high link throughput and to improve the spatial reuse by interference suppression.

I. Tomkos et al. (Eds.): BROADNETS 2010, LNICST 66, pp. 158–177, 2012.
© Institute for Computer Sciences, Social Informatics and Telecommunications Engineering 2012

Although smart antennas have been shown to significantly improve the spatial reuse (by interference suppression) in theory [1], relatively few works have focused on whether the promised gains are achievable in practice or the design of practical solutions to realize those gains. Interference suppression algorithms can be classified into two main groups, namely coordinated and uncoordinated. Coordinated beamforming algorithms [2], typically compute the best set of weight vectors in a coordinated iterative manner. These algorithms yield the best performance but are also the most complex. On the other hand, with uncoordinated beamforming algorithms, the beamformers are computed at each AP in isolation. A popular instantiation of this class is interference nulling through Zero-Forcing (ZF).

Interference suppression between smart antenna links requires the estimation of the channel both from the desired and interfering transmitters (i.e. APs) at each of the receivers (i.e. clients). When the estimates are fed back to the APs, a joint processing helps determine how each individual AP should adapt its transmissions to maximize the signal to the desired client while minimizing the interference to other clients. Thus, accurate channel estimation at the clients is critical to realize interference suppression. However accurate channel estimates are not readily available in legacy omni-directional clients. Further, even with multiple antenna clients, they are available only at the physical layer of a single link (e.g. 802.11n), but not at the higher layers where the decisions about joint beamforming or multi-link scheduling must be taken. Additionally, practical networks must accommodate a variety of client platforms (smart phones, VOIP phones, laptops, etc) from several different manufacturers and all of them may not provide the required information for taking medium access decisions. Given the above challenges, the key questions to be answered are: (i) *Can channel estimation be realized without requiring hardware changes at the clients?* and (ii) *Can we enable interference suppression and achieve spatial reuse in practical networks which comprise such clients?*

We establish that the answer to both the above questions is affirmative but relies on appropriate algorithm design for channel estimation and link scheduling. We showed in our previous work [3] that single-link channel estimation and beamforming is possible even with conventional clients using just received power measurements and no hardware/software changes [1]. However, in this work we first show that a straight-forward extension of that approach has poor accuracy and scalability when applied in a multi-link scenario. We design several mechanisms to ensure that the channel estimation using just RSSI measurements is both *accurate and scalable* in a multi-link scenario. Given accurate channel estimates, the next step toward realizing network level gains of interference suppression is link scheduling. While the large potential set of links in a dense AP deployment makes this problem especially challenging, we propose a simple and light-weight scheduler that selects the right subset of links to be concurrently active so that the aggregate network throughput is maximized. We show that the

---

[1] Received Signal Strength Indicator (RSSI) is readily provided by all cards without additional software requirements.

proposed scheduler is scalable. i.e. it provides benefits close to an optimal solution involving brute force search over all combination of links without incurring the exponential complexity with increasing number of links. We call our solution that integrates the above algorithmic components Light-weight Multi-Antenna Spatial Reuse (LSR). LSR performs both *accurate channel estimation and link scheduling without requiring changes at the clients* and keeps the overheads low compared to competitive approaches.

To evaluate the practical benefits of LSR, we develop a testbed of six 802.11g APs equipped with eight element antenna arrays and six software radio clients in an indoor office environment. We implement the multi-link channel estimation on the testbed and identify that the beamforming vectors computed with RSSI measurements are very close to those obtained with ideal channel measurements (with 95% correlation coefficient for over 90% of the locations profiled). Although the channel estimation itself was successfully implemented, we identified that realizing the complete 'interference suppression' gains involves addressing new practical challenges such as the inability of the hardware to change patterns fast and the power leakage from the transmit antennas. Despite these limitations, We evaluate the real potential of interference suppression, by collecting a large set of signal strength traces from our testbed. Our evaluation indicates that, LSR improves the median sum rate by up to 2.7x compared to single user beamforming strategies and by up to 2.3x compared to concurrent interference-unaware beamforming. *Interestingly, we observe that the median number of concurrent links to be scheduled in indoor WLANs to maximize network throughput with eight antenna APs is around 4.* This observation has significant system design implications and keeps the run-time complexity of LSR small for a significant fraction of the topologies.

The rest of this paper is organized as follows. Section 2 provides a brief background on beamforming with interference suppression and also discusses related work in this area. Section 3 describes the solution components and also summarizes the key properties of the solution. Section 4 presents a detailed performance evaluation using real-world traces. Section 5 discusses issues and Section 6 concludes the paper.

2   Background and Related Work

2.1   A Beamforming Primer

In a scenario with M APs each equipped with k antennas and N clients each with a single (omni-directional) antenna, the baseband channel model at client n is given by,

$$y_n = \sum_{m=1}^{M} \mathbf{h}_{mn}{}^T \mathbf{x}_m + z_n \tag{1}$$

where each column vector $\mathbf{h}_{mn} = [h_{mn1}, h_{mn2} \ldots h_{mnk}]^T$ denotes the channel between AP m and client n, $\mathbf{x}_m$ is the $k \times 1$ vector of transmitted signals from

AP m, y_n is the received signal and z_n is additive White Gaussian noise with zero mean and variance σ^2. The transmitted signal is related to the symbol (s_m) to be transmitted by a weight vector $\mathbf{w}_m$ as $\mathbf{x}_m = \mathbf{w}_m s_m$. By appropriately modifying $\mathbf{w}_m$, different beam patterns can be generated.

In directional beamforming Dir, the weights are set such that the beam patterns point a main lobe in a certain direction. Typically a fixed set of such beams (independent of the channel) are used to cover the the entire azimuth of 360 degrees. Such beams are known to be less effective indoors than outdoors due to multipath fading [1]. On the other hand, when the beam is adapted to leverage the multipath effects and maximize the SNR (Signal to Noise Ratio) at the receiver, the technique is called adaptive beamforming. When applied to a single link (which we refer to as Single User Adaptive Beamforming or SUA), the weights that optimize the received SNR are related to the channel gains $\mathbf{h}$ as $\mathbf{w} = \frac{\mathbf{h}*}{|\mathbf{h}|}$.

In a multi-AP setting, two types of beamforming are well known: (1) coordinated beamforming, where the APs share the channel estimates from each of their clients. (2) Uncoordinated beamforming where each AP only uses the channel estimates from itself to the other clients. While coordinated beamforming can provide higher gains than uncoordinated beamforming, it incurs more overheads due to joint computation of weight vectors. Consequently uncoordinated beamforming provides a good balance of performance and overheads making it desirable in practice.

Zero forcing (ZF) [1], is a popular uncoordinated beamforming method used for interference suppression. In ZF, the weight vectors are chosen by each AP such that the received signal power at the intended client is maximized subject to the constraint that the interference caused to the other clients is reduced to zero. The solution at each AP is related to the N channel vectors from that AP to the clients as described in [1]. For a 2 AP, 2 client case, the channel vectors from AP1 are given as $\mathbf{h_{11}}, \mathbf{h_{12}}$ and the vectors from AP2 as $\mathbf{h_{21}}, \mathbf{h_{22}}$. In this case, the weight vectors for AP1 is given as

$$w_1 = h_{11}^* - \frac{h_{12}^T h_{11}^*}{h_{12}^H h_{12}} h_{12}^* \qquad (2)$$

where ^{H} denotes the Hermitian transpose and * denotes conjugate. The weight vector for AP2 is computed similarly. Compared to single user beamforming , a rate improvement up to 2x can be obtained in a two link setting using ZF.

2.2   Related Work

Theory: There has been an abundance of theory and protocol works on smart antennas [1,4] in the areas of channel estimation, beamforming and scheduling. Theoretical solutions to channel estimation [5,6,7] require accurate measurement of the baseband symbols at the receiver. Further, they also assume that antennas can be switched to create new beam patterns very fast (within a burst of symbols) and/or assume complicated receiver designs that require prior knowledge of the channel covariance matrix or rely on reciprocity which is difficult in the presence of interference. Recently in [8], the problem of user selection and beamforming has been considered, where a single AP beamforms to multiple clients simultaneously. Later works [2,9] have also considered the case where multiple APs cooperate to beamform to multiple clients. All these solutions assume that perfect channel state information is available at the AP.

Practical solutions in indoor wireless networks: There has been relatively fewer works on practical solutions to use beamforming in indoor wireless networks. In [10], the authors presented a system for downlink MIMO transmission, whereas the work in [11] proposes a channel estimation algorithm for random beamforming. Both these works use custom built narrow bandwidth hardware. DIRC [12] uses a fixed set of steerable 'directional' beams (independent of the channel) to increase spatial reuse whereas we use beams adapted to the channels that enable more spatial reuse compared to schemes that use directional beams. Interference alignment and cancellation [13] optimizes the performance by aligning the transmissions from multiple APs. However, it requires multiple elements at the clients and accurate channel state information.

In our prior work [14], we studied single user adaptive beamforming using software radios. Recently in [3], we considered the benefits of single-user beamforming using commercial Wifi devices. Both these works are intended to improve single link performance, do not consider interference and cannot be used to improve spatial reuse in a multi-link scenario. In contrast, in this work we design new estimation and scheduling algorithms to enable multiple concurrent AP-client links by interference suppression.

3   Light-Weight Multi-antenna Spatial Reuse

3.1   Network Model

We consider indoor WLANs where the APs posses multiple antennas arrays using which they can manipulate their beams. The APs are connected by a high-bandwidth ethernet connection. The clients posses a single (omni-directional) antenna and follow the Wifi association model wherein a single AP can only communicate to a single client at a time on a fixed channel. The objective is to maximize the weighted sum rate of all clients, where the weights are adjusted based on some fairness model.

3.2   Solution Overview

In this section we present our solution for improving spatial reuse in high density wireless networks which leverages the interference suppression capabilities of APs equipped with multiple antennas. The overarching goal is to design a solution which does not have sophisticated and unrealistic requirements and can be deployed in a WLAN without significant changes at the clients. We call our solution Light-weight Multi-antenna Spatial Reuse solution (LSR).

LSR consists of two main components, namely a light-weight channel estimation scheme and a low-complexity beamforming and scheduling scheme. The first component of LSR is a technique to perform channel estimation in a multiple AP multiple client Wifi network using just RSSI measurements at the client devices. i.e. *LSR does not require any phase or baseband symbol measurement at the receiver.* Conventionally channel estimation involves using special training symbols at the transmitter and enhanced receivers that provide both the magnitude and phase of received symbols [1]. While this has been accomplished in the open-loop context in 802.11n receivers, it is still non-trivial to feed it to the APs and perform closed-loop beamforming. Additionally, legacy clients do not have sophisticated hardware to provide channel estimates. Combined with the large variety of Wifi clients (e.g. PDAs, laptops, smartphones, etc), current techniques leave a significant fraction of Wifi clients unable to leverage beamforming. In contrast to conventional estimation procedures, LSR uses an intelligent antenna excitation scheme that relates the RSSI to the channel gain magnitudes and the differential phases. While we introduced the idea of estimating beamforming coefficients for single AP beamforming in [3], it is unclear whether they can be applied to multi-link beamforming. We first show that a straight-forward extension of the single AP procedure would suffer from poor accuracy and scalability when applied to a multi-AP setting. Then, we introduce optimizations to accommodate multi-link channel estimation. The second component of LSR involves selecting the right set of links to perform joint beamforming. Here LSR incorporates a Zero Forcing beamformer and a novel scheduler that identifies the best subset of links to operate on, while keeping the overall complexity low.

3.3 LSR Channel Estimation

We first revisit the basic procedure for single link estimation [3] and describe its enhancement for multiple links.

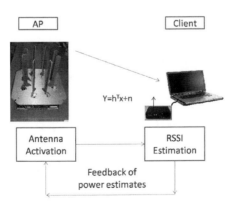

Fig. 1. LSR channel estimation

Single-Link channel estimation. We briefly summarize the idea of received power based channel estimation for single link beamforming that we presented in [3]. The key idea is to estimate 'differential' channel phases (instead of absolute channel phases) by employing *tandem activation of more than one antenna* and using received power estimates. Assuming a channel model given by 1, when a single antenna is activated at a time, the received power is dependent only on the channel magnitude and is given by $P_i = |h_i|^2$ (assuming that the transmit power is unity). Hence the information about the channel phase $arg(h_i)$ is lost when the power is computed. In contrast, by the tandem activation of more than one antenna element, the effects of the channel phases are also reflected in the received power in a manner that depends on the relative channel phases. i.e. when two elements i and j are activated simultaneously with equal weights (such that the transmitted power still adds up to unity), the received signal power can be computed as $P_{ij} = |h_i + h_j|^2$. Thus, for tandem activation, the received power P_{ij} is given as

$$P_{ij} = P_i + P_j + 2\sqrt{P_i.P_j}.cos(\theta_{ij}) \qquad (3)$$

where θ_{ij} is the *channel phase difference* between h_i and h_j. The resulting power at the client depends on the relative channel phase θ_{ij}. When $\theta_{ij} = 0$, the signals combine constructively causing the powers of the individual elements to add up. However, when $\theta_{ij} = 180$ the signals combine destructively causing the received power to be the difference of the powers transmitted from the individual antennas. Hence, the change in the received power across a strategic set of activations can be used to identify the relative channel phase between the channel gains by rewriting Equation 3 as

$$\theta_{ij} = \cos^{-1} \frac{P_{ij} - P_i - P_j}{2\sqrt{P_i.P_j}} \qquad (4)$$

By repeating this idea for pairs of antenna elements, the relative phases and the channel magnitudes can be obtained as described in [3].

Multi-link vs multiple single link estimation. In a M-AP N-client network, a straight-forward application of this procedure would be to perform the basic algorithm for each AP-client pair (All Pairs Estimation-APE). APE has the following issues. (1) The channel estimation for each AP-client pair would be separated significantly in time. Since interference suppression requires the channels to the different clients to be estimated as close in time as possible, the accuracy of the estimates could be affected. (2) The excitation overhead for APE increases proportional to MN. In contrast, by interleaving the estimation process across clients intelligently, the overhead in LSR is reduced significantly to be proportional to M. (3) In APE, the feedback overhead from each client (in packets) scales linearly with M. But in LSR, by using aggregated feedback the overhead is restricted to a few packets for practical AP densities. Thus LSR carefully considers these issues which are not addressed by APE.

Multi-Link Estimation and beamforming. A straight-forward extension of the above procedure to a multi-link scenario affects the accuracy of the estimates. Further it increases the time required for estimation and the feedback overheads. Hence, we develop additional mechanisms that must be designed into each step of the single-link solution [3] for efficient multi-link estimation.

i. Simultaneous multi-client measurement

As with single-link estimation, each one of the k elements at each AP is activated in isolation first. Following this, one antenna is designated as the reference and is activated with each of the remaining $k - 1$ antennas in tandem pairs. This step is performed by each AP one after another by transmitting beacon packets. All clients estimate the channels simultaneously from each AP, enabling the measurements to be consistent across links. This also reduces the overheads compared to exciting each AP-client pair at a time.

ii. Aggregated Feedback from clients to APs

Single link estimation involves feedback of $2k - 1$ received power values for the activations of step i. described previously. Instead of transmitting the feedback for each AP-client pair separately, the estimates from different APs are aggregated at each client into one or more packets and transmitted to the AP to which it is associated. An AP which receives the packet successfully broadcasts it on the ethernet backbone to the other APs so that they can extract the channel estimates required.

iii. Multi-link Ambiguity resolution

For the channel estimates between each AP-client pair, the magnitudes of the channel gains are obtained correctly. But the channel phases ϕ_{ij} (in radians) have an ambiguity due to the use of the cos^{-1} function in Equation 4. i.e. the correct θ_{ij} can be either of $\phi_{ij}, -\phi_{ij}, \pi - \phi_{ij}, -(\pi - \phi_{ij})$. The ambiguity is resolved by tandem activations with the estimates of Steps i and ii as described in [3] across each AP-client pair. As an additional optimization, the ambiguity resolution can also be performed by *applying the interference suppression weights* (instead of single link beamforming weights) across pairs of antennas so that the overhead of ambiguity resolution is reduced compared to that in [3].

Properties. The previously described channel estimation approaches uses assumptions about the channel coefficients and channel noise. While we experimentally showed that using power measurements provides single link beamforming benefits [3], here we provide the analytical reasoning for the effectiveness of the proposed solution for both single and multi-link beamforming. We briefly state the following properties and refer the interested reader to [15] for the details.

P1. Channel magnitudes and 'Differential phases' computed by LSR achieve the same beamforming benefits as using magnitudes and 'absolute' channel phases.

Conventionally beamforming requires accurate estimation of the channel vector **h** both in magnitude and phase. However, LSR uses differential phases measured using RSSI. We show analytically that the interference suppression benefits of LSR are close-to-ideal interference suppression benefits. We show how the weight vectors using absolute and differential phases differ only by a complex number whose magnitude is unity. Thus both the signal and interference powers are the same in both cases.

P2: For practical operating SNRs, thermal noise has minimal impact on the accuracy of LSR.

We explore how thermal noise affects RSSI based channel estimation. We show that for any AP-client pair, the differential phase estimate between two elements i and j when using RSSI measurements is related to the accurate differential phase and noise variance σ^2 as

$$\tilde{\theta}_{ij} = \cos^{-1} \frac{\cos\theta_{ij}.|h_i|.|h_j|}{\sqrt{(|h_i|^2 + \sigma^2))(|h_j|^2 + \sigma^2)}} \tag{5}$$

For practical Signal to Noise ratios (SNRs), the noise term is negligible compared to the signal term. Hence, we obtain $\tilde{\theta}_{ij} \dot{=} \theta_{ij}$.

The magnitude of the channel gains can also be obtained from the RSSI as $|\tilde{h}_i| = \sqrt{P_i}$ or $|\tilde{h}_i| = \sqrt{|h_i|^2 + \sigma^2}$. Again for practical SNRs, this can be simplified to yield $|\tilde{h}_i| \dot{=} |h_i|$. Thus, the effect of thermal noise on the accuracy of LSR is minimal as elaborated in [15].

3.4   Link Scheduling

Given a set of links, the above procedure estimates the channels using RSSI measurements at the desired and interfered clients that in turn helps achieve interference suppression. To achieve low complexity, we chose the ZF based beamforming solution, where each AP forces the interference power it causes to other clients to be reduced to zero[2]. Thus, given the channel vectors $\mathbf{h}_{mn}$ from AP m to client n, ZF solution maximizes $|\mathbf{h}_{mm}^T w|^2$ to the desired client m while minimizing the interference to client n, namely $|h_{mn}^T w|^2 = 0, \forall n \neq m$.

However, the design of a MAC solution would also require the determination of the set of links (scheduling) that must operate concurrently using ZF to maximize a desired system objective. To incorporate both throughput and fairness, we consider the popular weighted sum rate as the system objective to be maximized. For simplicity of discussions, consider a network with N co-channel APs and one client associated with each AP. The proposed solution will also apply to the case with multiple clients per AP. To determine which subset of links must operate concurrently a brute force search could be employed. However, it would need to evaluate the system objective for all combinations of n links, where $n \in [1, N]$. This results in a total of $\binom{N}{1} + \binom{N}{2}... + \binom{N}{N} = 2^N$ combinations, making it exponential in N. To keep the scheduling solution scalable, we propose a greedy algorithm to identify the set of concurrent links that runs in $O(N^2)$ time, while yielding a performance comparable to that of the exhaustive approach. Note

---

[2] We note here that other closed loop MU-MIMO strategies can also be used at this stage given that the channel estimates computed in LSR with RSSI are close to the actual channel estimates as we show later.

Algorithm 1. Link Scheduler for LSR

1: Run LSR to obtain the channel estimates for desired and interference links using RSSI measurements.
2: $\mathcal{L} \leftarrow$ Set of active links; $C = \emptyset$
3: **while** $C \neq \mathcal{L}$ **do**
4:     $\ell^* = \arg\max_{\ell \in \mathcal{L} \setminus C}$
            $\sum_{k \in C' : C \cup \ell} T(\rho_{k,C'}) - \sum_{m \in C} T(\rho_{m,C})$
5:     $\hat{S} = \sum_{k \in C'} T(\rho_{k,C'})$
6:     **if** $\hat{S} > S$ **then**
7:         $C \leftarrow C \cup \{\ell^*\}$
8:         $S = \hat{S}$
9:     **else**
10:        Exit
11:    **end if**
12: **end while**
13: Run $ZF(C)$ to obtain weight vectors $\mathbf{w}_\ell$, $\forall \ell \in C$
14: Execute $\mathbf{w}_\ell$, $\forall \ell \in C$

---

that, one could also optimize the greedy algorithms further to improve system performance. Our goal here is to provide a low complexity greedy scheduler that will help us evaluate the performance of our RSSI based interference suppression scheme (LSR) in a network-wide setting.

The algorithm (Algorithm 1) works as follows: First the channel estimates are obtained using RSSI measurements for all the desired and interfering links (step 1). The scheduler initializes the set of selected links C to an empty set initially (step 2). At each iteration, it grows the selected set C by adding the link from the remaining set $\mathcal{L} \setminus C$ that provides the highest increase in the system utility using the rate table $T(\rho, C)$ for a given set of SINRs ρ for links in C (steps 4-8). The iterations stop when the system utility cannot be increased any more by the addition of a link (steps 9-11). The scheduler then runs the zero-forcing based beamforming solution on the selected set of links C to obtain the weight vectors and executes them (steps 13-14). The while loop and step 4 contribute to the time complexity and is bounded by $\frac{N(N+1)}{2}$ in the worst case, which is $O(N^2)$.

Note that, the above algorithm does not require the division of the network topology into multiple contention domains to determine the set of concurrent links in each contention domain. Instead, by virtue of being greedy, it automatically leverages the natural spatial reuse available in the network, to determine links both within and across contention domains that can operate concurrently.

4   Performance Evaluation

4.1   Measurement Setup

We perform experiments in a testbed that consists of six APs and six clients deployed in an indoor office environment whose layout is shown in Figure 2. Each of the APs is a commercial 802.11 b/g AP (Phocus Array [16]), which has

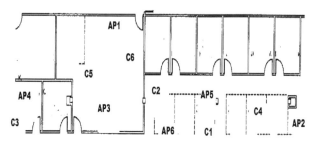

Fig. 2. Experimental Testbed

an eight element circular antenna array. Each client is a software radio which employs the Universal Software Radio Peripheral (USRP [17]) for the hardware and the GNURadio software [18] package along with the 802.11b code from [19]. The AP provides a command line interface to set specific beam patterns by writing weight vectors. We use this to implement the channel estimation component of LSR. The excitation steps of LSR are implemented as user level code on the Phocus Array.For every experiment, we also implement the complete channel estimation proposed in our previous work [14], which we refer to as 'perfect' channel estimates. In both LSR and our previous work, the first stage of channel estimation is performed concurrently. The ambiguity resolution is performed with the perfect channel measurement procedure first, immediately followed by LSR. We collect the channel estimate traces for both the schemes across every pair of AP and client, across physical locations and across time (multiple runs over several days).

We use the weight vectors for the 16 directional beams provided by the man-ufacturer [16]. For the competitive strategies ZF and SUA, we use the estimated channels to compute weight vectors. We compute the resulting Signal to Inter-ference plus Noise ratio (SINR) for each of these strategies and the data rate table for 802.11g systems for each link. This table maps an input SINR to a data rate from 6 Mbps to 54 Mbps and is well known in the rate control literature [20]. We compute the sum rate of the concurrent links as the final metric (i.e. we use equal weights in our weighted sum rate objective function).

We organize the evaluation into three classes, namely channel estimation in isolation, joint channel estimation and beamforming, integrated operation (which includes channel estimation, beamforming and the scheduling components).

4.2   LSR Channel Estimation in Isolation

RSSI being a quantized estimate of the received power, results in a quantization error that may affect LSR. To quantify the performance difference between using full precision power estimates and RSSI values, we run the channel estimation algorithm on a two AP-two client scenario using full (16 bit) resolution for power and then with RSSI expressed as an integer in dB. Since we are interested in the similarity in the direction between two vectors, we define the similarity Index (SI) between two vectors as

$$SI(a, b) = \frac{|a^H b|}{|a||b|} \tag{6}$$

SI is the cosine of the angle between the vectors a and b. An SI value of 1 indicates that the two vectors are similar (highly correlated) whereas a value close to zero indicates that they are not similar.

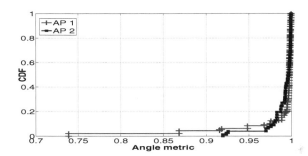

Fig. 3. Two Link Similarity Index

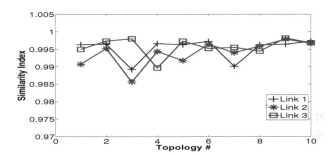

Fig. 4. Three Link Similarity Index

We first focus on a single pair of links in our testbed. We compute the weight vectors for zero forcing and determine the similarity index between the weight vectors computed using the ideal and RSSI measurements. The CDF of the similarity index for several runs of two link scenarios in our testbed is plotted in Figure 3. The figure reveals that the SI is very close to 1 for a majority of the cases and at most goes down to 75% still indicating a good correlation between the weight vectors using power and with RSSI.

We then explore if the weight vectors are also similar or more different for three link zero forcing. We select subsets of three links (with fixed AP-client association), and compute the three AP zero forcing vectors using both the perfect estimates and the estimates from LSR. For each link, we plot the similarity index (SI) in Figure 4. We observe from the figure that for all the 10 topologies, the similarity between the weight vectors is very high approaching 1. Thus both perfect estimates and using RSSI measurements yield zero forcing vectors which are highly correlated. Thus, LSR which requires RSSI measurements only, enables close to ideal weight computation for practical operating conditions.

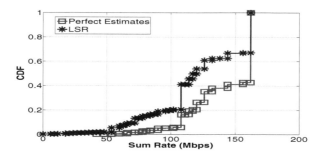

Fig. 5. CDF of sumrates

4.3   Joint LSR Channel Estimation and Beamforming

While our implementation of channel estimation operated successfully as described in Section 4.2, we encountered two practical challenges when implementing zero-forcing, (i) the inability of the hardware to update patterns quickly and (ii) power leakage from the transmit antennas at the APs. We believe that these can be overcome by better hardware and software designs in the future. Nevertheless, we evaluate the practical benefits of the interference suppression with LSR using realistic signal strength traces from our testbed. We consider the aggregate rate of concurrent links employing LSR, and compare it with other competing strategies.

Aggregate rate. We are interested in studying how the aggregate rate varies across different two link and three link topologies. For each of the two link runs, we choose two out of six APs and two out of six clients (yielding $\binom{6}{2} * \binom{6}{2} = 225$ topologies). We plot the CDF of the sum rates in Figure 6. The CDFs indicate that the distribution of rates is similar when both perfect and LSR estimates are used. Specifically, while more than 70% of the link configurations can sustain a data rate of 108 Mbps with perfect estimates, with LSR almost 60 % can sustain the same rate. The median rate is 108 Mbps, which is double the single link rate. Similarly, for the case of three links we study the performance over 400 topologies and plot the result in Figure 5. The resulting median rates are 162Mbps and 120 Mbps when using perfect estimates and LSR estimates. These results suggest that LSR yields significant benefits for a majority of indoor locations and is also close to the performance of zero forcing with ideal estimates.

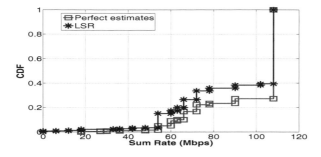

Fig. 6. Joint LSR channel estimation and beamforming: Two Link rates

Comparison of strategies. We are interested in analyzing the competitive advantage of LSR over other approaches. We consider the 225 link pairs (i.e two link topologies) for this evaluation. We compare with directional beamforming (Dir) [12] and adaptive beamforming (SUA) from an AP to its clients. Each of these strategies can be employed either in (1) a time division manner or (2) simultaneously across links. Activating multiple single user beamformed links simultaneously can yield a high sum rate if the channels of the users are well separated in vector space. Hence, for comparison, we consider the following four strategies Dir-TDMA, Dir-concurrent, SUA-TDMA, SUA-concurrent. We implement a search over all combination of beams with Dir to compare with an ideal implementation of [12].

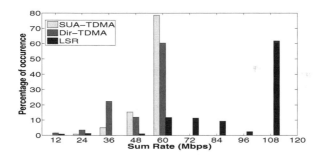

Fig. 7. Joint LSR channel estimation and beamforming: Strategies - TDMA

The histogram of the sum rates obtained with time division versions of these strategies is presented in Figure 7 and for the concurrent versions in Figure 8. From the figure, the following inferences can be made. (1) LSR outperforms both the TDMA approaches by a factor of 2 in the median sum rate. (2) For more than 80 % of the link pairs, LSR outperforms Dir-concurrent and SUA-concurrent. (3) The relative benefits of LSR are higher over SUA-concurrent than over Dir-concurrent since SUA-concurrent has lesser configuration flexibility than Dir-concurrent which can choose out of $16 * 16 = 256$ beam combinations.

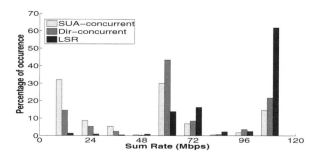

Fig. 8. Joint LSR channel estimation and beamforming: Strategies - Concurrent

4.4   LSR Integrated Operation

We consider an integrated operation of all components of LSR, namely the channel estimation, beamforming and scheduling.

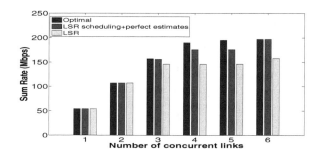

Fig. 9. LSR Integrated operations: Scalability of LSR

Scalability with number of concurrent links. We investigate how the performance benefits provided by LSR scale with the number of concurrent links as compared to ZF with perfect channel estimates. We feed in topologies with 2 link, 3 links, 4 links and so on upto 6 links.

The average sum rate for each case is plotted for optimal scheduling, greedy scheduling with perfect estimates and LSR in Figure 9. From the figure it is clear that the average rate for all three strategies is same for a small number of links. However, as the number of links increases, there is a degradation in rate due to the greedy nature of the algorithm employed in LSR. Further, when the number of links is large, the weight vector computation involves more channel vectors and the errors in the estimation could also affect the sum rate. However, the evaluation reveals the following surprising observation. The maximum degradation between optimal solution and LSR solution occurs around 5 links where the throughput is reduced from 195 Mbps to 146 Mbps. Although there is a degradation, we note that the performance of optimal Zero Forcing also begins to saturate around 4 links and the degradation does not increase further. Hence, LSR suffers minimal degradation while incurring much lesser complexity compared to optimal zero forcing.

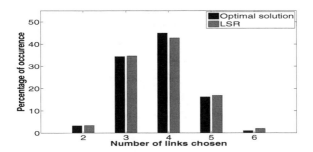

Fig. 10. LSR Integrated operations:# of links chosen

Comparison with optimal search and complexity. We investigate the run-time complexity of LSR under practical conditions by studying the impact of number of concurrent links and the sum rates achievable. The run-time complexity depends on the number of links at which the greedy algorithm terminates. If the optimal number of concurrent links is N, then the worst-case time complexity of $O(N^2)$ is always incurred by LSR. However, if the sum-rate optimal number of links is smaller than N, LSR incurs lesser complexity in practice. To study this, we generate $6! = 720$ topologies with 6 APs 6 clients from our traces by varying the AP-client association.

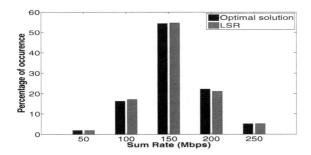

Fig. 11. LSR Integrated operations:Sum Rates obtained

For each topology, we determine the best sum-rate obtained by an exhaustive search of 2 links, 3 links and so on upto N links and the number of links that yields the best sum-rate. We then allow LSR to operate and determine the sum

rate and the number of operating links identified by LSR. The results are plotted
as histograms in Figure 10 and 11 for the optimal number of links and the sum
rate. The main observations are as follows: (1) *With eight antennas at each AP,
for more than 45 % of topologies, 4 concurrent links is the best* and for more than
35 % of the topologies activating 3 links yield the best rate. Thus the optimal
number of links is much less than the number of antennas at each AP. (2) *In
practical indoor deployments, the run-time complexity of LSR is likely to be lower
than that expected in theory and brute force scheduling incurs a large complexity
that is not justified.* (3) Around 55 % of topologies yield a sum rate around 150
Mbps. A very small number of topologies yields close to 250 Mbps and a smaller
set yields close to 50 Mbps. Thus, the association in multi-AP smart antenna
deployments is more important than their single antenna counterparts and a
range of benefits can be obtained based on the topology.

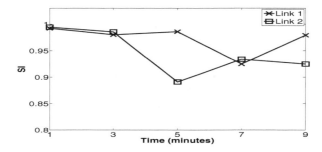

Fig. 12. Similarity index of weight vectors

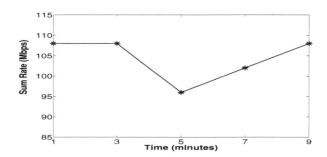

Fig. 13. Sum Rates vs. time

4.5   Impact of Channel Time Variation

We study the channel variation over time to understand how frequently beam
patterns must be adapted. To study this effect, we first estimate the channel and
compute weight vectors using the estimates. We then estimate the channel at a
subsequent time duration to see whether the previously computed weights can

be retainedin a two link scenario. We plot the Similarity Index between weight vectors computed at consecutive two minute intervals in Figure 12. It can be observed that the correlation is quite high for most of the time instants. The corresponding sum rates are plotted in Figure 13. It can be observed that as long as the correlation between vectors is greater than 95 %, the sum rate is retained at the maximum value of 108 Mbps. When transient fluctuations exist, the rate is reduced momentarily to 96 Mbps but is still quite close to the rate achieved with current estimates. We also note that we are constrained by the hardware in terms of how fast we can measure channels and write new patterns. With a kernel space implementation of LSR on the Phocus Array, we believe that the channel adaptation would be faster and the rate achieved would be closer to the rate obtained using accurate and timely channel estimates.

5 Discussion

- *Other beamforming and scheduling strategies:* While the proposed solution uses Zero Forcing and a greedy scheduling algorithm to obtain a good balance between complexity and performance, other alternatives to these could also be explored using the channel estimation component of LSR as is.
- *MIMO clients:* With the growing popularity of 802.11n, clients are likely to have more antenna elements. We believe that LSR can be extended to such clients and also combined with open-loop MIMO techniques for performance improvement.
- *Mobility:* We have considered primarily static clients in an indoor environment. While we believe that estimation and weight adaptation can be performed fast enough to account for indoor mobility, the design of the adaptation algorithm and its implementation are interesting directions to be explored.

6 Conclusions

In this work, we have developed LSR, a light-weight solution to obtain spatial reuse benefits in indoor wireless LANs equipped with smart antennas. The core components of LSR are: a scheme for multi-AP channel estimation which uses simple RSSI measurements, a Zero forcing beamformer which uses these estimates and a greedy link scheduler. We evaluate the solution using extensive traces collected from an indoor office environment. Our evaluation reveals that significant spatial reuse benefits can be obtained using LSR, and the median aggregate rate of the network improves up to 2.7x compared to related approaches.

References

1. Paulraj, A., Nabar, R., Gore, D.: Introduction to space-time wireless communications. Cambridge University Press (May 2003)
2. Skjevling, H., Gesbert, D., Hjorungnes, A.: Low-complexity distributed multibase transmission and scheduling. Eurasip Journal on Advances in Signal Processing (2008)

3. Lakshmanan, S., Sundaresan, K., Rangarajan, S., Sivakumar, R.: Practical beam-forming using rssi measurements on off the shelf wireless clients. In: ACM Internet Measurement Conference (November 2009)
4. Ramanathan, R.: On the Performance of Ad Hoc Networks with Beamforming Antennas. In: ACM MOBIHOC (2001)
5. Ieee 802.11n working group draft, http://www.ieee802.org/11
6. Li, Y., Winters, J.H., Sollenberger, N.R.: MIMO-OFDM for Wireless Communications: Signal Detection with Enhanced Channel Estimation. IEEE Transactions on Communication 50(9), 1471–1477 (2002)
7. Minn, H., Al-dhahir, N.: Optimal training signals for mimo ofdm channel estimation in the presence of frequency offset and phase noise. IEEE Transactions on Communications 54(10) (October 2006)
8. Yoo, T., Jindal, N., Goldsmith, A.: Multi-antenna broadcast channels with limited feedback and user selection. IEEE JSAC 25(7) (September 2007)
9. Chae, C.-B., Inoue, T., Mazzarese, D., Heath, R.W.: Non-iterative multiuser mimo coordinated beamforming with limited feedforward. In: IEEE ICASSP (April 2008)
10. Samardzija, D., Huang, H., Valenzuela, R.A., Sizer, T.: An experimental down-link multiuser mimo system with distributed and coherently-coordinated transmit antennas. In: IEEE ICC (2007)
11. Kecicioglu, B., Ozdemir, O., Torlak, M.: Opportunistic multiple antenna systems: Channel estimation and experimental results. In: IEEE ICC (2006)
12. Liu, X., Sheth, A., Kaminsky, M., Papagiannaki, K., Seshan, S., Steenkiste, P.: Dirc: Increasing indoor wireless capacity using directional antennas. In: ACM SIG-COMM (August 2009)
13. Gollakota, S., Perli, S.D., Katabi, D.: Interference alignment and cancellation. In: ACM SIGCOMM (August 2009)
14. Lakshmanan, S., Sundaresan, K., Khojastepour, M., Rangarajan, S.: Towards adaptive beamforming in indoor wireless networks: An experimental approach. In: IEEE Infocom (Miniconference) (April 2009)
15. Lakshmanan, S., Sundaresan, K., Khojastepour, M., Rangarajan, S.: Spatial reuse with smart antennas in indoor wlans (July 2009), http://www.nec-labs.com/~karthiks/papers/tr-lsr.pdf
16. Fidelity-comtech inc., http://www.fidelity-comtech.com
17. Ettus inc., http://www.ettus.com
18. Gnuradio project, http://www.gnuradio.org/trac
19. Adroit project, https://acert.ir.bbn.com/projects/adroitgrdevel
20. Ramachandran, K., Kokku, R., Zhang, H., Gruteser, M.: Symphony: Synchronous two-phase rate and power control in 802.11 wlans. In: ACM MOBISYS (2008)

A   Complexity and Overheads

In this section, we quantify the overheads incurred in LSR in terms of the number of excitations at the transmitter and the number of feedback bits. For an M AP-N client network, beamforming with interference suppression requires the estimates of MN channel vectors. The first stage involves $2k - 1$ excitations since this is completed in parallel at all the clients together. The ambiguity resolution step involves $4k - 4$ excitations per Ap-client pair. Hence, the total number of excitations can be shown to be $6k - 2$ per AP-client pair. The the number of receive observations that must be fed back is $3k - 2$. With B bits to represent each symbol [3], the total number of bits to be fed back from each client to each AP is $O_s = (3k - 2) * B$. Since the observations are aggregated, a single client sends $O_s = (3k - 2) * B * M$ bits.

In practice, with 8 antenna elements and 16 bit precision, the total number of excitations at each AP for each client is 43. Even with 20 bytes per excitation (the size of a control packet in 802.11), the number of bytes to be transmitted from the AP is 860 bytes. Since the excitation is in two stages, each AP would need about two packets per client for excitation. In a 6 AP 6 client environment, 12 packets per AP leads to 72 packets for the entire estimation procedure. The process for the entire network can be completed within one or two seconds. The total feedback overhead from a client to each AP is limited to 44 bytes (i.e 22 * 16 bits). Since multiple feedback packets can be aggregated, even with 6 APs, the feedback overhead per client is just 264 bytes, which is less than a normal 802.11 data packet. Thus, the overhead of LSR channel estimation is very small and can be easily accommodated in any deployment.

---

[3] For instance, the number of bits used to represent each baseband sample magnitude in the USRP is 16.

On the Scheduling and Multiplexing Throughput Trade-Off in MIMO Networks

Tamer ElBatt

Faculty of Engineering, Cairo University, Giza 12613, Egypt

Abstract. In this paper we explore the cross-layer MIMO-MAC resource allocation problem in interference-limited wireless networks. This is primarily motivated by the trade-off between maximizing the throughput of individual non-interfering links, using spatial multiplexing, and maximizing the spatial reuse of lower rate interfering links, using spatial multiplexing in conjunction with nulling. First, we formulate a cross-layer optimization problem that jointly decides the scheduling and MIMO stream allocation in order to maximize the average sum rate of a given set of single-hop links, subject to signal-to-interference-and-noise-ratio (SINR) constraints. Second, we characterize the problem as a non-convex integer programming problem which is quite challenging to solve. However, we show that under low SINR regimes, an approximate problem can be cast into a geometric programming formulation which is convex. Finally, we characterize the optimal solution for the case of two links and utilize the developed decision rules as a basis for a distributed iterative MIMO link scheduling (IMLS) algorithm that achieves significant gains for arbitrary number of links. Numerical results show that, for plausible scenarios, IMLS achieves more than 2-fold improvement over one-link-per-slot utilizing full spatial multiplexing gain.

Keywords: MIMO networks, convex optimization, scheduling, spatial multiplexing, interference nulling.

1 Introduction

Multiple-input multiple-output (MIMO) [1] is a major breakthrough in wireless communications that has received considerable attention in the point-to-point literature due to its substantial spectral efficiency and reliability advantages for the same power and bandwidth. Exploring the multiple access trade-offs of different MIMO schemes in multi-user settings, namely interference mitigation, spatial multiplexing (SM), and diversity, has received less attention. Thus, we focus on the MIMO-MAC resource allocation problem over the interference channel.

The problem of networking MIMO radios has started to receive recent attention in the literature [3, 4, 5, 6, 7, 8, 9, 10]. Exploiting the interference reduction advantages of smart antennas and reducing the MAC overhead constitute major thrusts. However, optimally allocating MIMO spatial streams in network settings has not received sufficient attention. This problem is motivated by a fundamental trade-off between scheduling and spatial multiplexing. In this paper, we analyze

I. Tomkos et al. (Eds.): BROADNETS 2010, LNICST 66, pp. 178–197, 2012.

this trade-off which reveals SINR-based decision rules that constitute a foundation for future MAC protocols. It constitutes a first step towards understanding the more general diversity-multiplexing-scheduling trade-off. Hence, our focus in this paper is on the trade-off, problem formulation, complexity and solution approach. Protocol design and performance comparison to other protocols lie out of the scope of this work and is a subject of future research.

Our contribution in this paper is three-fold: i) Formulating the cross-layer MIMO-MAC resource allocation problem, ii) Investigating convexity and casting an approximate problem into convex geometric programming, under low SINR and iii) Introducing Iterative MIMO Link Scheduling (IMLS) that demonstrates significant improvement over scheduling non-interfering links with full Spatial multiplexing gain.

First, we characterize the MIMO-MAC resource allocation problem as a non-convex integer programming problem which is quite challenging. Hence, we cast an approximate problem as convex geometric programming under low SINR. Next, we characterize the optimal policy for two links and employ the decision rules as a foundation for scheduling arbitrary number of MIMO links using IMLS. Finally, we present numerical results for plausible scenarios that not only confirm the trade-off at hand but also show the IMLS throughput gains.

The paper is organized as follows: In section 2, we discuss related work in the literature. We introduce the assumptions and formulate the problem in section 3. In section 4, we analyze the complexity of the problem and formulate approximate problems. Next, we develop SINR-based decision rules that characterize the optimal solution for two links and constitute the basis for IMLS in section 5. In section 6, we show performance results for a number of interference scenarios. Finally, conclusions are drawn in section 7.

2   Related Work

Recent work has focused on the design of MAC protocols that exploit the unique capabilities offered by networking MIMO nodes [3, 4, 5, 6, 7, 8, 9, 10]. [4] focuses on handling the non-negligible encoding and decoding delays caused by Lucent's V-BLAST [18]. It introduces mechanisms for reducing the MAC overhead (e.g. RTS/CTS) as well as parallel stop-and-wait ARQ scheme to remedy the per packet ACK. [5] explores the role of spatial diversity schemes (e.g. space-time coding (STC)) to combat fading and achieve robustness in MIMO-enabled ad hoc networks. [6] introduces distributed scheduling for MIMO ad hoc networks (DSMA) within the CSMA/CA framework where SM stream allocation depends on the transmitter-receiver distance. In [7], SM with antenna subset selection for data packet transmission is proposed. In [8], the authors compare the asymptotic network spectral efficiency in the presence and absence of channel state information (CSI) at the transmitters. In fact, the theoretical study in [8] motivated us to investigate cross-layer multiplexing-scheduling schemes that balance this trade-off. In [9], three MIMO MAC protocols are introduced, namely SRP, SMP and SRMP, however, the multiplexing-scheduling trade-off is not analyzed.

Unlike our approach, the interference model is not SINR-based and there are no insights as to which protocol is the best under what conditions.

This work extends upon our earlier work [11] in which we limited our attention to the simple case of two MIMO links without solving or analyzing the complexity of the general number of links case. In [12], we studied the problem of cross-layer diversity and scheduling optimization for reliable communications. Despite the fundamental differences between [12] and the problem at hand, which focuses on multiplexing and scheduling optimization for maximizing the average sum rate, both problems lend themselves to a somewhat similar solution approach which is quite interesting. This, in turn, calls for a unified framework for both problems which constitutes an entry point to the generalized scheduling-multiplexing-diversity problem in future work.

In [3], the authors present stream controlled multiple access (SCMA) for MIMO ad hoc networks. It focuses on SM and explores the gains of stream control and partial interference suppression. However, this work differs from [3] with respect to the following: i) Formulating a cross-layer optimization problem that formally captures the scheduling-spatial multiplexing trade-off, ii) Investigating complexity and formulating an approximate geometric programming problem and iii) Developing distributed SINR-based decision rules that are inspired by the optimal solution for two links and serve as the basis for iteratively scheduling the MIMO links using IMLS.

3   Joint MIMO-MAC Resource Allocation

3.1   Assumptions

We focus on the interference channel with K MIMO links involving $2K$ distinct stationary nodes. Two types of interference may arise; *Primary interference*, e.g. common receiver and self-interference. *Secondary interference* arises when a receiver, Rx, receiving from a particular transmitter, Tx, overhears other transmissions intended elsewhere. In this paper, we target the more challenging secondary interference while handling primary interference is considered complementary to this work and lies out of its scope.

Each node is supported by M transmit antennas and N receive antennas. We assume that the channel state information (CSI) is known only at the receiver, not at the transmitter. Hence, we focus on open-loop (OL), as opposed to closed-loop (CL), MIMO systems due to their practical relevance. We assume a pessimistic interference model which accounts for interference contributed by any transmitter at any receiver, no matter how small this interference is. This is justified by our focus on single-hop links in a neighborhood for the purposes of MAC analysis.

All nodes share a single frequency channel, time is divided into slots and the channel is assumed to be constant across the K slots under investigation. We assume fixed power (P) and modulation for all nodes. Accordingly, we focus on optimizing a single PHY variable, namely the number of spatial streams dedicated to SM, denoted X. In order to support SM in conjunction with interferer nulling, we assume a receiver structure that combines both SM receiver algorithms, which typically rely on multi-user detection (MUD), along with adaptive spatial nulling algorithms.

We adopt a Gaussian MIMO channel model where the channel matrix H is perfectly known at the receiver and is deterministic [1]. It is assumed to be an uncorrelated full-rank channel where $r(H) = min(M, N)$. The path loss follows exponential decay with distance, with a path loss exponent α. We model the receiver thermal noise as additive white Gaussian noise (AWGN), with power σ_n^2 dBm. The results of this paper can be extended to frequency-flat independent and identically distributed (*iid*) Rayleigh fading MIMO channels under high SINR since the open-loop capacity is given by $min(M, N)\ log\ SNR + O(1)$ which is similar to the capacity of the Gaussian MIMO channel in (1) below.

It has been shown in [13] that the open-loop capacity (or link spectral efficiency in bps/Hz) of a point-to-point link with M transmit, N receive antennas, a deterministic Gaussian channel with full rank matrix and a SM signaling scheme that attains full spatial multiplexing gain (SMG) (e.g. V-BLAST [2]) grows linearly with the channel rank,

$$C(SNR) = min(M, N)\ log(1 + SNR) \tag{1}$$

Thus, if we model interference as AWGN using the Gaussian approximation, then the link spectral efficiency in a multi-user setting can be approximated as,

$$R(SINR) \approx min(M, N)\ log(1 + SINR)$$

3.2 Problem Formulation

In this section, we formulate a cross-layer optimization problem that strikes a balance between activating high rate non-interfering links and simultaneously activating interfering lower rate links to maximize the average sum link rate. Our formulation studies K links over K slots to be able to compare to the baseline policy, namely one link with full SMG per slot.

Given K links and K slots, we define F as the optimization objective function that is given by the average sum link rate,

$$F = \frac{1}{K} \sum_{i=1}^{K} \sum_{j=1}^{K} R_{ij} \tag{2}$$

where i is the link index and j is the slot index. R_{ij} is the bit rate supported by link i in slot j and is approximated by,

$$R_{ij} = X_{ij}\ log(1 + SINR_{ij}) \tag{3}$$

where X_{ij} is the number of SM streams of link i in slot j and $SINR_{ij}$ is the SINR of link i in slot j and is given by,

$$SINR_{ij} = \frac{P_{ij}\ G_i^i\ G_r}{\sigma_n^2 + \sum_{k=1, k \neq i}^{K - \lceil \frac{N}{X_{ij}} - 2 \rceil} P_{kj} G_k^i} \tag{4}$$

Notice that $SINR_{ij}$ given in (4) is per SM stream, where a SM stream may include more than one data stream in case $X_{ij} < min(M, N)$. G_u^v is the path loss gain between the transmitter of link u and receiver of link v. $G_r = \frac{N}{X_{ij}}$ is the receiver array gain attributed to exploiting the CSI available at the receiver to null using the $\frac{N}{X_{ij}}$ streams within a single SM stream. Finally, the summation term in the denominator (interference) assumes interferers are spatially separated from the signal of interest to perfectly null the $(\frac{N}{X_{ij}} - 2)$ strongest interferers. This is a reasonable assumption in light of state-of-the-art beamforming algorithms [17]. For instance, the optimal beam former with L antennas can null up to $(L - 2)$ interferers using its $(L - 1)$ degrees of freedom (DoF) where a single DoF is utilized to detect the signal of interest.

The problem is formulated as a constrained optimization problem that maximizes F subject to SINR among other range constraints,

$$\textbf{P1}: \quad \max_{\underline{X}, \underline{P}} F \quad\quad\quad (5)$$

s.t.
$$SINR_{ij} \geq \beta \quad\quad \forall i, j$$
$$P_{ij} = \{0, P\} \quad\quad \forall i, j$$
$$1 \leq X_{ij} \leq min(M, N) \quad\quad \forall i, j$$
$$X_{ij} \quad Integer \quad\quad \forall i, j$$

where the optimization variables are $\underline{X} = [X_{ij}]$, vector of number of SM streams for link i in slot j and $\underline{P} = [P_{ij}]$, vector of binary variables representing the link-slot assignment for link i in slot j, such that $P_{ij} = P$ when link i is activated in slot j, otherwise $P_{ij} = 0$. β is a minimum requirement on the SINR that is necessary for successful reception.

4   Problem Complexity

4.1   Non-convexity of P1

Motivated by the recent advances in convex optimization and its applications to wireless communications [14], we investigate the convexity of P1. We examine three complexity aspects of the problem, namely the integer optimization variables X_{ij} and P_{ij}, concavity of objective function F and convexity of the SINR constraints. Afterwards, we introduce approximate formulations to show how efficiently the MIMO-MAC resource allocation problem can be solved.

The main challenges towards solving P1 stem from: i) The non-concavity of F attributed to the non-concavity of R_{ij} in the presence of interference [14], ii) The Bilinear Matrix Inequality (BMI) nature of the SINR constraints and iii) The integer optimization variables X_{ij} and P_{ij}. Hence, P1 is characterized as a *non-convex integer programming* problem which is quite challenging to solve.

4.2   Approximate Problems

First, we tackle the integer programming challenge. We relax variables X_{ij} and P_{ij} to be real and denote the continuous variable optimization problem subject to the same constraints as **P2**. This relaxation is typically used for solving integer programming problems and, hence, can be justified for our problem where a continuous optimization problem is solved in each iteration of the branch and bound algorithm.

Second, we examine the convexity of P2. Even though the SINR constraints are non-linear, as written, they can be re-written in a bilinear form as follows.

Lemma 1. *The SINR constraints are non-convex, bilinear with respect to the P_{ij} and X_{ij} optimization variables.*

Proof. The SINR constraints can be written as follows,

$$P_{ij} \, G_i^i \, N \; \geq \; X_{ij} \, \beta \, (\sigma_n^2 + \sum_{k=1, k \neq i}^{K - [\frac{N}{X_{ij}} - 2]} P_{kj} G_k^i) \qquad \forall i, j \qquad (6)$$

Re-writing it in the standard form $(f(x) \leq 0)$ yields,

$$g(P_{11}, P_{12}, ... P_{KK}, X_{ij}) =$$

$$\beta \, \sigma_n^2 \, X_{ij} + \beta \, X_{ij} \sum_{k=1, k \neq i}^{K - [\frac{N}{X_{ij}} - 2]} P_{kj} G_k^i \; - \; G_i^i \, N \, P_{ij} \; \leq \; 0 \; \; \forall i, j \qquad (7)$$

The first term of g is linear in X_{ij} and the last term is linear in P_{ij}. However, the summation in the middle term includes the product of P_{kj} and X_{ij} and, hence, is bilinear. In fact, the Hessian of g does not satisfy the second derivative condition of convexity $\nabla^2 g(\underline{P}, \underline{X}) \geq 0$ since it has a negative eigenvalue. Hence, we conclude that $g(\underline{P}, \underline{X})$ is non-convex, bilinear.

Unfortunately, BMI problems are known to be non-convex [19] and, moreover, there are no systematic procedures in the literature for solving BMIs. This adds even more complexity to the problem. Notice that the above result differs from prior results studying the convexity/linearlity of SINR constraints due to the following reasons. SINR convexity has been examined under different problems, e.g. [14] studied SINR convexity with respect to antenna weights in the transmitter beamforming problem. For power control problems, the SINR constraints are simply linear in the powers [15]. Another reason is due to our focus on the MIMO-MAC problem where optimization is with respect to two sets of variables, namely X_{ij} and P_{ij} $\forall i, j$. This gives rise to bilinear terms in $g(\underline{P}, \underline{X})$ as seen above which immediately suggests that g is no longer linear and examining convexity is in order.

In the rest of this section, we examine low and high SINR regimes in an attempt to circumvent the above hurdles.

We show that, under low SINR, P2 can be approximated to a convex geometric programming problem. The MIMO rate function becomes $R_{ij} \approx X_{ij} \, SINR_{ij}$, which yields problem **P3** maximizing $F = \frac{1}{K} \sum_{i=1}^{K} \sum_{j=1}^{K} X_{ij} SINR_{ij}$ subject to the same constraints of the continuous variable version of P1, namely P2.

Lemma 2. *Under low SINR, the objective function F in P3 is non-linear and non-concave.*

Proof. Under low SINR, F is approximated by,

$$F = \frac{1}{K} \sum_{i=1}^{K} \sum_{j=1}^{K} \frac{P_{ij} \, G_i^i \, N}{\sigma_n^2 + \sum_{k=1, k \neq i}^{K - [\frac{N}{X_{ij}} - 2]} P_{kj} G_k^i} \tag{8}$$

Notice that F is non-linear in P_{ij} and X_{ij} $\forall i, j$ due to their contributions in the denominator of each term in (8). Hence, examining concavity is in order. With respect to P_{ij}, individual terms as stated in (8) have the same structure as the SINR in classical power control problems, known to be non-concave [16]. Moreover, the terms in (8) monotonically decrease as X_{ij} increases. Hence, F in P3 is non-concave.

This, in turn, yields the following complexity result for P3.

Theorem 1. *Under low SINR, the approximate problem P3 is not convex.*

Proof. The result follows directly from the non-convexity of the SINR constraints shown in Lemma 1 and non-concavity of F shown in Lemma 2.

It should be noted that the low SINR approximation does not reduce P3 in its current form to a convex problem. This is in agreement with [16] which has to cast the SINR maximization problem into a geometric programming formulation to establish convexity. On the contrary, the low SINR approximation directly renders the problem of minimizing the sum of powers subject to rate constraints linear as shown in [15].

Even though P3 is not convex in its current form, an approximate problem can be cast into a geometric programming formulation similar to [16]. This is attributed to the fact that $\frac{1}{X_{ij} \, SINR_{ij}}$ is a posynomial function, where a function $f(x)$ is said to be posynomial if it takes the following form:

$f(x) = \sum_k c_k \, x_1^{a_{1k}} \, x_2^{a_{2k}} ... x_n^{a_{nk}}$ where $c_k \geq 0$ and a_{ik} is real. This yields a new objective function to minimize: $U = K \sum_{i=1}^{K} \sum_{j=1}^{K} \frac{1}{X_{ij} \, SINR_{ij}}$ that is posynomial.

However, this is an "approximate" problem since $U \neq F^{-1}$. Similarly, the SINR constraint can be re-formulated into a posynomial form in order to reach the approximate geometric programming problem P4 known to be convex,

$$\mathbf{P4}: \quad \min_{\underline{X}, \underline{P}} U \tag{9}$$

s.t.
$$SINR_{ij}^{-1} \leq \beta^{-1} \qquad \forall i, j$$
$$0 \leq P_{ij} \leq P \qquad \forall i, j$$
$$1 \leq X_{ij} \leq min(M, N) \qquad \forall i, j$$

Under high SINR, the problem turns out to be more challenging and cannot be approximated to convex geometric programming primarily because of the role of the stream allocation variables X_{ij} in breaking the posynomial structure of the objective function approximation. Accordingly, the MIMO rate function becomes logarithmic in the SINR, i.e. $R_{ij} \approx X_{ij} \, logSINR_{ij}$. We show next that this non-linear, non-convex problem (due to the BMI nature of the SINR constraints), denoted **P5**, cannot be approximated to geometric programming.

Theorem 2. *Under high SINR, problem P5 cannot be approximated to a geometric programming problem.*

Proof. The objective function F of P5 can be written as,

$$F = \frac{1}{K} \sum_{i=1}^{K} \sum_{j=1}^{K} X_{ij} \, logSINR_{ij} \tag{10}$$

$$= \frac{1}{K} \, log \prod_{i=1}^{K} \prod_{j=1}^{K} SINR_{ij}^{X_{ij}} \tag{11}$$

We propose to minimize a related function V, even though it is not exactly equivalent to maximizing F since $V \neq F^{-1}$.

$$V = \prod_{i=1}^{K} \prod_{j=1}^{K} \frac{1}{SINR_{ij}^{X_{ij}}} \tag{12}$$

The objective is to reach a posynomial function which facilitates geometric problem formulation. However, the role of X_{ij} as $SINR_{ij}$ exponent does not yield the posynomial structure. This confirms that, unlike P4, problem P5 cannot be cast into a geometric programming formulation and, hence, cannot be solved using convex optimization techniques.

In conclusion, approximate problems (P3 and P5) are not only non-convex but also require costly integer programming solvers. At best, P3 can be approximated to a geometric programming problem as shown in P4. It is evident by now that P1 cannot be solved in closed form and is quite challenging to solve numerically. Hence, in the next section, we take a drastically different approach towards this rather challenging problem. First, we focus on $K = 2$ links and characterize the optimal policy for problem P1 (based on [11]). In the rest of the paper, we shift our attention to introducing a low-complexity distributed algorithm, for scheduling arbitrary number of MIMO links, that is founded on the optimal decision rules for two links.

5   Iterative MIMO Link Scheduling (IMLS)

In this section, we first present SINR-based decision rules that characterize the optimal MIMO stream allocation and link scheduling for $K = 2$ links. These rules serve as the basis for IMLS which iteratively partitions the links over successive slots depending on the levels of interference.

5.1   Optimal Spatial Multiplexing and Scheduling for Two Links

In this section, we solve the problem for the simple case of two links which constitutes the basis for solving arbitrary number of links using IMLS in the next section. This greatly simplifies the scheduling sub-problem and, hence, facilitates solving the MIMO stream allocation sub-problem.

The decision rules derived in this section stem from the optimality of P1 and the SINR constraints. Next, we focus on these two conditions and their direct impact on optimizing the MIMO stream allocation (number of SM streams, X) and link scheduling (transmit or not with fixed power P).

For $K = 2$ links, the scheduling policy space collapses to two simple policies, namely Policy A: 1 link per slot and Policy B: 2 links per slot. Scheduling one of the links exclusively in the two slots violates the requirement that each link should be activated at least once over the K slots. Hence, the combinatorial complexity of scheduling vanishes. Furthermore, MIMO stream allocation for, typically, small M and N in state-of-the-art radios is solved using search which yields upper and lower bounds on X.

5.1.1 Lower Bound on X

In this section, we address the question which establishes a lower bound on X: When does policy B outperform policy A with respect to F? This can be written formally as,

$$F_B > F_A \tag{13}$$

where F_B denotes the average sum rate in the presence of interference from the other link and F_A denotes the average sum rate in the absence of interference. Next, we show how to quantify F_A. In this case, all MIMO spatial streams (i.e. SMG = $min(M, N)$) are utilized for improving the link rate through SM (e.g. V-BLAST [2] which achieves full SMG) and no nulling is needed. Based on the definition of C in (1) and the fact that under policy A each link transmits only in 1 slot, then it can be easily shown that,

$$F_A = \frac{1}{2} \sum_{i=1}^{2} C_i = \frac{1}{2}(C_1 + C_2) \tag{14}$$

Next, we quantify F_B where any link i is activated in any slot j among the two slots. Due to the presence of interference in each slot, a subset of MIMO streams (X) is dedicated to SM, and the remaining degrees of freedom at the receiver are dedicated to nulling the other interferer. Accordingly,

$$F_B = \frac{1}{2} \sum_{i=1}^{2} \sum_{j=1}^{2} R_{ij} = \frac{1}{2}(R_{11} + R_{12} + R_{21} + R_{22}) \tag{15}$$

Clearly, the interplay of interference and nulling and their effect on SINR under policy B (as opposed to SNR under policy A) and the associated smaller SMG X yields the outcome of which policy constitutes the optimal. The above formula could be simplified if we factor in the fact that interference under policy B, where all (two in this case) links are activated in each slot, is the same and does not vary from slot to slot. This inherent characteristic of policy B yields $R_{11} = R_{12} = R_1$, $R_{21} = R_{22} = R_2$ and, hence, we can drop the slot index and (13) can be re-written as,

$$R_1 + R_2 > \frac{1}{2}(C_1 + C_2) \tag{16}$$

Notice that different values of X_i may or may not satisfy the above condition. This is primarily attributed to the effect of X_i on the LHS since the RHS is independent of X_i. As X_i is increased from 1 to $min(M, N)$ (i.e. higher SMG), the LHS increases due to the role of the linear pre-log factor in (3). Our prime interest is to find the minimum value of X_i that satisfies (16) which constitutes the lower bound (LB) on X_i.

5.1.2 Upper Bound on X

In this section, we shift our attention to reception success which is governed by the SINR constraints in P1 and dictates the upper bound (UB) on X.

$$SINR_i \geq \beta \qquad\qquad \forall i \tag{17}$$

The RHS of (17) is independent of X_i whereas the LHS varies with X_i. It is straightforward to verify that as X_i decreases from $min(M, N)$ to 1 (i.e. more streams dedicated to nulling at the receiver), SINR increases. Our objective is to find maximum X_i that satisfies (17) and constitutes the UB on X_i.

The interplay of the upper bound and lower bound on X, yields the distributed SINR-based decision rules derived in the next section. Although these rules fully characterize the optimal solution for two links, they constitute only a sub-optimal solution for $K > 2$ due to comparing only two extreme scheduling policies: Policy A (1 link/slot) and Policy B (K links/slot) and leaving many other schedules unexamined. Nevertheless, we introduce in the next section a novel iterative MIMO link scheduling (IMLS) algorithm based on the SINR decision rules examined at individual receivers in a distributed fashion.

5.2   IMLS for Arbitrary Number of Links

5.2.1 Distributed Decision Rules

So far, we have focused on centralized optimization problems, namely P1 and its simplified two link version studied in section 5.1, that maximize a global objective function F.

In this section, we shift our attention to the distributed problem and extend the previous section to scenarios with arbitrary number of links. Given K slots, each link strives to maximize its aggregate rate over the K slots, i.e. the distributed objective function for each link is given by $F_i = R_i = \sum_{j=1}^{K} R_{ij}$.

This enables each receiver to autonomously find a solution, i.e. number of SM streams (X_i) and link activation (P_i), for its link and feed it back to its transmitter. Hence, the IMLS algorithm is distributed since it involves communication between the transmitter-receiver parties of each link with absolutely no inter-link communication. The knowledge of number of contending links K can be obtained through higher layers, e.g. topology control and routing mechanisms.

Next, we show how to develop the SINR-based decision rules for arbitrary number of links based on insights distilled from the two links case studied in section 5.1. For each link, we compare only two extreme scheduling policies to get a solution: Policy A: 1 link per slot and Policy B: K links per slot. The rationale behind this is two-fold. First, it greatly simplifies the problem as it eliminates the combinatorial complexity of the scheduling portion of the problem. Second, it opens room for distributed IMLS which iteratively packs links into different slots depending on the levels of interference. Along the same lines of section 5.1, we compare the performance of policies A and B for link i (i.e. $F_{iB} > F_{iA}$) as follows,

$$R_i > C_i \tag{18}$$

Since link i experiences same interference in all slots under policy B, i.e. $R_{i1} = R_{i2} = ... = R_{iK}$, (18) reduces to,

$$R_{i1} > \frac{C_i}{K} \tag{19}$$

This condition yields the LB_i on X_i.

The SINR constraint determines the UB_i on X_i which, along with LB_i, yield the following distributed decision rules:

Distributed Decision Rules executed at the receiver of link i:

- If $LB_i \leq UB_i$:

    Scheduling: Activate the K links in each of the K slots

    MIMO: SM with $X_i = UB_i$ streams

    Nulling with $\frac{N}{X_i}$ streams

- Else:

    Scheduling: Activate 1 link in each slot (TDMA)

    MIMO: SM with $X_i = min(M, N)$ streams

5.2.2 IMLS Description

Based on the distributed decision rules, we introduce an iterative MIMO link scheduling (IMLS) algorithm that achieves near-maximal link packing per slot. This is attributed to examining the feasibility of extreme policy B, which packs all K links to one slot and, if not, iteratively partitions it to smaller link subsets which are likely to be feasible under reduced interference conditions. This process proceeds in a *distributed manner* as described next.

Fig. 1 shows the flowchart of IMLS, executed at the receiver (Rx) of link i, to schedule K links over minimal number of slots, denoted s. The variable s denotes also the number of iterations until IMLS finds a solution starting from iteration $s = 0$. As indicated before, IMLS commences with K links which get partitioned over successive iterations to subsets denoted $K_s < K$ where $K_0 = K$. Accordingly, the time axis over which IMLS operates is partitioned to s slots. Each slot is preceded by a short *probing interval* where the K_s links examined in the sth iteration probe the wireless medium with short probing packets in order

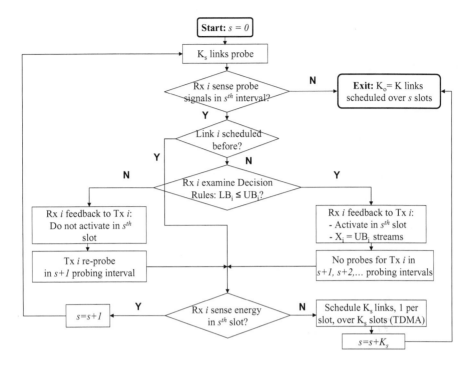

Fig. 1. IMLS Flowchart at Rx of link i to schedule K links over minimal number of slots, s

for receivers to individually examine the distributed decision rules. Hence, the sth IMLS iteration operates over the sth probing interval and s^{th} slot.

In essence, IMLS iteratively partitions a given set of links to find maximal subsets which can be activated simultaneously in consecutive slots. As shown in Fig. 1, it involves four conditional statements where the first and last ones are responsible for exit conditions, as illustrated later, whereas the third condition constitutes the core of IMLS. Given K_s links that probe the medium in iteration s, Rx i computes the LB and UB of X_i and compares them to decide whether it can be activated in the next slot or not. If $LB_i \leq UB_i$, then link i can survive the $(K_s - 1)$ interferers, i.e. achieve $SINR \geq \beta$ with $X_i = UB_i$ and $\frac{N}{X_i}$ streams for nulling. Hence, it can be activated in the sth slot and does not need to probe anymore. These Rx-based decisions are fed back to the transmitter (Tx) side for execution in future slots and iterations. If $LB_i > UB_i$, then no solution exists for link i at present interference levels and, hence, it should not transmit in the sth slot and should re-probe again in the $s + 1$ probing interval.

So far, we have described the fundamental operation of a single iteration. However, transition from iteration to another in a distributed manner is a major contributor to IMLS performance gains. Consider an arbitrary iteration with K_s probing links, the third condition (decision rules) would partition K_s into two subsets: i) Feasible Subset: which share slot s and do not need to re-probe the medium and ii) Infeasible Subset: which do not activate in slot s and need to re-probe in the next iteration. In fact, this latter group constitutes $K_{s+1} < K_s$ probing links of the next iteration. This yields our first key observation: *IMLS goes through another iteration iff the Infeasible Subset is non-empty.* In essence, if all links are feasible in iteration s, then no transmitters will re-probe the medium in iteration $s + 1$. This defines our exit condition in the first conditional statement, i.e. if an arbitrary Rx i does not sense a probing signal in the sth probing interval, it exits with its own scheduling and MIMO stream allocation solution along with the information that the K links are scheduled over s slots.

The second key observation stems from the other extreme, i.e. What if the K_s links probing in iteration s are all infeasible? This implies that those links cannot share the same slot and, hence, there is no need for more iterations under same interference conditions since it will not change the infeasibility result. Introducing criteria for further partitioning infeasible links lie out of the scope of this work. Instead, IMLS simply falls back to 1 link per slot for the K_s links, as suggested by the decision rules. This defines our exit condition in the last conditional statement, i.e. if any Rx i does not sense any transmission in the sth slot, it exits with its own scheduling and MIMO solution along with the s slots needed for the K links, where the last K_s slots are scheduled in a TDMA fashion.

Finally, the second conditional statement indicates that once Rx i finds a solution, say in iteration s, it does not need to re-probe or re-solve the problem any more, it just needs to keep track of the evolution of the algorithm for other links, via incrementing the iteration counter and examining the exit conditions. This is essential for all links to proceed synchronously over IMLS and exit with consistent results, irrespective of which iteration yields their individual solutions.

It is evident that IMLS is distributed since each link takes its link activation and MIMO stream allocation decisions independent of other links. The only communication needed is the feedback from each receiver to its respective transmitter. It should also be noted that if K is finite, the links are guaranteed to find a solution in a *finite* number of iterations. For the two extremes, namely K links are feasible and K links are infeasible, a solution is found in a single iteration. Under typical scenarios, interference decreases from iteration to another as we partition the links until iteration s has: i) $K_s = 1$ which is trivial, ii) $K_s > 1$ and feasible which activates the links in slot s and exits and iii) $K_s > 1$ and infeasible which yields a TDMA solution for the K_s links and exits. It can be shown that the worst case number of iterations for IMLS is $\frac{K}{2}$ which yields only two feasible links in each iteration, since two is the minimum number of links sharing a slot.

6   Performance Results

In this section, we present numerical results obtained using Matlab for: i) The Optimality regions for two MIMO links and ii) IMLS performance for arbitrary number of links.

6.1   Optimality Regions for K=2 Links

We consider two links where each link is supported with $M = N = 8$ antennas. For ease of exposition, we focus in this section on two symmetric links where the transmitter-receiver separation is 250m. In addition, the distances between each receiver and the other transmitter (interferer) are equal and denoted D. The parameter D is varied across different runs, from 500m to 5000m, in order to model varying levels of interference. The symmetry in this scenario gives rise to equal interference at both receivers and, hence, same solution for the MIMO-MAC problem. Accordingly, we focus our analysis on a single link and drop the link index i in X_i.

The transmit power per node, which can be split among different antennas, is fixed at $P = 20$ dBm. The minimum SINR requirement β is set to 5 dB. The path loss exponent is set to $\alpha=4$ and σ_n^2 is set to -90 dBm.

Table 1. Optimal Policies for Two 8x8 Symmetric MIMO Links

D (km)	# links per slot	LB on X	UB on X	Optimal X	Max. F (bps/Hz)
5	2	4	8	8	9.972
3	2	4	8	8	9.965
2	2	4	8	8	9.391
1.5	2	4	4	4	6.895
1	2	4	4	4	6.67
0.75	2	4	4	4	6.148
0.65	2	4	4	4	5.661
0.6	2	4	4	4	5.315
0.55	1	8	2	8	4.98
0.5	1	8	2	8	4.98

First, we compute the lower bound through examining the throughput constraint in (16) with X growing from 1 to 8. The minimum value for X that satisfies this constraint constitutes the lower bound. Table 1 shows the lower bounds obtained under gradually increasing interference levels due to reducing the receiver-interferer distance D. It is evident that the LB increases as interference increases which agrees with intuition. This is primarily attributed to the fact that higher interference yields lower SINR which makes it impossible for policy B to outperform policy A with small values of X.

Second, we compute the upper bound through examining the SINR constraint in (17) with decreasing number of SM streams, from $X=8$ to $X=1$. The maximum value of X that satisfies this constraint determines the UB. Again, Table 1 shows the UB while gradually increasing interference. Unlike the LB, the UB decreases as interference becomes more intense since more degrees of freedom are needed for nulling which, in turn, implies smaller and smaller SMG, X.

The decision rules in section 5.2 decide the optimal X. The first 3 rows in Table 1 exhibit optimality with slot sharing and $X=8$ due to negligible interference. For the next 5 rows, slot sharing with $X=4$ turns out to be the optimal due to increasing interference. Finally, for the last two rows, TDMA with $X=8$ yields the maximum average sum link rate.

Fig. 2 shows the trends of F and associated optimality regions for five MIMO-MAC resource allocation policies. The objective function F is plotted against $\frac{1}{D}$. Policy 1 represents TDMA with $X=8$ (corresponds to scheduling policy A) whereas policies 2 through 5 represent slot sharing with different values of X (correspond to scheduling policy B).

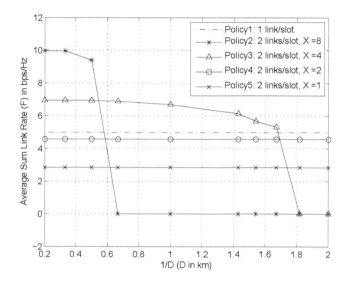

Fig. 2. Optimality Regions for Two Symmetric 8x8 Links

Notice that policy 1 performance does not vary with D since transmissions are interference-free. Policy 2 and 3 performance varies with D due to the impact of interference on the SINR and, hence, on the achievable link rate. Finally, policies 4 and 5 performance does not vary with D, despite the fact that these are slot sharing policies. The reason for this trend is attributed to the fact that these policies have small number of SM streams ($X=1,2$) which leaves sufficient spatial streams for the receiver to null the other interferer. Therefore, policies 4 and 5 completely null interference and, hence, experience no SINR variation with D.

In addition, the figure reveals different regions of optimality for different policies. For the leftmost region (D>1500 m), policy 2 achieves maximum F due to slot sharing while using the 8x8 MIMO for SM due to the negligible interference. For $600m < D < 1500m$, policy 2 fails to maintain the SINR constraint, due to interference buildup and, hence, its throughput falls sharply to zero. On the other hand, the less aggressive policy 3 assumes the optimal role for this region due to dedicating MIMO resources to nulling. Finally, as interference dominates for $D < 550m$, none of the slot sharing policies achieves the optimal and, interestingly, naive TDMA with $X = 8$ achieves maximum F. This suggests that contention-free TDMA is the only resort in case of high interference, where none of the links could guarantee their SINR minimum requirement β and still achieve high link rates.

Finally, it should be noted that policies 4 and 5 are not optimal in any region. This is attributed to the fact that these policies have small X (which reduces the SMG) and dedicate more resources than needed for nulling a lone interferer.

6.2   IMLS Performance for K>2 Links

In this section, we analyze the performance of IMLS. In particular, we compare three scheduling paradigms: i) Naive TDMA where 1 link is activated per slot, ii) Slot sharing and TDMA, denoted SS/TDMA, where only the first iteration of IMLS is executed for K links and the Feasible Subset is activated in a single slot whereas the Infeasible Subset is scheduled in a TDMA fashion without further iterations and iii) IMLS where multiple iterations activate different subsets of the K links over different slots.

We consider three scenarios, randomly generated, with K=10 8x8 MIMO links and simulation parameters similar to previous section. First, we analyze the scenario shown in Fig. 3 where the average Tx-Rx separation d is 248m and the average distance between any receiver and other transmitters (interferers) D is approximately 2393m. Link indices are written next to individual links in the figure. Large D yields low interference which permits receivers to suppress it via dedicating a subset of the spatial streams to nulling. In fact, this scenario turns out to be an extreme one where *all* receivers can share the same slot using the following stream allocations $\underline{X}$=[4 4 4 4 8 8 8 4 2], where X_i denotes stream allocation for link i. Hence, IMLS yields a solution after one iteration. Although this scenario does not represent the typical case in ad hoc networks, it reveals insights about the gains of cross-layer MIMO-MAC over scheduling high rate links with 8 SM streams in an interference-free manner. Using TDMA, the average sum link rate is given by $F_{TDMA} = 5.129 \; bps/Hz$ whereas $F_{IMLS} = 42.047 \; bps/Hz$. This confirms the profound impact of IMLS, that is almost 8-fold improvement over TDMA. This is attributed to low interference which not only permits activating the 10 links simultaneously but also using minimum number of spatial streams for nulling.

Second, scenario 2 in Fig. 4 exhibits higher interference since D is approximately 1739m and d is 258m. Therefore, interference cannot be resolved in a single iteration as in the previous example. Instead, IMLS takes four iterations. In the first iteration, only 3 out of 10 links (links 4, 8 and 10) are feasible using X = 8, 4, 2 streams, respectively. Next, IMLS attempts to solve the infeasible subset of $K_1 = 7$ links, namely 1, 2, 3, 5, 6, 7, 9 where $s = 1$. Reduced interference enables links 2, 3, 6 to become feasible using $X = 2, 2, 2$ streams respectively. For $s = 2$, IMLS attempts to solve the remaining infeasible $K_2 = 4$ links, namely 1, 5, 7, 9 where links 7 and 9 manage to share a slot under reduced interference.

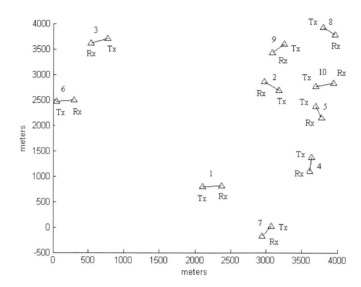

Fig. 3. Scenario1: 10 links with average receiver-interferer distance D=2393m and average Tx-Rx distance d=248m

Finally, links 1 and 5 are examined in the last iteration, however, they cannot share the same slot due to their high mutual interference, even in the absence of the other 8 links which have been already scheduled in previous iterations.

Next, we compare the performance of five policies, namely TDMA, SS/TDMA, IMLS and two variations of it. Under TDMA, the throughput performance $F_{TDMA} = 4.792\ bps/Hz$ whereas SS/TDMA achieves $F_{SS/TDMA} = 6.8632\ bps/Hz$, i.e. 43% improvement over TDMA. On the other hand, IMLS yields $F_{IMLS} = 8.32\ bps/Hz$, that is 73% improvement over TDMA and 21% improvement over SS/TDMA due to IMLS iterative nature which attempts to achieve near-maximal link packing per slot.

The following IMLS variations optimize its performance and address fairness respectively. The first variation is inspired by the observation that stream allocation (X) can be further optimized for a set of feasible links (e.g. links 4, 8, 10 for $s = 0$) under reduced interference, i.e. after eliminating interference from infeasible links who could not share slot 0 with these three links anyway. For instance, plain IMLS yields $X = 8, 4, 2$ for links 4, 8, and 10 respectively when all 10 links were transmitting. On the other hand, optimized IMLS, denoted IMLS1, re-examines the decision rules with these 3 links alone, once it decides their feasibility in iteration $s = 0$. This yields $X = 8, 4, 4$ for links 4, 8, and 10 respectively (notice the improvement in the SMG for link 10 due to the reduced interference). This results in $F_{IMLS1} = 10.1\ bps/Hz$, i.e. 21% improvement over plain IMLS and more than 2-fold improvement over TDMA with full SMG.

The second IMLS variation trades throughput for fairness, depending on how the K slots are assigned. The IMLS performance reported so far has been computed over K slots, where K is always greater than the number of iterations s upon IMLS completion as discussed earlier. This implies allocating more than one slot to each feasible link subset identified over IMLS iterations. If m links can share a single slot in iteration s, we assign those links m out of the K slots. Clearly, this could lead to overall throughput improvement over the K slots due to favoring highly packed slots, however, it could lead to unfairness with respect to lightly packed slots (e.g. link 1 in scenario 2 cannot share a slot with any other link and, hence, it is assigned only 1 out of K slots). An intuitive measure of fairness in this context is the difference between the maximum number of slots assigned to a link and the minimum number of slots assigned to a link, i.e. $f = \max_i (\#$ slots out of K assigned to link i) - $\min_i(\#$ slots out of K assigned to link i). As f gets far from 0, the scheduling algorithm becomes less fair. For scenario 2 above, $f = 3 - 1 = 2$, and hence plain IMLS exhibits low fairness.

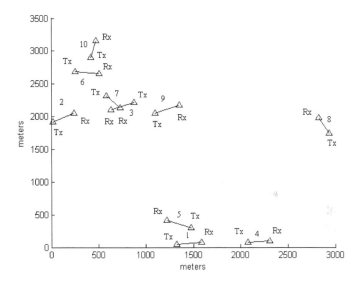

Fig. 4. Scenario2: 10 links with average receiver-interferer distance D=1739m and average Tx-Rx distance d=258m

An approach that achieves better fairness, at the expense of throughput loss, is to split the K slots equally among the different subsets of links identified in different iterations. For the example above, assigning two slots for each of the five link subsets identified in the four iterations yields $F_{IMLS2} = 7.14 \; bps/Hz$, i.e. 14% loss compared to IMLS. However, this is compensated with improved fairness since $f = 2 - 2 = 0$.

Finally, the scenario shown in Fig. 5 exhibits highest interference due to the role of $D = 490m$ and $d = 250m$. This yields no feasible links in the first iteration

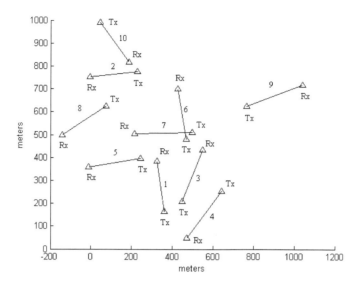

Fig. 5. Scenario3: 10 links with average receiver-interferer distance D=490m and average Tx-Rx distance d=250m

of IMLS. Accordingly, IMLS cannot proceed with partitioning the links based on their different slot sharing capabilities as illustrated earlier. Thus, TDMA yields modest performance of $F_{TDMA} = 5.11\ bps/Hz$. Extending IMLS to handle this scenario lies out of the scope of the paper and is a subject of future research.

7   Conclusions

We studied the problem of MIMO-MAC resource allocation for the MIMO interference channel. The prime motivation is to balance the trade-off between maximizing the throughput of individual non-interfering links, using spatial multiplexing, and maximizing the spatial reuse of lower rate interfering links, using spatial multiplexing in conjunction with nulling. We formulate a cross-layer optimization problem and characterize it as a non-convex integer programming problem which is quite challenging. However, we show that under low SINR regimes, an approximate problem can be cast into a convex geometric programming formulation. Finally, we characterize the optimal solution for two links and use the distributed decision rules as a basis for Iterative MIMO Link Scheduling (IMLS) that achieves significant gains for arbitrary number of links. Numerical results confirm the trade-off as well as show more than 2-fold improvement by IMLS over TDMA with maximum spatial multiplexing gain. This work can be extended along the following directions: i) Extend the formulation to the generalized diversity-multiplexing-scheduling trade-off and ii) Develop MAC protocols based on the decision rules and iterative MIMO link scheduling.

References

1. Paulraj, A.J., Gore, D., Nabar, R., Bolcskei, H.: An Overview of MIMO Communications-A Key to Gigabit Wireless. Proceedings of the IEEE 92(2) (February 2004)
2. Foschini, G.J.: Layered Space-Time Architecture for Wireless Communications in a Fading Environment when using Multiple Antennas. Bell Labs Technical Journal 1(2) (1996)
3. Sundaresan, K., et al.: A Fair Medium Access Control Protocol for Ad-hoc Networks with MIMO Links. In: IEEE INFOCOM (June 2004)
4. Redi, J., et al.: Design and Implementation of a MIMO MAC protocol for ad hoc networking. In: Proceedings of SPIE (2006)
5. Hu, M., Zhang, J.: MIMO Ad Hoc Networks: Medium Access Control, Saturation Throughput and Optimal Hop Distance Journal of Communications and Networks (December 2004)
6. Casari, P., et al.: DSMA: an Access Method for MIMO Ad Hoc Networks Based on Distributed Scheduling. In: ACM IWCMC (July 2006)
7. Park, M., et al.: Improving Throughput and Fairness of MIMO Ad hoc Networks using Antenna Selection Diversity. In: IEEE Globecom (2004)
8. Chen, B., Gans, M.: MIMO Communications in Ad hoc Networks. IEEE Transactions on Signal Processing 54(7) (July 2006)
9. Hamdaoui, B., Shin, K.: Characterization and Analysis of Multihop Wireless MIMO Network Throughput. In: ACM Mobihoc (September 2007)
10. Jaiswal, S.: MIMO Communication for Ad hoc Networks: A Crosslayer Approach M.Sc. Thesis, University of Massachusetts (May 2008)
11. ElBatt, T.: Towards Scheduling MIMO Links in Interference-limited Wireless Ad-hoc Networks. In: IEEE MILCOM (November 2007)
12. ElBatt, T.: Cross-layer Diversity and Scheduling Optimization for Interference Limited MIMO Ad hoc Networks. In: IEEE Globecom (December 2008)
13. Telatar, I.E.: Capacity of Multi-antenna Guassian Channels. European Transactions on Telecommunications (1999)
14. Luo, Z.-Q., Yu, W.: An Introduction to Convex Optimization for Communications and Signal Processing. IEEE Journal on Selected Areas in Communications 24(8) (August 2006)
15. Cruz, R.L., Santhanam, A.: Optimal Routing, Link Scheduling and Power Control in Multi-hop Wireless Networks. In: INFOCOM (2003)
16. Julian, D., Chiang, M., O'Neill, D., Boyd, S.: QoS and Fairness Constrained Convex Optimization of Resource Allocation for Wireless Cellular and Ad Hoc Networks. In: Proceedings of INFOCOM (2002)
17. Godara, L.: Application of Antenna Arrays to Mobile Communications, Part II: Beam-Forming and Direction-of-Arrival Considerations. Proceedings of the IEEE 85(8) (August 1997)
18. Wolniansky, P.W., Foschini, G., Golden, G., Valenzuela, R.: V-BLAST: An Architecture for Realizing Very High Data Rates Over the Rich-Scattering Wireless Channel In: ISSSE 1998 (September 1998)
19. Xiao, Y., Crusca, F., Chu, E.: Bilinear Matrix Inequalities in Robust Control: Phase I - Problem Formulation. In: MECSE-3-1996, Monash University (April 1996)

Efficient Resource Allocation Algorithm for Spatial Multiuser Access in MISO OFDMA Systems

Vasileios D. Papoutsis, Ioannis G. Fraimis, and Stavros A. Kotsopoulos

Wireless Telecommunications Laboratory,
Department of Electrical and Computer Engineering,
University of Patras, Rio, Greece 265 00
{vpapoutsis,ifraimhs,kotsop}@ece.upatras.gr

Abstract. The problem of user selection and resource allocation for the downlink of wireless systems operating over a frequency-selective channel is investigated. It is assumed that the Base Station (BS) uses many antennas, whereas a single antenna is available to each user and Orthogonal Frequency Division Multiple Access (OFDMA) is used as a multiple access scheme. The general mathematical formulation is provided but achieving the optimal solution has a high computational cost. For practical implementation, a suboptimal, but efficient algorithm is devised that is based both on Zero Forcing (ZF) beamforming and on spatial correlation and is less complex than other approaches. The algorithm maximizes the sum of the users' data rates subject to constraints on total available power and proportional fairness among users' data rates. Simulation results are provided to indicate that the algorithm can satisfy the fairness criterion. Thus, the algorithm can be applied to latest-generation wireless systems that provide Quality-of-Service (QoS) guarantees.

Keywords: MISO, OFDMA, resource allocation, Zero-Forcing, proportional fairness.

1 Introduction

OFDMA [1] is a multi-user version of the popular Orthogonal Frequency Division Multiplexing (OFDM) [2] digital modulation scheme. In OFDMA, multiple access is achieved by first dividing the spectrum of interest into a number of subcarriers and then assigning subsets of the subcarriers to individual users. OFDMA helps exploit multiuser diversity in frequency-selective channels, since it is very likely that some subcarriers that are "bad" for a user are "good" for at least one of the other users [3]. Because of its superior performance in frequency-selective fading wireless channels, OFDMA is the modulation and multiple access scheme used in latest wireless systems such as IEEE 802.16e (Mobile WiMAX).

In recent years, many dynamic resource allocation algorithms have been developed for the Single Input Single Output (SISO)-OFDMA systems. In [4] [5], the system throughput is maximized with a total power constraint and in [6] [7],

I. Tomkos et al. (Eds.): BROADNETS 2010, LNICST 66, pp. 198–212, 2012.
© Institute for Computer Sciences, Social Informatics and Telecommunications Engineering 2012

the total power consumption is minimized with constraints on the users' data rates. In [8]-[11], proportional fairness among the users' data rates and in [12] [13], the fulfillment of every user's data rate constraints are guaranteed in order to maximize the sum of the users' data rates. In [14], the sum throughput is maximized with long term access proportional fairness. Finally, in [15], system throughput is maximized but the resource allocation unit is not the subcarrier, as in previous algorithms [4]-[14], but a time/frequency unit (slot), in accordance with WiMAX systems.

An additional major advance in recent wireless systems is the use of Multiple Input Multiple Output (MIMO) transmission to improve communication performance. The capacity of the broadcast channel (downlink) has been studied extensively in [16] [17]. In fading environments MIMO technology offers significant increase in the data throughput and the link range without additional bandwidth or transmit power requirements by opening up multiple data pipes in the same frequency band of operation [3]. Because of these properties, MIMO systems have received increasing attention in the past decade.

When Channel State Information (CSI) is available to both the transmitter and the receiver, in general, in order to achieve transmission on the boundary of the capacity region, the BS needs to transmit to multiple users simultaneously in each subchannel, and needs to employ Dirty Paper Coding (DPC) [18]. An iterative algorithm for computing the sum data rate is presented in [19]. In [20] [21], DPC is combined with QR decomposition to completely eliminate the interference among transmitting users. However, DPC-based techniques have large implementation complexity. For this reason, suboptimal transmission methods with smaller complexity have been proposed.

Space Division Multiple Access (SDMA) using transmit beamforming has been proposed as a promising solution for resource allocation that retains the benefits of MIMO and is less complex than DPC-based techniques [22]. In SDMA, a group of compatible users share the common resources improving the efficiency of the system but transmitting to one user affects the transmission of all others. In order to separate users in downlink transmission, ZF transmit beamforming is used [23]. In [24], a suboptimal user selection and beamforming algorithm for the Multiple Input Single Output (MISO) case is proposed and the idea is extended to the MIMO case in [25] [26]. A more realistic scenario is described in [27], where per-antenna power constraints are applied. Moreover, in [28], a low complexity space-time-frequency scheduling is introduced and in [29], multiuser diversity in MIMO systems with antenna selection is analysed. Finally, in [30], a new user selection algorithm is proposed that offers considerable complexity savings.

MIMO related algorithms can be implemented in each subcarrier and by combining OFDMA with MIMO transmission, wireless systems can offer larger system capacities and improved reliability. The data rate maximization problem was first considered in [31], but SDMA was not enabled. In [32], the performance of [31] is challenged and in [33], the total power consumption is minimized. In [34], the system capacity is maximized but certain users may be completely shut off during a scheduling period. In addition, in [35], the priority of users is dynamically adjusted frame by frame and the aim in [36], is to maximize the MISO-OFDMA system throughput with the constraints of total available power and Bit Error Rate (BER) while supporting a kind of fairness among users.

In this paper, a user selection and resource allocation algorithm for multiuser downlink MISO-OFDMA systems is developed that is less complex than other approaches and incorporates fairness by imposing proportional constraints [8]-[11] among the users' data rates. The beamforming scheme of [24] [30] is applied in each subcarrier, where each user experiences flat fading [2], but the user selection procedure takes fairness into account. Simulation results sustain its effectiveness in distributing the sum data rate fairly and flexibly among users.

The remainder of the paper is organized as follows. A description of the MISO-OFDMA system model is introduced in Section 2, whereas the problem of sum data rate maximization using proportional data rate constraints is formulated in Section 3. The proposed algorithm is introduced in Section 4 and Section 5 contains the complexity analysis of the proposed algorithm and a complexity comparison with other algorithms. Simulation results, analysis and a comparison between the proposed algorithm and previous resource allocation schemes are provided in Section 6. Finally, Section 7 contains concluding remarks.

In the following, $(\cdot)^T$ denotes transpose, whereas $(\cdot)^*$ denotes conjugate transpose. $\mathbf{x}$ denotes a column vector, $\mathbf{A}$ denotes a matrix, and $\| \cdot \|$ represents the Euclidean norm. Finally, $[x]_+ = \max\{0, x\}$.

2   System Model

Consider an OFDMA downlink transmission with N subcarriers, T transmit antennas at the BS and K active users, each equipped with a single receive antenna. Also, let B be the overall available bandwidth, and $\mathbf{h}_{k,n} = [h_{k,n}^1 \; \ldots \; h_{k,n}^T]^T$ be the $T \times 1$ baseband equivalent gain vector of the channel between the BS and user k in subcarrier n. Thus, for each subcarrier n, the baseband equivalent model for the system can be written as

$$\mathbf{y}_n = \mathbf{H}_n \mathbf{x}_n + \mathbf{z}_n, \tag{1}$$

where

$$\mathbf{H}_n = [\mathbf{h}_{1,n} \; \mathbf{h}_{2,n} \; \ldots \; \mathbf{h}_{K,n}]^T$$

is a $K \times T$ matrix with complex entries, $\mathbf{x}_n = [x_{1,n} \ldots x_{T,n}]^T$ is the $T \times 1$ transmitted signal vector in subcarrier n, $\mathbf{y}_n = [y_{1,n} \ldots y_{K,n}]^T$ is a $K \times 1$ vector containing the received signal of each user, and $\mathbf{z}_n = [z_{1,n} \ldots z_{K,n}]^T$ is a $K \times 1$ vector denoting the noise that is assumed to be independent identically distributed (i.i.d.) zero-mean circularly symmetric complex Gaussian with covariance matrix $\sigma^2 \mathbf{I}_K$.

It is also assumed that the channel vectors are statistically independent and that their distribution is continuous. Hence, $\text{rank}(\mathbf{H}_n) = \min(T, K)$. Moreover, the practically important case where $K \geq T$ is considered. Hence, $\text{rank}(\mathbf{H}_n) = T$. The total transmitted power, in the entire OFDM symbol, is P_{tot} and equal power is allocated to each subcarrier. Hence, $\text{trace}[\mathbf{C}_n] \leq \frac{P_{tot}}{N}$, where $\mathbf{C}_n = \mathbb{E}[\mathbf{x}_n (\mathbf{x}_n)^*]$ is the covariance matrix of the transmitted signal $\mathbf{x}_n$.

Using only transmit beamforming, which is a suboptimal strategy, the following model is obtained. Let $\mathbf{w}_{k,n} = [w^1_{k,n}\ w^2_{k,n}\ \cdots\ w^T_{k,n}]^T$ be the $T \times 1$ beamforming weight vector for user k in subcarrier n. Then, the baseband model (1) can be written as

$$\mathbf{y}_n = \mathbf{H}_n \mathbf{W}_n \mathbf{D}_n \mathbf{s}_n + \mathbf{z}_n, \tag{2}$$

where

$$\mathbf{W}_n = [\mathbf{w}_{1,n}\ \mathbf{w}_{2,n}\ \cdots\ \mathbf{w}_{K,n}]$$

is the $T \times K$ beamforming weight matrix, $\mathbf{s}_n = [s_{1,n} \ldots s_{K,n}]^T$ is a $K \times 1$ vector containing the signals destined to each user, and

$$\mathbf{D}_n = \begin{pmatrix} \sqrt{p_{1,n}} & 0 & \cdots & 0 \\ 0 & \sqrt{p_{2,n}} & \cdots & 0 \\ \vdots & \vdots & \ddots & \vdots \\ 0 & 0 & \cdots & \sqrt{p_{K,n}} \end{pmatrix}$$

accounts for the distribution of the power allocated to subcarrier n among the K users. According to (2), the resulting received signal vector for user k in subcarrier n, is given by

$$y_{k,n} = \sum_{i=1}^{K} \mathbf{h}_{k,n} \mathbf{w}_{i,n} \sqrt{p_{i,n}} s_{i,n} + z_{k,n} =$$

$$= \mathbf{h}_{k,n} \mathbf{w}_{k,n} \sqrt{p_{k,n}} s_{k,n} + \tag{3}$$

$$+ \sum_{i=1,i\neq k}^{K} \mathbf{h}_{k,n} \mathbf{w}_{i,n} \sqrt{p_{i,n}} s_{i,n} + z_{k,n},$$

where the term in third line in (3) represents the multi-user interference caused by the simultaneous transmission of data to other users in subcarrier n. Concerning (3), a graphic representation of the MISO downlink beamforming block diagram is shown in Fig. 1.

3   Problem Formulation

ZF beamforming is a spatial signal processing by which the multiple antenna transmitter can null multiuser interference signals in wireless communications. It inverts the channel matrix at the transmitter in order to create orthogonal channels between the transmitter and the receiver. The beamforming vectors are selected such that $\mathbf{h}_{i,n} \cdot \mathbf{w}_{j,n} = 0$, for $i \neq j$, and (3) becomes

$$y_{k,n} = \mathbf{h}_{k,n} \mathbf{w}_{k,n} \sqrt{p_{k,n}} s_{k,n} + z_{k,n}.$$

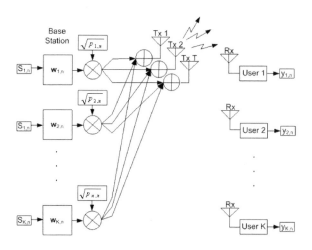

Fig. 1. MISO-OFDMA block diagram

It is then possible to encode users individually, and with smaller complexity compared to DPC. ZF at the transmitter incurs an excess transmission power penalty relative to ZF-DPC and the (optimal) MMSE-DPC transmission scheme. If $K \leq T$ and rank($\mathbf{H}_n$) = K, the ZF beamforming matrix is the pseudo-inverse of $\mathbf{H}_n$, namely

$$\mathbf{W}_n = \mathbf{H}_n^*(\mathbf{H}_n\mathbf{H}_n^*)^{-1}. \tag{4}$$

However, if $K > T$, it is not possible to use (4) because $\mathbf{H}_n\mathbf{H}_n^*$ is singular and low complexity SDMA approaches are required. In that case, it is necessary to select $t \leq T$ out of K users in each subcarrier. Hence, there are I possible combinations of users transmitting in the same subcarrier, denoted as A_i, where $A_i \subset \{1, 2, \ldots, K\}$, $0 < |A_i| \leq T$, where $|A_i|$ denotes the cardinality of set A_i, and $I = \sum_{l=1}^{T} \binom{K}{l}$.

Let a set of users $A_i = \{s_1, \ldots, s_t\}$, that produce the row-reduced channel matrix

$$\mathbf{H}_n(A_i) = [\mathbf{h}_{s_1,n} \ \mathbf{h}_{s_2,n} \ \cdots \ \mathbf{h}_{s_t,n}]^T$$

in each subcarrier. When ZF is used, the data rate of user $k \in A_i$, in subcarrier n, is given by [18]

$$r_{k,i,n} = \log_2(\mu_n c_{k,n}(A_i)), \tag{5}$$

where

$$c_{k,n}(A_i) = \{[(\mathbf{H}_n(A_i)\mathbf{H}_n(A_i)^*)^{-1}]_{k,k}\}^{-1} \tag{6}$$

and μ_n is obtained by solving the water-filling equation [37]

$$\sum_{k \in A_i} \left[\mu_n - \frac{1}{c_{k,n}(A_i)} \right]_+ = \frac{P_{tot}}{N}.$$

The power loading then yields

$$p_{k,i,n} = c_{k,n}(A_i) \left[\mu_n - \frac{1}{c_{k,n}(A_i)} \right]_+ , \forall k \in A_i.$$

By applying the conclusions above, the linear beamforming optimization problem, that performs user selection in each subcarrier and resource allocation in the entire OFDM symbol, can be formulated as

$$\max_{\rho_{k,i,n}, p_{k,i,n}} \frac{B}{N} \sum_{k=1}^{K} \sum_{n=1}^{N} \sum_{i=1}^{I} \rho_{k,i,n} r_{k,i,n} \tag{7}$$

subject to

$$\rho_{k,i,n} \in \{0, 1\}, \forall k, i, n$$

$$p_{k,i,n} \geq 0, \forall k, i, n$$

$$\sum_{k=1}^{K} p_{k,i,n} \leq \frac{P_{tot}}{N}, \forall n, i$$

$$\sum_{k=1}^{K} \rho_{k,i,n} \leq T, \forall n, i$$

$$R_1 : R_2 : \ldots : R_K = \gamma_1 : \gamma_2 : \ldots : \gamma_K$$

where $\rho_{k,i,n}$ is the subcarrier allocation indicator such that $\rho_{k,i,n} = 1$ if user $k \in A_i$ and A_i is selected in subcarrier n; otherwise $\rho_{k,i,n} = 0$, $k = 1, 2, \ldots, K$, $i = 1, 2, \ldots, I$ and $n = 1, 2, \ldots, N$. The total data rate for user k, denoted as R_k, is defined as

$$R_k = \frac{B}{N} \sum_{n=1}^{N} \sum_{i=1}^{I} \rho_{k,i,n} r_{k,i,n} \tag{8}$$

and $\{\gamma_k\}_{k=1}^{K}$ are the proportional data rate constraints.

The user selection and resource allocation under the fairness criterion (7) is an NP-hard combinatorial optimization problem [38] with non-linear constraints. The optimal solution can be obtained by exhaustive search of all possible user assignment sets in all subcarriers but the complexity is given by I^N, which is extremely complicated even for moderate K and N. The complexity becomes larger by not performing equal power allocation among subcarriers and by not restricting power allocation in each subcarrier to water-filling that, in contrast to the sum data rate case, is not necessarily optimal for the case of proportional fair data rates.

4   The Proposed User Selection and Resource Allocation Algorithm

In the following, a suboptimal, low-complexity user selection and resource allocation algorithm is proposed, that selects users independently in each subcarrier. The proposed algorithm is based on ZF beamforming and on spatial correlation between different users, denoting

$$\eta_{l,m} = \frac{|(\mathbf{h}_{l,n})^*\mathbf{h}_{m,n}|}{\| \mathbf{h}_{l,n} \| \| \mathbf{h}_{m,n} \|}, \ 0 \leq \eta_{l,m} \leq 1, \tag{9}$$

the spatial correlation between user l and user m in subcarrier n. The larger the $\eta_{l,m}$ is, the more power is required to eliminate the interference between users l, m, and the less sum data rate is achieved.

Let $\mathcal{U} = \{1, 2, \ldots K\}$ denote the set of indices of all K users and $A_i = \{s_1, \ldots, s_t\} \subset \mathcal{U}$ denote the set of t selected users ($|A_i| = t$, $t \leq T$) that share a subcarrier. The proposed algorithm iteratively selects users based on the spatial correlation (9) between the users who have already been selected in subcarrier n, for $n = 1, 2, \ldots, N$, and the remaining ones. In each iteration, it forms a set of candidate users, $\mathcal{Q}$, of size L drawn from the set $\mathcal{U} - A_i$. The members of $\mathcal{Q}$ have the smallest spatial correlation with the users of set A_i. The proposed algorithm comprises the following steps

1. **Initialization:**
   - Set $\mathcal{S} = \{1 \ldots N\}$, $R_k = 0$, $\forall k \in \mathcal{U}$, $\rho_{k,i,n} = 0$, $\forall k \in \mathcal{U}$, $i = 1, 2, \ldots, I$ and $n \in \mathcal{S}$.
   - Set $\{\gamma_k\}_{k=1}^K$, the proportional data rate constraints.
2. **While $|\mathcal{S}| \neq \emptyset$:**
   - Set $\mathcal{U} = \{1, \ldots, K\}$, $|A_i| = \emptyset$.
   - Find user k satisfying $\frac{R_k}{\gamma_k} \leq \frac{R_i}{\gamma_i}$ $\forall i, 1 \leq i \leq K$.
   - Find subcarrier $n = \arg\max_{j \in \mathcal{S}} \| \mathbf{h}_{k,j} \|$.
   - Set $t = 1$, $\rho_{k,i,n} = 1$, $A_i(t) = \{k\}$, and $\mathcal{U} = \mathcal{U} - \{k\}$.
   - Compute R_k, according to (5), (8).
   - For $t = 2$ to T:
     - For each $l \in A_i(t - 1)$ and $m \in \mathcal{U}$, compute $\eta_{l,m}$, according to (9).
     - Compute the average correlation between already selected users $A_i(t-1)$ and each candidate user $m \in \mathcal{U}$, according to equation $\overline{C}_m = \frac{\sum_{l \in A_i(t-1)} \eta_{l,m}}{|A_i(t-1)|}$.
     - Form the group, $\mathcal{Q}$, of candidates that contains the L users with the lowest values of $\overline{C}_m$, $m \in \mathcal{U}$.
     - Find a user, $s_t \in \mathcal{Q}$, such that

$$\sum_{k \in A_i(t-1) \cup \{s_t\}} r_{k,i,n} > \sum_{k \in A_i(t-1)} r_{k,i,n} \text{ and}$$

$$\left| \frac{R_{s_t} + r_{s_t,i,n}}{\gamma_{s_t}} - \frac{R_k}{\gamma_k} \right| \leq D, \ \forall k \in A_i(t - 1)$$

where D is a system parameter that indicates the relation between proportional fairness among the users' data rates and sum of the users' data rates.

- If user s_t is found, set $\rho_{s_t,i,n} = 1$, $A_i(t) = A_i(t-1) \cup s_t$, and $\mathcal{U} = \mathcal{U} - \{s_t\}$.
- Compute R_k, $\forall k \in A_i(t)$, according to (5), (8).
  - Set $\mathcal{S} = \mathcal{S} - \{n\}$.

3. **Output:**
   - The users' data rates: R_k, $\forall k = 1, \ldots, K$.
   - The subcarrier allocation indicator: $\rho_{k,i,n}$, for $k = 1, 2, \ldots, K$, $i = 1, 2, \ldots, I$, and $n = 1, 2, \ldots, N$.

The proposed algorithm allocates users and power separately in each subcarrier, but the sequence with which the subcarriers are considered is determined based on the data rates after each iteration. More specifically, the algorithm determines which of the K users is treated most "unfairly" after the last allocation step by calculating $\frac{R_k}{\gamma_k}$, $\forall k \in \mathcal{U}$. The only exception is the first iteration, when all users have zero data rates and any user can be chosen. After determining the user k, all available subcarriers are searched and n is chosen that maximizes the data rate of k if that user were to transmit alone in that subcarrier. Additional users are admitted to the subcarrier based on two criteria: 1) similar to [24] [30], the sum data rate in the subcarrier should increase, and 2) the newly admitted user s_t can achieve "fair" sum, OFDM-symbol, data rate compared to the sum data rate of the other users that have already been admitted to the subcarrier, according to system parameter D. The size of the set $\mathcal{Q}$ is set heuristically equal to $L = \min\{\mathcal{U}, T\}$, because it was shown to lead to good performance in most simulated cases. $A_i(t)$ means the allocation result of the t step. Therefore, at least one, and at most T users can be transmitting in the same subcarrier. Regardless of the number of users, the total power in each subcarrier is equal to $\frac{P_{tot}}{N}$.

5   Complexity Analysis

In order to analyze the computational complexity of the proposed algorithm, recall that K refers to the total number of users in the system and T refers to the number of transmit antennas at the BS. N on the other hand refers to the number of subcarriers, which is much larger than both K and T.

Initialization step of the proposed algorithm requires constant time. In the while loop, which runs for every subcarrier of set $\mathcal{S}$, the best user k among K users for N subcarriers is found, in the worst case scenario. Thus requires $O(KN)$ operations. After determining the best user k for subcarrier n, at most $T - 1$ other users are found for subcarrier n. In each one of the $t = 2$ to T steps, the average correlation $\overline{C}_m$ between each candidate user ($m \in \mathcal{U}$) and already selected users ($A_i(t-1)$) must be computed. The computation of spatial correlation $\eta_{l,m}$ for each pair (l, m) can be done within time $O(T)$, as it mainly requires an inner product and a division. Additionally, the computation of $\overline{C}_m$ needs time $O(KT)$ in the worst case scenario. Moreover, the evaluation of at most T data rates $r_{k,i,n}$ is required. In order to evaluate $r_{k,i,n}$, inversion of $\mathbf{H}_n(A_i(t-1) \cup s_t)\mathbf{H}_n(A_i(t-1) \cup s_t)^*$ (6) is required which can be done in time $O(T^2)$, for the worst case when T users are admitted to each subcarrier, using the matrix inversion lemma as described in [24]. Repeating this over at most L users $(s_t \in Q)$ in each one of the $t = 2$ to T steps, and over all subcarriers of set S, the complexity is obtained to be $O([KT + LT^2]TN)$. Given that $LT < K$, the complexity becomes $O(KNT^2)$. Thus the overall computational complexity of the proposed algorithm is $O(KNT^2)$.

As was mentioned before the complexity of exhaustive search for the optimal solution of the original problem is given by I^N, where $I = \sum_{l=1}^{T} \binom{K}{l}$. Alternatively, the complexity is $O(K^{NT})$ and is prohibitive even for moderate values of K, N, and T. The complexity of the algorithm described in [34] is $O(K^T N)$ while the complexity of the algorithm that is described in [24] for flat fading channels is $O(KT^3)$. Implementing it in each subcarrier, in order to compare it with our approach, its complexity becomes $O(KNT^3)$. In addition, the complexity of the algorithm proposed in [36] is $\sum_{n=1}^{N} \binom{K}{s_n}$, where $s_n = 1, 2, \ldots, T$. In the worst case scenario, where there are T users transmitting on each subcarrier, the complexity becomes $\sum_{n=1}^{N} \binom{K}{T}$ which is of order $O(K^T N)$.

It is easily observed that the proposed algorithm has a very dramatic reduction in complexity compared to $O(K^{NT})$ required by the exhaustive search. In addition it has similar complexity to [24] and smaller than [34] [36]. Table 1 summarizes the complexity of the algorithms mentioned above.

Table 1. Computational Complexity

Exhaustive Search	Proposed Algorithm	Algorithm in [24]	Algorithm in [34]	Algorithm in [36]
$O(K^{NT})$	$O(KNT^2)$	$O(KNT^3)$	$O(K^T N)$	$O(K^T N)$

6   Simulation Results

In this section, the performance of the algorithm is evaluated using simulation. The proposed algorithm is compared with the algorithm proposed in [24], applying it in each subcarrier, the existing greedy capacity maximization with prescreening [34] algorithm, the fairness based resource allocation [36] algorithm, Round Robin (RR) algorithm and the method that employs transmission, using Maximal Ratio Combining (MRC), only to the user with the strongest channel. In [24], it was suggested, via numerical examples, that the sum data rate of sub-optimal, ZF beamforming schemes can approach that of DPC even for a moderate number of users. However, an inherent drawback of the maximum sum data rate criterion is the lack of fairness, because certain users may be completely shut off during a scheduling period. This is dealt with by imposing

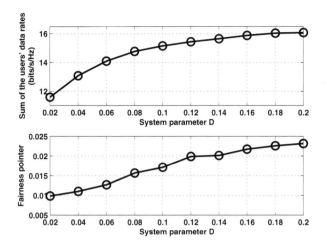

Fig. 2. Choice of system parameter

fairness criteria, such as the proportional data rate constraint [8]-[10] considered in this paper. In RR algorithm, each user is given a fair share of the channel resource regardless of the channel state. T users are selected in each subcarrier. Both equal power (EQ) allocation and water-filling (WF) power allocation over the parallel subchannels are considered.

In all simulations presented in this section, the frequency-selective channel consists of six independent Rayleigh multipath components (taps) for every downlink transmission path between any of the T transmit antennas and users. For each channel realization the proposed algorithm is used. As in [9], an exponentially decaying power delay profile is assumed, the ratio of the energy of the lth tap to the first tap being equal to e^{-2l}. A maximum delay spread of $5\mu s$ and maximum doppler of 30Hz is assumed. The channel information is sampled every 0.5ms to update the user selection and resource allocation. BS consists of $T = 4$ transmit antennas and the number of subcarriers is $N = 64$. The number of channel realizations is equal to 1000 and 100 time samples for each realization are used for each user.

For each channel realization, a set of proportional constants $\{\gamma_k\}_{k=1}^K$ are assigned to available users. It is assumed that these constants follow the probability mass function

$$p_{\gamma_k} = \begin{cases} 1 \text{ with probability } 0.5 \\ 2 \text{ with probability } 0.3 \\ 4 \text{ with probability } 0.2 \end{cases}$$

In Fig. 2, the performance of the proposed algorithm is shown for different values of system parameter D, when there are $K = 16$ available users in the system and $SNR = 15$. Fairness pointer indicates the maximum difference between users' data rates and respective fairness constraints. It is shown that as the system

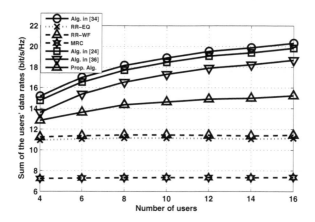

Fig. 3. Sum of the users' data rates vs number of users

parameter becomes larger, the sum of the users' data rates becomes larger too, but the fairness criterion is more relaxed. Thus, the system parameter indicates a tradeoff between sum of the users' data rates and accomplishing fairness between users' data rates.

Figs. 3 - 5, are shown for a fixed system parameter $D = 0.1$, which is chosen heuristically to ensure a reasonable trade off between sum of the users' data rates and accomplishing fairness between users' data rates. In Fig. 3, the number of users varies from 4-16 in increment of 2, while figs. 4, 5 are shown when all, $K = 16$, users are present in the system. In figs. 3, 5, $SNR = 15$.

In Fig. 3 it can be seen, the reasonable price being paid in order to guarantee fairness by using the proposed algorithm. As the number of users increases, the difference in sum data rates also increases because additional multiuser diversity is available to [24] [34] that only target sum data rate maximization. On the other hand, more users put more constraints to the proposed algorithm, because new users need to share the same resources. In addition, sum data rate of the proposed algorithm is significantly enhanced over both RR-WF and RR-EQ algorithm. MRC algorithm is the lower bound of the proposed algorithm as in MRC each subcarrier is allocated to only one user. Sum data rate of [36] is degraded compared with [24] [34] and enhanced over the other algorithms. This is because it imposes a kind of fairness between users' data rates.

The same conclusions can be drawn from Fig. 4, where the sum of the users' data rates is shown as a function of SNR. It can also been seen that MRC is a viable choice only in the low SNR regime.

In Fig. 5, fairness index F_p is a modified version of the one introduced in [9], and is defined as

$$F_p = \frac{(\sum_{k=1}^{K} \frac{R_k}{\gamma_k})^2}{K \sum_{k=1}^{K} (\frac{R_k}{\gamma_k})^2},$$

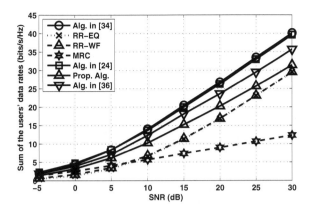

Fig. 4. Sum of the users' data rates vs SNR(dB)

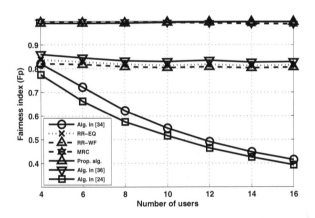

Fig. 5. Fairness index vs number of users

where F_p is a real number in the interval $(0, 1]$ with the maximum value of 1 for the case that the achieved data rate proportions among the users are the same as the predetermined set $\{\gamma_k\}_{k=1}^{K}$. Employing [24] [34], no guarantees are provided for the fairness between user data rates. In addition, as the number of users increases, fairness index degrades. RR-WF, RR-EQ and [36] experience almost the same fairness index regardless of the number of users. This is because these algorithms achieve approximately equal data rates among users. Both the proposed algorithm and MRC distribute the sum data rate very well among users, very close to the defined ideal data rate constraints which is the main point of this paper. However, MRC does not exploit the $T = 4$ degrees of freedom that are available in each subcarrier.

7 Conclusion

A fairness-aware user selection and resource allocation algorithm for the MISO downlink over frequency-selective channels was introduced. The algorithm is based on ZF beamforming and on spatial correlation (9) between users transmitting in the same subcarrier. It maximizes the sum of the users' data rates subject to constraints on total available power and proportional fairness among users' data rates. Although it is suboptimal, as was shown by simulations, the loss with respect to the unconstrained case where the only target is the maximization of the sum data rate is reasonable in order to achieve proportionality among users' data rates. Finally, the proposed algorithm is less complex than other approaches.

References

1. Andrews, J.G., Ghosh, A., Muhamed, R.: Fundamentals of WiMAX: Understanding Broadband Wireless Networking. Prentice-Hall (2007)
2. Nee, R.V., Prasad, R.: OFDM for Wireless Multimedia Communications. Artech House (2000)
3. Tse, D., Viswanath, P.: Fundamentals of Wireless Communication. Cambridge University Press (2005)
4. Jang, J., Lee, K.B.: Transmit power adaptation for multiuser OFDM systems. IEEE J. Sel. Areas Commun. 21(2), 171–178 (2003)
5. Li, G., Liu, H.: On the Optimality of the OFDMA Network. IEEE Commun. Lett. 9(5), 438–440 (2005)
6. Wong, C.Y., Cheng, R.S., Letaief, K.B., Murch, R.D.: Multiuser OFDM with Adaptive Subcarrier, Bit, and Power Allocation. IEEE J. Sel. Areas Commun. 17(10), 1747–1758 (1999)
7. Kivanc, D., Li, G., Liu, H.: Computationally Efficient Bandwidth Allocation and Power Control for OFDMA. IEEE Trans. Wireless Commun. 2(6), 1150–1158 (2003)
8. Mohanram, C., Bhashyam, S.: A Sub-optimal Joint Subcarrier and Power Allocation Algorithm for Multiuser OFDM. IEEE Commun. Lett. 9(8), 685–687 (2005)
9. Shen, Z., Andrews, J.G., Evans, B.L.: Adaptive Resource Allocation in Multiuser OFDM Systems With Proportional Rate Constraints. IEEE Trans. Wireless Commun. 4(6), 2726–2737 (2005)
10. Sadr, S., Anpalagan, A., Raahemifar, K.: Suboptimal Rate Adaptive Resource Allocation for Downlink OFDMA Systems. Intern. J. Veh. Techn. (2009)
11. Papoutsis, V.D., Fraimis, I.G., Kotsopoulos, S.A.: Fairness-aware resource allocation for the SISO downink over frequency-selective channels. In: IEEE Wireless Commun. and Networking Conf., Sydney, NSW, Australia (2010)
12. Zhang, Y.J., Letaief, K.B.: Multiuser Adaptive Subcarrier-and-Bit Allocation With Adaptive Cell Selection for OFDM Systems. IEEE Trans. Wireless Commun. 3(5), 1566–1575 (2004)
13. Mao, Z., Wang, X.: Efficient Optimal and Suboptimal Radio Resource Allocation in OFDMA System. IEEE Trans. Wireless Commun. 7(2), 440–445 (2008)
14. Ma, Y.: Rate-Maximization for Downlink OFDMA with Proportional Fairness. IEEE Trans. Veh. Techn. 57(5), 3267–3274 (2008)

15. Biagioni, A., Fantacci, R., Marabissi, D., Tarchi, D.: Adaptive Subcarrier Allocation Schemes for Wireless OFDMA Systems in WiMAX Networks. IEEE J. Sel. Areas Commun. 27(2), 217–225 (2009)
16. Goldsmith, A., Jafar, S.A., Jindal, N., Vishwanath, S.: Capacity Limits of MIMO Channels. IEEE J. Sel. Areas Commun. 21(5), 684–702 (2003)
17. Rhee, W., Cioffi, J.M.: On the Capacity of Multiuser Wireless Channels With Multiple Antennas. IEEE Trans. Inf. Theory 49(10), 2580–2595 (2003)
18. Weingarten, H., Steinberg, Y., Shamai, S.: The capacity region of the Gaussian MIMO broadcast channel. IEEE Trans. Inf. Theory 52(9), 3936–3964 (2006)
19. Jindal, N., Rhee, W., Viswanath, S., Jafar, S.A., Goldsmith, A.: Sum Power Iterative Water-Filling for Multi-Antenna Gaussian Broadcast Channels. IEEE Trans. Inf. Theory 51(4), 1570–1580 (2005)
20. Caire, G., Shamai, S.: On the Achievable Throughput of a Multiantenna Gaussian Broadcast Channel. IEEE Trans. Inf. Theory 49(7), 1691–1706 (2003)
21. Tu, Z., Blum, R.S.: Multiuser Diversity for a Dirty Paper Approach. IEEE Commun. Lett. 7(8), 370–372 (2003)
22. Sharif, M., Hassibi, B.: A Comparison of Time-Sharing, DPC, and Beamforming for MIMO Broadcast Channels with Many Users. IEEE Trans. Commun. 55(1), 11–15 (2007)
23. Spencer, Q.H., Swindlehurst, A.L., Haardt, M.: Zero-Forcing Methods for Downlink Spatial Multiplexing in Multiuser MIMO Channels. IEEE Trans. Signal Processing 52(2), 461–471 (2004)
24. Dimic, G., Sidiropoulos, N.D.: On Downlink Beamforming With Greedy User Selection: Performance Analysis and a Simple New Algorithm. IEEE Trans. Signal Processing 53(10), 3857–3868 (2005)
25. Yoo, T., Goldsmith, A.: On the Optimality of Multiantenna Broadcast Scheduling Using Zero-Forcing Beamforming. IEEE J. Sel. Areas Commun. 24(3), 528–541 (2006)
26. Shen, Z., Chen, R., Andrews, J., Health Jr., R., Evans, B.L.: Low Complexity User Selection Algorithms for Multiuser MIMO Systems with Block Diagonalization. IEEE Trans. Signal Processing 54(9), 3658–3663 (2006)
27. Yu, W., Lan, T.: Transmitter Optimization for the Multi-Antenna Downlink With Per-Antenna Power Constraints. IEEE Trans. Signal Processing 55(6), 2646–2660 (2007)
28. Fuchs, M., Galdo, G.D., Haardt, M.: Low-Complexity Space-Time-Frequency Scheduling for MIMO Systems With SDMA. IEEE Trans. Veh. Techn. 56(5), 2775–2784 (2007)
29. Zhang, X., Lv, Z., Wang, W.: Performance Analysis of Multiuser Diversity in MIMO Systems with Antenna Selection. IEEE Trans. Wireless Commun. 7(1), 15–21 (2008)
30. Karachontzitis, S., Toumpakaris, D.: Efficient and Low-Complexity User Selection for the Multiuser MISO Downlink. In: IEEE Personal, Indoor and Mobile Radio Commun. Symposium, Tokyo, Japan (2009)
31. Koutsopoulos, I., Tassiulas, L.: Adaptive Resource Allocation in SDMA-based Wireless Broadband Networks with OFDM Signaling. In: IEEE INFOCOM, New York, USA, vol. 3, pp. 1376–1385 (2002)
32. Tsang, Y.M., Cheng, R.S.: Optimal Resource Allocation in SDMA/Multi-Input-Single-Output/OFDM Systems under QoS and Power Constraints. In: IEEE Wireless Commun. and Networking Conf., Georgia, USA, vol. 3, pp. 1595–1600 (2004)

33. Zhang, Y.J., Letaief, K.B.: An Efficient Resource-Allocation Scheme for Spatial Multiuser Access in MIMO/OFDM Systems. IEEE Trans. on Commun. 53(1), 107–116 (2005)
34. Chan, P.W.C., Cheng, R.S.: Capacity Maximization for Zero-Forcing MIMO-OFDMA Downlink Systems with Multiuser Diversity. IEEE Trans. Wireless Commun. 6(5), 1880–1889 (2007)
35. Tsai, C.F., Chang, C.J., Ren, F.C., Yen, C.M.: Adaptive Radio Resource Allocation for Downlink OFDMA/SDMA Systems with Multimedia Traffic. IEEE Trans. Wireless Commun. 7(5), 1734–1743 (2008)
36. Kai, S., Ying, W., Zi-xiong, C., Ping, Z.: Fairness based resource allocation for multiuser MISO-OFDMA systems with beamforming. J. China Univ. of Posts and Telec. 16(1), 38–43 (2009)
37. Cover, T.M., Thomas, J.A.: Elements of Information theory. John Wiley & Sons, Inc., Hoboken (2006)
38. Ibaraki, T., Katoh, N.: Resource Allocation Problems-Algorithmic Approaches, M. Garey, Ed. MIT Press (1988)

Signaling Load Evaluations for Policy-Driven Cognitive Management Architectures

Kostas Tsagkaris, M. Akezidou, A. Galani, and P. Demestichas

University of Piraeus, Department of Digital Systems, Piraeus, Greece
{ktsagk,akezidou,agalani,pdemest}@unipi.gr

Abstract. Future networks will need to accommodate a significantly augmented user demand, mainly stemming from the wireless and mobile domains. This will stress network operators for developing mechanisms to confront the challenges and to leverage the opportunities posed by such a versatile radio environment. In particular, the situation calls for adaptive and flexible management paradigms that are able to dynamically manage network elements and terminals thus ensuring the great availability and efficient usage of spectrum and other radio resources. Framed within the above, this paper considers a cognitive management architecture, which is destined to the optimized management of future wireless networks and terminals operating in versatile radio environments and presents a performance evaluation methodology, which was set up for measuring the signaling loads that the operation of the architecture will bring in to the managed network.

Keywords: Cognitive management architecture, Functional entities, ASN.1, Signaling load.

1 Introduction

Future wireless networks will exhibit great levels of complexity and heterogeneity as a result of the (co-)existence of multiple and different kinds of radio access networks, technologies and the advent of new demanding user applications. Moreover, the introduction of flexible spectrum management concept and the adoption of cognitive capabilities to both networks and terminals, seem to be an efficacious response to this accrued complexity as well as a powerful enabler for the accomplishment of both users' and operators' goals. Therefore, the efficient operation of future wireless networks necessitates significant alterations in the way they are managed and call for the adoption and deployment of innovative and scalable management architectures. Such advanced, cognitive management architecture is the subject of this work. The adjective "cognitive" is used here to describe both the ability to operate in different spectrum bands in a dynamic and flexible manner and the possession of some intelligent processing and decision making ability e.g. based on learning.

In particular, the focus of this paper is placed on evaluating the signaling loads, with which the considered cognitive management architecture will burden the network that it manages. First, an evaluation methodology that takes into account and

I. Tomkos et al. (Eds.): BROADNETS 2010, LNICST 66, pp. 213–225, 2012.
© Institute for Computer Sciences, Social Informatics and Telecommunications Engineering 2012

analyzes the information that should flow in the interfaces of the architecture is described and secondly and mainly, signaling loads are calculated in various test cases and after applying the above mentioned methodology into an indicative operation scenario. These results are expected to influence the deployment of the management architecture in both legacy and future networks.

Actually, this cognitive architecture falls in the wider scope of the E^3 project [8] and comprises a variant of the Functional Architecture (FA) that has been proposed Interestingly, the proposed architecture has been actually elaborated within the Working Group 3 (WG3) of the Reconfigurable Radio Systems Technical Committee (RRS TC) [2][3]. It should be also mentioned that a relevant functional architecture, which proposes a policy-driven optimization of radio resource usage in heterogeneous wireless networks has been standardized within IEEE and in particular by the P1900.4 Working Group [9]. The elaborated architecture comprises a policy-driven management architecture that amalgamates features of the mentioned works.

Accordingly, the rest of this paper is structured as follows. In Section 2, the considered management architecture, the role and the operation of its functional entities are revisited. Section 3 describes the methodological steps we have followed in order to perform the signaling load evaluations, whereas results from the application of this methodology into indicative test cases are given in Section 4. Finally, the paper is concluded in Section 5.

2   Cognitive Management Architecture

The proposed cognitive management architecture consists of four functional entities that cater for different operational needs and goals and exchange proper information via the interfaces as shown in Fig. 1: (i) the Dynamic Spectrum Management (DSM) (ii) the Dynamic, Self-organizing Planning and Management (DSNPM), (iii) the Joint Radio Resource Management (JRRM), and (iv) the Configuration Control Module (CCM). The functional entities of the architecture may actually span across various network elements, access and core, and MTs, as well. What follows is a brief revisiting of the more thorough description of these functional, management entities given in [1][2].

2.1   Dynamic Spectrum Management (DSM)

The functionality of DSM concerns the spectrum management in medium and long term. Specifically, DSM is responsible: a) for the assignment of operating frequencies to RATs in specific time periods and specific geographical areas and derivation of corresponding directives for DSNPM operation (sent via MS interface), according with constraints for predefined spectrum assignment rules or spectrum utilization metrics and b) for the detection of long-term available frequency bands for sharing or trading with other network operators (NOs).

2.2   Dynamic, Self-organising Planning and Management (DSNPM)

DSNPM's responsibilities include (i) the management and reconfiguration of network elements, (ii) the detection of new elements, (iii) the provision of the essential configuration information of the managed RATs to MTs, for initial network connection, (iv) the derivation of policies for the managed MTs, (v) and the calculation of spectrum utilization metrics. DSNPM's objectives are accomplished by applying optimization functionality, enhanced with learning capabilities, thus strengthening the characterization of the architecture as "cognitive", based on received context and profiles information.

2.3   Joint Radio Resource Management (JRRM)

JRRM is distributed among network (n-JRRM) and MTs (m-JRRM) and is mainly responsible for jointly managing the radio resources belonging to heterogeneous RATs. It performs functionalities such as MT access selection based on requested QoS, radio conditions, user preferences and network policies, neighborhood Information provision for efficient discovery of available accesses, as well as QoS/bandwidth allocation/admission control.

2.4   Configuration Control Module (CCM)

CCM implements the decisions of DSNPM and JRRM in network elements and JRRM in MTs. Specifically, CCM, for both network elements (n-CCM) and MTs (m-CCM), is responsible for the implementation of all the stages of reconfiguration and all the possible related actions (e.g. software download), as well as the provision of the relevant information about the configuration capabilities of the network element or the MT, to the corresponding entity (DSNPM for network elements and m-JRRM for MTs).

3   Signaling Load Evaluation Approach

In this section, we analyze the methodology we have followed in order to evaluate the signaling loads induced in the considered cognitive network management architecture. It must be noted that this analysis is sound only in the case that the described functional entities reside in distinct network entities. Such an attempt to map these entities to the 3GPP LTE-SAE and its respective network interfaces, has been made for instance in [6].

Our purpose is to calculate the signaling loads in the interfaces of the architecture by characterizing the signaling loads that are needed to carry out a set of elementary procedures. Accordingly, the interfaces are first defined in terms of elementary procedures, which is a traditional way used for signaling and protocol analysis of interfaces, and is also the approach that has been followed within E^3 project [4] and inspired this study. Every single operation/scenario in the considered architecture is supposed to be built from a set of elementary procedures taking place in the interfaces of the architecture, thus the term "elementary".

Without loss of generality and in order to demonstrate our method, we follow a scenario-driven approach, that is an analysis based on its application to a specific scenario, a so-called "New spectrum assignment" scenario.

The scenario is described by the Message Sequence Chart (MSC) in Fig. 2. Generally speaking, the scenario considers the case that new frequencies are disposed by a regulator to NOs. The NO, the network of whom is used as reference in the sequel for the description of the operational scenario, requests new frequencies for specific Radio Access Technologies (RATs).

In this scenario, the following procedures have been determined with respect to the interfaces in which they appear. Each procedure is assigned with an index $i = 1, 2, 3...$ (see Table 1 for the value set of i). Moreover, the current methodology also includes the identification of the messages that constitute each of the defined procedures, due to the fact of lacking of a standardized architecture to work with (see Fig. 2).

The next important step is to study and describe the type and number of parameters that each of the messages must convey for satisfying the purpose for which the architecture has been designed for. In order to define the parameters per message, we followed an approach similar to the one we conducted in our studies in [9] for the 1900.4 standardized architecture. These parameters were determined mainly based on the authors' view and experience, albeit in alignment with the respective functionality in each of the functional entities i.e. with respect to the input data that is required for a function to be properly executed within an entity and to the output that the latter is expected to produce.

In the next step, we proceed with the calculation of the length of every message which actually derives as a summation of its constituent parameters' length values. In order to describe the syntax of the messages conveyed between the interfaces of the architecture in a formal way, thus facilitating calculations, we have used Abstract Syntax Notation One (ASN.1) [12]. ASN.1 is a standardised specification language that describes data structures for representing, encoding, transmitting, and decoding data. The part of representation of date concerns what is well known as "abstract syntax". The rest part concerns the so called "transfer syntax". Specifically, in the same standard, i.e. [12], a set of ASN.1 encoding rules, which describe various ways according to which the formatted data is transformed into bit-stream prior to being transmitted into the network, are also provided. These rules include among others, Basic Encoding Rules (BER), Canonical Encoding Rules (CER), Distinguished Encoding Rules (DER), XML Encoding Rules (XER), and Packed Encoding Rules (PER) [13][14][15] etc. The calculations presented later in this work have been conducted by assuming the Basic Encoding Rules (BER) [13]. Although this may not necessarily comprise the best choice to make, it is definitely in line with the primary objective of this work.

It should be also made clear that our intention is neither to define any management protocol nor to designate any possible encapsulation e.g. with respect to the transport part, but just to define messages and their respective parameters and an anticipated length as needed for our analysis. Accordingly, the calculations have been made by taking into account only the encoding overheads as a result of assuming the use of BER for encoding only the defined parameters and not any management protocol (i.e. in terms of Tag-Length-Value (TLV) encoding) and excluding any overheads due to the selection of a specific transport protocol.

An example of such calculation follows. We consider the *Spectrum Usage* procedure which takes place in MS interface by exchanging messages used by DSM in order to request and receive information for the current spectrum usage from DSNPM namely, SpectrumUsageRequest and SpectrumUsageResponse messages (see Table 2). In Table 2 the calculated bytes are given in two separate columns. The first column corresponds to the case that assumes BER-based encoding and the second assumes no encoding at all. As it can be observed, the loads obey some generic formulas comprising a combination of both variable and constant parts. The variable part reveals dependency of the signaling loads upon parameters, which are either specific to each procedure e.g. number of requested frequency bands, denoted as f in current message or more generic ones such as the number of MTs in the managed area.

The derived values correspond to the actual size of the parameters actually conveyed and can be assumed both with BER-based encoding and without encoding at all. The values are supposed to derive after some preliminary dimensioning work we have conducted for defining the limits of each parameter.

Last but not least, special care was taken for the case of the message used to convey the policy(-ies) from the network to mobile terminal(s) side. The term "policies" here refers to radio resource selection policies, which act as directives with the scope to assist MTs to achieve best connectivity. Policies can be characterized as the ability to provide the terminals with access selection information on which of the available accesses to use for a session. Then, MTs take into consideration those policies and finally they decide for their behavior based on their own strategy, being at the same time in compliance with the rules of DSNPM. The policies are formatted as rules of the well known Event-Condition-Action (ECA) type. Once again, the analysis for the formalization of the policy related message is based on ASN.1. In particular, we have been based on the ASN.1 formation of the RRS policies which are part of the in the information model proposed in 1900.4 standard [10][9]. That is to say a RRS policy is actually a statement of the following type: ON <Event> IF <Condition> THEN <Action> where traditionally, the event part specifies the signal that triggers the invocation of the rule, the condition part is a logical test that, if satisfied or evaluates to true, causes the action to be carried out, the action part consists of the actual execution of the modification/update on the resources.

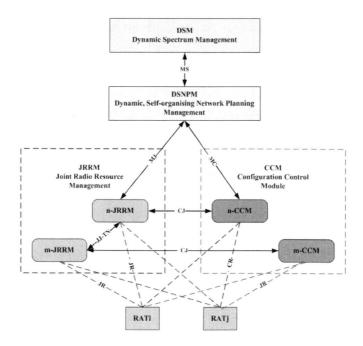

Fig. 1. Overview of Management Architecture

Table 1. Interfaces, procedures and parameters

Interface	Procedure i	Short Description	Messages
MS (DSM – DSNPM)	1	Spectrum Usage	*SpecrtumUsageRequest*
			SpecrtumUsageResponse
	2	Spectrum Assignment	*SpectrumAssignmentRequest*
MJ (DSNPM– n-JRRM)	3	Context Request	*ContextInfoRequest*
			ContextInfoResponse
JR (n-JRRM– RAT)	4	Configuration Request	*Context&ConfigurationRequest*
			Context&ConfigurationResponse
MC (DSNPM – n-CCM)	5	Reconfiguration Request	*ReconfigurationRequest*
	6	Reconfiguration Execution	*ReconfigurationExecutionNotification*
JJ-TN (n-JRRM– m-JRRM)	7	Status Info	*StatusInfoRequest*
			StatusInfoResponse
	8	Policy Derivation	*Policy*

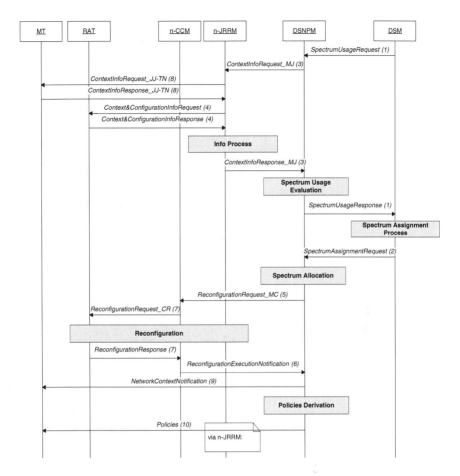

Fig. 2. Message sequence chart for the considered "New spectrum assignment" scenario

Table 2. Spectrum Usage Procedure (MS-Interface) (where *f* is the number of Frequency Bands)

Spectrum Usage (MS-Interface)			
Messages:	Content Parameters:	Bytes:	
Spectrum Usage Request DSM -> DSNPM	SpectrumBands ::= SEQUENCE OF FrequencyBand RatType ::= RatType	[3+10]*f 3	4*f 1
TOTAL:		3+13*f	1+4*f
Spectrum Usage Response DSNPM -> DSM	SpectrumInfo ::= SEQUENCE OF SEQUENCE{ frequencyBand FrequencyBand, operatingRAT PrintableString, pectrumUtilizationMetrics PrintableString OPTIONAL}	3+[2+57]*f 10 47 [47]	49*f 4 45 [45]
TOTAL:		3+59*f	49*f

4   Test Cases and Results

This section focuses on the actual performance evaluation part, which is used to provide some evidence on the signaling loads associated with the operation of the examined cognitive network management architecture in both the wired and the wireless (air) interfaces of the network.

4.1   Test Case 1: Generic Evaluations

In the first test case we proceed with evaluations of the signaling load by assuming a generic situation with input parameters as summarized in Table 3.

The total produced signaling load is depicted in Fig. 3. The volume at which the air and core parts contribute to this total load is also depicted in Fig. 4. In both figures, the results are depicted when assuming BER-based encoding and when not using encoding at all. In addition, the load per procedure is depicted in Fig. 5, whereas Fig. 6 depicts the signaling load as it appears in each of the interfaces of the architecture. Once again, the results are depicted for both BER-encoded and not encoded cases.

Table 3. Input parameter

Number of active mobile terminals	50
Number of FBSs	3
Number of RATs	2

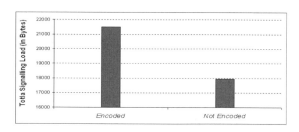

Fig. 3. Total produced signaling load (in bytes) – Test case 1

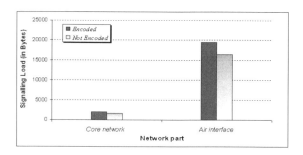

Fig. 4. Air and core signaling loads (in bytes) – Test case 1

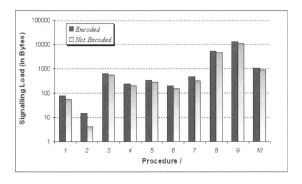

Fig. 5. Signaling load per procedure – Test case 1

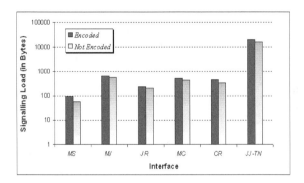

Fig. 6. Signaling load per interface – Test case 1

4.2   Test Case 2: Scalability Issues

A second test case has been set up in order to showcase scalability issues of the architecture. In particular, the goal is to show how the signaling load evolves in function to the number of RATs, of FBSs and of MTs in the managed network. Fig. 7 shows the evolution of signaling load with respect to the number of RATs that are participating in the operational scenario. In a similar way, Fig. 8 and Fig. 9 show the evolution of signaling load with respect to the number of FBSs and MTs in the managed area respectively considered in the operational scenario.

4.3   Test Case 3: Signaling Delays

In this test case we experiment with the signaling delays into the managed network. In particular, the objective is to give some evidence on the delay that the management operations will suffer as a result of the transmission of the produced management signaling information This delay is derived after dividing the volume of signaling

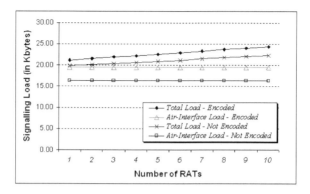

Fig. 7. Evolution of signaling load vs number of RATs – Test case 2

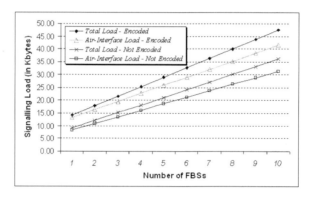

Fig. 8. Evolution of signaling load vs number of FBSs – Test case 2

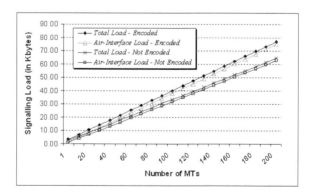

Fig. 9. Evolution of signaling load vs number of MTs – Test case 2

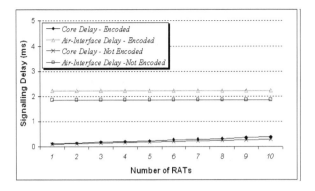

Fig. 10. Evolution of signaling delay vs number of RATs – Test case 3

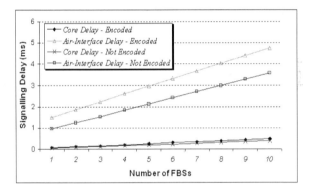

Fig. 11. Evolution of signaling delay vs number of FBSs – Test case 3

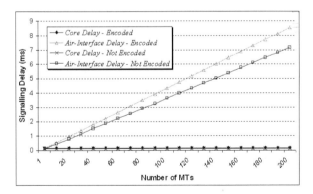

Fig. 12. Evolution of signaling delay vs number of MTs – Test case 3

load measured in each of the functional interfaces, with the capacity of the actual network link to which the specific interface may be implemented. For instance, the signaling load in the interface between DSNPM and n-JRRM, which could be mapped to the S1-MME interface in 3GPP LTE/SAE [6][7], could be conveyed by variant network, wired link types exhibiting different capabilities in terms of offered capacity. The evolution of signaling delays (in ms) with respect to the number of RATs, FBSs and MTs are shown in Fig. 10, Fig. 11 and Fig. 12. For these measurements we have assumed wired and wireless links offering 100Mbps and 70Mbps of capacity, respectively.

5   Conclusion and Future Work

The heterogeneity of future wireless networks requires a dramatic change in the current management operations. Framed within this statement, this paper considers a cognitive management architecture, which is destined to the optimized spectrum and other resource management of future wireless networks operating in versatile radio environments. In particular, the paper presents a performance evaluation methodology, which was set up for measuring the signaling loads that the operation of the architecture will bring in to the managed network. Results that were obtained from the application of the methodology to an indicative scenario were also presented and analyzed and show that the management architecture will not aggravate the overall network operation.

This paper will act as a solid basis for further investigation. First, a more complete set of scenarios will be studied and evaluated. Second, the periodicity of specific procedures-messages will be identified since it will give insight on the expected load that will regularly appear in the managed network as part of the rest legacy management/control procedures e.g. call setup, mobility etc. when designing and/or dimensioning the network. Last but not least, a mapping to existing transport protocols currently used for signaling purposes is also of high importance and will be subject to our future studies.

Acknowledgements. This work was performed in the project E^3 (www.ict-e3.eu) which has received research funding from the Community's Seventh Framework programme. The work is evolved in the context of UniverSelf and OneFIT (www.ict-onefit.eu <http://www.ict-onefit.eu/>) Projects. This paper reflects only the authors' views and the Community is not liable for any use that may be made of the information contained therein.

References

1. ETSI, TC RRS, Reconfigurable Radio Systems (RRS); Functional Architecture (FA) for the Management and the Control of Reconfigurable Radio Systems, Technical Report 102 682 v1.1.1 (July 2009)

2. Dimitrakopoulos, G., Demestichas, P., Saatsakis, A., Tsagkaris, K., Galani, A., Gebert, J., Nolte, K.: Functional Architecture for the Management and Control of Reconfigurable Radio Systems. IEEE Vehicular Technology Magazine 4(1), 42–48 (2009)

3. ETSI, TC RRS, Reconfigurable Radio Systems (RRS); Functional Architecture (FA) for the Management and the Control of Reconfigurable Radio Systems, Technical Report 102 682 v1.1.1 (July 2009)

4. E^3 Project Deliverable D2.3 Architecture, Information Model and Reference Points, Assessment Framework, Platform Independent Programmable Interfaces, Public dissemination (September 2009)

5. 3GPP TR 25.913 v9.0.0, Requirements for Evolved UTRA (E-UTRA) and Evolved UTRAN (E-UTRAN) (Release 9) (December 2009)

6. Kaloxylos, A., Rosowski, T., Tsagkaris, K., Gebert, J., Bogenfeld, E., Magdalinos, P., Galani, A., Nolte, K.: The E3 architecture for future cognitive mobile networks. In: Proc. 20th IEEE International Symposium on Personal, Indoor and Mobile Radio Communications (PIMRC 2009), Tokyo, Japan, September 13-16 (2009)

7. Nolte, K., Kaloxylos, A., Tsagkaris, K., Rosowski, T., Stamatelatos, M., Galani, A., Bogenfeld, E., Magdalinos, P., Tiemann, J., Arnold, P., Gebert, J., Von-Hugo, D., Alonistioti, N., Demestichas, P., Koenig, W.: The E3 architecture: Enabling future cellular networks with cognitive and self-x capabilities. in revision (minor) International Journal of Network Management, Wiley

8. FP7-EC ICT Project End-to-End Efficiency (E^3), https://www.ict-e3.eu

9. Buljore, S., Harada, H., Houze, P., Tsagkaris, K., Holland, O., Filin, S., Farnham, T., Nolte, K., Ivanov, V.: Architecture and Enablers for Optimised Radio Resource usage: The IEEE P1900.4 Working Group. IEEE Communications Magazine 47(1), 122–129 (2009)

10. IEEE Std 1900.4^{TM}-2009, IEEE Standard for Architectural Building Blocks Enabling Network-Device Distributed Decision Making for Optimized Radio Resource Usage in Heterogeneous Wireless Access Networks (January 2009)

11. Galani, A., Tsagkaris, K., Koutsouris, N., Demestichas, P.: Design and Assessment of Functional Architecture for Optimized Spectrum and Radio Resource Management in Heterogeneous Wireless Networks. International Journal of Network Management, Wiley (to appear)

12. ITU-T X.680: Information technology - Abstract Syntax Notation One (ASN.1): Specification of basic notation (2002)

13. ITU-T X.690: Information technology - Information technology – ASN.1 encoding rules: Specification of Basic Encoding Rules (BER), Canonical Encoding Rules (CER) and Distinguished Encoding Rules (DER) (2002)

14. ITU-T X.691: Information technology - Information technology – ASN.1 encoding rules: Specification of Packet Encoding Rules (PER) (2002)

15. ITU-T X.693: Information technology - Information technology – ASN.1 encoding rules: XML Encoding Rules (XER) (2001)

Image Quality Estimation
in Wireless Multimedia Sensor Networks:
An Experimental Study

Pinar Sarisaray Boluk[1], Kerem Irgan[2],
Sebnem Baydere[2], and A. Emre Harmanci[1]

[1] Istanbul Technical University, Istanbul, Turkey
pinar.sarisaray@bahcesehir.edu.tr, harmanci@itu.edu.tr
[2] Yeditepe University, Istanbul, Turkey
{sbaydere,kirgan}@cse.yeditepe.edu.tr

Abstract. Multimedia applications in wireless sensor networks
(WMSN) have stringent quality of service (QoS) requirements. In this
paper, we study image quality distortions due to packet losses in multi
hop WMSN. An experimental simulation and real testbed environment
has been setup to estimate the quality of the test images over 30,000
transmissions. Two scenarios are considered: in the first scenario, images
are watermarked with their replicas at the source node and an error concealment (EC) algorithm is employed at the sink. In the second scenario,
raw images are transmitted without any encoding. The empirical results
have revealed that there is a strong correlation between Peak-Signal-
To-Noise-Ratio (PSNR) values of the distorted images and packet loss
rate of the transmission route (PER). Moreover, the relationship is linear
when EC technique is used with an achievement over 25dB PSNR for
PER less than 0.6. This correlation is useful when designing QoS based
transport schemes.

Keywords: Image Transmission, Wireless Multimedia Sensor Networks,
WSN, TestBed, PSNR Estimation, Error Concealment, Watermarking.

1 Introduction

With the wireless multimedia sensor networks coming of age, a new field of
research is to investigate the use of multimedia sensors to monitor and transmit data in the form of image, video and audio. That is, many applications
necessitate efficient multimedia communication in sensor networks [1]. Due to
strict energy constraints of sensor nodes, majority of the studies are focused
on energy efficiency [2,3,4,5,6,7,5,8,9,10]. In [8], the authors present energy cost
comparisons associated with transmission of raw and jpeg compressed images
for a variety of processor-radio combinations. Their results show that depending
on the processor-radio combination, both compressed and uncompressed image transmission schemes may be among the most energy and time efficient

I. Tomkos et al. (Eds.): BROADNETS 2010, LNICST 66, pp. 226–241, 2012.

options. Moreover, works in [11] demonstrate that the complexity of popular image compression algorithms may lead to greater energy consumption than the transmission of the uncompressed image.

When transmitting images over WMSN the quality is constrained by packet losses due to failures and transmission errors. Even more, cumulative packet loss rate grows exponentially with respect to number of hops in multi hop settings. Packet loss tolerance of an image coded with classical compression algorithms (e.g., JPEG, JPEG2000, SPIHT) is very low [9]. Hence, in order to achieve required perceptual quality, reliable transport protocols, such as ARQ [12] or FEC [13] are needed at the intermediate nodes to deal with packet losses [14]. However, these transport schemes may not be suitable for WMSN due to their consequent delay and additional resource requirements. In this respect, error concealment (EC) approach has received particular attention as an effective mechanism that reconstructs the distorted multimedia data as closely as the original one without increasing the bandwidth demand as well as avoiding the burden of retransmissions and consequent delay [15]. Consequently, EC algorithms are promising candidates to alleviate packet losses due to errors and failures in WMSNs. In [16], we have shown that EC algorithm gives better delay and processing performance than FEC and ARQ methods in WMSN.

In this work, we elaborate on the effectiveness of the error concealment technique for the estimation of image quality in terms of PSNR. In spite of many studies related to energy efficiency, to the best of our knowledge, image quality performance and the impact of multi hop in WMSN is not well studied in the literature.

PSNR is a full reference metric which identifies the degree of distortions in an image by comparing the pixel values with the corresponding values in the original image. However, in networked multimedia applications, in order to measure the quality of the transmitted image, the original may not be available for referencing at the sink. The motivation behind this study is to find a correlation between a measurable network parameter; ie. dropped packets rate; and the PSNR value of the transmitted image so that the quality can be estimated at the sink.

A comprehensive set of simulations are carried out in two different settings; In the first setting, the EC algorithm is used for quality enhancement. In the second, raw images are simply transmitted without any encoding. The performance of these schemes is analyzed for singlepath and disjoint multipath transmission scenarios. The simulation results are also validated in a real testbed, which is shown in Figure 2.

The results indicate that there is a promising theoretical relationship between cumulative packet loss rate (PER) over the transmission path and the quality of the degraded image in terms of PSNR. Moreover, PSNR values are linearly correlated with PER when EC technique is used. Since mapping an application quality metric to a network parameter is useful when designing QoS algorithms, we believe that this relationship is worth for further investigation. The rest of the paper is organized as follows: Section 2 introduces the system model and the EC algorithm. Section 3 gives the analysis of transmission schemes in terms of packet loss rate. Section 4 describes simulation methodology. Section 4.1 present quality estimation results. Section 4.2 presents the performance analysis and real testbed results. Finally, Section 6 concludes with discussions and future work.

2   System Model

Figure 1 depicts the considered system, entailing two types of sensors; Type 1 C_i, i=1,2...W sensors are equipped with camera and Type 2 S_{ij}, i=1,2...W_1, j=1,2...W_2, sensors are simple routing sensors. C_i's and the sink's capability is higher than that of the S_{ij}'s in terms of energy, processing power, and storage capacity. $N_1 \times N_2$ 8-bit grayscale images are partitioned into $s \times s$ pixel macro-

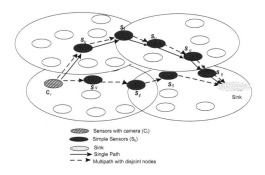

Fig. 1. General WMSN scenario

blocks at the source node. Each macro-block is transmitted in a separate network packet towards the sink over a single path or disjoint multipath. So the number of distinct data packets to be transmitted are $N = N_1 \times N_2/s^2$ per image. Two construction schemes are considered: in the first scheme, the images are transmitted in their raw form (NC) and in the second, images are encoded using the following error concealment (EC) algorithm.

2.1   EC Algorithm

The EC algorithm [1] employs a modified discrete wavelet transform (DWT) for embedding downsized replicas of original image into itself, thereby mitigating degradations in a backward-compatible scheme without increasing the total size of the data to be transmitted. Additionally, it corrects pixel and block losses due to transmissions using embedded replicas. We embed the replicas of the original

---

[1] An earlier version of this algorithm was presented at the 2007 IEEE/ACM International Symposium on Modelling, Analysis and Simulation of Computer and Telecommunication Systems (MASCOTS 2007) in part and was published in its proceedings.

Fig. 2. A view from testbed area

image's $M \times M$ macro-blocks in the sub-bands of the to-be-transmitted image, excluding LL (low-low) sub-bands, in order to limit the visual degradation. The host macro-blocks where replicas are embedded are chosen by using a shared-key-dependent pseudo-random sequence, so the extraction of the replicas is blind. If all of the replicas embedded in the sub-bands are lost, then each pixel in the lost macro-block is replaced by the median value of the sequence composed of non-zero values of neighboring macro-blocks' corresponding pixel. The detailed algorithm can be described as follows:

At the Source Nodes $\mathbf{C}_j$,

1. Capture the original image, I, with size of $N_1 \times N_2$ pixels.
2. If there are macro-blocks consisting of all 0's, then replace a pixel value in each of these macro-blocks with 1. This step facilitates fragile watermarking for error detection, and is inspired by work of Kundur et al [17].
3. Take l^{th} level pyramid-structured DWT of the original image I. Note that $k \geq l$, where k is the number of levels of the tree structured DWT.
4. Store each $(M/2^k) \times (M/2^k)$ macro-block of the tree structured DWT of the original image, namely replicas.
5. Scale each replica by the designated coefficient, then embed that scaled replica in each pyramid-structured wavelet sub-band, excluding LL ones, by using shared-key dependent sequence for each individual sub-band. Note that step 4 to 6 actualizes robust watermarking schema, which uses repeated watermark technique which is a modified version of the method studied by Kundur et al. [18].

6. Take inverse DWT (IDWT) of the watermarked image, namely IWM, and round the floating-point pixel values to the corresponding integer values.

At the Sink,

1. Read the received image, I_{rec}, and determine the lost pixels by searching blocks consisting of 0's. Thus, we utilize fragile watermarks in this step for error-detection.
2. Take l^{th} level pyramid-structured DWT of the received image I_{rec}.
3. By generating shared-key dependent random sequence, which was also used in the encoder, determine the location of lost pixels' replicas for each individual sub-band.
4. Multiply each replica with the known scaling coefficient used in encoder and take k^{th} level IDWT of the extracted replicas.
5. If there is more than one non-zero extracted pixels, take average of all those non-zero values, then place that average into the received image, I_{rec}, as the lost pixels. After this process is finished, the extracted image, I_{ext} is constructed.
6. Scan I_{ext} for lost blocks, which could not be healed. If there are still blocks consisting of all 0's, then replace them with the median value of the neighboring healthy blocks. After this process, the healed image I_{healed} is constructed in the sink.

2.2   Image Quality

In this study, image quality is measured as the mean squared error (MSE) value which is defined as

$$MSE = \frac{1}{N_1 \times N_2} \sum_{i}^{N_1} \sum_{i}^{N_2} \left[I(i,j) - \widehat{I}(i,j) \right]^2 \tag{1}$$

where $I(i,j)$ and $\widehat{I}(i,j)$ are the pixel values of the original and reconstructed images respectively. We use the following PSNR metric which is

$$PSNR(dB) = 20 \log_{10} \frac{2^n - 1}{\sqrt{MSE}} \tag{2}$$

where $n = 8$ for 8-bit grayscale images and $(2^n - 1)$ is the largest possible value of the signal.

3   Image Transmission Model

In this section, we provide an analysis of the packet loss rate (PER) for single path and disjoint multipath transport schemes in multi hop network.

Disjoint multipath transmission is employed to provide fault tolerance at the expense of increased bandwidth usage and processing overhead. In this scheme, captured images are transmitted through diverse paths to improve the perceptual quality of the received image at the sink. Disjoint multipath transmission scheme constructs n_p disjoint paths ($n_p = 2$ in our case). These parallel streams may independently suffer from node failures and channel impairments. Therefore, received redundant images may include both lost and correct pixel values. However, the likelihood of simultaneous losses on all paths is lower than losses a on single path. This probabilistic leverage facilitates an additional robustness of multipath transmission. Disjoint multipath scheme also utilizes a simple fusion algorithm namely *select max* on the sink. The algorithm performs fusion in the pixel value domain by selecting for each fused pixel the input coefficient with the largest absolute value. The block diagram of this operation is depicted in Figure 3.

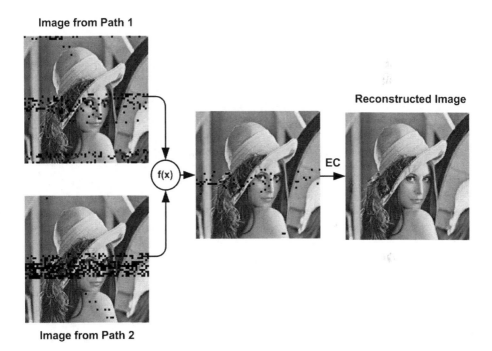

Fig. 3. An illustration of Error Concealment over Disjoint Multipath (ECDP)

3.1 Packet Loss Analysis

First, we start with the analysis of the simplest case, where there is a transmission over two parallel paths of two hops as depicted in Figure 4. For this case, packet loss means that the packet is lost on both paths. The packet carrying an image block is either lost on the first hop, which gives p, or it is not lost on the first

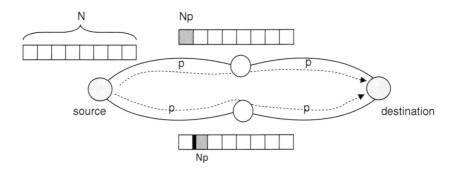

Fig. 4. Multipath transmission using two parallel paths

hop but lost on the second hop, which gives $(1-p)p$. Adding these probabilities, we get

$$PER_1^2 = (p) + ((1-p)p) = 2p - p^2 \tag{3}$$

PER_1^2 corresponds to the probability of loss over *two* hops for the *single* path case. We should multiply this probability by itself since we need to have simultaneous failures in two paths case. This yields:

$$PER_2^2 = (2p - p^2)^2 \tag{4}$$

Generalizing the above analysis, for n_p paths each with n_h hops we get

$$PER_{n_p}^{n_h} = [1 - (1-p)^{n_h}]^{n_p} \tag{5}$$

Hence, if we have N Blocks transmitted from the source towards the sink, the number of lost blocks x will be given as

$$x = N \cdot [1 - (1-p)^{n_h}]^{n_p} \tag{6}$$

4   Experimental Setup

We established an experimental setup to analyze the image quality for three transport variants:

1. No error concealment (NC)
2. Error Concealment over single path (EC)
3. Error Concealment over disjoint multipath (ECDP).

Scheme (I) is the simplest case selected as a baseline for performance improvement. In this scheme, we consider transmitting 256×256 pixels grayscale raw images tiled with 4×4 macro-blocks from source to destination on a single path, subject to certain channel and radio impairments. Scheme (II) employs the error

concealment algorithm on a single path. Scheme (III) employs the error concealment algorithm on two disjoint paths. In this scheme, a simple fusion algorithm
is applied to the replicas at the sink.

To study the effect of the physical layer on the quality of the transmitted
image we assumed a log log-normal shadow fading channel using NRZ encoding
and NCFSK modulation as proposed in [19]. From the model, packet error rate
p for distance d is obtained as follows:

$$p(d) = 1 - \left(1 - \frac{1}{2} \exp^{-\frac{\gamma(d)}{2}}\right)^{8f} \tag{7}$$

where f is the frame size, d is the transmitter-receiver distance,$\gamma(d)$ is the signal
to noise ratio (SNR).

We have conducted a comprehensive set of simulation experiments under Matlab to study the correlation between cumulative PER and PSNR values as presented in Section 4.1. We then conducted various performance tests to analyze
the effectiveness of the EC scheme for different network design forces. Finally,
we have validated our results on a real testbed with Tmote Sky wireless sensor
nodes as explained in Section 5.

In the simulation experiments, we used thirty different grayscale test images
of size 256×256 pixels for quality estimation. The results for only five different
images are given due to the size constraints in the graphics. However, the results
for the other images were similar to the ones that are presented.

4.1   Image Quality Estimation

For image quality estimation, thirty test images are impaired under a certain
percentage of the packet loss. Then, the quality of the impaired images are
evaluated in terms of PSNR for NC and EC schemes. A regression analysis is
performed on the results as follows:

For NC: first, PSNR values vs PER are drawn onto a scatter plot as shown
in Figure 5. The least-squares, fit through the points, are calculated by using
a logarithmic equation as a function of (x); i.e number of lost packets. The
regression equation for Lena image is calculated as:

$$PSNR_{NC} = -4,375ln\,(x) + \ 41,502 \tag{8}$$

Where the regression value that reflects the proportion of variation explained
by the regression curve for Lena image is 0.99. Since the same curve fitting with
close variations for all test images are obtained we can generalize the above
formula for NC as:

$$PSNR_{NC} = \alpha ln\,(x) + \ \beta \tag{9}$$

where α is a constant, which can be obtained through curve fitting over empirical
data and β is the reference quality value of the image in the case of a single block
loss. In the calculation of β, firstly, every possible single block of the image is

lost, then quality of the impaired image is calculated in terms of PSNR. Then β is acquired by taking the average of the PSNR values.

For EC: the effect of EC algorithm on the quality of the received image is evaluated by taking the same steps as explained above. Again, the results for five images are given in Figure 6. The regression equation obtained for Lena image (with proportion of variation 0.97) is given as:

$$PSNR_{EC} = -0,0032x + 31,63 \tag{10}$$

Due to similar behavior with close variations in all test images, the above equation can be generalized for EC as follows:

$$PSNR_{EC} = \alpha'x + \beta' \tag{11}$$

where β' is the quality of the watermarked image in case of a single block loss of the watermarked image and α' is a constant obtained from the empirical tests. As can be seen from the scatter plots and the equations (9) and (11),

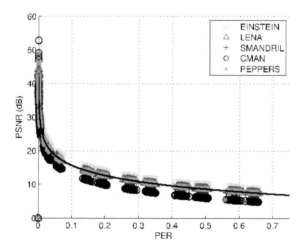

Fig. 5. Scatter plot of PSNR vs. PER and logarithmic least squares fitted curve for transmitted raw images

the relationship between the number of lost packets and PSNR is converted to a linear function with EC algorithm. Moreover, the algorithm achieves image quality over 25dB when PER is less than 0.6 for all test images.

The equations (9) and (11) can further be generalized for a multi hop path by replacing x with equation (6) as given below:

$$PSNR_{NC} = \alpha ln(N[1 - (1 - p)^{n_h}]^{n_p}) + \beta \tag{12}$$

$$PSNR_{EC} = \alpha'(N[1 - (1 - p)^{n_h}]^{n_p}) + \beta' \tag{13}$$

These equations are also verified with the testbed results in Section 5.

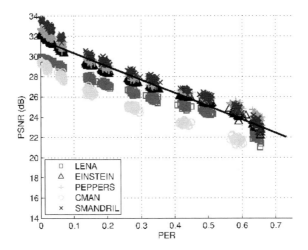

Fig. 6. Scatter plot of PSNR vs. PER and logarithmic least squares fitted curve for transmitted watermarked images

4.2 Performance Analysis

In this section, we present simulation and theoretical estimation results for NC, EC and ECDP schemes in terms of PSNR. For each test image, we run the simulations 50 times and obtain PSNR values together with the number of lost packets. We take the mean of these values as the result of the test. We then feed the number of lost packets to the equations (12) and (13) to obtain the corresponding theoretical estimation results. Estimated PSNR values are also plotted in the Figures so that the correlation between the real and estimated results can be seen.

Figure 7(a) shows the impact of the physical channel in terms of internode distances on the PSNR performance. The results show that NC scheme is the most susceptible scheme to channel impairments. It is also clear that NC scheme is not adequate to transmit images over WMSN. EC and ECDP schemes are more robust to packet losses. For EC scheme, PSNR slowly decreases from 34 dB to 25 dB for varying distances. Figure 7(b) illustrates the PSNR performances versus number of hops, when the distance between nodes is 6m. Range of improvement over NC is changing from 17 dB to 20dB when the distance between hops is 6m. Performance gain attained by integrating the EC and disjoint multipath transmission schemes is at most 4dB. Hence, the performance is not profoundly improved by ECDP.

5   Testbed

In order to verify the results of the simulations, we have established an indoor, 10-hops testbed by using 20 Tmote Sky sensor nodes [20]. We utilized TinyOS

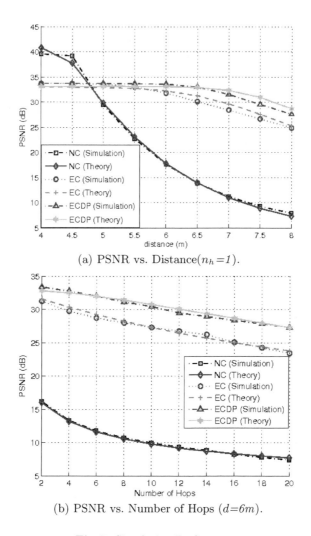

(a) PSNR vs. Distance($n_h = 1$).

(b) PSNR vs. Number of Hops ($d=6m$).

Fig. 7. Simulation Performance

v2.1 with nesC v1.3 [21] to realize a simple still-image transmission over a chain topology.

5.1   Node Deployment

We aim to achieve a clear line of sight between nodes and make them share the same communication medium to homogenize environmental effects on the communication channels. Therefore the tests are conducted inside a building with a large *atrium* as shown in Figure 2. Moreover, the nodes are partitioned into two groups (Group0 and Group1) and lined up vertically on thin linear sticks which are horizontally pointed out from the windows on the first floor, approximately 5m above from ground, with no obstacles between them. The distance between the groups is measured as 27m. The groups consist of five "hop couples" with intra and inter couple spacings of 4 and 17cm respectively. As depicted in Figure 8, the sticks equipped with the sensors nodes are positioned parallel to each other to complete a hypothetical rectangular area when looked from above. The output power of nodes is set to -3dBm. Each group is connected to a base station computer via self-powered USB hubs, in order to avoid performance variation due to power differences when they run on batteries.

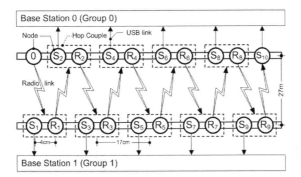

Fig. 8. Testbed Diagram

5.2   Image Transmission Setup

The actual image transmission scheme is as follows: A gray scale image, encoded with our EC algorithm, of 256x256 size is partitioned into 4x4 macro-blocks of 16B with extra 2B being used for the block offsets and sent over ten hops to the sink node. To make hop based PSNR comparisons accurately, it is necessary to get the packet loss patterns occurred in each hop at the same time, as conducting the tests on different time periods, and consequently on different diurnal conditions, causes dramatic changes in packet loss patterns. In the afternoon, for instance, we get very high PERs due to the noise induced by the crowd in the atrium, on the contrary, in the midnight we get low PERs. To satisfy these concurrency requirements, while transmitting an image over ten hops we record the intermediate results in each hop by using *snooping nodes*. In our image transmission scheme each hop consists of two nodes called *"hop couple"* which have the same node-id. In each hop couple, one of the nodes, called relay node (R_i, $i=0, 1 \ldots 9$), is used to send the incoming data to the other hop couple with consecutive node id via radio link, while the other node, called snooping node (S_i, $i=1, 2 \ldots 10$), is used to send the incoming data to the base station computer via USB link. There are only single nodes numbered with 0 and 10, as the source and the sink node respectively. The base station computers at each side records the image data along with RSSI (Received-Signal-Strength-Indicator) and LQI (Link-Quality-Indicator) values for each packet at each hop. To make more equitable comparisons of our EC algorithm for different images, the acquired image loss patterns are used as masks and projected to the other encoded test images, instead of repeating the tests for them. After the projections, the resulting images are decoded with our EC algorithm. The block diagram of this operation is given in Figure 9.

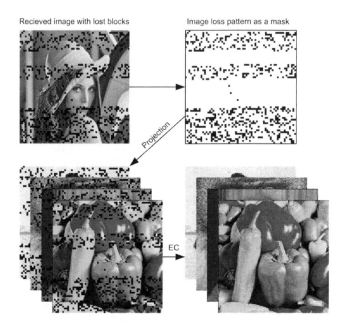

Fig. 9. Using image loss patterns as masks

The difficulties to establish a test setup for disjoint paths in a building with the requirements above, lead us to use another method to realize the tests for ECDP scheme. In this method, the tests taken place at the two different days are matched, and the images are fused as if they are coming from disjoint paths. Again, image loss patterns are extracted from the resulting images and projected to the other images as masks.

5.3   Testbed Results

We have conducted over 3000 image transmission tests spreading approximately 15 days. Over 30000 image loss patterns are gathered via 10 hops. The graphs, which show PSNR and PER relation for NC and EC scheme in Figure 10(a) and Figure 10(b), include all the results projected to five different images. It is obvious that the results of the real tests verify the simulation results depicted in Figure 5 and Figure 6. The results for EC scheme give us a threshold for PER as 0.6 to transmit an image within an acceptable quality.

To evaluate the effect of the number of hops on image tranmsission for all schemes, one-day-long tests within our result set are used. Only the tests from

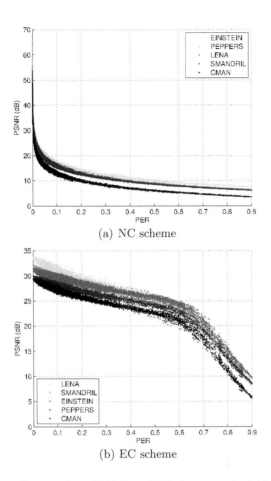

Fig. 10. Scatter plot of PSNR vs PER for on testbed ($d=27m$)

holiday days are used to avoid variance in packet loss patterns due to environmental changes. In the tests packet reception rates vary from 0.77 to 1.00. The values coming from real tests were applied to the equations (12) and (13) to obtain the theoretical results. Figure 11 shows the real results for all schemes combined with the theoretical calculations. Figure 12 represents the channel conditions of the testbed in terms of average LQI. Because the chosen channel conditions for the simulations are worse than the testbed conditions, the results are parallel to the simulations in short distances. The results of real tests again indicate the superior performance of EC scheme over NC scheme. And also by using ECDP scheme, a little gain can be achieved over EC scheme.

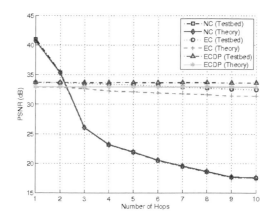

Fig. 11. PSNR vs Number of Hops on testbed $(d=27m)$

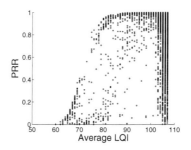

Fig. 12. PRR vs. Average LQI

6 Conclusion

We have shown that there is a correlation between PSNR values and the number of lost packets in a multi hop WMSN. Additionally, we have shown that when EC technique is used, PSNR value of the transmitted image is a linear function of the packet loss rate. Based on this theoretical relation, image quality requirements can be met by a transport protocol which statistically controls the cumulative packet error rate and guarantees the minimum required number of packets to be received at the sink.

We have also presented the effect of error concealment and multipath transmission on the quality of the raw images transmitted over WMSN. The simulation and real testbed results indicate that the EC algorithm is capable of restoring corrupted images, especially for high channel error conditions. Moreover, employing disjoint multipath transmission along with fusion at intermediate nodes brings further improvements on the received image quality.

References

1. Akyildiz, I., Melodia, T., Chowdhury, K.: A survey on wireless multimedia sensor networks. Computer Networks 51, 92–960 (2007)
2. Chow, K., Lui, K., Lam, E.: Efficient Selective Image Transmission in Visual Sensor Networks. In: IEEE 65th VTC, pp. 1–5 (2007)
3. Chen, M., Leung, V., Mao, S., Yuan, Y.: Directional geographical routing for real-time video communications in wireless sensor networks. Computer Communications 30, 3368–3383 (2007)
4. Dai, R., Akyildiz, I.F.: A spatial correlation model for visual information in wireless multimedia sensor networks. Trans. Multi. 11, 1148–1159 (2009)
5. Lee, H., Tessens, L., Morbee, M., Aghajan, H., Philips, W.: Sub-optimal Camera Selection in Practical Vision Networks through Shape Approximation. In: Blanc-Talon, J., Bourennane, S., Philips, W., Popescu, D., Scheunders, P. (eds.) ACIVS 2008. LNCS, vol. 5259, pp. 266–277. Springer, Heidelberg (2008)
6. Barr, K., Asanovic, K.: Energy-aware lossless data compression. ACM Transactions on Computer Systems (TOCS) 24, 291 (2006)
7. Wu, H., Abouzeid, A.: Energy efficient distributed JPEG2000 image compression in multihop wireless networks. In: IEEE ASWN, Citeseer, pp. 152–160 (2004)
8. Lee, D., Kim, H., Rahimi, M., Estrin, D., Villasenor, J.: Energy-efficient image compression for resource-constrained platforms. IEEE Transactions on Image Processing 18 (2009)
9. Pekhteryev, G., Sahinoglu, Z., Orlik, P., Bhatti, G.: Image transmission over IEEE 802.15. 4 and ZigBee networks. In: IEEE ISCAS, pp. 3539–3542 (2005)
10. Wu, H., Abouzeid, A.: Power aware image transmission in energy constrained wireless networks. In: ISCC, pp. 202–207 (2004)
11. Ferrigno, L., Marano, S., Paciello, V., Pietrosanto, A.: Balancing computational and transmission power consumption in wireless image sensor networks. In: IEEE VECIMS, p. 6 (2005)
12. Lin, S., Costello, D.: Error control coding: fundamentals and applications. Prenticehall, Englewood Cliffs (1983)
13. Zorzi, M.: Performance of FEC and ARQ error control in bursty channels under-delay constraints. In: 48th IEEE VTC, vol. 2 (1998)
14. Thomos, N., Boulgouris, N., Strintzis, M.: Optimized transmission of JPEG2000 streams over wireless channels. IEEE Transactions on Image Processing 15, 54–67 (2006)
15. Zhu, Q., Wang, Y.: Error Control and Concealment for Video Communication. In: Visual Information Representation, Communication, and Image Processing (1999)
16. Sarisaray, P., Gur, G., Baydere, S., Harmanc, E.: Performance Comparison of Error Compensation Techniques with Multipath Transmission in Wireless Multimedia Sensor Networks. In: 15th MASCOTS, pp. 73–86 (2007)
17. Kundur, D., Hatzinakos, D.: Digital watermarking for telltale tamper proofing and authentication. Proceedings of the IEEE 87, 1167–1180 (1999)
18. Kundur, D., Hatzinakos, D.: Toward robust logo watermarking using multiresolution image fusion principles. IEEE Transactions on Multimedia 6, 185–198 (2004)
19. Zuniga, M., Krishnamachari, B.: An analysis of unreliability and asymmetry in low-power wireless links. ACM Transactions on Sensor Networks (TOSN) 3, 7 (2007)
20. Crossbow, T.: TelosB Data Sheet, http://www.xbow.com/
21. Department, U.B.E.: TinyOS: An operating system for sensor networks, http://www.tinyos.net/

Detecting TCP Traffic Dynamical Changes in UMTS Networks

Ioannis Vasalos[1], Averkios Vasalos[2], and Heung-Gyoon Ryu[3]

[1] Newcastle University, UK
[2] University of Birmingham, UK
[3] Chungbuk National University, Korea
vasaloseng@googlemail.com, ecomm@cbu.ac.kr

Abstract. This paper presents a study of the methodology for the detection of congestion epochs and data transmission dynamical changes over mobile connections in the Universal Mobile Telecommunications System (UMTS) network. Dynamical changes in the data traffic occur in the Transmission Control Protocol (TCP), which is the protocol that regulates the data transmission inside the network. Using the concept of the recently introduced natural complexity measure of the Permutation Entropy (PE), the dynamical characteristics of the TCP inside the UMTS network are studied. It is shown that the PE can be effectively used to detect congestion epochs and the timely change in the dynamical pattern of the data transmission as regulated by the TCP. This is of crucial importance in order to prevent extended congestion epochs and the deterioration of the Quality of Service (QoS) in mobile networks.

Keywords: TCP, UMTS, Permutation Entropy, Data Traffic Dynamics, Network Congestion.

1 Introduction

Evolution in the field of communications has seen a phenomenal development in contemporary networks. Nowadays networks with different functional attributes and performance limits such as wired, wireless and mobile networks interoperate and form an extremely complex infrastructure. The emergence of this large scale network of networks has seen the formation of the Internet, which is one of the most complicated systems ever created. In particular UMTS networks, which are the latest generation of cellular mobile networks, amalgamate a wireless and wired infrastructure [1] in order to offer data services to the network's users. This heterogeneous network comprised by subnetworks with different fundamental architectures and different performance requirements is expected to function seamlessly allowing the smooth data traffic flow from the source to the destination node in order to offer users an increased QoS.

Teletraffic studies in wired communication networks [2] and mobile communication networks [3, 4] showed that during peak traffic time, chaos and

I. Tomkos et al. (Eds.): BROADNETS 2010, LNICST 66, pp. 242–255, 2012.

persistent oscillations appear through the network. The nature of these effects can be targeted on the Additive Increase Multiplicative Decrease (AIMD) dynamics of the Transmission Control Protocol (TCP) that networks use in order to offer a connection oriented reliable byte stream service. Crucially Veres and Boda [5] were the first to demonstrate how the TCP congestion control can show chaotic behaviour. Complementary research by Rao et al [6], analytically presented that TCP can generate bounded trajectories with a complicated attractor and its dynamics embed a tent like map for the update of the packet transmission window size, which generates chaotic dynamics. Relative research in mobile UMTS networks, as it is presented in [3, 4], showed that under increased traffic load in moderate radio conditions the TCP data traffic dynamics of Mobile Stations (MS) range from periodically stable to chaotic with a direct impact on the QoS of service of the network. Such impact is expressed by significantly decreased data throughputs, unfairness in resource allocation to the network users and increased delays in data application performance. Therefore timely detection of dynamical changes and of the appearance of chaotic dynamics in the UMTS network traffic profile is a crucial problem in order to maintain the network's integrity and guarantee the QoS as perceived from the users.

Research focused on the detection of anomalies of the network dynamics, among others, is presented in [7, 8] where space-time characteristics of congestion in large networks and the system behaviour relative to the levels of congestion is studied. A macroscopic level method is established to simulate a network of thousands of on-off traffic sources creating congestion in various locations of the network. The research is focused on how to locate network bottlenecks and how to detect possible Distributed Denial of Service (DDoS) attacks by studying the spatio-temporal traffic dynamics. Furthermore in [9] the phase transition between congested and non-congested phases in the Internet is studied to quantify the probabilities of network congestion according to the dynamic complexity of the Internet traffic. In [10] probability distributions of several network long-term traffic measures such as the source IP address, the destination IP address and data flow size are studied to create a unique fingerprint of the traffic profile of the network under consideration. In case this profile changes, as measured by the Information Entropy, anomalies in the network behaviour can be detected.

Methods presented above for the detection of dynamical changes in the network traffic regard macroscopic network models and require long-term observation of network dynamics. Therefore according to our literature review there is an open question for algorithms that can detect fast and efficiently real-time dynamical changes and anomalies in the traffic profile of communication networks. To answer this question in this paper the methodology of the Permutation Entropy (PE) is considered. In the seminal paper of Band and Pompe [11], the concept of the PE is introduced as a complexity measure for time series analysis. The methodology is verified in [12] to be a conceptually simple and computationally very fast algorithm for the quantification of the complexity of a time series produced by a complex system and the detection of dynamical changes in the time series of the system.

Following the aforementioned research [3, 4] on the chaotic dynamics developed in the traffic profile of the TCP traffic flow inside the UMTS network, research in this paper is focused on the quantification of the complexity and the detection of dynamical changes of the TCP traffic profile time series in the UMTS network. We propose the utilisation of the PE to detect dynamical changes and network anomalies in the TCP traffic flow. The framework of the methodology is based on the hypothesis that when normal traffic with fairness and QoS exist inside the network, the traffic profile should have a certain measure of complexity as determined by the PE. Consequently, possible variations of the PE could detect dynamical changes and anomalies inside the network. Such information along with the impact of this behaviour on the QoS of the UMTS network can be used as a real-time, computationally fast algorithm to detect anomalies in the network and provision the network in order to guarantee the QoS and ensure the network's functionality.

The remainder of this paper is organized as follows. Section 2 presents the TCP algorithm and its dynamical behaviour analysis. Additionally the motivation of the research on the UMTS network as the network currently used globally for mobile communications is explained. Section 3 introduces the concept of PE as a measure of time series complexity and Section 4 presents the network simulation model. Section 5 presents the results of the PE for characterisation of the complexity and the detection of dynamical changes in the TCP traffic flow time series along with the impact of dynamic complexity on the QoS of the network. Finally Section 6 concludes the paper.

2   TCP Dynamical Behaviour

TCP is the network protocol that provides a connection-oriented, reliable byte stream service over the Internet. Reliability in the TCP connection between the sender and the receiver in the network is guaranteed through a set of rules that for each packet sent by the sender the receiver acknowledges each packet sent. When packets are lost in the network the receiver using timer and packet sequence number information notifies the sender that packets that have not arrived on time are lost in the network. Fundamentally the TCP relies on two mechanisms to regulate the flow of data: flow control and congestion control. The flow control ensures that the sender does not overflow the receiver buffer and the congestion control ascertains that the sender does not congest the network by exceeding the connection bandwidth and the buffer space at the network's queues. Assuming large receiver buffers, the dynamics of TCP traffic are generated by the congestion control mechanism. Fundamentally the congestion control mechanism uses strict deterministic rules in order to regulate the transmission rate of the sender by controlling the congestion window $w(t)$. This is the maximum number of unacknowledged packets the sender can send to the destination before it stops and waits for an acknowledgment. From the congestion window, the throughput s of each TCP is specified by the number of packets over the Round Trip Time (RTT).

$$s(t) = \frac{w(t)}{RTT} \ . \tag{1}$$

RTT is the time from when a packet was sent from the sender until its acknowledgment was received. If a network is assumed with a total of N nodes and $n \in N$ number of queues with queue size q and $n \in N$ number of relative links with bandwidth B and propagation delay D, then the RTT is defined as the sum of propagation delays D and queuing delays $\dfrac{q^n}{B^n}$.

$$RTT = \sum_{n \in N} D^n + \frac{q^n}{B^n} \ . \tag{2}$$

The strict deterministic rules that define the data flow and the TCP dynamical behavior are categorized into four main dynamical modes. These are *slow-start, congestion-avoidance, Fast Retransmit/ Fast Recovery (FR/FR)* and *timeout* modes and form the Additive Increase Multiplicative Decrease (AIMD) congestion control mechanism. The detailed rules for each dynamical mode vary along with the version of the TCP used. In this paper the dynamical behavior of the TCP SACK protocol is studied. TCP SACK has being tested over various wireless networks [13, 14] to achieve the best throughput over wireless links. So it is the preferred version of the protocol to be used in the UMTS network modeled in this paper. A brief presentation of the four dynamical models is presented.

1) *Slow-start* mode: When a connection is initiated the TCP enters *slow-start* mode and the congestion window is increased very rapidly with an exponential rate being multiplied by 2 every RTT. This is modelled by

$$\frac{d}{dt} w(t) = \frac{\log 2}{RTT} w(t) \ . \tag{3}$$

2) *Congestion-avoidance* mode: When the congestion window reaches the advertised window of the receiver the system switches to congestion-avoidance mode. During congestion control the congestion window size increases linearly with an increase equal to the packet-size L every RTT

$$\frac{d}{dt} w(t) = \frac{L}{RTT} \ . \tag{4}$$

Slow start and congestion avoidance modes last until a drop or a timeout are detected. Detection of a drop leads the system to *FR/FR* mode, whereas the detection of a timeout leads the system to timeout mode.

3) *Fast Retransmit/Fast Recovery (FR/FR)* mode: When congestion occurs and packets are dropped, TCP SACK *FR/FR* mode immediately decreases the congestion window by half and immediately retransmits the missing segments. Once acknowledgements for the retransmitted packets arrive the sender leaves fast recovery mode and switches again to congestion avoidance mode. It has to be noted, that for our system, since selective acknowledgement is used in the protocol, for every

window of packets dropped TCP enters only one time fast recovery, since it knows exactly which packets are dropped. Considering w^{CA} as the last value of the congestion window in the congestion avoidance mode, the evolution of the congestion window is expressed as

$$w(t) = \frac{w^{CA}}{2} \,.$$

(5)

4) *Timeout mode*: Finally a timeout occurs when the retransmission timer of a packet sent expires. The congestion window is reset to 1, and *slow-start* as described before repeats.

In general apart from the initiation of the connection, TCP mainly operates between *congestion-avoidance* and *FR/FR* modes. *Timeout* and *slow-start* are used when severe packet losses occur in a network. The dynamics of the TCP algorithm can be described by two main dynamical modes. Mode 1 *congestion-avoidance* and mode 2 *FR/FR*. In mode 1 TCP starts sending packets with a rate proportional to the reception of acknowledgments from the receiver. Mode 2 is entered when packet loss occurs and the congestion window is halved. The TCP dynamics are due to the "gluing together" of mode 1 and mode 2 [6]. These are directly related to the level of traffic congestion inside the network, expressed by the number of TCP traffic flows sending traffic through the network and the packets buffered at the queues inside the network.

From [15] it is known that chaos is the aperiodic, long-term behaviour of a bounded system that exhibits sensitive dependence to initial conditions. As it is analytically and experimentally studied for a wired network in [6] and for a UMTS network in [3, 4], in case of stable RTT delays, dynamics alternate between congestion avoidance and *fast retransmit/fast recovery* mode in a stable cycle and hence create periodic trajectories. However when the traffic load increases, queues get congested much faster and multiple losses occur that makes the RTT exhibit large variations. When the RTT loses stability due to high levels of lost packets in the network the trajectories in one mode will enter the other generating bounded trajectories, which create aperiodic routes, which under circumstances can be chaotic.

2.1   TCP over UMTS

In mobile networks the problem of the complexity of the network dynamics is aggravated by the wireless nature of the system. As analysed in [3, 4] instability in the network is further invoked by the variable restricted wireless bandwidth, the user mobility and the interference of the physical environment. These inherent characteristics of the mobile network cause increased round trip time and increased packet loss probability, which is well-known to severely affect the throughput performance of the TCP. In UMTS the Radio Link Control (RLC) protocol is used to recover lost packets from the radio access network by using an Automatic Repeat Request (ARQ) algorithm. Although this minimises packet loss probability, it increases RTT because of the link layer retransmission of lost frames. Since the TCP protocol remains unchanged for wired and wireless applications, these fundamental parameters are not implemented in the protocol. Under such interference it is possible that TCP measures and adapts to congestion erroneously, inserting more instability to the network dynamics due to nonlinear chaotic behaviour and unpredictability due to stochasticity from packet losses in the whole system.

For the reasons discussed above it is very crucial to study the TCP behaviour inside the wireless system in order to quantify the complexity of the dynamics developed in the TCP traffic profile. Such knowledge would allow the creation of congestion control mechanisms able to detect changes in the network dynamics and act accordingly to control and suppress such anomalies inside the UMTS. In this paper we focus on the implementation of the PE for the quantification and detection of dynamical changes and postpone the discussion of mechanisms for the control of such phenomena for a future study.

3   Permutation Entropy Definition

Permutation entropy is introduced in the paper of Band and Pompe [11] as the methodology of transforming a time series of a dynamical system into a symbolic sequence. The method relies on the embedding theorem [15], which states that when a dynamical system has an attractor with box-counting dimension D_f the complete dynamical and topological properties of the original system can be studied from a single scalar time series using an embedding dimension $m > 2D_f$. In this case the TCP protocol is considered as the dynamical system, whose dynamical properties through the PE measurements will be studied from the single scalar time series of the congestion window. The methodology as presented in [11, 12] includes the embedding of a scalar time series creating vectors of the form $X_i = (x_i, x_{i+L}, \ldots x_{i+(m-1)L})$ where m is the embedding dimension, L is the delay time and $(m-1)L$ is the embedding window. In the scalar time series we consider all the $m!$ permutations. In order to create a symbolic sequence for any vector each real value of the X_i vector is rearranged in an increasing order and it is assigned to a symbolical corresponding j value with increasing order where $j = j_0, j_1, j_2, \ldots, j_{m-1}$. Finally a new vector X_j is created where each symbolical value of j is rearranged in the position of the original X_i vector. Hence as it is explained in [12] any vector X_i is uniquely mapped onto $j_0, j_1, j_2 \ldots j_{m-1}$, which is one of the $m!$ permutations of m distinct symbolical values $(0, 1, 2, \ldots, m-1)$. When each such permutation is considered as a symbol, the reconstructed trajectory in the m-dimensional space is represented by a symbol sequence. The Permutation Entropy (PE) is defined as a measure of the probabilities of the appearance of the permutations for each of the different $m!$ permutations. Considering the probability distribution for the appearance of distinct symbols as $P_1, P_2, \ldots P_l$ where $l \leq m$. The Permutation Entropy is defined as [11, 12]

$$H_m = -\sum_{j=1}^{l} P_j \ln P_j \ . \tag{6}$$

For example let us consider the embedded time series x= 10, 5, 7, 12, 4, 8, creating vectors X_i with three values. The vectors with three consecutive values that are created are: (10, 5, 7), (5, 7, 12), (7, 12, 4), (12, 4, 8). Following the methodology as described above, these correspond to the symbolic X_j vectors: (2, 0, 1), (0, 1, 2), (1, 2, 0), (2, 0, 1). Hence from eq. 6 the PE of order $m = 3$ is

$$H_3 = -\frac{2}{4}\ln\left(\frac{2}{4}\right) - 2 \cdot \frac{1}{4}\ln\left(\frac{1}{4}\right) \approx 1.0397 \ .$$

It is clear that for a completely random system where the time series of the system will be an Independent and Identically Distributed (i.i.d) sequence the probability distribution for any symbol would be $P_j = 1/m!$. Then for a sequence of values the PE would be $H_m = \ln(m!)$ which is the maximum value H_m can acquire. Accordingly when a time sequence has only a certain value sequence or a constantly decreasing or increasing time series the PE will be $H_m = 0$. In order to define a specific upper bound, H_m is normalized by $\ln(m!)$. Hence the range of values of the normalized Permutation Entropy H_m is $0 \le H_m \le 1$. This is verified in [11, 12] where application of the PE to an i.i.d sequence measured $H_m = 1$. Accordingly application of the PE to the chaotic time series data of the transient logistic chaotic map and the transient Lorenz chaotic attractor measured $H_m < 1$. In general the PE is a measure of the dynamics of the time series, and the more irregular the time series is, the larger value the PE acquires.

4   Methodology

In order to evaluate the dynamics of the TCP protocol inside the UMTS network, we select to measure each TCP's congestion window $w(t)$ as a representative of the protocol behaviour. The congestion window is directly related to the nonlinear equations that govern the TCP data rate and congestion avoidance. The network model is built using the OPNET□ modeller and consists of a typical UMTS network architecture [1]. The simulation parameters settings for the network model scenario are detailed in Table.1. The most important parameters for the research objectives include settings for the TCP algorithm, the radio-air interface, the QoS configuration and the RLC channel.

We focus our study on the scenario where 2 Mobile Stations (MSs) are considered to send information on the uplink using the TCP SACK, sending data files with the File Transfer Protocol (FTP) to an FTP server in the wired part of the network. In order to simulate a network with increased traffic load a drop-tail router inside the network is considered as a bottleneck in the network, served by a 200 kbps throughput link with a bottleneck queue of 40 packets. The simulations are run for 800 seconds.

Table 1. Simulation parameters settings values

Network Parameter	Setting
TCP	
TCP Flavour	SACK
Maximum TCP/IP Packet Size	1500 bytes
Maximum Received Window	65535 bytes
Initial Window	1
Radio-Air Interface	
Cell Pathloss Model	Outdoor to Indoor Pedestrian Environment
Shadow Fading Standard Deviation	10 dB
QoS Configuration	
QoS Traffic Class	Background class
Maximum Bit Rate (Uplink/Downlink)	128 kbps
RLC Channel Configuration	
RLC Mode (Uplink/Downlink)	RLC Acknowledged Mode
Packet Unit (PU) Segmentation	Yes
In-Sequence Delivery of PU	No
Transmitting/Receiving Window	32 PU

The objective of the simulation is to test the network under different levels of congestion inside the network, which have proportional levels of packet drops. This is because we want to study how the PE measures the complexity of the traffic profile time series relative to the occurring congestion; and if it can detect dynamical changes in the traffic profile due to the different levels of the occurring congestion. Therefore the router is considered to serve on-off background traffic from a source sending traffic through the bottleneck buffer using the UDP protocol. As shown in [16], use of 10% UDP traffic is adequate in order to ensure random packet loss in the router queues. The experimental procedure consists of increasing the level of background traffic from 40 to 80 kbps served by the router and examining the dynamic behaviour of the congestion window of each mobile station's TCP as well as QoS measurements of MS throughput inside the UMTS network.

In order to acquire the PE measurement from the time series of the TCP congestion window, initially the 800 seconds time series is partitioned into small vectors of data. The data blocks are embedded using the optimal embedding dimension m and delay time L, which are calculated using the methodology as presented in [17]. For the TCP time series presented in this paper the optimal embedding parameters are

$m = 6$ and $L = 10$. From the embedded vectors, the PE H_6 is calculated as a function of time according to the blocks of data considered. The variations of the PE are expected to detect changes and anomalies in the TCP congestion window time series.

5   Results

In Fig. 1 and Fig. 2 plots of the temporal evolution of the TCP congestion windows along with the complexity measure of the PE of MS1 and MS2 are respectively presented. Plots (a) and (b) in each figure correspond to different levels of congestion for on-off UDP background traffic of 40 and 80 kbps respectively. In the plots windows as indicated by the dashed vertical lines are drawn to indicate a change of the dynamics in the evolution of the congestion window. The windows are drawn to indicate when apparent dynamical changes occur inside the network.

As it is presented in Fig. 1.a, from the congestion window temporal evolution graphs for 40 kbps background traffic, apart from the initiation of the connection where *slow-start* is performed, the congestion windows of MS1 and MS2 evolve in a stable pattern. This is portrayed in the temporal evolution of the PE measurement, which for the complete time duration of the simulation acquires values around 0.2. Additionally one small increase in the congestion window for MS1 as shown in Fig. 1.a with a relative decrease in the PE around the window of 400-450 seconds is observed. A similar phenomenon occurs for MS2 in Fig. 2.a in the window of 600-640 seconds.

As congestion increases for 80 kbps background traffic, it is observed from Figs. 1.b of MS1 and Figs 2.b of MS2 that the congestion window temporal evolution becomes much more irregular. As congestion increases and more packet drops occur inside the network, the size of the congestion windows gets significantly decreased. From the windows drawn by the dashed vertical lines it is observed that when congestion increases and the dynamics of the congestion window become irregular a sharp increase in the PE is observed. As an example we refer to the window from 230-400 seconds as observed for MS1 in Fig 1.b where a sharp increase in the PE is measured. Respectively MS2 in the same time window gets a decrease in the PE and although a timeout occurs around 310 seconds much larger values of congestion windows are observed. This indicates that the MS2 will achieve a better throughput with an increased QoS in this time window.

Similar observations are made for all the plots in Fig. 1 and Fig. 2. In general a sharp increase in the PE indicates the onset of a congestion epoch inside the network with more irregularity in the time series of the congestion window and more packet drops inside the network. That is why in the case of 80 kbps background traffic the measurements of PE temporal evolution mainly vary from 0.3 to 0.4. Additionally the decrease in the PE captures the transition from an increased congestion epoch to a more stable congestion window evolution where larger congestion windows are observed. Hence it is concluded that the PE can capture anomalies and changes in the dynamics of the TCP traffic flow and can be used as a measure of complexity for the quantification of the dynamics of the TCP traffic flow. Additionally it is highlighted that measurements of the PE for the traffic flows is very fast. For each simulated 800 second TCP time series, the processing of the PE lasted for less than one minute on a 2.26 GHz laptop pc. This is a seminal advantage of the PE as it can be used for online traffic monitoring applications for real-time detection of congestion epochs inside the network.

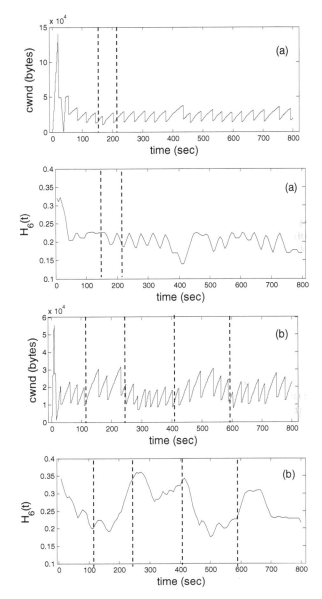

Fig. 1. MS1 temporal evolution of the TCP congestion window (cwnd) $w(t)$ and normalized Permutation Entropy H_p for background traffic of: (a) 40 kbps, (b) 80 kbps

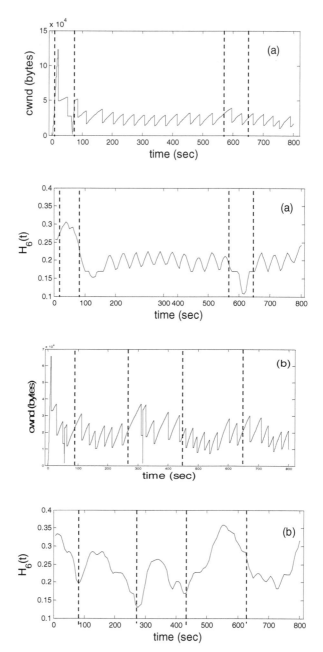

Fig. 2. MS2 temporal evolution of the TCP congestion window (cwnd) $w(t)$ and normalized Permutation Entropy H_p for background traffic of: (a) 40 kbps, (b) 80 kbps

The stable behaviour of the congestion windows for 40 kbps background traffic has a direct relation to the QoS as it is perceived from the average throughput for MS1 and MS2. As presented in Fig. 3.a both MSs average throughputs have close values along the temporal evolution of the simulation. Such a result indicates that both MSs use the network resources fairly and efficiently. On the contrary, as shown above from the PE measurements, the complexity of the dynamics of the congestion window increases as the traffic congestion increases at the simulations with background traffic of 80 kbps. As a consequence in Fig. 3.b MS1 has an average throughput reduced to around 20 kbps in comparison to MS2. Relatively in Fig. 3.c MS2 has an averaged throughput reduced to around 10 kbps in comparison to MS1. Therefore it is understood that the complex dynamics of the traffic profile have a direct impact on the QoS as perceived by the users in the network. Additionally loss of valuable radio resources of the UMTS network is observed as in both simulations MS1 is not transmitting packets up to its highest fair potential. This outcome is directly related with the appearance of chaotic dynamics that develop in the TCP traffic profile in congested networks as studied in [3, 4]. The chaotic dynamics are verified by the increased dynamic complexity as proved by the PE measurements.

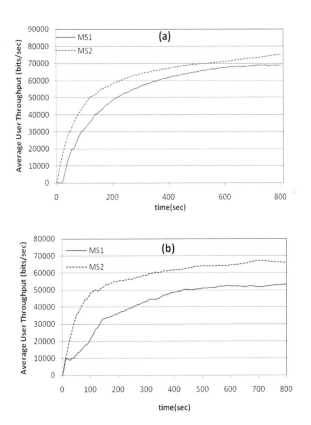

Fig. 3. Average MS1 and MS2 user throughput for background traffic of: (a) 40 kbps, (b) 80 kbps

6   Conclusions

This paper presented the feasibility of using the natural complexity measure of the PE in order to detect anomalies and dynamical changes in the temporal evolution of data transmission in UMTS networks. By analysis of the dynamics of the TCP traffic profile it is shown that the PE can accurately detect such dynamical changes using a computationally very quick algorithm. The PE is able to measure the complexity of the TCP time series as simulation results showed the increasing PE measurements relative to the increasing congestion levels in the network. Consequently the PE concept can be used for real-time monitoring of data traffic flows inside the UMTS, in order to prevent the prolonging of congestion epochs, or detect data traffic anomalies.

References

1. Walke, B.H.: Mobile Radio Networks, 2nd edn. Wiley, England (2002)
2. Pointon, C.T., Carrasco, R.A., Gell, M.A.: Complex Behaviour in Nonlinear Systems. In: Modelling Future Telecommunications Systems. BT Telecommunications Series, pp. 311–344. Chapman & Hall, England (1996)
3. Vasalos, I., Carrasco, R.A., Woo, W.L., Soto, I.: Nonlinear Complex Behaviour of TCP in UMTS Networks and Performance Analysis. IET Circuits Devices Syst. 2(1), 69–79 (2008)
4. Vasalos, I., Carrasco, R.A.: Dynamic Complexity of TCP in UMTS Networks and Performance Evaluation. In: IEEE ICWMC 2008, The Fourth International Conference on Wireless and Mobile Communications, pp. 253–259 (August 2008)
5. Veres, A., Boda, M.: The Chaotic Nature of TCP Congestion Control. In: IEEE INFOCOM, pp. 1715–1723 (March 2000)
6. Rao, N.S.V., Gao, J., Chua, L.O.: On Dynamics of Transport Protocols over Wide-Area Internet Connections. In: Kocarev, L., Vattay, G. (eds.) Complex Dynamics in Communication Networks, Springer Complexity 2005. Springer, Heidelberg (2005)
7. Yuan, J., Mills, K.: Exploring Collective Dynamics in Communication Networks. Journal of Research of the National Institute of Standards and Technology 107(2), 179–191 (2002)
8. Yuan, J., Mills, K.: Monitoring the Macroscopic Effect of DDoS Flooding Attacks. IEEE Trans. on Dependable and Secure Computing 2(4), 324–335 (2005)
9. Takayasu, M., Tretyakov, A., Fukuda, K., Takayasu, H.: Phase Transition and 1/f Noise in the Internet Packet Transport. In: Schreckenberg, M., Wolf, D.E. (eds.) Traffic and Granular Flow, pp. 57–67. Springer, Singapore (1998)
10. Nucci, A., Bannerman, S.: Controlled Chaos. IEEE Spectrum, 37–42 (December 2007)
11. Band, C., Pompe, B.: Permutation Entropy – A Natural Complexity Measure for Time Series. Phys. Rev. Lett. 88, 174102 (2002)
12. Cao, Y., Tung, W.W., Gao, J.B., Protopopescu, V.A., Hively, L.M.: Detecting Dynamical Changes in Time Series. Phys. Rev. E 70, 046217 (2004)
13. Vangala, S., Labrador, M.A.: The TCP SACK aware Snoop Protocol for TCP over Wireless Networks. In: IEEE 58th Vehicular Technology Conf., vol. 4(6-9), pp. 2624–2628 (October 2003)

14. Huang, J.J., Chang, J.F.: A New Method to Improve the Performance of TCP SACK over Wireless Links. In: IEEE 57th Vehicular Technology Conference, vol. 3, pp. 1730–1734 (April 2003)
15. Alli, K.T., Sauer, T.D.: Chaos an Introduction to Dynamical Systems. Springer, New York (1996)
16. Bohacek, S., Hespanha, J.P., Lee, J., Obraczka, K.: A Hybrid Systems Modeling Framework for Fast and Accurate Simulation of Data Communication Networks. In: ACM SIGMETRICS (June 2003)
17. Gao, J.B., Zheng, Z.M.: Direct dynamical test for deterministic chaos and optimal embedding of a chaotic time series. Phys. Rev. E 49, 3807–3814 (1994)

Binary Symmetric Channel Based Aggregation with Coding for 802.11n WLANs[*]

Xiaomin Chen, Vijay G. Subramanian, and Douglas J. Leith

Hamilton Institute, NUI Maynooth, Ireland
{Xiaomin.Chen,Vijay.Subramanian,Doug.Leith}@nuim.ie

Abstract. In this paper we present the first detailed theoretical analysis of the potential performance gains of adopting a BSC paradigm in 802.11 WLANs. Importantly, we also consider the multi-user channel aspect of a WLAN i.e. that transmissions are inherently broadcast in nature. We find that increases in network throughput of more than 100% are possible over a wide range of SNRs. These performance gains are achieved exclusively through software rather than hardware changes.

Keywords: binary symmetric channel, packet aggregation, superposition coding, multi-user channel.

1   Introduction

In this paper we consider the potential benefits of viewing the channel provided by an 802.11 WLAN as a binary symmetric channel (BSC), as opposed to a more conventional packet erasure channel (PEC). That is, rather than simply discarding corrupted frames, we consider viewing a received frame as a binary vector in which an unknown subset of bits have been "flipped". Although some bits are corrupted/flipped, we can often still extract useful information from corrupted frames thereby increasing the effective transmit rate between wireless stations. This is motivated by a number of observations.

Firstly, for 802.11a/g it has been shown in [1] using experimental measurements that even with a $10 - 30\%$ packet erasure rate typically only a small fraction (usually $< 1\%$) of the bits within corrupted packets are in error. Thus, although noisy, the corrupted packets potentially provide a reasonable channel through which we can transmit information. Modeling the bit error process as a BSC, a simple theoretical analysis (ignoring CSMA/CA features such as collision losses) indicates the potential for significant performance gains. For example, Fig. 1 compares the BSC throughput capacity versus the packet erasure throughput capacity for the set of modulations/rates available in 802.11a/g. See the next section for details on the calculations used to obtain this figure. It can be seen that throughput improvements of 100% or more are indicated over a wide range of SNRs.

---

[*] This material is based upon works supported by the Science Foundation Ireland under Grant No. 07/IN.1/I901.

I. Tomkos et al. (Eds.): BROADNETS 2010, LNICST 66, pp. 256–273, 2012.

Secondly, recent breakthroughs in efficient capacity-approaching error correction codes such as LDPC codes make these performance gains practically achievable. Since such coding would be introduced above the MAC layer, it is compatible with standard 802.11 hardware i.e. it requires only a software change and so the performance gains essentially come for "free".

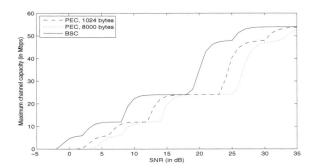

Fig. 1. 802.11a/g BSC and PEC capacities vs. SNR, Rayleigh physical channel. Packet erasure capacities are shown for frame sizes of both 1024 bytes and 8000 bytes.

Thirdly, this BSC paradigm dovetails with the trend towards greater decoupling of the unit of transmission (i.e. frames) used at the MAC/PHY layer from the unit of transmission (i.e. packets) used at the IP layer. For example, to maintain throughput efficiency at high PHY rates, the recent 802.11n standard [2] supports transmission of large frames formed by aggregating multiple packets together. This is because increasing PHY rates leads to faster transmission of the MAC frame payload, but overheads such as PHY headers and MAC contention time typically do not decrease at the same rate and thus begin to dominate the frame transmission time unless amortised across multiple packets, e.g. see [3]. A logical extension is to consider aggregation of packets destined to different receivers into a single MAC frame. Such multi-destination aggregation is currently the subject of much interest because we expect that often there simply may not be enough traffic to an individual destination to always allow large frames to be formed and the network efficiency quickly degrades when small frames are used. This scenario is particularly important for the higher PHY rates proposed for 802.11n [2] and when applications like VoIP [4,5], email and web-browsing are considered. Also, multicast traffic is expected to become increasingly important in WLANs in view of the escalating demand for real-time multimedia applications.

In [6,7] packet erasures are modelled assuming a bit-level BSC model, but the analysis is otherwise based on a packet erasure channel i.e. they do not consider the BSC paradigm of this paper. While [1] demonstrates that packets that fail the CRC check only have a few bits in error, the authors do not consider a BSC modeling paradigm and, in particular, the multi-user BSC paradigm that we are interested in.

Our contributions include:

- The first detailed theoretical analysis of the potential performance gains of adopting a BSC paradigm in 802.11 WLANs. This includes important 802.11 MAC features such as the framing overhead and the overhead of CSMA/CA contention and collisions.
- Consideration of the multi-user channel aspect of a WLAN in the context of the BSC paradigm, i.e. frame transmissions are inherently broadcast in nature and so may be received by multiple stations. We explore this for both unicast and multicast traffic. In the unicast case we consider, in particular, the potential performance gains of using a BSC paradigm for multi-destination aggregation.

2   Channel Models

We begin by reviewing the performance of the PHY layer modulation and FEC available in 802.11 a/g. Since 802.11n uses very similar modulation and FEC (adding a small number of additional OFDM tones and a new 5/6 code rate), our analysis carries over essentially unchanged for single antenna systems. We leave consideration of MIMO 802.11n systems as future work.

2.1   Packet Erasure Rate of Rayleigh Channel

The indoor fading environment is modelled as a Rayleigh channel. Assuming hard-decision Viterbi decoding is used, analytic expressions for the bit error rate (BER) when using each of the various 802.11a/g modulations are described in [8]. The analysis considers Nakagami-m fading channels, and we note that a Rayleigh channel corresponds to a Nakagami channel with $m = 1$. The demodulation BER needs to be adjusted to take account of the error correction provided by convolutional coding. As bit errors in the output of Viterbi decoder are no longer independent, for a packet erasure model, an upper bound on the packet erasure rate (PER) is given in [9] by $p_e = 1 - (1 - p_u)^L$, where L is the length of packet in bits, and p_u is the union bound on the first-event error probability of Viterbi decoding [10]. Fig. 2 shows the resulting PER versus SNR curves for each of the 802.11a/g transmission modes for a packet length of 1024 bytes. The channel capacity is $R \times (1 - p_e)$ at PHY rate R.

2.2   BSC Crossover Probability of Rayleigh Channel

The crossover probability p, i.e. the (symmetric) probability of a 1 being changed into 0 and *vice-versa*, is the probability of a bit error in a BSC model. An upper bound on the bit crossover probability is the sum of the expected number of erroneous bits for all possible incorrectly selected paths while performing Viterbi decoding, as described in [10]. For a binary-tree convolutional code, the expression for this upper bound is given by $\sum_{d=d_{free}}^{\infty} \beta_d p_2(d)$, where $p_2(d)$ is

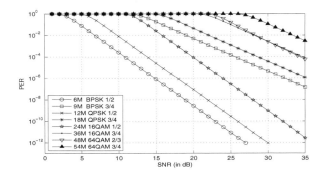

Fig. 2. Packet erasure rate (PER) vs. SNR, $L = 1024B$, Rayleigh channel

the probability that an incorrect path with Hamming distance d is selected, and β_d is the number of bit errors totaled over all paths with Hamming distance d. Fig. 3 shows the resulting crossover probability vs SNR curves for the 802.11a/g OFDM modulations/rates and a Rayleigh channel. The BSC capacity at PHY rate R is $R \times (1 - H(p))$, where $H(p)$ is the entropy function of a Bernoulli(p) random variable, i.e. $H(p) = -p \log_2(p) - (1 - p) \log_2(1 - p)$.

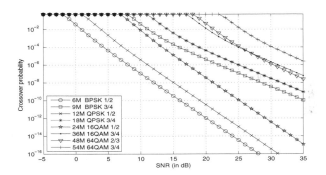

Fig. 3. Crossover probability vs. SNR, Rayleigh channel

The overall capacity curves shown in Fig. 1 are obtained by selecting the PHY modulation/rate R that maximises the capacity at each SNR. Note that these curves do not include the MAC layer framing overheads, contention time, collision losses etc. In the following sections we extend the analysis to include these overheads for both unicast and multicast traffic. We also extend the analysis to take account of the multi-user nature of the wireless channel, including multi-destination unicast aggregation.

3   Coding in Multi-user Channels

Owing to the broadcast nature of the wireless medium every transmission can be heard by all the receivers within the coverage area. However, the channel quality between the transmitter and every receiver, e.g. the access point (AP) and each client station in a WLAN, is generally different for every receiver, owing to a multitude of reasons such as differences in distance between the transmitter and receivers, obstacles such as walls when operating indoors and differences in the local interference environment. While the 802.11 standard allows transmissions to multiple receivers in one single frame, it constrains the bits transmitted in the same frame to use the same PHY modulation/rate. Hence, the state of the art in 802.11 WLANs is to send multi-user transmissions at the highest PHY rate which the client with the worst channel quality can support, so that all clients can decode the transmission; this is the recommendation for multicast traffic in the current 802.11 standards. Clearly, this is inefficient. One of the outcomes of our analysis is also the quantification of this inefficiency. Since the traditional approach drops packets once the CRC check fails, it is appropriately modelled as a PEC [11].

In contrast to PEC model, the BSC paradigm allows us to transmit information within a frame with different segments encoded with different levels of protection. In this manner we can transmit at different information rates to different destinations while using a single PHY modulation/rate exploiting developments in multi-terminal information theory [11].

The specific multi-user BSC paradigm we consider forms what is known as a physically degraded binary symmetric broadcast channel [11]. For this class of channels superposition coding [12] is known to be capacity-achieving. Superposition coding works by first picking an ordering of the users and constructing the code of every user based upon the codes of all the users before. Decoding starts from the last user for whom the decoder treats every other user's signal as noise. After the last user is decoded, its contribution is subtracted and the remaining users are decoded in a similar nested fashion. For a more concrete illustration of our particular setting, we limit the discussion to two classes of users where for illustration purposes we assume that class 2 experiences no errors and class 1 has a crossover probability $p \in (0, 1/2)$. We have a natural order in this setting where class 2 appears before class 1 in the encoding process. As mentioned earlier instead of partitioning a MAC frame into separate segments for each distinct message, in superposition coding the message (i.e. binary vector) U destined to class 1 and the message V destined to class 2 are summed, modulo 2, to yield the MAC frame body. The binary vector received by the class 1 user can then be viewed as message U corrupted by a bit flips due to a combination of channel noise and the summation with V. This is illustrated in Fig. 4. The message U destined to the class 1 user is first passed through a BSC with crossover probability β determined by the entropy of V. It is then transmitted over the physical BSC channel with crossover probability $p(R)$ at PHY rate R. The channel capacity for the class 1 user in bits per channel use is therefore

$$C_1 = 1 - H(\beta \circ p(R)) \tag{1}$$

where $\beta \circ p(R) = \beta(1 - p(R)) + (1 - \beta)p(R)$.

The channel capacity for the class 2 user is

$$C_2 = H(\beta) \tag{2}$$

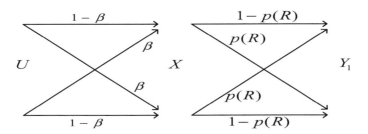

Fig. 4. Physically degraded binary symmetric broadcast channel

From the discussion above it is clear that superposition coding can be a complex operation. A simpler but demonstrably sub-optimal choice is a time-sharing based coding scheme [11]. In our setting with two classes of users, time-sharing based coding is such that each MAC frame is partitioned (i.e. time-shared) into one portion intended for class 1 and the other intended for class 2. Using the same setting that is illustrated above for superposition coding, it is clear that the portion intended for class 2 is noise-free and thus not protected. However, the portion intended for class 1 is protected by an error correction code that allows information to be extracted even when bits within the frame are corrupted; the information rate is obviously reduced compared to a noise-free channel. We assume an ideal code with coding rate matched to the BSC capacity. Since the aggregated frame is large, capacity-approaching codes, e.g. LDPC codes [13], exist.

In this paper we present a performance analysis of superposition coding, which is known to be capacity-achieving in multi-user BSC channels, and of the simpler time-sharing coding scheme. We will show in results that there is minimal loss of optimality in using the time-sharing coding scheme. For both schemes our analysis indicates the potential for substantial performance gains over the traditional packet erasure channel paradigm. To our knowledge, this is the first such analysis of multi-user coding in 802.11 WLANs.

4   Modelling Analysis

Consider a wireless network with an AP and two classes of client stations, with n_1 stations in class 1 and n_2 in class 2. The AP has N_{D1} downlink flows destined for n_1 class 1 stations and N_{D2} downlink flows for n_2 class 2 stations, in general

$N_{D1} \neq n_1$ and $N_{D2} \neq n_2$. We assume all stations in the same class have the same SNR. Class 1 is located far from the AP with low SNR such that stations in this class are subjected to noisy reception; while class 2 lies within a region where stations have high SNR and thus experience reliable reception at any of the available PHY data rates. The analysis can be readily generalised to encompass situations where each user station has a different SNR, but the two-class case is sufficient to capture many important features of WLAN performance.

To ensure a fair comparison amongst different schemes it is not sufficient to simply compare sum-throughputs. Rather we also need to ensure that schemes provide comparable throughput fairness, since an approach may achieve through-put gains at the cost of increased unfairness. In the following we take a max-min fair approach and impose the fairness constraint that all flows achieve the same throughput. Extension of the analysis to other fairness criteria is, of course, possible.

4.1   Unicast

The vast majority of network traffic is unicast, and contention between multiple stations, with associated collision losses and increased CSMA/CA countdown time, is the norm. For the unicast scenario we set $N_{D1} = n_1$ and $N_{D2} = n_2$. The AP aggregates these $N_{D1} + N_{D2}$ downlink flows into a single large MAC frame and then transmits it at a single PHY rate. Each client station also has an uplink flow for the AP.

For simplicity we assume that all stations are saturated, although the analysis could be extended to include unsaturated operation using, for example, the approach in [14]. We also assume uplink transmissions by client stations are immediately acknowledged by the AP (rather than, for example, using a block ACK). Similarly, we assume that downlink transmissions are immediately acknowledged by client stations and, to make our analysis concrete, we adopt the approach described in [15] which uses the orthogonality of OFDM subcarriers to allow a group of user stations to transmit feedback signals at the same time, and thereby ACK collisions are avoided. However, these assumptions really just relate to the calculation of the MAC overheads and our analysis could be readily modified to account for alternative acking mechanisms[1].

MAC Model. Transmissions by the AP are subjected to collisions with competing uplink transmissions, while transmissions by client stations are subjected to collisions with the AP and uplink transmissions from other client stations. In the packet erasure setting, transmissions by class 1 stations are also subjected to noise losses, while those in class 2 are assumed to have a high SNR channel and

---

[1] In particular, for operation on standard 802.11n hardware we might tunnel data packets for multiple destinations via multicast MPDUs aggregated into an A-MPDU (thereby achieving standards-compliant multi-destination aggregation) and generate appropriate acknowledgements either by modifying the receiver NIC driver or at the application layer.

thus not subjected to noise. For class 1 stations we therefore have the probability that a transmission fails (due to collision and/or loss) is

$$p_{f_1} = 1 - (1 - p_{c21})(1 - p_{e21}) \tag{3}$$

where p_{e21} is the probability that the packet is erased due to noise, and p_{c21} is the collision probability of a transmission from a class 1 station,

$$p_{c21} = 1 - (1 - \tau_1)^{n_1-1}(1 - \tau_2)^{n_2}(1 - \tau_0) \tag{4}$$

with τ_0, τ_1 and τ_2 being the attempt probability of AP, class 1 stations and class 2 stations, respectively. As the AP and class 2 stations have the same back-off probability (the probability that a transmission fails), according to Bianchi model [16], $\tau_0 = \tau_2$. The backoff probability for the AP or a class 2 station is

$$p_{f_2} = 1 - (1 - \tau_1)^{n_1}(1 - \tau_2)^{n_2} \tag{5}$$

The usual Bianchi [16] expression gives the relation between the attempt probability τ and the probability p_f that a transmission fails. However, we make use of expression (6) in [17] that builds upon the Bianchi expression taking into account a finite number of retransmission attempts and losses due to decoding errors.

Packet Erasure Channel. Similarly to the approach used in 802.11n A-MPDUs [2], we consider a situation where messages addressed to distinct destinations are aggregated together to form a single large MAC frame. We do not present results here without aggregation since the throughputs are strictly lower than when aggregation is used [3]. To keep our discussion concrete, we assume the frame format is as shown in Fig. 5. However, it is important to stress that this really just relates to the calculation of the MAC overheads and our analysis could be readily modified to account for alternative frame formats. In Fig. 5 a sub-header is prefixed to each IP packet to indicate its receiver address, source address and packet sequence information. An FCS checksum is used to detect corrupted packets. Since the sub-header already contains the receiver address, source address and sequence control, the MAC header removes these three fields, but keeps other fields unchanged from the standard 802.11 MAC header. For simplicity, we assume that the MAC header is transmitted at the same PHY rate as the PLCP header and thus can be assumed error-free in the following analysis, although we will relax this assumption in future work. The frame format is known to all user stations, so that each station can correctly locate its packet even if some bits in the frame are corrupted.

In the PEC scenario, the downlink transmission rate is determined by the worst client which has the lowest SNR, hence we have the downlink PHY rate R_1 used by the AP equal to the uplink PHY rate of class 1 stations R_{21} in order to meet the max-min fairness objective. For a given SNR and R_1, the union bound on the first-event error probability of Viterbi decoding is $p_u(R_1)$. The packet erasure rate of an uplink packet from class 1 stations $p_{e21}(R_1)$ is then

$$p_{e21}(R_1) = 1 - (1 - p_u(R_1))^{L_{21}(R_1)} \tag{6}$$

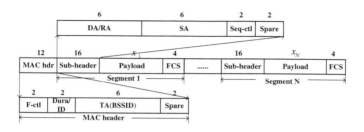

Fig. 5. Erasure channel frame format [2]

where $L_{21}(R_1)$ is the frame size in bits, given by

$$L_{21}(R_1) = DBPS(R_1) \times \left\lceil \frac{(x_{21}(R_1) + L_{machdr} + L_{FCS}) \times 8 + 6 + 16}{DBPS(R_1)} \right\rceil \quad (7)$$

where $DBPS(R_1)$ represents data bits per symbol at PHY rate R_1, $x_{21}(R_1)$ is the payload size in bytes of an uplink packet from a class 1 station, and L_{machdr} and L_{FCS} are the length in bytes of the standard MAC header and the FCS field. The expected payload delivered by an uplink packet of a class 1 station is

$$E_{pld_{21}}(R_1) = x_{21}(R_1)(1 - p_u(R_1))^{L_{21}(R_1)} \quad (8)$$

Let x_{22} denote the payload size in bytes of class 2 uplink transmissions. By assumption, uplink transmissions by class 2 stations are assumed to be loss free at all supported rates and so we may take the transmission rate $R_{22} = 54\text{Mbps}$. The expected payload of an uplink packet from a class 2 station at R_1 is

$$E_{pld_{22}}(R_1) = x_{22}(R_1) \quad (9)$$

Turning now to the AP, similar to the approach used in 802.11n, the aggregated MAC frame then consists of $N_{D1}+N_{D2}$ unicast packets. Let $x_{11}(R_1)$ and $x_{12}(R_1)$ denote the payload size in bytes to class 1 and class 2 stations at R_1 respectively. The length of a MAC frame L is thus

$$L = N_{D1}x_{11}(R_1) + N_{D2}x_{12}(R_1) + (N_{D1} + N_{D2})(L_{subhdr} + L_{FCS}) \quad (10)$$

where L_{subhdr} is the sub-header length. The expected payload delivered to a class 1 station in a downlink packet is

$$E_{pld_{11}}(R_1) = x_{11}(R_1) \times (1 - p_u(R_1))^{(x_{11}(R_1)+L_{subhdr}+L_{FCS}) \times 8} \quad (11)$$

The expected payload delivered to a class 2 station in a downlink packet is

$$E_{pld_{12}}(R_1) = x_{12}(R_1) \quad (12)$$

To equalize the throughput of each flow, we require

$$x_{12}(R_1) = x_{11}(R_1)(1 - p_u(R_1))^{(x_{11}(R_1)+L_{subhdr}+L_{FCS}) \times 8} \quad (13)$$

$$x_{22}(R_1) = x_{12}(R_1) \tag{14}$$

$$\tau_1(1 - \tau_2)(1 - p_u(R_1))^{L_{21}(R_1)} x_{21}(R_1) = \tau_2(1 - \tau_1)x_{22}(R_1) \tag{15}$$

For a given R_1 and a fixed L we can solve equations (10) and (13) to obtain x_{11} and x_{12}. As τ_0, τ_1 and τ_2 also depend on R_1, combining the expressions for τ_0, τ_1 and τ_2 from the MAC model with expression (15), we can solve to obtain $x_{21}(R_1)$.

To obtain the throughputs it remains to derive expressions for the expected duration of a MAC slot. There are four possible types of MAC slot. We consider each in turn.

– Type 1 - AP transmits: Observe that the duration of AP frames is larger than that of the client stations (due to aggregation). Hence, if the AP transmits during the slot, then regardless of whether it suffers from a collision the duration of the slot in μs is

$$T_{AP} = T_{phyhdr1} + T_{DN}(R_1) + T_{sifs} + T_{phyhdr} + T_{ack} + T_{difs} \tag{16}$$

where $T_{phyhdr1}$ is the PHY/MAC header duration for an aggregated frame; T_{phyhdr} is the standard PHY header duration; T_{sifs} and T_{difs} are respectively DIFS and SIFS durations. DIFS is the 802.11 distributed coordination function (DCF) interframe space, and SIFS is the short interframe space [2]. T_{ack} is the transmission duration of an ACK frame; $T_{DN}(R_1)$ is the transmission duration of a downlink MAC frame,

$$T_{DN}(R_1) = \lceil (L \times 8 + 6 + 16)/DBPS(R_1) \rceil \times 4 \tag{17}$$

– Type 2 - class 1 transmits: Observe that the duration of class 1 frames is larger than that of class 2 stations. Hence, if a class 1 station wins the transmission opportunity, and its transmission does not collide with a downlink transmission, but might collide with other uplink transmissions, the duration in μs is

$$T_{21} = T_{phyhdr} + T_{UP1}(R_1) + T_{sifs} + T_{phyhdr} + T_{ack} + T_{difs} \tag{18}$$

where $T_{UP1}(R_1)$ is the transmission duration of an uplink MAC frame from a class 1 station, given by

$$T_{UP1}(R_1) = 4 \times \lceil \frac{(x_{21}(R_1) + L_{machdr} + L_{FCS}) \times 8 + 22}{DBPS(R_{21})} \rceil \tag{19}$$

The probability that a collision occurs among uplink packets (not involving downlink packet) is

$$
\begin{aligned}
p_{CUP} = \quad & (1-\tau_0)\big(1-(1-\tau_1)^{n_1}(1-\tau_2)^{n_2} \\
& - n_1\tau_1(1-\tau_1)^{n_1-1}(1-\tau_2)^{n_2} - n_2\tau_2(1-\tau_2)^{n_2-1}(1-\tau_1)^{n_1}\big)
\end{aligned}
\tag{20}
$$

The probability that a collision occurs only among uplink packets from class 2 stations is

$$
p_{CUP2} = (1-\tau_0)(1-\tau_1)^{n_1}\big(1-(1-\tau_2)^{n_2} - n_2\tau_2(1-\tau_2)^{n_2-1}\big)
\tag{21}
$$

Hence, the probability that the duration is T_{21} is

$$
p_{T_{21}} = n_1\tau_1(1-\tau_1)^{n_1-1}(1-\tau_2)^{n_2}(1-\tau_0) + p_{CUP} - p_{CUP2}
\tag{22}
$$

– Type 3 - only class 2 transmits: If a class 2 station makes a transmission which does not collide with an AP or class 1 station transmissions, but might collide with uplink packets from other class 2 stations, the duration within a slot time in μs is

$$
T_{22} = T_{phyhdr} + T_{UP2}(R_1) + T_{sifs} + T_{phyhdr} + T_{ack} + T_{difs}
\tag{23}
$$

where $T_{UP2}(R_1)$ is the transmission duration in μs of an uplink MAC frame from a class 2 station,

$$
T_{UP2}(R_1) = 4 \times \Big\lceil \frac{(x_{22}(R_1) + L_{machdr} + L_{FCS}) \times 8 + 22}{54 \times 4} \Big\rceil
\tag{24}
$$

The probability that the duration is T_{22} is given by

$$
p_{T_{22}} = n_2\tau_2(1-\tau_2)^{n_2-1}(1-\tau_0)(1-\tau_1)^{n_1} + p_{CUP2}
\tag{25}
$$

– Type 4 - idle slot: If no transmission occurs, the duration is a PHY slot σ. This event occurs with probability

$$
p_{Idle} = (1-\tau_1)^{n_1}(1-\tau_2)^{n_2}(1-\tau_0)
\tag{26}
$$

Combining these yields the expected MAC slot duration,

$$
E_T = p_{Idle}\sigma + \tau_0 T_{AP} + p_{T_{21}}T_{21} + p_{T_{22}}T_{22}
\tag{27}
$$

The network throughput is then given by

$$
S(R_{21}) = \frac{N_{D1}X_1 + N_{D2}X_2}{E_T}
\tag{28}
$$

where

$$
X_1 = \tau_0(1-\tau_1)^{n_1}(1-\tau_2)^{n_2}E_{pld_{11}} + \tau_1(1-\tau_1)^{n_1-1}(1-\tau_2)^{n_2}(1-\tau_0)E_{pld_{21}}
\tag{29}
$$

$$
X_2 = \tau_0(1-\tau_1)^{n_1}(1-\tau_2)^{n_2}E_{pld_{12}} + \tau_2(1-\tau_1)^{n_1}(1-\tau_2)^{n_2-1}(1-\tau_0)E_{pld_{22}}
\tag{30}
$$

We select the downlink PHY rate R_1^* (equal to the uplink PHY rate of class 1 stations) from the set $\mathcal{R}$ of supported 802.11a/g rates so as to maximise this throughput given the channel SNR.

BSC Time-Sharing Coding. For the BSC paradigm we start by considering the simpler time-sharing coding scheme. As in the erasure channel case, MAC frames are constructed by aggregating two portions intended for the different classes of stations with the portion meant for class 1 stations coded (based on BSC crossover probability) and the remainder (for class 2 stations) being uncoded. Note that each portion is in itself composed of sub-frames meant for the different users. We also apply similar coding to protect uplink transmissions of class 1 stations to allow information to be recovered from corrupted uplink frames.

Let x_{11} denote the information payload size for a class 1 station and x_{12} for a class 2 station. Suppose a downlink PHY rate R_1 is chosen. The crossover probability for class 1 stations is $p(R_1)$ and the number of coded bits for x_{11} is $x_{11}/(1 - H(p(R_1)))$. To equalize the downlink throughputs of stations in both classes, we therefore require

$$x_{11}(R_1) = x_{12}(R_1) \tag{31}$$

Given a frame size L, we have that

$$L = N_{D1} \cdot \frac{x_{11}(R_1) + L_{subhdr} + L_{FCS}}{1 - H(p(R_1))} + N_{D2} \cdot (x_{12}(R_1) + L_{subhdr} + L_{FCS}) \tag{32}$$

and hence $x_{11}(R_1)$ and $x_{12}(R_1)$ can be solved. As downlink packets to class 1 stations are erasure-free in the BSC paradigm, the expected payload delivered to a class 1 station is $E_{pld_{11}} = x_{11}(R_1)$.

To equalize the uplink and downlink throughput from/to class 2 stations we require $x_{22}(R_1) = x_{12}(R_1)$. Since erasure-free frames are delivered, $p_{e21} = 0$ and $\tau_0 = \tau_1 = \tau_2$. Thus, to equalize the uplink and downlink throughput from/to class 1 stations we require $x_{21}(R_1) = x_{11}(R_1)$.

The uplink PHY rate of a class 1 station R_{21}^* is selected in terms of maximising its BSC capacity, i.e.

$$R_{21}^* = \arg\max_{r \in \mathcal{R}} \ r \cdot \left(1 - H(p(r))\right) \tag{33}$$

The expected duration in a slot time E_T and the network throughput $S(R_1)$ are derived in a similar manner to the erasure case. We select the downlink rate R_1^* so as to maximise the network throughput given the channel SNR.

BSC Superposition Coding. The MAC frames in this setting are constructed in two steps. Once a value of β has been determined, the V and U bit vectors are generated from the aggregated IP packets of each class. These are then added to generate the MAC frame. Despite the scheme being more complicated, the analysis with superposition coding is similar to the BSC time-sharing case. The main difference lies in the calculation of the downlink payload size.

Suppose the downlink PHY rate used by the AP is R_1, the downlink BSC capacity in bits per channel use between the AP and a class 1 station is

$1 - H(\beta \circ p(R_1))$, and that between the AP and a class 2 station is $H(\beta)$. The MAC frame body is formed by superimposing N_{D2} downlink unicast packets destined to class 2 stations to N_{D1} downlink unicast packets destined to class 1 stations. Let x_{11} denote the information payload size for a class 1 station, and x_{12} the information payload size for a class 2 station. Given the MAC frame size L, we have

$$L = \frac{N_{D1}(x_{11}(R_1) + L_{subhdr} + L_{FCS})}{1 - H(\beta \circ p(R_1))} = \frac{N_{D2}(x_{12}(R_1) + L_{subhdr} + L_{FCS})}{H(\beta)}$$

(34)

To equalize the downlink throughputs of stations in both classes, we require

$$x_{11}(R_1) = x_{12}(R_1)$$

(35)

Thus we find the relationship $N_{D1}H(\beta) = N_{D2}\left(1 - H(\beta \circ p(R_1))\right)$. The ratio N_{D1}/N_{D2} fixes the value of β. With the value of β determined, the downlink unicast payload size for each client station (class 1 or class 2) is then given by

$$x(R_1) = \max\left(\frac{LH(\beta)}{N_{D2}} - L_{subhdr} - L_{FCS}, 0\right)$$

$$= \max\left(\frac{L\left(1 - H(\beta \circ p(R_1))\right)}{N_{D1}} - L_{subhdr} - L_{FCS}, 0\right)$$

(36)

The uplink PHY rate of class 1 stations R_{21}^* is selected in the same manner as BSC time-sharing case. We also protect uplink transmissions using the ideal code. Again, the PHY rate R_1^* is chosen to maximise system throughput.

4.2   Multicast

In the multicast scenario that we consider, the AP multicasts only two downlink flows, which are aggregated into a large MAC frame. Flow 1 is communicated to n_1 class 1 stations and flow 2 is communicated to n_2 class 2 stations, respectively. There are no competing uplink flows. Therefore, we can compute the throughput using the analysis in Section 4.1 by setting the following parameter values: $N_{D1} = N_{D2} = 1$; $x_{21} = x_{22} = 0$; $p_{e21} = p_{c21} = 0$; $\tau_1 = \tau_2 = 0$; $\tau_0 = 2/(W_0 + 1)$, where W_0 is the minimum contention window size. The expected payload and MAC slot duration can be calculated using the same way as the unicast analysis, but for a multicast network, we consider per-station multicast saturation throughput,

$$S(R_1) = \frac{\tau_0 E_{pld11}(R_1)}{E_T(R_1)} = \frac{\tau_0 E_{pld12}(R_1)}{E_T(R_1)}$$

(37)

The optimal PHY rate R_1^* is selected to maximise the per-station throughput.

5   Performance

5.1   Unicast

We compare the throughput performance of the erasure channel and BSC schemes for the protocol parameters detailed in Table 1. Fig. 6 shows the sum-throughputs achieved by the different approaches for a network consisting of 20 client stations, 10 in class 1 and 10 in class 2. This is quite a large number of saturated stations for an 802.11 WLAN and suffers from a high level of collision losses. Comparing with Fig. 1, it can be seen that the throughput is significantly reduced due to the various protocol overheads and collisions that have now been taken into account. Nevertheless, the relative throughput gain of the BSC based approaches compared to the erasure channel approach continues to exceed 50% for a wide range of SNRs. BSC time-sharing coding achieves very similar performance to the more sophisticated superposition coding. Fig. 7 shows the corresponding result for a smaller number of client stations, 5 in class 1 and 5 in class 2. The overall throughput is higher than that with 20 stations because of the lower chance of collisions, and the gain offered by BSC approaches is even higher i.e. more than 75% over a wide range of SNRs.

Table 1. Protocol parameters used in simulations

T_{sifs} (μs)	16	L_{subhdr} (bytes)	16
T_{difs} (μs)	34	L_{FCS} (bytes)	4
Idle slot duration σ (μs)	9	L_{machdr} (bytes)	24
T_{ack} (μs)	24	CW_{min}	16
T_{phyhdr} (μs)	20	CW_{max}	1024
$T_{phyhdr1}$ (μs)	36	Retry limit	7

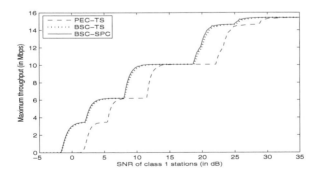

Fig. 6. Unicast maximum network throughput vs. SNR of class 1 stations, Rayleigh channel, $L = 8000$ bytes, with $n_1 = n_2 = 10$ stations

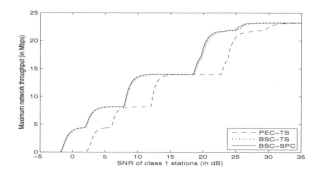

Fig. 7. Unicast maximum network throughput vs. SNR of class 1 stations, Rayleigh channel, $L = 8000$ bytes, with $n_1 = n_2 = 5$ stations

Fig. 8 illustrates how the number of stations affects these results. The decrease in network throughput with increasing number of stations is evident, as is the significant performance gain offered by the BSC schemes. For smaller numbers of stations (which is perhaps more realistic), the throughput gain offered by the BSC approaches is larger e.g. nearly up to 70% for 2 stations and falling to around 50% with 20 stations. The proportion of class 1 and class 2 stations can be

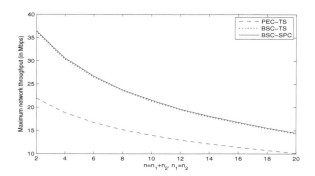

Fig. 8. Unicast maximum network throughput vs. varying total number of stations for a fixed proportion of class 2 stations $n_1 = n_2$, $SNR = 22$dB, $L = 8000$ bytes, Rayleigh channel

expected to affect the relative performance of the erasure and BSC schemes. This is because we now have multiple transmitting stations, and each station defers its contention window countdown on detecting transmissions by other stations. Since class 1 transmissions are of longer duration than class 2 transmissions, we expect that the network throughput will rise as the number of class 1 stations falls and indeed we find that this is the case. See, for example, Fig. 9 which plots the network throughput versus the varying proportion of class 2 stations while maintaining the total number of client stations constant as $n_1 + n_2 = 10$.

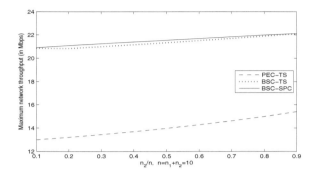

Fig. 9. Unicast maximum network throughput vs. varying proportion of class 2 stations for a fixed total number of stations $n_1 + n_2 = 10$, $SNR = 22$dB, $L = 8000$ bytes, Rayleigh channel

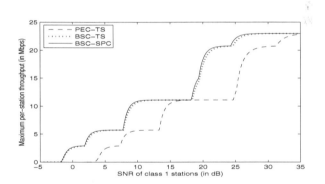

Fig. 10. Multicast per-station maximum throughput vs SNR of class 1 stations, $L = 8000$ bytes, Rayleigh channel, with $n_1 = n_2 = 10$ stations

5.2   Multicast

Fig. 10 shows the per-station multicast throughput for a network with $n_1 = 10$ class 1 stations and $n_2 = 10$ class 2 stations. The throughput is much higher than the unicast case as shown in Fig. 6 because of the absence of collisions among different stations. Nevertheless, both of the BSC schemes (time-sharing and superposition coding) continue to offer substantial performance gains over the erasure channel approach, increasing throughput by almost 100% over a wide range of SNRs. The superposition coding scheme performs slightly better than the time-sharing scheme, but the difference is minor. Fig. 11 shows the corresponding results with a larger MAC frame size of 65536 bytes, which is the maximum frame size allowed in the 802.11n standard. The performance gain

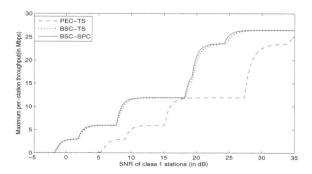

Fig. 11. Multicast per-station maximum throughput vs. SNR of class 1 stations, $L = 65536$ bytes, Rayleigh channel, with $n_1 = n_2 = 10$ stations

offered by the BSC approaches increases as the frame size is increased. Since the per-station multicast throughput is independent of the number of stations, we only show results for one value of n_1 and n_2.

6   Conclusions

In this paper we consider the potential benefits of viewing the channel provided by an 802.11 WLAN as a binary symmetric channel (BSC), as opposed to a more conventional packet erasure channel. That is, rather than simply discarding corrupted frames we consider viewing a received frame as a binary vector in which an unknown subset of bits have been "flipped". We present analysis results for both multicast and unicast traffic, taking account of important MAC layer overheads such as collision losses. Importantly, we also consider the multi-user channel aspect of a WLAN i.e. that transmissions are inherently broadcast in nature. We find that increases in network throughput of more than 100% are possible over a wide range of SNRs and that the much simpler time-sharing scheme yields most of these gains. To our knowledge, this is the first detailed analysis of multi-user BSC coding in 802.11 WLANs. We note that these performance gains involve software rather than hardware changes, and so essentially come for "free".

References

1. Lin, K., Kushman, N., Katabi, D.: ZipTx: Harnessing Partial Packets in 802.11 Networks. In: Proc. of ACM MobiCom 2008, San Francisco, pp. 351–362 (2008)
2. IEEE 802.11n-2009 - Amendment 5: Enhancements for Higher Throughput. IEEE-SA (2009)
3. Li, T., Ni, Q., Malone, D., Leith, D., Xiao, Y., Turletti, T.: Aggregation with Fragment Retransmission for Very High-speed WLANs. IEEE/ACM Trans. on Networking 17(2), 591–604 (2009)

4. Verkaik, P., Agarwal, Y., Gupta, R., Gupta, A.C.: Softspeak: Making VoIP Play Well in Existing 802.11 Deployment. In: Proc. of NSDI 2009, Boston, MA (2009)
5. Wang, W., Liew, S.C., Pang, Q., Li, V.O.K.: A Multiplexing-multicast Scheme that Improves System Capacity of Voice-over-IP on Wireless Lan by 100%. In: Proc. of ISCC 2004, Washington, DC, USA, vol. 2, pp. 472–477 (2004)
6. Zheng, Y., Lu, K., Wu, D., Fang, Y.: Performance Analysis of IEEE 802.11 DCF in Binary Symmetric Channels. In: Proc. of GLOBECOM 2005 (2005)
7. Zheng, Y., Lu, K., Wu, D., Fang, Y.: Performance Analysis of IEEE 802.11 DCF in Imperfect Channels. IEEE Trans. on Vehicular Technology 55(5), 1648–1656 (2006)
8. Simon, M.K., Alouini, M.S.: Digital Communication over Fading Channels, 2nd edn. Wiley-IEEE Press (2005)
9. Pursley, M.B., Taipale, D.J.: Error Propabilities for Spread-spectrum Packet Radio with Convolutional Codes and Viterbi Decoding. IEEE Trans. on Communications 35(1), 1–12 (1987)
10. Viterbi, A.J.: Convolutional Codes and Their Performances in Communication Systems. IEEE Trans. on Communications Technology 19(5), 751–772 (1971)
11. Cover, T.M., Thomas, J.A.: Elements of Information Theory, 2nd edn. John Wiley & Sons, Inc. (2006)
12. Bergmans, P.P., Cover, T.M.: Cooperative Broadcasting. IEEE Trans. on Information Theory IT-20(3), 317–324 (1974)
13. MacKay, D.J.C.: Information Theory, Inference and Learning Algorithms. Cambridge University Press, New York (2003)
14. Malone, D., Duffy, K., Leith, D.: Modeling the 802.11 Distributed Coordination Function in Nonsaturated Heterogeneous Conditions. IEEE/ACM Trans. on Networking 15(1), 159–172 (2007)
15. Dutta, A., Saha, D., Grunwald, D., Sicker, D.: SMACK - A Smart ACKnowledgment Scheme for Broadcast Messages in Wireless Networks. In: Proc. of SIGCOMM 2008 (2008)
16. Bianchi, G.: Performance Analysis of the IEEE 802.11 Distributed Coordination Function. IEEE Journal on Selected Areas in Communications 18(3), 535–548 (2000)
17. Ni, Q., Li, T., Turletti, T., Xiao, Y.: Saturation Throughput Analysis of Error-prone 802.11 Wireless Networks. Wiley Journal of Wireless Communications and Mobile Computing (2005)

An Impact of Cooperation and Altruism on Transmission

Andrey Garnaev, Irina Antonova,
Vsevolod Brekelov, and Natalia Marutenkova

Saint Petersburg State University, Saint Petersburg, Russia
garnaev@yahoo.com

Abstract. In wireless access, transmitter nodes need to make individual decisions for distributed operation and do not necessarily cooperate or bargaining with each other. We consider a single-receiver random access system of transmitters (users) with altruistic payoffs which are generalized weighted individual objectives of their throughput rewards, transmission energy costs and delay costs. We compare altruistical behaviour with selfish (Nash equilibrium), cooperative (Shapley vector) and bargaining behaviour (Nash bargaining solution). We produce criteria where altruistical behaviour is more profitable for a user than either selfish, or cooperative, or bargaining ones.

Keywords: ALOHA, Nash equilibrium, Shapley vector, altruistical behaviour, bargaining solution.

1 Payoffs without Altruism

Aloha [1] and slotted Aloha [2,4] have long been used as random distributed medium access protocols for radio channels. They are in use in both satellite as well as cellular telephone networks for the sporadic transfer of data packets. In these protocols, packets are transmitted sporadically by various users. If packets are sent simultaneously by more than one user then they collide.

In this paper we focus on the following Aloha protocol model formulated in [3]. It is assumed that multiple nodes randomly transmit packets with fixed probabilities to a common receiver. Each transmitter has a packet queue of infinite buffer capacity. We consider a synchronous slotted system, in which each packet transmission takes one time slot. We assume saturated queues with always availability of packets. Let p_i denote the transmission probability of node i from the set N of n transmitters. We assume multi-packet reception channels with possible packet captures. The packet transmission of node i is successfully received with probability $q_{i|J}$, if nodes in set J (including node i) transmit in the same time slot. Throughout the paper, we will specialize the results to the particular case of the classical collision channels with $q_{i|J} = 1$ for $J = \{i\}$ and $q_{i|J} = 0$ for $J \neq \{i\}$. Any selfish node i has the objective of choosing the transmission probability p_i to maximize the utility function u_i that reflects the difference between the throughput rewards and costs of transmission energy

I. Tomkos et al. (Eds.): BROADNETS 2010, LNICST 66, pp. 274–282, 2012.
© Institute for Computer Sciences, Social Informatics and Telecommunications Engineering 2012

and delay per time slot, i.e the utility of node i is defined as $u_i = r_i\lambda_i - e_i - d_i$, where λ_i is the throughput rate, namely the average number of successful packet transmissions per time slot, r_i is the reward for any successful packet transmission, e_i is the average transmission energy cost per time slot and d_i is the average delay-type cost per time slot. We will focus on two users game. Node (user) i transmits a packet with probability p_i and it is successfully received with probability $q_{i|i}$, if the other node decides not to transmit, or captured with probability $q_{i|12}$, if the other node also transmits in the same time slot. We assume $0 \le q_{i|12} \le q_{i|i} \le 1$ for $i = 1, 2$. We also assume that throughput rate for user i is given as follows $\lambda_i = p_i(p_{\hat{i}}q_{i|12} + (1 - p_{\hat{i}})q_{i|i})$, the average transmission energy cost e_i per time slot is permanent and equals E_i, and the average delay-type cost per time slot d_i is proportional of failed transmission with coefficient D_i. Thus, the payoff to users are given as follows:

$$
\begin{aligned}
u_1(p_1, p_2) &= r_1 p_1(p_2 q_{1|12} + (1 - p_2)q_{1|1}) \\
&\quad - D_1(1 - p_1 + p_1(1 - p_2 q_{1|12} - (1 - p_2)q_{1|1})) \\
&\quad - E_1 p_1, \\
u_2(p_1, p_2) &= r_2 p_2(p_1 q_{2|12} + (1 - p_1)q_{2|2}) \\
&\quad - D_2(1 - p_2 + p_2(1 - p_1 q_{2|12} - (1 - p_1)q_{2|2})) \\
&\quad - E_2 p_2.
\end{aligned}
$$

This game is equivalent to the following bimatrix game $M = (A, B)$ with two pure strategies: to transmit (T) and do not transmit (N), where

$$
A := \begin{array}{c} \\ \mathrm{T} \\ \mathrm{N} \end{array}
\begin{array}{c} \begin{array}{cc} \mathrm{T} & \mathrm{N} \end{array} \\
\begin{pmatrix} R_1 q_{1|12} - E_1 - D_1 & R_1 q_{1|1} - E_1 - D_1 \\ -D_1 & -D_1 \end{pmatrix} \end{array}
$$

and

$$
B := \begin{array}{c} \\ \mathrm{T} \\ \mathrm{N} \end{array}
\begin{array}{c} \begin{array}{cc} \mathrm{T} & \mathrm{N} \end{array} \\
\begin{pmatrix} R_2 q_{2|12} - E_2 - D_2 & -D_2 \\ R_2 q_{2|2} - E_2 - D_2 & -D_2 \end{pmatrix} \end{array}
$$

with

$$R_1 = r_1 + D_1, \quad R_2 = r_2 + D_2.$$

This game always has Nash equilibrium in pure strategies and its form is determined by the fact whether the transmission by both users or each of them separately is too expensive or accessible for them, namely, as it is given in Table 1.

Thus, in particular the case where it is too expensive to transmit for both users simultaneously, but transmission is preferable for each of them separately turns out to be very competitive since two pure Nash equilibrium (T, N) and (N, T) arise simultaneously. This situation takes place under the following conditions:

$$q_{1|12} < E_1/R_1 < q_{1|1} \text{ and } q_{2|12} < E_2/R_2 < q_{2|2}. \tag{1}$$

Table 1. Nash equilibrium

E_1/E_2	$\leq R_2 q_{2\vert 12}$	$\in [R_2 q_{2\vert 12}, R_2 q_{2\vert 2}]$	$\geq R_2 q_{2\vert 2}$
$\leq R_1 q_{1\vert 12}$	(T,T)	(T,N)	(T,N)
$\in [R_1 q_{1\vert 12}, R_1 q_{1\vert 1}]$	(N,T)	$(N,T), (T,N)$	(T,N)
$\geq R_1 q_{1\vert 1}$	(N,T)	(N,T)	(N,N)

Besides for the case (1) a mixed Nash equilibrium $((p_1, 1-p_1), (p_2, 1-p_2))$ exists where

$$p_1 = \frac{1}{q_{2\vert 2} - q_{2\vert 12}} \left(q_{2\vert 2} - \frac{E_2}{R_2} \right),$$

$$p_2 = \frac{1}{q_{1\vert 1} - q_{1\vert 12}} \left(q_{1\vert 1} - \frac{E_1}{R_1} \right)$$

with payoffs

$$(v_1^s, v_2^s) = (-D_1, -D_2).$$

In spite of quite competitive situation the payoffs for mixed strategies coincide with payoffs for pure strategies where both users have just chosen do not to transmit at all which is quite senseless since, of course, they have a chance to improve their payoff.

2 Comparing Selfish, Cooperative and Bargaining Solutions

In the strong competitive situation (1) with two equilibrium cooperative and bargaining approach can be applied to improve user's outcome.

First we consider the Shapley solution of the bargaining problem. To do so, we note that our bimatrix game can be present as $M = (A, B)$ where

$$A = \begin{array}{c} T \\ N \end{array} \begin{array}{cc} T & N \\ \begin{pmatrix} T_{11} - D_1 & T_1 - D_1 \\ -D_1 & -D_1 \end{pmatrix} \end{array},$$

$$B = \begin{array}{c} T \\ N \end{array} \begin{array}{cc} T & N \\ \begin{pmatrix} T_{22} - D_2 & -D_2 \\ T_2 - D_2 & -D_2 \end{pmatrix} \end{array}$$

with

$$T_i = q_{i\vert i} R_i - E_i,$$
$$T_{ii} = q_{i\vert 12} R_i - E_i, i = 1, 2.$$

Then, in the new notation the conditions (1) are equivalent to the following ones:

$$T_{11} < 0 < T_1 \text{ and } T_{22} < 0 < T_2. \tag{2}$$

Also, note that the Pareto optimal boundary is just the line segment L joining two points: $(T_1 - D_1, -D_2)$ and $(-D_1, T_2 - D_2)$.

The security levels (maxmin) for users are given as solution of two zero-sum games with matrix A and B. Clearly, under condition (1) (N, T) is the saddle point for zero-sum game with matrix A and (T, N) is the saddle point for zero-sum game with matrix B. Thus, the security level is $(-D_1, -D_2)$ which presents status quo point (x_*, y_*). Thus, to find Shapley solution we have to find the point (x, y) maximizing

$$T := (x - x_*)(y - y_*) = (x + D_1)(y + D_2)$$

with

$$y = -\frac{T_2}{T_1}x + \frac{T_1 T_2 - D_1 T_2 - D_2 T_1}{T_1}$$

for $x \in [-D_1, T_2 - D_2]$. Then we have the following result.

Theorem 1. *The Shapley solution for the bargaining problem (v_1^b, v_2^b) is given by*

$$v_1^b = \frac{T_1}{2} - D_1 = \frac{1}{2}(R_1 q_{1|1} - D_1) - D_1,$$

$$v_2^b = \frac{T_2}{2} - D_2 = \frac{1}{2}(R_2 q_{2|2} - D_2) - D_2.$$

Besides, bargaining solution a cooperative approach can be applied to deal with competitive situation (1). Namely, the users have cooperatively to maximize the joint payoff

$$v = v_1 + v_2,$$

so, to solve the following optimization problem:

$$\max_{p_1, p_2} v.$$

It is clear that the the cooperative problem has the following optimal strategies $(p_1^c, 1 - p_1^c)$, $(p_2^c, 1 - p_2^c)$ where

$$p_1^c = \frac{T_2}{T_1 - T_{11} + T_2 - T_{22}},$$

$$p_2^c = \frac{T_1}{T_1 - T_{11} + T_2 - T_{22}}$$

with joint payoff

$$v^c = \frac{T_1 T_2}{T_1 - T_{11} + T_2 - T_{22}} - D_1 - D_2.$$

This payoff they can share, for example, according to Shapley vector which is given in the following theorem.

Theorem 2. *The Shapley vector for the cooperative solution* $\varphi = (\varphi_1, \varphi_2)$ *is given as follows:*

$$\varphi_1 = \frac{T_1 T_2}{2(T_1 - T_{11} + T_2 - T_{22})} - D_1,$$

$$\varphi_2 = \frac{T_1 T_2}{2(T_1 - T_{11} + T_2 - T_{22})} - D_2.$$

We can compare the bargaining and cooperative solution estimating the difference of the corresponding total payoffs, i.e. $v = v_1^b + v_2^b - v^c$. It is clear that

$$v_1^b + v_2^b - v^c$$
$$= \frac{T_1 + T_2}{2} - \frac{T_1 T_2}{T_1 - T_{11} + T_2 - T_{22}}$$
$$= \frac{T_1^2 + T_2^2 - (T_1 + T_2)(T_{11} + T_{22})}{T_1 - T_{11} + T_2 - T_{22}}$$
$$> (\text{by } (2)) > 0.$$

Thus, the bargaining approach can essentially increase the quality of the network as a whole. To estimate what it can bring to a user we have to investigate the difference of corresponding payoffs, so values $v_1^b - \varphi_1$ and $v_1^b - \varphi_1$. It is clear that

$$v_1^b - \varphi_1 = \frac{T_1 - T_2 - T_{11} - T_{22}}{T_1 - T_{11} + T_2 - T_{22}} T_1,$$

$$v_2^b - \varphi_2 = \frac{T_2 - T_1 - T_{11} - T_{22}}{T_1 - T_{11} + T_2 - T_{22}} T_2.$$

Thus, by (2) we have the following result.

Theorem 3. *(a) If*

$$T_{11} + T_{22} \leq T_1 - T_2 \leq -T_{11} - T_{22}$$

then both users benefits from bargaining approach compare to cooperative one,
(b) if

$$T_1 - T_2 > -T_{11} - T_{22}$$

then only user 1 benefits from bargaining approach compare to cooperative one,,
(c) if

$$T_1 - T_2 < T_{11} + T_{22}$$

then only user 2 benefits from bargaining approach compare to cooperative one,.

3   Payoffs with Altruism

In this section we consider the other way of user's cooperation where in behavior of users some altruism presents, namely, in payoff each user takes into account payoff of the other one with some weights (say, normalized by 1), namely, the user payoffs are given as follows:

$$u_1^J = \alpha_1 u_1 + \alpha_2 u_2, \quad u_2^J = \beta_1 u_1 + \beta_2 u_2.$$

where $\alpha_i, \beta_i \in [0, 1]$.

Then the game has the following bimatrix form $M = (A, B)$ with

$$A = \begin{array}{c} \\ T \\ N \end{array} \begin{array}{cc} T & N \\ \left(\begin{array}{cc} \alpha_1(T_{11} - D_1) + \alpha_2(T_{22} - D_2) & -\alpha_2 D_2 + \alpha_1(T_1 - D_1) \\ -\alpha_1 D_1 + \alpha_2(T_2 - D_2) & -\alpha_1 D_1 - \alpha_2 D_2 \end{array} \right) \end{array}$$

$$B = \begin{array}{c} \\ T \\ N \end{array} \begin{array}{cc} T & N \\ \left(\begin{array}{cc} \beta_1(T_{11} - D_1) + \beta_2(T_{22} - D_2) & -\beta_2 D_2 + \beta_1(T_1 - D_1) \\ -\beta_1 D_1 + \beta_2(T_2 - D_2) & -\beta_1 D_1 - \beta_2 D_2 \end{array} \right) \end{array}.$$

For this game we have that

(a) (N, N) is a Nash equilibrium if $T_1 \leq 0$ and $T_2 \leq 0$,
(b) (T, T) is a Nash equilibrium, if $\alpha_1 T_{11} + \alpha_2 T_{22} \geq \alpha_2 T_2$ and $\beta_1 T_{11} + \beta_2 T_{22} \geq \beta_1 T_1$,
(c) (N, T) is a Nash equilibrium, if $\alpha_1 T_{11} + \alpha_2 T_{22} \leq \alpha_2 T_2$ and $T_2 \geq 0$,
(d) (T, N) is a Nash equilibrium, if $\beta_1 T_{11} + \beta_2 T_{22} \leq \beta_1 T_1$ and $T_1 \geq 0$.

Also, if

$$T_1 \geq 0, T_2 \geq 0, \beta_1 T_{11} + \beta_2 T_{22} \leq \beta_1 T_1 \text{ and } \alpha_1 T_{11} + \alpha_2 T_{22} \leq \alpha_2 T_2 \qquad (3)$$

besides two pure Nash equilibrium (T, N) and (N, T), the game has a mixed Nash equilibrium $((p_1, 1 - p_1), (p_2, 1 - p_2))$ where

$$p_1 = \frac{\beta_2 T_2}{\beta_1(T_1 - T_{11}) + \beta_2(T_2 - T_{22})},$$

$$p_2 = \frac{\alpha_1 T_1}{\alpha_1(T_1 - T_{11}) + \alpha_2(T_2 - T_{22})}$$

with the corresponding payoffs

$$v_1^J = \frac{\alpha_1 \alpha_2 T_1 T_2}{\alpha_1(T_1 - T_{11}) + \alpha_2(T_2 - T_{22})} - \alpha_1 D_1 - \alpha_2 D_2,$$

$$v_2^J = \frac{\beta_1 \beta_2 T_1 T_2}{\beta_1(T_1 - T_{11}) + \beta_2(T_2 - T_{22})} - \beta_1 D_1 - \beta_2 D_2.$$

So, in the competitive situation the payoffs for mixed strategies is greater than the payoffs for pure strategies where both users have just chosen do not to transmit at all which tells that taking into account interest of the opponent can improve the work of network even in selfish scenario of user's behaviour. Also. it is interesting that in the competitive cases (2) and (3) the domain (T_{11}, T_{22}) for altruistical payoff contains the corresponding domain for the selfish payoffs, that produces some extra advantage.

The following results allow to tell when altruistical behavior even is more profitable for users than selfish one.

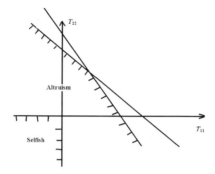

Fig. 1. Areas of competitive solution for selfish and altruistical payoffs

Theorem 4. *Let (2) hold. Then*

$$v_1^J \geq v_1^s, \quad v_2^J \geq v_2^s.$$

if and only if

$$\frac{\alpha_1 \alpha_2 T_1 T_2}{\alpha_1 (T_1 - T_{11}) + \alpha_2 (T_2 - T_{22})} \geq (\alpha_1 - 1)D_1 + \alpha_2 D_2,$$

$$\frac{\beta_1 \beta_2 T_1 T_2}{\beta_1 (T_1 - T_{11}) + \beta_2 (T_2 - T_{22})} \geq \beta_1 D_1 + (\beta_2 - 1)D_2,$$

In particular, for small delay costs D_1 and D_2 or where there are no these costs at all (so, $D_1 = D_2 = 0$), the altruistical behavior is more profitable for users than selfish one.

The following theorem compares selfish altruistical behavior with cooperative one (note, that to escape bulky formulas here we consider only the case where there are no delay costs at all).

Theorem 5. *Let $D_1 = D_2 = 0$. Then*

$$v_1^J \geq v_1^c, \quad v_2^J \geq v_2^c.$$

if and only if

$$\alpha_1(1 - 2\alpha_2)(T_1 - T_{11}) + \alpha_2(1 - 2\alpha_1)(T_2 - T_{22}) \geq 0,$$
$$\beta_1(1 - 2\beta_2)(T_1 - T_{11}) + \beta_2(1 - 2\beta_1)(T_2 - T_{22}) \geq 0.$$

In particular,
(a) if

$$\alpha_1, \alpha_2, \beta_1, \beta_2 \geq 1/2$$

then selfish altruistical behavior always more profitable than cooperative one.
(b) if

$$\alpha_1, \alpha_2, \beta_1, \beta_2 < 1/2$$

then cooperative one is more profitable than selfish altruistical behavior.

Similarly we can compare altruistical behavior with cooperative solution.

Theorem 6. *Let $D_1 = D_2 = 0$. Then*

$$v_1^J \geq v_1^b, \quad v_2^J \geq v_2^b.$$

if and only if

$$2\alpha_1\alpha_2 T_2 \geq \alpha_1(T_1 - T_{11}) + \alpha_2(T_2 - T_{22}),$$
$$2\beta_1\beta_2 T_1 \geq \beta_1(T_1 - T_{11}) + \beta_2(T_2 - T_{22}).$$

In particular, if $\alpha_1, \beta_2 < 1/2$ then bargaining one is more profitable than selfish altruistical behavior.

The Pareto optimal boundary is just the line segment L joining two points: $(-\alpha_1 D_1 + \alpha_2(T_2 - D_2), -\beta_1 D_1 + \beta_2(T_2 - D_2))$ and $(-\alpha_2 D_2 + \alpha_1(T_1 - D_1), -\beta_2 D_2 + \beta_1(T_1 - D_1))$. The security level is $(-\alpha_1 D_1 - \alpha_2 D_2, -\beta_1 D_1 - \beta_2 D_2)$ which presents status quo point (x_*, y_*). Thus, to find Shapley solution for the bargaining problem we have to find the point $(x, y) \in L$ maximizing

$$T := (x - x_*)(y - y_*) = (x + \alpha_1 D_1 + \alpha_2 D_2)(y + \beta_1 D_1 + \beta_2 D_2)$$

where

$$y = -\frac{\beta_1 T_1 - \beta_2 T_2}{\alpha_1 T_1 - \alpha_2 T_2} x + \frac{(\beta_1\alpha_2 - \beta_2\alpha_1)(D_1 T_2 + D_2 T_1 - T_1 T_2)}{\alpha_1 T_1 - \alpha_2 T_2}$$

Theorem 7. *The Shapley solution for the bargaining problem (v_1^{Jb}, v_2^{Jb}) is given by*

$$v_1^{Jb} = \frac{\alpha_1\beta_2 - \alpha_2\beta_1}{2(\beta_2 T_2 - \beta_1 T_1)} T_1 T_2 - \alpha_1 D_1 - \alpha_2 D_2,$$
$$v_2^{Jb} = \frac{\alpha_2\beta_1 - \alpha_1\beta_2}{2(\alpha_2 T_2 - \alpha_1 T_1)} T_1 T_2 - \beta_1 D_1 - \beta_2 D_2.$$

4   Discussion

In this paper we considered a single-receiver random access system of transmitters (users) with altruistic payoffs which are a generalized weighted individual objectives of their throughput rewards, transmission energy costs and delay costs. We compared altruistical behaviour with selfish (Nash equilibrium), cooperative (Shapley vector) and bargaining behaviour (Nash bargaining solution). We produced criteria where altruistical behaviour is more profitable for a user than either selfish, or cooperative, or bargaining ones.

Finally we note that as the other altruistical payoffs for users we could take weighted fairness utility ([5]), namely, the user altruistical payoffs could be given as follows:

for $\alpha \neq 1$

$$u_1^F = \alpha_1 \frac{u_1^{1-\alpha}}{1-\alpha} + \alpha_2 \frac{u_2^{1-\alpha}}{1-\alpha},$$

$$u_2^F = \beta_1 \frac{u_1^{1-\alpha}}{1-\alpha} + \beta_2 \frac{u_2^{1-\alpha}}{1-\alpha}$$

and for $\alpha = 1$

$$u_1^F = \alpha_1 \ln(u_1) + \alpha_2 \ln(u_2),$$

$$u_2^F = \beta_1 \ln(u_1) + \beta_2 \ln(u_2).$$

Here we just briefly produce the mixed equilibrium strategies for the plot where there are no delay costs D_1 and D_2 at all (so, $D_1 = D_2 = 0$). Then the mixed Nash equilibrium $((p_1, 1 - p_1), (p_2, 1 - p_2))$ is given as follows:

for $\alpha = 1$

$$p_1 = \frac{\alpha_1 T_2}{(\alpha_1 + \alpha_2)(T_2 - T_{22})},$$

$$p_2 = \frac{\beta_2 T_1}{(\beta_1 + \beta_2)(T_1 - T_{11})},$$

for $\alpha \neq 1$

$$p_1 = \frac{T_2}{T_2 - T_{22}} \frac{T_1 - (T_1 - T_{11})p_2}{T_1 - \left(1 - \frac{\beta_1\alpha_2}{\beta_2\alpha_1}\right)(T_1 - T_{11})p_2},$$

$$\frac{\beta_1\alpha_2}{\beta_2\alpha_1} \frac{(T_1 - T_{11})p_2}{T_1 - (T_1 - T_{11})p_2} = \frac{1}{T_2 - T_{22}} \left(\frac{\alpha_2}{\alpha_1} \frac{(T_2 - T_{22})p_2^{1-\alpha}}{(T_1 - (T_1 - T_{11})p_2)^{1-\alpha}}\right)^{1/\alpha}.$$

References

1. Abramson, N.: The Aloha system – another alternative for computer communications. In: AFIPS Conference Proceedings, vol. 36, pp. 295–298 (1970)
2. Altman, E., El Azouzi, R., Jimenez, T.: Slotted Aloha as a game with partial information. Computer Networks 45, 701–713 (2004)
3. Sagduyu, Y.E., Ephremides, A.: A Game-Theoretic Analysis of Denial of Service Attacks in Wireless Random Access. Journal of Wireless Networks 15, 651–666 (2009)
4. Roberts, L.G.: Aloha packet system with and without slots and capture, Tech. Rep. Note 8, Stanford Research Institute, Advance Research Projects Agency, Network Information Center (1972)
5. Altman, E., Avrachenkov, K., Garnaev, A.: Generalized Alpha-Fair Resource Allocation in Wireless Networks. In: Proc. of the 47th IEEE Conference on Decision and Control (CDC 2008), Cancun, Mexico, pp. 2414–2419 (2008)

Multicast Routing in Hierarchical Optical Networks Using Collection-Distribution Networks
(An Invited Paper)

Onur Turkcu[1], Suresh Subramaniam[2], and Arun K. Somani[1]

[1] Department of Electrical and Computer Engineering
Iowa State University, Ames, IA 50011
{onurturk,arun}@iastate.edu
[2] Department of Electrical and Computer Engineering
The George Washington University, Washington, DC 20052
suresh@gwu.edu

Abstract. Emerging optical networks have hierarchical architectures with varying capabilities at different levels. Moreover, many applications nowadays require multicast (one-to-many) connections. We propose a network model that has such a hierarchical architecture which is designed for multicast connections. We develop a multi-stage routing scheme which solves the routing problem in different levels of the network for multicast connections. The network model consists of three levels: collection, core and distribution networks. We adopt the light-trail model in collection-distribution networks which is a convenient way to carry multicast connections. Connection points between the core and collection networks are the edge routers which groom several multicast connections destined to the same distribution network. We evaluate two call acceptance criteria, namely *best effort* and *all-or-none* corresponding to total or partial multicast service, respectively. We show using simulations that our multi-stage routing algorithm with light-trails and edge-grooming improves the performance in the hierarchical network model.

Keywords: multicasting, light-trails, hierarchical optical networks, routing algorithms.

1 Introduction

The design of optical networks depends on the geographical area coverage which leads to classification into two main categories, namely long-haul or metropolitan area networks. Long-haul networks operate as backbones of nation-wide networks covering large land masses. On the other hand, metropolitan area networks are employed in smaller geographical regions such as cities. Switching technologies and lightpath termination capabilities may differ as well as the wavelength conversion and e-grooming capabilities according to the design of the network.

I. Tomkos et al. (Eds.): BROADNETS 2010, LNICST 66, pp. 283–301, 2012.
© Institute for Computer Sciences, Social Informatics and Telecommunications Engineering 2012

As new network architectures are evolving, applications that utilize the network are also changing. Applications such as video-on-demand, teleconferencing, etc. are all multicast in nature. Multicast connections are defined as one-to-many with a source node transmitting to several destination nodes. Multicasting can be achieved by utilizing light-trees which is a single hop connection from one source to multiple destinations [1]. Light-trees are created using optical wavelength splitting at intermediate nodes and related routing problems involve calculation of light-trees on a certain wavelength based on the network state.

Connections with sub-wavelength bandwidth requests result in under-utilization of the capacity of wavelengths. In order to overcome this deficiency, traffic grooming combines several connections together in the electronic or optical domain and transmits them on a single lightpath. Traffic grooming is widely studied in the literature [2]. This topic is also considered for multicast connections in [3].

Light-trail technology, proposed in [4], achieves traffic grooming in the optical domain using a uni-directional bus. Every node on a light-trail can transmit to every downstream node. Since each node transmits on a different time slot, time sharing of the available bandwidth is achieved. A *convener* node initiates the light-trail which is terminated by a *terminator* node. Connections that can be carried to/from the intermediate nodes depend on the light-trail architecture adopted [5]. Source Light-Trails (SLTs) allow transmission only from the convener node to all downstream nodes, whereas in Destination Light-Trails (DLTs) only the terminator node receives and every other node can transmit to it. In general Light-Trails (LTs), every node can transmit to its downstream nodes on the light-trail. Performance evaluation of all light-trail models and other grooming strategies is done in [6]. A testbed for demonstrating light-trails is developed and evaluated in [7].

Several graph models for routing and wavelength assignment with light-trails are proposed in [5,8] considering unicast connections. Light-trails also offer a convenient way for carrying multicast connections since any node in the downstream of a convener node can access the same time slot. In [9], given a set of already established light-trails in the network, the authors introduced graph formulations to optimally find the minimum number of light-trails to carry a multicast connection for mesh networks. They also present an optimal greedy heuristic achieving the same objective for ring topologies.

Network Description. In this paper, we consider a heterogeneous network architecture consisting of a long-haul core network connecting several metropolitan area (access) networks (see Fig. 1). We divide the access networks into *collection* and *distribution* networks (CDNs) since they carry out those tasks. This type of architecture fits well into the emerging fiber optic network designs today since network carriers employ access networks at cities and the communication between cities is carried on the core backbone. Collection network is where source nodes are located and distribution network distributes the corresponding data to their destinations. We note that some of the connections may be local, i.e., the destination nodes are within the same network. The rest of the connections are global as they travel through the core network to reach other CDNs.

A similar network model has been investigated in [10] where the multicast routing problem is studied for a core network with light splitting capabilities. The authors developed an auxiliary graph model to represent the logical topology consisting of light-trees in the core network. They provided algorithms for finding the set of light-trees to carry a multicast connection depending on various design objectives. Different from [10], we also consider the routing problem in CDNs besides the routing in the core network. The solutions we provide for CDNs and core network can be solved independently for each network.

We develop distributed routing algorithms for core network and CDNs to find the route of a multicast or unicast connection. We assume light-trail technology is available at CDNs which are connected to the core network through a single node which we call as the *edge* node. We provide an effective solution in CDNs for multicasting using light-trails. The core network carries only lightpaths and several connections from a collection network to the same distribution network can be groomed at the edge node. Our goal is to find a multicast route that uses minimal network resources in terms of transceivers and wavelengths at each network considered. Our performance metric is the requested multicast bandwidth blocking probability(RMBbp) which captures both the bandwidth and size of multicast call under dynamic traffic model. DLTs/SLTs are used at collection/distribution networks, respectively. Each access network can be used for collection or distribution depending on the multicast call and each of them may also contain local traffic. Therefore, we commonly use LTs for CDNs.

The rest of the paper is organized as follows. In Section 2, we describe the network model. In Section 3, we introduce our routing algorithm together with the graph model for light-trails adapted from [5]. We provide a routing algorithm for the core network in Section 4. We then present numerical results in Section 5 and conclude the paper in Section 6.

2   Network and Traffic Model

The network model is shown in Fig. 1. There are Γ CDNs numbered from 1 to Γ. A CDN d consists of N_d nodes connected with L_d bidirectional links (two fibers in opposite directions). Let Ω_d denote the set of nodes in d. The set of nodes in all such networks is denoted by $\Omega = \Omega_1 \cup \Omega_2 \cup \ldots \cup \Omega_\Gamma$. Light-trail technology is enabled at these nodes having T transmitter/receiver pairs (transceivers). The edge node of CDN d is denoted by E_d which is the connecting point to the core network. An edge node has T transceivers dedicated to the core network and T transceivers dedicated to the corresponding CDN.

The core network consists of N_c nodes and L_c bidirectional links. LTs are not available in the core network and nodes other than the edge nodes do not have any transceivers. Therefore, multihopping and traffic grooming is not possible within the core network except at the edge nodes.

Multicast connection m is initiated from a source node and it has D_m destinations. We choose D_m uniformly randomly between 1 and max_d where max_d is the maximum possible number of destinations for a multicast connection. When $D_m = 1$, the connection request is unicast. The source node and destination nodes are chosen uniformly randomly from the set $\Omega \setminus \{E_1, E_2, \ldots, E_\Gamma\}$ without picking the same node twice. Let bw_m be the bandwidth request of m. We then have the following definitions for a connection request m.

- S : The source CDN that contains the source node s of m.
- Δ : Set of CDNs that include at least one destination of the request. It consists of elements δ_i $(1 \le i \le |\Delta|)$
- Y_d : The set of destinations of m in CDN d. Y_S includes the edge node E_S of the source network. $|Y_d|$ is the size of this set.

Multicast connections arrive at the network according to a Poisson process with a total arrival rate of ρ and they have exponential holding time with mean 1. Upon a connection request arrival, we try to find a route for the multicast connection in the core network and CDNs based on the auxiliary graph model in [5]. The algorithm we propose in Section 3 tries to find the best route for the multicast connection that uses minimum network resources. We consider two interconnection models: 1) the overlay model in which a connection is first routed across the virtual topology (consisting of already established LTs and lightpaths) and then on the physical topology if needed; and 2) the peer model in which a connection can use both layers [5].

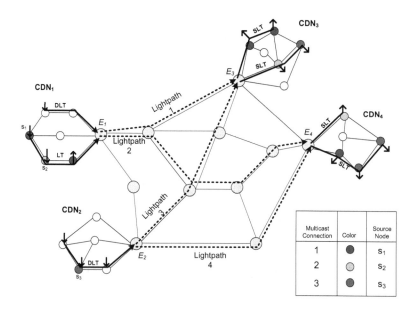

Fig. 1. Network model with several light-trails

We divide the general network routing problem into three sub-problems as follows:

1. **Routing Problem 1 (Collection network):**
   Routing the multicast connection from source node s to every node in Y_S using light-trails.
2. **Routing Problem 2 (Core network):** Routing the multicast connection from E_S to every E_{δ_i} for $1 \leq i \leq |\Delta|$ using lightpaths.
3. **Routing Problem 3 (Distribution networks):**
   For every δ_i in Δ, routing the multicast connection from E_{δ_i} to every node in Y_{δ_i} using light-trails.

Upon a multicast call arrival, we run the routing algorithms for every access network δ_i in Δ and the core. For routing problems 1 and 3, we develop a routing algorithm that runs on the auxiliary graph of [5]. For problem 2, we create another auxiliary graph and develop our core routing algorithm. We consider two call acceptance criteria as explained in the following section.

2.1   Call Acceptance Criteria

The first criterion accepts the call to the network only if connections to every destination in every CDN can be established. This can be described as a *all-or-none* criterion and can be used for certain type of applications in the network. For example, in a teleconference request between several users, it would be unacceptable if one or more of the users cannot connect to the teleconference from one lecturer. In this case, the source node should be able to the edge node E_S and every other destination in Y_S. The core network should be able to establish connections to every CDN that include destinations and also all of those CDNs should be able to establish connections to every destination within. Otherwise, the call is blocked and dropped.

   The previous criteria may not be the best strategy depending on the application. For example, in a video-on-demand application several customers requesting the same video are connected with a multicast call. In such a scenario, even if some of the destinations cannot be reached, we would still like to serve the remaining customers. Therefore, the goal of the network operator should be to serve as many customers as possible offering a partial multicast service. We call this call acceptance criterion as the *best-effort* criterion and the corresponding routing scheme as best-effort routing. In this case, each CDN δ_i in Δ tries to establish connections to as many destinations in Y_{δ_i} as possible. Each CDN can be reached if the core network can support a connection to its edge node and also source CDN can support a connection between the source node s and the edge node E_S. The multicast call is established for every such destination that can be reached and the remaining destinations are blocked. In the extreme case that none of the destinations can be reached, the entire call is blocked and dropped.

2.2   Performance Metric

The common performance metric blocking probability is insufficient to evaluate the network performance for multicast calls since it does not capture the size of the multicast request and its bandwidth. In this paper, we propose to use a new metric called *requested multicast bandwidth blocking probability* (RMBbp) which captures both those attributes. We first calculate the sum of the product of number of blocked destinations and their requested bandwidth. For example, for a multicast call request m with D_m destinations and bw_m bandwidth, this product is $B_m \times bw_m$, where B_m be the number of blocked destinations of m. We divide this sum to the total sum of the product of number of destinations and their bandwidth over all multicast requests (e.g., sum of every $D_m \times bw_m$) to get the RMBbp. This metric also allows us to fairly compare the two call acceptance criteria. For *all-or-none* criterion, B_m is equal to D_m for the blocked multicast calls.

Even though, best-effort scheme is expected to have a better RMBbp performance, we note that partial service of multicast calls may result in lower ratio of *totally-accepted* multicast calls compared to the all-or-none scheme. By accepting partial multicast requests, the network may not be able to accommodate future multicast calls totally which it would have otherwise. If the difference between the two cases is high, it would not be a favorable result for the best-effort scheme. In order to evaluate this, we calculate the metric called *not-totally-accepted* multicast call ratio which equals to the sum of *partially-accepted* (or blocked) and *totally-blocked* multicast call ratios for the best-effort scheme to compare it with the *blocked* call ratio of all-or-none.

3   Routing in the CDN

We first describe the routing algorithm for CDNs according to the *all-or-none* call acceptance criterion. At the end of the section, we explain how the algorithm is modified for the *best-effort* criterion. The auxiliary graph in [5] is shown in Fig. 2 for a particular CDN. This is a multilayer graph consisting of $W + 3$ layers and each of the first W layers corresponds to one wavelength. Layers $W + 1$ and $W + 2$ represent the virtual topology (VT) which is defined by the already established light-trails in the network. Subnodes that are on the left/right side of the main node are input/output nodes, respectively. The arcs between the output subnode of node i to the input subnode of node j ($1 \leq i, j \leq N_d$) on wavelength layer w is created based on the availability of that wavelength in that direction of the link. Layer $W + 3$ is the grooming layer. For CDN d, this graph contains $2WN_d + 6N_d$ subnodes. This model supports all the three light-trail architectures, i.e., SLT, DLT, and LT by allowing only the architecture-specific arcs in the VT layer.

We call the nodes that are already transmitting/receiving a connection using a transmitter/receiver on a light-trail as *active nodes*. Therefore, upon a new call arrival, the active nodes that belong to either the source or destination of

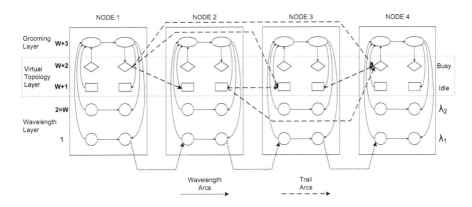

Fig. 2. Auxiliary graph model

the multicast call can accommodate the new call without the addition of new transceivers. We make proper cost assignment for the arcs that connect to a subnode in the virtual topology layer of the graph depending on whether the node is active or not in the light-trail. BUSY layer of the VT corresponds to nodes that are active and IDLE layer corresponds to nodes that are not active.

When multihopping from one light-trail to another is allowed in the VT layer, the light-trail model can perform additional traffic grooming [5]. The technology required for multihop light-trails is also explained in [11]. Now we give an example to illustrate how multihopping can give a route using fewer transceivers for a multicast connection. In Fig. 3(a), initially 3 light-trails are established in the CDN. There is a new multicast connection request between edge node E and two destination nodes 2 and 4. LT2 is established between E and 4. Node 2 is on LT2, however it is not active (i.e., not using a receiver to receive a connection). Suppose that there is enough capacity in the LTs to accommodate the new connection. If multihopping is not allowed and we suppose that this new multicast connection is established on LT2, we would need to use an additional receiver at node 2. In the multihopping case, we can use LT1 to connect E to node 4 without the need of an additional receiver. In the second hop, we can use LT3 from node 4 to node 2 which again does not require any additional transceiver. Overall, if we use multihopping with LT1 and LT3, we can establish the multicast connection without requiring any new transceivers.

Minimum Steiner Tree (MST) algorithms are generally used to solve multicasting problems [9]. The solution finds the minimum cost tree including all the nodes in a given set within a graph. However, MST algorithms cannot be applied to our case since the tree solution may not be valid for the following reason. Splitting at a node in one of the wavelength layers would require wavelength splitting capability which is not considered in our model. We show this case in Fig. 4(a). Splitting of the tree from a node in the VT layer would correspond to transmission of two new light-trails for which there may not be enough transceiver resources as shown in Fig. 4(b).

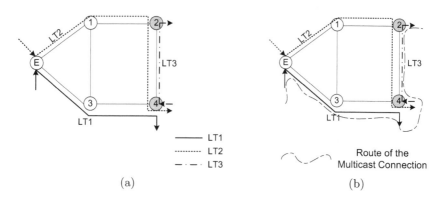

Fig. 3. Illustrative example: (a) Light-trails in the CDN before multicast connection request arrival, and (b) The route chosen for the connection

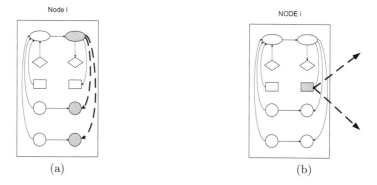

Fig. 4. Illustration of possible MST solutions that contradict our network model with splitting at (a) wavelength layer, and (b) VT layer

Since a direct tree calculation to cover all of the nodes in the multicast session is not possible, we propose a greedy heuristic that creates light-trails sequentially to cover as many destination nodes as possible in each iteration. The routing decision for the remaining nodes in each step depends on the light-trails created in the previous step. Initially, we create the auxiliary graph for the CDN, we calculate the shortest paths using Dijkstra's algorithm to all of the nodes from the source node of the connection or from the edge node for collection or distribution networks, respectively. In the overlay model, we first run Dijkstra's algorithm on the VT and grooming layers and if a path for the multicast connection is not found, we run it on the wavelength and grooming layers. For the peer model, we run Dijkstra's algorithm on the entire graph.

For each of the destination nodes d_j on Y_{δ_i}, we trace the shortest route to calculate the number of other destination nodes that are already active on the light-trails that d_j uses. We denote the set of active nodes along the path to destination node d_j by I_j and $|I_j|$ is the size of this set. We find the node with the maximum $|I_j|$ and denote that node by d_z. We first establish the connection from source to destination d_z on the path calculated using existing light-trails or creating new light-trails. Along this path, other destinations in I_j that coincide with the already active nodes are also covered. Before the second iteration, the auxiliary graph is updated and we run the shortest path algorithm again.

We note that established light-trails from the previous step may result in shorter paths for the remaining destinations that are not covered yet. This does not yet affect the bandwidth of these trails in our simulation. We again find d_z within the remaining destinations and route the connection. The algorithm stops when all of the destination nodes in the CDN are covered. Whenever one of the remaining destinations becomes unreachable as calculated by the shortest path algorithm, we block the call. We note that while calculating I_j we exclude those nodes that are already covered. We call this algorithm Greedy Multicast Routing (GMR) algorithm and we show its steps in Algorithm 1. The function Dijkstra$(s, \delta_i, \text{Model})$ finds the shortest path from the source node s to every destination within CDN δ_i. The parameter Model is set to OV1 or OV2 for routing on the virtual or physical links, respectively, in overlay model and it is set to PEER for the peer model.

3.1   Modified GMR Algorithm for Best-Effort Routing

Until now, we assumed the call acceptance criteria was *all-or-none*. Now, we modify the GMR algorithm for *best-effort* criterion. The difference is that we do not stop the routing algorithm whenever one of the destinations cannot be reached. After every run of Dijkstra's algorithm, we find the destination d_z with the maximum value of $|I_z|$, that is also reachable (e.g., $dist(z) < \infty$). We connect the destination d_z and update the auxiliary graph and go back to step of Dijkstra's run. In this way, we continue to connect to the other reachable destinations until each destination d_j in Y_{δ_i} is either unreachable or already connected (e.g., $d_j \in \Phi$). Modified GMR algorithm returns the number of destinations $b_{m,i}$ that are blocked in CDN δ_i.

4   Routing in the Core Network

Recall that only lightpaths can be established in the core network. However, the edge node that terminate the light-trails on a collection network can electronically groom several multicast connections together on a lightpath if they share a common distribution network. We call this capability as the edge grooming (EG) model. The auxiliary graph we generate for the core network is similar to the auxiliary graph for CDNs except that several arcs are different. Note that multihopping is possible in the core network using an edge node as an intermediate node which is allowed with this graph. When a lightpath is created between two nodes, there is an arc created between the output node of the source to the

---

input   : Auxiliary Graph G; source node s and set of destination nodes Y_{δ_i} in
CDN δ_i

output: Routing and wavelength assignment for the multicast connection

1 *Initialization*: $\Phi \longleftarrow \emptyset$, $Trails \longleftarrow \emptyset$;

3 **while** $\Phi \neq Y_{\delta_i}$ **do**

4 | *Run Dijkstra's algorithm to find the shortest path from s to every node in*
      δ_i;

5 | **if** *Model is Overlay* **then**

6 | | Dijkstra $(s, \delta_i, \text{OV1})$;

7 | | **if** $\exists d_j \in Y_{\delta_i} \setminus \Phi$ *s.t.* $dist(j) = \infty$ **then**

8 | | | Dijkstra $(s, \delta_i, \text{OV2})$;

9 | | **endif**

10 | **else**

11 | | Dijkstra $(s, \delta_i, \text{PEER})$;

12 | **endif**

13 | $Path_j$: shortest path for $d_j \in Y_{\delta_i}$ with length $dist(j)$;

14 | **if** $\exists d_j \in Y_{\delta_i} \setminus \Phi$ *s.t.* $dist(j) = \infty$ **then**

15 | | Block the call;

16 | | Update the Graph G back to the initial state;

17 | **endif**

18 | $Path_j$ is on the LTs $tr_1, tr_2, ...,tr_{H_j}$ where H_j is the number of hops;

19 | **for** $d_j \in Y_{\delta_i} \setminus \Phi$ **do**

20 | | Calculate I_j by tracing $Path_j$;

21 | **end**

22 | *Finding the maximum*: $z = \arg\max_j |I_j|$;

23 | *Route the connection to d_z*;

24 | *Along $Path_z$, connect every node $i \in I_z$* ;

25 | **for** $h \leftarrow 1$ **to** H_j **do**

26 | | $Trails = Trails \cup tr_h$

27 | **end**

28 | *Update G without allocating bandwidth for LTs $(\forall tr \in Trails)$*;

29 | $\Phi = \Phi \cup I_z$

30 **end**

31 Update G by allocating bandwidth of LTs $(\forall tr \in Trails)$ used;

Algorithm 1. Pseudocode for the Greedy Multicast Routing (GMR)algorithm

input node of the destination in the VT layer. This arc enables the grooming of an incoming connection request to the existing lightpath.

A tree-based solution is still not possible since there is no light splitting in the core network. We take the connection requests one by one from the destination CDNs $|\Delta|$, and first route the connection between E_S and E_{δ_1}. We run Dijkstra's shortest path algorithm on the auxiliary graph. If there is a connection in the virtual topology between E_S and E_{δ_1} with enough capacity to carry the call, then the call is groomed into that lightpath. If a path is found, a lightpath is established between E_S and E_{δ_1} and the auxiliary graph is updated. For the other nodes, we follow the same procedure by first running the shortest path algorithm. The steps of the Core Network Routing (CNR) algorithm are shown in Algorithm 2.

---

input : Auxiliary Graph G_c; source edge node E_S and set of destination edge nodes E_{δ_i} for every CDN δ_i in $|\Delta|$

output: Routing and wavelength assignment for the multicast connection in the Core network

1 **for** $i \leftarrow 1$to$|\Delta|$ **do**
2   **if** *Model is Overlay* **then**
3   Dijkstra $(E_S$, Core, OV1$)$;
4   **if** $dist(E_{\delta_i}) = \infty$ **then**
5   Dijkstra $(E_S$, Core, OV2$)$;
6   **end**
7   **else**
8   Dijkstra $(E_S$, Core, PEER$)$;
9   **end**
10   **if** $\exists \delta_j \; j \geq i \; s.t. \; dist(E_{\delta_j}) = \infty$ **then**
11   Block the call;
12   Update the G_c back to the initial state;
13   **end**
14   Route the connection to E_{δ_i};
15   Update Auxiliary graph G_c;
16 **end**

Algorithm 2. Pseudocode for Core Network Routing (CNR) algorithm

4.1   Modified CNR Algorithm for Best-Effort Routing

In the best-effort routing, our goal is to maximize the total number of connected destinations. Therefore, for a multicast call m we first want to establish light-paths to the CDNs with higher number destinations. For this purpose, we sort the CDNs with descending order with respect to $|Y_{\delta_i}|$'s. Assume that the ordered CDNs are $\delta_1, \delta_2, \ldots, \delta_\Delta$. We try to establish lightpaths to the edge nodes of CDNs in this order. If we cannot establish a connection for δ_i, we move to next CDN δ_{i+1}. Whenever the edge node of E_{δ_i} is reachable from the source edge node E_S, we run the modified GMR algorithm for δ_i. However, if GMR returns that all destinations are blocked (i.e., $b_{m,i} = |Y_{\delta_i}|$), then the connection between E_S and E_{δ_i} is not established. We note that modified CDR algorithm runs after the GMR algorithm for source CDN S confirms that the source node s is connected to the edge node E_S.

5   Simulation Results

We ran simulations to evaluate the performance of our routing algorithm. The number of call arrivals denoted by $num\_arrivals$ is 10^5 or 10^6 depending on the blocking probability range observed. We use an additional initialization period of 10^4 trials at the beginning of the simulation. We show the 95% confidence intervals on the curves which are calculated over 10 intervals with $num\_arrivals/10$ call arrivals each. For each interval, the period before that interval acts as its initialization period. The Erlang load on the network is denoted by ρ. The core network topologies are the well-known NSFNet and Arpanet. Four CDNs are created randomly having 4, 5, 6, and 7 nodes and their edges nodes are randomly chosen out of the nodes of the core network. The maximum number of destinations in a multicast session (max_d) is 8. The capacity of a wavelength is 10 units. The bandwidth request of a multicast session is a randomly chosen integer between 1 and 3. We assume the light-trails established at CDNs are all LTs (as opposed to SLTs or DLTs). The number of wavelengths W in the system is 16.

In order to see the performance gain achieved by GMR and CNR algorithms separately, we compare our results with two additional cases. In the first case, we restrict CDNs to establish only lightpaths (LPs) to see the performance gain achieved by using LTs. We use the same routing algorithm (GMR) for LPs by modifying the auxiliary graph as follows. In VT layer, the only connections created in this case are between the end nodes of an LP. We note that traffic grooming and multihopping is possible with LPs, too. In the second case, we do not allow edge grooming for the connections through the core network to see the performance gain achieved using edge grooming with our algorithm CNR. We call the case with no edge grooming as NEG. Therefore, the three models that we evaluate are: LT-EG, LP-EG, and LT-NEG. We also compare to call acceptance criteria of best effort and all-or-none, denoted as BE and AoN, respectively.

We first plot RMBbp vs. load in Fig. 5 for both topologies with 20 transceivers per node (i.e., $T = 20$) under overlay model. For both AoN and BE, we see that LT-EG is better than LP-EG with lower loads in Fig. 5(a) for the NSFNet. Specifically, for $\rho = 50$ the difference is more than an order of magnitude. As the load increases the performance gap between LT-EG and LP-EG narrows down. Light-trails offer more savings by better utilizing the bandwidth of a wavelength at lower loads. Blocking for LT-NEG is much higher than that for the other two cases. Therefore, we conclude that even if we have light-trails available at CDNs, NEG causes a bottleneck in the overall network performance. We note that with the best effort curves have lower RMBbp as expected. The RMBbp of BE gets less than the half of AoN and this improvement stays similar over the observed load range. In Fig. 5(b), we observe a similar behavior for Arpanet. In the load range observed, the performance difference between LT-EG and LP-EG is very close to that of NSFNet. Similarly, the gap increases as the load becomes smaller. The BE curves shows the improvement obtained using best-effort scheme and

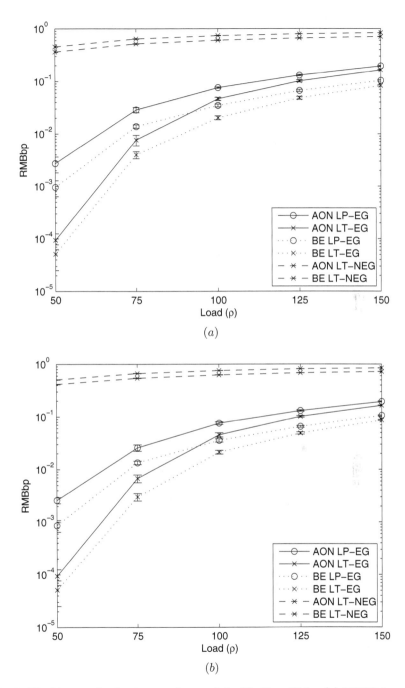

Fig. 5. Blocking vs. load using overlay model with $T = 20$ for (a) NSFNet, and (b) Arpanet as core network

the difference between the BE and AoN curves for LT-EG gets even higher with lower loads. Our recommendation is to see LTs in CDNs with the best-effort criterion to achieve the best performance.

We next compare the best effort and all-or-none schemes in order to evaluate the ratio of the *totally-accepted* calls (i.e., $B_m = 0$). For this purpose, we show the the ratio of the *not-totally-accepted* calls (partially accepted or totally blocked) in BE scheme to the total number of trials. For AoN, we show the *blocked* call ratio. As shown in Fig. 6(a) for the NSFNet, not totally accepted call ratio for BE is almost the same with the blocked call ratio of the AoN. Thus, the partial multicast service (i.e., best effort) does not degrade the performance in terms of totally accepted call ratio. It just have a slightly higher *not-totally-accepted* call ratio than the *blocked* call ratio of AoN. In other words, it has a slightly lower totally-accepted call ratio than AoN. We also note that totally-blocked calls constitute a very small portion of the *not-totally-accepted* calls. In most cases, BE scheme is able to provide a partial multicast service than rather blocking the entire call. We plot the same metrics in Fig. 6(b) for Arpanet. The ratio of *not-totally-accepted* for BE is again very close to the *blocked* call ratio of AoN which is a similar result to NSFNet. Thus, our conclusion is that BE criterion offers the best service without deteriorating the service for totally-accepted calls.

We next plot RMBbp vs. number of transceivers (T) in Fig. 7 for overlay model. In Fig. 7(a), we see that blocking decreases with increasing T for all curves, as expected. With higher T, the blocking difference between LT-EG and LP-EG becomes higher with either BE or AoN. More transceivers allow more traffic grooming capabilities at the intermediate nodes along a light-trail. The difference between the BE LT-EG and AoN LT-EG curves stays the same the whole range of T. This shows that the performance improvement with best effort over all-or-none does not change with the number of transceivers. The same can be said about BE LP-EG and AoN LP-EG curves. Blocking improvement with higher transceivers is also higher in the case of Arpanet as seen in Fig. 7(b). Difference between LT-EG and LP-EG curves is close to an order of magnitude with $T = 20$. Our conclusion is that the use of light-trails in CDNs is more advantageous with larger number of transceivers and best effort scheme is recommended with any number of transceivers.

5.1   Comparison of Overlay and Peer Models

In this section, we plot RMBbp vs. load for both overlay and peer models in order to compare the two in Fig. 8(a) for the all-or-none scheme. We note that LT-EG and LP-EG in peer model have similar performance with LT-EG being slightly better, and they are both much better than both overlay cases. Peer model enables even LP-EG to use many multihopped paths which results in a similar performance to LT-EG's. LT-EG curve is just slightly better than the LP-EG curve. Therefore, having LTs is not advantageous over having LPs in the peer model since the resources of the network can be utilized more efficiently. However, traffic grooming may be expensive and sometimes limiting. In Fig. 8(b), we plot

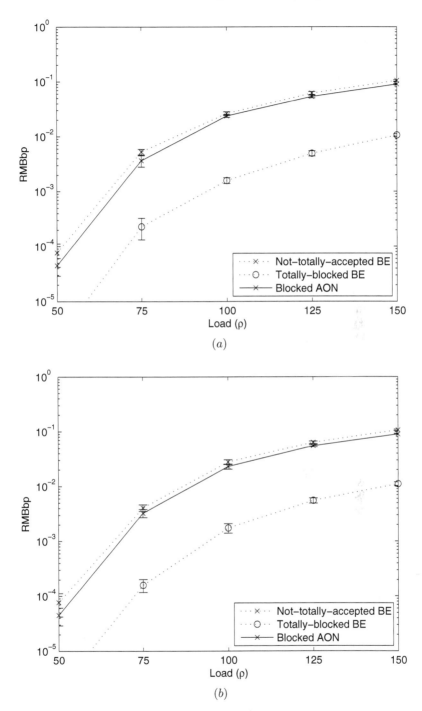

Fig. 6. Blocking vs. load using overlay model with $T = 20$ for (a) NSFNet, and (b) Arpanet as core network

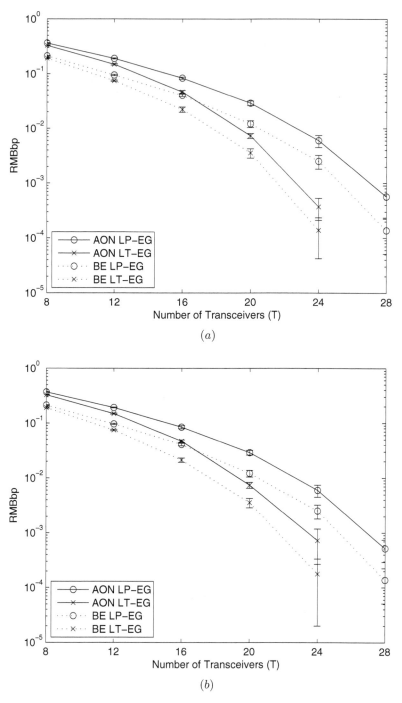

Fig. 7. Blocking vs. T using overlay model with $\rho = 75$ for (a) NSFNet , and (b) Arpanet as core network

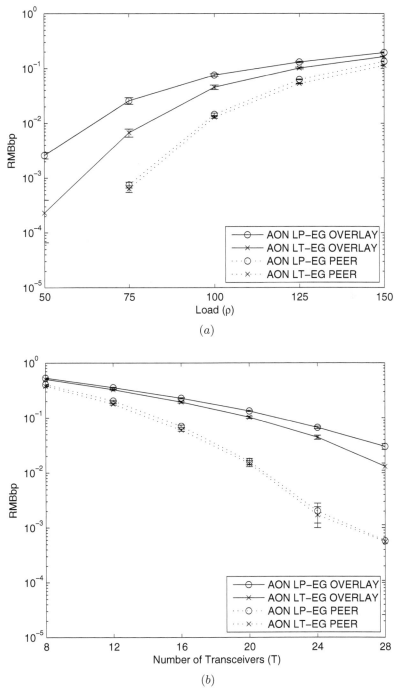

Fig. 8. Blocking vs. (a) ρ for $T = 20$, and (b) T for $\rho = 100$ with Arpanet as core network

RMBbp vs. T. Difference between the peer model curves and the overlay model curves first increaseswith higher T until $T = 24$. After that point, the blocking decreases slowly for the peer model. In the peer model, transceivers are utilized very well because of many multihopping opportunities. However, performance starts getting limited by the availability of wavelengths with higher T. Peer model offers a much better performance either with light-trails or lightpaths at the expense of higher information exchange to make the physical topology information available at higher layer.

6   Conclusion

We considered a hierarchical network model with collection/distribution networks (CDNs) employing light-trails and attached to a core network. Edge nodes that are the connecting points between the core network and CDNs perform grooming. We investigated the multi-stage routing problem for multicast connections in this network model and proposed routing algorithms for the core network and CDNs. The multicast routing algorithm in CDNs calculates the route using the existing light-trails or creates new light-trails to accommodate the multicast call with minimal network resources. We considered two call acceptance criteria, namely best-effort and all-or-none and we introduced a new performance metric called *requested multicast bandwidth blocking probability (RMBbp)* to evaluate the performance. We showed using simulations that the use of light-trails improves the performance compared to lightpaths, and grooming at the edge nodes is crucial for better performance. Partial multicast service with the best effort criterion improves the RMBbp and it does not deteriorate the performance significantly for totally serviced calls. Our overall recommendation is to use partial multicast service with the best effort criterion and utilize light-trails technology in CDNs.

Acknowledgment. The research reported in this paper funded in part by the Jerry R. Junking Endowment at Iowa State University, NSF projects CNS 0626741 and 0915795. Any opinions, findings, and conclusions or recommendations expressed in this material are those of the author(s) and do not necessarily reflect the views of the National Science Foundation (or another funding agency).

References

1. Sankaranarayanan, S., Subramaniam, S.: Comprehensive performance modeling and analysis of multicasting in optical networks. IEEE J. Sel. Areas Comm. 21(9), 1399–1413 (2003)
2. Zhu, H., Zang, H., Zhu, K., Mukherjee, B.: A novel generic graph model for traffic grooming in heterogeneous WDM mesh networks. IEEE/ACM Trans. Netw. 11(2), 285–299 (2003)

3. Ul-Mustafa, R., Kamal, A.E.: Design and provisioning of WDM networks with multicast traffic grooming. IEEE J. Sel. Areas Comm. 24(4), 37–52 (2006)
4. Gumaste, A., Chlamtac, I.: Light-trails: A novel conceptual framework for conducting optical communications. In: Proc. HPSR, pp. 251–256 (June 2003)
5. Balasubramanian, S., Somani, A.K.: Design algorithms for path-level grooming of traffic in WDM metro optical networks. OSA J. Optical Networking 7(8), 759–782 (2008)
6. Balasubramanian, S., Somani, A.K.: A comparative study of path level traffic grooming strategies for wdm optical networks with dynamic traffic - invited paper. In: Proc. ICCCN, pp. 267–272 (August 2008)
7. Vanderhorn, N., Balasubramanian, S., Mina, M., Weber, R.J., Somani, A.K.: Light-trail testbed for metro optical networks. IEEE Communications Magazine 43(8), S5–S10 (2005)
8. Ye, Y., Woesner, H., Grasso, R., Chen, T., Chlamtac, I.: Traffic grooming in light trail networks. In: Proc. GLOBECOM (November-December 2005)
9. Li, Y., Wang, J., Gumaste, A., Xu, Y., Xu, Y.: Multicast routing in light-trail WDM networks. In: Proc. GLOBECOM (November–December 2008)
10. Zhu, Y., Patel, A.N., Jue, J.P.: A novel graph model for dynamic multicast flow aggregation in optical networks. In: Proc. ICC (June 2009)
11. Gumaste, A., Wang, J., Karandikar, A., Ghani, N.: Multihop light-trails MLT - a solution to extended metro networks. In: Proc. ICC (June 2009)

Future Proof Next Generation Access Networks -- The Case for FTTH

Wolfgang Fischer

Cisco Europe
wfischer@cisco.com

Abstract. The insatiable demand for more and more bandwidth lets access bitrates in broadband networks grow exponentially at a rate of about 50% year-over-year. None of the copper-based wireline access technologies will be able to cope with this demand in the long term. Also wireless networks see similar growth and require higher and higher backhaul speeds. There is industry-wide consensus that only fiber-based access networks will be able to support this growth. It can be expected that the new generation of passive infrastructure will experience the same lifetime as today's copper-based infrastructure. Therefore, it is of vital importance that this infrastructure will be built in a way that it is as flexible as possible, supporting future applications and technologies without costly upgrades, while still being affordable at the time of deployment.

1   Introduction

Broadband access has many facets today with wireline (e.g., DSL, cable, Ethernet, PON, etc.) and wireless (e.g., WiFi, WiMaX, 3G, LTE etc.) technologies being abundant. Within the physical limits of the respective media all these technologies have evolved to higher and higher bitrates over the last two decades. Typical access bitrates (i.e., the physical bitrates in the access network for Internet subscribers) have consistently grown by about 50% year-over-year on average. Using available data and extrapolating them into the future, 100Mbit/s can be seen as a typical access bitrate around 2014, and 1Gbit/s would be typical in 2019 (see Fig. 1). Many stakeholders even believe that this projection is rather conservative. In a number of networks, e.g., in Sweden, Netherlands, or Hongkong, 1Gbit/s is already state of the art. This consideration is supported by a significant increase in video-related applications over broadband networks which go far beyond the usual TV-related applications, and which will be characterized by higher definition, symmetrical bitrate requirements, ultra-high-speed bursts for non-real time video applications, and multiple streams per household. High-Definition video cameras have become affordable for the masses, and the efficient transport of the content created by them is one of many factors which continue driving bitrate growth.

There is widespread agreement in the industry that only direct Fiber to the Home (FTTH) will allow all of these applications to be supported in the longer term, with wireless technologies being an indispensable complement providing mobility.

I. Tomkos et al. (Eds.): BROADNETS 2010, LNICST 66, pp. 302–313, 2012.

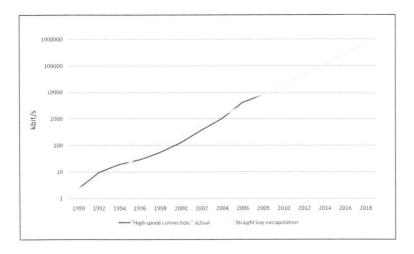

Fig. 1. Exponential growth of Broadband access bitrates (Source: Graham Finnie, HeavyReading)

2   Topology vs. Technology

While there is agreement about the need for fiber-based access networks, there is an ongoing debate about the best architecture for these networks, both in terms of the topologies of the fiber infrastructures as well as the technologies for transporting data over those fibers.

The two most fundamental types of topologies are Point-to-Multipoint and Point-to-Point.

Point-to-Multipoint topologies with multiplexing devices in the field are deployed in order to be used by one of the standardized Passive Optical Network (PON) technologies (EPON, GPON) and their evolutions, by Active Ethernet (Fiber to the Building, Fiber to the Curb), or by WDM-PON. The common fiber is shared and all subscribers connected to a tree use the same technology.

Point-to-Point topologies provide dedicated fibers between the Central Office / POP and the subscriber. As there is a dedicated transparent medium a wide choice of transport technologies is available. All currently existing point-to-point FTTH deployments use Ethernet (100BASE-BX10 or 1000BASE-BX10) over single fibers, but this can be mixed with other transmission schemes for business applications (e.g., FiberChannel, SDH/SONET, …), and even with PON technologies by placing the passive splitters into the POPs. Upgrades and modifications of a transmission technology can be performed on a subscriber-by-subscriber basis.

		Technology		
		Ethernet	TDM-PON (GPON, EPON, DPON, XG-PON, 10GEPON)	WDM-PON
Topology	P2P	Ethernet P2P	PON P2P	N.A.
	P2MP	Active Ethernet	PON P2MP	WDM-PON

Dedicated medium

Shared medium

Fig. 2. Classification of FTTH architectures

Fig. 2 shows a classification of FTTH architectures in terms of fiber topologies and technologies.

Ethernet P2P and PON P2MP are the classical architectures in the context of FTTH. Active Ethernet is used mainly for Fiber-to-the-Building (FTTB) or Fiber-to-the-Curb (FTTC) deployment models.

PON P2P has become more popular recently as a way to combine some aspects of P2P topologies and PON technology, by placing the splitter in the central office. This, however, sacrifices the benefit of fiber savings in P2MP architectures. TDM-PON will always constitute a shared-medium architecture, even with a P2P topology as the port on the OLT is shared. Thus, most of the well-known characteristics of shared media remain.

WDM-PON is an emerging architecture which promises to provide dedicated connectivity over a P2MP infrastructure by providing pairs of wavelengths per customer on the fiber tree. WDM PON on a P2P fiber infrastructure makes no practical sense.

From a civil engineering perspective the structure of the fiber plant for Point-to-Point fiber deployments are identical to that of Point-to-Multipoint. From the POP location feeder fibers are deployed towards some distribution point in the field either in some underground enclosure or a street cabinet. From this distribution point individual drop fibers are laid towards each individual household. The difference between both structures is only the number of feeder fibers. As fiber densities in the feeder and drop part are very different, often different cabling techniques are employed, depending on the specific circumstances.

Cabling techniques include classical cables and blown fiber in microducts. Classical cables can either be directly buried or accommodated in ducts for larger flexibility. In the feeder part deployments can be greatly facilitated not only by existing conventional ducts, but by other rights of way, like sewers, tunnels, or other available tubes. Thus, in most cases the higher number of feeder fibers in point-to-point topologies do not pose any major obstacle for these installations.

3   The Case for Point-to-Point Topologies

Access to the telephone network has always been provided via dedicated copper lines into every household. Initially, these lines were dimensioned for voice communication with frequencies up to 3.4kHz. Technological progress during the past 30 years has enabled a rapid increase of transmission rates over this classical medium. With VDSL2 the physical limits of this medium have now been reached with frequencies on the medium reaching up to 30MHz over short distances. This evolution would not have been possible if the passive infrastructure had contained technology specific components (in fact, in the US the loading coils in the copper plant have caused challenges to the DSL introduction in many places).

The structure of the access network has also allowed to easily unbundle the local loop, and to create competition among access network providers. This competition has largely contributed to increased access bitrates at lower and lower prices.

For the deployment of new fiber-based access networks for consumers (Fiber to the Home – FTTH) during the past few years there has been an intense discussion whether they should be built in the same way as the copper-based networks, in a Point-to-Point topology, or whether the high capacity of fibers would rather imply a Point-to-Multipoint structure, which allows savings of fibers and optical interfaces. Nonetheless, they could provide relatively high bitrates for every customer. For this purpose optical splitters are introduced in the passive infrastructure, which restrict its use to a class of technologies – Passive Optical Networks (PON). These technologies were developed initially at a time when fibers and optical interfaces were still very expensive. These arguments have become largely irrelevant through mass production of fibers, cables with very high fiber counts (e.g., 720 fibers in a cable with 16mm diameter), and very cost effective optical interfaces.

The economic lifetime of a passive infrastructure will be more than 40 years. During this period novel applications will be developed, enabled by the high transmission bitrates, and we will see innovative fiber-based transmission technologies which will allow higher and higher speeds at lower and lower cost. Technology specific components in the passive infrastructure will restrict the degrees of freedom for these developments.

Dedicated fibers allow to provide individual, virtually unlimited speeds for each customer. Changing technologies for one customer does not cause technology changes for the other subscribers as is the case with P2MP architectures.

The P2P topology allows access to individual fibers to every household allowing potentially the same kind of physical unbundling as in copper networks. National regulators are split about the question whether a physical unbundling of the access network will be required to enable competing service providers access to the passive infrastructure. The joint usage of such an infrastructure, however, can be of high commercial interest and allow investment sharing into a common physical network by multiple providers. For example, in Switzerland bilateral agreements between the incumbent operator and individual utilities have been signed about co-investments into passive infrastructures in a P2P topology.

Furthermore, the European Commission has set the criteria for state aid in broadband networks within their Community Guidelines for the application of State aid rules in relation to rapid deployment of broadband networks:

"... whatever the type of the NGA network architecture that will benefit from State aid, it should support effective and full unbundling and satisfy all different types of network access that operators may seek (including but not limited to access to ducts, fibre and bitstream). ..."

In the POP the fibers arriving from the outside plant are terminated on an Optical Distribution Frame (ODF) as the fiber management solution which allows to flexibly connect any customer to any port on switches or splitters in the POP. Due to the large number of fibers to be handled in a POP the density of such a fiber management solution has to be very high in order to minimize real estate requirements. Fig. 3 shows a high-density ODF that allows to handle more than 2300 fibers in a single rack. For illustration purposes it is positioned next to a rack with active equipment.

Take rates in FTTH projects typically take some time to ramp up and usually stay well below 100%. The fiber management allows a ramp up of the number of active ports in sync with the activation of customers. This minimizes the number of unused active network elements in the POP and enables a slow ramp up of the investments.

Fig. 3. High-density fiber management solution (source: Huber&Suhner)

The emergence of 4G radio access networks is another driver for fiber deployment in the access network.

FTTH deployment will create major synergies with the rollout of these 4G networks because subscriber densities and base station densities in an area are positively correlated. This means that in urban areas where FTTH is deployed with priority also sufficient fiber can be made available for the large number of base stations.

As base stations have different connectivity requirements from residential customers – primarily clock synchronization – their connectivity should not be merged with that for residentials in a P2MP infrastructure.

4   The Case for Ethernet Technology

4.1   Transmission Technologies

After many years of technological debate Ethernet has emerged as the most prevalent transmission technology for virtually every application, from home networking to backbone networks. This is due to its conceptual simplicity, its support of a variety of different media – coaxial cable, shielded / unshielded twisted pair, single / dual multi-mode / single-mode fiber – and its scalability. There are Ethernet versions available, starting at 2Mbit/s on a shared coaxial cable up to 100Gbit/s on a fiber pair. Backwards compatibility has been largely maintained, leading to the ubiquitous 10/100/1000Mbit/s auto-sensing interfaces in homes and offices.

This ubiquity has led to the emergence of very cost-effective components for transmission and switching of Ethernet frames, and to a huge market for Ethernet equipment.

Recognizing the need for Ethernet in Service Provider access networks IEEE had established the IEEE 802.3ah working group already in 2001, creating a standard for "Ethernet in the First Mile (EFM)". Besides standards for OAM, Ethernet over copper and EPON, two standards for Fast Ethernet and Gigabit Ethernet over Single-Mode Single-Fiber were created.

The EFM standard was approved and published in 2004, and was included into the base IEEE 802.3 standard in 2005.

The specifications for the transmission over Single-Mode Single-Fiber are called 100BASE-BX10 for Fast Ethernet and 1000BASE-BX10 for Gigabit Ethernet. Both specifications are defined for a nominal maximum reach of 10km.

For the separation of the directions on the same fiber wavelength-division duplexing is employed, such that for each of the bitrate classes two specifications for transceivers are defined, one for "Upstream", i.e. from the CPE towards the POP and one for "Downstream", i.e., from the POP towards the CPE.

The following table provides the fundamental optical parameters of these specifications.

Table 1. Ethernet transmission technologies for FTTH

Description	100BASE-BX10-D	100BASE-BX10-U	1000BASE-BX10-D	1000BASE-BX10-U
Transmit direction	Downstream	Upstream	Downstream	Upstream
Nominal transmit wavelength	1550nm	1310nm	1490nm	1310nm
Minimum range	0.5m to 10km			
Maximum channel insertion loss	5.5dB	6.0dB	5.5dB	6.0dB

In order to cope with requirements not considered in the standard the market also offers optical transceivers with non-standard characteristics.

Some types can bridge significantly longer distances, e.g., for deployments in rural areas.

As the nominal transmit wavelength of 100BASE-BX-D (1550nm) is the same as the standard wavelength for video overlays in PON systems, transceivers exist which can transmit at 1490nm which allows to insert an additional signal at 1550nm carrying an RF-modulated video overlay signal on the same fiber using off-the-shelf video transmission equipment (see Fig. 5).

4.2   Operational Considerations

Traffic Management

For obvious reasons all communication networks are oversubscribed, starting at the uplink interface of the access network element. In shared media architectures oversubscription already occurs in the access network based on appropriate Media Access Control (MAC) protocols. Management of oversubscription in packet networks requires queueing and priority mechanisms. As a general rule, such queueing and priority implementations in switches and routers can be made significantly more sophisticated and effective than those based on MAC protocols. Using a dedicated port per fiber, therefore, removes the need for a MAC protocol in the access network, and it removes also an additional point of congestion to be managed within the entire context of traffic management.

Access network elements follow fast innovation life cycles and are replaced or upgraded in regular intervals which are much shorter than the lifetime of the fiber. Therefore, any bottlenecks in the active infrastructure can be removed on a regular basis, but this should not have any impact on the passive access infrastructure.

Security

A dedicated port on a dedicated fiber is inherently secure because the information transmitted over it can only be received at either end of the fiber, and it will not be shared, by default, with any other subscriber in the same access network domain. This inherent security, therefore, obviates the need for encryption on the fiber which is a necessary function in any shared medium architecture.

A failed ONT / CPE device connected to a dedicated fiber cannot impact the traffic of any other subscriber because any unplanned behaviour can be detected by the associated switch port in the POP, and the port can be deactivated until the defect is repaired. This property also eliminates denial of service attacks which can be launched by malicious users in shared medium architectures by deliberately jamming the signals.

CPE Deployments

For the deployment of the CPEs – either simple ONTs with integrated Ethernet switches, or more sophisticated routed Home Access Gateways – the service providers have the choice of two different scenarios.

- They own and install the CPE by themselves and also test the integrity of the transmission. In this case the subscriber has no need to touch the fiber in any way but only connects his home network to the subscriber-facing interfaces of the CPE.
- They can drop-ship the CPEs to the subscribers and have them connect their CPEs via optical patch cables to optical wall outlets. This requires more confidence in the subscribers' capabilities to handle optical fibers. Eventually, this will also allow CPEs to be distributed over retail channels.

While there are operational pros and cons for either solution, with Ethernet over dedicated fibers in no case is there any security risk involved in having the subscriber handle the fiber. Any potential problem is strictly confined to this particular subscriber's access line. One of the main questions in this context is rather whether the savings from self installation can compensate the higher cost of support calls.

Trouble-Shooting

Optical Time Domain Reflectometry (OTDR) mechanisms are used to determine any discontinuities or reflections in the fiber plant. OTDR transmits light pulses into the fiber, and the timing and intensity of the reflections indicates the location and the nature of any problem. In a point-to-point deployment the fiber is visible on its entire length from the POP to the subscriber, which greatly facilitates trouble-shooting of the fiber plant, compared to point-to-multipoint architectures which create ambiguous results for the reflections coming from the drop fibers.

Power Budget Planning

The Ethernet transmission technologies typically employed for point-to-point connectivity provide sufficient margin, even at the nominal maximum distances, such that a substantial number of splices and connectors can be accommodated without exceeding the maximum channel insertion loss. This facilitates the planning of the outside plant and allows for some aging of the passive components.

4.3   Support for Video Broadcast

IPTV-based video solutions provide superior features over simple broadcast solutions and have, therefore, become an indespensable part of any triple-play offering. Quite frequently, however, there is a need to provide RF video broadcast overlays in order to support existing TV sets in the subscribers' households. In splitter-based P2MP architectures this is typically accomplished by providing an RF video signal, compatible with cable TV solutions, over an additional wavelength at 1550nm. In Ethernet P2P installations this can be achieved by two different approaches, depending on the possibilities for fiber installation:

- In the first approach an additional fiber per customer is deployed in a tree structure (see Fig. 4) and carries only an RF video signal that can be fed into the inhouse coax distribution network. In this case the split factors (e.g. ≥ 128) exceed those typically used for PONs so that the number of additional feeder fibers is minimized.

- In the second approach a video signal is inserted into every point-to-point fiber at 1550nm. Fig. 5 shows how the RF video signal carried by a dedicated wavelength from a Video-OLT is first split into multiple identical streams by an optical splitter and then fed into each point-to-point fiber by means of diplexers. Mechanically, this solution is implemented in structures similar to Optical Distribution Frames. On the customer side the wavelengths are separated, the 1550nm signal converted into an RF signal for coax distribution, and the 1490nm signal made available on an Ethernet port.

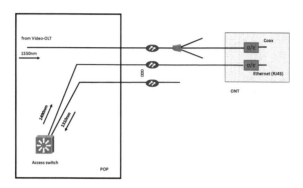

Fig. 4. RF video overlay using a second fiber per subscriber, deployed in a P2MP structure

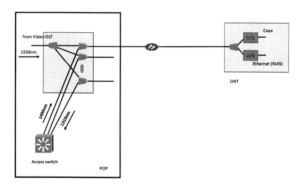

Fig. 5. Insertion of RF video signal into P2P fibers

In both cases the CPE/ONT devices comprise two distinct parts:

- a media converter which takes the RF signal on 1550nm and converts it into an electrical signal that drives a coax interface,
- and an optical Ethernet interface into an Ethernet switch or router.

In the single-fiber case the signals are separated by a diplexer built into the CPE, while in the dual fiber case there are individual optical interfaces for each fiber.

4.4   Support for Wireless Base Stations

To support the backhaul of traffic from wireless base stations tight clock synchronization is required. This can be achieved by special Ethernet interfaces with capabilities like Synchronous Ethernet (SyncE) or Precision Time Protocol (PTP) according to IEEE1588. As these capabilities incur cost which is not required to connect residential or business customers they are provided by dedicated linecards or systems.

5   Cost Considerations

5.1   Capital Cost

FTTH deployment involves a number of different cost components that can each be individually optimized. However, it is important to understand the relative contribution of each component and, thus, the relative saving potential. Fig. 6 shows a typical cost distribution for greenfield FTTH deployments.

This graph confirms what intuitively could be expected: civil works comprise almost 70% of the total initial capex. Obviously, this is the cost component where saving efforts have the largest effect. Therefore, usage of every potential right-of-way solution should be considered in order to reduce this component. As already mentioned earlier this comprises existing ducts, sewers, tunnels, ...

With 6%, respectively 2% the fiber and other passive optical elements only contribute a very small part to the capex. Therefore, the saving potential from these components is very limited.

Active network elements are the second largest component with 12% contribution. Independent of the particular technology employed, this is a component where technological progress will continue to bring down per-port cost. In the case of Ethernet point-to-point architectures the access switches in the POPs are usually derived from systems that are deployed in very large quantities in Enterprise networks. Therefore, their cost benefit very strongly from manufacturing volumes which are significantly larger than they would be in the case of Service-Provider-only equipment. Furthermore, their technological evolution can be more broadly funded which leads to rapid innovation cycles and cost reduction.

It is also interesting to consider the distribution of cost for the infrastructure deployment. Swisscom have determined that 85% of the cost is in the drop segment and the inhouse segment of the network. Only 15% account for the feeder and the central office segment. As the former two segments are the same for each topology the saving potential from a P2MP topology, therefore, is very limited.

Based on detailed business case analyses with European Service Providers some typical values for the cost differences between point-to-point and point-to-multipoint deployments have been derived. In those cases where just sufficient duct space in the feeder plant was available to deploy the smaller cables for point-to-multipoint architectures, but not enough for point-to-point, the cost premium for Ethernet point-to-point could run up to 25% because of the need for additional civil works.

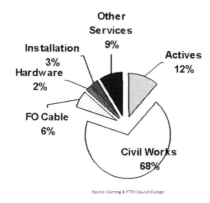

Fig. 6. Typical initial capex distribution for green-field FTTH deployments

Experience with real deployments, however, implies that this situation occurs far less frequently than situations where there is either no duct shortage, or where civil works have to be carried out because either all the ducts are occupied by other cables, or in greenfield scenarios where no infrastructure is available in the first place. In those cases the cost premium for point-to-point deployments usually stays below 5%. This difference can be mainly attributed to the more extensive fiber management in the POPs.

It can be expected that these initial small project cost differences will be overcompensated, over the lifetime of the fiber plant, by the inherent benefits of point-to-point deployments (flexibility, upgradability, fiber plant maintenance, …).

5.2   Operating Cost

Operating cost are a multi-faceted subject. Most of these cost items are not specific to any particular access technology, like marketing, subscriber acquisition, subscriber management, …

It is very difficult, though, to quantify operational cost differences. Therefore, we try to identify qualitatively the technology and architecture dependent aspects that can impact the operating cost of an FTTH access network.

Aspects which are favourable for Ethernet point-to-point deployments are mainly due to the relative simplicity of the architecture, as there are

- Ease of traffic management
- No encryption
- Ease of troubleshooting the physical layer
- Easy upgrade to higher speeds / new technologies on a per-customer basis.

Certainly, there are also some operational disadvantages of Ethernet point-to-point deployments:

- More real estate in the POP location due to the more extensive fiber management
- Slightly higher space requirements for the active equipment, although for typical penetration rates the difference is rather small as only active subscribers require

switch ports, in contrast to point-to-multipoint architectures where the first subscriber on a tree requires the allocation of an OLT port
- Higher power consumption in the POP as every active subscriber is connected to a dedicated port, although also this aspect is mitigated by the penetration rate, and technological advances will continue to reduce power consumption.

6   Summary

The need for Fiber to the Home is largely undisputed. The discussion is focused now on the timing, the business models, and the right architectures.

Synergies can be created with the backhaul connectivity of wireless base stations.

A variety of architectures for FTTH are available, each with its particular pros and cons. Access fiber deployment will form the basis of a new infrastructure which holds the promise to last for the next 40...50 years. This longevity should lead to deployment models which are technology agnostic and allow the maximum flexibility for the introduction of novel technologies and the support of new business models.

Point-to-Point architectures meet all these requirements at a very small initial capex premium.

On the technology side Ethernet is the most mature approach with its scalability, security and ubiquity. Recent developments provide also support for clock synchronization required by wireless base stations.

Throughput-Delay Trade-Offs
in Slotted WDM Ring Networks

Thomas Bonald[1], Raluca-M. Indre[2], Sara Oueslati[2], and Chloe Rolland[2]

[1] Telecom ParisTech, France
[2] Orange Labs, France

Abstract. We analyse the throughput-delay trade-offs that arise in an optical burst-switched slotted WDM ring, where each node can transmit and receive on a subset of the available wavelengths. Specifically, we compare SWING, an access control scheme that combines opportunistic transmission and dynamic reservations, with a purely opportunistic aceess scheme. By means of analysis, we highlight the shortcomings of the opportunistic scheme in terms of load balancing and fairness. We then evaluate the performance of both schemes by simulation under several traffic scenarios and show that SWING yields the best throughput-delay trade-off.

Keywords: Optical Burst Switching, WDM ring, MAC protocol, dynamic reservation, throughput, delay.

1 Introduction

Increasing internet traffic volumes and the growing ubiquity of broadband access solutions (FTTx) challenge the simple use of over-provisioning in future metropolitan area networks (MAN). Most of today's MANs employ circuit-switching at the wavelength level [14] and have limited flexibility in handling traffic variability. An alternate switching paradigm, Optical Burst Switching (OBS), allows statistical multiplexing of data at the burst level, thus improving bandwidth utilization and network scalability.

This paper addresses the issue of resource access control in a burst-switched WDM metro ring. We are particularly interested in comparing the performance of SWING [6], a novel MAC protocol that combines opportunistic access and dynamic slot reservation, with that of a reference, purely opportunistic scheme, from a throughput and delay perspective.

The topic of resource access control in slotted WDM rings has drawn considerable research attention in recent years. Most of the existing proposals aim at providing a certain degree of fairness among the network nodes. A great number of these proposals are based on the idea that each station is allowed to emit up to a certain quota of packets in a dynamically or statically determined cycle [3,9,10,4]. The main drawback of these schemes is that the quota has to be large enough to ensure an efficient utilization of the ring, which implies a large interval

I. Tomkos et al. (Eds.): BROADNETS 2010, LNICST 66, pp. 314–327, 2012.

between the transmission periods for each station and leads to potentially unacceptable packet delays. Some proposals rely on a connection-oriented reservation strategy [2,1], where the ring is divided in multiple reservation frames in which consecutive slots can be used to transmit long packets without segmentation. Finally, a solution based on virtual circuit allocation has been investigated in [7], where a centralized reservation scheme is deployed.

In this paper, we analyze SWING, a distributed reservation protocol that aims at seizing all available transmission opportunities, while ensuring fair resource allocation. The underlying dynamic reservation mechanism is original in many ways. Firstly, no reservation quota is imposed, which makes it more flexible. Secondly, the reservations are not connection-oriented, allowing a station to use a reserved slot for any destination. Lastly, it allows spatial reuse of reserved slots, thus enhancing bandwidth utilization.

This work builds on a previous paper [6], where SWING is presented in detail and its stability condition and throughput efficiency evaluated under the restrictive assumption of a single wavelength. The present study extends [6] by considering the impact of tunable transmitters and fixed receivers on network stability and performance. It turns out that the property of throughput optimality established for the opportunistic transmission scheme in [6,12] is lost in the more realistic context of multiple wavelength channels. A thorough performance evaluation is carried out by means of analysis and simulations, the latter being realised in a multiservice context, with two service classes. The results highlight the interesting throughput-delay trade-off achieved by SWING, compared to the opportunistic scheme.

The paper is organized as follows. Section 2 presents the network architecture and the access protocols. The traffic model and performance metrics are described in Section 3. Section 4 presents the throughput analysis of the opportunistic scheme, focusing on load balancing and fairness issues. Section 5 is devoted to the simulation results, that show the throughput-delay trade-offs achieved by the opportunistic and dynamic reservation schemes. Section 6 concludes the paper.

2   System

This section presents the network architecture, the scheduling mechanism as well as the considered access protocols.

2.1   A Slotted WDM Ring

The network is a slotted WDM ring, which actually consists of two counter rotating fiber rings, one of which is used for backup in case of failure. We consider here the operation of a single ring. The ring consists of $N + 1$ nodes linked with optical fibers, as illustrated by Figure 1 for $N = 6$. A particular station, say station 0, corresponds to the *hub* that connects the ring to the Internet. The other N nodes are *access stations* connecting end-users to the ring. Each node is an optical packet add/drop multiplexer (OPADM) capable of transmitting and receiving data on W wavelengths. Control information (occupancy of each wavelength, destination of each packet, reservation state when applicable) is sent via control packets on an out-of-band channel. One control packet is associated to every time slot.

Each node i is equipped with t_i tunable transmitters, $t_i \in \{1, \ldots, W\}$, and with a set of fixed receivers, $r_i \subset \{1, \ldots, W\}$; it can thus simultaneously transmit data on any t_i distinct wavelengths and receive data on a fixed subset r_i of the wavelengths. Throughout the paper, we assume that in each time slot, the hub can transmit and receive on all wavelengths simultaneously i.e., $t_0 = W^1$, $r_0 = \{1, \ldots, W\}$) while all other nodes can transmit and receive on a single wavelength (i.e., $t_i = |r_i| = 1$ for all $i \neq 0$). The received wavelengths are allocated in a cyclic manner from node 1 to node N, as shown in Figure 1. In the numerical examples, we consider either $W = 2$ or $W = 4$, which is compliant with the current economical and technological constraints [17].

Time is slotted so that there are S slots circulating on the ring at the speed of light, visiting nodes in a cyclic manner in the order $1, \ldots, N$. Slots have a fixed duration, 10 μs, which is taken as the time unit throughout the paper. Each slot on each wavelength channel may carry at most one optical burst. The size of an optical burst is thus given by the slot duration times the transmission speed on each wavelength, that is 12.5 KB for a transmission speed of 10 Gbit/s.

When a slot arrives at node i, all packets contained in this slot on the subset of wavelengths r_i and destined to node i are received and extracted from the corresponding wavelengths. In addition, node i can transmit up to t_i packets in this slot, depending on the queued packets and the occupancy state of the wavelengths, as described below.

2.2 Scheduling

Each node i maintains a queue of optical bursts per destination. At the arrival of each slot, if several wavelengths are unoccupied, the next wavelength to be used for transmission is selected using the reverse round robin policy, where wavelengths are scanned cyclically in the order $W, \ldots, 1$. Among the destinations that can receive on the selected wavelength, the next queue to be served is also selected using reverse round robin scheduling (this reverse order tends to favor longer paths, see [6] for details). This process stops once t_i queues have been served or no other queue can be served, and resumes at the arrival of the next slot.

---

[1] Since the number of transmitters is equal to W, the hub is actually equipped with *fixed-tuned* transmitters. However, for the sake of generality, we maintain the notation t_0.

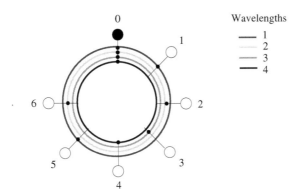

Fig. 1. Ring of $N = 6$ nodes with $W = 4$ wavelengths and fixed receivers $r_0 = \{1, 2, 3, 4\}$, $r_1 = \{1\}$, $r_2 = \{2\}$, $r_3 = \{3\}$, $r_4 = \{4\}$, $r_5 = \{1\}$, $r_6 = \{2\}$

2.3 Access Protocols

In the described network architecture, all nodes implement two MAC sub-layers: adaptation and transport. The adaptation sublayer is in charge of assembling variable-size data packets into fixed-size optical bursts. This is done by means of a timer-based burst-assembly mechanism proposed in [5].

The transport sub-layer is responsible for providing ressource access control for the network nodes. In the following, we consider two different schemes at the transport sub-layer: a purely opportunistic scheme and SWING, a dynamic reservation scheme that allows on-demand slot reservation. In the opportunistic scheme, nodes seize every opportunity to use an idle slot in order to send a waiting optical burst. In such a scheme, nodes compete for access to the ring without any control beyond the packet scheduling policy described above.

In SWING, each node reserves slots when necessary and preempts the reservations of other nodes in order to preserve fairness, as explained in the following. The packet scheduling policy is still the one described in §2.2. A wavelength k is considered free by node i in slot n if this slot carries no burst and is either:

- *unreserved* (opportunistic transmission);
- *reserved for node i*, which means the reservation made by node i in the previous cycle has not been preempted;
- *reserved for another node and spatially reusable*, i.e. node i can send an optical burst to node j on a reserved slot as long as node j is not downstream from the node that reserved the slot.

All reservations held by node i on slot n are then released.

The reservation scheme is fully distributed. Each node i maintains a counter $c_{ij}(k)$ of the number of reservations node j has made on each wavelength k over slots $1, \ldots, n-1$, where n is the current slot. Note that these counters are local visions of the reservation status and, in general, are different from one station to another.

A maximum number t_i of new reservations are attempted by node i on slot n if the pending reservations are not sufficient to clear all queues of node i. To determine whether the number of pending reservations of node i, namely $\sum_{k=1}^{W} c_{ii}(k)$, is sufficient, the burst scheduling algorithm is *virtually* run on all queues for each wavelength k, assuming that $c_{ii}(k)$ slots are available on wavelength k and no other slot is available. The algorithm stops either when there are no more pending optical bursts in the queues or when all reserved slots have been used. Reservations are attempted on wavelengths r_j associated with queues j that still have waiting bursts when the algorithm stops. Node i requests the reservations on unreserved wavelengths and preempts the reservations made by other nodes, if allowed; the preemption of a reservation held by node j on wavelength k is allowed if and only if node i has fewer pending reservations, that is if $c_{ii}(k) < c_{ij}(k)$.

3   Model

This section presents the traffic characteristics and the performance metrics used throughout the paper.

3.1   Traffic Characteristics

Packets are assumed to arrive according to a Poisson process of intensity λ. Although this assumption is known to be incorrect in local area networks [16,19], it is reasonable in the metropolitan and wide area networks we are interested in [8]. Traffic is indeed shaped by the transmission speed of end systems and access queues; typical peak rates of end-to-end data flows do not exceed a few hundred Mbit/s while the transmission speed on each wavelength of the ring is equal to 10 Gbit/s. The multiplexing of a large number of such flows typically leads to Poisson packet arrivals.

Let p_{ij} be the associated traffic matrix, with $p_{ii} = 0$ for all i: an incoming packet has source i and destination j with probability p_{ij}. We denote by $\lambda_{ij} = \lambda p_{ij}$ the packet arrival rate on the source-destination pair (i, j) and by $\lambda_i = \sum_j \lambda_{ij}$ the total packet arrival rate at node i.

3.2   Throughput Metric

A key criterion for MAC efficiency is its ability to fully use the transmission and reception capabilities of each node. Formally, this can be expressed as the following stability issue, which is reminiscent of those arising in the performance analysis of ad-hoc networks [13] and switching fabrics [15].

Nodes are indexed by integers modulo N. We refer to link l as that connecting node l to node $l + 1$, for all $l = 1, \ldots, N$. We denote by $[i, j]$ the set of nodes between node i and node j, that is the set $\{i, \ldots, j\}$ if $i \leq j$ and the set $\{i, \ldots, N\} \cup \{1, \ldots, j\}$ otherwise. For the network to be stable, in the sense that all queues (i, j) remain finite, it is necessary that traffic does not exceed the transmission and reception capabilities of each node, namely:

$$\forall i, \quad \lambda_i < t_i \tag{1}$$

and

$$\forall l, \ \forall r \subset \{1, \ldots, W\}, \qquad \sum_{i,j:l\in[i,j],r_j\subset r} \lambda_{ij} < |r|. \tag{2}$$

We say that the network is *throughput-optimal* if these conditions are also sufficient for stability.

In view of (1) and (2), it is natural to define the *load* as:

$$\rho = \max \left(\max_i \frac{\lambda_i}{t_i}, \max_{l,r\subset\{1,\ldots,W\}} \frac{1}{|r|} \sum_{i,j:l\in[i,j],r_j\subset r} \lambda_{ij} \right). \tag{3}$$

The optimal stability condition can then be simply written as $\rho < 1$. In general, the actual stability condition is more restrictive, say $\rho < \theta$ with $\theta \leq 1$. We refer to θ as the throughput efficiency, which depends both on the considered MAC and on the traffic matrix. Throughput optimality is equivalent to the equality $\theta = 1$.

3.3 Delay Metric

Data packet delay is another key performance metric. We estimate the probability that the queueing delay of any packet exceeds some threshold, taken equal to two cycle times ($2S$ slots). This delay is supposed to be sufficient for the dynamic reservation scheme to work out since one cycle is needed before a node can benefit from its reserved slot.

4 Throughput Analysis of the Opportunistic Scheme

To analyse the performance of the opportunistic scheme, we consider in this section a simple burst-level model where bursts (instead of packets) arrive according to Poisson processes.

4.1 Load Balancing Impairment

The opportunistic scheme was proven to be throughput-optimal for a single wavelength [12,6]. It turns out that this property is lost for multiple wavelengths, as shown by the example of Figure 2 with $N = 2$ nodes, $W = 2$ wavelengths. Recall that the hub station (i.e., station 0) can simultaneously receive and transmit on all wavelengths such that $r_0 = \{1, 2\}$ and $t_0 = 2$ when $W = 2$. The access nodes are able to transmit on all wavelengths ($t_1 = t_2 = 1$) but they can receive on a single predefined wavelength ($r_1 = \{1\}$ and $r_2 = \{2\}$). Assume that there is traffic only on source-destination pairs $(1,0)$ and $(2,1)$. In view of (1)-(2), the optimal stability condition is given by:

$$\lambda_1 < 1 \quad \text{and} \quad \lambda_2 < 1.$$

It is achieved by forwarding all traffic of the source-destination pair $(1,0)$ on wavelength 2, so that the traffic of the source-destination pair $(2,1)$ can fully use wavelength 1. Unfortunately, node 1 is not aware of the traffic matrix and thus cannot make the optimal decision; in view of the scheduling policy described in §2.2, it chooses wavelength 1 or 2 alternately, resulting in the actual stability condition:

$$\lambda_1 < 1 \quad \text{and} \quad \frac{\lambda_1}{2} + \lambda_2 < 1.$$

In the homogeneous case, i.e. $\lambda_1 = \lambda_2 = \lambda/2$, this reduces to the inequality $\lambda < 4/3$ whereas the optimal stability condition is $\lambda < 2$. The throughput efficiency θ is thus equal to $2/3$ in this case.

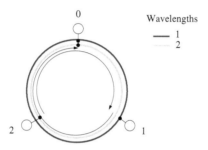

Fig. 2. A simple traffic scenario where opportunistic transmission is suboptimal

We generalize this toy example to the case $N \geq W$. We still consider that there is traffic only on source-destination pairs $(N,1)$ and $(i,0), i \in \{1,...,N-1\}$. We consider the homogeneous case in which $\lambda_i = \lambda/N$ for all $i \in \{1,...,N\}$. Nodes $1,...,N-1$ alternately choose one of the W wavelengths, thus limiting the transmission opportunities of node N on wavelength 1. Stability is defined by the capacity of wavelength 1 on link N. From (2) and (3) we obtain the throughput efficiency of the opportunistic scheme:

$$\theta = \frac{N}{N + W - 1}.$$

Table 1 shows the corresponding throughput efficiencies for different values of W and N. Since the traffic on source-destination pair $(N,1)$ decreases with the number of nodes N , the fraction of slots required by station N also decreases, leading to a better throughput efficiency. Similarly, efficiency decreases with W . Under SWING access control, the dynamic reservation scheme forces nodes $1,...,N-1$ to use wavelengths $2,...,W$, yielding throughput-optimality (i.e., $\theta = 1$).

Table 1. Throughput efficiency θ of the opportunistic scheme in the studied scenario

N	4	6	8	10
$W = 2$	0.80	0.85	0.88	0.90
$W = 4$	0.57	0.67	0.72	0.77

4.2 Fairness Impairment

We study a scenario in which there is traffic only from the access nodes to the hub, namely $\lambda_{i0} = \lambda/N$ for all $i \neq 0$. We refer to this scenario as *hub uplink*. There are W wavelength channels in the network. When no access control is implemented, the amount of free slots available to each node depends on the node's position on the ring. Indeed, the stations preceeding the hub are more likely to suffer from slot starvation, in particular station N. It is this station that will drive the stability of the network. In the following, we analyze the characteristics of the waiting queue corresponding to node N.

We model our ring network as a system of two waiting queues. The first queue is an aggregation of the waiting queues associated to stations $1, \ldots, N-1$. The second queue corresponds to station N's waiting queue. At each station, clients arrive according to a Poisson process of rate $\lambda_a = \sum_{i=1}^{N-1} \lambda_{i0}$ and $\lambda_b = \lambda_{N0}$, respectively. For both queues, the service rate μ corresponds to the arrival rate of free time slots. Our network can thus be reduced to a single-server queueing system as shown in Figure 3. Under opportunistic access, the stations succeeding the hub will have privileged access to the free slots meaning that the first queue has priority over the second.

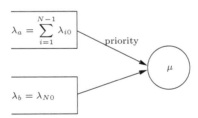

Fig. 3. Single-server priority queueing system

We consider the worst case scenario in which the first queue has *preemptive priority* over the second one (Figure 4). Using the generating function of the stationary distribution of the second queue, we express the tail asymptotics of the *number of clients* in the second queue (see [18] for more details):

$$P(Q_b = n) \sim \frac{1-\rho}{\rho_b}(\rho^2 - \rho_a)\rho^{n-1}, \qquad (4)$$

where $\rho_a = \lambda_a/\mu$, $\rho_b = \lambda_b/\mu$ and $\rho = \rho_a + \rho_b$.

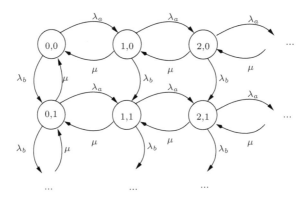

Fig. 4. Markov chain for a single-server preemptive priority queueing system

If we limit the second queue size to 25 clients[2] and we consider the network to be stable if the packet loss rate is less than 2%, then (4) can be used to compute the maximum sustainable load. Table 2 gives the maximum sustainable load for different values of N and for $W = 4$. We note that the lack of fairness of the opportunistic scheme can lead to efficiency losses as high as 10%.

Table 2. Throughput efficiency θ of the opportunistic scheme in the hub uplink scenario

N	4	6	8	10
Analysis	1.00	0.88	0.90	0.92
Simulation	0.99	0.90	0.91	0.93

5   Simulation Results

This section presents the results of our data packet-level simulations which were conducted on a multiservice network supporting two classes of service: real-time and best-effort.

5.1   Simulation Parameters

The number of slots S is taken equal to 100, corresponding to a cycle time of 1 ms for a typical slot duration of 10 μs. Each simulation run lasts 10^6 cycles. For throughput performance, we need to decide if the network is stable or unstable at the end of the simulation, for any given load ρ. To this end, we chose to limit each queue size to 100 MTU packets (each node has 2 queues, one for each class of service). We consider the network to be stable as long as the packet loss rate is less than 2% at each queue. We have verified that the results are not very sensitive to these parameters.

---

[2] This corresponds to a total queue size of 200 MTU packets which is also the value considered in the simulations of §5.

We assume real-time packets to have absolute priority over best-effort packets (see [5] for details). Real-time packets arrive according to a Poisson process, while best-effort packets arrive according to a *batch* Poisson process, with a batch size uniformly distributed between 1 and 16 packets. We consider 10% of the traffic to be real-time traffic. The packet size distribution is given by 60% of 40B packets (minimum transmission unit) and 40% of 1500B packets (maximum transmission unit), for both real-time and best-effort packets.

We simulate the access protocols described in §2.3 where data packets are aggregated into optical bursts using a timer-based burst assembly mechanism.

5.2 Traffic Scenarios

In order to evaluate throughput-delay performance in typical traffic conditions, we consider the following three traffic scenarios, depicted by Figure 5:

Local Scenario: All traffic is local in the sense that there is no traffic originating from or going to the hub, yielding:

$$\forall i, j \neq 0,\ i \neq j, \quad \lambda_{ij} = \frac{\lambda}{N(N-1)}$$

Hub Scenario: All traffic originating from node $i \neq 0$ is destined to the hub. Referring to "upstream" as the traffic destined to the hub and to "downstream" as the traffic originating from the hub, the traffic matrix is characterized by a single parameter α representing the fraction of upstream traffic:

$$\forall i \neq 0, \quad \lambda_{0i} = \frac{\lambda(1-\alpha)}{N}, \quad \lambda_{i0} = \frac{\lambda\alpha}{N}.$$

P2P Scenario: There is some traffic between any pair of nodes (i, j) and traffic is symmetric in the sense that $\lambda_{ij} = \lambda_{ji}$ for all $i, j, i \neq j$, which is representative of peer-to-peer traffic. The traffic matrix is characterized by a single parameter β representing for any node $i \neq 0$ the fraction of local traffic, that is the fraction of traffic originating from all nodes $j \neq 0$:

$$\forall i \neq 0, \quad \lambda_{0i} = \lambda_{i0} = \frac{\lambda(1-\beta)}{2N},$$

$$\forall i, j \neq 0,\ i \neq j, \quad \lambda_{ij} = \frac{\lambda\beta}{2N(N-1)}.$$

Unless otherwise specified, we take $\alpha = \beta = 20\%$.

Fig. 5. Considered traffic scenarios (from right to left): local, hub and P2P (hub station represented in black)

5.3   Results

Throughput. Figure 6 gives the throughput efficiency with respect to the number of nodes N (other than the hub) in the three traffic scenarios of §5.2, for W = 4 wavelengths, for both SWING and the opportunistic scheme. The throughput efficiencies of the two schemes are fairly similar and are higher than 0.75, regardless of the considered scenario. Note that efficiency is slightly higher for $N = 6$ for both schemes. In this case, wavelengths 1, 2 carry more traffic than wavelengths 3, 4 (see Figure 1), which reduces the number of limiting ressources and increases the maximum throughput.

As shown in [6], in the case of a single wavelength, the opportunistic scheme is throughput optimal while SWING experiences efficiency losses due to the reservations which limit possibilities for opportunistic transmission. In the case of multiple wavelength channels where each node can transmit and receive on a subset of the available wavelengths, the efficiency of the opportunistic scheme

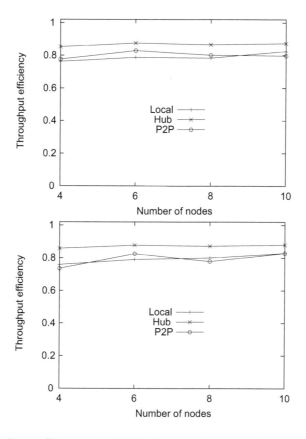

Fig. 6. Throughput efficiency of SWING (top) and opportunistic scheme (bottom) against the number of nodes N in the local, hub and P2P scenarios

decreases because of its poor load balancing over the wavelengths and lack of fairness, as explained in Section 4. Despite the efficiency loss due to the reservation scheme, SWING is able to achieve the same level of throughput efficiency as the opportunistic scheme, while ensuring fairness.

Delay. Figure 7 shows the probability that the queueing delay of a data packet exceeds 2 ms, for both SWING and the opportunistic scheme for $N = 8$ nodes plus the hub. Delays of best effort traffic are low as long as the load is less than the maximum sustainable load θ, for both access protocols in all traffic scenarios.

We further notice that the opportunistic scheme experiences low delays for real-time traffic in both local and hub scenarios. However, this is not the case in the P2P scenario, where delays of real-time traffic are significant for $\rho > 0.8$. This is a direct consequence of the opportunistic scheme's absence of access control. As seen in §4.2, depending on its position on the ring, a node may be

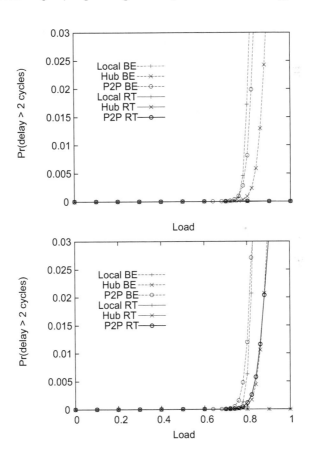

Fig. 7. Delay performance of SWING (top) and opportunistic scheme (bottom) in the local, hub and P2P scenarios in a ring of $N = 8$ nodes

starved from free slots on a specific wavelength that serves a given destination. The node is then unable to satisfy the corresponding queue, which leads to high delays for both real-time and best effort traffic. It turns out that such situations occur more often in the P2P scenario due to the joint effect of high traffic coming from and going to the hub and local traffic exchanged among access nodes.

We notice that SWING is able to guarantee low delays for real-time traffic even at high network loads in any of the considered traffic scenarios. Indeed, the overall probability that real-time packets wait longer than 2 ms is close to 0. For instance, only 5 out of 10^6 real-time packets wait longer than 2 ms at load $\rho = 1$ in the P2P scenario. As for the opportunistic scheme, over 7% of real-time packets will wait longer than 2 ms under the same traffic conditions.

6   Conclusion

In this paper we have analysed the throughput-delay trade-offs that arise in slot-ted WDM rings for a purely opportunistic transmission scheme and for SWING, a dynamic slot reservation protocol. We have highlighted the throughput subop-timality of the purely opportunistic scheme as well as its fairness impairments in the context of multiple wavelength channels. The results of our simulations have shown that the dynamic reservation scheme of SWING ensures fairness while maintaining high throughput efficiency. Unlike the opportunistic scheme, SWING is able to guarantee low delays for high priority traffic under any of the considered traffic scenarios.

Future work is focused on analysing throughput-delay trade-offs arising in other network topologies. We also intend to investigate fairness in the context of WDM ring interconnection.

Acknowledgements. The authors would like to thank Alain Simonian for his contribution to the analytic part of this work, in particular on the considered priority queueing system.

References

1. Ajmone Marsan, M., Bianco, A., Leonardi, E., Morabito, A., Neri, F.: SR3: a Bandwidth-Reservation MAC Protocol for Multimedia Applications over All-Optical WDM Multi-Rings. In: Proc. INFOCOM (1997)
2. Bengi, K., van As, H.R.: QoS Support and Fairness Control in a Slotted Packet-Switched WDM Metro Ring Network. In: Proc. GLOBECOM (2001)
3. Bianco, A., Cuda, D., Finochietto, J., Neri, F.: Multi-MetaRing Protocol: Fairness in optical packet ring networks. In: Proc. ICC (2007)
4. Bianco, A., Cuda, D., Finochietto, J.M., Neri, F., Piglione, C.: Multi-Fasnet Proto-col: Short-Term Fairness Control in WDM Slotted MANs. In: Proc. GLOBECOM (2006)
5. Bonald, T., Indre, R.-M., Oueslati, S., Rolland, C.: On Virtual Optical Bursts for QoS Support in OBS Networks. In: Proc. of ONDM (2010)

6. Bonald, T., Oueslati, S., Roberts, J., Roger, C.: SWING: Traffic capacity of a simple WDM ring network. In: Proc. of ITC 21 (2009)
7. Cadere, C., Izri, N., Barth, D., Fourneau, J.M., Marinca, D., Vial, S.: Virtual Circuit Allocation with QoS Guarantees in the ECOFRAME Optical Ring. In: Proc. ONDM (2010)
8. Cao, J., Cleveland, W.S., Lin, D., Sun, D.X.: Internet Traffic Tends Toward Poisson and Independent as the Load Increases. In: Nonlinear Estimation and Classification. Springer, New York (2002)
9. Carena, A., De Feo, V., Finochietto, J., Gaudino, R., Neri, F., Piglione, C., Poggiolini, P.: RingO: An experimental WDM optical packet network for metro applications. IEEE JSAC 22(8) (October 2004)
10. Cidon, I., Ofek, Y.: Metaring: A full-Duplex Ring with Fairness and Spatial Reuse. In: Proc. INFOCOM (1990)
11. Chiaroni, D.: The French RNRT ECOFRAME project: packet technology perspectives in metro networks. In: APOC 2008 (2008) (invited presentation)
12. Dantzer, J.-F., Dumas, V.: Stability Analysis of the Cambridge Ring. Queueing Systems: Theory and Applications 40(2) (2002)
13. Ephremides, A., Tassiulas, L.: Stability Properties of Constrained Queueing Systems and Scheduling Policies for Maximum Throughput in Multihop Radio Networks. IEEE Trans. on Automatic Control 37, 1936–1949 (1992)
14. Herzog, M., Maier, M., Reisslein, M.: Metropolitan Area Packet-Switched WDM Networks: A Survey on Ring Systems. IEEE Communications Surveys and Tutorials 6(2), 2–20 (2004)
15. Keslassy, I., McKeown, N.: Analysis of Scheduling Algorithms That Provide 100% Throughput in Input-Queued Switches. In: Proc. Allerton Conference on Communication, Control, and Computing (2001)
16. Leland, W.E., Taqqu, M.S., Willinger, W., Wilson, D.V.: On the self-similar nature of Ethernet traffic (extended version). IEEE/ACM Transactions on Networking 2(1), 1–15 (1994)
17. Matisse Networks, EtherBurst: Optical Packet Transport System, White Paper (2008)
18. Miller, R.G.: Priority Queues. The Annals of Mathematical Statistics 31(1) (1960)
19. Paxson, V., Floyd, S.: Wide area traffic: the failure of Poisson modeling. IEEE/ACM Transactions on Networking 3(3), 226–244 (1995)

Profiling TCP Traffic
in Optical Burst Switching Networks

Kostas Ramantas and Kyriakos Vlachos

Computer Engineering and Informatics Department & Research Academic
Computer Technology Institute, University of Patras, Rio, Greece
{ramantas,kvlachos}@ceid.upatras.gr

Abstract. The efficient transmission of TCP traffic over OBS networks is a challenging problem, due to the high sensitivity of TCP congestion control mechanism to losses. In this paper, a traffic profiling scheme is proposed for gathering TCP flow statistics, which are used to estimate steady-state performance of TCP traffic over OBS networks. The burst assembly unit, in parallel to the assembly process, can inspect TCP traffic, keeping traffic statistics that can be used for throughput estimations. In this paper, we detail the traffic profiling and estimation mechanism and also provide analytical and simulation results to assess its performance.

Keywords: TCP profiling, traffic measurement, Optical Burst Switching, Burst Assembly.

1   Introduction

The transmission of TCP traffic over OBS [1], has been extensively studied in the related literature. Various burst assembly and burst scheduling algorithms have been proposed [2] to enhance the efficient transmission of TCP over OBS networks, but it still remains an open problem, since the (relatively) high burst loss ratio experienced in OBS networks is incompatible with TCP congestion control mechanism. It has been observed that burst losses have a significant impact on the TCP end-to-end performance, as shown in [3], [4]. In particular, TCP transmission over OBS networks suffers from the high number of segments that are lost, upon a single burst drop. This typically results in many sources timing out and which will subsequently enter a slow start phase. This may also result in synchronizing TCP transmissions with an imminent effect on link utilization, [5]. Further, the introduction of an unpredictable delay, challenges the window mechanism used by TCP protocol for congestion control. In this work, we focus on TCP flow profiling in OBS networks, which can provide insights regarding user-perceived performance, and serve as a basis for capacity planning.

TCP flow profiling is extremely useful, as TCP traffic represents a dominant and at the same time very predictable part of internet workload. According to recent internet measurement studies [8], TCP protocol is responsible for over 95% of total bytes

I. Tomkos et al. (Eds.): BROADNETS 2010, LNICST 66, pp. 328–340, 2012.

transmitted. Additionally, it has been established that internet workload is heavy-tailed and a large part of network capacity is dedicated to long-lived file transfers. Most of this traffic is mainly P2P file exchanges and web file transfers, as well as online video connections over HTTP (i.e. Youtube). Moreover, as shown in [7], the TCP throughput of large transfer TCP flows over OBS, collapses to a single fixed operating point (called equilibrium) enabling the accurate prediction of aggregate TCP throughput in a single OBS link. However, aggregate throughput statistics have a limited value, since they only reflect the network state when traffic measurements are taken. Network operators are mainly interested in flow-level statistics, exported for example by enterprise routers through Cisco Netflow protocol [6]. Flow-level statistics can provide insights for user-perceived performance, and they are useful for network management and capacity planning. Estimating flow-level statistics is a resource-intensive process, as it involves specialized monitoring equipment that captures packets from monitored flows and extracts statistics. Typically, a small percentage of the original network flows is monitored, denoted as "flow sample". There is a lot of research done on sampling TCP flows [14], and optimally estimating flow statistics from flow samples [15], a process that is called "inversion".

In this paper, we propose a TCP flow profiler for OBS networks, which performs on-line estimation of active TCP flow statistics, as well as network parameters like burst loss ratio and round trip time. The rest of the paper is organized as follows. Section II discusses predictability issues of long-lived TCP traffic, while Section III presents the in detail the TCP traffic profiler architecture. Finally, Section IV presents performance evaluation results, obtained through simulations using ns-2.

2   TCP Traffic Profiling in OBS Networks

In this section, the main issues and challenges are discussed, for collecting TCP traffic statistics in OBS networks. In principle, collecting detailed traffic information for active TCP connections provides an intimate traffic knowledge, which can serve as a basis for traffic engineering. Flow-level metrics like flow size distribution, number of active flows, and average throughput are useful for network management and capacity planning.

2.1   Collecting Traffic Statistics in OBS Networks

For gathering flow-level traffic statistics, a monitoring system is required, that stores and constantly updates a record of sampled flows. Cisco Netflow [6] is an example of such system, deployed in commercial enterprise-class routers. For gathering network-wide traffic statistics, a node with access to all packets transmitted is needed. In OBS networks, this node can be the burst assembler. Burst assembler is well suited for gathering traffic statistics, having access to all packets received at the edge node. Packet headers have to be examined, before being assigned to the appropriate burst assembly queue, assuming that a separate queue for each source-destination pair is kept. Thus, keeping traffic statistics does not bear a significant overhead for edge nodes, provided that very short-lived TCP connections are filtered-out.

It has to be noted that in real-world networks, long-lived TCP flows constitute both the dominant (in terms of bytes transmitted) and the most predictable part of network traffic. Internet workloads are regarded to be heavy-tailed [13], i.e. their flow length distribution Z follows a probability distribution such that the right tail has power-law decay, or:

$$P[Z > z] \sim z^{-a}, \qquad z \to \infty. \tag{1}$$

Long-lived flows, also known as "elephant flows", are responsible for 80% of the overall bytes transmitted. This has been verified by recent internet measurement studies in [8], where it has been found that the majority of data transmissions over the internet is due to large file transfers, online video downloads over HTTP (i.e. YouTube) and P2P file exchanges. On the other hand, the average size of data transmitted from interactive Web request is fairly small, in the order of 26–30 kB, with a small contribution the aggregated throughput and a high degree of burstiness. To this end, it becomes clear that it is preferable to filter-out short-lived flows and gather statistics solely for long-lived TCP flows. This requires the profiler to effectively distinguish short-lived from long-lived flows, and can be carried out by defining a *flow lifetime threshold* θ, that is intuitive and easy to implement.

In what follows, we focus on the TCP traffic predictability issues, and argue that formula-based TCP throughput estimation for long-lived TCP traffic is a viable solution.

2.2   Predictability of Long-Lived TCP Flows in OBS Networks

The feedback control mechanism of TCP protocol is a well known mechanism for introducing a degree of predictability in TCP traffic. TCP flows are prevented from transmitting at the full link capacity, to avoid saturating the network, and they can only transmit as many packets as their congestion window (*cwnd*) allows. Newly arrived flows have to "probe" for network capacity, by starting their transmission with a *cwnd* of 1, and which is doubled in every lossless round. TCP flows ultimately reach steady state (or congestion avoidance state) after the first segment loss is detected, which corresponds to network equilibrium. In such a case, all flows fairly share the available bandwidth.

TCP congestion avoidance algorithm operates in a purely deterministic way, while TCP window in an idealized scenario follows a periodic "saw tooth" profile. This traffic pattern is common to all TCP implementations that only differ in the fast recovery phase, with a small contribution in the overall throughput.

It has been established in [9] that traffic dynamics of large transfer TCP flows can be accurately estimated by making use of appropriate performance modeling formulas. This is due to the fact that long-lived flows' congestion window ultimately converges to a steady state, reaching equilibrium. In [7] the authors show that they can accurately predict the network fixed point (i.e. the steady state input rates of long-lived TCP flows) over an OBS link. Formula based throughput estimation requires up-to-date measurements of burst loss ratio p, flow round trip time (RTT) and segment per burst distribution. Studies on TCP predictability have concluded that accuracy is negatively impacted by unpredictable queuing delays in congested paths. This results in fluctuating RTTs and affects the accuracy of the TCP performance estimation formulas. However, due to the bufferless nature of OBS networks, large transfer TCP flows over OBS are expected to be very predictable. The accuracy of TCP bandwidth estimation depends on the accuracy of the estimated network parameters, like burst loss ratio, as well as TCP flow statistics like flow access rates and access delays.

3   TCP Flow Profiler Architecture

In this section, the profiler architecture is presented, as well as how flow statistics are formed from a subset of active flows, called the *flow sample*. Flow sampling is employed for limiting the consumption of resources required to extract flow statistics from traffic measurements, which would be prohibitive if all packets and flows were taken into account. Thus, it follows that the flow statistics from unsampled flows must be extracted from the sampled flow statistics. In this work, unbiased estimation of flow statistics is achieved by selecting the flow sample independently of measured statistics (unbiased selection). As an example, for performing an unbiased estimation of flow length distribution, sampled flows are selected independently of the flow length. Consequently, the statistics of the sampled flows are expected to converge to the ones of the unsampled flows, as the number of sampled flows approaches the overall number of active flows.

In what follows, a TCP flow profiler is designed, which is integrated with the burst assembly process. Its goal is to provide running online measurements of flow and network performance metrics. These metrics are constantly updated, so that they don't become outdated. Being in the middle of the flow end-to-end path, the flow profiler has access to all segments transmitted from TCP sources assigned to the burstifier, and it is able to inspect TCP segment headers without incurring excessive overheads. It does not have information on TCP segments lost before the burst assembly process, or on internal TCP sender state (like congestion window). The profiling module proposed here performs an estimation of the following metrics:

- Burst loss ratio
- Number of active long-lived TCP flows
- TCP performance variables (round trip time and access rate)
- Steady-state TCP throughput.

Passive estimation techniques are used in our profiler for compiling flow statistics, as opposed to active estimation techniques, where probing sessions are initiated by the profiler. Passive techniques allow monitoring of a large number of flows in a diverse set of network paths without interfering with traffic flows. Most of the metrics can't be estimated in a stateless manner. In order to compile flow statistics, a table of flow records, indexed by *flowID* must be maintained. A representative, unbiased flow sample has to be stored in this flow table, so that traffic statistics of the sampled flows match the traffic statistics of the unsampled flows. Usually, the traffic sample is a small percentage of the overall flow population (typically less that 1%) as the overall number of flows assigned to a burstifier is in the order of millions.

In the proposed scheme, TCP profiler divides active flows in sampled and un-sampled ones according to the flow sampling rate 1/N, which denotes that only 1 in N flows is sampled on average. For every packet that is received by the burstifier, the profiler determines if the packet will be retained and whether a flow record is active for it's flowID. If a flow record is active, the flow statistics are updated on the reception of the packet. If not, it instantiates a new record with the packet's flowID. The primary constraints of flow-level profilers are the memory bandwidth and memory size limitations, since millions of flows can be assigned to a single monitoring device. The memory bandwidth of DRAMs utilized in typical Netflow capable routers [6] is not sufficient to lookup the flowID of all incoming packets, thus a small sampling rate is used. To cope with this problem, in [16] an alternative profiling architecture was proposed, based on fast SRAMs. However, SRAMs are expensive and come in very small sizes as compared to DRAMs – thus being capable of storing a smaller flow sample.

In this work, we employ hash-based sampling technique, which avoids memory lookup for packets belonging to unsampled flows, resulting in large memory bandwidth savings. According to this technique, the profiler calculates a hash value for the flowID of every packet received, i.e. $h = f(flowID)$, which is normalized in the interval $h \in [0,1]$. Since hash algorithms are designed with an objective to evenly distribute a stream of (possibly correlated) values, the hash value is uniformly distributed and thus can serve as an unbiased criterion of flow selection. Thus, if $h \leq 1/N$, with 1/N the flow sampling rate, the flow is sampled or else it is not.

The abovementioned selection technique is unbiased and efficient, since one can track as many flows as the DRAM memory bandwidth allows, and accordingly set the value of the sampling rate. Additionally, since in OBS networks the burst assembler has to inspect packet headers in order to assign them to the appropriate queue, this technique only adds-up a few clock cycles overhead per received packet. Similar works that calculate hashes of received TCP packet *flowIDs* were able to track millions of flows at line speeds [10].

The efficiency of the abovementioned technique can be further enhanced by filtering out slow flows. One-packet long TCP flows have a disproportionally large frequency, owing to HTTP protocol (clients send http requests to web servers encapsulated in a single packet). To avoid wasting resources for storing one-packet flows, in the proposed scheme, new records for slow flows (i.e. flows with a single data packet in a burst) are not created.

3.1   Burst Loss Ratio Estimation

The estimation of the burst loss ratio is carried out using the signaling messages received by the edge router's control unit. For every dropped burst the core node returns a message (BHP_DROP) to the edge router to report the loss. This is communicated to the profiler, which stores a bit vector of bursts successfully transmitted (denoted with '0') and bursts lost (denoted with '1'). Bit values X_k are assumed independent Bernoulli random variables that take value '1' with a probability equal to the burst loss ratio. The burst loss ratio is thus estimated as the sum of '1' values in the vector divided by the vector length W. Thus, the burst loss ratio is defined as:

$$p = \frac{\sum_1^W X_k}{W}. \tag{2}$$

For the online estimation of burst loss ratio, we use the well known sliding window averaging technique that discards aging values, older than the vector length. According to this technique, proposed in [11], for packet loss ratio estimation, given that X_k is the kth bit value of the vector corresponding to the kth burst transmission and W is the vector length, a running estimation of burst loss ratio is obtained by:

$$\hat{X}_{i+1} = \frac{1}{W} \sum_{k=i-W+1}^{i} X_k. \tag{3}$$

The vector length W is calculated based on the desired accuracy, using the analytic model proposed in [11]. The estimated burst loss ratio error for a vector length W, a real burst loss ratio p and a confidence interval of 95% is derived as:

$$e = \frac{1.96\sqrt{p(1-p)/W}}{p}. \tag{4}$$

Thus, for a burst loss ratio of 1% and an error rate of 0.002, this corresponds to a bit vector length of 4.000 values, which is the one used in our experiments.

3.2   Access Rate and RTT Estimation

Flow access rate depends on the bottleneck link across the path from the sender to the edge router, for which the burstifier has no knowledge. It can be estimated by finding the maximum number of segments that a flow injects in a burst. Thus, it requires estimating segment-per-burst ratio for the sampled flows, throughout their duration while retaining its maximum value. Then, the flow access rate for flow-i, denoted as r_i, can be estimated as:

$$r_i = \frac{MAX\{SPB_i\} * MSS}{T_{MAX}}. \tag{5}$$

Where SPB is the segment-per-burst ratio, MSS is the maximum segment size and T_{MAX} is the burst assembly time. With respect to the round-trip time of the sampled flows, it can be easily estimated at the flow setup phase during the three-way handshake period, a procedure detailed in [12]. The profiler must keep track of the time each control packet was received (SYN, SYN-ACK and ACK), which allows the direct computation of the Profiler-to-Server and Client-to-Profiler round trip times. The flow RTT is estimated as the sum of these two values.

3.3   Long Lived Flows Threshold

For distinguishing flows into long and short lived, we define a threshold in the flow length, where length refers to the number of packets transmitted until the flow concludes its transmission. If the observed flow length is smaller than the threshold, denoted with θ, then it is classified as short lived – otherwise it is classified as long-lived. It has been mentioned previously that steady-state throughput of large file transfers constitutes a significant part of internet traffic, while long-lived flow dynamics are very predictable. Thus, we may set threshold θ as the expected flow length of the first packet loss. After the first loss, the flow will enter the congestion avoidance phase. This approach is much more efficient than passively estimating TCP state of individual active flows, a process which is TCP implementation dependent and very computationally intensive. In contrast, the proposed technique is more straightforward, easy to implement, and it is implementation-agnostic, as it assumes an idealized congestion window evolution. It assumes that TCP flows begin their transmission with a congestion window of one segment that doubles per lossless round, while after the first segment loss the flows enter the congestion avoidance state, in which they stay until they conclude their transmission. Fast retransmit/fast recovery and Time-Out phases are not taken into account, as they have a minimal effect on TCP performance for small burst loss ratios.

The expected number of packets transmitted until the first loss, which serves as the long-lived flow threshold, is estimated analytically. In an OBS network packet losses are correlated, due to the assembly of multiple packets in a single burst. Thus, packet loss ratio is not identical to the burst loss ratio. One burst loss carrying at least one packet of a flow in the slow-start phase is enough to agitate the flow to its congestion avoidance (steady-state) phase, regardless of the number of assembled packets carried by the burst. Assuming that burst losses in OBS networks are independent events, the probability of transmitting k bursts before a loss occurs and assuming a burst loss ratio p is:

$$P[B = k] = (1 - p)^k p. \tag{6}$$

The number of segments that are assembled in a single burst denoted as SPB (segments-per-burst ratio) depends on the flow access rate, the burst assembly period and also by the flow congestion window. Thus, the number of segments transmitted before the first loss occurs can be approximated as:

$$E[P] = S * E[B] = S * \sum_{0}^{\infty} (1 - p)^k p = \frac{SPB}{p}. \tag{7}$$

The value SPB/p is equal to the TCP Triple Duplicate Period (TDP) over OBS, derived from [3]. Alternatively, for flows that had no loss before saturating their local capacity, the bandwidth-delay product $r_i * RTT_i$ can be used as a threshold, where both values are estimated by the profiler for flow-i. For a typical burst loss ratio of 1% and a value of $SPB=4$, the long-lived flow threshold corresponds to 400 segments. This value is considerably higher than the average HTTP request size, and thus can successfully serve as a definite criterion of differentiation.

Next, we argue that in heavy-tailed workloads like the ones in the internet, the majority of bytes are transmitted after this threshold has been reached, i.e. in the steady-state phase. In [13], web traffic is classified in web requests, shown to follow a heavy-tailed distribution with parameter $\alpha = 1.21$ and web file transfers shown to follow a heavy-tailed distribution with heavier tail weights, and $\alpha = 1.1$. Due to the heavy-tailedness of the workload, long-lived flows are very likely to continue being active a long time after they have been identified as such, i.e. long after they have exceeded the long-lived flow threshold. Heavy-tailed flow length distribution Z has the following fundamental property:

$$\lim_{z \to \infty} \Pr[Z > z + k \mid Z > z] = 1.$$ (8)

This denotes that for flows with a long duration $(z \to \infty)$ the probability of transmitting k extra bytes before concluding their transmission is large, i.e. $\Pr[Z > z + k] \to 1$ as $z \to \infty$. In other words, the longer the flow duration is, the higher it's expected residual life is. As an example, assuming that file sizes follow Pareto distribution, with an index parameter $a = 1.1$, then assuming that the flow reached the threshold θ, its *Mean Residual Life* (i.e. the expected number of bytes the flow is expected to transmit before concluding its transmission) is [17]:

$$MRL(\theta) = \frac{1}{1 - \alpha} \theta = 10 * \theta.$$ (9)

Thus, flows characterized as long-lived, transmit more than 90% of their file size after having reached threshold θ, in the steady-state phase.

3.4 Long-Lived Flow Counting

In the proposed architecture, the number of active long-lived flows that have been assigned to the burstifier, along with their TCP state has to be known. A sampled flow is regarded active as long as it's *flowID* is stored in the flow table. The *flowID* is inserted after the first packet from the flow is received at the burstifier, and it is removed after a time threshold of inactivity (few RTTs). Thus, the number of active sampled flows is the number of distinct *flowIDs* in the flow table. In addition, the number of active sampled long-lived flows, is the number of distinct *flowIDs* exceeding threshold θ, as defined in previous section. This is a valid assumption, since the proposed TCP profiler architecture guarantees unbiased selection of the flow sample. Sampled flows have a fixed probability of being selected, irrespective of their duration or their ON period. This can be formulated as (following the same rationale as in [14]): Assuming that the number of active long-lived flows at a given time on the network is NF_{LL}, each one of them (due to unbiased selection) is modeled with an independent Bernoulli random variable w_i with a selection probability of $1/N$. The expected number of selected flows (assuming a selected flow contributes '1' to the sum) is:

$$\widehat{NF}_{LL} = N * \sum_{i=1}^{Nf} wi.$$ (10)

where NF_{LL} is the number of steady-state flows and N is the inverse the sample rate. Thus, the true number of active long-lived flows converges to the number of sampled long-lived flows multiplied by N, i.e. the above equation performs an unbiased estimation of the number of long-lived flows. Regarding the variance of the estimation, it is bounded by the number of active long-lived flows on the system (NF_{LL}) as well as the profiler sampling ratio $1/N$. Specifically, the standard error of the estimation is:

$$\frac{\sqrt{Var(\widehat{NF}_{LL})}}{NF_{LL}} = \sqrt{\frac{N}{NF_{LL}}}. \tag{11}$$

It can be seen that the estimator variance is small and can be made arbitrarily small when a high sample ratio is used.

3.5   Estimating Aggregated Steady-State Throughput

The goal of the steady-state throughput estimation process is to calculate the aggregated steady-state throughput of file transfers, based on TCP traffic statistics at the flow level. TCP throughput calculations are based on network parameters and flow statistics as estimated by the profiler, such as round-trip delay and segments-per-burst distribution. By constantly updating these, the steady-state throughput is estimated, taking into account potential changes to the number of active TCP flows, network state etc. This approach is advantageous for achieving fast conversion times caused by sudden state changes. TCP flow profiling and estimation of the network parameters allows pro-active network management, capacity planning and ultimately enhancing network performance and improving bandwidth utilization.

The performance of a single TCP flow over OBS has been analyzed in [3] giving closed formulas for estimating steady-state throughput for a given burst loss ratio, RTT and number of segments-per-burst. Here, we derive steady-state TCP throughput, assuming that the burst loss ratio, the segments-per-burst distribution and RTT statistics are evolving over time, and are constantly updated by the profiler.

The steady state throughput of a single TCP flow in an OBS network with a known number of segments per burst (*SPB*) and round trip time (RTT) and a known burst loss ratio *p* is obtained by the formula:

$$B(SPB, RTT) = \sqrt{1.5 * SPB} \bigg/ RTT * \sqrt{p}. \tag{12}$$

Assuming different RTTs and access rates per TCP flow, with *SPB(i)* being the empirical distribution of segments per burst, and *RTT(i)* being the distribution of round-trip times, we calculate the average TCP steady-state throughput over OBS as:

$$\bar{B} = E\left[\frac{1}{RTT}\right] * E\left[\frac{\sqrt{1.5 * SPB}}{\sqrt{p}}\right]. \tag{13}$$

Or equivalently:

$$\bar{B} = \left(\frac{1}{RTT}\right) \sum_{i=1}^{\infty} P\{SPB = SPBi\} * \frac{\sqrt{1.5 * SPBi}}{\sqrt{p}} * MSS . \tag{14}$$

Both $\overline{(1/RTT)}$ value and segment-per-burst distribution $SPB(i)$ are estimated by the traffic profiler, and so is burst loss ratio p. Coupled with the measured number of steady-state flows at time t, $N_F(t)$, the above formula can provide a constantly updated estimate of aggregated TCP steady-state throughput over OBS, denoted by R(t):

$$R(t) = N_F(t) * \bar{B} . \tag{15}$$

4   Profiler Evaluation

The TCP profiler was evaluated with simulations using ns-2 platform. A simple 3-node topology was used, consisting of two edge routers, denoted as E1 and E2 interconnected via a single core router, denoted as C. Clients are assigned to edge node E1 and initiate file transfers on servers assigned to E2. The modeled OBS network uses JET protocol for resource reservations. Burst assembly process is performed at the edge nodes, using a timer-based aggregation algorithm (T_{MAX}) with a time threshold of 3ms. The network round trip time was set equal to 15ms, while all clients had a uniformly distributed access delay in the interval [0,2] ms and a uniformly selected access rate of 20Mb, 50Mb and 100Mb. A realistic traffic scenario was modeled, that consists of TCP connection requests, whose arrivals follow Poisson distribution and their sizes are drawn from Pareto distribution. The traffic profile is representative of typical internet workloads, with many short-lived TCP connections representing web requests, and fewer long-lived file transfers, responsible for the 90% of the overall bytes transmitted. In what follows, numerical results are based only on long-lived flows, since short flows spending their lifetimes in the slow-start phase were filtered-out by the profiler.

The exact parameters of the each file transfer were estimated by the profiler, which was evaluated with three different sampling rates, $\{1/2, 1/10, 1/20\}$. In what follows, we present experimental results comparing real and estimated TCP flow parameters for all sampling rates.

Figure 1 displays the evolution of the aggregated steady-state TCP throughput. It can be seen that the estimator's output closely follows the measured real value of the steady-state throughput, especially for high sampling rates, relying solely on the running estimation of burst loss ratio, number of active flows and flow-level statistics. Additionally, as expected, higher sampling rates yield more accurate throughput estimations.

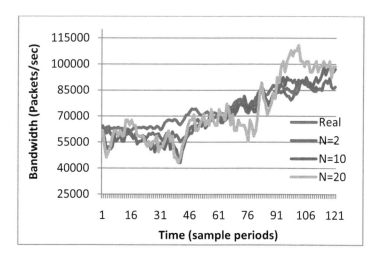

Fig. 1. Estimated versus true steady-state throughput, for different sample rates

Figure 2 displays the estimated number of active flows. Again, the estimated number of flows closely follows the real number of active flows while estimation accuracy improves with the increase of sampling rate. It must be noted however that the number of flows lacks the burstiness of TCP throughput and thus it is less sensitive to the selection of the flow sampling rate.

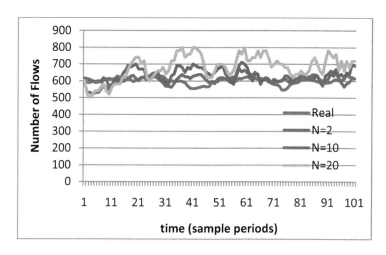

Fig. 2. Number of active flows estimation

Finally, for the characterization of the estimator's accuracy we have calculated the Cumulative Density Function (CDF) of the Relative Error of the estimation (see Figure 3) as well as the Coefficient of Variation (CoV) metric and the Root Mean Square Error (see Table 1), as an indication of the variance of the estimator.

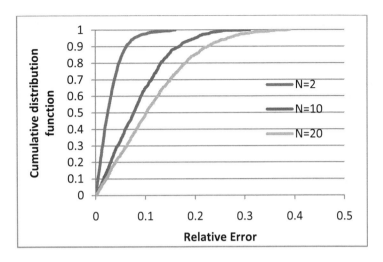

Fig. 3. Relative Error cumulative density function

Table 1. Estimator standard error

	p=0.5	p=0.1	p=0.05
Coefficient of Variation (CoV)	0,037	0,10	0,17
Root Mean Square Error (RMSE)	2945	8147	11326

5   Conclusions

In this paper, a TCP profiler has been designed for OBS networks, which is capable of estimating aggregated TCP throughput. The profiler operation relies solely on the running estimations of burst loss ratio, number of active flows and flow-level statistics like segments-per-burst distribution and RTT. These are used to estimate steady-state performance of TCP traffic over OBS networks. Simulation results have shown that the proposed scheme adequately profiles flow dynamics with a low accuracy variation and a low mean absolute error value.

Acknowledgements. The work described in this paper was carried out with the support of the BONE-project ("Building the Future Optical Network in Europe"), a Network of Excellence funded by the European Commission through the 7th ICT-Framework.

References

1. Qiao, C., Yoo, M.: Optical burst switching (OBS)-A new paradigm for an optical internet. J. High Speed Networks 8(1), 69–84 (1999)
2. Li, J., Qiao, C., Xu, J., Xu, D.: Maximizing throughput for optical burst switching networks. IEEE/ACM Transactions on Networking, TON (2007)

3. Yu, X., Qiao, C., Liu, Y., Towsley, D.: Performance evaluation of TCP implementations in OBS networks. Technical Report 2003-13, CSE Dept., SUNY, Buffalo (2003)

4. Yu, X., Li, J., Cao, X., Chen, Y., Qiao, C.: Traffic statistics and performance evaluation in optical burst switched networks. IEEE/OSA Journal of Lightwave Technology 22(12), 2722–2738 (2004)

5. González, O., Guidotti, A.M., Raffaelli, C., Ramantas, K., Vlachos, K.: On transmission control protocol synchronization in optical burst switching. Photonic Network Communication 18(3), 323–333 (2009)

6. Cisco Systems, NetFlow services and applications, White Paper (2000)

7. Cameron, C., Le Vu, H., Choi, J., Bilgrami, S., Zukerman, M., Kang, M.: TCP over OBS - fixed-point load and loss. Optics Express 13(23), 9167–9174 (2005)

8. Maier, G., Feldmann, A., Paxson, V., Allman, M.: On dominant characteristics of residential broadband internet traffic. In: Proc. ACM IMC (2009)

9. He, Q., Dovrolis, C., Ammar, M.: On the predictability of large transfer TCP throughput. In: ACM SIGCOMM (2005)

10. Schuehler, D.V., Lockwood, J.W.: TCP splitter: A TCP/IP flow monitor in reconfigurable hardware. IEEE Micro (2003)

11. Yajnik, M., Moon, S.B., Kurose, J., Towsley, D.: Measurement and modeling of the temporal dependence in packet loss. In: IEEE INFOCOM (1999)

12. Jiang, H., Dovrolis, C.: Passive estimation of TCP round-trip times. In: ACM SIGCOMM (2002)

13. Park, K., Kim, G., Crovella, M.: On the relationship between file sizes, transport protocols, and self-similar network traffic. In: Proc. IEEE ICNP (1996)

14. Duffield, N., Lund, C., Thorup, M.: Properties and prediction of flow statistics from sampled packet streams. In: Proceedings of the 2nd ACM SIGCOMM Workshop on Internet Measurment (2002)

15. Tune, P., Veitch, D.: Towards optimal sampling for flow size estimation. In: Proceedings of the 8th ACM SIGCOMM (2008)

16. Estan, C., Varghese, G.: New directions in traffic measurement and accounting: Focusing on the elephants, ignoring the mice. ACM Transactions on Computer Systems (2003)

17. Luo, S., Li, J.H., Park, K., Levy, R.: Exploiting Heavy-Tailed Statistics for Predictable QoS Routing in Ad Hoc Wireless Networks. In: IEEE INFOCOM (2008)

A Fault-Tolerant Multipoint Cycle Routing Algorithm (MCRA)

David Lastine, Suresh Sankaran, and Arun K. Somani

Department of Electrical and Computer Engineering
Iowa State University, Ames, Iowa 50011
{dlastine,sankaran,arun}@iastate.edu

Abstract. In this paper we propose a new efficient fault tolerant multipoint routing algorithm for optical networks. The routing for a multipoint request is accomplished by finding a bidirectional cycle simple or nonsimple including all nodes that are participating in the multipoint session. Each link can be used only once. Use of a cycle ensures that a single link (or node in case of simple cycle) failure does not interrupt the session except the failed node if it was part of the multipoint session. Determining the smallest cycle with a given set of Multi-point (MP) nodes is a NP-Complete problem. Therefore, we explore heuristic algorithms to determine an appropriate cycle to route multipoint connections. We allow non-simple cycles to route requests as they use fewer resources than simple cycles in some cases. We also provide an ILP formulation for routing multipoint request and compare its results with the output of our best heuristic algorithm. On Arpanet for over 80% of the time, our best heuristic is able to find a cycle that is within 1.2 times that of the optimal.

Keywords: Cycle routing algorithm, Multipoint Communication, Multicasting, Fault Tolerant Routing.

1 Multipoint Connection Problem

Multipoint (MP) to Multipoint communication is the transmission of information from all source nodes to all destination nodes. The sources and destinations form a subset of nodes in the network. We shall refer to them as multipoint (MP) nodes. Currently there exist many applications such as multimedia collaborations, video conferencing and shared workspaces which require MP to MP services. The increasing number of users of these applications necessitates a fiber-optic based optical network that can satisfy the bandwidth needs per request. However, failures in fiber-optic lines happen as frequently as every couple of days. This motivates us to explore fault aware MP routing.

The challenge in providing efficient protection to multipoint to multipoint communication is to recognize that it provides more opportunities for resource sharing than distinct entities of multicast communication. The relationship between multipoint and multicast is analogous to the situation between multicast

I. Tomkos et al. (Eds.): BROADNETS 2010, LNICST 66, pp. 341–360, 2012.

and unicast. Consider implementing a fault tolerant multicast connection as a set of fault tolerant unicast connections. While this would be feasible, connections for different destinations would independently reserve capacity on every link they use, even when a link is common between them. Multicast specific routing strategies avoid this redundant reservation. All multipoint routing algorithms try to avoid redundancies that would be incurred by repeatedly using multiple unicast strategies.

1.1   Multicast Protection Scheme

MP to MP connection is a generalization of multicast. It is equivalent of a multiple multicast request. Significant work has been done for protecting and restoring multicast connections in light tree, little work has been done on efficient protection of multipoint request. In [1] multicast tree protection is classified into the following categories: path-based, segment-based, tree-based, p-cycle based, and ring-based protection.

Most of the existing approaches route a multicast light tree that is protected by another tree or a cycle of some type. The idea of using a cycle to both route and protect a multicast request has received little attention in the literature. The idea is considered in [2]. The paper considers routing dynamic multicast connection using a cycle in NSF network. If their algorithm fails to find a cycle, they classify it as a blocked connection. We note that the lowest blocking probability reported for the network is 0.1, which is rather high.

We in this paper, solve the general problem of MP to MP connection using a cycle-based approach. Since this problem has received little attention in literature, for comparison we review the multicast protection schemes below.

A straightforward approach to protect a multicast tree is to compute a link-disjoint or arc-disjoint backup tree providing 1+1 dedicated protection [3] but this protection scheme consumes excessive resources. Although it may not be always possible to find an arc-disjoint backup tree once a primary tree has been discovered, it may be possible to protect each segment in the primary tree by finding a segment-disjoint path. Two protection schemes called Optimal Path Pair-based Shared Disjoint Segment(OPP-SDS-H) and Optimal Path Pair-based Shared Disjoint Path(OPP-SDP) have been proposed in [4] and the results suggest OPP-SDP outperforming SDS protection scheme. In dynamic multicast session, Link Based-Shared protection algorithm (LB-SPDM) is shown to perform better in terms of blocking probability than OPP-SDP [5]. Since OPP-SDP is a failure-independent method which looks for only one protection path for each working path for any link failure on that path, it makes the protection path unable to share wavelengths with working path unlike in failure dependent LB-SPDM protection.

The use of p-cycles and multicast trees to provide protection for dynamic multicast connections is considered in [6] and [7]. Several ways to place p-Cycles are examined in [8] and their resource usage and computation speed are compared. In [9] the blocking of multicast trees is examined for three different p-cycle placement scenarios. They consider placing the p-cycles without knowledge of the traffic, placing p-cycles dynamically as traffic arrives, and a hybrid scenario. Researchers in [10] analyzed a p-cycle based light-tree protection (ESHT) for combined node and link failure recovery. The capacity efficiency of this heuristic is close to OPP algorithm, while the blocking performance is in between OPP-SDP and OPP-SDS. The advantage of p-cycle based approach is faster restoration speed because p-cycle are pre-cross-connected.

[1] evaluated the performance of node-and-link protecting p-cycle based approach, tree-protecting p-cycle based approach and the OPP based approach. It is found that efficiency-score based heuristic algorithm of node-and-link protecting p-cycle outperforms the other heuristic algorithms. These protection strategies are shown to be efficient when applied for single multicast request but how to extend them efficiently to multipoint request is unclear.

1.2   Multipoint Protection Scheme

In this paper, we propose to route the multipoint request in a bidirectional cycle with UPSR like protection. We explore fault tolerant MP routing by establishing cycles to support MP requests. In order to provide a single link fault tolerance to a MP connection, there needs to exist a path from each node to all other nodes participating in the MP communication that does not use that link. A bidirectional simple or non-simple cycle satisfies this property if no link is reused. Since we only allow reusage of nodes and not links for a request, a single link failure does not disconnect the MP connection in a bidirectional cycle. This is done by having the transmitting node send its' traffic in both directions as shown in Figure 1(a) where node s_1 is transmitting. The transmitting node is responsible for ensuring the signal is dropped, once it has completed the loop. Receiving nodes listen to the incoming signal from both directions. In fault free operation a receiver will receive the same information twice and can either ignore the duplicate information or can use it for verification. When a fault occurs, as shown in Figure 1(b), then all nodes still receive the transmitted information, but only once. In this case, verification is not possible, but information is available at the destination.

By this kind of protection scheme, we eliminate the cost of a dedicated disjoint backup path and reduce latency since the traffic is transmitted in both the directions. When we compare with other protection mechanisms like dual multipoint tree and p-cycle, the multipoint cycle based protection scheme has the advantages that no loss of traffic occurs and the fault location need not be identified. This is true irrespective of which node is transmitting. Hence MP to MP protected connection is established.

1.3   Multipoint Connection Cycle

To route a multipoint connection, the network receives request to create a cycle involving a set of nodes participating in multipoint session. The cycle may

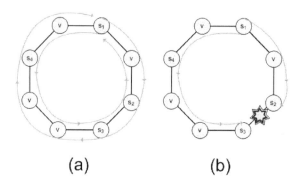

(a)   (b)

Fig. 1. Media Access Control Protocol

contain additional nodes as required due to the network topology, while containing all the nodes that are part of the request. If such a cycle cannot be established, then the request is rejected and the connection is blocked.

Finding the smallest cycle that includes a specified set of nodes is a hard problem. We formally define a decision version of the Cycle Based Routing (CBR) problem as follows.

CBR Problem: Given a graph $G(V, E)$, where V denotes the set of nodes and E denotes the set of edges in the graph, an integer k, $S \subseteq V$ as a subset of nodes, is there a simple or non-simple cycle graph $P(V(P), E(P)) \subseteq G$, where $V(P)$ is the set of nodes in P and $E(P)$ is the set of edges in P such that $S \subseteq V(P)$ and $|E(P)| \leq k$?

This problem is hard. Therefore, we develop heuristic algorithm to determine an appropriate cycle to route a multipoint connection. The evaluation of our heuristic is performed by routing many randomly generated requests on randomly generated networks. The number of nodes considered varies between twenty and sixty five nodes. We assume that networks consisting of more than sixty five nodes will have their routing performed in a hierarchical fashion. It is generally accepted that blocking is kept low by using a minimum amount of networking resources per request. To explore how efficiently our heuristics utilize resources we analyze different variations of the algorithm and compare the best performing heuristic them with the optimal results of an ILP.

2   Network Graph Model

The network is modeled using a connected graph $G(V, E)$. V is the set of vertices representing nodes in the network. E is the set of edges $(u, v) \in E$ where $u, v \in V$. An edge (u, v) represents the physical link that allows communication between nodes u and v. Links are assumed to have capacity which can take the values of 1 or 0 depending on availability or non-availability.

3   Multipoint Cycle Routing Algorithm (MCRA)

One application of CBR problem is in multipoint communication. $S \subseteq V$ is a set of nodes, which participate in a multipoint session. In this paper, we develop a multipoint cycle routing algorithm (MCRA). For this purpose, we associate costs with nodes. This cost is modeled as a binary variable. For non-MP nodes the cost is always one, for MP nodes we have considered two scenarios; in one scenario the cost is set to one and in the other the cost is set to zero. Since links are used only once we assume that links have no costs.

Since finding an optimal cycle is hard, we use simple heuristic algorithm to find a cycle. Our algorithm to find a fault tolerant cycle to route the MP request consists of multiple phases.

3.1   First Phase Algorithm

In the first phase, we consider all pairs of MP-nodes and compute a shortest distance path between each MP-node pair in the graph. We examine all these shortest paths, the one that includes the largest number of MP-nodes is recorded as the Initial $P(T)$. If there are more than one, we select the first one discovered.

One way to compute the shortest paths is to create the shortest path tree for each node $s_i \in S$. The shortest path tree is created by the function $D(s_i)$ (pseudo code for this function is not included as we simply use a variation of Bellman-Ford where we consider nodes not edges to be weighted). The function $M(s_j)$ retrieves a shortest path from destination s_j to source s_i (pseudo code for this function is also not provided as it is simply a tree traversal algorithm). Out of all the shortest paths in $|S|$ trees, the one with many MP-nodes is recorded as Initial $P(T)$ as shown in Figure 2 as Initial $P(T)$.

3.2   Second Phase Algorithm

In the second phase, a new segment passing through a yet to be added MP-node is inserted in between the two multipoint end nodes of Initial $P(T)$. It is done by considering each yet-to-be-covered MP-node and finding the segment to connect between multipoint end nodes in Initial $P(T)$. The segment is computed using the function $Find - Segment$ as described later on. While finding this segment, by assigning the link capacity to zero we do not use any of the links already present in Initial $P(T)$. We choose the best segment, that has many uncovered MP-nodes, to insert into Initial $P(T)$. This closes Initial $P(T)$ to form a cycle.

Figure 2 shows the second phase computation. For each uncovered MP node s_i, we calculate a segment $s_j- > s_i$ and $s_i- > s_k$. All edges except those on $P(T)$ are considered available. The set of segments $s_j - s_i - s_k$ (shown as dotted line) is selected for insertion for which $s_j - s_i - s_k$ has maximum number of uncovered MP nodes. Notice that a MP node on $P(T)$ can also belong to segment in $s_j - s_i - s_k$ but it does not count towards uncovered MP nodes.

MCRA algorithm

Input: Graph G, Subset S
Output: $P(T)$ - Self Protecting Multipoint Communication Cycle
$P(T) = NULL; P = NULL;$
//Phase 1 starts
foreach $s_i \in S$ **do**
 | $D(s_i)$; creates shortest path tree rooted at s_i
 | **foreach** $s_j \in S; j > i$ **do**
 | | $P = M(s_j)$; Finds the path from s_j in the tree
 | | **if** # of MP nodes in P > # of MP nodes in $P(T)$ **then**
 | | | $P(T) = P$;
 | | **end**
 | **end**
end
$\forall e \in P(T)$ capacity(e) = unavailable;
//Phase 1 ends - Phase 2 starts
$subpath = NULL; Bestpath = NULL;$
$s_j = FirstnodeP(T);$
$s_k = LastnodeP(T);$
foreach $s_i \in S$ and $s_i \notin P(T)$ **do**
 | $subpath = Find_segment(P(T), G, s_i, s_j, s_k);$
 | **if** # of uncovered MP nodes in subpath > # of MP nodes in Bestpath
 | **then**
 | | $Bestpath = subpath$; pick new segment
 | **end**
end
if $Bestpath == NULL$ **then**
 | return $NULL$; request blocked
end
Insert $BestpathinP(T)$; P(T) becomes a cycle
//Phase 2 ends - Phase 3 starts
$subpath = NULL; BestSubpath = NULL;$
while $S \nsubseteq P(T)$ **do**
 | **foreach** $s_i \in S - P(T)$ **do**
 | | $subpath = Select - Segment(s_i, GraphG);$
 | | **if** # of uncovered MP nodes in subpath > # of MP nodes in
 | | BestSubpath **then**
 | | | $BestSubpath = subpath$; pick new segment
 | | **end**
 | **end**
 | **if** $BestSubpath == NULL$ **then**
 | | return $NULL$; request blocked
 | **end**
 | Insert $BestSubpath$ into P(T);
end
Return P(T); *//Phase 3 ends*

Select-Segment

Input: $s_i \in S$ and $s_i \notin P(T)$, Graph G
Output: $BestSubpath$
$BestSubpath = NULL;$
foreach *consecutive* $s_j, s_k \in P(T)$, $s_j, s_k \in S$ **do**
  | $subpath = Find - Segment(\text{P(T)}, s_i, s_j, s_k, \text{Graph } G);$
  | **if** $s(subpath) > s(BestSubpath)$ **then**
  | | $BestSubpath = subpath;$
  | **end**
end

Find-Segment

Input: $P(T)$, s_i, s_j, s_k, Graph G
Output: $Subpath$
$Subpath = Find - Segment - Helper(P(T), s_i, s_j, s_k, \text{Graph } G);$
if $Subpath = NULL$ **then**
  | $Subpath = Find - Segment - Helper(P(T), s_i, s_k, s_j, \text{Graph } G);$
  | switches order of nodes
end
return *subpath*;

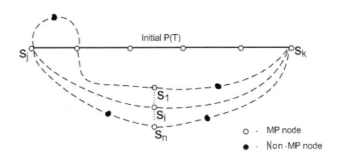

Fig. 2. Example of Phase 2

3.3 Third Phase Algorithm

In the third phase, each of the remaining MP-nodes are inserted into the cycle $P(T)$. New segments are selected after considering all remaining MP-nodes and all possible segments (a path between two consecutive MP-nodes s_j and s_k on $P(T)$) such that an uncovered node $s_i \in S - V(P(T))$ can be included between nodes s_j and s_k. A node s_i is inserted by replacing the path between nodes s_j and s_k on $P(T)$ by a segment that includes s_i. Each rerouting enables inclusion of one or more uncovered MP-nodes in $P(T)$. This is depicted in Figure 3.

Find-Segment-Helper

Input: $P(T)$, s_i, s_j, s_k, Graph G
Output: *Subpath*
Set $s_k.Cost = |V|$;
$D(s_j, G)$; Builds a shortest path tree rooted at s_j
$P_1 = M(s_i)$; Find shortest path between s_i and s_j
Set $s_k.Cost = 1$;
$\forall e \in P_1 \;\; capacity(e) = 0$;
Set $s_j.Cost = |V|$;
$D(s_k, G)$;
$P_2 = M(s_i)$;
Set $s_j.Cost = 1$;
$\forall e \in P_1 \;\; capacity(e) = 1$;
if $P_1 = NULL$ or $P_2 = NULL$ **then**
| return $NULL$;
end
else
| return $P_1 \bigcup P_2$;
end

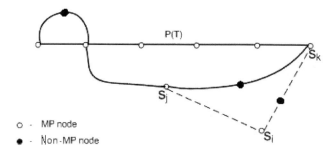

Fig. 3. Example of Phase 3

No link that is used in $P(T)$ is available to compute segment $s_j - s_i - s_k$ (shown as dotted line) except the links on path $s_j - s_k$ in $P(T)$.

The candidate segments for a specific uncovered node are found by calling the function $Select - Segment$. One uncovered MP-node s_i and the current $P(T)$ are input to $Select - Segment$. The best segment to insert MP-node s_i and the location in $P(T)$ between nodes s_j and s_k is returned by $Select - Segment$ function.

$Select - Segment$ Function $Select - Segment$ is responsible for finding the best new segment that includes s_i in $P(T)$. It performs the necessary work to loop over all the consecutive MP-nodes pairs on $P(T)$ starting with one pair of MP-nodes s_j and s_k to include node s_i. It does so by considering every segment of $P(T)$, i.e., a path between two consecutive MP-nodes on $P(T)$, and checks if the path can be replaced by a new segment containing the node s_i. $Select - Segment$ uses a function $Find - Segment$ to find the new segment.

$Find - Segment$ Function $Find - Segment$ is used to find a short, low cost segment passing through node s_i between nodes s_j and s_k. Recall that MP nodes are assigned cost 0 and other nodes are assigned cost 1. we later experiment with other cost models too. The arguments for this function are the current $P(T)$, Graph G, node s_i - a MP-node to be included in $P(T)$, and the two consecutive MP-nodes s_j and s_k on $P(T)$ such that the path between them is to be replaced to insert node s_i.

For each s_i, function $Find-Segment$ is called p times by the function $Select-Segment$, where p is the number of MP-nodes currently in $P(T)$. Then the segment with the least cost and the most MP-nodes is selected to be inserted into $P(T)$. The maximum value of p can be at most $|S| - 1$. When finding a segment a currently used link is not allowed to be used again.

3.4   Detailed Example

Figure 4 depicts the three phases of execution of our heuristic algorithm to find a cycle in Arpanet for a multipoint request of consisting of nodes in set $S = \{2, 5, 13, 14, 17, 19\}$. The top of the figure shows the segment found in the first phase is and it is $\{2, 4, 11, 13, 17\}$. This segment includes three of the nodes from S.

This example was produced by our implementation. Recall that there may be more than one shortest path between a pair of nodes in a given graph. Different numbering of nodes and processing steps could lead to many valid executions of the Bellman-Ford algorithm. The outcome will be different based on which shortest path is found by a particular implementation of the Bellman-Ford algorithm. In the example graph there are several shortest paths between nodes 2 and 19. The shortest path algorithm may find the path $\{2, 1, 3, 7, 10, 19\}$. This path has only two nodes from S while the Initial $P(T)$ selected by our algorithm has three nodes from S. There exists a shortest path $\{2, 4, 11, 13, 17, 19\}$ between nodes 2 and 19. This path has four nodes from S. If this had been the path found by our implementation then it would have become the Initial $P(T)$. However, this did not happen to be the path found by our shortest path algorithm.

The middle of the figure shows the second phase of the execution where a segment $\{2,5,6,7,10,19\}$ is added to form a cycle. This segment includes two previously uncovered MP-nodes of S i.e. 5 and 19.

The bottom of the figure shows the third phase of execution where connection between nodes 17 and 19 has been replaced by the non-simple path $\{17, 19, 16, 15, 14, 20, 19\}$. The segment is non-simple since node 19 is both one

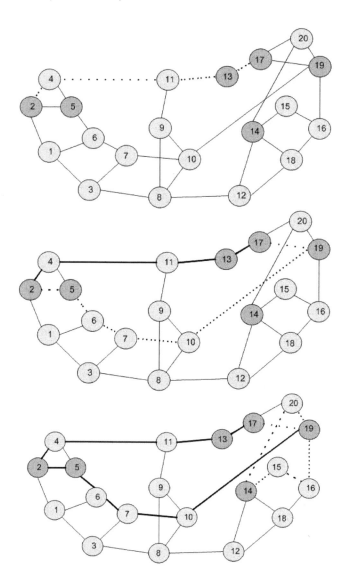

Fig. 4. Step 1, 2 and 3 for Cycle Routing Algorithm

of its' end point and appears in its middle. The segment also happens to include the link that connected 17 and 19 in the previous step. This happened because the algorithm found path {19, 16, 15, 14} and then found {17, 19, 20, 14}. Notice this is not optimal cycle but all nodes have been included. The non-optimality can be observed by noting there exists paths {17, 20, 14} and {19, 16, 15, 14} which could have been used to create a simple cycle using one less link. Since all nodes in S have been included the algorithm terminates.

3.5   Special Cases

In order to give a clear explanation of the execution of our algorithm, we omitted details relating to a couple of special cases in algorithm description. Case 1: It

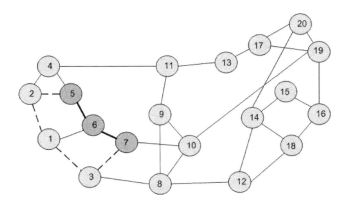

Fig. 5. Example of Special Case 1

is possible for all MP nodes to be included in the path found in Phase I. If this happens then there are no uncovered MP nodes to include when closing the cycle. In this case we simply find the shortest path between the two end nodes of Initial $P(T)$ or report failure if there is no such path.

Figure 5 shows the example of Special Case 1. The MP-nodes in the network are $\{5, 6, 7\}$. The Initial $P(T)$ (solid line) includes all the MP-nodes in its path $\{5, 6, 7\}$. Since all the MP-nodes are covered, our heuristic algorithm finds the shortest path $\{5, 2, 1, 3, 7\}$ between end MP-nodes of Initial $P(T)$ and the algorithm terminates.

Case 2: Sometimes the selection of the Initial $P(T)$ creates a situation where the cycle cannot be closed. Instead of reporting failure in this case we start inserting uncovered MP nodes. Inserting new nodes may free up critical resources allowing the formation of a cycle. If we could not close the cycle initially, we check if the cycle can be closed after each insertion of a new segment.

The example for Case 2 is shown in Figure 6. The Initial $P(T)$ is the path $\{1, 2, 3, 9, 17, 23, 24, 25\}$. Since the links in Initial $P(T)$ cannot be reused, this disconnects the graph preventing the completion of a cycle. When MP node 13 is inserted between MP nodes 2 and 24, the edge between nodes 9 and 17 becomes available. This reconnects the graph allowing for the cycle to be created.

4   Variations of MCR Heuristics Algorithm

To explore the impact on optimality by various design features of our heuristic algorithm, we considered four variations of algorithm MCRA. The variations are

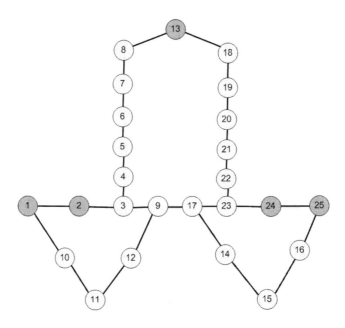

Fig. 6. Example of Special Case 2

obtained by using different node cost and adjusting when the cycle is likely to be closed. The cycle closing can be adjusted by skipping Phase 2 and considering the segments between end nodes of P(T) as part of the segments found between consecutive multipoint nodes in Phase 3.

We use notation ij to describe the four variations of the heuristic algorithm. Index i takes binary value of 0 or 1 whereas Index j takes a value of Y or N. Index i describe the assigned node cost function and Index j describe the inclusion of Phase 2. The four cases are as follows.

- $0Y$ - Multipoint nodes have cost 0 and the other nodes have cost 1. Phase 2 is included.
- $0N$ - Multipoint nodes have cost 0 and the other nodes have cost 1. Phase 2 is skipped.
- $1Y$ - The cost of both multipoint and non-multipoint nodes are same. Phase 2 is included.
- $1N$ - The cost of both multipoint and non-multipoint nodes are same. Phase 2 is skipped.

In Section 7, we analyze the performance of these four variations of our heuristic algorithm in terms of average cycle length and percent blocking in different graph types.

5   ILP Formulation to Find Multipoint Cycles

This section describes an ILP that solves the multipoint cycle routing problem. In most of this paper we have treated the network graph as undirected. In formulating the ILP it was more convenient to assume directed edges. This does not give rise to inconsistencies, since a directed cycle can be converted to a bidirectional cycle by including the edge between nodes in the cycle that go in the direction opposite to the selected edges.

We solved the multipoint cycle problem using an ILP that minimizes the number of edges in the cycle. This is accomplished by the objective function given as in Equation 1. The set of edges found as output should satisfy the following three constraints: edges traveling in opposite directions cannot be used, the selected edges form a cycle, and all S nodes are included in the cycle. The last property is enforced by a flow constraint. The selection problem is related to the flow constraint by requiring that the flow only uses selected edges. The constraints for controlling the flow are written in terms of the following variables and constants, which are indexed over the set of edges $e \in E$ in the network as well as nodes $n, m \in V$ in the network.

The constant values used to specify the ILP are as follow.

$$j_n \quad = \quad \begin{cases} |S| - 1 \text{ for one arbitrary } s_0 \in S \\ -1 \text{ for } s_n \in S, s_n \neq s_0 \\ 0 \text{ for } v_n \in V, v_n \notin S \end{cases}$$

$$d_{e,n} \quad = \quad \begin{cases} -1 \text{ for entering node } n \text{ from edge } e \\ 1 \text{ for leaving node } n \text{ from edge } e \end{cases}$$

$$x_{e,n,m} = \begin{cases} 1 \text{ if edge } e \text{ connects nodes } n \text{ and } m \in V \\ 0 \quad \text{otherwise} \end{cases}$$

The variables and the values they may take are as follows.

$$f_e \quad = \{ \text{ flow on edge } e$$

$$l_e \quad = \begin{cases} 1 \text{ if link } e \text{ is selected} \\ 0 \quad \text{otherwise} \end{cases}$$

Objective Function

$$Minimize \sum_{e=1}^{|E|} l_e \tag{1}$$

The constraints for the ILP are given below:

We setup a flow problem that can only be satisfied if all S nodes are connected by selected links.

$$\sum_{e=1}^{|E|} d_{e,n} f_e = j_n \tag{2}$$

The selected number of incoming links equals the selected number of out going links. This forces the selected links to form one or more cycles. Satisfying the flow problem in 2 forces the selection to be a single cycle.

$$\sum_{e=1}^{|E|} d_{e,n} l_e = 0 \tag{3}$$

Both the edges between a node pair n,m cannot be selected at the same time.

$$\sum_{e=1}^{|E|} x_{e,n,m} l_e \leq 1 \tag{4}$$

If the connectivity enforcing flow uses edge e, then l_e will show that it has been selected. Since the amount of flow is just a book keeping device for checking connectivity, l_e is scaled by the largest possible flow size.

$$|V| l_e \geq f_e \tag{5}$$

We have used this ILP to find the average cycle length for set of random requests in Arpanet and the comparison with that of best performing heuristic is shown in later section.

6   Random Graph Generation for Heuristic Evaluation

To evaluate our algorithms, we have generated random graphs with the following characteristics. Fault-tolerant connections are not possible in 1-connected graphs; hence we needed to ensure that the random graphs are at least 2-connected. We achieve this 2-connectedness by starting with a Hamiltonian cycle passing through all the nodes. Forcing a graph to have a Hamiltonian cycle is a stronger condition than necessary to create a 2-connected graph. Since we start with a Hamiltonian cycle in all the random graphs, a solution always exists to any multipoint request. This characteristic of random graph helps us evaluating the performance of our algorithm. This is because a cycle solution always exists. The blocking cases reported in later section are due to the failure of our algorithm.

We assumed that the physical distance between nodes affects the probability of placing a link between them. Nodes are randomly placed inside a 20x20 grid. On top of this Hamiltonian cycle, we add the rest of the links in the graph randomly with probability given by Equation 6 following the Waxman model. In Equation 6, s and d are nodes, $D(s,d)$ is the distance between the nodes computed by using their coordinates in the grid. α and β are parameters that can be adjusted.

$$P(s,d) = \beta e^{\frac{-D(s,d)}{L\alpha}} \tag{6}$$

The parameters α and β can be adjusted to control the expected density and the average link length of a generated graph. Consider a graph of n nodes and kn edges. We consider a graph as sparse if k is about two, medium density if $k = (2 + \log_2 n)/2$ and dense if $k = n \log_2 n$. To achieve a target density the values of α and β must depend on the selected value of n. We specify six types of graphs in terms of link density and length, as discussed in Table 1. Values of α and β used to realize the target link density and lengths for 64 node Type 0 to Type 5 networks are also given in the table.

Table 1. Graph Types With α, β for Sixty Four Node Networks

Type	Density	Length	α	β
0	sparce	short	0.2	0.2
1	sparce	long	0.8	0.05
2	medium	short	0.2	0.57
3	medium	long	0.8	0.15
4	dense	short	0.2	0.8
5	dense	long	0.8	0.27

7   Numerical Analysis

In this section, we will analyze the performance of four variations of our heuristic algorithm in different types random graphs, based on cycle length and percent blocking as evaluation metrics. We consider one algorithm to be best performing which has least percent blocking and cycle length close to the best solution found by all variations of our algorithm.

All four variations are executed on six types of random networks (sample size of 12 for each type mentioned in Table 1) of size 65 nodes for 10,000 requests each of which had 10 multipoint nodes. The average length of cycle generated by these variations for all the networks is shown in Figure 7. The variations $1N$ and $0N$ outperform other two heuristic variations in terms of cycle length, but it can be seen from Figure 8 that the blocking performance is too high in comparison to other algorithms. High blocking percentage nulls the advantage of getting smaller cycle length using $1N$ and $0N$ algorithms. Since success rate of the request is an important criteria for any algorithm, the algorithms $0Y$ or $1Y$ are preferred as they have lower blocking percentage although the average cycle length is slightly more than that yielded by $0N$ and $1N$ algorithm. We notice that node cost attribute have minimal impact on the average multipoint cycle length in all random networks.

The performances of four variations of heuristic algorithm are analyzed for these six types of networks and also for different network sizes. The average cycle length generated by all four variations of heuristic in six types of random graphs increases with the network size. This is because for large networks, multipoint

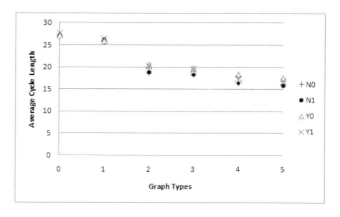

Fig. 7. Average Cycle length for 65 nodes Network

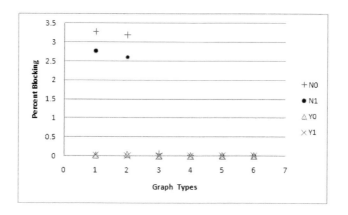

Fig. 8. Blocking Percentage for 64 nodes Network

nodes can be distributed far from each other. Figure 9 depicts that variation $0N$ gives the lowest average cycle length for most network sizes in case of sparse link density (Type 0). For networks with link density medium or higher, variation $0Y$ gives longer cycle length for most network sizes.

Figure 10 shows the average cycle length of all four variations for Type 5 network. The cycle length proportionate to the network size characteristic of algorithm persists for all types of random graphs. Since Type 5 networks have denser link distribution, the maximum cycle length tends to be smaller than that of Type 0 networks.

Figure 11 shows that in case of sparser (Type 0 and Type 1) and medium link density (Type 2 and Type 3) networks the variations $0N$ and $1N$ have many blocked requests whereas the blocking percentage of $0Y$ and $1Y$ algorithms is very close to zero. For dense (Type 4 and Type 5) networks, there is no blocking

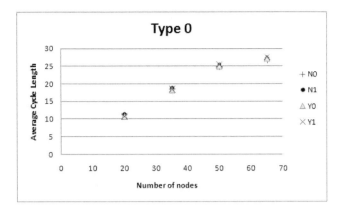

Fig. 9. Average Cycle Length for Type 0 Network

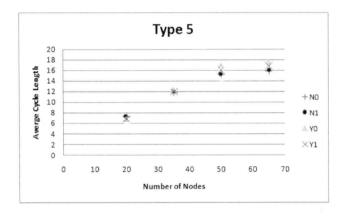

Fig. 10. Average Cycle Length for Type 5 Network

for all variations of algorithms. $1Y$ algorithm always finds a solution for large 65-node networks of all types except for Type 0.

Since the blocking percentage of the algorithms $0N$ and $1N$ is very high for sparser networks (Type 0) and the cycle length found by $1Y$ algorithm does not differ much from $0N$ and $1N$ algorithms, we will be considering $1Y$ algorithm to compare with the optimal results founds by ILP. The reason for selecting $1Y$ over $0Y$ is that we have a done studies of their relative performance for dynamic traffic and $1Y$ had lower blocking. Hence $1Y$ is our recommended heuristic.

7.1 Comparison between Heuristic and ILP

An idea commonly employed by routing algorithms is that a request should be routed with the minimum amount of resources possible. Integer Linear Program (ILP) is used to find optimal routes for some randomly generated requests.

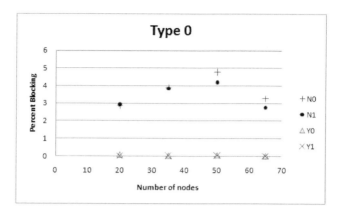

Fig. 11. Blocking Percentage for Type 0 Network

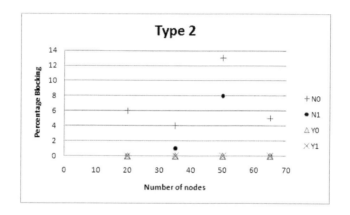

Fig. 12. Blocking Percentage for Type 0 Network

We use CPLEX to solve our ILP. A thousand requests are randomly generated and then routed using ILP. The requests are also routed using our MCRA algorithm. For each of these thousand requests, the ratio is found between the cycle lengths of heuristic and ILP. All results in this section are for Arpanet (20 Nodes, 31 Links). Arpanet has a Hamiltonian cycle so there exists a solution to any possible multipoint request.

This experiment is repeated for requests with different number of multipoint nodes, which are five, seven, nine and eleven. The curves are marked as $S5$, $S7$, $S9$, and $S11$ in Figure 13 respectively for 5,7,9,11 MP-node cases. The list of cycle length ratios of each experiment is sorted and displayed in Figure 13. The X-axis refers to thousand requests used in the experiment and the Y-axis refers to their cycle length ratios. When a quarter of the nodes are multipoint

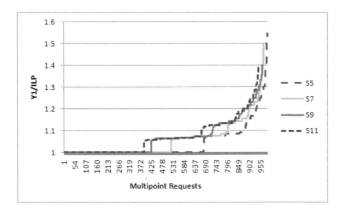

Fig. 13. Ratio Of Cycle Lengths Y1:ILP

nodes $(S = 5)$, optimal resource usage occurred for more than 50% of the total requests. When just over half the nodes in the network are multipoint nodes, optimal resource usage occurred over thirty percent of the time. The figure shows that heuristic $(1Y)$ algorithm yielded performance within a factor of 1.2 of the optimal performance over 80% of the time. Requests, where the MCRA failed to find a cycle, are obviously not included in the Figure 13.

8   Conclusion

Multipoint communication can be protected in such a way that single link failures are automatically restored by the communication protocol without the time consuming process detecting and reacting to the link failure. This is accomplished by forming a bidirectional cycle inside a mesh network and transmitting both directions along the cycle. In this paper we developed a multipoint cycle routing algorithm (MCRA) and provided various heuristic to find a cycle including nodes wishing to form the multipoint session along with a small number of extra nodes. The small number of extra nodes is forced by the network topology. Since we are trying to control the computational complexity of the algorithm, the number of extra nodes included in the cycle are not minimal. We compared the performance of our algorithm to the results of an ILP with the same set of random requests on Arpanet. The algorithm yielded performance within a factor of 1.2 of the optimal performance over 80% of the time.

Acknowledgements. Research funded in part by NSF project CNS 0626741, a Department of Education GAANN Fellowship, and the Jerry R. Junkins Endowment at Iowa State University. Any opinions, findings, and conclusions or recommendations expressed in this material are those of the author(s) and do not necessarily reflect the views of the National Science Foundation (or another funding agency). We would like to thank Onur Turkcu for helpful discussion during the project.

References

1. Zhang, F., Zhong, W.: Performance Evaluation of Optical Multicast Protection Approaches for Combined Node and Link Failure Recovery. Journal of Lightwave Technology 27(18), 4017–4025 (2009)
2. Khalil, A., Hadjiantonis, A., Ellinas, G., Ali, M.: Pre-planned multicast protection approaches in wdm mesh networks. In: 31st European Conference on Optical Communication, ECOC 2005, 25-29, vol. 1, pp. 25–26 (2005)
3. Ramamurthy, S., Sahasrabuddhe, L., Mukherjee, B.: Survivable WDM mesh networks. Journal of Lightwave Technology 21(4), 870 (2003)
4. Singhal, N., Sahasrabuddhe, L., Mukherjee, B.: Provisioning of survivable multicast sessions against single link failures in optical WDM mesh networks. Journal of Lightwave Technology 21, 11–21 (2003)
5. YuQing, G., Beijing, C.: Protecting Dynamic Multicast Sessions in Optical WDM Mesh Networks
6. Wen-De Zhong, F.: Applying p-Cycles in Dynamic Provisioning of Survivable Multicast Sessions in Optical WDM Networks. In: Conference on Optical Fiber Communication and the National Fiber Optic Engineers Conference, OFC/NFOEC 2007, pp. 1–3 (2007)
7. Feng, T., Lu, R., Zhang, W.: Intelligent p-Cycle Protection for Multicast Sessions in WDM Networks. In: Proc. ICC, vol. 8, pp. 5165–5169 (2008)
8. Zhang, F., Zhong, W., Jin, Y.: Optimizations of p-Cycle-Based Protection ofOptical Multicast Sessions. Journal of Lightwave Technology 26(19), 3298–3306 (2008)
9. Zhang, F., Zhong, W.: Performance evaluation of p-cycle based protection methods for provisioning of dynamic multicast sessions in mesh WDM networks. Photonic Network Communications 16(2), 127–138 (2008)
10. Wen-De Zhong, F.: p-Cycle based tree protection of optical multicast traffic for combined link and node failure recovery in WDM mesh networks. IEEE Communications Letters 13(1), 40–42 (2009)

Failure Presumed Protection (FPP): Optical Recovery with Approximate Failure Localization

János Tapolcai*

Dept. of Telecommunications and Media Informatics,
Budapest University of Technology and Economics, Hungary
tapolcai@tmit.bme.hu

Abstract. This paper investigates failure recovery mechanisms for optical network with a very high reliability requirement, where a novel framework of network failure recovery, called Failure Presumed Protection (FPP), is proposed. Our scheme aims to perform 100% failure restoration using only an approximate location of the failed links identified from the connection status information available at each network node.

Keywords: In-Band Failure Localization, Failure Dependent Protection, Restoration, Shared Protection, Shared Risk Link Group.

1 Introduction

Failure Independent Protection (FIP) mechanisms, such as dedicated and shared protection, are widely accepted approaches where the protection switching is performed without any knowledge of the failed network elements. With these approaches simple and fast failure recovery can be achieved for single link failures by sacrificing a significant amount of bandwidth for protection. The rest of the failures, including operational errors, power outage, and even DOS attack, etc., could hit the network for multiple links/nodes. These failures are often modeled by a *Shared Risk Link Group* (SRLG), which is a group of network elements subject to a risk of simultaneous failure.

Protecting the SRLG failures is expected to serve as the solution for possibly achieving the highest level of end-to-end availability guarantee. Under such circumstances, the optical layer protection scheme may not be able to guarantee 100% restorability for the connections against the failures of all listed SRLGs. Allocating two or more protection routes for each connection under FIP mechanism could be infeasible due to the sparsely meshed network topology and consumption of additional spare capacity, even with the employment of shared protection.

---

* This work was supported by High Speed Network Laboratory (HSNLab) and the Hungarian Scientific Research Fund, OTKA Grant No. T-67651. The author is grateful for the financial support of Magyary Zoltn postdoctoral program of Foundation for Hungarian Higher Education and Research.

I. Tomkos et al. (Eds.): BROADNETS 2010, LNICST 66, pp. 361–368, 2012.

Failure Dependent Protection (FDP) [1] was reported in contrast with FIP, where in case of a failure event the *switching node* of an interrupted connection restores the connection according to where the failure event occurs in the network. With FDP, more than one protection paths are pre-planned for each connection, where upon a failure, the nodes responsible for traffic switchover initiate restoration the affected connections by activating one of the protection paths/segments to restore the connections, according to the failed network elements. The merits of FDP against FIP mainly lie in better achievable capacity efficiency and flexibility to sparse network topologies. Note that, the protection paths of a FDP connection may traverse through one or a number of common links with the working path. Therefore, the protection paths should not be totally disjoint from the working path, and the working capacity along the interrupted connections could be possibly reused during the recovery. Such a protection strategy is supposed to be the most efficient especially when spare capacity sharing is allowed [2,3].

Failure localization is considered as a very difficult job due to the transparency in the optical domain along with various design requirements [4]. *Out-of-band all-optical monitoring* via a set of dedicated pre-cross-connected lightpaths has been considered as an effective approach to achieve fast failure localization in all-optical backbones. In the past, several monitoring structures, including m-cycles, m-paths, and m-trails, etc., have been extensively studied. Detailed comparison and descriptions can be found in [5]. In contrast, *in-band monitoring* solutions rely on operational lightpaths only to localize any failure occurring in the network. Compared to traditional in-band monitoring solutions we allow some ambiguity in localizing the failed links and instead FDP protection is adapted to cope with imprecision in failure localization. The new framework is called *Failure Presumed Protection* (FPP). To the best of our survey, the concept of FDP has never been adopted and exercised in any study based on the general definition of SRLGs.

With our in-band failure localization method, each node collects the alarm triggers by the connections traversing through it, and according to this information, each network node can approximate the location of failed network elements and activate some pre-planned protection routes to recover the interrupted connections. In particular, we focus on the case where the working capacity originally reserved by a connection can be reused only by its protection paths during the failure restoration, in which a compromise will be initiated between the precision of failure localization and the amount of information exchange.

The rest of the paper is organized as follows. In Section 2 we give a short overview on the failure dependent protection schemes. In Section 3, we present the proposed path restoration framework, Failure Presumed Protection (FPP), where each node presumes the location of the failed network elements according to the local in-band connection status information available at each node. In Section 4, we evaluate and compare the performance of each FPP scheme with the previously reported counterparts.

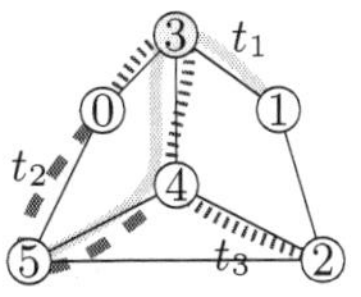

SRLGs	t_1 t_2 t_3
(3,4)	1 0 1
(1,3)	1 0 0
(5,4)	1 1 0
(0,5)	0 1 0
(0,3)(2,4)	0 0 1
∅(1,2)(5,2)	0 0 0

SRLGs	t_2
(0,5)(5,4)	1
∅(1,2)(5,2)	0
(3,4)(1,3)	
(0,3)(2,4)	

(a) Topology and working lightpaths. (b) Alarm code table at node 4 (ACT^4) of FPP^{OD}. (c) ACT^4 of FPP^{ED}.

Fig. 1. Rough failure localization based on connection status information, where each link is an SRLG

2 Failure Presumed Protection (FPP)

In our framework we consider an online routing problem, without any knowledge of future request arrivals and without applying prediction based routing on the statistics of the past requests. Bi-directional connections and links are considered in the network.

2.1 Approximate Failure Localization

Each node n monitor a set of J_n connections $t_1, t_2, \ldots, t_{J_n}$, which are the lightpaths passing through or terminating the node in optical networks. Upon a failure, each lightpath traversing the failed SRLG will generate an alarm. At each node an alarm code $[a_1, a_2, \ldots, a_{J_n}]$ can be formed after all the alarms are collected, where $a_j = 1$ means that lightpath t_j alarms, and $a_j = 0$ otherwise. Let the failure of SRLG $\mathscr{S}$ at node n results an alarm code denoted by $a(\mathscr{S}, n)$. Fig. 1 shows an example with three connections t_1, t_2, t_3 corresponding to node 4. If SRLG of link $(3, 4)$ fails, both lightpaths t_1 and t_3 will alarm to produce the alarm code $[1, 0, 1]$ at node 4. At the same time, if there is any failure along SRLG of links $(0, 3)$ and $(4, 2)$ both result an $[0, 0, 1]$ alarm code, and thus the location of the failure cannot unambiguously identified, just presumed. Finally there is no information at node 4 on the failure of SRLGs containing links $(1, 2)$ and $(5, 2)$, because they all result $[0, 0, 0]$ alarm code similarly to the no failure case. Each network node n computes its own alarm code table (ACT), which maintains all the possible alarm codes that could be resulted at the network controller. Each row of the ACT is assigned to a group of SRLGs with the same alarm codes. Let us denote the set of SRLGs with the same alarm code a by $\mathcal{R}_n^a$ at node n. In such a way node n will be able to obtain a rough location of the failed network elements by matching the alarm code in its own alarm code table, denoted by ACT^n. The precision of the failure localization intuitively depends on the number of rows and the size of $\mathcal{R}_n^a$ $\forall a$.

The size of the alarm code equals to the number of monitored connections at each node, which strongly influences the precision of failure localization. The status of a connection can be monitored at node n, if node n can capture (local) alarm messages on the failure of the connection. We consider two architectures for capturing the local alarm messages

FPP^{OD} where the failure of a connection is *detected at optical layer*. Each port of the optical cross connects is equipped with an optical signal power monitor. A failure along the lightpath will issue loss of light (LoL) alarm messages at each transient network nodes. See Fig. 1(c) as an example of ACT for FPP^{OD} architecture.

FPP^{ED} where the failure of a connection is *detected only at electrical layer* at the terminal nodes of each lightpath. Thus, the transient network nodes along the working route cannot monitor the status of the connection. See Fig. 1(b) as an example of ACT for FPP^{ED} architecture.

2.2   System and Problem Formulation

By considering each SRLG with multiple network elements, there are two impacts upon solving the survivable routing problem compared with the case where there is a one-to-one mapping between each link/node and a SRLG. First, the survivable routing problem becomes NP-hard; second, the number of SRLGs could be largely increased, which makes the amount of shareability information of protection routes increased accordingly. The shareability information is stored in *spare provision matrix* (SPM) [6], where entry (i, j) is the amount of restoration traffic is routed on link i in case of failure of SRLG j.

The routing problem is formulated as follows. Given a network topology represented with an undirected graph $G(V, E)$ with a set of *links* E and *nodes* V, where $|E|$ and $|V|$ are the number of links and nodes in G. Each SRLG of the original network can be represented by a set of links in the transformed graph. Furthermore, we are given the source node s and the destination node d of the new demand for bandwidth b. The unreserved free capacity along link j is denoted as $f_j \ \forall j \in E$. The amount of shared capacity (i.e., the capacity reserved for protection routes) along link j is denoted as $v_j \ \forall j \in E$. SPM is denoted as $\underline{S}$ and it is a $|E| \times |SRLG|$ matrix. The entry (i, j) of $\underline{S}$ (denoted as $s_{i,j}$, where $i = 1 \dots |E|$, $j = 1 \dots |SRLG|$) is the amount of non-sharable spare capacity along link i of the protection path (denoted as P) if the working path (denoted as W) *involves in* the j-th SRLG.

In FPP to each row of the ACT at node n (having alarm code a) optionally a *protection route* is assigned, denoted by P_n^a. In case of failure for each connection a *restoration action plan* is determined based on the protection route. The restoration plan describes the actions needed for resolving the failure situation for single connection, which includes releasing the failed segment of working path (called span) and allocating a new protection route. When a failure occurs in the network alarm codes at each node are generated and in each ACT the corresponding protection routes are looked up and restoration action plan is determined for each connection.

2.3   Connection Setup in FPP

When a new connection demand arrives, the goal of the survivable routing process is to allocate a single working path W for each connection, and add protection routes to some rows of the ACTs at either nodes s or d, such that either node s or d activates protection route for W in case of every single SRLG failure interrupting W.

We propose two steps connection setup (a.k.a. *two-step-approach*), where first the working path is established and in the next step the protection routes are calculated and signaled. Two step is favored for its simplicity, efficiency, and its main drawback, the trap-topology problem [7], can be solved for FDP and almost always for FPP. In trap problem the network has such an unfortunate topology that after the shortest working path is chosen, finding an SRLG disjoint protection path fails; however, with a joint optimization an SRLG disjoint working and protection paths can be found.

In the first step working path W is selected, such that the feasible condition for selecting link j for working path W is that $f_j \geq b$ for all links $j \in W$. Such working path can be calculated with Dijkstra's algorithm in a graph with links $f_j \geq b$. Next, the ACT is updated in each node involved in W and a new ACT, denoted by ACT^{new}, is determined for calculating the protection route.

After ACT^{new} is determined, protection routes are calculated for each row of ACT^{new} involved in working path W. A row of ACT^{new} with alarm code a is involved in W if the failure of the corresponding SRLGs interrupts W. Let us denote the set of SRLGs with the same alarm code a in ACT^{new} by $\mathcal{R}^a_{new}$. Let the failure of SRLG $\mathcal{S}$ listed with an alarm code denoted by $a(\mathcal{S}, new)$ in ACT^{new}. To protect single SRLG failure of the new connection, we take each row of ACT^{new} involved in W one by one, and calculate a protection route which satisfies the following properties. Let us denote the alarm code of the selected row by a and the corresponding protection route by P^a.

1. the protection route P^a is disjoint from the SRLGs with common alarm code a, i.e. $P^a \cup j = \emptyset$ for all SRLG $j \in \mathcal{R}^{a(\mathcal{S}, new)}$,
2. the protection route P^a has sufficient restoration capacity for the protection of the working routes affected by any single failure of $j \in \mathcal{R}^{a(\mathcal{S}, new)}$. Formally, the amount of spare capacity required along the protection route P^a assigned to the set of SRLGs denoted by $a(\mathcal{S}, new)$ is $b - v_i + \max_{\forall j \in a(\mathcal{S}, new)} s_{i,j}$, except for the common segments with W. Thus for all link $i \in P^a$ the feasible condition is

$$f_i \geq b - v_i + \max_{\forall j \in a(\mathcal{S}, new)} s_{i,j}.$$

Each protection route can be calculated with Dijkstra's algorithm by erasing the links not satisfying the above mentioned properties from graph G in the same way as protection paths were calculated in [6].

Obviously, the proposed approximate failure localization does not work in an empty network, and requires a certain amount of operating connections. However, for lightly loaded networks the capacity efficiency may not be a serious issue and dedicated link protection can achieve very high service reliability.

2.4   Connection Release in FPP

One of the main difficulties in FPP is that connection release is far not that simple than in traditional resilience mechanisms. On the other hand, connection release is not a time critical process, which weight against fast connection setup, great capacity efficiency and a superb flexibility in service reliability. The difficulty comes from the fact that network connections rely on each other. If a connection is released its status information no longer available, thus every later connection, that rely on this information should re-calculate their protection routes. Unfortunately, in some instance the status information of the releasing connection is so important that, without it some later connection would not be able to protect the failure of every SRLG they required to. We call this phenomenon as *blocked at release*. In this case, either the connection release is postponed, or the later problematic connections are protected with any other protection mechanism. Even if the connection release is postponed, its protection routes can be released, and its working bandwidth can be reduced to a minimum value.

3   Simulation Results

Extensive simulation is conducted to explore the performance of each protection scheme and routing algorithm. A call request is completed if there is a working path and any single SRLG failure can be protected. Otherwise, we regard the incoming request as being blocked. The simulations are conducted on four different network topologies, see Table 1 for details. The average distance is the average hop distance between every node-pairs of the network. A dynamic traffic pattern is generated as indicated by the traffic matrix with Interrupted Poisson Process arrival times and exponential holding times.

Three different protection methods are compared: Shared Dual-link Protection (*SDP*) with two-step-approach, where the working path is shortest path routed, while in the second step two disjoint protection paths are calculated with Suurballe's algorithm. We take simple sharing rule of backup capacity and do not specify any activation order among the protection paths. Failure Presumed Protection (*FPP*) with two different architectures: superscript ^{OD} or ^{ED} is added for optical/electrical layer failure detection, respectively. The corresponding routing problem was implemented with the two-step-approach as described in Section 2.3.

Table 1. Reference networks

name	nodes	average distance	max distance	nodal
German	17	2.69853	6	3.05882
European	22	2.46753	5	4.09091
Usa	26	3.30769	8	3.23077
North American	39	4.20513	10	3.12821

In the simulations the flexibility of each protection scheme on adopting to extreme conditions was investigated. In order to measure the capacity efficiency as well, the link capacities were set small at the beginning of the simulation and were proportionally increased to allow routing the requests with a minimal amount, such that each connection can fit into the network. If the blocking was not due to the lack of capacity, each link capacity remains with the same value. Since FPP cannot deal with networks without traffic, therefore an initial network state was calculated routing 1000 demands without protection.

In the simulation the list of SRLGs contains every single and dual links and 1000 demands were routed. In SDP three link disjoint path was established for each connection. It provided on an average 60% of blocking, which is mainly because none of the networks were 3-connected. FPP_s^{OD} over performed SDP by routing averagely 50% of the connection requests. The amount of reserved network resources depends on the number of connections routed, thus a higher blocking leads to a lower link capacity scaler. On Fig. 2(a) the link capacity scaler and the blocking probability of each simulation was illustrated. The results of the same network was connected with lines, while each symbols represents different protection scheme. Methods with smaller value on blocking probability and link capacity are preferred. Compared to dedicated and shared protection FPP^{ED} and FPP^{OD} is able to route more demands and at the same time it provides a better sharing of protection resources.

On Fig. 2(b) the same simulation was repeated; however, after 100 demands every dual links, every dual node and link, and every dual nodes failure were added as SRLGs to the network. Protecting every dual links and nodes failure in 2-connected network topologies is an even harder task due to the significant

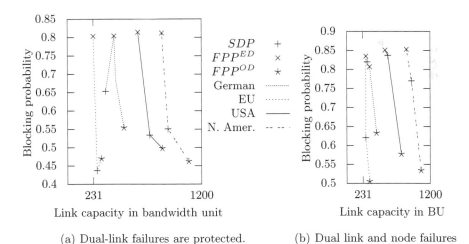

(a) Dual-link failures are protected.

(b) Dual link and node failures are protected.

Fig. 2. Overall comparison of link capacity and the related blocking probability values when dual-link failures are protected

increase in the number of SRLGs. It results in a higher blocking for all methods. Despite the bad conditions FPP^{OD} was able to successfully route an average of 50% of all the demands protecting dual link and node failures.

4   Conclusions

In this paper the problem of establishing highly fault tolerant connections was investigated. The goal was to protect the connection for every listed failure patterns, which is called Shared Risk Link Groups (SRLGs). These SRLGs may be extreamly long with many and arbitrary network elements, while the connectivity of today's backbone network is usually very limited. Our goal was to break through this conflict and propose a routing method, which can highly adopt to the network topology and provide the highest level of service reliability. We assume in-band monitoring which can partially localize the failed network elements at each switching node. In such an environment the switching node activates one of its protection paths depending on the failed network elements. We propose a framework, named Failure Presumed Protection (FPP), where the switching node can presume the location of the failure by processing all of the retransmitted alarm messages. Finally, with simulation the benefits of FPP framework was proved.

References

1. Ramasubramanian, S., Harjani, A.S.: Comparison of failure dependent protection strategies in optical networks. Photonic Network Communications 12(2), 195–210 (2006)
2. Grover, W., Doucette, J., Clouqueur, M., Leung, D., Stamatelakis, D.: New options and insights for survivable transport networks. IEEE Communications Magazine 40(1), 34–41 (2002)
3. Martin, R., Menth, M., Canbolat, K.: Capacity requirements for the one-to-one backup option in mpls fast reroute. In: Proc. BroadNets, San Jose, CA (October 2006)
4. Tomkos, I.: Dynamically reconfigurable transparent optical networking based on cross-layer optimization. In: ICTON 2007, vol. 1, pp. 327–327 (2007)
5. Wu, B., Ho, P.-H., Yeung, K., Tapolcai, J., Mouftah, H.: Optical layer monitoring schemes for fast link failure localization in all-optical networks. IEEE Comm. Surveys & Tutorials (2010)
6. Liu, Y., Tipper, D., Siripongwutikorn, P.: Approximating optimal spare capacity allocation by successive survivable routing. In: Proc. IEEE INFOCOM, Anchorage, Alaska, pp. 699–708 (2001)
7. Xu, D., Xiong, Y., Qiao, C., Li, G.: Trap avoidance and protection schemes in networks with shared risk link groups. IEEE Journal of Lightwave Technology (2003)

Static Multipoint to Multipoint Buses Placement in Transparent Optical Networks

Benaissa El-Khattar[1,2], Nicolas Le Sauze[1], and André-Luc Beylot[2]

[1] Alcatel-Lucent Bell Labs France (ALBLF), Nozay, France
[2] IRIT-ENSEEIHT Toulouse, France
{benaissa.el_khattar,Nicolas.Le_Sauze}@alcatel-lucent.com,
beylot@enseeiht.fr

Abstract. We propose a node architecture supporting the packet-oriented multipoint to multipoint (MP2MP) transparent optical passive buses. The main goal of the bus concept is to minimize costs by maximizing resources utilization in transparent optical mesh networks. We first formulate the problem of MP2MP passive optical bus placement (OBP) as an ILP problem with linear constraints in case of static traffic demands. We propose next a heuristic named Maximizing Resources Utilization (MRU). We use further the MRU dimensioning with two traffic models. We compare the concept of MP2MP bus to the multipoint-to-point (MP2P) passive optical bus and an active MP2MP bus (MP2MP with online optical packet erasing) called also Optical Packet Switching (OPS). We finally derive conclusions from the numerical results on the performance of both the passive and active MP2MP optical and the MP2P bus as well as on the MP2MP passive bus and the OPS active one.

Keywords: Optical Bus, Dual Optical Bus, MP2MP, MP2P, OPS, packet-oriented, passive, active, bus placement, statistical multiplexing, ON/OFF traffic.

1   Introduction

In transparent optical networks, the bandwidth requested by a traffic stream can be much lower than the capacity of a lightpath [1], which may result in large underutilization of optical resources. Efficient grooming of low-speed connections onto high-capacity lightpaths may be therefore required to improve network throughput and reduce network cost.

Several approaches of intermediate grooming have been investigated for transparent optical networks with the general principle to allow intermediate nodes to access a light path in the optical domain, without re-passing through electronic domain. The first approach called optical packet switching (OPS) [2], supposes that an intermediate node on a lightpath is able to drop and erase, in the optical domain, packets destined to it. The second one called indifferently multipoint-to-point (MP2P) traffic aggregation, MP2P optical buses or distributed aggregation (DA) supposes that intermediate nodes are not able to erase packets in the optical domain but to only detect availabilities on the resource and fill it on the fly [3] leading to a set of

I. Tomkos et al. (Eds.): BROADNETS 2010, LNICST 66, pp. 369–384, 2012.
© Institute for Computer Sciences, Social Informatics and Telecommunications Engineering 2012

multipoint-to-point (MP2P) unidirectional bus. Another approach named super lightpath or P2MP optical bus supposes that the edge node of a lightpath broadcasts its traffic to all intermediate nodes [4]. Finally, the approach called optical dual bus represents an optimal combination of MP2P and P2MP buses partially described in [5]. Intermediate electronic grooming is also a solution for the mentioned problem, but with this solution the network is no longer transparent.

In this paper, we evaluate the MP2MP optical bus concept [6] in transparent mesh networks. Another concept called "Light Trail", similar to a MP2MP bus and burst-oriented (not packet-oriented) was previously investigated [7]. The light trail concept uses a control channel to establish rapid connections and to avoid collision between nodes sharing a light trail. Therefore, the light trail is connection-oriented in contrast with a MP2MP bus, which is entirely connection-less and packet-oriented.

We propose a new ILP formulation of the MP2MP optical bus placement problem for minimizing the number of required wavelengths. Next, we propose a heuristic named MRU to solve this problem. For the evaluation and network dimensioning, we use two traffic models. The first model is a simple model taking into account the average bandwidth of traffic demands. The second model is the ON/OFF flow model [8] allowing taking into account the statistical multiplexing effect, when multiplexing individual traffic flows onto a single optical resource at different grooming places. We finally compare, for the two traffic models, the proposed MP2MP aggregation to the OPS and MP2P approaches according to the minimum number of resources (lightpaths, transmitters: Tx and receivers: Rx) required to route a given traffic through a given network. This minimum is the performance criterion used for the comparison of different types of optical buses in this paper. A theoretical framework to calculate the statistical multiplexing gain for a single bus in the case of uniform traffic demand is also proposed.

2   MP2MP Optical Bus

An optical bus is a lightpath that can be accessed by its intermediate nodes in the optical domain without passing through the electronic domain. An optical bus consists of a lightpath and intermediate nodes generating traffic (Ethernet frames for example) and accessing the lightpath.

The MP2MP optical bus feature enables full bus sharing among several access nodes. Instead of limiting access to the bus on intermediate nodes only for writing (as in MP2MP case), each node can have an access to a bus for both reading and writing according to the availability. In a MP2MP aggregation, the bus can be shared by multiple connections that have several destinations instead of a single destination for a MP2P bus. Intermediate nodes access the bus in a similar way as in MP2P and use a simple Medium Access Control (MAC) protocol based on void/null detection [9]. Figure (1) depicts different optical buses compared in this article.

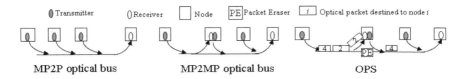

Fig. 1. An illustration of the compared optical busses

3   Node Architecture

3.1   Physical Layer

The node must allow wavelength routing and sharing in a MP2MP manner, controlling the access to the MP2MP bus and on demand MP2MP buses reconfiguration (Bus set up/tear down, add nodes to bus and delete nodes from bus). This architecture must also allow a fair access to the bus and finally, it must allow also classical point-to-point (P2P) lightpath [1] to establish circuit P2P connections if the flow value between two nodes is close to the bandwidth capacity C (Gb/s).

The node architecture comprises optical multiplexers (Mux) and de-multiplexers (Demux), tunable transmitters (Tx) and receivers (Rx), carrier sensing device (CS) or MAC introduced in [9], tunable burst mode receivers (BM-Rx) and transmitters (BM-Tx). Note that in appropriate cases, a burst mode receiver can be used both to receive and detect the void/null as a MAC device (BM-Rx/CS). The node architecture also comprises optical couplers, variable optical attenuators (VOA) to terminate optical MP2MP busses and 2×2 optical switches to reconfigure the busses (only slow reconfiguration is required). Figure (2) shows an optical node supporting MP2MP optical buses. This architecture can be implemented differently, but the more important is that such architecture should be more flexible to allow optical MP2MP buses setup and reconfiguration as well as optical circuit switching. The proposed architecture is scalable and extended easily to an N inputs and N outputs one.

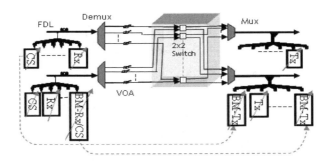

Fig. 2. A node Architecture supporting MP2MP optical buses

3.2   Data Link Layer

In the case of MP2MP bus, the access to the wavelength is controlled, as in MP2P bus, by a simple MAC layer presented in [9]. In addition to a simple Carrier Sense Multiple Access with collision avoidance, the bus fairness is controlled by the TCARD protocol [10]. In this paper, we do not propose any modification to these control mechanisms, as TCARD is also applicable for a fair access between nodes sharing an optical MP2MP bus.

4   Static Optical M2MP Bus Placement: An ILP Formulation

The problem of static optical bus placement is described in [6]. This problem is to find, for a given configuration of traffic, the optimal placement of the different buses. For our study, the cost function is supposed to be the number of buses (wavelengths) required to satisfy a given traffic configuration. The inputs of this problem are:

The physical topology (number of node (N) and physical shortest path between node i and j), the traffic matrix ($T(s,d)$) and the wavelength capacity C. The wavelength capacity C will be equal to 10 Gb/s in our study. From those inputs we define the parameters L and H as follow.

$$L(i, j, k) = \begin{cases} 1 \text{ if node } k \text{ is an intermediate node of the bus } (i, j) \\ 0 \text{ otherwise} \end{cases} \tag{1}$$

$H(s,d)$: is the hop-distance (in number of links) of the shortest path between nodes s and d. The optical buses will be constructed in a shortest path manner.

We define the variable λ, that indicates if a MP2MP bus is used or not by a traffic demand, as follow.

$$\lambda(s, d, i, j) = \begin{cases} 1 \text{ if the bus } (i, j) \text{ is used by the demand } T(s, d) \\ 0 \text{ otherwise} \end{cases} \tag{2}$$

Under these assumptions, the OBP problem can formulated as follow:

$$\min_{\lambda(i,j,s,d)} \sum \lambda(i, j, i, j)$$

Subject to :

$$\begin{array}{lll}
(C1) & \sum_{s,d} \lambda(i, j, s, d) = \delta_{T(i,j)} & \forall i, j \\
(C2) & \lambda(i, j, s, d) = 0 & \text{if } (L(s, d, i) = 0 \text{ or } L(s, d, j) = 0) \\
(C3) & \lambda(i, j, s, d) = 0 & \text{if } H(s, i) \geq H(s, j) \\
(C4) & \sum_{i,j} \lambda(i, j, s, d) T(i, j) \leq C & \forall(s, d) \\
(C5) & \lambda(i, j, i, j) \geq \lambda(s, d, i, j) & \forall i, j, s, d
\end{array} \tag{3}$$

.

Constraint $C1$ explains the fact that a traffic demand $T(i,j)$ use one and only one optical bus. $C4$ is the bus capacity constraint and $C5$ explains the fact that if an optical bus (i,j) is used, it is necessarily used by the traffic demand $T(i,j)$. $C2$ and $C3$ are considered as inputs constraints of the problem, because $C2$ explains that, if a node i or a node j is not an intermediate node to the optical bus (s,d), the traffic demand T(i,j) will not use the bus (s,d) and $C3$ is the constraint explaining that if the orientation of the demand T(i,j) is opposite to the bus (s,d), this demand will not use the bus (s,d).

Theorem 1. The OBP problem is NP-hard.

Proof 1. The Bin Packing Problem (BP) can be reduced to the OBP since the OBP has more constraints (BP has only the two constraints C1 and C4). Hence the OBP problem is NP-Hard.

Since, the OBP is NP-hard, the complexity of an exact resolution algorithm is exponential and the problem is inaproximable. This complexity is one of the key motivations for a heuristic approach to solve the static MP2MP OBP problem.

We propose a heuristic that we name MRU (Maximizing resource utilization). The pseudo-code of the MRU is described by the Algorithm 1. The principle of this heuristic is to prioritize the flows $T(s,d)$ which have the farthest hop-distance $H(s,d)$ between their nodes source and destination. Unlike the MTA algorithm used for MP2P buses [11], MRU allows intermediate nodes to receive data in a given lightpath, it can assign, therefore, a traffic demand $T(i,j)$ to a lightpath (s,d) even if j is not equal to d.

Algorithm 1 The pseudo-code of the heuristic MRU

1. Reorder the connection requests $T(s,d)$ in descending order of $H(s,d)$.

2. For each connection request $T(s,d)$:

    (a) If $T(s,d)$ is not satisfied :

        i. Establish the bus (s,d) to satisfy $T(s,d)$.

        ii. Insert the intermediates MP2P connections $T(i,d)$ in the bus (s,d) in descending order of $H(i,d)$.

        iii. Insert, in the bus (s,d), the others intermediates connections $T(j,k)$ if there is sufficient bandwidth (in descending order of $H(j,k)$).

3. Route the traffic requests in the constructed topology.

---

5   Network Dimensioning, Results and Comparison

5.1   MRU Compared to Optimal Solution

In this part, we compare the performance of the heuristic MRU to the optimum obtained by the numerical solver CPLEX [12]. We use the 6-nodes network (small

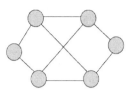

Fig. 3. A six node network

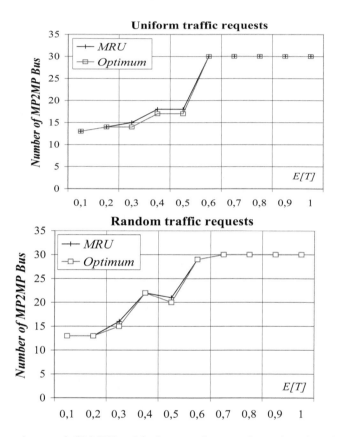

Fig. 4. A six node network (b) MRU and Optimum performance in number of required MP2MP buses

size) network presented on figure 3. We consider a traffic model based in the average bandwidth of each demand T(s,d). It means that the value T(s,d) gives the time-averaged bandwidth of the demand T(s,d). We define the parameter $\overline{T}$ as the averaged and normalized (to the wavelength capacity C) bandwidth value of all the traffic demand:

$$\overline{T} = \frac{\sum_{s,d} T(s,d)}{(Number\ of\ non-zero\ traffic\ demands\ T(s,d)) \times C} . \qquad (4)$$

We consider uniform and random traffic scenarios. In the uniform scenario, the demand T(s,d) have the same value for all (s,d) (s≠d). And in the random one, demands T(s,d) are randomly generated following an uniform distribution.

It is noteworthy that all traffic demand will be considered sub-lambda (T(s,d)<C) in this part to be accommodated in an optical bus. Because if a traffic demand is non sub-lambda (T(s,d)≥C) we can not accommodate it in an optical bus, but in this case we can break it into two components: the first one is composed of static lightpath while the second one is sub-lambda (part 5.3.4) . From any traffic demand matrix T we can create a traffic demand matrix T_1 that all its elements $T_1(s,d)$ are sub-lambda.

Figure 4 shows that, in this case, the performance of the heuristic MRU are very close to the optimum. In both uniform and random traffic scenarios, the relative error of MRU does not exceed 7%. We conclude that the heuristic MRU can be used to achieve near-optimum performance and thus, we will use it in this paper to map the demands to different MP2MP approach.

5.2   Average Bandwidth Model Network Modeling

In this part, we consider, as in part 5.1, an unicast traffic matrix T and only the "random" scenario. It is noteworthy that the MP2MP architecture will have additional benefits in case of multicast traffic, thanks to its full drop and continue feature. The network dimensioning is achieved by evaluating the saving rate of the minimum required resources (Tx, Rx and lightpath) to satisfy a given traffic demand in each approach compared to the classical transparent P2P networks.

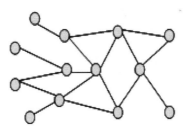

Fig. 5. Network Topology

In our simulation, we use a topology representative of a typical metropolitan network Fig 5. Fig 6. reports the proportion of transceiver saving per node and the reduction of the number of lightpaths in the different approaches compared to the classical transparent case.

$\overline{T}$	percent transceivers per node saving			percent reduction of light path number		
	MP2P	MP2MP	OPS	MP2P	MP2MP	OPS
0.05	25%	50%	50%	49%	77%	77%
0.1	25%	48%	50%	49%	76%	77%
0.15	25%	43%	47%	49%	73%	75%
0.2	25%	38%	43%	49%	70%	73%
0.25	24%	34%	39%	48%	65%	69%
0.3	23%	30%	34%	46%	60%	65%
0.35	21%	26%	29%	42%	53%	58%
0.4	18%	22%	25%	36%	46%	52%
0.45	16%	19%	22%	32%	41%	46%
0.5	14%	17%	19%	27%	36%	40%
0.55	8%	10%	11%	16%	22%	26%
0.6	4%	6%	6%	9%	13%	16%
0.65	2%	3%	3%	4%	7%	8%
0.7	1%	1%	1%	1%	2%	2%
0.75	0%	0%	0%	0%	0%	0%

Fig. 6. Results and comparison

The performance results show that, an average transceivers saving of 15%, 23% and 25% compared to the classical approach is obtained by the MP2P, MP2MP and OPS approaches respectively. We have also an average number of lightpaths reduction of respectively of 31%, 43% and 46%. Furthermore, given the properties of the MP2MP and OPS architecture, where connections to different destinations could be aggregated in the same lightpath on the contrary to the MP2P approach, the number of transceivers and lightpaths required to satisfy all traffic requests is reduced, for all $\overline{T}$ values (Fig 6.).

It is very important to note that, despite the lack of on line packet erasing features in MP2MP approach, its performances are close to those of the OPS. In general, Fig 6. shows average savings of 2% on the number of transceivers and 3% on the number of lightpaths comparing MP2MP and OPS, while the maximum difference is 5% on both criteria. As a result, the proposed MRU algorithm has a resources saving efficiency close to the OPS case without using optical erasing devices that require very faster re-configurability and more complex control [2].

Analyzing results of the Fig 6., we can define three different areas: In the case of a small E[T] (less than 20%), OPS and MP2MP have similar performance, and gains compared to MP2P are very significant (around 50% on transceivers and 25% on lightpaths). In this optimistic case, MP2MP advantageously compete with OPS, having similar performance and a reduced complexity. In the pessimistic case ($\overline{T}$ higher than 60%), the performance of all approaches compared to the classical transparent network becomes low, and those approaches may be more questionable. Typical such case may occur in core networks where previous metro network segments enabled to bundle enough traffic to effectively have traffic demands close to the wavelength granularity. In the intermediate case ($\overline{T}$ is in the interval [25%, 55%]), which is a probable scenario in a metropolitan network, a difference arises between OPS and MP2MP, but this difference remains limited and not exceeds 5%. As a result, the simplicity of passive devices and control mechanisms of the MP2MP approach make it very competitive.

5.3   The Flow Model

In this part, we use the "buffer-less" flow model based on two-states (ON/OFF) Markov sources described in [8]. Each source is described by its utilization ratio (or activity rate) ρ and its peak rate a. The overall traffic model is then characterized by the wanted Grade of Service (GOS) determined by the expected overflow probability ε. Under those assumptions, we can fully characterize a traffic demand T(s,d) by the number N(s,d) of ON/OFF sources, supposed to be identical and independent, that compose it. We consider the two previous traffic scenarios (Uniform and Random).

5.3.1   Inputs and Performance Metrics

The inputs will be the same as in the part 5.2, but we will define another parameter $\overline{m}$, that will replace the parameter $\overline{T}$, as the averaged (to the number of traffic demand T(s,d)) number of N(s,d) multiplied by $a\rho$ to obtain the average network throughput and normalized by the wavelength capacity :

$$\overline{m} = \frac{\sum_{s,d} N(s,d)}{(Number\ of\ non-zero\ traffic\ demands\ T(s,d))} \times \frac{a\rho}{C} . \tag{5}$$

In the uniform traffic scenario, $\overline{m}$ becomes equal to (N(s,d)aρ/C). In both scenarios m= $\overline{m}$ C.

Some useful parameters for uniform traffic scenario:

•   N(C,m) : Represents the maximum number of demands T(s,d) having each one an average rate of m that can be multiplexed in a wavelength.
•   K(m): Represents the number of demands T(s,d) having each one an average rate of m that are effectively multiplexed in a given bus.
•   Ke(m): The number of demands T(s,d) having each one an average rate of m passing through the link number #e. This parameter is considered only for the OPS case.

We will define also some performance metrics to compare the three bus concepts:

•   ΔG1 (resp ΔG2): The difference between the gain obtained with MP2MP and MP2P (respectively OPS and MP2MP) compared to the classical transparent point to point (P2P) lightpaths networks. Those gains are expressed in percent and represent the savings in terms of transceivers and lightpaths. ΔG1 and ΔG2 are simulated for two dimensioning scenarios (statisical and deterministic multiplexing) combined with two traffic scenarios (uniform or random traffic). The deterministic multiplexing allocates an amount of resource equal to the sum of bandwidths required for each demand and thus causes an over dimensioning of the network. The deterministic multiplexing is similar to a perfect circuit dimensioning. The statistical multiplexing corresponds to a dimensioning that takes into account the effect of traffic burstiness when a bus is shared between several nodes.

• g(K(m)): the statistical multiplexing gain obtained for K(m) traffic demands multiplexed on a given bus and having each one a mean bit rate of m (in Gb/s). The statistical multiplexing gain represents the percent of bandwidth gained when the spatial reuse (statistical multiplexing) is taken into account. In practice, this gain is very difficult to formulate. So, this gain will be formulated, for each type of bus, as the relative bandwidth gain of a statistical dimensioning compared to a deterministic dimensioning. Let $BW_{det}(K(m))$ be the bandwidth reserved in the bus for K(m) traffic demands when a deterministic multiplexing is made, and $BW_{stat}(K(m))$ the same value of bandwidth but in case of a statistical dimensioning, the gain g(K(m)) can thus be expressed as:

$$g\left(K(m)\right) = 1 - \frac{BW_{stat}\left(K(m)\right)}{BW_{det}\left(K(m)\right)}. \tag{6}$$

The statistical multiplexing gain is not used to compare the three buses, but only to compare, for a given bus, a statistical and a deterministic multiplexing. The criteria used to compare the three bus concepts are only the difference of gain ΔG1 and ΔG2.

5.3.2 Buses Modeling

The optical buses MP2P and MP2MP will be modeled by a single resource shared between K(m) traffic demands. But for the OPS, because of existence of online optical packets erasing devices, a bus can't be modeled by a single resource, in this case we will model each link e by a single resource shared between Ke(m) traffic demands. Figure 7 highlights the different bus modeling.

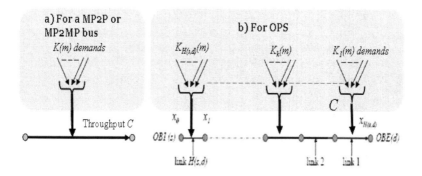

Fig. 7. Buses and traffic demands modeling

5.3.3 Local Derivation of Performance

In this part, we propose a theoretical approach to compute the defined performance metrics for one optical bus (MP2P, MP2MP or OPS), in the case of uniform traffic scenario. This theoretical approach will help us to understand the performance obtained by simulation. We will compute, the performance criteria g(K(m)) for the three bus MP2P, MP2MP and OPS.

K(m) and Ke(m) derivation:

To compute the value of K(m) and Ke(m) for a given bus, we'll start by computing the value of N(C,m) for both deterministic multiplexing (Circuit multiplexing) and statistical multiplexing case. Let BWeq(m) be the bandwidth required by a traffic demand having an average throughput m. BWeq(m) is the equivalent bandwidth given by the Guérin's formula:

$$BW_{eq}(m) = m + \alpha(\varepsilon)\sqrt{ma(1-\rho)} .$$ (7)

With α(ε) is given by the following approximation:

$$\alpha(\varepsilon) \approx \sqrt{-2\ln(\varepsilon) - \ln(2\pi)} .$$ (8)

In the deterministic multiplexing case (Circuit), the bandwidth required for a number of traffic demands is the sum of bandwidth required by each demand. Therefore, for an uniform traffic, the maximum number (N(C,m)) of traffic demand that can be multiplexed in a wavelength having a capacity C is:

$$N(C,m) = \left[\frac{C}{BW_{eq}(m)} \right] .$$ (9)

where [x] is the integer part of x.

In the statistical multiplexing case, N(C,m) is computed differently. The bandwidth required for q traffic demands having each one an average throughput of m is BWeq(mq):

$$BW_{eq}(mq) = mq + \alpha(\varepsilon)\sqrt{mqa(1-\rho)} .$$ (10)

And since the value of the required bandwidth of q traffic demands should be lower than C (BWeq(mq)≤C) , the value of N(C,m) is thus, the maximum value of q with BWeq(mq)≤C:

$$N(C,m) = \max\left\{q / BW_{eq}(mq) \le C\right\}$$

$$= \left[\frac{\left(\sqrt{4C + \alpha(\varepsilon)^2 a(1-\rho)} - \alpha(\varepsilon)\sqrt{a(1-\rho)}\right)^2}{4m}\right].$$

(11)

Once the value of N(C,m) is obtained, we can now compute the value of Ke(m) and K(m) for the three buses concepts:

- • For a MP2P bus (s,d) having a distance H(s,d), there are H(s,d) traffic demands having d as destination. So, since the number of traffic demands K(m) multiplexed in a MP2P bus should not exceed N(C,m) we have :

$$K(m) = \min(N(C,m), H(s,d)).$$

(12)

- In the MP2MP bus, the number of traffic demands (uniform traffic demands) that belong to the bus is:

$$\binom{H(s,d)+1}{2} = \frac{(H(s,d)+1)H(s,d)}{2}.$$

(13)

So, in this case K(m) is expressed as follow :

$$K(m) = \min\left(\binom{H(s,d)+1}{2}, N(C,m)\right).$$

(14)

- In the OPS case, only Ke(m) will be computed. Let Ne be the number of possible traffic demands in link e. Ne is computed as follow: While this origin of link #e is node $x_{H(s,d)-e}$ and its destination is $x_{H(s,d)-e+1}$ (Fig. 7), Ne is the sum of the number of demands destined to each node belonging to { $x_{H(s,d)-e+1}$, ..., $x_{H(s,d)}$} and having an origin located upstream to $x_{H(s,d)-e}$ (in Se = {x_0 , x_1 ,..., $x_{H(s,d)-e}$}):

$$\begin{aligned} N_e &= size(S_e) \times size(D_e) \\ &= e(H(s,d)-e+1) \end{aligned}.$$

(15)

were size{X} is the number of elements of set {X}. Once the number of possible traffic demands in a link e, Ne, is computed, we can now give easily the number Ke(m):

$$K_e(m) = \min(N(C,m), eH(s,d)-e+1).$$

(16)

Bus statistical multiplexing gain g(K(m)) computing:

In this part we will represent two statistical multiplexing gains. The first one, *Local gain*, is the gain obtained by multiplexing individual flows (ON/OFF sources) in the node level. This is independent of the fact that an optical bus concept is used or not. The second gain, g(K(m)), defined previously, is the gain obtained by the multiplexing of K(m) traffic demands on the bus. To compute the Local gain for M(M>>1) multiplexed individual ON/OFF source, we use the same formula as in (1), but the sum of bandwidth required for each ON/OFF source ($BW_{det}(M)$) will be only Ma (Number of ON/OFF source × peak rate). The bandwidth required $BW_{stat}(M)$ in the statistical multiplexing for M ON/OFF sources is given by the Guérin's formula: $BW_{stat}(M)=BW_{eq}(Ma\ \rho)$, now the Local gain is:

$$Local\ gain = 1 - \frac{BW_{eq}(Ma\rho)}{Ma}. \qquad (16)$$

To compute the gain g(K(m)) we will distinguish two cases:

- Case of MP2P or MP2MP bus: In this case we use the formula (6), with $BW_{det}(K(m))$ and $BW_{stat}(K(m))$ are expressed as follow:

$$\begin{array}{rcl} BW_{stat}(K(m)) & = & BW_{eq}(K(m)m) \quad and \\ BW_{det}(K(m)) & = & \sum BW_{eq}(m) = K(m)BW_{eq}(m) \end{array} \qquad (17)$$

- Case of OPS: In this case, formula (6) is also used but $BW_{det}(K(m))$ and $BW_{stat}(K(m))$ will be expresses as follow:

$$\begin{array}{rcl} BW_{stat}(K(m)) & = & \displaystyle\sum_{e=1}^{H(s,d)} BW_{eq}(K_e(m)m) \quad and \\ BW_{det}(K(m)) & = & \left(\displaystyle\sum_{e=1}^{H(s,d)} K_e(m)\right) BW_{eq}(m) \end{array} \qquad (17)$$

Results of figure 8 show that the bus statistical multiplexing gain is better for a MP2MP bus, but it becomes quickly the same for all buses type and becomes low when $\overline{T} > 25\%$. The reason is that, when the requested bandwidth per traffic demand increases, the number of traffic requests K(m) (resp Ke(m)) that can be multiplexed in a bus (resp in a link) decreases until being the same for the three buses types. We conclude from those results that, the statistical multiplexing in the optical layer has significant benefits in sparse areas and limited benefits in dense ones.

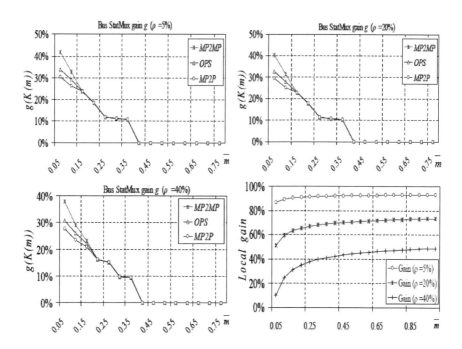

Fig. 8. Local and Bus statistical multiplexing gain (H(s,d)=4, ε=10⁻⁶ and a=50Mb/s)

Results show also that the variation of the utilization ratio of the ON/OFF sources ρ, that characterizes the traffic burstiness, does not significantly affect the bus statistical multiplexing gain g(K(m)). For example, when ρ passes from 40% to 5%, the bus statistical multiplexing gain increases very slightly (~3%). The reason for this is that the gain obtained from the traffic burtiness variation is mainly represented in the local gain (for example, when ρ passes from 40% to 5%, the local multiplexing gain increases significantly of about 77%).

5.3.4   Network Dimensioning

This part is independent from the local computing, but some conclusion from the local computing part will be used to explain some simulation results. For this part we keep the same network topology as in 5.2. We represent in this part the variations of the difference of gain ΔG1 and ΔG2 for different scenarios as a function of $\overline{m}$. The algorithm used in the MP2MP dimensioning is the heuristic MRU. This part compares effectively the three buses performance (Costs saving: number of buses (lightpath) and transceivers).

Figure 9 shows that, the difference between MP2MP and MP2P is significant in some cases, but the difference between OPS and MP2MP remains always limited. It is also shown that, when the statistical multiplexing effect is taken into account, the difference between MP2MP and MP2P increases slightly but the difference between OPS and MP2MP decreases slightly compared to a deterministic multiplexing.

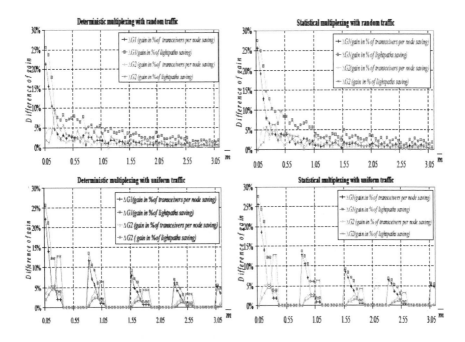

Fig. 9. Difference between the three buses (a=50 Mb/s, ρ=40% and ε=10⁻⁶)

The explication is the fact that, the statistical multiplexing effect is more favorable to MP2MP (figure 8). So, the conclusion given with an average bandwidth traffic model in part 5.2 remains valid and is consolidated with a flow model. Results show also that the difference between the three approaches decreases as the average bandwidth $\overline{m}$ requested by traffic demands increases, because when the bandwidth requested by a traffic demand becomes high, only a small number of demands can be placed in a bus in all cases and thus the difference between the buses decreases.

6   Conclusion

In this paper we investigate the problem of minimizing cost while maximizing resource utilization in transparent optical networks. We proposed an architecture supporting MP2MP packet-oriented optical bus to address this problem. Next the problem of MP2MP bus placement and planning has been investigated and a heuristic was introduced to solve it. This heuristic has been evaluated and compared to the optimal solution under a small size topology.

MP2MP passive bus placement heuristic has been implemented and evaluated trough simulations in a more realistic transparent optical network topology. Simulation results show that the MP2MP bus combined with the proposed heuristic algorithm leads to significant optimization with respect to the MP2P approach.

MP2MP approach can also achieve performance close to those of the OPS, and thus remains very competitive compared to OPS thanks to its passives and simple devices. A further work is to compare it to all the existing buses and evaluate it in a multilayer network.

Acknowledgements. This work was partially supported by the CELTIC TIGER 2 project.

References

1. Chlamtac, I., Faragó, A., Zhang, T.: Lightpath (wavelength) routing in large WDM networks. IEEE J. Selected Areas in Communications 14(5), 909–913 (1996)
2. Dittmann, L., et al.: The European IST Project DAVID: A Viable Approach Toward Optical Packet Switching. IEEE J. Selected Areas in Communications 21(7), 1026–1040 (2003)
3. Bouabdallah, N., Dotaro, E., Ciavaglia, L., Le Sauze, N., Pujolle, G.: Distributed aggregation in all-optical wavelength routed networks. In: IEEE Conference on Communications (ICC), pp. 1806–1810. IEEE Press (2004)
4. Mellia, M., Leonardi, E., Feletig, M., Gaudino, R., Neri., F.: Exploiting OTDM technology in WDM networks. In: IEEE International Conference on Computer Communications (INFOCOM), pp. 1822–1831. IEEE Press (2002)
5. Le Sauze, N., et al.: A Novel, Low Cost Optical Packet Metropolitan Ring Architecture. In: 27th IEEE European Conference on Optical Communications (ECOC), pp. 66–67. IEEE Press (2001)
6. Dorgeuille, F., Le Sauze, N., El Khattar, B., Ciavaglia, L., Dotaro, E., Zami, T.: Dual Optical Bus for Efficient Aggregation and Backhauling Networks and Potential Extensions. Bell Labs Technical Journal 14(4), 243–264 (2010)
7. Chlamtac, I., Gumaste, A.: Light-Trails: A Solution to IP Centric Communication in the Optical Domain. In: Ajmone Marsan, M., Corazza, G., Listanti, M., Roveri, A. (eds.) QoS-IP 2003. LNCS, vol. 2601, pp. 634–644. Springer, Heidelberg (2003)
8. Guérin, R., Ahmadi, H.: Equivalent Capacity and Its Applications to Bandwidth Allocation in High-Speed Networks. IEEE J. Select. Areas Commun. 9(7), 968–981 (1991)
9. Ciavaglia, L., Le Sauze, N., Dotaro, E., Popa, D., Nguyen, V.H.: Performance Assessment of Carrier-Grade Optical Ethernet Metropolitan Ring. In: 9th OptoElectron. and Commun. Conf./3rd Internat. Conf. on Optical Internet (OECC/COIN 2004). IEEE Press (2004)
10. Bouadallah, N., Beylot, A.-L., Dotaro, E., Pujolle, G.: Resolving the fairness issue in bus-based optical access networks. IEEE J. Select. Areas Commun. 23(8), 1444–1457 (2005)
11. Bouabdallah, N., Pujolle, G., Perros, H.: Multipoint-to-point light paths in all-optical networks: Dimensioning and cost analysis. Performance Evaluation 65(3-4), 262–285 (2008)
12. Ilog, http://www.ilog.com/products/cplex/

Ambient Intelligence in Network Management

Mary Luz Mouronte[1,2], Pilar Cano[2], and Miguel Ángel Fernández[1,2]

[1] Universidad Carlos III, Universidad 30,
28911 Madrid, Spain
[2] Telefónica Investigación y Desarrollo, Emilio Vargas 6,
28043 Madrid, Spain
`mmouront@it.uc3m.es, mlml@tid.es`

Abstract. This paper presents a technical method for solving the main provisioning problems on transmission networks automatically: communications, naming, misalignments, etc. This solution incorporates users' experience and business knowledge in expert agents which execute specific actions on the Network Management System (NMS) when an error occurs. The human intervention is reduced so that OPEX and network management are improved.

This paper gives an overview of the NMS of Telefónica España (GEISER), where the described method is applied. The framework has been verified in the actual network scenario while new features have been validated with simulated requests and tested on a real testbed.

Keywords: Network Element (NE), Network Element Manager (NEM), Network Management System (NMS); Network failures, Ambient Intelligence (AmI), OPerational EXpenditure (OPEX).

1   Introduction

A NMS of the transmission network is a combination of hardware and software used to monitor and control all the equipment in the network. In particular, the provision function is responsible for setting up the circuits or path routes. This paper proposes a method to improve the provision from a NMS whose main problems are the communication failures and the errors by inconsistency of entities.

Specifically, this paper applies the technical procedure to NMS of Telefónica España (GEISER). This NMS is a unified network management solution which provides end to end view and homogenous functions across different vendors. Furthermore, it executes all business processes related to the transmission network and its services: network creation, circuit provisioning, network supervision and performance monitoring. This NMS manages Synchronous Digital Hierarchy (SDH), Ethernet over SDH and Wavelength Division Multiplexing (WDM) networks. The operation is highly complex: it handles over 36.000 Network Elements (NES), which belong to different providers [1] [2], so it has a large number of procedures which are used by over 500 operators.

For all these reasons, when a failure occurs, the operators spend a vast amount of time to solve it. This paper presents a technical method to solve the main provisioning problems. This solution incorporates users' experience in expert agents which execute specific actions on the NMS without reducing its performance, achieving less human

I. Tomkos et al. (Eds.): BROADNETS 2010, LNICST 66, pp. 385–397, 2012.

intervention, OPEX reduction and reliability improvement [3]. The described method is based on the Ambient Intelligence (AmI) issue.

AmI represents an intelligent service system to enhance operations. It provides a context aware system, which uses unobtrusive computing devices that improve people's life and work quality by acknowledging their needs, requirements and preferences and thus acting in some way on their behalf [4].

The rest of the paper is organized as follows: section 2 discusses relevant related work, section 3 gives an overview about the NMS of Telefónica España (GEISER) and also about the most important problems in the network provisioning, section 4 goes on to describe the approach to solve these problems automatically, section 5 summarizes the results while section 6 describes main conclusions and evolution areas.

2   Related Works

The architecture of a NMS has several management layers. Each layer has its own functions and is connected with its upper or lower layer through interfaces [5]. Users control an specific network domain [6]. and the NMS must have all required services for its management [7], during the execution of these services different errors can happen.

There is no previous works on applications using expert agents to solve provision problems on the transmission network from a NMS. Nevertheless, similar methods have been developed in others areas such as:

- Manufacturing and supplying chains where the solution consists of a community of autonomous, intelligent, and goal oriented units which cooperate and coordinate their decisions to reach a global goal [8].
- Smart home where the AmI concept is implemented to show how simple devices may be networked and how several tasks may be automated to get an intelligent health management [9].

3   Overview

The Transmission Network is a strategic Telefónica España asset. It is a multi-vendor network and carries all kinds of services:

- Imagenio (IPTV)
- ADSL/FTTH, IP Services, Ethernet VLAN
- POTS, GSM, GPRS, etc
- Leased Circuits.

The NMS of Telefónica España manages SDH, Ethernet over SDH and WDM networks. Its main features are:

- Network model based on standards like ITU-T G.803, ITU-T G.805, ITU-T G.709, complemented with the extensions required to support Telefónica's business.
- It provides unified network management, independent of vendors.
- It connects to the vendor Network Element Managers (NEMs). The interaction with the plant is carried out using the northbound interfaces that the NEMS offers. The NEMs interact with the Network Equipments (NE).

- End to end control of the whole transmission network.
- Complete functional support in the following areas: fulfillment (network creation and circuit provisioning), network supervision and performance monitoring.
- Simple and intuitive user interface, based on well-known web technologies, which allows accessing the NMS from any point of the Telefónica corporate network, defines operating profiles adapted to each user and enforces a strict security policy. An essential requirement of the system is to reduce the training time of new users.
- Connection to corporate systems of Telefónica España in order to automate most routine tasks for creation and provisioning of the network. Its main goals are: to shorten the time needed to solve network issues and to reduce the frequency of human interventions in operational processes. The interconnection with the Telefónica corporate uses MQ-Series.

The NMS processes:

- 130.000 alarms per day and correlates to 4.000 root alarms/300 network troubles,
- 1000 fulfillment requests (network creation, circuit provisioning) per day.

The NMS is used by 500 users.

Different functions are integrated in the NMS:

- Circuit provisioning: this function sets up the circuits or path routes: SDH (2 Mbps and 34 Mbps), Ethernet: (2 Mbps, 10 Mbps and 100 Mbps). It also maintains the consistency in the inventory, the alignment with the corporate repositories and with the NEMS. The NEMS belong to different vendors.
- Network creation: it executes operations over the NEMS regarding NES, cards, circuits, paths and physical links. In particular: SDH Path (155 Mbps, 622 Mbps, 2, 5 Gbps, 10 Gbps, 40 Gbps, 100 Gbps); SDH Circuits (155 Mbps, 622 Mbps, 2, 5 Gbps, 10 Gbps and 40 Gbps) and Ethernet circuits (1 Gbps, 10 Gbps and physical links: 155 Mbps, 622 Mbps, 2, 5 Gbps, 10 Gbps and 40 Gbps). This function maintains the consistency in the inventory, the alignment with the corporate repositories and with the NEMs.
- Inventory: this function maintains the network repository in NMS and carries out the tasks of auditing and discovery.
- QoS: this utility executes operation about network quality assurance and the Service Level Agreements SLAS.
- Surveillance: this function carries out automatic alarm correlation, root cause identification, end to end view and protection against "alarms floods".

The NMS is a system constructed around standards based network model, supported by an ORACLE DBMS, with a business logic layer that allows interacting with the core applications through a CORBA bus. The NMS works as a centralized system, with a primary machine of 16 CPUs, another one of 4 for the mediation with the plant and three more for users' access.

In this paper the proposed solution is applied to the main provisioning problems although it may be extended to all troubles that happen in the fulfillment.

The circuit provisioning requires high performance and efficiency. The NMS must process a large number of requests with high success percentage at the first attempt and understand the different kinds of requests: setting up, elimination, modifying, restoration and rerouting.

NMS receives the provisioning requests from a corporate repository where allocation tasks are performed. It is joined to different NEMs which interact with the NES to build the SubNetwork Connections (SNC) which are necessary to set up the circuits. Fig.1 represents the architecture of the system.

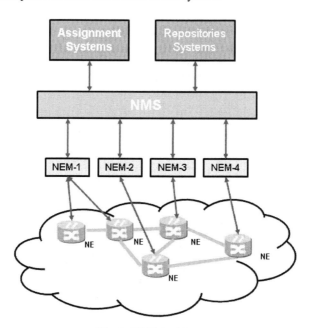

Fig. 1. NMS Architecture

The NMS deals with an average of 520 provision requests daily, with a 70% success rate at first attempt. Each request is split in different operations over the NEs which be included in the route (build/elimination of SNC, build/elimination of Subnetwork Connection Protections (SNCP), build/elimination of Virtual Circuits (VC), configurations of Link Capacity Adjustment Scheme (LCAS), etc.). These operations are executed on the NEMs.

Different problems have been identified in network provisioning, they are described bellow: Internal error, NE communication, Entity does not exist, Entity already exists, Unknown owner identifier, Busy entity, Processing failure, Functionality not supported, NMS communications and others.

3.1 Current Status of Network Errors Management

Vendors offer catalogues about the errors in the NEMs and the NEs. The failures in the operations have been analyzed monthly and a small subset of errors is repeated regularly:

1.   Internal error: it refers to communication internal errors in the NMS.
2.   NE communication: these errors are related to the absence or rejection connection between the NEM and the NE.
3.   Entity does not exist: it is a data misalignment problem, the NMS does not have the same entity that the NEM.
4.   Entity already exists: it represents a data misalignment problem, this error occurs when NMS tries to create an existing entity in the NEM.
5.   Unknown owner identifier: it represents a naming problem, this failure occurs when the NMS does not have the data to operate on the NEM.
6.   Busy entity: this error occurs when NMS tries to occupy some entity which exists in the NEM; it represents a data misalignment problem.
7.   Processing Failure: these errors are internal of NE (e.g. Management Information Base (MIB) in wrong state).
8.   Functionality not supported: this error occurs when NMS requests a not supported operation to NEMs.
9.   NEM communication: It is a communications problem between the NMS and the NEMs.

Fig. 2 shows the average frequency of each error pattern in the daily operation over the network. Nine patterns are the most frequent (90%). The pattern "Unknown owner identifier" is in first place.

When the operator finds any of these errors, he can adopt different solutions to solve it:

1.   Retry: failure is expected to be sporadic and the user repeats the action.
2.   Do it locally: the user implements the action directly in the NEM which produces a misalignment between the NMS and the NEM.

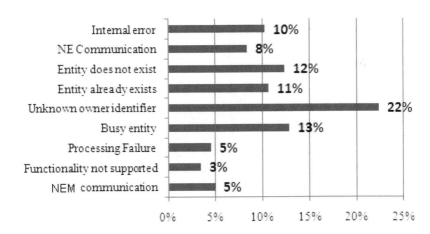

Fig. 2. Percentage of each class error over the total failures. In a month, the specific error average has been calculated in daily operation and its percentage has been considered over the total failures.

3.   Align and retry: the operator can solve the problems by mean of specific actions in the NMS in order to align data (for instance, update the owner identifiers and then repeat the action).

4.   Notices: the user send a notice to technicians to solve the problem.

On a month operators have been observed while working and they often solve errors in the NEMs directly. This practice produces data misalignments which will cause new failures in the future. The Fig. 3 shows the misalignment caused by this way of resolving errors. If operators do not solve errors in the NEMs then they must execute several procedures in the NMS and spend a vast amount of time to solve failures. It is shown in Fig. 4.

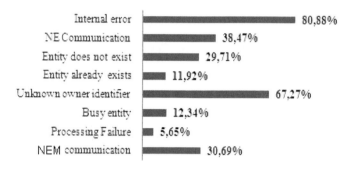

Fig. 3. Percentage of misalignment produced by resolution of each class error over the total failures. The average of misalignment by the resolution of each error has been calculated in the daily operation and its percentage has been considered over the total failures in a month.

3.2   Correct Network Errors Management

The correct actions to solve the errors are:

- Internal error: the operation should be tried again after a while.
- NE communication: all operations related to the NE with communications problems should be stopped until the situation is recovered. If the problem persists then a report with information about the failure has to be sent to technicians.
  - NEM communication: the actions to be done are similar to the ones in NE communication error case, but the failure affects to all the operations on the NE connected with the NEM.
  - Processing Failure: a report with information about the failure has to be sent to the technicians.
  - Functionality not supported: the operator must be warned about it.
  - Owner identifier unknown: in the NMS, all operations on the same NE should wait for the adaptation of owner identifiers.
  - Entity does not exist: it is necessary to compare the data on the NEM and on the NMS which allows the operator to solve the misalignment.

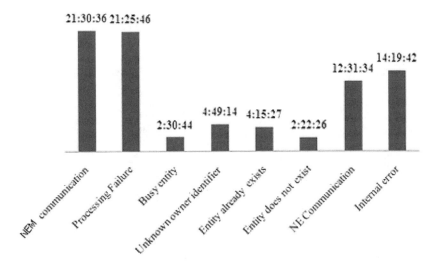

Fig. 4. Average time for solving each failure. The time is expresed as hh:mm:ss.

- Entity already exists: it is necessary to audit the situation to solve the problem.
- Busy entity: it is necessary to remove any residual entity in the network.

4   Solutions

The proposed solution in this paper, allows supervising and executing actions on the NMS automatically as soon as a failure occurs. The architecture of the solution is shown in Fig 5. It uses ORACLE mechanisms and C Language Integrated Production System (CLIPS).

CLIPS is an open source expert system tool developed by NASA-Johnson Space Centre. It is fast, efficient, free and updated and supported by the original author, Gary Riley [8]. CLIPS has been designed to facilitate the development of software to model human knowledge or expertise through rules, facts, functions and even object-oriented programming. Besides, CLIPS is designed for full integration with other languages [11].

The components in the architecture are: expert agents (Event Manager and Action Manager) and a Knowledge Base which contains different rules.

Expert Agent: *Event Manager*

In NMS, a trigger is fired by an error and it writes an event in an ORACLE queue, such information is collected by mean of SQL*Net [12] and processed by *Event Manager.*

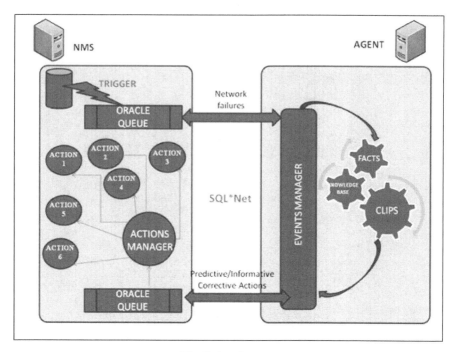

Fig. 5. Arquitecture

This event has the following format:

```
<date>|<id action>|<id operation>|<failure
description>|<equipment>|<NEM>
```

Instance:

```
<17/06/2010 13:46:53|283214|153292|Failure: Q3:
OmisCnf::errProcessingFailure|B.ET0050TX01:TTSF16S
3:1662|INICIAL.GER:NM_NR7.0:105>
```

Event Manager does the following tasks:

• Read and send an event to an inference engine, which is written in CLIPS, where it is processed as a fact. It is not necessary to modify event information.

Instance:

```
        (defrule processing-failure; this rule establishes
if the type of failure is "Processing Failure"
        ?h1 <- (message (equipment ?equipment) (error
?error & 21068|21177|22052) (id_action ?id_action) (NEM
?NEM) (times 1))
```

```
        =>
        (printout t "CLIPS: Equipment " ?equipment "has
received a Processing Failure. Code: "?error crlf)
        (printout t "CLIPS: Send action type 3" crlf)
        (printout t (send_action (str-cat
"3||"?equipment"|"?NEM"|"?id_action)) crlf); To put
incidence
        (retract ?h1)):
```

- The inference engine decides the necessary actions to be sent to the *Event Manager* which sends information to an ORACLE queue through SQL*Net, where it will be processed by the *Action Manager*. The actions have the following format:

```
[<type of action>|<description>|<equipment>|<NEM>|<list
of actions>]
```

Instance:

```
Action: Retry
   [1||B.ET0050TX01:TTSF16S:18||231385]
```

Expert Agent: *Action Manager*

The *Action Manager* processes the instructions generated by the inference engine and interacts with the NMS to perform the suitable actions. This expert agent does the following tasks:

- Read the actions from ORACLE queue.
- Execute the specific procedures in NMS.

Knowledge Base

It contains different kinds of rules:

- Correlation rules: to establish relations between the facts and construct new ones.
- Decision rules about the actions: to determine the specific criteria to shoot actions.
- Metacontrol: to establish priorities in the rules according to their relevance.

The described architecture allows decoupling of the integration layer (ORACLE queues) from the business logic layer (management of rules and execution of corrective actions). In this way, This is an independent solution from the NMS which supervises and makes decisions based on users' experience. It does not interfere in normal NMS workflow.

5   Solutions

An experimental prototype aimed to test and validate the improvement in network provisioning has been prepared.

The rules of business knowledge have been implemented in CLIPS and they include the corrective actions to be performed when the NMS finds a network error.

Once the business knowledge has been modelled, the trigger has been prepared, the ORACLE queues have been configured and all processes have been implemented, which can be seen in Fig. 5, a set of provision requests were prepared to send them to the NMS. Such requests were processed by the NMS which sent the associated operations to NEMs. A set of 100 requests were prepared which result in 700 operations on the network. Of these 100 requests, 70 finished successfully at first attempt. However, the other 30 had problems and some of its operations cannot be executed successfully on the NEM. These 30 requests were integrated by 210 operations on the network, of which 70 ended unsuccessfully. Table 1. shows the distribution of these 70 errors.

The 70 identified problems were sent to our architecture and the agent took the associated decisions. These decisions were:

- Internal error: the agent tried again the 7 occurrences of this error. These redone operations finished successfully every time. Those new attempts were made 10 minutes after the error occurred.
- NE Communication: there were 7 occurrences of this error, 3 of them happened in the same NE and the other 4 in another one. From the first error in the NEs, operations were stopped by the agent. The two NEs were isolated from the NMS, and communication was recovered 23 minutes later. After that, these 7 operations were sent again by the agent and they finished successfully.

Table 1. Error Distributions

Error	Times
Internal error	7
NE Communication	7
Entity does not exist	7
Entity already exists	7
Unknown owner identifier	18
Busy entity	7
Processing Failure	4
NEM Communication	5
Functionality not supported	2
Another errors	6

- Entity does not exist: there were 7 occurrences. In all cases the agent decided to execute the audit procedure automatically in order to compare the situations in the NEM and in the NMS. The agent showed the results to the user. The misalignments were solved.

- Entity already exists: the agent had the same behaviour as in the previous case.
- Unknown owner identifier: in the 18 occurrences, the agent decided to execute the procedure for updating the information. 4 NEs were affected. The procedures ran in parallel and finished in 7 minutes. Eventually, the agent decided to retry the operations which ended successfully.
- Busy entity: the results for this case were similar to the misalignment cases.
- Processing failure: in the 4 occurrences, the agent decided to send a notification to a technician in order to review the state of the equipment.
- EMS Communications: the 5 occurrences happened in the same NEM. When the first failure occurred the agent decided to stop the operations on the NEM and retried them a time later, once the communication was reestablished. The operation finished successfully.
- Functionality not supported: in the 2 occurrences, the NMS could not program a loop in a port because this operation was not supported on the interface with the NEM. Both problems were unrecoverable, so that the agent decided not to do anything.
- Other errors: these errors did not have a regular frequency. No specific actions were planned.

The prototype solved 90% of errors automatically and its actions did not cause other failures. It contained 102 rules, 88 of them were correlation and decision rules and 14 were metacontrol rules. The operations finished successfully in a short time, as we see in Table 2. This table also shows the spent time by the operators at the present.

All errors in network provisioning can be included in the definitive solution by extending the knowledge base with new rules, in this way, all problems would be solved automatically.

6   Conclusions and Future Works

This paper described a technical method for automatic solving fulfillment problems on the transmission network. In particular, this procedure is applied to network provisioning. This solution is based on expert agents who detect failures and solve them by means of users' experience.

Table 2. Results

Error	Average Time with Agent (hh:mm:ss)	Previous Average Time (hh:mm:ss)
Internal error	00:10:23	14:19:42
NE Communication	00:23:12	12:31:34
Entity does not exist	00:40:34	2:22:26
Entity already exists	00:40:34	4:15:27
Unknown owner identifier	00:43:28	4:49:14
Busy entity	00:24:21	2:30:44
Processing Failure	15:45:28	21:25:46
NEM Communication	00:20:15	21:30:36

The solution uses different technologies to build an AmI environment which provides greater efficiency in the operations on the transmission network and reduces the OPEX because when a failure occurs, the operators do not have to spend so much time solving it.

This method can be applied to other areas:

- Adaptive graphical user interface: it is possible to detect user preferences for developing adaptive intelligent user interfaces [13] [14].
- To correct data in repositories: a right inventory SDH, Ethernet, and WDM components is complicated because many operations are necessary due to the multilayer hierarchy in these networks. Sometimes information is corrupt in data repositories. These situations could be solved by mean of expert agents based on users' experience.

Acknowledgments. We thank our department colleagues their support in the development, especially Alfonso Badillo Llada and Francisco Javier Ramos Gutiérrez.

References

1. Mouronte, M.L., Benito, R.M., Cárdenas, J.P.: Complexity in Spanish optical fiber and SDH transport networks. Computer Physics Communications 180(4), 523–526 (2009)
2. Santiago, A., Cárdenas, J.P., Mouronte, M.L., Feliu, V., Benito, R.M.: Modeling the topology of SDH networks. International Journal of Modern Physics C 19(12), 1809–1820 (2008)
3. Chan, V.: Optical network architecture from the point of view of the end user and cost. IEEE Journal on Selected Areas in Communications 24(12), 1–2 (2006)
4. Gasson, M., Warwick, K.: D12.2: Study on emerging AmI technologies, Future of Identity in the Information Society FIDIS Deliverables, European Union (2007)
5. Song, H., Xu, Y., Gui, X., Zhang, J., Gu, W.: Design and implementation of intelligent optical network management system. In: Proceedings of ICCT, pp. 625–628 (2003)
6. Mir, M., Banerjee, A., Mao, L., McGinnis, E., Sheikh, H., Galimberti, G., Jerphagnon, O., Ati, R., Liem, S., Gyurek, R., Tatipamula, M., Gerstel, O.: A GMPLS-controlled multi-vendor optical network demonstrating a variety of switching, control, and protection mechanisms. In: 31st European Conference. Optical Communication ECOC, vol. 2, pp. 215–216 (2005)
7. Verdi, F.L., Magalhães, M.F., Cardozo, E., Madeira, E.R., Welin, A.: A service oriented architecture-based approach for interdomain optical network services. Journal of Network and Systems Management 15(2) (2007)
8. Industrial Adoption of Agent-Based Technologies, http://www.inf.udec.cl/~atkinson/cursos/electivos/mas/Papers/APLICA-industrial.pdf
9. Ambient Intelligence and Home Networking for Wellness Management and Home Automation, http://www.ercim.eu/publication/Ercim_News/enw47/korhonen.html
10. http://en.wikipedia.org/wiki/CLIPS

11. CLIPS User's guide. Version 6.20,
    `http://clipsrules.sourceforge.net/documentation/v624/ug.pdf`
12. `http://www.orafaq.com/wiki/SQLNet_FAQ`
13. Mourlas, C., Germanakos, P.: Intelligent user interfaces: Adaptation and personalization systems and technologies. Information Science Reference (2009)
14. Nasoz, F., Lisetti, C.L.: Affective user modelling for adaptive intelligent user interfaces. In: HCI Intelligent Multimodal Interaction Environments, pp. 421–430 (2007)

Using MPLS-TP for Data-Center Interconnection

Ashwin Gumaste, Chirag Taunk, Sarvesh Bidkar, Deval Bhamare, and Tamal Das

Department of Computer Science and Engineering,
Indian Institute of Technology, Bombay, Mumbai, India - 400 076
ashwing@ieee.org,
{chiragtaunk,sarvesh,deva,tamaldas}@cse.iitb.ac.in

Abstract. Data center interconnectivity is particularly very important and essential for emerging applications such as cloud computing and financial trading. Current data center architectures are built using Ethernet switches or IP routers - both with significant cost and performance deficiencies. We propose for the first time, extending MPLS-TP into the data-center. To this end, a new look-up protocol for MPLS-TP is proposed. Autonomic communication within the data center is possible using our look-up protocol that enables fast creation and deletion of LSPs. The MPLS-TP based data-center that is architected in this paper leads to performance betterments over both IP and Ethernet. To this end, a comprehensive simulations model is also presented. Operations within the data-center using MPLS-TP are also extended to inter-data-center operations using LSP setup across a core network. OAM and performance issues are investigated.

1   Introduction

The growth of data traffic and web services has put excessive stress on current network infrastructure. Emerging applications are typically web-based and these imply the need for distributed storage and processing across the Internet – leading to the proliferation of the data-center. The data-center is becoming an important network infrastructure from the perspective of application virtualization as well as resource consolidation. A typical data-center consists of servers, storage elements and very fast switches. The latter is the key to making the data-center a success – interconnecting memory modules to servers as well as to the rest of the Internet is an efficient way. The interconnection must support the ability to provide virtualization and consolidation – amongst servers, amongst memories and across supported applications. Apart from being able to meet carrier class requirements, the switches should also be able to support high-bandwidth volume cross-connect, at low energy needs and provide low-latency guarantees. Mapping applications that reside in network attached storage (NAS) devices as well as those running at servers is daunting on account of the inability to migrate easily when one considers typical data-center tasks such as load balancing, etc. Typical network interconnection fabrics are based on complex IP-routers or MPLS LSRs. The use of high-end IP-MPLS equipment has been known to be an overkill [1]. Particularly from both cost and performance standpoints, the use of IP/MPLS routers is not necessarily justified. The closed domain of the data-centers along with the proximity of network elements

I. Tomkos et al. (Eds.): BROADNETS 2010, LNICST 66, pp. 398–410, 2012.

within the data-center implies that use of IP/MPLS routers leads to significant routing overhead, which can otherwise be achieved by simple switches, provided they can guarantee service differentiation (QoS support) and Carrier-Class features (OAM&P support). To alleviate this problem, there have been proposals [2,3] to use Ethernet switches [4] for data-center support. The strong emphasis on carrier-class support means using transport-oriented versions of Ethernet – Carrier-grade Ethernet transport platforms. Amongst the two version of carrier-grade Ethernet, the MPLS-TP (transport profile) has gathered significant attention recently, especially when compared with the Ethernet-bridging based PBB-TE (Provider Backbone Bridged Traffic Engineering) standard.

In this paper, we propose the use of MPLS-TP [6-14] as an architectural technology for use in the data-center. To this end, we use MPLS-TP in conjunction with our earlier proposed Ethernet transport technology called "Omnipresent Ethernet" [5] or OEthernet for short. The OEthernet technology uses network interconnection patterns as aids in creating a communication framework (for switching, routing and transport). In the OEthernet framework, any network graph is converted to a binary graph. This leads to binary routing and source routing – two well-known concepts in interconnection systems. However, to make these pragmatic, we propose the use of binary addresses as MPLS-TP labels. This leads to a system, whereby forwarding of MPLS-TP packets is instantaneous – without the need for a lookup table, as the corresponding bits of a label signify to which port a packet would be forwarded to. The binary forwarding mechanism when applied to an MPLS-TP framework solves the larger question of the control plane for the data-center. The resultant is an autonomic data-center, where LSP setup and tear down are accomplished through the OEthernet control plane, and forwarding is entirely based on binary addresses and source routing. The use of OEthernet mechanism with MPLS-TP makes MPLS-TP a plausible alternative for the data-center. Moreover, simulation results show significant cost, latency and energy efficiency improvements with our approach when compared with other solutions.

This paper is organized as follows: Section II is a primer on MPLS-TP while Section III describes OEthernet –for the data-center. Section IV describes the use of MPLS-TP using OEthernet from the perspective of the data-center. Section V focuses on numerical evaluation, while Section VI concludes the paper.

2   MPLS-TP Primers

MPLS was developed to focus on improving the cost and performance issues associated with core IP routers. MPLS has proved successful in carriers' converged IP/MPLS core networks. However, MPLS is an expensive technology due to the higher cost of managing the routers in the core networks. Also, MPLS is not fully-optimized for transport functions such as guaranteed QoS, protection, deterministic end-to-end delay, leading to new extensions that meet the transport needs. MPLS-TP based networks are more deterministic with the addition of features like traffic engineering, end-to-end QoS, full protection switching and fast restoration. Being a packet-based technology, MPLS-TP simplifies the networks as well as reduces the CAPEX and OPEX.

MPLS-TP is aimed to provide fault management (fault identification, fault isolation, fault recovery, resiliency), configuration management (generating statistics of configuration of network resources, updating the records), accounting management, performance management (utilization, error rate) and security management.

MPLS-TP supports bi-directional label switched paths (LSP). MPLS-TP provides end-to-end connection-oriented transport. It also provides end-to-end path protection and QoS with operation administration and maintenance (OAM) support. MPLS-TP OAM functionality is independent of the dynamic control plane, offering the services using only the data plane.

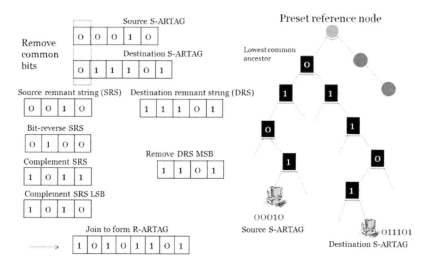

Fig. 1. Omnipresent Ethernet Architecture and Addressing

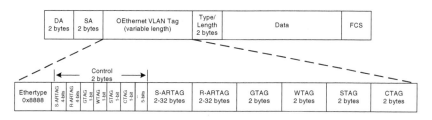

Fig. 2. OEthernet Frame Format

3　Omnipresent Ethernet in the Data-Center

Carrier Ethernet has been the new buzzword for metropolitan networks – with active worldwide deployments. Carrier Ethernet is currently available in two flavors – from the IEEE the 802.1ah/802.1Qay (PBB/PBB-TE) and from the IETF the MPLS-TP with 5+ separate drafts under circulation. We proposed the Omnipresent Ethernet [5] or OEthernet technology as a solution to Carrier Ethernet showing superior performance. In particular, the OEthernet solution is more scalable, has lower latency, supports multipath service provisioning and consumes lower energy as compared to PBB-TE/MPLS-TP variants.

OEthernet was proposed as an end-to-end solution for communication without the use of IP or more blatantly with the sole use of Ethernet and the optical layer [5]. It has since then been investigated to provide multiple communication paradigms leading to benefits such as low latency, low cost, superior service support, lower energy requirement and resiliency [15]. Note that OEthernet has been proposed as a stand-alone communication paradigm, and we extend this to the domain of Carrier Ethernet technology, particularly from the perspective of MPLS-TP.

The OEthernet concept involves converting any network topology to a binary graph – by the addition of "dummy" nodes to smoothen-out all the nodes, resulting in a system where each node is a 1×2 interconnection element [5]. A binary graph leads to binary routing *i.e.* the facilitation of source routing with binary addresses. A single bit can now tell a node (1×2 switch) whether to go left or right. A node only has to process $(2\log_2 N)$ bits in an $N \times N$ switch. Further, there is no need for any lookup. Each node is assumed to have its address – a binary value that determines its route from a preset node in the binary graph.

Communication in the OEthernet framework: A source node has access to the destination node's binary address through a procedure called the *Ethernet Nomenclature System* (ENS) that is central to the working of the OEthernet framework. Note that the ENS is not required in MPLS-TP – all one needs is to use OEthernet addresses for LSRs and binary values of the addresses are now embedded in MPLS-TP LSPs.

To compute the route from the source to the destination, the source node uses the procedure described next. The source node examines both binary addresses (of itself and the destination). This is done by aligning the two addresses MSB onwards. All the leading *common* bits (if any) are then discarded. What remains are the source and destination remnant binary strings. We have now isolated the lowest common ancestor for the source and the destination nodes. The next step is to do a 1's complement on the source remnant string – this enables us to obtain a string that would guide a frame *from* the source to the lowest common ancestor. Recall that the original source binary address enabled a frame to be guided from the preset reference node to the node under consideration – and we now want to go in the opposite direction, *i.e.* towards the reference node. But instead of going all the way, we desire to stop at the lowest common ancestor. The next step is to flip the LSB of the source remnant string. The LSB of the source remnant string is used to indicate to the 1×2 switch at the lowest common ancestor as to what it should do with the incoming frame. The source remnant string with its 1's complemented bits and the last bit further complemented is now conjoined to the destination remnant string to create a *route-binary-string* as shown in Fig. 1.

In the case of OEthernet without MPLS-TP, we make use of the IEEE 802.1Qay but with minor differences resulting in significant performance improvements. Four key features distinguish the IEEE 802.1Qay from LAN/switched **Ethernet:** (1) Absence of MAC learning. (2) Turning off of Spanning Tree Protocol (STP). (3) The customer frames with or without VLAN tags are mapped to service provider tag (STAG and then the ITAG) – which is further mapped to the BTAG and BMAC, thereby allowing encapsulation of the entire frame in a service provider frame and (4) Frames are forwarded based on a service provider BTAG in conjunction with a BMAC address. In the OEthernet case [5], we adopt this methodology (of turning OFF STP, disabling MAC learning) and allowing the use of multiple stacked VLAN tags in an Ethernet frame as our basic protocol data unit (PDU) for OEthernet. Further, five kinds of tags are proprietarily defined as follows: Source Address-Route TAGs or S-ARTAGs, Route ARTAGs or R-ARTAGs, Granularity Tags or GTAGs, Type Tags or TTAGs and Window-TAGs or WTAGs [15]. The S-ARTAG is a series of VLAN tags stacked together and contains information pertaining to the address of the node (*i.e.* the route from the preset reference node to the node). A single S-ARTAG can have 12 entries as its VID and hence can support a binary tree of diameter 12. If however, the binary tree has a larger diameter, then multiple S-ARTAGs can be stacked together. The R-ARTAG is a series of VLAN tags that carries route information – a binary string indicating the route from the source node to the destination node. The R-ARTAG is the most important tag for forwarding the frame. Each 1×2 switch examines just 1 bit in the R-ARTAG (based on the method below) and forwards the frame to one of its output ports. The frame format for the OEthernet frame is shown in Fig. 2.

From the perspective of MPLS-TP, our approach is to induct binary addresses as labels. An MPLS-TP LSP is now defined by its route from a source node to the destination node. Labels can be stacked together similar to MPLS-TP with each label depicting a path from the corresponding intermediate source node to an intermediate destination node. Shown in the Fig. 3 is a set of MPLS-TP LSPs that are stacked to provide an integrated LSP from the source to the destination. Shown in Fig. 4 is corresponding label stack that provides for the LSPs.

Working: The creation of the MPLS-TP LSPs using OEthernet concepts is explained in Section IV. We now discuss how to use the created MPLS-TP LSPs in a network. At an intermediate node, the topmost label is examined. The 20-bit address is analyzed as follows: the first 4 bits are called *pointers* – they indicate which bit amongst the 16-remaining bits in the shim, should the switch begin to work on. If the value of the first 4-bits is 1111, then the label is popped; the next label would have the first 4-bits set to 0000 as it is "fresh" implying that is has yet not been considered upon. The MPLS-TP LSR would then consider the next $\log_2 N$ bits, for an N-port LSR. The LSR would also update the first 4-bits to mark the $(\log_2 N + 1)^{th}$ bit, so that that next switch can begin consideration of the binary label. The last label in the stack is pushed into the stack after "last-label-preprocessing". As part of last-label-preprocessing, the first 4-bits of the bottommost label are changed from 0000 to a value that determines the number port count of the last LSR – the one that is the destination node. This value $(15 - \log_2 N)$ will tell the LSR that it is the destination node, and to send the packet to the requisite destination port.

Switching: At an LSR, there is no requirement for a lookup table. All that the LSR does, is to receive the packet correctly (usually done through cyclic redundancy check at layer-2) and then isolate the correct $log_2 N$ bits corresponding to the LSR. Once these bits have been isolated, the LSR forwards the packets based on the value of the

$\log_2 N$ bits. There is no lookup required to compare the value of the label – thus saving energy and time, reducing latency and maintaining wire-speed operation.

Note: Label swapping in the MPLS sense is not supported – the MPLS packet is created at the source node with multiple labels. It is assumed that the source node has the global topology of LSPs. This assumption is valid when we consider that (1) the data-center is a relatively closed domain and (2) without the knowledge of global LSP topology, it is not possible to enable end-to-end QoS support at the transport layer.

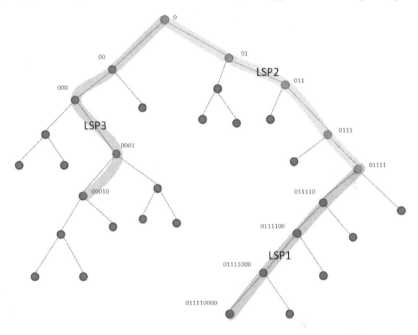

Fig. 3. LSPs in MPLS-TP using OEthernet addressing scheme

LSPs	S-ARTAG (Ingress)	S-ARTAG (Egress)	R-ARTAG
LSP1	011110000	01111	111
LSP2	01111	0	0001
LSP3	0	00010	1010

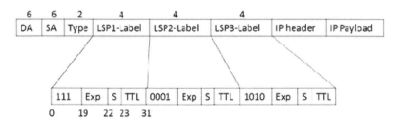

Fig. 4. Labels using MPLS-TP and OEthernet addressing scheme

4   Implementing MPLS-TP in the Data-Center

In this Section, we discuss the creation of MPLS-TP LSPs using OEthernet technology, as well as the implementation of MPLS-TP within the data-center. A generic data-center is shown in Fig. 5. Observe that the topology of the data-center resembles a star network – several servers and NAS units are interconnected to a gateway through the star topology. There are multiple methods to implement such a star network – as a hierarchical tree, or generic shuffle-exchange architecture [16]. We will present an approach to convert a given data-center interconnection model into a binary tree. Subsequently, we will show how to implement MPLS-TP within the data-center.

We first create a binary tree. For this purpose, the topology is discovered by the Network Management System (NMS) [17]. The gateway of the data-center that connects the data-center infrastructure to the rest of the Internet now becomes a default point of access.

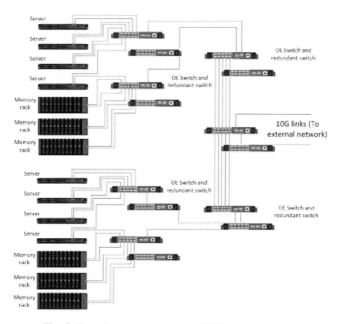

Fig. 5. Generic data-center using OEthernet switches

The following algorithm is run by the NMS in a breadth first search manner:

```
for ∀N
    if D(N)<1x2,
        replace N with N″
    end
end
```

The two variables D and N'' are defined as follows: $D(.)$ is an operator that denotes the degree of a node, while N'' converts any node with degree of connectivity greater than 1×2 to a set of nodes such that each node has a degree of connectivity 1×1 or 1×2. Upon converting every node in the tree to a binary-node, we apply the following algorithm to break cycles and create a tree.

```
is-cycle:=sort cycle()
       while is-cycle ≠ Ø
              break (cycle(i))
                     is-cycle=is-cycle-i
                     refresh is-cycle()
                     increment (i)
       end
```

In the snippet above, we sort all the cycles in the graph according to their sizes in terms of number of edges and call this set as *is-cycle*. We disconnect the first cycle (the largest one), in the set *is-cycle*. We refresh the set *is-cycle()* to check if any cycles persist. If another cycle continues to persist despite the break of the previous cycle, we break the next largest cycle, and again check if any further cycles exist (after refreshing the set *is-cycle()*. The algorithm ensures that every cycle is broken with the disconnection of the minimal number of edges. To break a cycle, we choose the edge that causes *maximum damage* to the cycle. To do so, each edge in every cycle is given a weight. The weight corresponds to the number of cycles that the edge would break, if removed. In the break cycle statement, we hence break the edge with the highest weight.

The next step is to add binary addresses to a node. Giving the root an address of "0", we traverse to every leaf, appending a "0"bit to the existing address of the ancestor if the current node is right of its immediate ancestor, or append a "1" if the node is left of the immediate ancestor. Hence the two descendants of the root would have addresses of 00 and 01 respectively.

Subsequent to this, we create LSPs. For the creation of LSPs, each edge node has to perform binary-specific penultimate hop-popping operation – contrary to the generic MPLS-TP requirements. However, this is allowed as the Management End Points (MEPs) in the OEthernet case continue to be the source and destination node, thereby facilitating complete connectivity and fault tolerance operation.

At the edge nodes of the tree, i.e. the leaves we have to interface the edge LSRs with the servers and NASs. Likewise, at the root, we have to interface the data-center to the rest of the Internet. Since the binary addressing and routing are internal to the data-center, we need to facilitate a mechanism at both the gateway of the data-center as well as the leaves (edge LSRs) so that the global addresses can be mapped to local binary addresses. This translation between globally unique IP-addresses to locally relevant binary addresses is done by an edge logic structure that in the OEthernet parlance is called as the "Thin Ethernet Logical Layer" or TELL. The TELL is a table that contains mapping between a destination IP address (typically IPv6) to a corresponding LSP or R-ARTAG from the OEthernet perspective. In the case of the OEthernet network as shown in [15], the mapping is between the IP addresses/MAC addresses or even HTTP URLS to S-ARTAGs, since the framework supports multi-layer communication. However, in the case of the MPLS-TP data-center, the mapping has to be only between the IP addresses and the S-ARTAGs. The edge LSRs create LSPs by examining the TELL table as shown in Fig. 6.

LSP Creation: We will consider how the LSPs are created inside an MPLS-TP supported data-center from the perspective of both communication from the edge nodes as well as from the core of the Internet (through the gateway).

At edge nodes: All the edge nodes are assumed to have at least one LSP to the gateway. An incoming packet whose prefix is beyond the scope of the data-center is encapsulated with labels that would enable it to reach the gateway (root) node. All such out-of-scope packets imply that the destination is outside the data-center.

IPv6	LSP ID	Label 1 (20 bit value)	Label 2 (20 bit value)	Label 3 (20 bit value)
2010:0db8:3c4d:0015:0000: 0000:abcd:ef12	LSP1	0000110110 1000000000	0000011000 1000000000	0000111101 0110000000
2010:0db8:3c4d:0015:0000: 0000:ad13:cd13	LSP2	0000100100 1000000000	0000011110 1000000000	0000100000 1000000000
2010:0db8:3c4d:0015:0000: 0000:abc1:0011	LSP3	0000100010 1100000000	0000101100 0001100000	0000110010 1000100000

Fig. 6. An example of a populated TELL Table

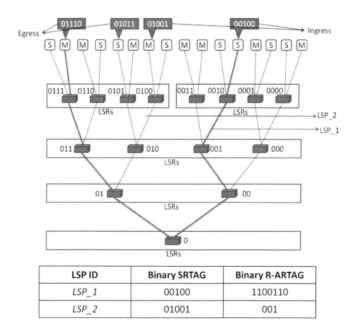

LSP ID	Binary SRTAG	Binary R-ARTAG
LSP_1	00100	1100110
LSP_2	01001	001

Fig. 7. MPLS-TP data-center and label creation

At the gateway: The TELL table at the gateway implements the mapping between incoming IP requests and outgoing LSPs. While we assume at least one LSP to each leaf (from the gateway), this assumption is not always practical for very large sized networks. The gateway using global LSP information then selects a set of multiple stacked LSPs (and hence a stack of labels) that would guide the incoming packet to the requisite destination node (leaf). Multicasting is handled using the multicaster logic used for OEthernet in [5, 15]. For multicasting, the lowest common ancestor for all the multicast nodes creates LSPs to each destination and replicates packets to each such LSP. In a future work, we also consider the creation of a multicast LSP tree, though this requires intelligence at intermediate nodes for selective multiplication.

LSP Consolidation: As mentioned earlier, it is not always possible to have LSPs from the gateway to every leaf. Likewise, for inter-leaf communication, especially to support virtualization, virtual machine migration etc. it is not possible to have LSPs set up between every pair of leaves within the data-center. Hence, we use the concept of multiple LSPs within the data-center by using label stacking (see Fig. 3 for example).

5   Simulation Model and Results

We performed an extensive discrete event simulation (DES) to evaluate the performance of our proposed data-center interconnection mechanism using Omnipresent Ethernet encoded in MPLS-TP. In the model, we assume 70% of the leaves to be NAS and 30% to be servers (processors). All the leaves have Gigabit Ethernet interfaces. The number of leaves is varied from 1000 to 1 million. Traffic requests arrive at the gateway as service jobs and these are to be transported to the leaves or within the leaves (inter-leaf communication) or from the leaves to the gateway. LSPs are set up ahead in time for the major routes. There are 4-levels of QoS supported by the network. Each LSP also defines with it a granularity that can be implemented using a token bucket rate-limiter function. Our interest is to measure the performance of the MPLS-TP architected data-center using OEthernet concepts as compared to native data-centers using MPLS, MPLS-TP (standard) as well as IP routers. Requests arrive following a Poisson distribution and are characterized by a general holding time (since the data-center is a specialized part of the network – most requests are heavily granular, as opposed to regular arrivals that are exponentially distributed). Load is computed as the ratio of the total consumed bandwidth in the network, as opposed to the total bandwidth that the network can provide, resulting in a range of [0,1].

Shown in Fig. 8 is a viewgraph of latency versus load for a data-center of size 1000 nodes (leaves). For comparison, we measured the performance of data-centers with IP routers, conventional MPLS and MPLS-TP (without OEthernet technology) using the same traffic and the same topology. Observe the almost 3-orders of difference in the delay values between any of the other technologies and our proposed data-center architecture. The measurements are taken as average latency over all the source-destination pairs and at time-ensemble, (1000 runs at the same load value). The MPLS-TP architecture using OEthernet does not require any lookup table and the maintenance of a global LSP database further facilitates faster switching. As can be seen in Fig. 8, the latency of our proposal is consistently better than all the other conventional technologies. This advantage is very important from the data-center perspective given that it is said that a 1-millisecond latency difference can cause a financial trading house over 100-million USD in a fiscal year.

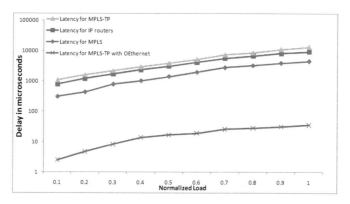

Fig. 8. Latency results for a 1000-node data-center

To demonstrate scale, the latency measurements are taken for a larger (1-million node) data-center. The measurements are consistent as can be seen in Fig. 9, whereby the latency difference between our proposal and existing technologies is easily 2-3 orders of magnitude. The superior performance of OEthernet when encapsulated within the MPLS-TP domain adds significant functionality flavor to MPLS-TP from the data-center perspective.

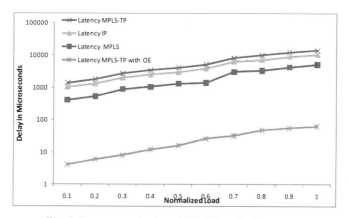

Fig. 9. Latency results for a 1000,000-node data-center

Shown in Fig. 10 is a viewgraph of energy consumption for an MPLS-TP network as compared to the energy consumption for our proposal. The MPLS-TP network requires more processing at each LSR. It can be concluded that the energy requirement is directly proportional to (1) the latency of the protocol – more the time spent at a node, more the energy consumed due to processing. and (2) lookup table size – larger the table, more the energy required. Base values for energy consumption are assumed as shown in [5, 15]. On an average, there is a 72% energy saving using our proposal as opposed to a generic MPLS-TP scheme. It should also be noted that the energy consumption for IP-routers and MPLS LSRs is significantly more than that when we use MPLS-TP and hence not shown in the viewgraph.

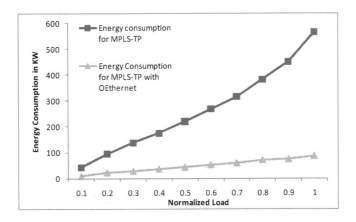

Fig. 10. Energy Efficiency comparison between MPLS

6   Conclusion

The fast proliferation of data-center technology has implied a need for a scalable, acceptable and economical protocol for interconnection between servers, NAS and switches. We propose the use of MPLS-TP to architect the data-center. However, instead of using native MPLS-TP, we propose the use of our earlier proposed Omnipresent Ethernet technology as an enabler for faster switching, lower energy consumption and better scalability within the data-center. The OEthernet technology, through the use of binary and source routing when plugged into MPLS-TP creates a very fast, efficiency and lower-energy consuming network – especially suited for the data-center. These performance results justify the use of OEthernet technology within an architected MPLS-TP data-center.

References

1. Gumaste, A., Antony, T.: Data Center Networking and Cloud Computing - A Networking Overview, Embedded Technology Brief (2009)
2. Shpiner, A., Keslassy, I.: A switch-based approach to throughput collapse and starvation in data centers. In: 18th International Workshop on Quality of Service (IWQoS), June 16-18 (2010)
3. Farrington, N., Rubow, E., Vahdat, A.: Data Center Switch Architecture in the Age of Merchant Silicon. In: 17th IEEE Symposium on High Performance Interconnects, August 25-27 (2009)

4. Ibanez, G., Carral, J.A., Garcia-Martinez, A., Arco, J.M., Rivera, D., Azcorra, A.: Fast Path Ethernet Switching - On-demand, efficient transparent bridges for data center and campus networks. In: IEEE Workshop on Local and Metropolitan Area Networks (LANMAN), May 5-7 (2010)

5. Gumaste, A., Mehta, S., Arora, I., Goyal, P., Rana, S., Ghani, N.: Omnipresent Ethernet— Technology Choices for Future End-to-End Networking. Journal of Lightwave Technology 28(8) (April 2010)

6. Niven-Jenkins, B., Brungard, D., Betts, M., Sprecher, N., Ueno, S.: Requirements of an MPLS Transport Profile. IETF RFC 5654 (2009)

7. Bocci, M., Bryant, S., Frost, D., Levrau, L., Berger, L.: A Framework for MPLS in Transport Networks. draft-ietf-mpls-tp-framework-12 (2010)

8. Busi, I., Allan, D.: Operations, Administration and Maintenance Framework for MPLS-TP based Transport Networks. draft-ietf-mpls-tp-oam-framework-08, September 17 (2010)

9. Koike, Y., Paul, M.: MPLS-TP OAM Maintenance Points. draft-koike-ietf-mpls-tp-oam-maintenance-points-01, March 8 (2010)

10. Sprecher, N., Farrel, A.: Multiprotocol Label Switching Transport Profile Survivability Framework. draft-ietf-mpls-tp-survive-fwk-06, June 20 (2010)

11. Bocci, M., Swallow, G.: MPLS-TP Identifiers. draft-ietf-mpls-tp-identifiers-0, March 8 (2010)

12. Takacs, A., Fedyk, D., He, J.: OAM Configuration Framework. draft-ietf-ccamp-oam-onfiguration-fwk[A1], January 28 (2010)

13. Zhang, F., Wu, B., Dai, X.: LDP Extensions for MPLS-TP PW OAM configuration. draft-zhang-mpls-tp-pw-oam-config-00, October 15 (2009)

14. Sprecher, N., Bellagamba, E., Weingarten, Y.: OAM Analysis. draft-ietf-mpls-tp-oam-analysis, July 04 (2010)

15. Gumaste, A., Mehta, S., Vaishampayan, R., Ghani, N.: Demonstration of Omnipresent Ethernet - A Novel Metro End-to-End Communication System Using Binary + Source Routing and Carrier Ethernet. Journal of Lightwave Technology 28(4), 596–607 (2010)

16. Mysore, R.N., Pamboris, A., Farrington, N., Huang, N., Miri, P., Radhakrishnan, S., Subramanya, V., Vahdat, A.: PortLand - A Scalable Fault-Tolerant Layer 2 Data Center Network Fabric. In: Proceedings of the ACM SIGCOMM Conference, Barcelona, Spain (August 2009)

17. Gumaste, A.: Deciphering omnipresent ethernet: An all ethernet communication system - the control plane. In: 12th International Conference on Transparent Optical Networks (ICTON), June 27-July 1 (2010)

A G.984 GPON Exhibiting Multi-wavelength Protocol Functionalities

Ali Gliwan, Pandelis Kourtessis, and John M. Senior

Optical Networks Group,
Science and Technology Research Institute (STRI)
University of Hertfordshire, Hatfield, UK
{A.Gliwan,P.Kourtessis,J.M.Senior}@Herts.ac.uk

Abstract. A Gigabit Passive Optical Network (GPON) upstream-map frame-format enhancement has been developed to accommodate dynamic multi wavelength (DMW) transmission over splitter-based GPONs. Accordingly network functionality has been supported by means of an algorithm, managing bandwidth allocation among utilised wavelengths in a dynamic two dimensional protocol. Modelling of the performance characteristics of the DMW-GPON topology in OPNET has demonstrated a minimum of 100 Mbit/s bandwidth provision for each of 32 Optical Network Units (ONUs) with a maximum 0.085 s packet delay for the worst performing lower service level agreement (SLA) ONUs.

Keywords: DBA, DWA, WDM, GPON, DMW.

1   Introduction

Scalability of standard GPON [1] topologies to larger split ratios would result in increased upstream polling waiting-time that could be intolerable for real-time services. The application of wavelength division multiplexing (WDM) to assign each ONU a unique point-to-point (P2P) logical connection with the optical line termination (OLT) provides a solution for reducing the polling waiting time and relaxing the bandwidth requirements on optical and electrical components. At present coarse WDM operation over the currently deployed splitter-based PONs has been proposed by means of the GPON band enhancement, defined by the ITU-T [2].

The application of extended band overlay has been demonstrated over a standard GPON topology and provided an ideal interim solution for smooth, dynamic and on-demand capacity upgrade [3]. It was achieved in [3] by reviewing the upstream and downstream frame format maps and consequently developing a new protocol based on the dynamic bandwidth allocation (DBA) algorithms previously developed for single-wavelength GPONs. To adapt and extend these algorithms for coarse WDM operation, extra fields were incorporated into the GPON frame format {ITU-T, 2004 #74}. Both the grant and the report packets used to establish communication between the OLT and ONUs were reconfigured to support dynamic multi-wavelength operation. Out of the twelve bits, in the Flags-field of the GPON upstream map frame format, the six unused

I. Tomkos et al. (Eds.): BROADNETS 2010, LNICST 66, pp. 411–417, 2012.
© Institute for Computer Sciences, Social Informatics and Telecommunications Engineering 2012

reserved bits were utilised by assigning four bits to express the ONU's operating wavelength for proceeding cycles and two bits to specify the packet type (e.g. whether it is a control packet or data packet as shown in Fig. 1).

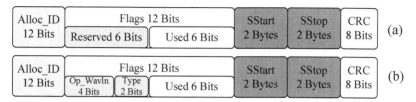

Fig. 1. Upstream map frame format, (a) Single-wavelength GPON, (b) DMW- GPON

The wavelengths utilised by each ONU for data transfer could be defined during the ONU's registration stage by means of each ONU reporting its supported wavelengths to the OLT [3]. To demonstrate the maximum transmission time-slot utilisation for each operating wavelength and consequently provide reduced packet delay, a scheduling algorithm was developed that prioritises user transmission according to traffic status.

2   The Dynamic Multi-wavelength Protocol

The DMW protocol aims to increase the upstream bit-rate by introducing dynamic allocation of bandwidth concurrently in the wavelength and time domains. This has been initially achieved by developing the dynamic minimum bandwidth (DMB) algorithm [4, 5] and modifying the GPON frame format to support multi-wavelength operation. The DMB algorithm facilitates three SLAs to assign each ONU with a guaranteed minimum bandwidth, to satisfy their basic service requirements, plus an additional allocation of extra bandwidth on demand based on the assigned SLA. In the DMW algorithm presented here a fourth service level is introduced to comply with modern service level provisioning [6] and to provide greater user experience and network flexibility. In addition, an extra upstream wavelength, bringing the total to five, is introduced with respect to previous DMW developments [3] to scale-up wavelength assignment in view of the ITU-T G.984.5 standard [2].

During ONU registration, the OLT "requests" from each ONU to confirm their supported wavelength(s). This is crucial to distinguish between different network sectors and bandwidth provision status among ONUs. Consequently, the OLT assigns the upstream bandwidth available in each polling-cycle in three stages. In the first stage, and after having received the requested bandwidth from each ONU, the OLT calculates a safety margin as shown in Fig. 2. The purpose of this approach is to process the maximum cycle time for bandwidth allocation independently for each wavelength, allowing for more accurate population of the polling cycles with considerable decrease in idle time slots. The safety margin is determined by considering the overall ONU minimum bandwidth requirement and the ONU SLA contracts. In that manner, the OLT allocates ONU bandwidth by means of the individual total network capacity depending on the time and wavelength measures ($R_{Available}$), as seen in equation (1).

$$R_{Available} = \sum_{\lambda=0}^{n} R_{Max}^{\lambda} - \text{Safety margin} \qquad (1)$$

The maximum allowed bandwidth for ONU$_i$ ($B_{allowed}^{t}$) is then assigned according to the DMB algorithm [4, 5] as in equation (2).

$$B_{allowed}^{t} = \begin{cases} B_{req}^{ONUi} & if & B_{req}^{ONUs} \langle R_{Available} \\ \\ B_{max}^{t} & if & B_{req}^{ONUs} \rangle R_{Available} \end{cases} \qquad (2)$$

where:

R_{Max}^{λ} is the maximum bit-rate for wavelength λ

B_{req}^{ONUi} is the requested bandwidth by ONU$_i$

B_{req}^{ONUs} is the total requested bandwidth by the network ONU$_s$

B_{max}^{t} is the maximum allowed bandwidth for SLA (t)

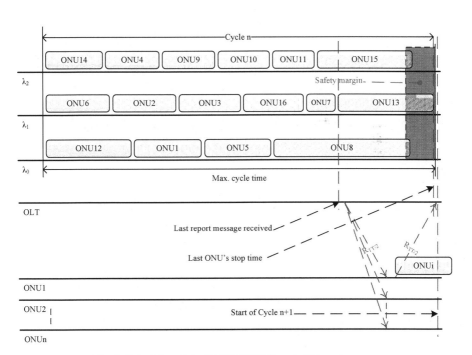

Fig. 2. Principles of the DMW-GPON bandwidth assignment

Random distribution of ONU traffic among the different wavelengths could potentially result in exceeding the maximum available cycle-time. Progressively the DMW OLT specifies the three highest ONU allocated bandwidths, since three wavelengths are utilised in the current algorithm, and positions them at the end of each cycle as shown in Fig. 2.

As a result the network throughput is increased by decreasing adjacent cycle idle times, resulting from delays associated with processing the report and grant messages by the OLT and the associated round trip time (RTT). The remaining ONU bandwidths are assigned to wavelengths in order, from high to low, starting at λ_{up0} and finishing at λ_{up2}.

This process allows the OLT to guarantee that the last ONU time-slot in λ_{up2} can fit within the safety margin as shown in Fig. 2. This approach potentially produces a shorter polling cycle length, a reduction in the ONU upstream packet waiting-time in proceeding cycles, and hence increased network utilization. Although the DMW algorithm deals successfully with adjacent cycle idle times, the network wavelengths are not always evenly populated resulting in idle times within each cycle, as seen primarily in Fig. 2 for λ_{up0} and λ_{up2}. To resolve this situation, before sending the gate message to the ONUs, the OLT will allocate any remaining available bandwidth for each wavelength to its assigned ONUs according to their SLA as seen in Fig.3.

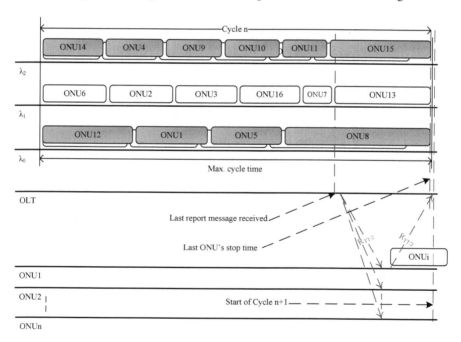

Fig. 3. DMW-GPON with extra bandwidth assignment

Fig. 3 portrays the finalised bandwidth allocation for each ONU in orange on top of the initial allocation in yellow to demonstrate the protocol enhancement. This step leads to a better bandwidth utilisation and reduces the mean packet delay of the system.

3   Simulation Results

To investigate the performance of the DMW protocol a FTTH oriented GPON network was modelled using the OPNET v.14.5 platform with Pareto self-similar traffic with typical Hurst parameter of 0.8, 1.24416 Gbit/s upstream data-rate, 2.488 Gbit/s downstream data-rate, and 32 ONUs. The latter were organised to implement service level agreement diversity with 4 ONUs assigned at SLA_0, 4 ONUs at SLA_1, 8 ONUs at SLA_2, and 16 ONUs at SLA_3 from high SLA to low respectively, simulating progressive network usage. In particular a 96 bits GPON guard-time between ONU traffic was considered, a 2.0 ms maximum cycle time, 20 km link lengths between the OLT and ONUs, and as explained in the previous section, 3% of the maximum cycle time utilised as a safety margin.

Comparing the DMW-GPON performance, with that of the DMB-GPON, as shown in Fig. 4, the overall network capacity of the former is confirmed to have been increased by a factor equal to the number of wavelengths employed.

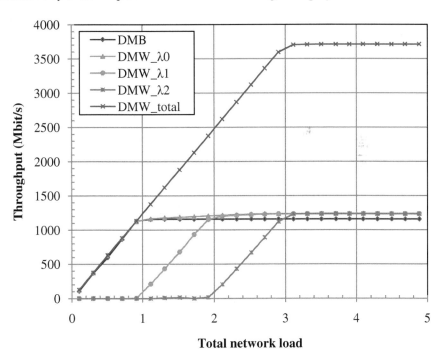

Fig. 4. Throughput against total network load for DMB and DMW

Although such a characteristic was rather expected, it was achieved with the simultaneous increase in each DMW wavelength throughput by 70 Mbit/s compared to the DMB network. It has also been achieved at the provision of 100 Mbit/s minimum transmission rate per ONU, for 32 ONUs, as opposed to 30 Mbit/s basic bandwidth per ONU in the DMB-GPON. This imposes a reduction in idle time between cycles. In addition, the use of the 3% safety margin has not limited each wavelengths' throughput, in contrast to the single wavelength DMB capacity, due to the more effective utilisation of the available time slots.

In another performance evaluation measure, while the mean packet delay for all SLAs utilising a single wavelength exceeds 0.1 s, when the total network load achieves one wavelength capacity at 1.24 Gbit/s, the DMW protocol provides notably decreased packet delay. Corresponding figures indicate 0.003 s delay up to the point the total network load reaches three wavelengths capacity. Shown in Fig. 5, this characteristic allows for the non obstructive transmission of interactive applications since it satisfies the recommended one-way delay requirement for these applications as defined by the ITU-T G.1010 [7].

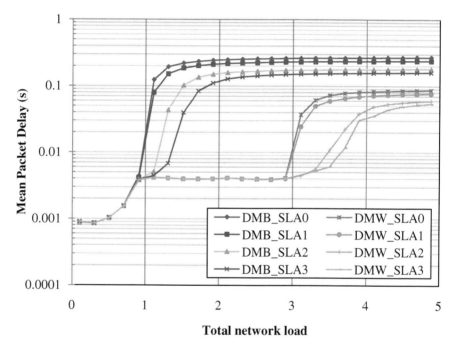

Fig. 5. Mean packet delay against total network load for DMB and DMW GPON

The DMW protocol therefore allows for real time service provisioning at the stringiest requirements of service provisioning such as conversational voice and videophone, at increased basic bandwidth to 100 Mbit/s and increased ONU volume. Even at higher network load, the lower service level DMW ONUs displaying the greatest delay still maintain delay figures below 0.1 s which provides scope for further scalability to ONU provision and for service advancements.

4   Conclusions

A DMW algorithm methodology and the corresponding protocol enhancements have been presented to accommodate multi-wavelength operation over splitter-based GPONs by means of smoothly upgrading the existing single-wavelength network infrastructure. This upgrade has been achieved by utilising additional bits in the frame fields of the GPON upstream format map to define the operating wavelength and packet type transfer for each ONU. The performance benefits of the multi-wavelength operation include aggregating transmission bit-rates of 3.70 Gbit/s in the presence of three wavelength signals and 32 ONUs, 100 Mbit/s minimum bandwidth per ONU and a considerable reduction in mean packet delay in comparison to a single wavelength GPON topology. The 0.003 s packet delay at typical network utilisation rates and the worst case 0.085 s equivalent at heavy loading allow for the continuous communication of the highest specification interactive services and a scope for additional network upgrade in services, ONU penetration and reach capabilities.

References

1. ITU-T.: G.984.2 Gigabit-capable Passive Optical Networks (G-PON): Physical media dependent (PMD) layer specification, ITU-T (2003)
2. ITU-T.: G.984.5 Enhancement band for gigabit capable optical access networks, ITU-T (2007)
3. Gliwan, A., Chang, C.H., Shachaf, Y., Kourtessis, P., Senior, J.M.: Upstream Format Map Enhancements for Multi-Wavelength GPONs. In: 13th European Conference on Networks and Optical Communications (NOC), Krems, Austria, pp. 75–82 (2008)
4. Chang, C.H., Kourtessis, P., Senior, J.M.: GPON service level agreement based dynamic bandwidth assignment protocol. IET Electronics Letters, 1173–1174 (2006)
5. Chang, C.H., Alvarez, N.M., Kourtessis, P., Lorenzo, R.M., Senior, J.M.: Full-Service MAC Protocol for Metro-Reach GPONs. Journal of Lightwave Technology, 1016–1022 (2010)
6. Super-Fast Cable Broadband, http://www.virginmedia.com
7. ITU-T.: G.1010 End-user multimedia QoS categories, ITU-T (2001)

A Novel QoS Provisioning Scheme for OBS Networks

Shavan K. Askar, Georgios Zervas, David K. Hunter, and Dimitra Simeonidou

School of Computer Science and Electronic Engineering
University of Essex, Colchester CO4 3SQ
skaske3@essex.ac.uk

Abstract. This paper presents Classified Cloning, a novel QoS provisioning mechanism for OBS networks carrying real-time applications (such as video on demand, Voice over IP, online gaming and Grid computing). It provides such applications with a minimum loss rate while minimizing end-to-end delay and jitter. ns-2 has been used as the simulation tool, with new OBS modules having been developed for performance evaluation purposes. Ingress node performance has been investigated, as well as the overall performance of the suggested scheme. The results obtained showed that new scheme has superior performance to classical cloning. In particular, QoS provisioning offers a guaranteed burst loss rate, and delay unlike existing proposals for QoS implementation in OBS which use the burst offset time to provide such differentiation. Indeed, classical schemes increase both end-to-end delay and jitter. It is shown that the burst loss rate is reduced by 50% reduced over classical cloning.

Keywords: QoS provisioning, Optical Burst Switching, Cloning.

1 Introduction

Optical Burst Switching (OBS) is an effective technology for the next generation optical Internet that aims to address the increasing bandwidth required by Internet users [1]. OBS is a good tradeoff between traditional Optical Circuit Switching (OCS), which is relatively easy to implement but suffers from poor bandwidth utilization and coarse granularity, and Optical Packet Switching (OPS) [2], which has a good bandwidth utilization and fine granularity but is difficult to implement because of the immaturity of current optical technologies [3]. In OBS networks, the basic switching entity is a burst. Prior to transmission of a burst, a control packet is created and immediately sent toward the destination in order to set up a buffer-less optical path for the corresponding burst. After an offset delay time, the data burst is transmitted without waiting for an acknowledgement from the destination node. The optical path exists only for the duration of a burst [4].

There has been a rapid increase in the volume of traffic from new applications (such as video on demand, Voice over IP, online gaming or Grid computing) which have real-time and/or bandwidth constraints. Hence, service differentiation must be provided for such applications in order to reduce the loss rate while maintaining the lowest possible end-to-end delay. Accordingly, the high burst loss probability evident

I. Tomkos et al. (Eds.): BROADNETS 2010, LNICST 66, pp. 418–428, 2012.
© Institute for Computer Sciences, Social Informatics and Telecommunications Engineering 2012

in OBS networks has become a critical issue that must be addressed in order to enable real deployment of OBS networks [5-7]. Most existing research in this area can be categorized into one of the mechanism shown in Fig. 1.

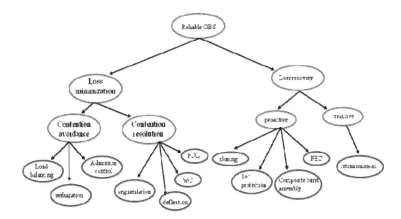

Fig. 1. OBS Mechanisms for loss reduction

The mechanisms shown in Fig. 1 are used for loss reduction in OBS networks – they are categorized into loss recovery and loss minimization techniques. Loss recovery mechanisms can be divided into sub-categories – reactive and proactive mechanisms – while loss minimization approaches are subdivided into contention resolution and contention avoidance schemes. In fact, each of these techniques has its advantages as well as its disadvantages, but all of them seek to reduce the loss rate in OBS networks. Contention avoidance aims at preventing the occurrence of contention, while contention resolution focuses on resolving contention that already exists. The most well-known contention resolution schemes are wavelength conversion [8, 9], fiber delay line (FDL) buffering [10] and deflection routing [11, 12]. Another technique called burst segmentation proposes segmentation of contended bursts [13, 14], and dropping only part of each one.

Contention resolution appears to be a very tempting solution to the problem of contention in OBS networks, however there are a number of implementation problems: 1) wavelength conversion is an immature technique which is still very expensive to implement, 2) FDL's are bulky and they merely offer fixed delays which generally reduce channel utilization because they generate voids between scheduled bursts, 3) deflection routing suffers from the problem of endless loops as well as the possibility of insufficient offset time for rerouted bursts, 4) burst segmentation is still very complicated to implement. Reactive loss recovery is a retransmission scheme where burst retransmission is possible in the event of contention [15, 16]. Many factors hinder its implementation; firstly, very large buffers are required in ingress nodes in order to implement retransmission. Also, although retransmission may be practical in LAN's, it is not useful in MAN's or WAN's because of their higher latency, which also requires larger buffers in order to implement retransmission. Finally, a notification protocol is required to notify edge nodes of burst losses, which generates additional load on the control channel. To overcome these problems we propose a new scheme for QoS provisioning with real-time applications – Classified Cloning – which is inspired by the basic cloning scheme [17]. In this paper we investigate the use of cloning to reduce packet loss. Research in this area is limited, with contradictions in the results from different studies [17-20]. However, it has been shown that the existing drawbacks of burst retransmission, such as the large buffer size and increased control traffic, can be avoided through cloning, yielding lower mean packet delay.

The rest of this paper is organized as follows: Section 2 provides a brief overview of the existing cloning scheme. Section 3 introduces our proposed scheme and a novel ingress node design. Section 4 evaluates the performance of the proposed Classified Cloning Scheme and compares the performance with the existing Basic Cloning Scheme. Section 5 concludes the paper.

2   Existing Cloning Schemes

In this section the existing Burst Cloning Scheme [17] is referred to as the Basic Cloning Scheme (BCS), while our proposed scheme will be referred as the Classified Cloning Scheme (CCS); the latter can provision traffic with higher priority QoS. In both the original BCS and our proposed Classified Cloning Scheme (CCS), the original copy of a burst is referred to as the "original burst", and the duplicate copy as the "cloned burst". Similarly, the traffic corresponding to the original and cloned bursts is referred as "original" and "cloned" traffic respectively. The node at which cloning is performed is referred to as the "cloning node".

In BCS, one or more cloned bursts can be made from each original burst and sent simultaneously; if one or more of these bursts arrive at the destination, the original burst is considered to be successful. On one hand, if more copies are made for a particular burst then it is less likely to be lost. On the other hand, if more copies are made overall, more cloned traffic is added to the network, which then actually increases the overall probability of burst loss.

A comparison has been made between a retransmission recovery scheme and a cloning scheme [18]. It was found that the drawbacks of the existing retransmission mechanism such as the use of large buffers and increased control channel traffic can be avoided through the use of cloning. Accordingly, lower average packet delay value was delivered.

In [19] each core node has the burden of determining whether cloned bursts have been lost or not, in order to decide whether another cloned burst must be produced. To do this, two assumptions are made. Firstly, it is assumed that each cloned burst arrives at a particular core node before its corresponding original burst. Secondly, it is assumed that there is enough time between receiving the original BHP and receiving the corresponding data to check the status of the received cloned bursts. In fact, implementing cloning in the core nodes is not recommended due to the complexity of implementing a database there, which must be accessed when every burst is received to determine whether each cloned burst has been lost. Indeed, cloning was originally proposed as a low cost alternative to the solutions mentioned in the Introduction, which require expensive hardware.

3   The Proposed Classified Cloning Scheme

The major side effect of burst cloning is increased network load, although BCS introduces a traffic isolation mechanism which allows original bursts to preempt reservations made by cloned bursts. The optical links on average carry twice the original load, or more, since some studies suggest making more than one copy of each original burst. However, having as many cloned bursts can be counterproductive because the probability of contention often actually increases due to the overall increase in traffic. To the best of the authors' knowledge, the use of cloning for QoS provisioning has not yet been suggested, and all research in this area has involved cloning all traffic in the network [17].

In our proposed CCS we seek to avoid cloning all incoming traffic because otherwise, the network will be heavily loaded by cloned traffic without much effective reduction in burst loss. The consequent low reduction in loss rate with BCS arises because of the low priority assigned to cloned traffic in order to provision class isolation. Many studies attempt to overcome this by implementing cloning in a core node, or by making many copies of each original burst.

By using the edge nodes for cloning and applying cloning only to UDP traffic, which possibly makes up 10% of the total, there is not a major effect on the network load; however the loss rate is reduced considerably. The reduction in loss rate benefits UDP-based applications because they are time-critical, and recovery from burst loss should therefore be immediate. Furthermore, the ETE delay is maintained because unlike BCS, no extra offset time is added before each burst. Fig. 2 shows the proposed edge node design; we have designed a classifier in the ingress node which classifies incoming IP packets depending on their type of service into either Serv 1 or Serv 2 packets (Serv 1 is for best effort while Serv 2 is for real-time applications). There are two buffers: the primary buffer aggregates all traffic (Serv 1+ Serv 2) while the secondary buffer aggregates traffic from real-time applications only (Serv 2). The secondary (cloning) buffer receives IP packets forming Serv 2 traffic, but only when the offered load is low or medium. This is implemented through the write enable (WE) signal, which goes low to enable writing if RT (Real-Time) and TRG (TRiGger) signals both become high. RT goes high if the IP packet belongs to Serv 2 traffic while the TRG signal is activated if the offered load is low or medium. The classifier classifies incoming IP packets according to their destination egress node. After aggregating IP packets in this way, there are two types of burst (namely original bursts and cloned bursts), which both have the same priority and are sent to the egress node which then segregates received bursts and drops duplicates where necessary.

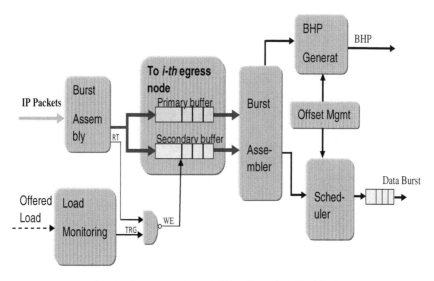

Fig. 2. Edge-ingress node model for Classified Cloning Scheme

4   Simulation and Analysis

The ns-2 simulator has been used to evaluate our proposed cloning scheme. New OBS modules have been developed to support the proposed concepts. Simulations took place on the 19-node NSF network topology of Fig. 3. A list of functionalities and simulation decisions made are shown below:

- the mean burst size is 125KBytes,
- the core nodes are bufferless,
- the wavelength continuity constraint is applied, and
- the OBS control plane supports JET (Just Enough Time).

Furthermore, in the absence of a detailed traffic model, we assume that the bursts which are generated at the network edge are described by a Poisson process, the traffic is distributed over the network uniformly, and all routes are established by a shortest path routing algorithm with the number of hops as the metric. In addition, bursts are assembled using hybrid threshold-timeout, with both timeout and size thresholds being used to obtain the best of both schemes.

Fig. 4 shows burst loss in the ingress node versus offered load. Fig. 5 shows the average delay and jitter versus the offered load, which arises because of aggregation in each edge node. Existing research does not consider loss at the ingress node when evaluating burst loss, moreover, many existing publications don't show jitter at the edge node; in fact, the edge node aggravates jitter, thus influencing the performance of the whole network. The jitter and delay values in Fig. 5 obtained are the average values for the corresponding offered load.

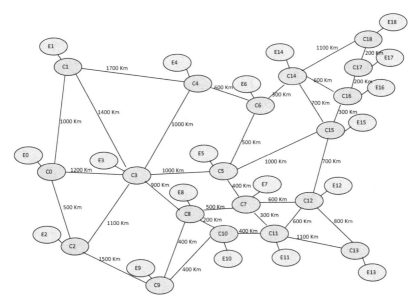

Fig. 3. A 19-node NSF network topology with real physical distances between the nodes

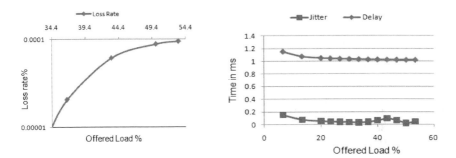

Fig. 4. Edge node loss rate versus the offered load

Fig. 5. Edge node delay and jitter versus offered load

Fig. 6 shows the Cumulative Distribution Function (CDF) of the jitter values with offered loads of 6.66%, 19.9%, 26.6%, and 33.3%, while Fig. 7 will shows offered loads of 39.9%, 46.6%, and 53.3%; two figures are provided in the interest of clarity. With a 6.66% offered load, the jitter is greater than with the other scenarios; with such a low level of incoming traffic, bursts are shaped with long interarrival times, even although hybrid aggreation is used. Hence with a low volume of incoming traffic, most of the generated bursts arise after the burst generation algorithm has timed out, even with hybrid aggregation – this is confirmed by Fig. 6, where no burst is of the maximum size. In Fig. 6, 93% (73%) of the generated bursts have jitter values below

0.4 ms (0.2 ms), with an offered load of 6.66%, which is acceptable with this low load. However, as the level of incoming traffic increases, jitter decreases (i.e. when the offered loads are 19.9%, 26.6%, and 33.3%). Out of these three scenarios, there is the greatest jitter with a load of 19.9% for the reasons discussed above, so that 98%, 87%, and 62% of the generated bursts have jitter vlaues of 0.2 ms, 0.1 ms, and 0.05 ms or less respectively. The CDFs of the jitter values at 26.6% offered load show that 93%, 73%, and 49% of the generated bursts have jitter values of 0.1 ms, 0.05 ms, and 0.025 ms or less respectively, while with a 33.3% offered load, 96.5%, 81%, and 56% of the generated bursts have jitter values of 0.1 ms, 0.05 ms, and 0.025 ms or less. Indeed, Fig. 6 shows that in general, jitter decreases as offered load decreases. However, there is a trade-off to be made when choosing burstification parameters, because a higher load will, in consequence, increase the edge loss rate as shown in Fig. 4.

Fig. 7 shows the CDFs for jitter at offered loads of 39.9%, 46.6%, and 53.3%. For jitter less than 1 ms, the CDFs are 92.4%, 93%, and 98.14% for offered loads of 39.9%, 46.6%, and 53.3% respectively while for jitter values less than 0.05 ms, the CDFs are 43%, 29.7%, and 73% with offered loads of 39.9%, 46.6%, and 53.3%.

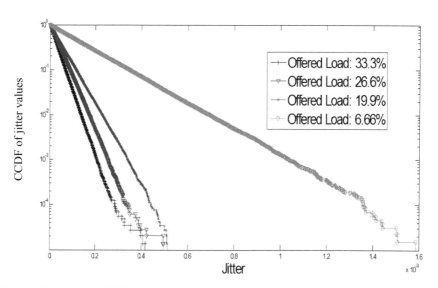

Fig. 6. CCDF (i.e. 1 - CDF) of Burst Jitter at 6.66% , 19.9%, 26.6%, and 33.3% offered loads

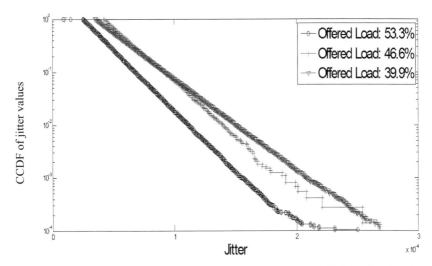

Fig. 7. CCDF (i.e. 1 - CDF) of Burst Jitter at 39.9%, 46.6%, and 53.3% offered loads

In order to conduct a comprehensive investigation of ingress node performance, the generated burst sizes must be studied in detail. Fig. 8 shows the CDFs of the generated burst sizes under different offered load scenarios, in order to provide further insight into the burst generation process. The Figure shows how the burst sizes increase as incoming load increases, and these results can be used to facilitate choosing suitable burstification parameters in order to enhance ingress node performance. Existing studies on choosing burstification parameters appear to be contradictory when specifying how to choose the maximum threshold value. Some studies suggest generating longer bursts in order to reduce control packet processing in core nodes, hence reducing the loss rate, while others argue that longer bursts increase the probability of preemption by other bursts because they occupy the link for longer It has also been claimed that bursts of equal length generated by ingress nodes will reduce the probability of loss due to contention [7, 21, 22]. As we already mentioned, we used hybrid aggregation because we sought a trade-off between loss, delay, and jitter at the ingress node when considering the burst loss rate arising in the network overall.

Fig. 9 shows the improvement in loss rate with real-time applications under the proposed Classified Cloning Scheme. The loss rate for Serv 2 applications has been reduced by more than 50% over the Basic Cloning Scheme. Because cloned traffic is sent with same priority as the original traffic, the loss rate for Serv 1 traffic increases due to the increased probability of contention arising from the additional cloned Serv 2 traffic. However real-time applications typically produce 10% of the total traffic, therefore, the loss rate with Serv 1 increases very slowly with CCS as shown in Fig. 10.

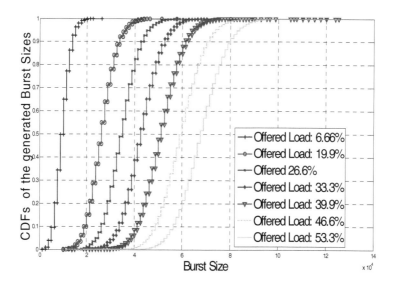

Fig. 8. CDF of generated burst sizes at different offered loads

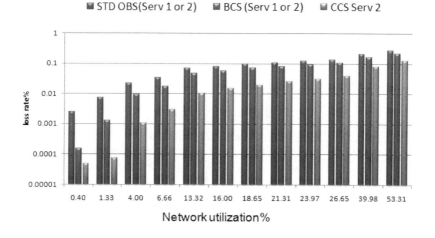

Fig. 9. Loss rate versus network load for standard OBS, BCS, and CCS

However, Serv 1 applications don't have jitter, delay and loss rate constraints. Providing that no extra offset time is added to the original traffic with CCS, Serv 2 bursts have lower ETE delay than with BCS. Applying cloning at the edge node to real-time UDP traffic does not affect network load appreciably, while it nevertheless reduces the burst loss rate considerably. The reduced loss rate benefits UDP-based applications by providing immediate burst loss recovery through CCS. Furthermore, the ETE delay is preserved because unlike BCS, no extra offset time is added to the original traffic.

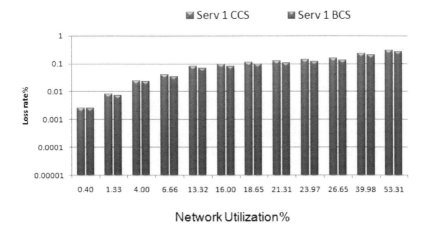

Fig. 10. Comparison of Serv 1 loss rate between BCS and CCS

5   Conclusion

This paper introduced a novel QoS provisioning scheme –Classified Cloning – for OBS networks. The ns-2 simulator was used as the simulation tool, with OBS modules being developed and compiled into the ns-2 simulator to evaluate the proposed mechanism. For real-time traffic, the results show a 50% reduction in burst loss rate over BCS. Additionally, evaluation of ingress node performance has shown the jitter, delay and loss rate values produced due to aggregation inside the edge-ingress node. The Classified Cloning Scheme outperforms BCS and the classical QoS provisioning mechanisms in OBS for three reasons: firstly, it retains the same delay as without cloning because the Classified Cloning Scheme does not use an extra offset time for class isolation; secondly, it implements immediate loss recovery for real-time applications; thirdly, it does not need extra hardware or optical splitting because classified cloning is implemented in the ingress node. We conclude that the proposed CCS scheme is a viable and realistic alternative to QoS provisioning schemes because it doesn't add extra offset time, and furthermore it offers significant improvements in reduction of burst loss rate.

References

1. Qiao, C., Yoo, M.: Optical Burst Switching (OBS) - A New Paradigm for an Optical Internet. Journal of High Speed Networks 8(1), 69–84 (1999)
2. Bianco, A., et al.: Design of optical packet switching networks. In: GLOBECOM, New York, vol. 3, pp. 2752–2756 (2002)
3. Perros, H.G., Rouskas, G.: Techniques for optical packet switching and optical burst switching. IEEE Communications Magazine 39, 136–142 (2001)

4. Luo, J., et al.: ROBS: A novel architecture of Reliable Optical Burst Switching with congestion control. Journal of High Speed Networks 16, 123–131 (2007)
5. Simeonidou, D., et al.: Dynamic Optical-Network Architectures and Technologies for Existing and Emerging Grid Services. Journal of Lightwave Technology 23, 3347–3357 (2005)
6. Xu, H., Fan, G.: Analysis of the burst loss rate in OBS rings with depth limited optical buffers. Journal of High Speed Networks 16, 341–351 (2007)
7. Vargas, T.R., Guerri, J.C., Sales, S.: Optimal Configuration for Size-Based Burst Assembly Algorithms at the Edge Node for Video Traffic Transmissions over OBS Networks. Building, 130–133 (2008)
8. Olmos, J.J.V., et al.: Optical node with time-space-and-wavelength domain contention resolution, deflection and dropping capability. Optics Express 14, 11545–11550 (2006)
9. Rosberg, Z., et al.: Analysis of OBS Networks With Limited Wavelength Conversion. IEEE/ACM Transactions on Networking 14, 1118–1127 (2006)
10. Pedro, J., et al.: Efficient Optical Burst-Switched Networks using only Fiber Delay Line Buffers for Contention Resolution. Networks (2006)
11. Hsu, C., Liu, T., Huang, N.: Performance analysis of Deflection Routing in Optical Burst Switched Networks. In: Proceedings, IEEE INFOCOM (2002)
12. Wang, X., Morikawa, H., Aoyama, T.: Deflection routing protocol for burst switching WDM mesh networks. In: Proc. SPIE/IEEE Terabit Optical Networking: Architecture, Control, and Management Issues, pp. 242–252 (2000)
13. Vokkarane, V.M., Member, S., Jue, J.P.: Prioritized Burst Segmentation and Composite Burst-Assembly Techniques for QoS Support in Optical Burst-Switched Networks. IEEE Journal on Selected Areas in Communications 21, 1198–1209 (2003)
14. Vokkarane, V.M., Jue, J.P., Sitaraman, S.: Burst Segmentation: An Approach For Reducing Packet Loss In Optical Burst Switched Networks. Time, 2673–2677 (2002)
15. Hirota, Y., Tode, H., Murakami, K.: A Study on RWA Cooperation Method Considering Retransmission. IEIC Journal 106(208), 55–60 (2006)
16. Kwak, K.J., Coffman, E.: Retransmission in OBS networks with fiber delay lines. In: Fourth International Conference on Broadband, Communication, Networks, and Systems, BROADNETS 2007 (2007)
17. Huang, X., Vokkarane, V.M., Jue, J.P.: Burst Cloning: A Proactive Scheme to Reduce Data Loss in Optical Burst-Switched Networks. Science, 1673–1677 (2005)
18. Vokkarane, V.M., Zhang, Q.: Forward Redundancy: A Loss Recovery Mechanism for Optical Burst-Switched Networks. Wireless and Optical Communications Networks, IFIP, 5 (2006)
19. Um, T.-W., et al.: priority based duplicate burst transmission in obs. ETRI 30 (2008)
20. Maach, A., Hafid, A.S., Belbekkouche, A.: Burst Loss Reduction schemes in Optical Burst Switching Networks. Network, 256–262 (2008)
21. Watagodakumbura, C., Praluyanto, H.: Composite Burst Assembly and Lower Real-Time Class Utilization Threshold in Optical Burst Switching As Means of Overcoming Effects of Self-Similarity. ITNG (2007)
22. Casoni, M., Luppi, E., Merani, M.L.: Impact of Assembly Algorithms on End-to-End Performance in Optical Burst Switched Networks with Different QoS Classes. In: IEEE/SPIE Third Workshop on Optical Burst Switching 2004, San Jose, CA (October 2004)

Enabling Multimode Wireless Access Networks Using Remote Radio Heads

Georgios Kardaras[1], Jose Soler[2], and Lars Dittmann[2]

[1] Radiocomp ApS
Krakasvej 17, 3400 Hillerød, Denmark
gka@radiocomp.com
[2] Networks Technology & Service Platforms Group
Department of Photonics Engineering,
Technical University of Denmark, 2800 Kgs. Lyngby, Denmark
{joss,ladit}@fotonik.dtu.dk

Abstract. The deployment of 4G networks is spreading rapidly providing mobile broadband services to the public. 4G technologies are designed to overlay existing 3G networks enabling reusability of several network components. In this way, the coexistence of 3G/4G standards is facilitated. This paper describes the advantages of using distributed base station architectures to provide multimode capabilities. In particular, it focuses on the radio unit, commonly known in industry as remote radio head. Multimode radio units capable of operating according to different wireless standards (WCDMA, LTE and WiMAX) can be proven extremely beneficial for operators especially in terms of operational and maintenance cost. Moreover, remote radio heads can enable effective spectrum management and allocation of radio resources. This is achieved through the advanced software configurability they provide and a flexible control and management plane. Switching between wireless standards becomes easily feasible through firmware upgrading. Finally, real-time configuration of radio functionalities, such as transmit power, receiver gain, carrier frequency, channel bandwidth and others result in a modular software defined radio platform.

Keywords: software defined radio, multimode radio, optical fibre, 4G communication, WiMAX, LTE.

1   Introduction

The demand for high speed broadband wireless access at low prices has been explosive the past years. Modern cell-based broadband wireless standards such as WiMAX and LTE are capable of fulfilling this demand. However, the cost of upgrading infrastructure is massive. Distributed base station architectures are able to resolve this challenge to an extent through the multimode capabilities they provide. Deploying this type of architectures allows operators to support multiple wireless standards sharing the same radio platform. This is achieved by separating physically the baseband from the radio functionalities combined in a base station design.

I. Tomkos et al. (Eds.): BROADNETS 2010, LNICST 66, pp. 429–434, 2012.

This paper concentrates on the remote radio unit, known as remote radio head. The benefits and limitations of this network component are described as far as multi-standard support, maintenance and upgrading are concerned. Firstly, the concept of distributed base station architectures is presented. The top-level design is briefly described and the major interfaces are discussed. The next step is to analyze more specifically the functionalities of remote radio head and the reasons they can facilitate multimode operation in modern wireless access networks.

2   Delivering Wireless through Fiber

In distributed base station architectures the two major network components are the baseband server and the remote radio head unit. The base station server is connected to the remote radio head through an optical fiber. This enables the remote radio head to be situated up to 15km away from the base station server adding substantial flexibility to network designing. The optical link is used to distribute modulated baseband wireless data of any standard to the remote radio head which is placed on the antenna tower very close to the antenna unit. This is possible because of its relatively small size and low weight. In average a remote radio head weights less than 15 kilograms and its size does not exceed 20x30x50cm, making it easy to install or replace.

On the contrary, in conventional base station architectures the RF wireless signals reach the antenna sites through copper feeders. This approach is expensive in power losses and signal attenuation. It is estimated that over 25% of power is consumed before being radiated over the air [5]. In addition, space for hosting and cooling the base station in the surroundings of the antenna tower is also necessary. This results in increased capital and operational expenditure.

Architectures based on remote radio heads exploit the advantages of radio over fiber systems (high bandwidth, low signal attenuation, lightweight materials) providing at the same time the necessary interfaces for remote control and management. In this way, the result is a fully configurable software defined radio node able to adapt in real-time to specific network requirements. It is agnostic to the wireless standard used, since the baseband data travelling over the fiber are already modulated. Therefore, the same radio hardware platform can be reused for multiple wireless standards after the necessary software upgrade.

However, necessary prerequisite for distributed architectures to function properly is the definition of a protocol between the baseband server and the remote radio head. In particular, there are two initiatives defining the appropriate interfaces and restrictions. The Open Base Station Architectures Initiative (OBSAI) and the Common Public Radio Interface (CPRI) have been introduced and supported independently by different network equipment vendors [7, 8].

These protocols provide a reliable communication link between the two nodes on the physical layer. They incorporate several functionalities enlisted in Table 1. As expected, multimode is supported by defining various mapping schemes for GSM/EDGE, WCDMA, WiMAX and LTE. Additionally, multiple antenna carriers are defined in the same frame for multi-standard multi-carrier radio transmission.

In this way, spectrum can be divided and managed efficiently according to operator's needs and regulations. In addition, another important feature of CPRI and OBSAI is the fact that they provide a dedicated Ethernet channel for the control and management of the remote radio head node. This means that the radio unit can be configured and monitored on an air-frame basis, for example every 5 or 10ms depending on the standard. This minimizes the response and adaptation time the radio hardware needs to enable new configurations. Thanks to this "embedded" control and management channel, a separate channel for control purposes through another type of cabling is no longer necessary. Both user data and control data are enhanced in the CPRI or OBSAI frame and transmitted through the optical fiber.

Table 1. Physical Layer for Distributed base station architectures

Protocol	Functionalities
OBSAI/CPRI	Electrical and optical signalling
	Synchronization and clock recovery
	Timing information and network topology
	Framing
	Delay calibration
	Reliable forwarding of baseband data
	Control management plane for remote radio head nodes

3   Functional Decomposition

It is essential to describe the way functionalities are decomposed between the baseband server and the remote radio head to clearly understand how and why multimode radio access is facilitated. The baseband server is responsible for providing interfaces to the backhaul network from one side and the remote radio head to the other side. It provides the same digital functions with a conventional base station including the control and management of the remote radio head. These functions involve backhaul transport, channel coding, interleaving, modulation, MIMO management and others. The difference with conventional base station is that all analogue and radio frequency functions, such as filtering, frequency conversion, and amplification have been moved to the remote radio head. Table 2 gives an overview of this functional decomposition specific for WiMAX applications.

Based on the functionalities a remote radio head incorporates, we observe that it is a transparent node, independent of the wireless standard used. However, it needs to be configured for supporting different channel bandwidths, sample rates and antenna carrier frequencies [2]. The configuration of the mentioned system parameters is done purely through software. Switching between standards is feasible as well as their coexistence in different antenna carrier frequencies. In this way, spectrum can be managed efficiently based on traffic characteristics, user demand or geographical constraints. The multimode and multi-carrier properties of remote radio heads become a very useful tool for operators, since they provide full control over the assigned spectrum.

However, there are some factors which limit the multimode operation of remote radio heads. The first concerns the multiplexing technique defined by the wireless standard. More specifically, WiMAX specifications define Time Division Duplex (TDD) as the multiplexing technique to be used. On the other hand, the multiplexing technique for LTE can be either TDD or Frequency Division Duplex (FDD), allowing even more flexibility. Remote radio heads can only support one multiplexing technique at a time. In case of TDD applications, the transmit and receive paths share the same RF frequency but transmission and reception take place in different time slots, defined by TDD switching. This has several advantages with most important the asymmetrical downlink and uplink data speeds. This means that the downlink and uplink speeds can be dynamically adjusted according to network or user equipment requirements. Allocating bandwidth in this flexible manner can save radio resources and optimize network planning. In case of FDD applications, the remote radio head is equipped with RF components tuned to operate in different transmit and receive carrier frequencies separated by a guard band to minimize interference. It becomes obvious that multimode radio operation is not feasible in case the multiplexing technique varies. However, it is commonly accepted that operators customize the standards according to their strategies, choosing a multiplexing technique suitable for their network.

Table 2. Functionalities of baseband server and remote radio head for TDD WiMAX applications [8]

Baseband server Functionalities		Remote Radio Head Functionalities	
Downlink	Uplink	Downlink	Uplink
Remote Radio Head control and management		Channel filtering	
Backhaul transport		D/A conversion	A/D conversion
MAC layer		Digital up conversion	Digital down conversion
Channel coding	Channel decoding	Control of antenna carriers	Automatic gain control
Interleaving	Deinterleaving	Carrier multiplexing	Carrier demultiplexing
OFDMA Modulation	OFDMA Demodulation	Power amplification	Low noise amplification
MIMO management		TDD switching	
Signal measurements		RF filtering	

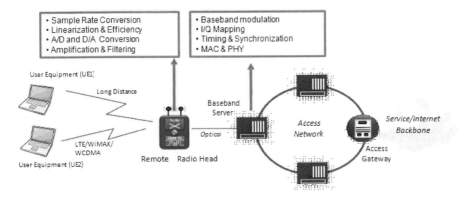

Fig. 1. Overview of distributed base station architecture

The second limitation also originates from the RF hardware platform. This restriction concerns the front-end RF filtering. These filters are precisely tuned to specific RF frequencies. This allows the remote radio head not to cause interference to adjacent frequency bands or being interfered by them. The range each front-end filter covers depends on the specification of the component and it cannot be modified dynamically during operation. This range defines the number of antenna carrier frequencies a remote radio head can provide. For example, a 50MHz front-end filter tuned at 2.5GHz could theoretically provide carrier frequencies between 2.48GHz and 2.52GHz, supposing that the channel bandwidth of the transmit signal is 10MHz. This constraint forces remote radio head vendors to design different modules for each frequency variant. Multimode operation is affected in case the operator decides to maintain persistent radio frequencies for each wireless standard. However, spectrum management can be substantially facilitated by the fact that user equipment is designed to scan several frequency bands, until it discovers the one where it can become operational.

4   Conclusions

This paper discussed the use of distributed base station architectures for enabling multimode capabilities in modern wireless access networks. In particular, the advantages provided by remote radio heads are described. This approach combines the benefits of radio over fiber and software defined radio systems. The distributed nodes are interconnected via optical fiber which offers flexibility in terms of network topology, bandwidth, power loss and interference. Moreover, the remote radio unit can be monitored and configured real-time through the protocols defined, CPRI and OBSAI. Another essential characteristic is that it remains agnostic to the wireless standard used. This allows reusing the same radio platform for different 3G/4G applications by performing only software upgrades. In this way, operators are able to shape strategies and introduce policies for managing spectrum and allocating radio resources. Additionally, the flexibility remote radio heads provide results in a smooth and cost-effective migration to new technologies.

References

1. Gomes, N.J., Alphones, M.M.A., Cabon, B., Mitchell, J.E., Lethien, C., Csörnyei, M., Stöhr, A., Iezekiel, S.: Radio- over-fibre transport for the support of wireless broadband services. Journal of Optical Networking 8(2) (February 2009)
2. Kardaras, G., Lanzani, C.: Advanced multimode radio for wireless and broadband communication. In: IEEE European Wireless Technology Conference, pp.132–135 (2009)
3. Strasser, M.: FTTA Fibre-to-The-Antenna - Technology Change in Mobile Communications, HUBER+SUHNER Switzerland Whitepaper,
   http://www.hubersuhner.com
4. Arranz, M.: Head of 2G Product, The Vodafone Commitment on Energy, Nokia World Event (December 2008),
   http://events.nokia.com/nokiaworld08/assets/pdf/
   Miguel_Arranz.pdf
5. Alcatel-Lucent Corporation, Eco-sustainable wireless solutions (2009),
   http://www.alcatel-lucent.com
6. Rigby, L., Boppana, D.: Simplifying Simultaneous Multimode RRH Design" ALTERA Whitepaper (2009),
   http://www.altera.com/literature/wp/
   wp-01097-arria-ii-gx-multimode-rrh.pdf
7. Open Base Station Architecture Initiative (OBSAI) specifications,
   http://www.obsai.com
8. Common Public Radio Interface (CPRI) specifications, http://www.cpri.info

Network Topology Visualization and Monitoring for Multi-hop Wireless Networks

Roberto Riggio[1], Matteo Gerola[1], Antonio Francescon[1], Andrea Zanardi[1],
Tinku Rasheed[1], and François Jan[2]

[1] CREATE-NET, Via Alla Cascata 56/D, 38123, Povo, Trento, Italy
name.surname@create-net.org
[2] France Telecom, R&D Division, 22300, Lannion, France
francois2.jan@orange-ftgroup.com

Abstract. Multi-hop wireless systems represent a viable means for deploying access networks covering medium-size areas with limited investment, making use of commodity hardware and freely available software suites. At the same time, management of such networks represent an overly complex task, due to the joint effect of the time-varying nature of the radio channel, user mobility and the inherently distributed nature of the system. A number of solutions are currently researched, whereby network management functionalities get embedded within the wireless network itself. A common building block of such approaches is represented by a monitoring framework able to bring the relevant network-level information to the decision points. In this paper, we present a distributed network monitoring toolkit, specifically developed for wireless multi-hop networks. The toolkit allows network administrators to monitor the status of the network as well as to plan and execute active measurement campaigns. Information is stored in a distributed network-wide repository and is accessible through a web interface.

Keywords: wireless networks, network management, network monitoring, mesh architecture.

1 Introduction

Wireless Mesh Networks (WMNs) provide many advantages over traditional wireless networks, such as robustness, greater coverage, low up–front costs and ease of deployment. Despite this, several critical issues need to be addressed in order to turn WMN into a commodity [1] solution for Wireless Internet Service Providers (WISP) operated deployments. In particular, for some usage scenarios, dedicated network control and management appliances may prove impractical due to either cost and/or architectural reasons. As a result, in the last few years, a tendency emerged to distribute network management functionalities within the network itself [2,3,4,5,6]. The effective deployment of such solutions requires a scalable signaling channel for gathering network status information and conveying it to the relevant decision points, as well as a controller–less network

I. Tomkos et al. (Eds.): BROADNETS 2010, LNICST 66, pp. 435–449, 2012.

management paradigm where network control and management functionalities are embedded into the network elements themselves (i.e. the access points or mesh routers).

In this paper, we present *OBELIX*, a distributed network monitoring toolkit specifically tailored for infrastructure multi-hop wireless networks, such as IEEE 802.11-based WMNs. The monitoring toolkit is designed to support domain specific knowledge and incorporates appropriate reasoning logic to detect and diagnose faulty network conditions in addition to being capable of performing necessary root cause analysis and autonomic recovery decisions for network administration purposes or for applications. OBELIX enables network administrators to manage network performance, find and solve network problems, and plan for network growth. Its main features are:

- *Adjustable level of pervasiveness.* OBELIX supports different levels of participation in the monitoring efforts. While in traditional network monitoring solutions such as SNMP [7], the function performed by each device is hard–coded at system deployment time, OBELIX exploits a monitoring overlay where each node's participation in the monitoring efforts (i.e. its role) can be dynamically changed at run–time to adapt to changing conditions (e.g., addition of new nodes in the network, nodes becoming unreachable due to faulty links).
- *Interoperability with legacy solutions.* Legacy network management tools are supported through an SNMP interface. The SNMP protocol is used to interact with already deployed SNMP Agents as well as to convey the gathered network state information to an existing SNMP–compatible network management system.
- *Ubiquitous network management.* OBELIX includes an advanced web-based Management Dashboard that allows network administrators to both monitor and manage the network from anywhere using just a web browser. Such Dashboard provides the network administrator with a synthetic representation of the network status in order to enable quick and efficient troubleshooting of critical situations.

The rest of the paper is structured as follows. Section 2 provides an overview of related work and of the state-of-the-art in the field. Section 3 describes the design principles and the implementation choices around which OBELIX has been built. The system architecture is introduced in Sec. 4. The implementation details and the outcomes of an experimental campaign, obtained from a small-scale testbed implementation, are reported in Sec. 5. Finally, Sec. 6 concludes the paper discussing a number of open issues and future extensions.

2   Related Work

A large set of protocols exists to support network and network devices management. Common solutions include SNMP [7], ICMP [8], netconf [9], and capwap [10]. However, most of such tools are designed around centralized architectures meaning that each node participating to the network runs a process which gathers information about the current network state. When a problem is recognized, the running process sends alerts to some management entities. Upon receiving these alerts, the management entities are programmed to react by taking some actions (e.g., operator notification, event logging, system reboot/shutdown, etc.). Management entities can also poll end-stations to check the values of certain variables.

In particular, Single Network Management Protocol (SNMP) represents the most widely used protocol for building monitoring applications [11]. Formally, SNMP is an application layer protocol developed in order to standardize the exchange of management information between network devices. From an SNMP perspective, a network is constituted by a set of managed device (devices which are monitored to gather information on their status), agents (software running on managed devices) and a network management system (software running on managers, i.e., nodes managing the network). The network-level parameters and quantities monitored are termed Managed Object (MO). An example of a MO is the radio channel being used on a given wireless interface. Management information is viewed by SNMP as a collection of Managed Objects, organized as a virtual information repository, called Management Information Base (MIB). Each device participating in an SNMP–managed network maintains a MIB, which is accessed using SNMP. Managers can query the MIB asking for information on a given MO. SNMP uses UDP connections for exchanging data among entities in the monitoring system. While in v2 of the standard, an interface was specified for enabling communication among managers, SNMP is inherently centralized in nature. With OBELIX, we aim at creating a distributed and effective architecture which is SNMP-compatible in order to provide backward compatibility with existing network management systems. In practice, the points at which we will aggregate network information will provide an SNMP–compatible interface, while the processes for gathering and replicating information will not rely on the methods specified in SNMP.

A Distributed Architecture for Monitoring Mobile Networks (DAMON) is introduced in [12]. DAMON relies on agents within the network to actively monitor network behaviour and to send this information to data repositories. DAMON's generic architecture supports the monitoring of any protocol, device, or network parameter. VISUM [13] is a distributed framework for monitoring wireless networks. Data, collected by agents distributed over several host, is gathered at a centralized repository and can be exploited by a visualization tool. In [14], the authors propose a novel monitoring framework capable of dynamically tuning the granularity of the data collection procedures according to some observed events (e.g. threshold crossing). Albeit showing adaptive characteristics from a data gathering perspective, the proposed systems still relies on centralized storage and processing of information. In contrast to the aforementioned works, our approach relies on a fully distributed repository to maintain the global network state and to make it available to all the nodes running network management tasks.

3   System Design

In this section, the three pillars *Adjustable level of pervasiveness*, *Interoperability with legacy solutions*, and *Ubiquitous network management*, upon which OBELIX has been designed are discussed and the implementation choices are introduced.

3.1   Adjustable Level of Pervasiveness

Typical network management solutions, such as SNMP, rely on a centralized architecture, whereby network management tasks are carried out on a per-device basis by the network administrator. Such a solution results in poor spatial reuse of the wireless medium, congestion of routes to the network controller, and excessive load at the repository itself. OBELIX moves away from this highly centralized approach to network management by embedding management functionality (data analysis and aggregation) into the network itself and by distributing the network state information among the nodes participating in the monitoring efforts improving the availability of the managed information without disrupting network services.

OBELIX supports different levels of participation in the monitoring efforts by the nodes in the WMN. Such participation can be conceptually classified into two categories:

- *Information gathering.* Monitoring agents (Taps in the following) running within a mesh router gather the local network state either by sniffing the traffic flow in their neighborhood (passive approach) as well as by performing on-demand/periodic measurements (active approach).
- *Information analysis.* The local network state information gathered by the Taps is periodically sent to a set of management daemons (Sinks in the following) and exploited to maintain a global view of the network.

It is worth pointing out that information gathering and information analysis are to be considered as two separate, yet non-mutually exclusive functionalities. As a matter of fact, any node in the WMN can support a single functionality, both, or none at all. In the latter case, information about the state of a network devices can only by inferred through passive sniffing from neighboring Taps. Network state updates are delivered by the Taps to the Sinks in the form {`key`, `value`} pairs, where:

- the `key` field uniquely identifies the managed object;
- the `value` field holds the actual value of the managed object;

Managed Objects are defined as Global or Local through a configuration file. The former identifies pieces of information that have a network-wide scope, i.e. the geographical position of the network devices, while the latter is used to identify pieces of information that are cluster or node specific, i.e. the number of bytes transmitted over an interface.

3.2   Interoperability with Legacy Solutions

Interoperability with other network management tools will be provided by means of an SNMP-compatible interface. The SNMP protocol will be used to convey management information between Sinks and existing network management systems. An additional HTTP interface will be developed in order to allow the web-based management dashboard to interact with the network Sinks. This section will detail the information exported by network Taps and network Sinks.

3.3   Ubiquitous Network Management

The Web-based OBELIX Management Dashboard allows network administrators to both monitor and manage the network from anywhere using just a web browser. Such Dashboard supports a combined reactive/proactive approach to network monitoring:

- *Reactive.* Aims at detecting a fault only after it occurs by passively studying its effects on the network. In this case, the Tap will send a failure event (e.g. a node leaves the network or is out of order) to its Sink. Such an event will be logged and made available to the network administrator through the Dashboard.
- *Proactive.* Exploits temporal trends of the monitored properties in order to foresee potential failures and isolate fluctuating behaviors. In this case, the Sink receives regular network state updates from its Tap and from neighboring Sink (e.g. high link utilization or low battery level) and take the appropriate actions (e.g. report a possible congestion situation).

4   System Architecture

The building blocks of the OBELIX toolkit and their relationships are sketched in Fig. 1. It consists of three main blocks, the Tap, the Sink, and the Management Dashboard; their detailed description follows. It is worth noticing that, unlike traditional SNMP–based systems, where the NMS continuously polls every managed device, in our architecture, network state updates are transmitted by the Taps to the Sinks periodically and only if required (i.e. if there has been a change in the state of a managed object).

4.1   Tap

The Tap is a software process running in each managed device. A Tap has local knowledge of the network. Such a knowledge is collected and published an the asymmetric group communication system which implements the OBELIX Signaling layer. The local network state is collected using a modular based information gathering back-end. Domain-specific information (e.g. routing tables, link status, etc.) are collected by specialized plugins and presented to the Tap using a protocol agnostic representation. The following plugins are currently supported:

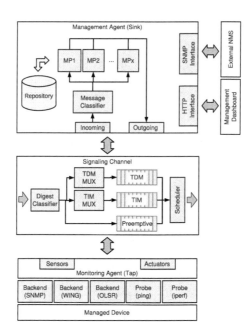

Fig. 1. OBELIX architectural components: Tap, Sink, Signalling Layer, Dashboard, and their interactions

- Routing WING plugin. Use to provided support for the WING routing protocol. WING [15] is a DSR-like routing protocol derived from the Roofnet [16]
  project by the MIT and optimized for network scalability and throughput
  rather than for supporting mobility. Wing extends the original protocol by
  adding support for multiple radio interfaces and for link quality routing using
  either the ETX, the ETT, ot the WCETT metric [17].
- Routing OLSR plugin. The Optimized Link State Routing Protocol (OLSR)
  is a level-3 routing protocol optimized for mobile ad-hoc networks, but can
  also be used on other wireless ad hoc networks.
- Probe Ping/Iperf plugins. Allows network administrators to plan, execute
  and retrieve network measurements campaigns using the Ping/IPerf utility.
  Measurements campaign can be planned for execution at a certain time.
  Results of the campaign are available trough the web interface after the
  campaign has terminated.

4.2   Sink

The Sink is a software process running on a subset of the nodes composing the
WMN. A Sink has global knowledge of the network state, which is stored on
a shared repository. Such a repository is made accessible to the Management
Dashboard through an HTTP interface. At bootstrap, Taps selects one Master
Sink for their normal operations and zero, one or more Slave Sinks to be used if
the Master Sink fails.

The repository is implemented in the form of a distributed database and provides a WMN-wide knowledge base. The data model for the shared repository is reported in Fig. 2 as UML Class Diagram describing the data model. The SQLite database has been chosen to implement the OBELIX data model. The data model can be easily extended in order to gather additional information. As a matter of fact, the actual data model currently used by the OBELIX Monitoring Toolkit is entirely defined in a set of configuration files. New Managed Objects can be defined by the network administrator. In such a case, an helper script which effectively gathers the information from the managed device must be provided.

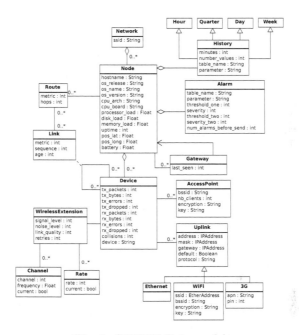

Fig. 2. OBELIX Data model

It is worth noticing that user-defined extensions are not mandatory and can thus be deployed only on a sub-set of the nodes participating the WMN. On the other hand, all nodes in an OBELIX-managed network are required to implement at least the data model reported in Fig. 2.

4.3   Signaling Layer

The OBELIX signaling layer is implemented in the form of a scalable asymmetric publish/subscribe system where messages are differentiated according to their temporal properties. For example, consider a requirement such as tracking the network topology in real-time. If topology information from the network is not delivered for processing in a timely manner, the resulting view of the network can be inaccurate. On the other hand, another requirement could be to monitor the amount of traffic forwarded by a node without any constraints on time. Based on their temporal properties, network state updates generated by the Taps can be classified into three categories:

- *Preemptive Message.* Alarms generated by the monitoring daemons that require immediate forwarding. Examples of Preemptive Messages include notification of a node going off–line, communication links becoming congested or fluctuating.
- *Time Dependent Message (TDM).* Delay sensitive message that can tolerate a fixed transmission delay. Examples of TDM include link state updates, number of users currently associated to a CPE etc. Since such network state updates are typically small in size, they can be aggregated at intermediate hops in order to improve the wireless medium utilization.
- *Time Independent Message (TIM).* Delivered on a best effort fashion only where and when the network bandwidth is not required by other applications. These kind of messages are expected to be larger in size than TDMs (transmission logs, extended link utilization statistics, etc.). With respect to this kind of messages, the monitoring tool is expected to support proper data fragmentation procedures in order to handle TIMs that are larger than the networks maximum transmit unit (MTU). A possible choice is to take direct advantage of the packet fragmentation capabilities already provided by the IP protocol.

In order to control the amount of signaling traffic exchanged over the signaling, OBELIX supports several levels pervasiveness:

- *Non-pervasive.* Collection of the network state is done by a single network element, which implements both Information Gathering and Information Analysis functionalities, while the other nodes in the network implement only Information Gathering functionalities. Such an approach is conceptually equivalent the an SNMP-based network management architecture where a single network element periodically interrogates network devices and revives alarms and events. In this setup administrative tasks are simplified in that all the information are already available at a single point. On the other hand, having a single global repository results in a poor spatial reuse of the wireless medium and introduces a single point of failure in the system.
- *Fully pervasive.* Collection and analysis of the network state is done by every node in the network. Such an approach effectively creates a distributed repository holding the global network state information where every node has a global knowledge of the network. While delivering the highest level of resilience to network failures, this setup is characterized by an high signaling overhead in that network state updates must be circulated among all the node participating in the monitoring efforts.
- *Hybrid.* The degree of pervasiveness of the previous solution can be minimized by limiting the nodes implementing Information Analysis functionalities, i.e. the Sinks, and by grouping the nodes implementing Information

Gathering functionalities, i.e. the Taps, into clusters. In this configuration, each cluster is composed by a variable number of Taps and one Sink, which acts as cluster head.

In the latter scenario, the one supported by default by OBELIX, Sinks have a complete knowledge about the state of the nodes in their cluster, while information about other clusters is limited to Global Managed Objects. Such an architecture allows for several degrees of pervasiveness by simply changing the ratio between the Taps and the Sinks and by tagging Managed Objects as either Global or Local. A typical configuration for a WMN would involve Taps deployed in each node and Sinks deployed only on the network gateways. Likewise, only information such as the geographical position of the devices and their default route to the mesh gateways would be tagged as Global. This is due to the fact that most of the traffic in a WMN flows through a set of pre-determined, non-mobile and fully-capable nodes (the mesh gateways).

4.4 Management Dashboard

The global network state information made available by the Sinks is exploited by the Management Dashboard in order to provide the network administrator with a powerful web-based network management interface. In particular each Sink implements an HTTP interface which can be exploited to send queries and commands to gather the value of a Managed Object or to request the execution of configuration and monitoring actions.

The dashboard is implemented in the form of a web application exploiting AJAX as enabling technology. The rationale behind this choice is to move as much of the computation on the client side as possible, while still using Web-based technologies allowing the access from any host. In fact, common mesh routers are characterized by relatively limited computing power in terms of both processor speed and RAM. On the other hand, clients are typically characterized by powerful processors equipped with adequate memory.

Due to these architectural choices, it is possible to deploy the Management Dashboard on any mesh router in the network as well as on an external machine. In the latter case, the machine hosting the Management Dashboard must have access to the HTTP interface exported by one of the Sinks. Security is handled using the HTTP authentication facilities provided by the web server.

The Dashboard provides the network administrator with a synthetic representation of the network status in order to enable quick and efficient troubleshooting of critical situations. The Dashboard supports the following features:

- *Display topological and geographical information.* A Google Maps-based interface is exploited. If no geographical information is available, a simple graphical representation of the network topology (with randomly placed nodes) is provided. Network administrator(s) can navigate the graphical representation of the network in order to identify critical spots and to gather detailed information about the managed devices.

- *Provide detailed reports of the network's performance.* The dashboard allow the network administrator(s) to sort the collected data by protocol, device, and other factors. Performance trends and network resources utilization pattern trends can be used to identify nodes with intermittent connections that need attention.
- *Raise accurate alarms.* Network administrator(s) are notified when there is a significant network event, such as a node going off-line, a gateway connection failing, etc. These functionalities are implemented within the Sink and are exported using either emails or an RSS feed.
- *Support network profiling.* Network administrator(s) are empowered with a set of tools to run real-time bandwidth and latency test. In this scenario, the Dashboard is expected to act as a remote front-end to traditional network probes such as: iperf, ping, etc. A detailed report of the measurement campaign is made available through the Dashboard after the tests have been completed. Traffic traces pre-processing is performed on the server-side (i.e. where they are collected) in order to lower the network usage.
- *Implement administrative tasks.* The Dashboard allows network administrator(s) to implement administrative tasks. For example, the Dashboard allows to modify the value of configuration parameters, such as the frequency of an hotspot, or to change the role of a node in the monitoring overlay as well as to deploy firmware updates to all the nodes automatically.

5   Evaluation

In this section, we report the outcomes of some experimental tests conducted using a prototypical implementation of OBELIX over a small-scale (15 nodes) wireless mesh network testbed. Our goals for this OBELIX-monitored mesh deployment were twofold. On the one hand we wanted to validate the design and implementation of the toolkit in a realistic environment by tracking the topology of the network in real-time. On the other hand we wanted to perform a set of measurements campaigns using the probing facilities provided by the toolkit itself.

5.1   Implementation Details

The OBELIX distributed monitoring toolkit is implemented in Python, a lightweight interpreted programming language. Signaling traffic is exchanged over an asymmetric scalable group communication system that allows the different entities involved in the monitoring efforts to communicate with one another supporting the entire monitoring life-cycle. Within a single OBELIX–monitored node, up to three distinct software processes can be active at any given time: the *sink*, the *tap*, and the *communication channel*. The latter effectively implements the message scheduling and processing on an hop-by-hop basis.

All nodes in the OBELIX overlay run the *communication channel* process. Nodes that are also publishers and subscribers of monitoring information will also run the *tap* and the *sink* processes, respectively. Albeit not exploited during our measurement campaign, a node can implement only data dissemination functionalities by running just the *communication channel* process. Standard TCP and UDP sockets are used to enable communications among processes. Such a feature may prove useful in a scenario where we are not interested in information coming from every device, yet we want to take advantage of their forwarding capabilities. Internet sockets are used to enable inter–process communications.

Messages being dispatched by the *communication channel* are composed by a header and a body. The header is used to indicate how and where a message should be delivered and the body provides information and commands to the destination entity. The header includes, among the other information, source and destination address, together with an indication of the type of message it carries (necessary for ensuring appropriate processing at the Sinks). Our goals for this Obelix-monitored WMN deployment were twofold. On the one hand we wanted to validate the design and the implementation of the toolkit in a realistic environment by tracking the topology of the network in real-time and by performing a set of measurements campaigns using the probing facilities provided by the toolkit itself.

5.2   Experimental Settings and Configuration

The software prototype has been experimentally evaluated over a real–world IEEE 802.11–based mesh testbed built using off–the–shelf components and consisting of 15 multi–radio mesh routers deployed across three floors of a typical office building. Mesh routers are built around three different hardware platforms, namely the PCEngines ALIX 2C2 (500MHz x86 CPU, 256MB of RAM) processor board, the PCEngines WRAP 1E (233MHz x86 CPU, 128MB of RAM) processor board and the Gateworks Cambria GW2358-4 (667MHz ARM CPU, 128MB of RAM). Each node is equipped with two IEEE 802.11a/b/g wireless interfaces (Atheros chipset) with RTC/CTS disabled. Routers employ the Open-WRT operating system, a Linux distribution specifically tailored to embedded devices. Routing is implemented using the Click modular router [18].

5.3   Results

In the scenario accounted in the paper, the OBELIX Dashboard is hosted by the nodes acting as mesh gateways. The network administrator can then connect to any of them from using a regular web browser in order to monitor the status of the network and/or to perform administrative tasks.

Figure 3 shows the Home Page of the Obelix Dashboard. As it can be seen, the interface is partitioned into three panes. The left pane lists the nodes currently available in the network indicating whenever the node is a mesh gateway (double-arrow marker) or a mesh router (round marker). Sink (S) and Tap (T) status is also indicated. The central pane is completely dedicated to the Google Map used to display the real-time network topology. Finally the right pane is used to display contextual information relative to the currently selected node. The interface is highly interactive, as for example, selecting one node on the left pane with a single click will center the map on the node and will display the local information about the same node on the right pane (no additional traffic is generated on the network for this operation). On the other hand, a double click on a node's marker will load both the local and the global information thus generating additional traffic over the network.

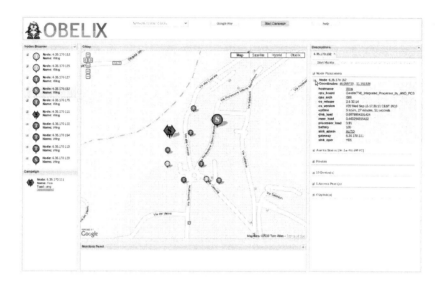

Fig. 3. The OBELIX Dashboard: the three panes home page. The dashboard is hosted by the mesh gateways and is accessible using any recent web browser.

The Dashboard can also be used in order to analyse the historical trends for any OBELIX-monitored network object (i.e. transmitted or received packets, signal-to-noise ratio, CPU or memory load, etc) in a graphical form. Figure 4 shows the pop-up through which the network administrator can select the attributes to be visualized. It is worth noticing that these parameter are constantly monitored by each Sink in an OBELIX-monitored network. The sampling period and the number of samples to be stored and user-configurable parameters. For example, in the default configuration the CPU load is sampled every minute and the last 60 samples are stored by each Sink. On top of this statistic, both the hourly and the daily averages are computed and, respectively, the last 24 and 30 samples are stored by each Sink.

OBELIX allows the network administrator to plan and execute network wide measurement campaigns using the embedded network probing facilities. The current version of OBELIX supports two types of network probes: *ping* and *iperf*. The former tool (*ping*) allows the user to performs simple connectivity and round–trip–time measurements campaigns, while the latter tool (*iperf*) allows the user to perform more complex tests involving throughput, jitter and exploiting either UDP or TCP as transport technology.

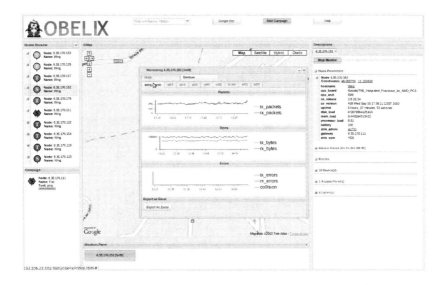

Fig. 4. The OBELIX Dashboard: monitoring historical trends. This figure reports the amount of traffic that traversed the mesh interface in the last hour. The graphs are update in real–time.

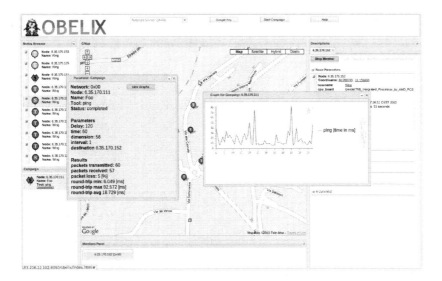

Fig. 5. The OBELIX Dashboard: planning and executing network wide measurement campaigns. This figure shows the results of a campaign exploting the *ping* tool. Results can be exported in CSV format for further processing.

6   Outlook and Future Work

In this paper, we have introduced a distributed network monitoring toolkit specifically tailored for infrastructure multi-hop wireless networks, such as IEEE 802.11-based Wireless Mesh Networks. Design choices have been made to accommodate the peculiarities of wireless multi-hop networks, in terms of adaptivity, robustness and efficiency requirements. The proposed framework has been prototyped and experimentally evaluated on a 15–nodes wireless mesh network.

As future research directions we plan to exploit concepts and techniques borrowed from the information–centric networking domain in order to make the entire monitoring framework address-agnostic, as well as to use cross–layer techniques in order to handle the replication of global monitoring information across multiple sinks leveraging knowledge on the underlying wireless technology employed.

References

1. Bruno, R., Conti, M., Gregori, E.: Mesh Networks: Commodity Multihop Ad Hoc Networks. IEEE Communications Magazine 43(3), 123–131 (2005)
2. Pavlou, G.: On the evolution of management approaches, framework and protocols: A historical perspective. Journal of Network and Systems Management 15, 425–445 (2007)
3. Mortier, R., Kiciman, E.: Autonomic network management: Some pragmatic considerations. In: Proc. of ACM SIGCOMMM, Pisa, Italy (2006)
4. Dobson, S., Denazis, S.G., Fernández, A., Gaïti, D., Gelenbe, E., Massacci, F., Nixon, P., Saffre, F., Schmidt, N., Zambonelli, F.: A survey of autonomic communications. ACM Trans. Auton. Adapt. Systems 1(2), 223–259 (2006)
5. de Souza, J.N., Strassner, J.: Self-organization and self-management in communications as applied to autonomic networks. Computer Communications 31(13), 2935–2936 (2008)
6. Gonzalez Prieto, A., Dudkowski, D., Meirosu, C., Mingardi, C., Nunzi, G., Brunner, M., Stadler, R.: Decentralized in-network management for the Future Internet. In: Proc. of IEEE ICC – Communications Workshops, Dresden, Germany, pp. 1–5 (2009)
7. Stallings, W.: Snmp and snmpv2: the infrastructure for network management. IEEE Communications Magazine 36(3), 37–43 (1998)
8. Postel, J.: Internet control message protocol, IETF RFC 0792 (September 1981), http://www.ietf.org/rfc/rfc0792.txt
9. Enns, R.: Netconf configuration protocol, IETF RFC 4741 (December 2006), http://www.ietf.org/rfc/rfc4741.txt
10. Montemurro, M., Stanley, D.: Control And Provisioning of Wireless Access Points (CAPWAP), IETF RFC 5415 (March 2009), http://www.ietf.org/rfc/rfc5415.txt
11. Case, J., Fedor, M., Schoffstall, M., Davin, J.: A simple network management protocol, IETF RFC 1157 (May 1990), http://www.ietf.org/rfc/rfc1157.txt
12. Ramachandran, K., Belding-Royer, E.M., Almeroth, K.C.: DAMON: A distributed architecture for monitoring multi-hop mobile networks. In: Proc. of IEEE SECON, Santa Clara, California, USA (2004)

13. Ho, C.C., Ramachandran, K.N., Almeroth, K.C., Belding-Royer, E.M.: A scalable framework for wireless network monitoring. In: Proc. of WMASH, Philadelphia, Pennsylvania, USA (2004)
14. Raghavendra, R., Acharya, P., Belding, E., Almeroth, K.: Antler: A multi-tiered approach to automated wireless network management. In: IEEE INFOCOM Workshops, Phoenix, AZ, USA (2008)
15. Granelli, F., Riggio, R., Rasheed, T., Miorandi, D.: WING/WORLD: An Open Experimental Toolkit for the Design and Deployment of IEEE 802.11-Based Wireless Mesh Networks Testbeds. Eurasip Journal on Wireless Communications and Networking 2010 (2010)
16. Bicket, J., Aguayo, D., Biswas, S., Morris, R.: Architecture and Evaluation of an Unplanned 802.11b Mesh Network. In: Proc. of ACM MOBICOM, Cologne, Germany (2005)
17. Draves, R., Padhye, J., Zill, B.: Comparison of Routing Metrics for Static Multi-Hop Wireless Networks. In: Proc. of ACM SIGCOMM, Portland, Oregon, USA (2004)
18. Kohler, E., Morris, R., Chen, B., Jannotti, J., Kaashoek, M.F.: The Click modular router. ACM Transaction on Computer System 18(3), 263–297 (2000)

Handover Performance Evaluation
in WiMAX Mobility Scenarios

Mihai Constantinescu and Eugen Borcoci

University Politehnica of Bucharest, Romania
{mihai.constantinescu,eugen.borcoci}@elcom.pub.ro

Abstract. In the context of mobility management and cross-layer design and optimization for multimode wireless access networks, the paper presents the simulation campaign done to construct a multidimensional decision space for WiMAX parameters, in order to identify the sets of configuration parameters with major impact into the handover process for the IEEE 802.16e mobile station. Simulation results could then be used by cross-layer optimization algorithms to increase the handover performance, from the application point of view.

Keywords: WiMAX, hard handover, mobility management, cross-layer optimization.

1 Introduction

The globalization of culture and economy are mixing and opening new standpoints emphasizing that knowledge is a real strength in the competitive world. Concepts such as connectivity, mobility and Quality of service have now rooted in the routine. Mobility expands connectivity and allows service continuity. The process of handover, commonly described as transfer of a data session or an ongoing call from one network channel to another, is essential to mobility and started as a way to overcome the cell range limitations and balance the number of users inside the same area.

IEEE 802.16/WiMAX family of standards and specifications introduces the mobility as an important feature to increase the usability of the WiMAX technology in the context of Broadband Wireless Access (BWA). The IEEE 802.16d [1] is defined for fixed terminals, while IEEE 802.16e [2] adds the mobility and power management support. Additionally, the WiMAX Forum [3] [4] extends the framework, by defining the reference models and procedures, including the IEEE 802.16 technology in a complete end to end architectures. WiMAX Forum reference model defines three tiers: the first is the wireless interface – IEEE 802.16 between the Subscriber fixed or Mobile Stations SS/MS and Base Station (BS); the second is the Access Services Network (wireline or wireless - implemented) linking several Base Stations (BS) to one or several ASN Gateways (ASN-GW) – the latter having a double functional role both in the data and control plane; the third part is Connectivity Services Network (Home or visited one). On this architecture, several types of mobility can been encountered: micro-mobility (solved at Layer two - L2) ,

I. Tomkos et al. (Eds.): BROADNETS 2010, LNICST 66, pp. 450–459, 2012.

intra or inter BS, but preserving the same anchor (in ASN-GW) and macro-mobility (inter-ASN or Inter-CSN). The latter is solved by cooperation between L2 mobility and Mobile IPv4/v6 [3] [4]. The basic scope of the IEEE 802.16 is the L2 mobility.

The standard IEEE 802.16e [2] defines three L2 HO types: Hard Handover (HHO), Fast Base Station Switching (FBSS) and Macro Diversity handover (MDHO). The basic (mandatory) one is the HHO, where the MS is logically linked to a single (serving) BS at each time instance. When the MS is moving it can switch to another BS by performing a „break before make" sequence of actions, i.e., it breaks the connection with the serving BS and then reconnects to a new (target) BS by performing all phases necessary phases for a network entry. While HHO involves a gap in the connection (and this will be reflected in a decrease of the corresponding throughput at application level), this is the most simple in terms and implementation and largely used in practice. The HO is decided at MS or network level and is performed following scanning actions [2]; it is executed after the signal strength from neighbor's cell exceeds with a given amount the signal level from the current cell.

While FBSS and MDHO are more performant (especially for seamless HO needs) they are more complex and costly. However, optimizing the HHO performance raises difficult problems of very complex interactions of a large set of parameters for 802.16e entities (at L1, L2 layers). Therefore analytical model cannot be defined and solved, but only very simplified ones. On the other side, the intelligence of the lower PHY and MAC layer of 802.16 creates the possibility of cross-layer optimization, usable to enhance HHO performance. Simulations based on realistic complex models can help.

SMART-Net Project. The work on mobility presented in this paper has been perform within a European research project SMART-Net (SMART-antenna multimode wireless mesh Network) having among its objectives studies and experimentations on hybrid mesh networks, including mobility issues. SMART-Net project is developing a heterogeneous access network solution incorporating multi-radio access technologies (RAT) and smart antennas to offer advanced wireless broadband solutions, [5] and [6]. This paper is focused on defining a a multidimensional decision space based on major WiMAX HHO parameters and their effects on HHO performance. A complex HHO-oriented simulation models are defined, with parameters modified step by step, in order to capture the exact behavior of the system and to define and to quantify the effect of each parameter modification to the overall performance. Analyzed parameters are related to PHY and MAC, together with environment parameters (distance, mobile speed, network topology). The effects on HHO performance are measured both at L2 level and at application level (throughput, delay, etc.). Simulation results could then be used to construct a database to guide some cross-layer optimization algorithms deciding upon HO trigger.

The paper is organized as follows: the Section 1 presents some related work. The Section 2 defines the HHO mobility issues to be studied in the paper. The Section 3 describes the simulation models, with comparative results of simulation analyzed on Section 4. Section 5 outlines the utilization of the simulation results toward mobility management and cross-layer optimization. Conclusion, open issues and future work are shortly outlined in the Section 6.

2   Related Work

Zhong et al. proposed a scheme for reducing unnecessary association procedure by evaluating mobile locations. That scheme offers application QoS requirements and can reduce the total handover latency [8].

A new downlink handover priority scheduling algorithm for different scheduling services is proposed in [8], aiming to provide lossless handovers and QoS.

A pre-coordination mechanism (PCM) for supporting fast handover in WiMAX networks is presented in [9]. This goal is achieved by measuring the distance between the BS and the MSS and predicting the time of handover occurs, and thus pre-allocating available resources for handover usages.

A MAC Layer solution to guarantee the demanded bandwidth and supporting a higher possible throughput between two WiMAX end points during the handover is described in [10], along with a PHY and MAC layers scheme to maintain the required communication channel quality for video streams during handover.

Barolli et al. presented a new handover system based on fuzzy logic [11]. That system uses 3 parameters for handoff decision: the change of signal strength of the present Base Station (BS), signal strength from the neighbor BS, and the distance between Mobile Station (MS) and BS.

3   IEEE 802.16 Handover Mobility Issues in Smart-Net and Cross-Layer Optimization

The simulations goal was to study in a large set of simulations the influence of different PHY and MAC parameters together with external parameters (distance, mobile speed) on application throughput, HO delay, and serving BS. The HO studied is HHO MS initiated. This is the simplest one, in terms of implementation, and actually is the only one defined in the IEEE 802.16 standard as mandatory for equipments. Two types of mobility: micro/macro, horizontal/vertical were considered, with HHO using MIPv4 and ASN-Anchored Mobility, in order to fulfill the SMART-Net project objectives related to WiMAX mobility.

A moving MSs may get current knowledge about its environment, by its scanning activity and through dialogue with the serving BS. If the MS "sees" in its geographical neighborhood several other BSs (apart from the serving BS) then it should take the decision if, when and to which new BS to perform the HO. The most simple decision is to perform HO whenever the SNR seen from other BSs is better than that of the serving BS. However each HHO action can determine a relative longer - in time - loss of connectivity (seconds), during HHO. A cross-layer optimization approach may improve the performance related to HO actions.

The results obtained after running simulations with a large combination of parameters can be organized in a database and then used in a   cross-layer optimization (PHY-MAC) approach, to offer guiding data to algorithms/policies for MS to decide when to perform or not. This is applicable when the MS is currently located in an environment where based on scanning activity it "sees", several BSs (different from the serving BS) as possible targets for HO, but it still has enough SNR seen from the serving BS, in order to sustain the current service flows. Then the MS can apply one of the following policies:

- Delay the HHO decision until the SNR seen from the serving BS is too low for sustaining its throughput of current flows, despite that some other BSs offer better SNR in comparison with the serving BS. Such actions can reduce the number of unnecessary HOs and have two benefices: first, avoid real-time flows interruptions (provoked by HHO) and increase the mean throughput.

- Apply a hysteresis threshold. This is used to select BSs as that are suitable candidates for the target BS in a HO. When finding the candidate BSs, the MS may compute the difference between the CINR(or SNR) of the serving BS and the CINR (or SNR) of the potential target BS .The value of this attribute (Multitarget Hysteresis threshold) specifies the minimum amount by which the CINR/SNR of potential target BS must exceed that of the serving BS. The value of this attribute must be less than the value of the Handover Threshold Hysteresis that triggers the HO.

- Use a SMART-Net antenna in directional mode instead of omnidirectional mode. Replacing an Omni-directional antenna by a smart one is impacting on many network mechanisms. The antenna systems need to be appropriately controlled by the MAC layer based on requests issued from higher layers of the stack. Such control is required for pointing in the right direction at the right time according to scheduling, routing and other mechanisms. However, such mechanisms should use optimal sets of WiMAX parameters, as determined from the multidimensional decision space, previous created using complex simulations. These mechanisms are not treated in the paper, being the scope of the next phases of SMART-Net project [5][6].

4   Simulation Models

The simulation was performed with OPNET v14.5 and v.16 [12]. Multiple network topologies were used: linear and random round trajectory, omnidirectional and 3 sectors BS antennas.

Basic Scenario Description (Linear Topology and Linear Trajectory, Macro-Mobility). The basic configuration contains a network composed of six BSs. The scenario uses MIPv4 as method to solve inter-BS mobility (Fig.1). The BS0 plays additionally the role of Home Agent (HA) and the other BSs the roles of Foreign Agents.

The MS has a linear trajectory along the above 6 BSs, moving from BS0 towards BS5, with constant but different speeds (5, 10, 15, 20, 25 m/s). The six BSs use the same frequency resource, thus some overlapping of cells and interference exists. The application flow is supposed to a 64kb/s UGS like flow – generated by an application server and flowing in download direction, from the server to a subscriber MS.

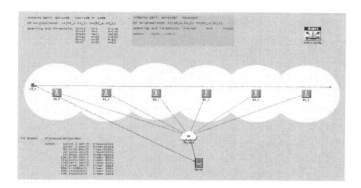

Fig. 1. Basic linear topology in IEEE 802.16 simulation scenarios

While moving the MS performs (depending on conditions and preconfigured settings) multiple HOs among BSs. The main parameter of interest for the application is the throughput variation (gaps in the real time flow) and mean values. These should be optimized by proper configuration of the MS behavior.

Heterogeneous Topology and Random Trajectory. In this scenario, the MS has a pseudo round random trajectory along 6 BSs located in a heterogeneous way. (Fig.2).

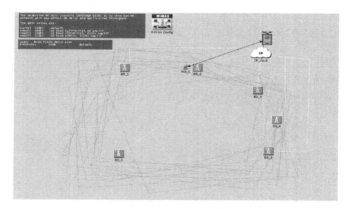

Fig. 2. Random topology in IEEE 802.16 simulation scenarios

The application flow is still a 64kb streaming download from an application server. The MS has two different speed sets: low speed - 1, 2, 3, 4, 5m/s (3.6, 7.2, 10.8, 14.4, 18km/h) and high speed - 10, 20, 30, 40 50m/s (36, 72, 108, 144, 180km/h). The MS antenna gain value has been selected as 14dBi, and for the BS antenna gain was 15dBi.

MIP Mobility with 3 Sectors BS. A set of simulations with sectored antenna on BS was performed, in order to study the combined effects of different parameters, (antenna gain, channel type, hysteresis threshold, multi-target hysteresis threshold, Tx power for BS and MS, etc.) on mobility performance, in comparison with the results from heterogeneous topology and random walk scenarios.

Network topology and configuration shown in Fig. 3, consists from: 3 BS with 3 sectors antenna ; 1 MS with omni-directional antenna; MS antenna gain: -1dBi (isotropic) – scenarios 01,02, 03 and 04; 16dBi (omni-directional) – scenarios 05, 06, 07 and 08. MIP Home Agent configured on BS_A; 128Kbps bidirectional voice flux configured between MS and Voice server; Multipath –vehicular; Pathloss: vehicular type A; Scanning threshold = 1dB; HO threshold hysteresis/Multi-target HO threshold range: 0dB/0dB – scenario 01 and 05; 5dB/0dB – scenario 02 and 06; 10dB/5dB – scenario 03 and 07; 15dB/5dB – scenario 04 and 08.

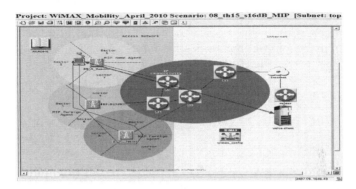

Fig. 3. MIP Mobility_BS 3 sectors topology in IEEE 802.16 simulation scenarios

ASN Anchored Mobility Scenarios-3 Sectors BS. The simulation scenario has the same network topology as MIP- 3 sectors BS scenario, the difference consists in the replacement of MIP with an ASN Gateway and in the configuration of 3 bidirectional tunnels, each of them connected one BS to the ASN-GW (Fig. 4).

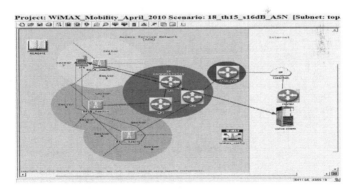

Fig. 4. ASN Anchored Mobility_BS 3 sectors topology in IEEE 802.16 simulation scenarios

The main configuration parameters are: 3 BS with 3 sectors antenna ; 1 MS with omni-directional antenna; MS antenna gain: -1 dBi (isotropic) – scenarios 11,12, 13 and 14; 16 dBi (smart antenna, unidirectional) – scenarios 15, 16, 17 and 18; ASN_GW tunnel configured on BS_A, BS_B and BS_C; 128 Kbps bidirectional voice flux configured between MS and Voice server; Multipath –vehicular; Pathloss: vehicular type A; Scanning threshold = 1dB; HO threshold hysteresis/Multi-target HO threshold range: 0dB/0dB – scenario 11 and 15; 5dB/0dB – scenario 12 and 16; 10dB/5dB – scenario 13 and 17; 15dB/5dB – scenario 14 and 18.

5   Comparative Simulation Results

This section presents samples of a large set of simulation sessions where several parameters are varied (MS speed, scanning threshold, neighborhood components, BS or MS antenna gain, scanning interleaving parameters, type of modulation/coding, etc. The purpose is as declared to observe what parameters and how much can influence the performance in HHO cases.

Mobile IP and ASN anchored mobility effects on Application Throughput, MS antenna gain -1 dB and 16 dB are presented in comparative mode (Fig. 5).

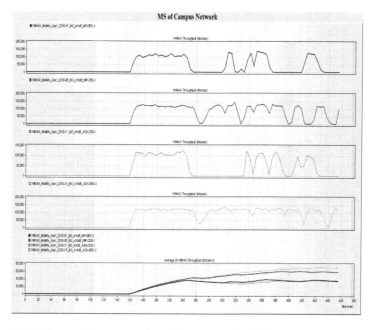

Fig. 5. Comparative average throughputs, scenarios 01-05-11-15, ASN/MIP

As expected, ASN anchored mobility provide a better throughput and lesser gaps with respect to Mobile IP. Clearly better results are obtained for antenna gain 16 dB toward -1 dB.

Fig. 6 and Fig. 7 show the effects of BS power threshold on throughput, for ASN, respectively MIP scenarios.

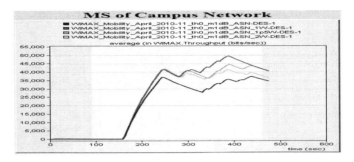

Fig. 6. Effects of BS power threshold (0.5-2W) on throughput, ASN_BS 3sectors

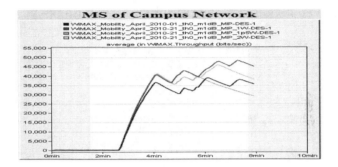

Fig. 7. Effects of BS power threshold (0.5-2W) on throughput, MIP_BS 3sectors

The power increase produces a non-monotonic effect on the HO performance and consequently on averaged throughput measured at application level. It is seen that there is an optimum of power at BS which is P= 1W, while for 0.5, 1.5, 2W the results are worse. The decrease in throughput at higher TX power is due to higher interference produced in the regions crossed by the MS (see the trajectory). An important conclusion is that one should correlate the TX power with the antenna gain and geographical positions in order to get good results. Another important result is that the effect is the same (qualitatively) for ASN mobility case and for MIP mobility case.

A comparison between ASN and MIP related to combined BS power and MS antenna gain effects is presented in Fig. 8.

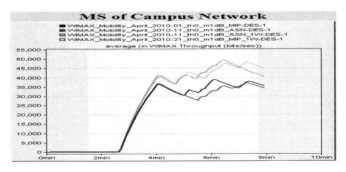

Fig. 8. Comparison ASN_MIP 0.5-1W, MS antenna gain -1dB_16dB - _BS 3sectors

The graphics clearly show that the TX appropriate power value adjustment is important (the average throughput for Ptx=0.5 W is only 60% of that obtained with Ptx= 1W).

An important result is that the MS antenna gain has a more dominant influence than BS power, so optimal results could be achieved using a smart antenna on MS, instead of increasing the BS power.

The temporal throughput and average throughput diagrams show a significant improvement both for MIP and ASN mobility cases while is a second order factor. Also, the ASN anchored mobility has a better result than MIP, as expected, due faster HO.

6   Conclusions on WiMAX Mobility Simulations

The extensive experiments described above and performed on various configurations for studying the mobility in IEEE 802.16/WiMAX mobility can be summarized in some conclusions as below:

- Micro-mobility (ASN-GW anchored) is clearly to be preferred versus micro plus macro-mobility (MIP) in terms of handover performance ; much faster handover can be obtained in the first case;
- A large set of parameters can influence the HO performance (topology, relative geographical distances Tx Power of BS and MS, MS trajectory, MS speed, interference, types of antennas (omni-directional, sectored, directional) antenna gain, scanning threshold, hysteresis threshold, etc. These makes the problem of optimizing the HO a multi-criteria problem and it is non-convex one; therefore local and context dependent can be only done;
- Antenna gain is a primary factor to influence the HO performance;
- Tx Power is a secondary factor influencing the HO performance;
- Adjusting the scanning threshold by cross layer optimization can reduce the HO delays;
- Combined adjustment of hysteresis threshold and scanning threshold can produce a better performance.

7   Conclusion and Future Work

This paper presents the simulation campaign done to identify the sets of configuration parameters in the IEEE 802.16e mobile station, in order to help the cross-layer optimization decision-taking algorithms, applied during scanning and hard handover activities. Given the limited space of the paper, we present only a few simulation result examples (taken out from a large set of simulations performed), in order to highlight the cases when the related parameters have a major influence to the HO performance. Future work will be done to study how these parameters could be used by cross-layer mechanisms to allow a coordination of smart antenna beam selection with the network topology [13], which, together with some signaling protocols on applications layers, will provide a seamless HO from the application point of view. A cross-layer mechanism for seamless HO for multimedia applications was proposed in [14], and further study for network topology awareness on MS level is under progress.

References

1. IEEE Standard for Local and metropolitan area networks, Part 16: Air Interface for Fixed Broadband Wireless Access Systems, IEEE Standard 802.16-2004 (2004)
2. Air Interface for Fixed and Mobile Broadband Wireless Access Systems: Amendment 2: Physical and Medium Access Control Layers for Combined Fixed and Mobile Operation in Licensed Bands, Standard IEEE P802.16e-2005 (2006)
3. WiMAX Forum, WiMAX End-to-End Network Systems Architecture – Stage 3: Detailed Protocols and Procedures (August 2006)
4. WiMAX Forum NWG, WiMAX Forum Network Architecture, Stage 2: Architecture Tenets, Reference Model and Reference Points, Release 1.0.0, March 28 (2007)
5. Wendt, S., Kharrat-Kammoun, F., Borcoci, E., Selva, B., Tonnerre, A., Hamadani, E.: D2.1 – Requirements and Specifications of SMART-Net Target Scenarios, ICT European FP 7 SMART-Net project, February 24 (2010), https://www.ict-smartnet.eu
6. Wendt, S., Kharrat-Kammoun, F., Borcoci, E., Cacoveanu, R., Lupu, R., Hayes, D.: ID2.4b – Network Architecture and System Specification, ICT European FP 7 SMART-Net project, internal WP2 deliverable, February 24 (2010), https://www.ict-smartnet.eu
7. Zhong, L., Liu, F., Wang, X., Ji, Y.: Fast Handover Scheme Based on Mobile Locations for IEEE 802.16e Networks. Wireless Communications, 1757–1760 (2007)
8. Fehri, H., Chitizadeh, J., Yaghmaee, M.H.: A Novel Downlink Handover Priority Scheduling Algorithm for Providing Seamless Mobility and QoS in IEEE802.16e BWA System. Communications and Mobile Computing, 227–231 (2009)
9. Chen, J., Wang, C., Lee, J.: Pre-Coordination Mechanism for Fast Handover in WiMAX Networks. In: The 2nd International Conference on Wireless Broadband and Ultra Wideband Communications (AusWireless 2007), p. 15 (2007)
10. Jerjees, Z., Al-Raweshidy, H.: Handover Optimization for Video Applications in WiMAX. Next Generation Mobile Applications, Services and Technologies, 189–196 (2009)
11. Barolli, L., Xhafa, F., Durresi, A., Koyama, A.: A Fuzzy-Based Handover System for Avoiding Ping-Pong Effect in Wireless Cellular Networks. In: Parallel Processing - Workshops, pp. 135–142 (2008)
12. OPNET Technologies, February 24 (2010), http://www.opnet.com
13. Wendt, S., Hamadani, E., Fazel, S., Mostafavi, M., Borcoci, E., Cacoveanu, R., Constantinescu, M., Enescu, A., Ciochina, S., Baraev, A., Rashid, T., Hayes, D., Kharrat-Kammoun, F., Selva, B., Tonnerre, A., Hamadani, E.: D4.3b - Performance Analysis of SMART-Net protocols and functionalities ICT European FP 7 SMART-Net project, July 24 (2010), https://www.ict-smartnet.eu
14. Constantinescu, M., Borcoci, E.: A SIP-Based Cross-Layer Optimization for WiMAX Hard Handover. In: International Conference Communications 2010, Bucharest, Romania, June 10-12 (2010)

RAT Selection Optimization in Heterogeneous Wireless Networks

Angelos Rouskas[1], Pavlos Kosmides[2],
Anastassios Kikilis[3], and Miltiades Anagnostou[2]

[1] Department of Digital Systems, University of Piraeus,
Karaoli kai Dimitriou Str. 80, 18534 Piraeus, Greece
`arouskas@unipi.gr`
[2] School of Electrical and Computer Engineering, National Technical University of Athens,
Heroon Polytechneiou Str. 9, 15773 Zografou, Athens, Greece
`{pkosmidi,miltos}@central.ntua.gr`
[3] Department of Information and Communication Systems Engineering,
University of the Aegean, 83200 Karlovassi, Samos, Greece
`akikilis@aegean.gr`

Abstract. While wireless access networks are rapidly evolving, constantly increasing both in coverage and offered bandwidth, the vision for Next Generation Wireless Networks (NGWNs) encompasses a core network incorporating various Radio Access Technologies (RATs) in a unified and seamless manner. In such an environment, providers with multi-RAT technologies will aim at the maximization of the satisfaction of their subscribers, while attempting to avoid overloading their subsystems. In this paper we deal with the network selection problem in a multi-RAT environment where users are equipped with multimode terminals. We introduce a utility-based optimization function and formulate the problem of allocating user terminals to RATs as an optimization problem under demand and capacity constraints. This problem is recognized as NP-hard and we propose an optimal Branch and Bound (BB) algorithm, as well as a greedy heuristic which exploits a metric that measures the utility gained versus the resource spent for each allocation. BB manages to significantly reduce the search procedure, while greedy produces optimal allocation results similar to BB but with very low computational cost.

Keywords: Next Generation Wireless Networks, network selection, optimization, Branch and Bound.

1 Introduction

Cellular networks have developed significantly in the past decade from voice-mainly 2G systems to voice and data 3G networks, mainly suitable for high coverage but with relatively low to higher bandwidth. On the other hand, Wireless LAN technology has emerged as an omnipresent technology, offering very high bandwidth compared to

I. Tomkos et al. (Eds.): BROADNETS 2010, LNICST 66, pp. 460–472, 2012.

cellular networks but significantly lower coverage. Apart from the aforementioned technologies, other wireless systems have also emerged, such as 802.16 [1], DVB and HSPA [2] [3].

NGWNs will be characterized by even higher bandwidth, e.g. LTE [4], along with the coexistence of various RATs. 3GPP has already developed a series of documents to deal with the 3G-WLAN coexistence, while the IEEE 1900.4 standard [5] describes the architecture and protocols for distributed decision making to optimize radio resource usage in heterogeneous wireless networks. In a multi-RAT environment, various issues are about to arise mainly due to such coexistence. According to the concept of being Always Best Connected (ABC) [6], the notion of "Best" can be represented by the satisfaction a user gains by using the network. In ABC networks, user satisfaction will become an important variable to successful network operation, since technological and market advancements will make it much easier for a user to migrate from one RAT to another within a single or multiple cooperating providers even on session level basis.

In this paper we examine the network selection problem, which deals with the assignment of each terminal to the most suitable RAT and is similar to well-known NP-hard problems, such as the Knapsack and the Generalized Assignment Problems [7]. We follow the approach in [8] and formulate it as an optimization problem which attempts to maximize a utility-based objective function under requirement and capacity constraints. We develop a Branch and Bound (BB) algorithm and a Greedy heuristic which exploits the special characteristics of the problem. It turns out that the Greedy heuristic behaves quite well compared to the BB under various traffic loads with significant computational savings.

The rest of this paper is organized as follows. In the next section we illustrate some related works. In Section 3, we briefly outline the system model of our study and formulate the optimization problem of access selection in multi-RAT environments. In Sections 4 and 5 we present the BB and the Greedy algorithms, while in Section 6 we present our simulation results. The paper is concluded in Section 7.

2   Related Work

There has been numerous works that deal with the Network Selection problem in different ways. For example, in [9] users are assigned to subsystems, in order to minimize blocking probability and at the same time maximize the system capacity, while the formulation is done according to the Online Bin-Packing Problem. In a similar context, the authors in [10] study resource allocation in the context of ABC using the Knapsack Problem formulation. The overall goal is to maximize the users' utility, while taking their preferences and satisfaction into account, through a quality-to-utility mapping.

A thorough study on the utility theory to define an appropriate decision mechanism in the frame of the access network selection was made by the authors in [11] who proposed new single-criterion and multi-criteria utility forms to best capture the user satisfaction and sensitivity facing up to a bundle of access network characteristics. In [12], the authors point out the need of the existence of a Common Radio Resource

Management (CRRM) as a fundamental part of the upcoming next generation wireless systems. They formulate the problem as a Generalized Access Selection Problem (GASP) and expose the optimization criteria that define the solution. They also formulate a Strict version of the Access Selection Problem (SASP) and in order to obtain the solution they use a heuristic strategy based on a Genetic Algorithm (GA).

In [13], users' allocation is compared to a competition among group of users in different service areas to share the limited amount of bandwidth in the available wireless access networks. Eventually the problem is formulated as a dynamic evolutionary game where the evolutionary equilibrium is considered to be the solution to this game. Finally, in [14] the authors cast the problem as a non-cooperative game where users and access networks act selfishly according to their objectives while in [15] bandwidth allocation and admission control algorithms are presented based on the bankruptcy game.

3   System Model and Problem Formulation

A representation of the entities involved in the scope of this paper is depicted in Fig. 1. We assume that there is a specific server responsible for collecting all necessary measurements and reaching the required decisions, such as the CRRM entity described in [12]. Upon arrival, the users' requests are forwarded to the CRRM whose optimization module is responsible for assigning each user to an available RAT, or even allocating different portions of its requested rate to various RATs.

Although the case of multiple providers can be formulated accordingly, we assume one provider offering network services, through a set of N RATs. Users arrive dynamically and are allocated resources from some RAT for a limited period of time, and then depart, releasing the occupied resources from that RAT. We denote the currently available data rate capacity of RAT j as C_j, $j = 1,...,N$. We assume that each user i declares upon arrival its data rate requirements R_{Di}, along with $S_i \subset \{1,...,N\}$, the preferable set of RATs, mainly to exclude some of the available RATs. Without loss of generality we assume that $S_i = \{1,...,N\}$. When admitted to some RAT j, user i may be assigned rate R_{ij} at that RAT, which may be less or equal to the requested rate R_{Di}.

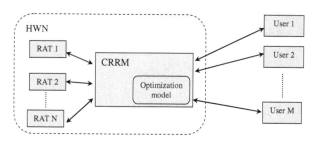

Fig. 1. Network selection model

To capture the gratification level of user i when served by some RAT j, we use *utility function* $U(R_{ij},R_{Di})$, which measures the normalized satisfaction of user i by taking into account the rate R_{ij} assigned at RAT j compared to the rate requested by the user. Thus, when a user gets exactly the rate requested, the utility should be high, while if the user is not accepted at some RAT the corresponding utility should be low. Users can then be differentiated by the way utility varies with respect to the rate assigned with normalized values ranging from zero (if zero rate is assigned) to one (if the requested rate is assigned). Below we define three different kinds of users:

- Linear-Expectation users (LEU) gain satisfaction that grows proportionally to the rate assigned. In this case, we assume that the utility function is a linear function of the rate assigned.
- High-Expectation users (HEU) are willing to spend a large amount of money but are very demanding regarding the level of service they get. In this case, the utility function should produce very low utility values, when they are assigned low rates compared to the rates requested, and should gradually increase only when the rates assigned approach the values of their requests.
- Between the two extremes we can define a class of users that are less demanding than HEU but more demanding than LEU. We will refer to these users as Mid-Expectation users (MEU).

We use the following utility functions for LEU, MEU and HEU users, respectively:

$$U_{LEU}\left(R_{ij},R_{Di}\right)=\frac{R_{ij}}{R_{Di}} \ ,$$

$$U_{MEU}\left(R_{ij},R_{Di}\right)=\left(\frac{R_{ij}}{R_{Di}}\right)^{2} \ ,$$

$$U_{HEU}\left(R_{ij},R_{Di}\right)=\left(\frac{R_{ij}}{R_{Di}}\right)^{4} \ .$$

The plots of these functions are also shown in Fig. 2. For example, if a HEU is requesting a rate of 256Kbps and the possible rates at some RAT are 128Kbps and 256Kbps, depending on the prevailing network conditions, the corresponding utility gain is 0.0625 and 1.00 when the lower or higher rate is assigned, respectively.

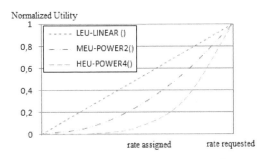

Fig. 2. Utility functions for LEU, MEU and HEU users

We can now formulate the network selection problem as follows:

$$maximize \qquad \sum_{i=1}^{M}\sum_{j=1}^{N}U(R_{ij},R_{D,i})$$

$$\sum_{i=1}^{M}x_{ij}\cdot R_{ij}\leq C_j, \qquad j=1,...,N \tag{1}$$

$$\sum_{j=1}^{N}x_{ij}\cdot R_{ij}\leq R_{D,i}, \qquad i=1,...,M \tag{2}$$

$$\sum_{j=1}^{N}x_{ij}\leq 1, \qquad i=1,...,M \tag{3}$$

$$x_{ij}=\begin{cases}1, & if\ user\ i\ is\ assigned\ to\ RAT\ j \\ 0, & otherwise\end{cases} \quad i=1,...,M,\ j=1,...,N \tag{4}$$

Equations (1) and (3) stand for the capacity constraints and the requirement constraints, respectively, while x_{ij} is an indicator variable that prohibits users from getting rate from more than one RATs. This policy corresponds to a scenario where no more than one hardware interface can be open at each multimode terminal. Finally, we assume that, even if a RAT supports more than one possible rates for user i of some class requesting rate R_{Di}, the problem is formulated after the final decision on the offered rate $R_{ij}\leq R_{Di}$ is taken based on the current traffic conditions at that RAT.

4   Branch and Bound

BB is designed to treat the above optimization problem under the last assumption of the previous section, namely when the rate and the corresponding utility gained by each RAT j for a specific user request i are known in advance and form two $M\times N$ matrices $R=[R_{ij}]$ and $U=[U_{ij}]$. The algorithm takes as input these two matrices and vector $C=[C_j]$ with the available capacity of each RAT and its goal is to find, among all the possible assignments, the optimal assignment of all user requests to RATs which maximizes the utility function. Assuming that every user $i=1,...,M$ can, theoretically, connect to every RAT $j=1,...,N$, all possible assignments form a feasible state space of N^M states.

A search algorithm starts developing the feasible solutions tree by creating all possible assignments of users to RATs, examining users one by one and considering user i at step i, $i=1,...,M$. The algorithm keeps track of all the feasible assignments in the form of paths along the solution tree. It begins by assigning the first user to all possible RATs, thus creating the first N paths which are stored in set S_1. At the next step, it attempts to extend the N existing paths, by adding to each existing path one new assignment of the current step user to one of the N RATs, thus creating $N\times N$

paths which are stored in set S_2. This exhaustive procedure will finally create the full state space of N^M paths stored in S_M. It is obvious that an exhaustive search is intractable and thus we employ a branch-and-bound technique to limit our search and avoid the extension of some of the existing paths of set S_{k-1} at step k.

The main condition for avoiding the unnecessary extension of some paths is based on the following idea. It is not necessary to further extend a path of set S_{k-1} if the sum of the utility gained up to step $k-1$ for that path and the maximum possible utility that can be obtained from the next $M-k+1$ steps is less than the utility gained up to step $k-1$ by some other path in S_{k-1}. More formally, at step k of the algorithm we can define an upper bound $\bar{U}_k$ of the maximum utility which may be achieved in the remaining steps $k+1, ..., M$ of the algorithm as:

$$\bar{U}_k = \sum_{i>k} \max_j (U_{ij}) . \tag{5}$$

Note that this is an upper bound which may not be achievable because the corresponding solution path may not be feasible due to some other problem constraint. If we now denote by $U_k^{(p)}$ the utility gained from path p of set S_k, including the assignment during step k, then the extension of path p is excluded from the next steps of the algorithm if the following inequality holds:

$$U_k^{(p)} \leq \max_q U_k^{(q)} - \bar{U}_k . \tag{6}$$

Indeed if this inequality holds for path p, then the total possible achievable utility including the remaining steps of the algorithm will be less than the utility already gained by some other path q without considering the remaining steps of the algorithm.

Additional checks for reducing the number of paths to extend at step k of the algorithm are imposed by the capacity constraints of (1). According to these, at step k the extension of some path p of set S_{k-1} is performed for RAT j only if the existing RAT capacity is greater than or equal to rate R_{kj}. If we denote by $C_j^{(k,p)}$ the capacity consumed by RAT j in path p until step $k-1$, then the extension of path p, by assigning user k at RAT j, is excluded if the following inequality holds:

$$R_{kj} > C_j - C_j^{(k,p)} .$$

We will use the example below to illustrate the behavior of BB algorithm, where we assume that there are $N=2$ RATs and $M=3$ users. The data in the following matrices which are fed as input to the algorithm are used only for the sake of the example:

$$U = \begin{bmatrix} 1 & 3 \\ 1 & 2 \\ 1 & 1 \end{bmatrix}, R = \begin{bmatrix} 1 & 1 \\ 1 & 1 \\ 1 & 1 \end{bmatrix}, C = \begin{bmatrix} 2 \\ 2 \end{bmatrix}$$

We can construct the upper bound $\bar{U}_k$, $k=1,...,M$ in advance as follows:

$$\left[\max_j U_{ij}\right] = \begin{bmatrix} 3 \\ 2 \\ 1 \end{bmatrix} \quad and \quad \left[\bar{U}_k\right] = \begin{bmatrix} 3 \\ 1 \\ 0 \end{bmatrix}$$

Each node of the solution tree is represented at step k by a triplet $[a_i],[C_j\text{-}C_j^{(k,p)}],U_k^{(p)}$. $[a_i]$ is the 1x3 allocation vector, whose values denote the RAT user i is allocated to, and corresponds to some path p. $[C_j\text{-}C_j^{(k,p)}]$ is the 1x2 vector of the remaining capacity in each RAT, while $U_k^{(p)}$ is the utility gained so far if allocations are made as shown in the allocation vector.

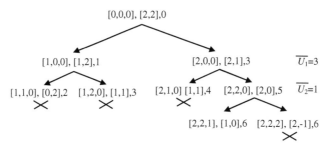

Fig. 3. Branch and Bound algorithm example

As we can see in Fig. 3, if the first user is allocated at the first RAT [1,0,0] at step 1, and the second user is allocated at the first RAT [1,1,0] as well at step 2, then the total utility gained so far at step 2 is 2. However, the best that we could achieve at step 2 is $\max_q U_k^{(q)} = 5$, in case both users are allocated to the second RAT and the maximum utility that the algorithm can achieve in the remaining third step is $\bar{U}_2 = 1$. Thus the path corresponding to allocation [1,1,0] is not further extended because (6) holds for that path. The same inequality holds also for the paths corresponding to allocations [1,2,0] and [2,1,0] and these paths are excluded from further expansion in step 3.

Finally, at the last step we illustrate how the capacity constraint is violated if the third user is allocated to the second RAT and thus this solution is excluded from the feasible set, rendering an optimum solution with allocation vector [2,2,1] and total utility value 6.

5   Greedy Heuristic

BB significantly reduces the computational cost compared to the exhaustive search procedure, and is useful for obtaining optimum solutions to compare with other non-optimal algorithms. Nevertheless, its time complexity, even for small problem instances, is prohibitive for problems which require finding a solution within reasonable time limits, as the one studied in this paper. Thus, it is necessary to devise heuristics that are computationally efficient and can produce near-optimum solutions.

Our greedy heuristic exploits the special characteristics of the problems and favors allocations of users to RATs that produce higher utility values, with relatively low RATs capacity consumption. The algorithm uses the ratio *utility gained per resource used* $\gamma_{ij} = U_{ij}/R_{ij}$ which is actually a measure of the utility that will be gained if user i is allocated to RAT j. So, instead of favoring allocations with high utility values, this heuristic favors allocations which yield higher values for this metric. Ties are resolved by favoring the allocation with the higher utility value.

The algorithm takes as input the same $M \times N$ matrices U and R and RAT capacity vector C and initially computes the $M \times N$ ratios γ_{ij}, which are then sorted in a list in decreasing order of their values. The algorithm performs the allocation of the users to RATs in M steps, each step consisting of the following two phases:

Phase 1: the first element γ_{ij} in the list of ratios is picked, and a check whether capacity constraints are violated is performed. If RAT j has greater capacity than R_{ij}, then user i is allocated to RAT j, the available capacity of RAT j is reduced by R_{ij}, and the algorithm proceeds to the second phase. Otherwise, user i cannot be allocated to RAT j, γ_{ij} is removed from the list and the algorithm repeats phase 1.

Phase 2: the remaining list of ratios is searched, and all the remaining γ_{il} ratios for user i that has been previously allocated to RAT j are removed from the list, $l \neq j$.

This procedure is repeated M times until all M users are assigned to RATs, or the available capacities of all RATs are too low to accept a user. Since there are M users to assign and the length of the initial list is $M \times N$, the time complexity of this heuristic is bounded by $O(M^2 \times N)$.

6   Simulation Results

Apart from BB and Greedy, we developed two Bin-Packing heuristics for comparing the efficiency of our algorithms. The first one is a variation of the First Fit (FF) strategy, while the second one is a variation of the Worse Fit (WF) strategy. Instead of using any utility based criterion for selecting the most appropriate RAT, both algorithms base their decisions only on rate requests and existing RAT capacities. FF assigns users to the first RAT that has enough capacity to accommodate the user requests, while WF assigns users requests to the RAT which will have the largest available capacity after the allocation.

We consider a wireless environment composed of 2 different RATs, RAT-1 and RAT-2, with capacities 256kbps and 512kbps, respectively. We assume that each incoming user requests 128kbps and may be allocated part of the rate requested depending on the prevailing network conditions and the RAT which is hosting the request. In this way, we can simulate different situations, where RATs cannot support the total requested rate, either due to RAT technology constraints or due to network traffic or inefficient channel conditions.

Table 1, summarizes the several combinations of rates assigned and utility gains under the different scenarios used in our study. Three different network conditions were considered. Depending on the probability of being fair or bad the network conditions can be distinguished as propitious, balanced or ominous. When network conditions are fair the rate allocated is 64kbps at RAT-1 and 128kbps at RAT-2. Thus, RAT-1 supports only half of the requested rate, even when conditions are good, and this assumption is mainly due to RAT technology constraints. On the contrary, when network conditions are bad the arriving user gets only 32kbps (64kbps) if allocated to RAT-1 (RAT-2). This assumption is made mainly because network traffic is high or channel conditions are bad.

Table 1. Rates assigned and utilities gained under different network conditions

	Fair - 70%		Bad - 30%	
Propitious Network Conditions	Fair - 70%		Bad - 30%	
Balanced Network Conditions	Fair - 50%		Bad - 50%	
Ominous Network Conditions	Fair - 30%		Bad - 70%	
RAT	RAT-1	RAT-2	RAT-1	RAT-2
Rate Assigned	64	128	32	64
LEU-Utility gained	0.5	1	0.25	0.5
MEU-Utility gained	0.25	1	0.0625	0.25
HEU-Utility gained	0.0625	1	0.003906	0.0625

Each user request is statistically categorized as arriving when network conditions are fair or bad, and this statistical outcome is used as input to the algorithms. According to Table 1, if for example a HEU arrives when ominous network conditions prevail, there is 70% chance the network conditions to be bad and 30% chance to be fair. If the user is statistically categorized as arriving when bad networks conditions prevail, then the utility gained is 0.003906 if assigned at RAT-1 and 0.0625 if assigned at RAT-2.

We estimate the efficiency of BB in reducing the number of necessary searches until the optimum solution is found, by measuring the total number of nodes examined, compared to the total number of tree nodes examined by an exhaustive search procedure. In Table 2 we present the results on the pruning performed by BB until the optimum solution is found when we run the BB algorithm for each of the three kinds of users in every possible network condition. We do not include results for number of users below 8 because the reduction is negligible for very light traffic load. As we can see, significant reductions in the search procedure start to appear when the number of users exceeds 9. In any case, when the system is fully loaded the saving of BB climb up to 20% and more, reducing efficiently the number of the extended paths. However, when the system is overloaded, BB's reduction of the search space is extremely high but the actual number of nodes examined remains quite high as well and cannot performed in real time.

Table 2. Total number of tree nodes examined

Number of Users	8	9	10	11	12	13	14	15	16	17	18
Exhaustive search	510	1022	2046	4094	8190	16382	32766	65534	131070	262142	524286
Propitious Network Conditions											
LEU-BB	469	862	1514	2680	4429	6889	10090	15029	22348	28657	30401
LEU-Reduction (%)	8	16	26	35	46	58	69	77	83	89	94
MEU-BB	470	862	1590	2755	4504	6942	9987	14656	18733	19521	19582
MEU-Reduction (%)	8	16	22	33	45	58	70	78	86	93	96
HEU-BB	495	951	1753	3081	5138	8113	12081	16716	20663	21425	21486
HEU-Reduction (%)	3	7	14	25	37	50	63	74	84	92	96
Balanced Network Conditions											
LEU-BB	498	977	1902	3673	7020	13249	23170	37371	54614	69577	73429
LEU-Reduction (%)	2.4	4.4	7	10	14	19	29	43	58	73	86
MEU-BB	486	912	1603	2844	5002	8630	12024	16453	21384	21522	21522
MEU-Reduction (%)	4.7	11	22	31	39	47	63	75	84	92	96
HEU-BB	495	951	1693	2678	4426	7455	12560	20837	24659	24707	24708
HEU-Reduction (%)	2.9	7	17	35	46	54	62	68	81	91	95
Ominous Network Conditions											
LEU-BB	504	1000	1925	3692	6583	11637	20083	33380	44806	55783	61476
LEU-Reduction (%)	1.2	2.2	5.9	9.8	20	29	39	49	66	79	88
MEU-BB	494	966	1848	3452	5380	8505	13244	19667	26811	32489	32494
MEU-Reduction (%)	3.1	5.5	9.7	16	34	48	60	70	80	88	94
HEU-BB	509	1005	1371	2060	2447	3063	4013	4071	4137	4184	4189
HEU-Reduction (%)	0,20	1.7	33	50	70	81	88	94	97	98	99

Fig. 4, 5 and 6 depict the total utility gained by each algorithm examined (BB, Greedy, FF, WF) under increasing traffic load, for every different class of users (LEU, MEU, HEU) and every network condition assumed. The results obtained by BB are optimal and are used to evaluate the performance of the other heuristics. Greedy produces very good results like BB at low, medium and high traffic loads, and this is justified by the metric used for sorting the user requests. The metric attempts to maximize the utility gained per capacity used and yields optimal results in the above example scenarios. On the other hand, FF and WF allocate user requests following the same pattern and behave relatively worse, since they do not take into consideration the corresponding utilities, but instead take into account only the rate requests and the available capacity at each RAT.

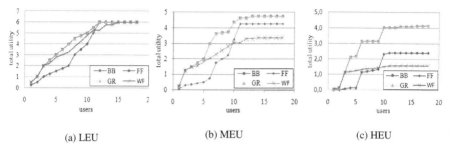

(a) LEU   (b) MEU   (c) HEU

Fig. 4. Total utility under ominous network conditions

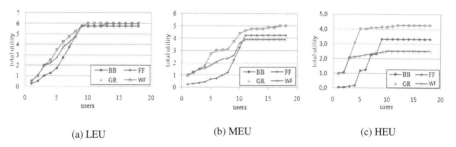

(a) LEU   (b) MEU   (c) HEU

Fig. 5. Total utility under balanced network conditions

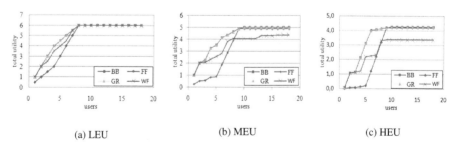

(a) LEU   (b) MEU   (c) HEU

Fig. 6. Total utility under propitious network conditions

7   Conclusions

In this paper we presented our work on the study of a multi-RAT environment. Specifically, we focused on the network selection problem where users are equipped with multimode terminals. We formulated this problem as an optimization problem and introduced a utility-based optimization function. We proposed an optimal Branch and Bound algorithm and a greedy algorithm which exploits a metric that measures the utility gained versus the resource spent for each allocation. In order to verify their efficiency, we compared them against two simplified algorithms based on the Bin-Packing problem, the First Fit and the Worse Fit algorithms. Our results showed that BB significantly reduces the search procedure and that the greedy heuristic is very efficient in achieving allocations of users to RATs that maximize utility values as BB does with much lower computational cost. However, even though the pruning of BB seems to be quite high for the settings of our simulation scenario, further investigation is necessary to reveal the dependency of the BB algorithm behavior on the parameters of the problem, namely the utility functions, RAT capacities and available RAT rates, and network conditions.

References

1. Wang, F., Ghosh, A., Sankaran, C., Fleming, P., Hsieh F., Benes S.: Mobile WiMAX systems: performance and evolution. IEEE Commun. Mag. (2008)
2. ETSI EN 302 304 V1.1.1 In: Digital Video Broadcasting (DVB); Transmission System for Handheld Terminals (DVB-H) (2004)
3. Modlic, B., Sisul, G., Cvitkovic, M.: Digital dividend – Opportunities for new mobile services. In: ELMAR 2009 International Symposium (2009)
4. Furuskar, A., Jonsson, T., Lundevall, M.: The LTE radio interface - key characteristics and performance. In: Personal, Indoor and Mobile Radio Communication (PIMRC 2008) (2008)
5. IEEE Standard for Architectural Building Blocks Enabling Network-Device Distributed Decision Making for Optimized Radio Resource Usage in Heterogeneous Wireless Access Networks, IEEE Std 1900.4-2009
6. O'Droma, M., Ganchev, I., Morabito, G., Narcisi, R., Passas, N., Paskalis, S., Friderikos, V., Jahan, A., Tsontsis, E., Bader, F., Rotrou, J., Chaousi, H.: Always Best Connected" Enabled 4G Wireless World. In: IST Mobile and Wireless Communications Summit (2003)
7. Martello, S., Toth, P.: Knapsack problems: algorithms and computer implementations. John Wiley & Sons, Inc., New York (1990)
8. Kikilis, A.A., Rouskas, A.N.: Formulation of optimization problems of access selection in next generation wireless networks. In: Proceedings of the 3rd International Conference on Mobile Multimedia Communications, MobiMedia 2007, Nafpaktos, Greece (2007)
9. Mariz, D., Cananea, I., Sadok, D., Fodor, G.: Simulative analysis of access selection algorithms for multi-access networks. In: International Symposium on a World of Wireless, Mobile and Multimedia Networks (2006)
10. Gazis, V., Houssos, N., Alonistioti, N., Merakos, L.: On the complexity of Always Best Connected in 4G mobile networks. In: Proc. of IEEE Vehicular Technology Conference, VTC (2003)
11. Nguyen-Vuong, Q.-T., Ghamri-Doudane, Y., Agoulmine, N.: On utility models for access network selection in wireless heterogeneous networks. In: Network Operations and Management Symposium (NOMS 2008) (2008)

12. De Sousa Jr., V.A., De O.Neto, R.A., De S. Chaves, F., Cardoso, L.S., Pimentel, J.F., Cavalcanti, F.R.P.: Performance of Access Selection Strategies in Cooperative Wireless Networks using Genetic Algorithms. In: Proceedings of the 15th World Wireless Research Forum Meeting (WWRF'15), Paris, France (2005)
13. Niyato, D., Hossain, E.: Dynamics of Network Selection in Heterogeneous Wireless Networks: An Evolutionary Game Approach. IEEE Transactions on Vehicular Technology 58(4) (2009)
14. Cesana, M., Malanchini, I., Capone, A.: Modelling network selection and resource allocation in wireless access networks with non-cooperative games. In: 5th IEEE International Conference on Mobile Ad Hoc and Sensor Systems, pp. 404–409 (2008)
15. Niyato, D., Hossain, E.: A cooperative game framework for bandwidth allocation in 4G heterogeneous wireless networks. In: IEEE International Conference on Communications, pp. 4357–4362 (2006)

Real-Time Inter-domain Handover Re-authentication Protocol

Radu Lupu[1], Eugen Borcoci[1], Dan Galatchi[1], and Tinku Rasheed[2]

[1] University Politehnica of Bucharest, Bucharest, Romania
[2] CREATE-NET, via alla cascata 56D. Povo, 38123 Italy
{rlupu,eborcoci,dgalatchi}@elcom.pub.ro,
tinku.rasheed@create-net.org

Abstract. Several statistics achieved to date on the Internet attacks have shown that one of the major causes for their proliferation is the scarce deployment of entity authentication mechanisms. Providing seamless support for real-time applications during the inter-domain handover procedure is one of the issues that still hinder the adoption of the network entity authentication service. In this paper, we focus on the design of a novel handover re-authentication protocol that can allow overcoming the current state. Furthermore, we also define the overall requirements for the underlying class of cryptographic methods which shall be used to implement our protocol. Thereafter, we present the preliminary results that were achieved on the re-authentication protocol validation.

Keywords: Authentication, real-time handover, wireless networks.

1   Introduction

The definition and integration of the security measures within the communication network infrastructure from its early stages of design represents a important task and challenge in recent times. In this paper, we focus on the design of the terminal handover re-authentication service for hybrid wireless mesh networks (composed of WiFi and WiMAX interfaces) [1]. In recent times, considerable research work has been performed or still in progress, in the field of handover re-authentication protocols and architectures, with notable results [4],[5],[7],[11],[12],[21],[23]. But, the inter-domain re-authentication of entities with support for real-time applications is still an open issue. Most of the re-authentication solutions proposed implied at least one transaction with the home domain (over Internet) during the handover process [6], which in turn increased significantly their latency (hundreds of milliseconds) and make them to be improper for real-time applications. Empirically, it has been shown in this case, that 90% of the latency is due the communication over Internet with the home domain [6]. Consequently, several proactive and reactive techniques were researched in order to avoid communication with the home domain during the handover process. However, all of these solutions experience some major drawbacks, such as: increased number of trust relationships required and domino effects [5],[11],

I. Tomkos et al. (Eds.): BROADNETS 2010, LNICST 66, pp. 473–482, 2012.

increased processing power due the use of asymmetric cryptographic mechanisms, or require seamless public-key infrastructures deployments [21].

We claim that our solution can overcome these limitations due a different approach which relies on the use of the re-authentication key derivation method with some special cryptographic properties. The main properties of our re-authentication protocol are:

- minimal inter-domain re-authentication latency (comparable with a local authentication) due to the re-authentication key (AK) derivation method;
- robustness with respect to the connectivity issues of the communication path in between visiting and home domains, through delegation of the re-authentication server role from home domain to the visiting domain. The connectivity issues are considered a common event within the networks with dynamic topology;
- low communication complexity through the use of the identity-based mechanisms;
- lower processing complexity through the use of symmetric techniques for more frequent events (e.g. within re-authentication mechanism), and asymmetric techniques for less frequent events (e.g. whenever a new re-authentication key is derived). It is expected, this property will enable the protocol to be run even on the mobile nodes with modest resources;
- completely avoids the costs entailed by the public-key certificates infrastructure management;
- minimize number of trust relationships involved by the re-authentication procedure (for instance, no trust relationships are required in between the current domain and its neighbors);
- prevents the domino effect, whenever one of the security architecture components is compromised.

The paper is organized as follows: Section II discusses the overall security architecture including a definition of the main functional components and their interactions in order to achieve the (re-) authentication services required. The proposed re-authentication protocol is specified in Section III. Thereafter, key derivation method design requirements and properties are outlined. Furthermore, we shortly describe how the re-authentication key material shall be managed. Section IV defines the validation process that we carried out on the re-authentication protocol to prove its security properties. This paper ends with Section V that concludes on the current status of the work and points out the future works.

2   The Security Architecture

In this section, we depict the security architecture for which our authentication protocol was initially designed. This security architecture was proposed as solution for implementation of the entity authentication, authorization and access control functionalities for the hybrid wireless mesh access network developed within the SMART-Net project [1]. According to the overall SMART-Net business model and network architecture, the security architecture design fits the two separate security administration domains corresponding to the RANP (Radio Access Network Provider) and BANP (Backhaul Access Network Provider) access networks, as defined in [1]. Due to the similarity of the RAN (Radio Access Network) and BAN (Backhaul Access Network) network functionalities, the security architecture design for RAN is analogous to the one for BAN (see Figure 1). Our security architecture design relies on the underlying 802.1x model (see [25]) due its extensibility and flexibility properties. These properties provide our solution the capabilities required to operate on hybrid and dynamic L2 network environments.

More specifically, our solution can work over either 802.11 or 802.16 infrastructures; and it allows partial auto-reconfiguration of the stakeholders' role (supplicant-authenticator) according to the network infrastructure modifications and allows security parameters negotiation (e.g. cryptographic algorithms). Most of these properties are due the integration of the EAP protocol within the 802.1x security model. Moreover, this model facilitates the local centralization of the management of the entities' credentials.

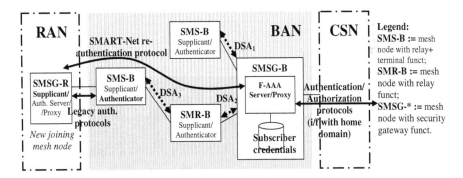

Fig. 1. The overall BAN's security architecture

In the following, we point out the main BAN's security architecture components and their roles:

- All wireless mesh nodes (e.g. SMS-B, SMR-B as shown in Figure 1) shall be capable to play supplicant, as well as, authenticator role in order to allow incremental buildup of the secure hybrid mesh infrastructure, while network entities are joining/leaving the infrastructure;
- One amongst the BAN mesh nodes has been assigned the security gateway role (denoted here SMSG-B). It is in charge with the BAN's security policy enforcement and control. SMSG-B can play either the role of a backend (re-) authentication and authorization server (F-AAA module) for subscribers /authenticated terminals, or the proxy role for authentication and authorization of the visiting network entities that enter the network for the first time. The mobile network entities shall be a priori registered and theirs credentials stored in a database that is accessible to the security gateway. For the case of real-time inter-domain handover, the SMSG-B should have the required functionality to allow efficient re-authentication procedures to be run locally, as much as possible.

Also, the SMSG-B entity is responsible for obtaining authorized connectivity service from the upstream network, on behalf of all mesh nodes within its RAN/BAN;

- Both dynamic (DSA) and static (SSA) security associations will be used to implement cryptographic-based security services. For enabling authentication service, it is assumed that each entity SMS-B or SMSG-B shares a pre-established SSA with the corresponding backend authentication server placed within the home domain. This SA is defined at the time of device (i.e. SMS-R/B, SMR-R/B or SMSG-R/B) registration to some domain. In addition, SSAs are pre-established in between SMSG-B (AAA modules) from several BAN domains, to ensure AAA's protocol security. DSAs are established by means of (re-)authentication protocols according to the 802.1x security model. Mainly, the DSAs are used to deploy security services upon a hop-by-hop security model (for authentication, integrity and confidentiality of data plane packets).

For the specification of the functional components interaction, we considered the scenario illustrated in Figure 1, where a new mesh node (denoted here SMSG-R) is joining the BAN mesh network. In order to support intra/inter-domain handover applications the interactions run according to HOKEY [7],[9] standard. Therefore, the SMSG-B is additionally assigned the re-authentication server role (a.k.a. ERP server).

In the case where the SMSG-R enters the network for the first time (i.e. it has no security context updated), it will be authenticated and authorized through the complete authentication procedure run with the SMSG-B within home domain, via SMS-B as authenticator. If SMSG-R is a visitor of the current BAN domain, the local SMSG-B shall play the role of a proxy F-AAA server. Otherwise, SMSG-R has already been (re-) authenticated and (re-) authorized within another BAN domain (i.e. it has updated security context) and subsequently will be re-authenticated and reauthorized at the current BAN using our optimized re-authentication procedure (specified in the next section), via SMS-B authenticator. This time, the local SMSG-B shall play the role of the re-authentication server. To assure proper operation of our re-authentication protocol a security context pre-distribution protocol shall run on the interface between local SMSG-B (F-AAA module) and home SMSG-B (H-AAA module). In the case of a successful (re-) authentication, the supplicant module located on SMSG-R and the authenticator module located on the physical adjacent SMS-B entity will run a legacy authentication protocol (e.g. "4-way Handshake") to check each other the claimed identity and establish a new DSA for securing the radio link that connects them. Eventually, the SMS-B is instructed by the SMSG-B to grant connectivity services to the SMSG-R entity.

3   SMART-Net Re-authentication Protocol

In this section, we specify a new authentication protocol optimized to support real-time applications during the handover process. It is designed to run in between the mobile node/subscriber (e.g. SMSG-R) and the re-authentication server (SMSG-B). The main objectives of our re-authentication protocol are:

- mutual authentication of principals;
- authentication key (material) synchronism verification and notification;
- master session key establishment (MSK).

This protocol combines asymmetric with symmetric cryptographic techniques to benefit the advantages of both schemes. The paradigm for its performances is the use of symmetric cryptographic algorithms, for computing authentication mechanisms, with the authentication key derived using an asymmetric method with the overall properties outlined below.

The proposed re-authentication protocol (see Figure 2) belongs to the class of "challenge-response" protocols with the time variable parameter of type nonce (e.g. random number). Both of the principals generate independently a nonce value with two objectives: to guarantee the protocol messages are fresh and to contribute to the master session key establishment. The last is required to avoid the master session key control by one principal, to guarantee its freshness and to enable PFS property (Perfect Forward Secrecy). Optionally, the protocol messages can provide an identification mechanism for principals, which is useful for authentication key derivation method.

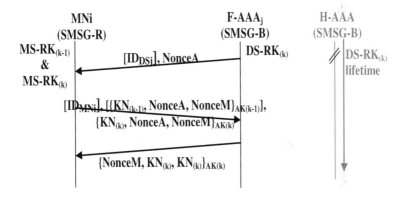

Fig. 2. the SMART-Net re-authentication protocol

In order to assure continuity of the re-authentication service during the re-authentication key management procedure, our protocol was designed to operate simultaneously with two successive authentication keys, associated to the time intervals (k-1) and (k). Moreover, each authentication key is assigned an identifier, named KN (k-1) and KN (k) respectively, to be used by the key re-synchronization mechanism. The identifiers are uniquely defined and distributed by the authentication server located in the home domain of the SMSG-R (see the next section). This way, if either authentication component {KN(k-1), NonceA, NonceM}_AK(k-1) or {KN(k), NonceA, NonceM}_AK(k) is valid (see the second message), then SMSG-B entity declares the SMSG-R as genuine. Each key identifier points to the authentication key to be used for validation of the corresponding authentication component. On the other side, SMSG-R relies on the last message to check the SMSG-B entity is authentic.

The first identifier in the last message points to the authentication key used by SMSG-B and the second identifier notify the SMSG-R about the most recent authentication key known by SMSG-B. Whenever the SMSG-R finds out this way a new authentication key have been established it starts (in parallel with the user data transfer) a complete authentication procedure with the authentication server in home domain, in order to obtain this key. If none of the authentication keys is known by SMSG-B, the protocol fails and the SMSG-R shall initiate the complete authentication procedure with the authentication server within the home domain. The transmission of the last message in this case is optional since its integrity cannot be verified.

After successful mutual authentication, the master session key can be derived independently by principals according to the following formula:

$$MSK\ (k) = hash\ (NonceA, NonceM, AK(k))$$

Thereafter, the MSK (k) is securely transferred toward the authenticator entity (typically an access point) and eventually the legacy local authentication protocol is run in between SMSG-R and SMS-B.

The Re-authentication Key Cryptographic Derivation Procedure

The real-time inter-domain re-authentication solution we proposed in this paper relies on the pre-distribution technique of the authentication key material from home domain to each subscriber entity (e.g. SMSG-R) and re-authentication server (e.g. SMSG-B) within each potential visited BANs, before the arrival of the mobile subscriber entity. The main hurdle to overcome was the issue of figuring out in advance what is the next visited BAN; and vice-versa, what is the next visiting mobile subscriber.

The key idea was to decouple to some extent the authentication key material from (subscriber entity, re-authentication server) pair. Therefore, we defined two components for deriving the authentication key: generic key material (generated and distributed by home domain authentication server) and local key material (known locally, such as identifiers of the principals). The main advantage of using generic key material is that it can be pre-distributed to all re-authentication servers and subscribers, before any tentative of association. Moreover, while the aim of the generic key material is to ensure the authenticity of the derived key and to supply the entropy, the local key material cryptographically binds the resulting authentication key to some (subscriber, re-authentication server) pair. In addition, a special cryptographic derivation method has been defined.

For maintaining the derivation method independent from the underlying cryptographic mechanisms, we will not specify in detail this method, but we point out below its overall design requirements:

- the authentication key derived has sufficient entropy to guarantee the required security level;
- the derivation transformation has one-way property;
- to guarantee the peer entities shall independently compute the same authentication symmetric key;

- (to prevent impersonation attacks) to guarantee the generic key material of some entity (subscriber or re-authentication server) cannot be used to compute neither the generic key material nor the authentication key corresponding to another entity or pair (subscriber, re-authentication server), respectively.

For a given pair of principals, we denote MS-RK and DS-RK the generic key material of the subscriber and the re-authentication server respectively. Further, we have considered the principals' identification information, denoted IDMN and IDDS as the local key material. Therefore, assuming the values of MS-RK, DS-RK, IDMN and IDDS are defined within the domain Zn, we have searched to figure out two functions f and g such that the following holds:

$$f, g : Z_n \times Z_n \rightarrow Z_n,$$
$$g(f(RAND, IDDSj), IDMNi) = g(f(RAND, IDMNi), IDDSj)$$

where f is the generic key material derivation function MS-RK = f(RAND, IDMNi), DS-RK = f(RAND, IDDSj). RAND is a random value parameter in Z_n. g is the authentication key derivation function: AK = g(MS-RK, IDDSj) = g(DS-RK, IDMNi).

Re-authentication Key Material Distribution

Since the DS-RK key material is used by re-authentication server to compute the authentication key of all subscribers of the same home domain, its lifetime is critical. Consequently, the DS-RK is periodically updated by the authentication server in the home domain of those subscribers. A secured AAA protocol can be used to push this key material toward all target domains. The period of DS-RK update depends on the cryptographic mechanisms involved by the authentication key derivation transformation, and the frequency of its use. Once the DS-RK is updated, the MS-RK key material should also be updated. In this regard, the re-authentication server is responsible to notify (through re-authentication protocol) the subscriber SMSG-R about the new MS-RK. Subsequently, the subscriber we'll start the complete authentication procedure to pull the MS-RK directly from the authentication server within home domain. Therefore, a counter-based mechanism for key material identification was defined. Thus, each time a new generic key material is generated, also the new value of the counter is associated with that material, denoted KN(k). To ensure the authentication service continuity while keeping the authentication key distribution mechanisms simple, both the subscriber SMSG-R and the re-authentication server SMSG-B shall maintain always only the two most recent generic key materials. On the other side, the distribution of the local key material may take place directly between the principals. In our implementation, we assumed a re-authentication protocol mechanism for such a distribution of the principals' identification information. Alternatively, any legacy lower layer mechanism may be used, optionally with identity confidentiality guarantees if required.

4   SMART-Net Re-authentication Protocol Security Properties Validation

We chose to use AVISPA (Automated Validation of Internet Security Protocols and Applications) simulation-based tool for verification of the security properties of the SMART-Net AA protocol we designed. The AVISPA tool was developed within the European funded research project AVISPA [24], and comprises a suite of applications for building and analyzing EFSM-based (Extended Finite State Machine) formal models of security protocols that are specified using HLPSL (High-Level Protocols Specification Language) language. The AVISPA tool allows to easily achieve fully automatic security properties verification using four complementary formal assessment techniques, implemented by the back-ends analyzers it comes with: OFMC (On-the-Fly Model Checking), CL-AtSe (Constraint-Logic-based Attack Searcher), SATMC (SAT-based Model Checker) and TA4SP (Tree Automata-based analyzer for Security Protocols).

In this regard, we have built the formal model of the re-authentication protocol behavior. Thereafter, we specified the security requirements in terms of authentication and confidentiality goals. Since the HLPSL is a role-based language, we had to specify the actions of each authentication principal as a module, but the attacker that is predefined, according to the Dolev-Yao model [3] (i.e. it is capable to drop, replay, delay, decrypt/encrypt and forge packets by mean of the inferred keys). The simulation assumptions were: all the communications are carried out through attacker participation, the attacker can act as an intermediate entity (e.g. MITM attack model) or as a peer entity, the cryptographic/hash algorithms are known by the attacker (see Kerckhoff's principles), the identities and location of the principals are known to the attacker. As a result of the re-authentication subsystem analysis, we have defined two more representative simulation scenarios:

> −mobile mesh node knows two successive (valid) re-authentication keys (AK(k-1) and AK(k));
> −mobile mesh node knows a single (valid) re-authentication key (AK(k))

At the time this paper was written, the HLPSL formal model we built had already been assessed according to the inter-domain handover scenario proving that our re-authentication protocol can successfully fulfill the security goals. In other words, our re-authentication protocol is SAFE with respect to: the secrecy of the session key (formalized as confidentiality goal on AK (k)) and the replay threats (formalized as authentication message goals on temporal variables).

5   Conclusion and Future Work

This paper presents the preliminary results of a (re-)authentication protocol and its architecture design, developed for hybrid wireless mesh networks. We presented the main design requirements that enabled our solution to sustain real-time inter-domain handover re-authentication applications. Our approach relied on the pre-distribution of the re-authentication key material and the key derivation method, in order to decrease the inter-domain re-authentication latency at the values similar to the local intra-domain solutions. The overall properties of the key derivation transformation have been outlined. At the moment of writing this paper, an AVISPA-based simulation model of the re-authentication protocol had already been built and the preliminary security properties verification has been successfully passed.

The ongoing future work is to build an OPNET/NS2 simulation model to evaluate the proposed security architecture and related mechanisms' performance, in terms of delay and traffic overhead (i.e. scalability). Since the identification mechanism provided by our re-authentication protocol cannot guarantee the confidentiality of principals' identity, new solutions are presently researched to overcome this issue.

Acknowledgements. The authors would like to thank the European Commission for funding our research work in the framework of the SMART-Net project IST-2008 223937-STREP.

References

1. Wendt, S., Kharrat-Kammoun, F., Borcoci, E., Cacoveanu, R., Lupu, R., Hayes, D.: Network architecture and system specification, SMART-Net project IST-FP7 223937 (October 2009)
2. Menezes, A., van Oorschot, P., Vanstone, S.: Handbook of Applied Cryptography. CRC Press (October 1996)
3. Dolev, D., Yao, A.: On the security of Public-Key Protocols. IEEE Transactions on Information Theory 2(29) (1983)
4. Calhoun, P., Montemurro, M., Stanley, D.: Control and Provisioning of Wireless Access Points (CAPWAP) Protocol Specification, IETF, RFC 5415 (March 2009)
5. Komarova, M.: Fast authentication and trust based access control in heterogeneous wireless networks, Ph.D. Thesis (May 2008)
6. Mishra, A., Shin, M., Arbaugh, W.: An Empirical Analysis of the IEEE 802.11 MAC Layer Handoff Process
7. Clancy, T., Nakhjiri, M., Narayanan, V., Dondeti, L.: Handover Key Management and Re-Authentication Problem Statement, IETF, RFC 5169 (March 2008), http://www.ietf.org
8. Narayanan, V., Dondeti, L.: EAP Extensions for EAP Re-authentication Protocol (ERP), IETF, RFC 5296 (August 2008), http://www.ietf.org
9. Hoeper, K., Ohba, Y.: Distribution of EAP based keys for handover and re-authentication, IETF, draft-ietf-hokey-key-mgm-06 (April 2009), http://www.ietf.org
10. Clancy, T.: Secure Handover in Enterprise WLANs: CAPWAP, HOKEY and 802.11r
11. Huang, P.J., Tseng, Y.C.: A Fast Handoff Mechanism for IEEE 802.11 and IAPP Networks
12. Chen, J.J., Tseng, Y.C., Lee, H.W.: A Seamless Handoff Mechanism for IEEE 802.11 WLANs Supporting IEEE 802.11i Security Enhancements
13. Bournelle, J., Laurent-Maknavicius, M., El Mghazli, Y., Giaretta, G., Lopez, R., Ohba, Y.: Use of Context Transfer Protocol (CXTP) for PANA, draft-ietf-pana-cxtp-01 (March 2006), http://www.ietf.org

14. Ohba, Y.: Pre-authentication support for PANA, draft-ietf-pana-preauth-06 (June 2009), `http://www.ietf.org`
15. Forsberg, D., Ohba, Y., Tschofenig, B., Yegin, A.: Protocol for carrying authentication for network access (PANA), RFC 5191 (May 2008), `http://www.ietf.org`
16. Lupu, R., Borcoci, E., Mirzadeh, S., Hamadani, E., Rasheed, T.: D3.5a: Security and Privacy Requirements, SMART-Net project IST 223937 (April 2009)
17. Farell, S., Volbrecht, J., Calhoun, P.: AAA Authorization Requirements, RFC 2906, IETF (August 2000)
18. Aboba, B., Beadles, M.: The network identifier, RFC 2486, IETF (January 1999)
19. Vollbrecht, J., Calhoun, P., Farell, S., et al.: AAA Authorization Framework, RFC 2904, IETF (August 2000)
20. Lupu, R., Stanciu, M.: Authentication and authorization architecture for hybrid mesh networks. In: Conf. Int. Communications 2010 (Iunie 2010)
21. Long, M., Wu, C-H., David Irwin, J.: Localized Authentication for Wireless LAN Internetwork Roaming
22. Lin, X., Ling, X., Zhu, H., Ho, P.H., Shen, X.: A novel localised authentication scheme in IEEE 802.11 based wireless mesh network. Intl. Journal Security and Networks 3(2) (2008)
23. Hong, Z., Rui, H., Man, Y.: A novel fast authentication method for mobile network access (2004)
24. AVISPA, `http://www.avispa-project.org`
25. IEEE-SA Standards Board, Port-based Network Access Control, IEEE Std. 802.1x-2001 (October 2001) ISBN 0-7381-2626-7

A Comparative Study of Impairments Aware Optical Networks Planning Tools

Siamak Azodolmolky[1], Marianna Angelou[1], Ioannis Tomkos[1], Annalisa Morea[2],
Yvan Pointurier[2], and Josep Solé-Pareta[3]

[1] Athens Information Technology, Athens, Greece
{sazo,mang,itom}@ait.edu.gr
[2] Alcatel-Lucent, Bell Labs, France
annalisa.morea@alcatel-lucent.com, yvan@ieee.org
[3] Universitat Politècnica de Catalunya Catalunya, Barcelona, Spain
pareta@ac.upc.edu

Abstract. Transparent and translucent optical networks are widely considered as the prime candidates for the core network technology of the future. These networks provide ultra high speed end-to-end connectivity with high quality of service (QoS) and resilience to failures. This will be achieved through appropriate network planning techniques. A downside of transparency, however, is the accumulation of physical layer impairments over long distances, which are difficult to mitigate using purely physical-layer techniques. Considering the impact of physical layer impairments on network planning and operation has received considerable attention from research community. A novel physical layer impairment aware network planning tool is presented in this paper. Its performance is quantitatively compared with results obtained by a state-of-the-art tool under a common network scenario. The differences between the two planning approaches are illustrated and discussed.

1 Introduction

The evolution trend of optical networks is a transformation towards higher capacity and lower cost core optical networks [1]. Operators also expect the optical networks to become more agile in order to meet their requirements in terms of fast and automatic reconfiguration. Transparent optical net- working is one of the main trends toward network agility, as it incorporates routing and wavelength mechanisms, which are agnostic to the modulation format and/or transmission rates. Transparent networks can also contribute to lower power consumption and heat dissemination by avoiding the uncondi- tional use of regenerators at each network node. However, a downside of transparency, is the accumulation of physical layer impairments over long distances, which are difficult to mitigate using physical-layer related techniques. In optical networks, bandwidth is allocated in the form of lightpaths (i.e., a route and a wavelength). Physical layer impairments accumulate as light propagates through a lightpath.

I. Tomkos et al. (Eds.): BROADNETS 2010, LNICST 66, pp. 483–490, 2012.

Due to large coverage of core optical networks, some lightpaths may not be feasible due to an unacceptable final bit error rate (BER) at the destination node. This issue is critical in the planning phase of the network and for the control plane functionality during network operation. Therefore, in order to increase the speed of lightpath establishment, it can be useful to avoid repeated, unsuccessful attempts by enhancing the control plane with an RWA process, which is aware of the impact of physical layer impairments and considers the quality of transmission (QoT) requirements.

To materialize the vision of transparent optical networks, while offering efficient resource utilization and strict quality of service guarantees based on certain service level agreements, the core network should efficiently provide high capacity, fast and flexible provisioning of lightpaths, high reliability, and integrated control plane functionalities.

Considering the physical layer impairments in the network planning phase gives rise to a set of offline Impairments Aware Routing and Wavelength Assignment (IA-RWA) [2] and regenerator placement algorithms. During the planning phase, the traffic demand is already known, enabling the network designer to perform the resource allocation task upfront. To the best of our knowledge this is the first comparative study, in which two different network planning tools (DICONET [3] impairment aware network planning tool (IANPT) and DIA- MOND [4]) with different approaches regarding the consider- ation of the physical impairments are quantitatively compared using a common network scenario and physical constraints framework.

In this work we compare the behavior of two design tools. The DICONET IANPT tool utilizes an accurate but compu- tationally expensive QoT estimator to return network designs with fewer regenerators and physically longer lightpaths than DIAMOND.

This paper is organized as follows. In Section II the descrip- tion of two network planning tools (i.e., DICONET IANPT and DIAMOND) are presented. The comparative simulation study and its setup is described in Section III. The obtained results and discussions are presented in Section IV and Sec- tion V draws the conclusions of this work.

2   Impairments Aware Network Planning Tools

The main functionality of a network planning tool is to receive a traffic demand set along with the network description (topology and/or physical layer) as inputs and to compute a list of lightpaths and possibly some regenerator locations to serve the demand set. An IANPT considers the impact of physical layer impairments while solving the RWA problem. The key building blocks of the DIAMOND and DICONET IANPT tools, which are considered in our comparative studies, are depicted in Fig. 1.

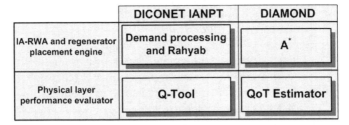

	DICONET IANPT	DIAMOND
IA-RWA and regenerator placement engine	Demand processing and Rahyab	A*
Physical layer performance evaluator	Q-Tool	QoT Estimator

Fig. 1. Structure of DICONET IANPT and DIAMOND

The Q-Tool and Rahyab [5] are two key components of the DICONET IANPT. The Q-Tool is a QoT estimator that com- bines most of the dominant physical impairments of a WDM system into a single figure of merit (the Q-factor). Given all the necessary topological, physical layer characteristics, and cur- rent network state, the Q-Tool estimates the Q-factor of a set of lightpaths. The Q-Tool estimates the distortion-induced eye closure that defines the impact of the combined effect of Self Phase Modulation (SPM), Chromatic Dispersion (CD) Filter Concatenation (FC) and Polarization Mode Dispersion (PMD). It also considers the impairments that introduce degradations at the amplitude levels, i.e. Amplified Spontaneous Emission noise (ASE), Cross Phase Modulation (XPM), and Four Wave Mixing (FWM).

The Rahyab module of IANPT receives a demand set, in the form of triplets source, destination, and number of lightpaths and computes corresponding lightpaths for it. The IANPT initially processes the demand set. In case that some of the demands cannot be served transparently, the regenerators will be deployed and the corresponding demands will be transformed into a set of transparent demands. In this step the regenerators will be put in some of the network nodes to make sure that the end-to-end QoT of the signal is acceptable after intermediate regeneration. Thus, the transformed demand set only includes the demands that can be served in transparent mode. After this initial step the IA-RWA engine of IANPT serves the transformed demand set sequentially. The Rahyab module performs a demand pre-processing step and then serves them sequentially. It generates a pool of candidate lightpaths for each demand and from this pool selects the one, which introduces the minimum impact (in terms of QoT) on the currently established lightpaths [5].

DIAMOND is a planning tool that searches for a lightpath between two nodes in a network by means of a layered network graph [4]. The path search is iterative and places a re- generator or wavelength converter whenever it is required (due to QoT or wavelength continuity constraints, respectively). The chosen path is the one having the lesser cost, which is obtained considering the link lengths and the eventual cost associated to intermediary regenerators. The path search is a heuristic based on the A* algorithm [4]. The traffic demands are considered in the arrival order and they are routed sequentially. A demand is blocked whenever there is no available resource, in terms of either available wavelengths in the fiber or regenerators in an intermediate node. The Q-factor is estimated by a polynomial function (QoT-estimator) considering the accumulation of the main effects degrading the signal propagation, such as ASE, CD and PMD, FC and nonlinearities. This QoT estimator considers the worst case impact of non-linear impairments due to active neighboring channels. More information about such Q-estimator is in [4]. To consider estimation uncertainties associated to an estimate, a fixed margin is added to the estimated Q-factor [6]. DIAMOND utilizes a path search heuristic based on the A* algorithm, considering the resource availability and minimum usage of regenerators [4]. During the path search the QoT validation is performed and if the shortest path is not able to have a QoT higher than a certain threshold, while a longer path does, the longer path will be chosen. The same technique is also utilized for the wavelength assignment. In order to guarantee the feasibility of a candidate lightpath, the QoT-estimator considers the worst case scenario for all connections, i.e. all neighbor channels are present.

DICONET IANPT finds the optimum lightpath from the set of candidate lightpaths, considering the degradation due to neighboring lightpaths. The optimum lightpath is the one that introduces the minimum QoT degradation on already established lightpaths. Rahyab intensively uses the Q-Tool to evaluate the QoT of the already established lightpaths in order to admit or reject a new demand. This means that Q-Tool is less pessimistic than the DIAMOND QoT estimator and can enable saving of regenerators. The main advantage of DIAMOND is its computation speed, while DICONET IANPT requires more time to compute the optimum solution.

3   Simulation Setup

We selected Deutsche Telekom's national network (DTNet) for our simulation studies. This network has 14 nodes and 23 bidirectional links, with an average node degree of 3.29 and average link length of 186 km. The physical characteristics of DTNet is shown in Fig. 2. We define the offered load in the network as the ratio between the number of lightpath demands divided by the number of pairs of nodes in the network. The unit traffic load corresponds to the demand set where there is on average a lightpath request between each pair of (distinct) source-destination. We studied three traffic load values (i.e. 0.3, 0.6 and 0.8), corresponding here to the establishment of 56, 110 and 146 lightpaths. In Fig. 3 the Q factor value (computed by Q-Tool) of 10 shortest paths between all possible pairs of the nodes is depicted. Without considering the impact of other established lightpaths, there is no lightpath with a length longer than 1500 km and acceptable QoT. There are short lightpaths with Q value lower than threshold (Region 1) and long lightpaths with acceptable Q values (Region 2). This demonstrates the benefit of IA-RWA engines, which are able to find long but feasible lightpaths.

4   Results

IANPT and DIAMOND served all demands without any blocking for all loads. IANPT served all demands without any generator and there was no need to transform the demand set as a result of initial step of IANPT as described in Section II.

Parameter	Value
Input power	-4 (SSMF), 3 (DCF) dBm
Pre-dispersion compensation	-85 ps/nm
Span length	70 km
Dispersion parameter	17 (SSMF), 80 (DCF) ps/nm/km
Attenuation	0.23 (SSMF), 0.4 (DCF) dB/km
PMD	0.1 ps/(km)$^{1/2}$
Channel spacing	50 GHz
Amplifier noise figure	6 dB
Mean under compensated dispersion	80 ps/nm per span
Q-factor threshold	15.5 dB (BER=10^{-9} without FEC)
Line rate	10 Gbps
Number of channels per fiber	16

Fig. 2. Physical characteristics of DTNet

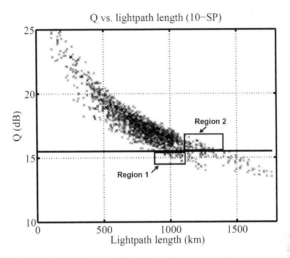

Fig. 3. Benefit of IA-RWA and different solution spaces

However DIAMOND computed a need for 2 and 6 regener- ators for load values 0.6 and 0.8 respectively. This is mainly due to the QoT estimator, which is utilized in DIAMOND. The QoT estimator considers the worst case scenario to consider the impact of neighboring channels and therefore the QoT estimation is more pessimistic than DICONET Q-Tool. Indeed DIAMOND utilizes a path search heuristic to find a lightpath with minimum number of regenerators and acceptable QoT value. However, wavelength blocking can occur, which is alleviated by wavelength conversion using regenerators. The Rahyab module of IANPT intensively invokes the Q-Tool to evaluate the performance of each candidate lightpath in order to guarantee the minimum QoT impact of the new lightpath on the currently established ones. Therefore the computation time of IANPT is very high compared to DIAMOND. The computation time of IANPT for load 0.3 was 9 hours while DIAMOND computes the results in 563 ms. The cumulative distribution function of the lightpath length for different loads is depicted in Fig. 4. The distribution of the lightpaths length, is presented in Fig. 5 for all 3 demand sets combined. We can observe from these two figures that the diverse routing engine of IANPT could find longer feasible lightpaths com- pared to DIAMOND. The average length of the lightpaths in DIAMOND is

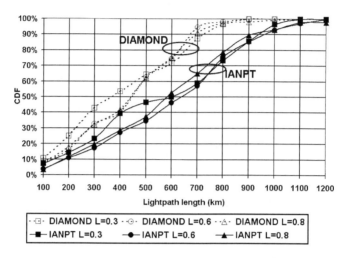

Fig. 4. CDF of lightpath length for different loads

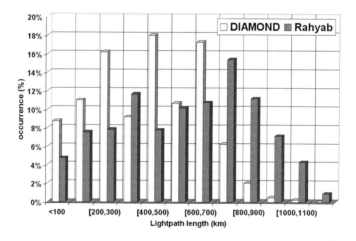

Fig. 5. Distribution of lighpaths length

419 km and 572 km for IANPT. Almost all computed lightpaths by DIAMOND have a length lower that 900 km. IANPT only considers the active lightpaths in order to admit or reject a demand, while DIAMOND (and in particular the QoT estimator) considers a worst case scenario, in which all neighboring lightpaths are active. As argued in Fig. 3 IANPT can find longer feasible lightpaths compared to DIAMOND. Fig. 6 presents the distribution of wavelength us- age by DIAMOND and IANPT for a particular demand set (i.e. Load=0.3). Rahyab utilizes an adaptive wavelength

assignment approach, in which the wavelength of the candidate lightpath is selected in a way that it introduces the minimum impact on the currently established lightpaths. DIAMOND finds a lightpath with fewer regenerators. The A* routing engine of DIAMOND and the wavelength assignment mechanism rely on the QoT estimator to guarantee the acceptable QoT of the selected lightpath. The Rahyab wavelength usage pattern is adaptive along the available channels per links depending on the network state and some channels are not assigned to any lightpath. We also observed that for the given demand sets on average the first 10 channels on the links were sufficient for both planning tools to serve 80% of the demands.

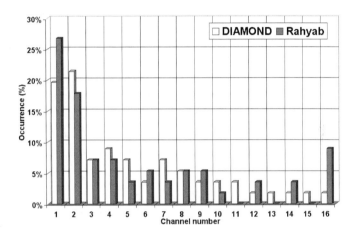

Fig. 6. Frequency of channel usage (Load=0.3)

IANPT and DIAMOND rely on different QoT estimators as depicted in Fig. 1. In order to evaluate the quality of the solutions of these tools, we fed the solution of each tool for each demand set to the IANPT's Q-Tool. The average Q value of DIAMOND's solutions is 4% better than IANPT. The average Q-factor of DIAMOND's solution (over three demand sets) is 28 dB. This is mainly due to the fact that DIAMOND routing module selects shortest paths in general to admit or reject a lightpath.

5   Conclusions

The evolution trend of optical networks introduces a need for intelligent and impairments aware network planning tools. DICONET IANPT and DIAMOND are two tools that address this issue. The IANPT adopt an approach, which results in lower number of regenerators and longer feasible lightpaths compared with DIAMOND. However the computation time and complexity of DIAMOND is much lower that IANPT, at the expense of a higher number of required regenerators.

Acknowledgments. The authors would like to thank the EU ICT FP7-DICONET project for funding this work.

References

1. Berthold, J., Saleh, A.A.M., Blair, L., Simmons, J.M.: Optical networking: Past, present, and future. J. Lightw. Technol. 26(9), 1104–1118 (2008)
2. Azodolmolky, S., Klinkowski, M., Marin, E., Careglio, D., Solé-Pareta, J., Tomkos, I.: A survey on physical layer impairments aware routing and wavelength assignment algorithms in optical networks. Elsevier Computer Networks 53(7), 926–944 (2009)
3. Azodolmolky, S., et al.: A dynamic impairment aware networking solution for transparent mesh optical networks. IEEE Commun. Mag. 47(5), 38–47 (2009)
4. Morea, A., Brogard, N., Leplingard, F., Antona, J., Zami, T., Lavigne, B., Bayart, D.: QoT function and A* routing: an optimized combination for connection search in translucent networks. Journal of Optical Networking 7(1), 42–61 (2008)
5. Azodolmolky, S., Pointurier, Y., Angelou, M., Solé-Pareta, J., Tomkos, I.: An offline impairment aware RWA algorithm with dedicated path protec- tion consideration. In: Proc. IEEE/OSA OFC/NFOEC, OWI1 (March 2009)
6. Leplingard, F., Morea, A., Zami, T., Brogard, N.: Interest of an adaptive margin for the quality of transmission estimation for lightpath establishment. In: Proc. IEEE/OSA OFC/NFOEC, OWI6 (March 2006)

Elastic Bandwidth Allocation in Flexible OFDM-Based Optical Networks

(Invited Paper)

Konstantinos Christodoulopoulos

Computer Engineering and Informatics Department,
University of Patras, and Research Academic Computer Technology Institute, Patra, Greece
`kchristodou@ceid.upatras.gr`

Abstract. Orthogonal Frequency Division Multiplexing (OFDM) has recently been proposed as a modulation technique for optical networks, because of its good spectral efficiency, flexibility, and tolerance to impairments. We consider the planning problem of an OFDM optical network, where connections are provisioned for their requested rate by elastically allocating spectrum using a variable number of OFDM subcarriers and choosing an appropriate modulation level taking into account the transmission distance. Using algorithms developed in our previous works, we evaluate the spectrum utilization gains that can be obtained by utilizing the elastic bandwidth allocation of OFDM, when compared to a traditional WDM network.

Keywords: Spectrum flexible networks, Optical OFDM, planning (offline) problem, Routing Modulation Level and Spectrum Allocation.

1   Introduction

The continuous growth of consumers IP traffic in combination with emerging high-rate applications, such as video on demand, high definition TV, cloud computing and grid applications require a cost-effective and scalable networking infrastructure. To meet the increasing capacity requirements, recent innovations in optical communication systems, including advanced modulation formats and digital equalization in the electronic domain, have enabled per-channel bandwidths of 40 and 100 Gbps with improved transmission distance in traditional fixed-grid single carrier WDM networks [1].

Although wavelength routed WDM networks offer well-known advantages, they still exhibit a major drawback due to their rigid and coarse granularity. Currently, wavelength-routed networks require full allocation of a wavelength to a connection even when the traffic between the end nodes is not sufficient to fill the entire capacity. Wavelength level granularity leads to inefficient capacity utilization, a problem expected to become even more significant with the deployment of higher capacity WDM networks (i.e., systems of 40 and 100 Gbps per channel).

The need for flexibility and efficiency requires an adaptive network that would have a fine granularity so as to elastically provide the required capacity to sub- or

I. Tomkos et al. (Eds.): BROADNETS 2010, LNICST 66, pp. 491–500, 2012.

super-wavelength demands. Approaches such as optical burst switching (OBS) and optical packet switching (OPS) that meet these requirements can only be viewed as long-term solutions since their enabling technologies are not yet mature [2][3].

Recently, Orthogonal Frequency-Division Multiplexing (OFDM) has been proposed as a modulation technique in optical networks [4]-[6]. Optical OFDM distributes the data on several low data rate subcarriers (multi-carrier system). The spectrum of adjacent subcarriers can overlap, since they are orthogonally modulated, increasing the transmission spectral efficiency. Moreover, optical OFDM can provide fine-granularity capacity to connections by the elastic allocation of low rate subcarriers according to the connection demands. Enabling technologies, such as bandwidth-variable (BV) transponders and bandwidth-variable WXCs, have been demonstrated in Spectrum-sLICed Elastic optical path network ("SLICE") [7]-[9].

To achieve high spectral flexibility a bandwidth-variable OFDM transponder generates an optical signal using just enough spectral resources, in terms of subcarriers with appropriate modulation level, to serve the client demand. Since, typically, the OFDM signal is generated at the RF domain, many transmission properties can be determined, enabling the choice of the number of modulated bits per symbol of the subcarriers. To establish a connection, every BV WXC on the route allocates a cross-connection with sufficient spectrum to create an appropriately sized end-to-end optical path (see figure 1).

The use of optical OFDM as a bandwidth-variable and highly spectrum-efficient modulation format can provide scalable and flexible sub- and super-wavelength granularity, in contrast to the conventional, fixed-grid WDM network. However, this new concept poses additional challenges on the networking level, since the routing and wavelength assignment (RWA) algorithms of traditional WDM networks are no longer directly applicable. A connection requiring capacity larger than that of an OFDM subcarrier has to be assigned a number of contiguous subcarrier slots for increased spectral efficiency (remember that OFDM uses overlapping orthogonally modulated adjacent subcarriers). In this context, the wavelength continuity constraint of traditional WDM networks is transformed to a spectrum continuity constraint. Also, note that in OFDM many properties of the transmitted signal are determined in the electrical domain and can be managed by software. A feature that is particularly important for further increasing the flexibility and efficiency of an OFDM network is the choice of the number of modulated bits per symbol for each subcarrier (or for the set of subcarriers corresponding to a connection). To address these issues, new Routing, Modulation Level and Spectrum Allocation (RMLSA) algorithms as well as appropriate extensions to network control and management protocols have to be developed.

The problem of planning a flexible OFDM-based optical network has only recently received some attention. The spectrum allocation problem in an OFDM-based core network, in a slightly different setting than the one considered here, has been examined in [11]. In particular, the authors in [11] use shortest path routing and do not account for the requirement of contiguous spectrum allocation for the OFDM subcarriers. An OFDM-based access network (OFDMA) and OFDMA sub-wavelength spectrum assignment to form fixed-grid WDM wavelengths are presented in [12]. The planning of an opaque point-to-point OFDM-based network with adaptive modulation levels based on transmission distance restrictions has been examined in [13]. A comparison of the number of transponders required to design a bandwidth flexible OFDM network using fixed 50 GHz spaced grid to that of a traditional 50 GHz fixed-grid and rigid bandwidth WDM network is presented in [14]. Although not yet studied in depth, the flexibility of OFDM is also expected to offer significant benefits in a dynamic network environment with time-varying connection rates as well as in dynamic restoration scenarios.

We consider the planning phase (offline problem) in OFDM-based elastic optical networks, where we are given a traffic matrix with the requested transmission rates of all connections. Our objective is to serve the connections and minimize the utilized spectrum under the constraint that no spectrum overlapping is allowed among these connections. To serve the connections efficiently, we exploit the two degrees of flexibility provided by OFDM, namely, the elastic spectrum allocation and the modulation level adaptation. In our previous works [17][18], we have formulated the Routing Modulation Level and Spectrum Allocation (RMLSA) problem and presented various algorithms to solve it; ranging from combinatorial optimization algorithms based on integer linear programming (ILP) formulations and a heuristic algorithm that sequentially serves the connections, combined with appropriate ordering policies and simulated annealing. Using these algorithms, we present here a short study in which we evaluate the spectrum utilization benefits that can be obtained by the flexible utilization of bandwidth enabled by OFDM, when compared to a typical, fixed-grid WDM network.This instruction file for Word users (there is a separate instruction file for LaTeX users) may be used as a template. Kindly send the final and checked Word and PDF files of your paper to the Contact Volume Editor. This is usually one of the organizers of the conference. You should make sure that the Word and the PDF files are identical and correct and that only one version of your paper is sent. It is not possible to update files at a later stage. Please note that we do not need the printed paper.

We would like to draw your attention to the fact that it is not possible to modify a paper in any way, once it has been published. This applies to both the printed book and the online version of the publication. Every detail, including the order of the names of the authors, should be checked before the paper is sent to the Volume Editors.

2   OFDM-Based Optical Network

In this section we shortly present the basic elements of the elastic OFDM optical network envisaged in our study.

In OFDM, data is transmitted over multiple orthogonal subcarriers. This technology has been widely implemented in various systems, such as wireless local area network (LAN) and asymmetric digital subscriber line (ADSL). Recently, research efforts have focused on an optical version of OFDM (OOFDM) as a means to overcome transmission impairments [4]-[6]. In addition to the advantages that stem from the low symbol rate of each subcarrier and the coherent detection that both help

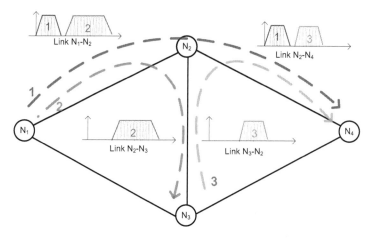

Fig. 1. Spectrum flexible OFDM-base optical network

to mitigate the effects of physical impairments, OFDM also brings unique benefits in terms of spectral efficiency, by allowing the spectrum of adjacent subcarriers to overlap thanks to their orthogonal modulation. Moreover, OFDM enables elastic bandwidth transmission by allocating a variable number of low-rate subcarriers to a transmission.

OFDM provides an additional degree of flexibility as described next. Typically, digital signal processing (DSP) are used at the transmitter and the receiver, to create the OFDM signal in the RF domain, while I-Q modulators and corresponding receivers are used to upconvert/downconvert the signal to the optical domain [6] [13]. Digital processing provides the capability to adapt many properties of the transmitted signal, in contrast to hardware implementations of 10/40/100 Gbits transponders in traditional WDM networks. In particular, each OFDM subcarrier can be modulated individually using, for example, single bit per symbol binary phase-shift keying (BPSK), QPSK (2 bits per symbol), 8QAM (3 bits per symbol), or 16QAM (4 bits per symbol), etc., while using the same I-Q modulator for the transmission. In contrast, in traditional WDM networks, changing the modulation level/ format would require the use of a different transponder [15].

The choice of the modulation level has to take into account the required Quality of Transmission (QoT) of the connection. A common assumption in optical OFDM ([9][13][14]) is that the transmission distance of the optical path is the sole QoT factor of interest. Transmissions over shortest optical paths are able to utilize higher modulation levels. Under this assumption, we can find the higher modulation level that can be used over a path if we are given its length.

A related issue is the choice of the spectral and capacity characteristics of the subcarriers. For example, consider a 50 Gbps connection that is served by an OFDM optical path consisting of 10 subcarriers, 5 GHz spaced, using QPSK to transmit 5 Gbps per subcarrier. Assume also that we can use a shorter path that supports 16 QAM modulation format with acceptable QoT, using 10 subcarriers of 2.5 GHz and 5Gbps each, or 5 subcarriers of 5 GHz and 10 Gbps each, or another combination.

In the literature [9][13] and our previous works [17][18], it is assumed that a subcarrier always utilizes a constant spectrum F GHz, irrespectively of the modulation format. Thus, for constant subcarrier spectrum F, the capacity of the subcarrier is defined by the modulation level choice.

Based on the above, a connection requesting a specific rate has two degrees of flexibility, the modulation level and the spectrum. Once these have been determined, the signal transmitted over the optical path is routed through bandwidth variable wavelength cross-connects (BV WXCs) towards the receiver. In this routing process, only the spectrum domain is essential. Every bandwidth variable WXC on the route allocates a cross-connection with the corresponding spectrum to create an appropriate-sized end-to-end optical path. To do so, the BV WXC has to configure its spectral switching window in a contiguous manner according to the spectral width of the incoming optical signal. MEMS or liquid crystal-based wavelength-selective switches (WSSs) can be employed as bandwidth variable WXC switching elements [10]. To avoid interference effects between adjacent optical paths, appropriate spectrum separation, implemented by spectrum guardbands, is required [9].

2.1   Transmission Rate Service Guarantees

Although the transmission rate of a connection may fluctuate with time, from the operators' perspective the network has to be planned to guarantee the service of a connection for a requested rate. This translates to the requirement for non-overlapping spectrum allocation to all connections for their requested rates. Although planning a network in this way may result in some waste of resources, when the connections under-utilize their provisioned bandwidth, there are still major gains that can be obtained over the traditional WDM networks.   These gains include (i) the high spectrum efficiency because of the orthogonally modulated overlapping subcarriers, (ii) the fine granularity at the low-rate subcarrier level, (iii) the adaptable modulation level, (iv) impairment tolerance due to OFDM properties, and (v) a possible reduction in power consumption by partially deactivating the transmitters, adjusting them to the rate at a specific time. Note that, at a specific time, unused spectrum could be shared and allocated to connections that surpass their requested transmission rates or to best-effort traffic, but this spectrum will be de-allocated when the initially provisioned connection requires it.

Additional gains in spectrum efficiency can be obtained by network planning based on time scheduling, using information on the traffic time-variations, or by allowing overlapping spectrum allocation based on stochastic traffic models. For example, connections with transmission rates that are complementary in time, in the sense that when the rate of a connection increases, the opposite tends to happen to that of another one, could be served by shared spectrum slots. The operational phase of the network, where online algorithms are used to serve dynamic traffic, is also an interesting and future topic of study.

2.2   RMLSA Requirements

Routing and wavelength assignment (RWA) algorithms devised for fixed grid WDM systems are not applicable to OFDM networks, even when the modulation level is fixed. To see that note that the OFDM routing and spectrum allocation (RSA) problem can be transformed into a typical RWA formulation, by viewing a subcarrier in the RSA problem as a wavelength of equal capacity in the RWA problem. Although a typical RWA algorithm is able to find a route for a connection requiring a number of subcarriers (wavelengths in the RWA context), the wavelengths that will be found by the RWA algorithm are not generally going to be contiguous. Allocating contiguous subcarriers is crucial in OFDM networks, since the spectrum of adjacent subcarriers must overlap to enable higher spectral efficiency.

Moreover, the majority of RWA algorithms proposed in the literature utilize variables and constraints that depend on the number of wavelengths, which in a typical WDM network seldom exceeds 80, beyond which the operators have to install additional fibers per link. The high number of OFDM subcarrier limits the applicability of traditional RWA algorithms. Finally, in the RMLSA problem, we also have to choose a modulation level per subcarrier and connection. This problem in a slightly different setting has been recently examined for mixed line rate (MLR) WDM systems [15].

From the above discussion it is clear that RMLSA requires the development of new algorithms that will (i) serve a connection utilizing a contiguous and elastic spectrum, (ii) formulate the problem using variables and constraints that do not depend on the number of subcarriers, and (iii) enable the choice of the modulation level for each connection.

In our previous works [17][18] we have developed such algorithms. We have presented an optimal combinatorial optimization algorithm and a decomposition approach (that breaks the problem into (a) routing and modulation level allocation and (b) spectrum allocation) based on integer linear programming (ILP) formulations. We have also presented a sequential heuristic algorithm that uses a pre-ordering phase and then a heuristic RMLSA algorithm designed for serving single demands, to sequentially serve all the demands one-by-one.

3   Spectrum Efficiency Study

We evaluate the spectrum utilization benefits that can be obtained through the elastic allocation of bandwidth of the envisioned OFDM-based optical network when compared to a typical fixed-grid WDM network.

For planning the OFDM network we used the simulated annealing meta-heuristic with 1000 iterations presented in [18]. We assume that a subcarrier utilizes F=5 GHz spectrum, single bit per symbol modulation (BPSK) capacity per subcarrier is C=2.5 Gbps, and the required guardband G=2 subcarriers. Regarding OFDM adaptive modulation levels we assume that BPSK can be used for transmissions up to 3000km, QPSK can be used up to 1500 km, etc. using the half distance law of [13]. For the RWA we used the LP-relaxation algorithm of [16], and we do not consider interference physical impairments, but when we utilize a mixed line rate (MLR) WDM system (Fig. 4) we use transmission reach constraints. We used the generic DT topology of Fig. 2 and a realistic traffic matrix for this network provided for 2009, as reported in deliverable D2.1 in www.diconet.eu/deliverables.asp. In this matrix, the average rate between nodes is around 15 Gbps. We uniformly scaled this realistic traffic matrix so as to obtain traffic matrices up to 8 times larger than the reference matrix of 2009.

Fig. 2. The generic DT network topology, with 14 nodes and 46 directed links

In the experiments presented in Fig 3 we assume that the WDM network uses 40 Gbps wavelengths with QPSK in a 50 GHz grid. Thus, when QPSK is used in both OFDM and WDM networks, they both have equal spectrum efficiency per 50 GHz WDM wavelength. As mentioned, OFDM provides two flexibility degrees: (i) the elastic spectrum allocation and (ii) the adaptive modulation level. At light loads, the elastic spectrum allocation (first degree of flexibility) is quite efficient due to the finer granularity of the OFDM network, and yields high spectrum gains. As the load increases the gains from the elastic spectrum allocation decrease, since the finer granularity of the OFDM network (5 Gbps as opposed to 40 Gbps) is not that important. Although the spectrum gains of the elastic spectrum allocation decreases as the load increases, this is compensated by the improving effects of the adaptive modulation level (second degree of flexibility) that become more dominant at heavy load. At heavy load high-rate connections are served over shorter paths using higher modulation levels, improving the spectrum efficiency of the OFDM network. This, yields significant spectrum utilization gains as the load increases.

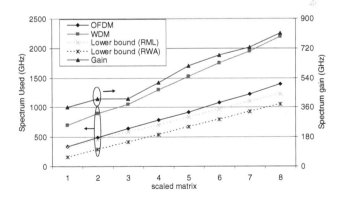

Fig. 3. Spectrum utilization of a 40 Gbps WDM network with spectral efficiency per wavelength (50 GHz) of 0.8 bit/s/Hz and an OFDM-based network with flexible spectrum allocation and adaptive modulation levels

In Fig. 4 we the compare the OFDM with a mixed-line rate (MLR) WDM system. For the WDM network we assumed that 10 Gbps, 40 Gbps, or 100 Gpbs wavelengths are able to transmit with acceptable quality up to 3000 km, 1500 km, and 500 km, respectively. The modulation level restrictions of the OFDM-based network were as previously, resulting in almost the same spectral efficiency per wavelength as the WDM network for the same transmission distance. Comparing the results of Fig. 3 and Fig. 4 we see the improvements obtained in the WDM network when utilizing MLR (the performance of OFDM is the same in both figures). Still, the performance of OFDM with flexible spectrum allocation and adaptive modulation levels is superior and the spectrum improvements are maintained even for heavy traffic loads. Note that adapting the modulation level in the OFDM network can be performed by software, while in the MLR WDM network changing the wavelength capacity requires the utilization of different transponders, constraining the adaptability to traffic changes.

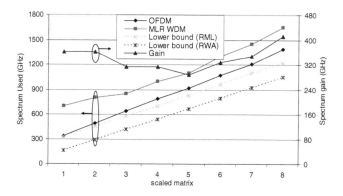

Fig. 4. Spectrum utilization of a mixed-line rate (MLR) WDM network with wavelength capacity of 10, 40 and 100 Gbps and an OFDM-based network with flexible spectrum allocation and adaptive modulation levels

An OFDM network would have better spectral characteristics per wavelength than a WDM network, because of the overlap of adjacent orthogonally modulated subcarriers. Moreover, due to low subcarrier rates, the reach of the OFDM network is expected to be higher than that of a WDM network. These attributes were not used in the above study, but instead we assumed similar spectral and reach characteristics for both OFDM and WDM networks in order to evaluate the gains that can be obtained by OFDM flexibility. When these characteristics are taken into account, combined with the flexibility benefits as presented here, the performance advantages of an OFDM-based network would be even more pronounced.

4   Conclusions

Optical OFDM is receiving recent attention as a spectrum-efficient modulation format that can provide elastic bandwidth transmission. We considered the problem of planning an OFDM-based optical network where connections are provisioned based on their requested transmission rate and assuming no spectrum overlapping between them. OFDM provides two degrees of flexibility, namely, elastic spectrum allocation and modulation level adaptation. Our results showed that the OFDM-based network has significant spectrum benefits over a typical fixed-grid WDM network, indicating that the OFDM architecture offers a promising solution for future high capacity transport networks.

References

[1] Berthold, J., Saleh, A.A.M., Blair, L., Simmons, J.M.: Optical networking: Past, present, and future. IEEE/OSA J. Lightw. Technol. 26(9), 1104–1118 (2008)

[2] Yoo, S.J.B.: Optical Packet and Burst Switching Technologies for the Future Photonic Internet. IEEE/OSA J. Lightw. Technol. 24(12) (2006)

[3] Chen, Y., Qiao, C., Yu, X.: Optical burst switching: A new area in optical networking research. IEEE Network 18(3), 16–23 (2004)

[4] Shieh, W., Yi, X., Tang, Y.: Transmission experiment of multi-gigabit coherent optical OFDMsystems over 1000 km SSMF fiber. Electron. Lett. 43, 183–185 (2007)

[5] Lowery, A., Du, L.B., Armstrong, J.: Performance of Optical OFDM in Ultralong-Haul WDM Lightwave Systems. IEEE/OSA J. of Lightw. Technol. 25(1), 131–138 (2007)

[6] Armstrong, J.: OFDM for Optical Communications. IEEE/OSA J. Ligthw. Technol. 27(3) (2009)

[7] Jinno, M., Takara, H., Kozicki, B., Tsukishima, Y., Sone, Y., Matsuoka, S.: Spectrum-efficient and scalable elastic optical path network: architecture, benefits, and enabling technologies. IEEE Commun. Mag. 47(11) (2009)

[8] Kozicki, B., Takara, H., Yoshimatsu, T., Yonenaga, K., Jinno, M.: Filtering Characteristics of Highly-Spectrum Efficient Spectrum-Sliced Elastic Optical Path (SLICE) Network, OFC (JWA43) (2009)

[9] Jinno, M., Kozicki, B., Takara, H., Watanabe, A., Sone, Y., Tanaka, T., Hirano, A.: Distance-Adaptive Spectrum Resource Allocation in Spectrum-Sliced Elastic Optical Path Network. IEEE Commun. Mag. 48(8) (2010)

[10] Ryf, R., Su, Y., Moller, L., Chandrasekhar, S., Xiang, L., Neilson, D., Giles, C.: Wavelength blocking filter with flexible data rates and channel spacing. IEEE/OSA J. Lightw. Tehcnol. 23(1) (2005)

[11] Zheng, W., Jin, Y., Sun, W., Guo, W., Hu, W.: On the Spectrum-Efficiency of Bandwidth-Variable Optical OFDM Transport Networks, OFC (OWR5) (2010)

[12] Wei, W., Hu, J., Qian, D., Ji, P.N., Wang, T., Liu, X., Qiao, C.: PONIARD: A Programmable Optical Networking Infrastructure for Advanced Research and Development of Future Internet. J. Lightw. Technol. 27(3) (2009)

[13] Bocoi, A., Schuster, M., Rambach, F., Kiese, M., Bunge, C., Spinnler, B.: Reach-Dependent Capacity in Optical Networks Enabled by OFDM, OFC (OMQ4) (2009)

[14] Klekamp, A., Rival, O., Morea, A., Dischler, R., Buchali, F.: Transparent WDM network with bitrate tunable optical OFDM transponders, OFC (NTuB5) (2010)

[15] Nag, A., Tornatore, M., Mukherjee, B.: Optical Network Design With Mixed Line Rates and Multiple Modulation Formats. IEEE/OSA J. Lightw. Tehcnol. 28(4) (2010)

[16] Christodoulopoulos, K., Manousakis, K., Varvarigos, E.: Offline Routing and Wavelength Assignment in Transparent WDM Networks. IEEE/ACM Transactions on Networking 18(5) (2010)

[17] Christodoulopoulos, K., Tomkos, I., Varvarigos, E.: Spectrally/Bitrate Flexible Optical Network Planning. In: ECOC 2010 (2010)

[18] Christodoulopoulos, K., Tomkos, I., Varvarigos, E.: Elastic Bandwidth Allocation in Flexible OFDM-Based Optical Networks. IEEE/OSA Journal of Lightwave Technology 29(9) (2011)

Evaluation of Effect of Network Energy Consumption in Load Distribution across Data Centers

Harumasa Tada[1], Makoto Imase[2], and Masayuki Murata[2]

[1] Faculty of Education, Kyoto University of Education
[2] Graduate School of Information Science and Technology, Osaka University

Abstract. Recently, the consumption of a considerable amount of energy by data centers has become a serious problem, and there are many researches aiming at the reduction of this energy consumption. However, previous researches intend to reduce only the energy consumed inside data centers. To the best of our knowledge, there are few researches on load distributuion that focus on the network energy consumption arising from the communication across data centers. In this study, we consider the energy consumption of the network as well as that of the data centers in the request distribution across geographically distributed data centers. By using various conditions, we calculate the overall energy consumption of two request distribution policies—one respects the network energy consumption, and the other does not. By comparing these two policies, we examine the condition under which the network energy consumption is worth considering.

Keywords: Cloud Computing, Electricity Cost, Optimization, Simulated Annealing.

1 Introduction

Recently, cloud computing has become popular, and the demand of data centers is increasing rapidly. On the other hand, modern data centers consume considerable amount of energy because of the performance improvement of the servers. The reduction in the electricity cost is one of the great concerns for data centers.

There are many researches on performance control and load distribution intended to reduce a data center's electricity cost. The basic approaches to this cost reduction include turning off redundant servers or using the dynamic voltage/frequency scaling (DVFS) of CPUs, according to the measured current load or the estimated future load [1–5]. These appraches are integrated with the load distribution to the servers [6–8]. Other researches focus on the energy consumption of disks or the memory of servers [9–12]. Moreover, recent researches on load distribution focus on the energy consumption of the cooling equipment in data centers [13–15].

These researches are aimed at reducing the amount of energy consumed in a data center. On the other hand, large organizations such as Google and Yahoo!

I. Tomkos et al. (Eds.): BROADNETS 2010, LNICST 66, pp. 501–517, 2012.

operate multiple data centers. These centers are geographically distributed for the purpose of the provision of service to worldwide customers or the improvement of service availability upon system failure. Data transfer among such data centers involves the energy consumption of network devices such as routers or switches. To the best of our knowledge, there are few researches on load distribution intended to reduce the network energy consumption across data centers.

However, the amount of communication across geographically distributed data centers seems to increase rapidly. For example, Google has many data centers around the world and is performing large-scale distributed processing on self-constructed systems [16–18]. Moreover, many companies including Yahoo! are using Hadoop, the opensource implementation of a large-scale distributed file system. The use of such systems that are premised on data distribution is expected to grow rapidly, and therefore, the network traffic across data centers will increase in the future. Moreover, we consider that in order to reduce the energy cost of data centers, the task transfer to remote data centers has to be carried out frequently. Recently, data centers are often located in the countryside for the reduction of the energy cost. For example, some data centers are located in the cold district in order to reduce the energy consumed for cooling [19]. Other data centers are located near the power plant to reduce the power transmission cost [20]. Moreover, one of the reasons why container data centers [21] are attracting attention is that they can move easily according to the variation in the operation cost, including the energy cost. In general, such data centers are located far away from the place of the computing demand. Therefore, tasks need to be transferred via a network.

There is a research on request distribution intended to reduce the energy cost for geographically distributed multiple data centers. Le *et al.* [22] proposed a method for reducing the electricity cost consumed by servers or the cooling equipments in data centers. Their method exploits the difference in the electricity prices of areas where data centers are located and the variation in the electricity price with respect to time. However, Le's method does not consider the network energy consumption when requests are transferred to data centers. Therefore, it is possible that requests are forwarded to distant data centers whose electricity cost is low, and the overall electricity cost increases.

In this study, we consider the energy consumption of the network as well as that of the data centers in the request distribution across geographically distributed data centers. By using various conditions, we calculate the overall energy consumption of two request distribution policies—one respects the network energy consumption, and the other does not. By comparing these two policies, we examine the condition under which the network energy consumption is worth considering.

The rest of this paper is organized as follows: In section 2, we mention the related works. In section 3, we explain the problem discussed in this paper and the request distribution policies. In section, 4, we compare the two policies—one respects the network energy consumption, and the other does not. We conclude the paper in section 5.

2   Related Works

There have been many researches to reduce the energy consumption of data centers, and various methods have been proposed. These methods control the energy consumption of a data center according to the center's load. The ultimate goal is to make the energy consumption of a data center proportional to its load.

Early researches proposed schemes that turn off redundant servers or use the dynamic voltage/frequency scaling (DVFS) function of CPUs in order to reduce the energy consumption while preserving the throughput [1,2]. Pinheiro *et al.* [1] proposed a method for changing the number of servers that are turned on (active servers) according to the current load. Elnozahy *et al.* [2] integrated the control of the operating voltage of the CPU and the method proposed in [1]. The drawback of the on/off scheme is the coarse granularity of the control of the energy consumption (in the unit of servers) and the effect of the DVFS is limited to the energy consumption of CPUs.

The following researches consider the service level agreement (SLA) or quality of service (QoS) and propose methods that aim at ensuring that the processing time of the requests meets the deadline as well as preserving the throughput [3–5]. Sharma *et al.* [3] proposed a method that for controlling the frequency of the CPU in order to maintain synthetic utilization that is defined to process the requests before the deadline. Rusu *et al.* [4] proposed a method for controlling the CPU frequency of each server on the basis of prediction of the processing time made by keeping a track of the processing time of the processed requests. Chen *et al.* [5] proposed two methods and compared them. One determines the CPU frequency of each server by solving the optimization problem whose constraint is the processing time estimated using the queuing model. The other changes the CPU frequency of each server dynamically using the feedback control based on the measured processing time. Although the deadline is essential in most of the real world services, meeting the deadline causes some inefficiency in the energy consumption.

Recent researches consider a relatively detailed model and introduce load distribution to servers [6–8]. Heath *et al.* [6] proposed the request distribution method for heterogeneous data centers, including different types of servers. Their method uses the model that reflects the variations in the characteristics of the CPUs and disks of different servers. Rusu *et al.* [7] proposed a method for heterogeneous data centers. Their method determines the number of active servers and the request distribution to these servers on the basis of the measured value of energy consumption. Chen *et al.* [8] proposed a method for data centers that provide connection-intensive services. Their method determines the number of active servers and the request distribution to these servers in order to reduce the energy consumption while avoiding the service not available (SNA) error and server-initiated disconnection (SID). Elaborate control based on realistic models contributes to the reduction of energy consumption. However, the trade off between its effect and its implementation cost need to be considered.

As other approaches, some methods that focus on the server components other than the CPU are proposed [9–12]. In a Google data center, at its peak time, the

DRAM occupies 30% of the total energy consumption and the disk occupies 10% while the CPU occupies 33% [23]. This fact implies that the methods focusing on memories and disks are promising for reducing the energy consumption of data centers. Gurumurthi *et al.* [9] proposed a method that modulates the disk rotation speed to reduce the energy consumption. Zhu *et al.* [10] proposed a cache replacement algorithm to reduce the energy consumption of disks. Ganesh *et al.* [11] argue that log-structured file systems can extend the time for which the disks stop in order to reduce the energy consumption. Li *et al.* [12] proposed a method that switches the operation modes of memories and disks in order to reduce the energy consumption. In order to make the server energy consumption proportional to the server load, it is essential to consider components other than the CPUs. However, this approach often results in an ad hoc method depending on a particular implementation of servers.

Recent researches have focused on the load distribution to servers in order to reduce the energy consumption by the cooling equipment [13–15]. Since servers that consume a considerable amount of energy produce a large amount of heat, the cooling equipment also requires considerable energy to cool the servers. Moreover, recently, because of a high density implementation of servers, the heat density of data centers is increasing and the energy required for cooling is rapidly increasing. Therefore, it will be important to reduce the energy required for cooling the servers in the future. Moore *et al.* [13] introduced a metric called heat recirculation factor (HRF) which expresses the amount of heat recirculation in a data center, and proposed a load distribution method based on HRF. Bash *et al.* [14] proposed a method that allocates a high load to servers placed in an area where the cooling efficiency is high in a data center in order to reduce the energy consumption for cooling. Tang *et al.* [15] proposed a task scheduling method that allocates tasks to equalize the inlet temperature of servers using a detailed model of the heat recirculation in a data center. Since the cooling is responsible for a significant portion of the energy consumption in today's data center [23], the importance of researches on cooling is increasing.

3   Request Distribution That Respects Network Energy Consumption

3.1   System Model

We extend the model introduced by Le *et al.* [22]. Figure 1 shows our system model. The system includes several front-ends, several data centers, and a single scheduler.

The transfer of a request is as follows: First, a client sends a request to a front-end. The front-end that receives the request selects a data center to forward the request. The data center that receives the request processes it and returns the result to the front-end. Then, the front-end forwards the result to the client.

The front-ends distribute requests to data centers according to certain fractions. These request fractions are updated periodically according to the variation

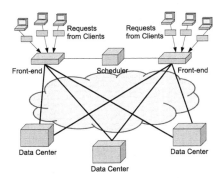

Fig. 1. System Model

in the request arrival rate. The period during which the request fractions are fixed is called an *epoch*. At the beginning of an epoch, the scheduler determines the request fractions for each front-end. In order to calculate the request fractions, the scheduler can use the information about the network and all the data centers. Moreover, the scheduler is periodically notified of the expected request arrival ratio by the front-ends. The details of the calculation of the request fractions are mentioned in the following sections.

3.2   Problem Overview

The problem that we deal with in this study is the determination of the fraction of requests that should be directed to each data center in order to minimize the total energy consumption of the data centers and the network. The energy consumption is measured on a daily basis. That is, the *accounting period* is one day. In the calculation of the request fraction, the following constraints must be taken into account. First, the peak request arrival rate of each data center cannot exceed the capacity of the data center. The *capacity* of a data center means the maximum number of requests that it can process in 1s. Second, the service has a single SLA that should be satisfied. The SLA is expressed as (L, P) which means that ratio of requests that are processed within time L to the total number of requests that arrive in a day should be more than P. The request processing time, which is measured at the front-end, is the time from forwarding a request to receiving its result. This implies that the communication delay between a client and a front-end does not affect the request processing time.

3.3   Assumptions about Energy Consumption

The energy consumption of a data center is the sum of the energy consumption of the servers, local network devices, cooling equipment, and so on. As mentioned in section 2, there are many methods to reduce the energy consumption of data centers. By applying these methods, we can control the energy consumption of the data center according to its load. In this study, we consider the ideal situation in which the energy consumption of a data center is proportional to its load. However, we must take into account that a data center consumes a fixed amount of energy irrespective of its load; we call this energy the *base energy*.

The energy consumption of a network is a sum of the energy consumption of network devices such as routers and switches, and devices for signal transfer such as amplifiers. The reduction of the network energy consumption has attracted attention recently, and there is a pioneering research [24]. However, the relation between the load and the energy consumption is still unclear. In this study, we consider the ideal situation in which the network energy consumption is proportional to the amount of traffic. We do not consider the network base energy because there is traffic that is unrelated to our system on the network.

On the basis of the above observations, we make the following assumptions.

1. A data center consumes a fixed amount of energy irrespective of the number of processed requests.
2. In addition to (1), a data center consumes the energy proportional to the number of processed requests per unit time.
3. The average amount of traffic between a front-end and a data center for requests is proportional to the number of forwarded requests per unit time.
4. The network energy consumption between a front-end and a data center is proportional to the average amount of traffic of (3). That is, we do not consider the energy consumption of the traffic that is unrelated to our system.

3.4   Problem Formulation

We formulate the problem mentioned in section 3.2 as an optimization problem.

Table 1 shows the parameters used in the formulation. In the table, t represents an epoch. Most parameters are the same as those used in [22]. We have replaced the parameters of monetary energy costs (\$) with those of energy consumptions (kWh) and introduced the variable h that represents a front-end. Figure 2 depicts an example of the parameters.

$$OverallEC = \sum_t \sum_h \sum_i (f_{hi}(t) LT_h(t) EC_{hi}) \tag{1}$$

$$\forall t \forall h \forall i \, f_{hi}(t) \geq 0 \tag{2}$$

$$\forall t \forall h \sum_i f_{hi}(t) = 1 \tag{3}$$

$$\forall t \forall i \sum_h (f_{hi}(t) LR_h(t)) \leq LC_i \tag{4}$$

$$\frac{\sum_t \sum_h \sum_i (f_{hi}(t) LT_j(t) CDF_i(L, offered_i(t)))}{\sum_t \sum_h LT_h(t)} \geq P \tag{5}$$

Table 1. Parameters (EC stands for "energy consumption")

Symbol	Meaning
$f_{hi}(t)$	Ratio of requests to be forwarded from frontend h to center i
$OverallEC$	Total EC (kWh)
EC_{hi}	Avg. EC (kWh) of a request forwarded from frontend h to center i
a_i	Avg. EC (kWh) of a request at center i
b_{hi}	Avg. network EC (kWh) of a request forwarded from frontend h to center i
LC_i	Load capacity (reqs/s) of center i
$LR_h(t)$	Expected peak service rate (reqs/s) at frontend h
$LT_h(t)$	Expected total service load (#reqs) at frontend h
$offered_i(t)$	$\sum_h (LR_h(t) \times f_{hi}(t))$ (reqs/s)
$CDF_i(L, offered_i)$	Expected ratio of requests that complete within L time, given $offered_i$ load

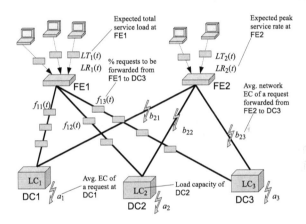

Fig. 2. Example of Parameters

The objective function to minimize is the total energy consumed for an entire day (formula (1)). However, the base energy is not included in formula (1) because it is not changed by the request distribution. If the monetary energy cost is used as the objective function instead of the energy consumption, formula (1) can be easily modified.

Constraints are shown as formulas (2)–(5). Formula (2) shows that the request ratio from any front-end to any data center should not be negative. Formula (3) shows that all requests that arrive at the front-end should be allocated to some data center. Formula (4) shows that the peak request arrival ratio of a data center should not exceed its capacity. Formula (5) shows that the SLA (see section 3.2) should be satisfied, that is, the ratio of requests that are processed within time L to the total number of requests that arrive in a day should be more than P.

3.5 Optimization Policy

In this study, we consider two optimization policies. Policy DC+Net respects the energy consumption of data centers and the network. Policy DConly respects the energy consumption of only the data centers. The difference in these policies is the definition of EC_{hi} included in objective function (formula (1)), which is shown as formulas (6) and (7).

$$\text{Policy DC+Net:}\quad EC_{hi} = a_i + b_{hi} \tag{6}$$

$$\text{Policy DConly:}\quad EC_{hi} = a_i \tag{7}$$

3.6 Instantiation of Parameters

The parameters of the optimization problem of section 3.4 are given as follows:

On the basis of assumptions stated in section 3.3, it can be inferred that the energy consumption per request at data center i and the network energy consumption per request for a pair of front-end h and data center i, denoted by a_i and b_{hi} respectively, are constants.

The request arrival rate differs for each front-end and varies with time. Therefore, the peak request arrival rate and the total service load of front-end h in epoch t, denoted by $LR_h(t)$ and $LT_h(t)$ respectively, are given as functions of epoch t.

We define $CDF_i(L, \mathit{offered}_i)$ as follows:

$$CDF_i(L, \mathit{offered}_i) = \begin{cases} 1 \ (\mathit{offered}_i \leq LC_i) \\ 0 \ (\mathit{offered}_i > LC_i) \end{cases} \tag{8}$$

Formula (8) shows that unless the load of data center i exceeds its capacity, all requests arrived that arrive at i are processed before their deadline, including the communication delay. This implies that as long as the constraint shown as formula (4) is satisfied, the constraint shown as formula (5) is also satisfied.

4 Evaluation

In order to examine the condition under which the network energy consumption should be considered, we applied two policies DC+Net and DConly mentioned in section 3.5 to various conditions and compared the energy consumption.

4.1 Methodology

We consider a system having three front-ends $FE1 \sim FE3$ and five data centers $DC1 \sim DC5$.

By using various parameter settings, we calculated and compared the total energy consumption of DC+Net and DConly. The term "the total energy consumption" refers to the total amount of energy consumed by all data centers and the network except for the base energy. The total energy consumption is calculated as follows: For each policy, we solve the optimization problem mentioned in 3.4 to determine the request fractions for all front-ends. Then, we calculate the whole-day energy consumption of each policy according to the request fractions determined above by assuming that the requests arrive at each front-end at the predicted rate. The calculated value is the lower limit of the energy consumption for each policy.

4.2   Solving the Optimization Problem

As in [22], we use the simulated annealing (SA) technique to solve the optimization problem. We use 1-hour epochs and divide a day into 24 epochs.

A state in SA, denoted by s, is defined as follows:

$$s = \{f_{hi}(t) \mid h \in FE, i \in DC, t \in EP\}$$

FE, DC, and EP represent the sets of all front-ends, all data centers, and all epochs, respectively.

Table 2 shows the pseudocode of SA that we used. $exp(x)$ denotes the exponential function. $Energy(s)$ is a function that returns the energy consumption in state s according to formula (1) in section 3.4. $Rand()$ is a function that returns a random actual number from 0 to 1. $Neighbor(s)$ is a function that returns a neighbor of state s. A neighbor of s is calculated as follows: First, $x \in FE$, $y, z \in DC$, and $u \in EP$ are selected randomly such that $f_{xy}(u) \in s$, $f_{xz}(u) \in s$, and $f_{xy}(u) \geq 0.1$. Then, a neighbor of s is made from s by subtracting 0.1 from $f_{xy}(u)$ and adding 0.1 to $f_{xz}(u)$. Table 3 shows the parameter setting of SA.

4.3   Parameter Settings

Request Arrival Rate. The request arrival rate of a front-end varies with time. In this study, we use the request arrival rate used in [22], which is shown in figure 3.

We use the same request arrival rate for three front-ends but shift -3 h, 0, and $+6$ h, respectively, reflecting different time zones in which front-ends are placed.

Capacity of Data Centers. We set the same capacities (200 reqs/s) for all data centers. Note that the total amount of capacities of five data centers is larger than the sum of peak request arrival rates of three front-ends. This implies that data centers are never overloaded as long as requests are distributed appropriately. This is a necessary condition for obtaining a solution of the optimization problem that meets the constraint of formula (4) in section 3.4.

Table 2. Pseudocode of SA

$s \leftarrow S_{init}$; $e \leftarrow Energy(s)$; $tp \leftarrow TP_{init}$
$s_{best} \leftarrow s$; $e_{best} \leftarrow e$
for $l = 1$ to L
    $s_{new} \leftarrow Neighbor(s)$
    $e_{new} \leftarrow Energy(s_{new})$
    if $e_{new} < e_{best}$ **then**
        $s_{best} \leftarrow s_{new}$; $e_{best} \leftarrow e_{new}$
    if $e_{new} < e$ **then**
        $s \leftarrow s_{new}$; $e \leftarrow e_{new}$
    else if $Rand() < exp((e - e_{new})/tp)$ **then**
        $s \leftarrow s_{new}$; $e \leftarrow e_{new}$
    $tp \leftarrow tp * C$
return s_{best}

Table 3. Parameter Setting of SA

Symbol	Meaning	Value
S_{init}	Initial state	$f_{hi}(t) = 0.2$ for any h, i, t
TP_{init}	Initial temperature	1000
C	Parameter to control temperature drop	0.999
L	Number of iterations	10000

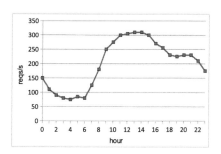

Fig. 3. Request Arrival Rate

Variations of Energy Consumption of Data Centers. In this study, we consider a situation in which there is variation in the energy consumption per request of data centers.

Table 4 shows the result of SPECpower_ssj2008 [25], a benchmark test of the power efficiency of servers. This tells us that there is a great difference between the power efficiency of a new server and that of an old one. In this study, as the metric of the variation in multiple values, we use the ratio of the maximum value and the minimum value, which we call the *max-min ratio*. For example, the max-min ratio in table 4 is approximately 51.2.

Table 4. SPECpower_ssj2008 Results

Server name	ssj_ops/W	Hardware Availability
HP ProLiant DL380 G4	45.2	Sep-2004
HP ProLiant SL2x170z G6	2316	Oct-2009

We used four settings, denoted by $d0 \sim d3$, of the energy consumption of data centers. The ratio of the energy consumption values of the data centers in each setting is shown in table 5. $d0$ is the case in which the energy consumption values of all data centers are the same and the max-min ratio is 1. In the case of $d1$, $d2$, and $d3$, the max-min ratios are 2.6, 5, and 25 respectively. Note that the sum of the values of the five data centers is the same for all settings. This implies that when the requests are distributed uniformly to all data centers, the total energy consumption is the same at any setting.

Table 5. Variation in Data Center Energy Consumption

ID/DC	DC1	DC2	DC3	DC4	DC5
d0	9	9	9	9	9
d1	5	7	9	11	13
d2	3	6	9	12	15
d3	1	2	5	12	25

Variation in Energy Consumption of Network. The energy consumption of the network depends on the location of the front-end and the data center. The energy consumption is low if they are close and high if they are far apart. In order to reflect this fact, we set different values of energy consumption per request for each pair of a front-end and a data center.

In order to determine the variation in the energy consumption of the network, we referred to the variation in the hop counts in a real network. We believe that the hop count is related to the energy consumption of the network since it represents the number of network devices that the packets pass through. Fei *et al.* [26] measured the hop counts from a host at UCLA to various sites on the Internet and reported that the maximum hop count was 27. On the basis of this fact, we used four settings, denoted by $n0 \sim n3$, of the energy consumption of the network. They are shown in table 6. $n0$ is the case with no variation, and its max-min ratio is 1. In the case of $n1$,$n2$, and $n3$, the max-min ratios are 2.6, 5, and 25 respectively.

Ratio of Energy Consumptions of a Data Center and the Network. The result of the comparison between DC+Net and DConly is significantly affected by the ratio of the energy consumption between a data center and the network. Of course, it is desirable that this ratio is close to the ratio in the real world. However, it is very difficult to measure the energy consumption of a

Table 6. Variation in Network Energy Consumption

ID	FE/DC	DC1	DC2	DC3	DC4	DC5
	FE1	9	9	9	9	9
n0	FE2	9	9	9	9	9
	FE3	9	9	9	9	9
	FE1	5	7	9	11	13
n1	FE2	12	8	5	8	12
	FE3	13	11	9	7	5
	FE1	3	6	9	12	15
n2	FE2	13	8	3	8	13
	FE3	15	12	9	6	3
	FE1	1	2	5	12	25
n3	FE2	18	4	1	4	18
	FE3	25	12	5	2	1

real network. Instead, we determined this ratio on the basis of the ratio of the energy consumption between a server and a router. According to the report of Principled Technologies Inc. [27], a server with Intel Xeon 5160 CPU processed 40461 requests/s in WebBench benchmark [28]. Unfortunately, neither the model name nor the energy consumption of the server is found in this report. Instead, we use the specification of Hitachi HA8000/130 server that has the same CPU, whose maximum energy consumption is 611 W. Using these value, we calculated the energy consumption per request to be approximately 15 mJ. On the other hand, Chabarek *et al.* [29] performed experiments using routers and measured the relation of the number of processed packets and the energy consumption. They reported that Cisco GSR 12008 router consumed 770 W when it processed 540,000 packets/s. That is, the energy consumption per packet was 1.4 mJ. Considering that the processing of a single request requires multiple packets and a packet passes multiple routers to reach the destination, we conclude that the difference in the energy consumption per request between a server and the network is not considerable in the case of WWW services. Based on this observation, we used three patterns of the ratio (2:1, 1:1, and 1:2) of the average energy consumption of a data center and the network.

4.4 Results

In this section, we show the calculated total energy consumption of DC+Net and DConly. In the following graphs, the x-axis shows the setting of the energy consumption of the data centers ($d0 \sim d3$) and the network ($n0 \sim n3$), which are shown in tables 5 and 6. The y-axis shows the total energy consumption of each policy, which is divided by the total energy consumption when the requests are distributed uniformly to all data centers, which is denoted by EQUAL.

Figure 4 shows the result when the ratio of the energy consumption of the data centers and the network is 2:1. Unless the data center energy consumption values are the same (setting $d0$), the difference in the total energy consumption

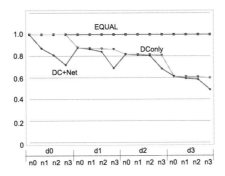

Fig. 4. Data Center:Network=2:1

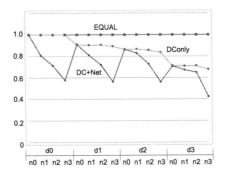

Fig. 5. Data Center:Network=1:1

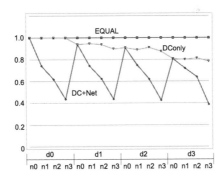

Fig. 6. Data Center:Network=1:2

between DC+Net and DConly is very small in the case of settings $n1$ and $n2$. In this case, since the data center energy consumption is dominant, the effect of considering the network energy consumption is relatively small. When the network energy setting is $n3$, DC+Net outperforms DConly by more than 15% in the case of settings $d1 \sim d3$. Since in the case of setting $n3$, the variation

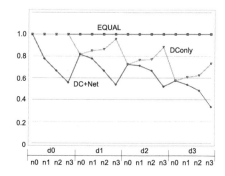

Fig. 7. Data Center:Network=1:1(half load)

in the network energy consumption is significantly large, the network energy consumption is worth considering even if the data center energy consumption is relatively large.

Figure 5 shows the result when the ratio of the energy consumption of the data centers and the network is 1:1. Unless the network energy setting is $n0$, DC+Net outperforms DConly significantly. This result shows that the network energy consumption should be considered in this case.

When the data center setting is $d3$, DC+Net outperforms DConly with more than 10% only in the case of setting $n3$. On the other hand, when the data center setting is $d1$, DC+Net outperforms DConly by more than 10% in the case of settings $n1 \sim n3$. This result shows that the network energy consumption should be considered when the variation in the energy consumption of the data centers is small. This is because when the variation in the energy consumption of the data centers is small, the choice of a data center makes little difference to the energy consumption of the data centers, and therefore, the effect of the network energy consumption becomes relatively large.

By comparing the case in which the network energy consumption is uniform and the data center energy consumption varies widely (setting $d3$ with $n0$) and the case in which the data center energy consumption is uniform and the network energy consumption varies widely (setting $d0$ with $n3$), we observe that DC+Net shows low energy consumption in the latter case. As shown in tables 5 and 6, the max-min ratios of the energy consumption of settings $d3$ and $n3$ is the same. Therefore, considering that the average energy consumption values of the data centers and the network are the same, we conclude that the effect of the variation in the network energy consumption is larger than that of the data center energy consumption. This is because the optimization of the network energy consumption has more options than that of the data center energy consumption. The data center energy consumption of a request is the same irrespective of a front-end that sends the request. In terms of the data center energy consumption, there are some data centers to which no requests should be forwarded. However, when the total load is heavy, some requests have to be forwarded to such data centers and the total energy consumption worsens. On the other hand, the network energy consumption of a request varies depending on the front-end that sends the request. In terms of the network energy consumption, every data center can receive requests from "near" front-ends. Therefore, even when the total load is heavy, the total energy consumption can be improved by the optimization considering the network energy consumption.

Figure 6 shows the result when the ratio of the energy consumption of the data centers and the network is 1:2. Irrespective of the variation in the energy consumption of data centers, in the case of all settings $n0 \sim n3$, DC+Net outperforms DConly by more than 10%. This result implies that it is essential to consider the network energy consumption in this case. In particular, in the case of setting $n3$, DC+Net outperforms DConly by more than 50% in the case of settings $d0 \sim d3$. This result shows that the effect of the network energy consumption is dominant.

Figure 7 shows the result when the ratio of the energy consumption of the data centers and the network is 1:1 and the total load is set to half of the default value. In the case of setting $n0$, in which the network energy consumption is uniform, the total energy consumption values of both DC+Net and DConly improve by 10%–20% as compared to those shown in figure 5. This is because when the load is considerably less than the data centers' capacity, many options are possible with respect to the choice of data centers; this enhances the effect of optimization. On the other hand, in the case of settings $d1 \sim d3$, the total energy consumption of DC+Net at setting $n3$ is 30%–40% lower than at setting $n0$ while that of DConly at setting $n3$ is 15%–30% higher than at setting $n0$. This result shows that when there are many options with respect to the choice of data centers, the penalty of ignoring the network energy consumption during the request distribution becomes relatively large.

On the basis of the above results, we argue that the network energy consumption should be considered in optimization if at least one of the following conditions is satisfied. Note that if some conditions are satisfied simultaneously, the effect of the network energy consumption will increase even if each condition is not sufficiently satisfied.

1. The average energy consumption of the network is equal to or larger than that of the data centers.
2. The max-min ratio of the energy consumption of the network is larger than 20.
3. The max-min ratio of the energy consumption of data centers is smaller than 3.
4. The total load is smaller than 50% of the total capacity of data centers.

5   Conclusions

The reduction of the energy consumption of data centers has been an important research topic. Recently, the energy consumption of the network is attracting considerable attention. In this study, we focused on the request distribution across geographically distributed data centers. We compared two optimization

policies—one respects the network energy consumption, and the other does not—
and examined the condition under which the network energy consumption is
worth considering.

Our evaluations are based on the total energy consumption values calculated
in the case of optimization. Since these values are estimated under an ideal
condition, they differ from the real energy consumption. In real systems, the
policy that is good for optimization does not necessarily show good performance
because of unexpected events, e.g., the unexpected increase in the number of requests. We do not consider such unexpected conditions because the scope of this
study is the effectiveness of considering the network energy consumption. Nevertheless, robustness, the property to maintain a good performance even under
unexpected conditions, is one of the important metrics for request distribution
methods. Evaluation in a more realistic environment is our future work.

References

1. Pinheiro, E., Bianchini, R., Carrera, E., Heath, T.: Load balancing and unbalancing
   for power and performance in cluster-based systems. In: Workshop on Compilers
   and Operating Systems for Low Power, vol. 180, pp. 182–195 (2001)
2. Elnozahy, E., Kistler, M., Rajamony, R.: Energy-Efficient Server Clusters. In: Fal-
   safi, B., VijayKumar, T.N. (eds.) PACS 2002. LNCS, vol. 2325, pp. 179–196.
   Springer, Heidelberg (2003)
3. Sharma, V., Thomas, A., Abdelzaher, T., Skadron, K., Lu, Z.: Power-aware QoS
   management in web servers. In: Proceedings of the 24th IEEE International Real-
   Time Systems Symposium, p. 63 (2003)
4. Rusu, C., Xu, R., Melhem, R., Mosse, D.: Energy-efficient policies for request-
   driven soft real-time systems. In: Euromicro Conference on Real-Time Systems,
   ECRTS 2004 (2004)
5. Chen, Y., Das, A., Qin, W., Sivasubramaniam, A., Wang, Q., Gautam, N.: Managing server energy and operational costs in hosting centers. ACM SIGMETRICS
   Performance Evaluation Review 33(1), 303–314 (2005)
6. Heath, T., Diniz, B., Carrera, E., et al.: Energy conservation in heterogeneous
   server clusters. In: Proceedings of the Tenth ACM SIGPLAN Symposium on Principles and Practice of Parallel Programming, p. 195. ACM (2005)
7. Rusu, C., Ferreira, A., Scordino, C., Watson, A., Melhem, R., Mossé, D.: Energy-
   efficient real-time heterogeneous server clusters. In: Proceedings of RTAS, pp. 418–
   428 (2006)
8. Chen, G., He, W., Liu, J., Nath, S., Rigas, L., Xiao, L., Zhao, F.: Energy-aware
   server provisioning and load dispatching for connection-intensive internet services.
   In: Proceedings of the 5th USENIX Symposium on Networked Systems Design and
   Implementation, pp. 337–350. USENIX Association (2008)
9. Gurumurthi, S., Sivasubramaniam, A., Kandemir, M., Franke, H.: DRPM: dynamic
   speed control for power management in server class disks. In: Proceedings of the
   30th Annual International Symposium on Computer Architecture, p. 181. ACM
   (2003)
10. Zhu, Q., David, F., Devaraj, C., Li, Z., Zhou, Y., Cao, P.: Reducing energy con-
    sumption of disk storage using power-aware cache management (2004)
11. Ganesh, L., Weatherspoon, H., Balakrishnan, M., Birman, K.: Optimizing Power
    Consumption in Large Scale Storage Systems. In: Proceedings of the 11th USENIX
    Workshop on Hot Topics in Operating Systems, HotOS 2007 (2007)

12. Li, X., Li, Z., Zhou, Y., Adve, S.: Performance directed energy management for main memory and disks. ACM Transactions on Storage (TOS) 1(3), 380 (2005)
13. Moore, J., Chase, J., Ranganathan, P., Sharma, R.: Making scheduling gcool h: Temperature-aware workload placement in data centers. In: Proceedings of the USENIX Annual Technical Conference, pp. 61–75 (2005)
14. Bash, C., Forman, G.: Cool job allocation: Measuring the power savings of placing jobs at cooling-efficient locations in the data center. In: 2007 USENIX Annual Technical Conference on Proceedings of the USENIX Annual Technical Conference, pp. 1–6. USENIX Association (2007)
15. Tang, Q., Gupta, S., Varsamopoulos, G.: Energy-efficient thermal-aware task scheduling for homogeneous high-performance computing data centers: a cyber-physical approach. IEEE Transactions on Parallel and Distributed Systems, 1458–1472 (2008)
16. Ghemawat, S., Gobioff, H., Leung, S.: The Google file system. ACM SIGOPS Operating Systems Review 37(5), 43 (2003)
17. Chang, F., Dean, J., Ghemawat, S., Hsieh, W., Wallach, D., Burrows, M., Chandra, T., Fikes, A., Gruber, R.: Bigtable: A distributed storage system for structured data. In: Proceedings of the 7th USENIX Symposium on Operating Systems Design and Implementation, OSDI 2006 (2006)
18. Dean, J., Ghemawat, S.: Map Reduce: Simplified data processing on large clusters. Communications of the ACM-Association for Computing Machinery-CACM 51(1), 107–114 (2008)
19. Data Center Knowledge, Google's Chiller-less Data Center (2009), http://www.datacenterknowledge.com/archives/2009/07/15/googles-chiller-less-data-center/
20. Information Week, Google In Oregon: Mother Nature Meets The Data Center (2007), http://www.informationweek.com/blog/main/archives/2007/08/google_in_orego.html
21. Hamilton, J.: Architecture for modular data centers, Arxiv preprint cs/0612110 (2006)
22. Le, K., Bianchini, R., Martonosi, M., Nguyen, T.: Cost-and Energy-Aware Load Distribution Across Data Centers. In: Workshop on Power Aware Computing and Systems, HotPower 2009 (2009)
23. Barroso, L., Hölzle, U.: The datacenter as a computer: An introduction to the design of warehouse-scale machines. Synthesis Lectures on Computer Architecture 4(1), 1–108 (2009)
24. Mahadevan, P., Sharma, P., Banerjee, S., Ranganathan, P.: A Power Benchmarking Framework for Network Devices. In: Fratta, L., Schulzrinne, H., Takahashi, Y., Spaniol, O. (eds.) NETWORKING 2009. LNCS, vol. 5550, pp. 795–808. Springer, Heidelberg (2009)
25. Standard Performance Evaluation Corporation, SPECpower_ssj (2008), http://www.spec.org/power_ssj2008/
26. Fei, A., Pei, G., Liu, R., Zhang, L.: Measurements on delay and hop-count of the internet. In: IEEE GLOBECOM 1998-Internet Mini-Conference (1998)
27. Principled Technologies, WebBench performance on quad-core and dual-core dual-processor servers (2006), http://www.principledtechnologies.com/clients/reports/Intel/X5355WebBench1106.pdf
28. WebBench, http://cs.uccs.edu/~cs526/webbench/webbench.htm
29. Chabarek, J., Sommers, J., Barford, P., Estan, C., Tsiang, D., Wright, S.: Power awareness in network design and routing. In: IEEE INFOCOM (2008)

Green Wireless Networks
through Exploitation of Correlations
(Invited Paper)

Frank Oldewurtel and Petri Mähönen

RWTH Aachen University, Institute for Networked Systems
Kackertstrasse 9, D-52072 Aachen, Germany
fol@inets.rwth-aachen.de

Abstract. Energy-efficient wireless networks are essential to reduce the effect of global warming and to minimize the operational costs of future networks. In this paper we investigate approaches exploiting spatial correlations that offer a high potential to significantly decrease the total energy consumption thus enabling "green" wireless networks. In particular, we analyze the impact of distributed compression and optimized node deployments on the energy-efficiency of networks. Furthermore, we present results on the operational lifetime of networks which is often a major performance criterion from applications' perspective.

Keywords: green networking, energy consumption, spatial correlation, distributed compression, deployment strategies.

1 Introduction

Information and communication technologies (ICTs) are a contributor to the global energy consumption. Increasing demands of energy is foreseen in future since intensified use and extended availability of ICTs is expected. Power generation through regenerative but also fossil technologies causes greenhouse gas emissions. Climatologists determined that primarily accumulated carbon dioxide (CO_2) forms a shield in the earth's atmosphere that prevents heat radiated away from earth [1]. Thus, carbon dioxide advances the global warming that beyond doubt will have strong negative impact on the societies world-wide. It has been estimated that ICTs contribute around 2-2.5 % of global greenhouse gas emissions already in the year 2007 with a strong trend to increase [2].

Although wireless networks are responsible for only a minor share of CO_2 emissions they have shown exponentially increasing energy consumption figures, doubling almost every four years. In addition, providing communication services on a world-wide scale would consume about 40 % of the current global power generation capabilities if western standards are targeted [3]. In addition to minimizing the environmental impact of industry, network operators show strong interest for economical reasons since the expenses for energy tend to increase,

I. Tomkos et al. (Eds.): BROADNETS 2010, LNICST 66, pp. 518–533, 2012.
© Institute for Computer Sciences, Social Informatics and Telecommunications Engineering 2012

while the revenues in bandwidth tend to decrease. Furthermore, energy conservation can also lead to improved performance in terms of operational lifetime of networks if those consist of nodes that are battery-operated.

Within the communications and networking sector a trend towards improved energy-efficiency, thus reducing the CO_2 footprint, has been identified. The most common energy reduction approaches target the hardware components and the power management of nodes and entire networks. Additionally, significant energy savings can be achieved if two other concepts are taken into account. First, improvements are possible if the amount of data to be communicated between nodes is reduced [4–7]. Second, gains can be achieved through optimisation of the applied node deployment strategies [8–11]. Both concepts considered in this work rely on the energy-efficient exploitation of spatial correlations and are complementary. Although we focus on the spatial domain, in principle also the temporal domain offers great potential. Spatial correlations are often inherent to networking scenarios taken from the wide field of data gathering applications. For example, for monitoring and surveillance purposes various correlation properties in the phenomenon under observation can be assumed.

Previous works often seek to decrease energy consumption either by trading off communication vs. signal processing costs or shifting computational complexity between transmitter and receiver. However, not all works thoroughly take into account the overall net energy balance including entire signal processing costs, see, for example, [6, 7, 11–13]. It is therefore of strong interest to minimize the *total energy* consumed, which includes the energy consumed in terms of communication as well as the energy sacrificed for the extra signal processing. Those additional costs occur due to the use of data reduction techniques offering the actual benefits.

In this study we present results on the analysis of the total energy consumed by a clustered wireless network. We consider lossless distributed compression on the lowest level in the hierarchy of nodes since we can make use of synergy effects if most of the data is reduced where it is originated. In addition, the net energy balance of our proposed approach is provided. Furthermore, different node deployment strategies are evaluated since the location of nodes has a strong impact on the energy consumption and operational lifetime of the network.

The remainder of the paper is structured as follows. In Section 2 we explain the lossless distributed compression scheme in detail. Section 3 briefly describes the system model including the node deployment models used for topology generation. In Section 4 we present the net energy balance taking into account the total energy consumed. Section 5 provides extensive simulations results and the energy-efficiency analysis of the considered wireless networks. Network lifetime is investigated in Section 6 since it is often a major performance criterion in the case of battery-operated networks. Finally, Section 7 draws conclusions.

2   Distributed Compression

In wireless networks observations of neighbouring nodes can be seen as spatially correlated discrete sources. The source information consists of blocks of v

symbols (bits) that are compressed into the same number of blocks of u symbols each, with $u < v$. Thus, the packet sizes are reduced prior to the transmission while the overall number of packets is kept constant. We denote the probability density function of the random source X by $p(x)$. Let $H(X)$ denote the information entropy which is the measure of the uncertainty associated to the source X. The Shannon source coding theorem states the limits on the achievable code rate R_x for lossless data compression described by $R_x \equiv \frac{u}{v} \geq H(X)$, where v and u denote the block lengths of the information word and of the code word, respectively.

One way of exploiting the spatial correlation of, for example, two neighboring nodes X and Y is through joint compression based on inter-node information exchange. If the nodes are allowed to communicate with each other, they could avoid the transmission of any redundant information, leading to the total compression rate R equal to the joint entropy $H(X, Y)$ [14]. The strong drawback is that this comes at the expense of energy and substantial communication overhead. The traditional way for separate encoding avoiding any inter-node communication is to compress at the total rate $R = H(X) + H(Y)$. Since we assume spatial correlation, $H(X) + H(Y)$ is always greater than $H(X, Y)$ and thus this approach is suboptimal and not considered further. Hence, the question arises what we will loose in compression efficiency if the costly inter-node communication is not allowed. This question has been answered by the fundamental information-theoretic result obtained by Slepian and Wolf [15]. The theorem states that there is theoretically no loss in performance if the joint distribution quantifying the node correlation structure is known. The Slepian-Wolf theorem defines the achievable rate regions for two sources and is given by

$$R_x \geq H(X|Y),$$
$$R_y \geq H(Y|X),$$
$$R = R_x + R_y \geq H(X, Y), \tag{1a}$$

where $H(\cdot|\cdot)$ and $H(\cdot, \cdot)$ are the conditional entropy and the joint entropy, respectively.

The source nodes do not communicate with each other and directly send their compressed observations to a central node (such as cluster head or gateway) which performs joint decoding. Hence, we actually reduce computational complexity of the source nodes and increase the computational complexity of the usually more powerful central node without sacrificing performance. Distributed compression can save energy by compression while preserving accuracy [16]. Furthermore, this approach is independent on the modality of the observed data.

We implement the source encoder as simple and energy-efficient matrix multiplication. The entropy tracking algorithm estimates the underlying joint probability density function $p(x, y)$ of the observations obtained by the source nodes which describes the correlation structure. Based on $p(x, y)$ we can determine the conditional information entropy

$$H(X|Y) = -\sum \sum p(x, y) \log p(x|y). \tag{2}$$

The previous works follow rather idealistic assumptions in terms of communication and network topology. Furthermore, the energy consideration is often highly abstracted and does not consider practical issues at sufficient depth. In this work, we study various effects on the performance of distributed compression in more realistic topologies. A sophisticated phenomenon model flexibly generating sensed phenomena with widely varying correlation structure is applied. For thorough and realistic evaluation we make use of a detailed framework that includes a Gilbert-Elliot error model and an energy model allowing even bit-level evaluation. Our network analysis considers the signal processing costs associated with distributed compression including entropy tracking capability and packet header overhead. The evaluation of more realistic deployment models leads to the identification of the best fitting deployment strategy in relation to the characteristics of the phenomena under study.

3   System Model

3.1   Phenomenon Model and Spatial Correlations

In this study we make use of synthetically generated and spatially correlated data fields $h(x, y)$ [17]. The model used is independent on the node density, the number of nodes or the topology. Any correlation structure can be taken into account by varying the parameters controlling the statistical structure of $h(x, y)$ which gives great flexibility. One important parameter that can be varied is the correlation distance $r_{\max}$. If the distance between data elements of the phenomena is more than $r_{\max}$, then they cannot be directly derived from each other. The generated data sampled from the model shows good correspondence when statistically compared with experimental data. It assumes an underlying stationary process that has any unique first-order distribution. This model is more general and more realistic than the commonly used jointly Gaussian model which makes it a suitable choice for our purposes.

3.2   Deployment Model

The node deployment model consists of the specification of the total number of nodes N, and the coordinates $(x_i, y_i)_{i=1}^N$ of the individual nodes. We assume a fixed region A with area $|A|$ and that the coordinates are defined by a *random point process* (PP) [18]. The simplest example of such a PP is the (homogeneous) Poisson PP for which the coordinates are distributed uniformly and independently on the region under study, and N is a Poisson random variable with parameter $\lambda|A|$. Here λ is called the *intensity* of the process, with units of points per unit area. The Poisson assumption might be convenient but unfortunately a rather unrealistic one. Hence, the need arises to develop and apply improved and more realistic models to make more reliable statements about real wireless networks. For more details on enhanced deployment models the reader is referred to [9]. In order to study the effects of different network realisations we have chosen three suitable deployment models. The first model we study is the Poisson PP for comparison purposes. The second and third are clustered models called the Thomas PP and the Matern PP.

The Thomas process [19] is based on a Poisson PP of intensity λ_T which is used to generate *cluster centers*. Then each parent or cluster center point is replaced by a cluster of points. The number of points in each cluster l_i is a Poisson distributed random variable with mean value μ_T,

$$\text{Prob}_{l_i}(l_i) = \frac{\mu_T{}^{l_i}}{l_i!} e^{-\mu_T}. \tag{3}$$

The locations of nodes (x, y) in each cluster are sampled from a two-dimensional (symmetric) normal distribution with variance σ_T^2 and the mean located at the cluster center,

$$\text{p}_{x,y}(x, y) = \frac{1}{2\pi\sigma_T^2} \exp\left(-\frac{x^2 + y^2}{2\sigma_T^2}\right). \tag{4}$$

Another example of a cluster process is the Matern point process. As for the Thomas PP, the number of parent points are distributed according to a Poisson process with intensity λ_M. The number of cluster members in each cluster is also sampled from a Poisson distribution with mean μ_M. The only difference lies in how the cluster points themselves are distributed. While for the Thomas PP a normal distribution is used, the cluster points of a Matern PP are uniformly distributed over a disc of radius R_M with the respective parent point as the center. Again, the parent points do not occur in the resulting realisation of the point process.

All introduced models can be conveniently described by up to three parameters. These parameters can easily be adjusted in order to create different models of the same class of point processes. For comparison reasons we have to ensure that all deployment models exhibit the same overall area density λ_A. Hence, the condition $\lambda_A = \lambda = \lambda_T \cdot \mu_T = \lambda_M \cdot \mu_M = \text{const.}$ needs to be always fulfilled.

3.3 Communication Model

In terms of communication we assume that each node has an omni-directional transmission range and utilizes erroneous links. For modeling error characteristics a widely used model is the "Gilbert-Elliot bit error model" [?, 20, 21]. This model is fundamentally based on a two-state Markov model that takes bit error bursts into account. In the case of packet errors, generated by this model, at maximum three retransmissions are initiated. In our simulations we observe an overall average packet error rate of ≈ 0.1 per scenario. We apply practical distributed compression achieving high energy-efficiency through exploitation of spatial correlations in the phenomena under study [4,5,8]. Here distributed compression is performed clusterwise and based on node pairs where the compressing node is a cluster member and the reference node is its cluster head. In terms of mobility the nodes are quasi-stationary at known positions and the overall network density is constant in all cases. In our simulations we focus on the closest-to-center of gravity scheme meaning that the cluster member with the minimum

Euclidean distance to the cluster center is selected as cluster head. For analysis of further cluster head selection schemes, see, for example, [5]. Throughout the scenarios the shortest path multihop routing protocol is applied.

4   Derivation of the Net Energy Balance

Let T_x and R_x denote the transmission and reception energies per bit, respectively. For the derivation of the net energy balance we also take into account the packet header overhead and the additional energy consumption due to the compression-related signal processing such as encoding, joint decoding and entropy tracking. While E_c accounts for the energy consumed for encoding, E_d stands for the decoding energy. The entropy tracking algorithm is executed each observation cycle once and consumes the energy denoted as E_t.

Let $D(i)$ denote the set of all descendent nodes of node i that belong to the same cluster. Furthermore, let $D_h(i)$ denote the set of all descendent nodes of node i that are cluster members belonging to any other cluster. Using the indicator function $\mathbf{1}_m(i)$ that is set to 1 if node i is a cluster member and 0 otherwise, we can define the energy consumption of a node i as follows:

$$
\begin{aligned}
e_i = \mathbf{1}_m(i) & \left[kE_c + (kc_in+p)T_x + (T_x+R_x)\sum_{j\in D(i)}(kc_jn+p) \right] \\
& + \left(1 - \mathbf{1}_m(i)\right)\left[E_t + |D(i)|kE_d + R_x\sum_{j\in D(i)}(kc_jn+p) \right. \\
& \left. + (kn+p)\left[|D(i)|T_x + |D_h(i)|(T_x+R_x)\right] \right],
\end{aligned} \tag{5}
$$

where n is the number of uncompressed bits and c being the used code rate which is always equal to the conditional information entropy $c = H(X|Y)$ of the considered node pair. The number of compressed bits thus becomes $c \cdot n$. Additionally, each packet consists of a constant number of packet header bits denoted by p and a payload consisting of a number of compressed or uncompressed phenomena observations k.

In order to analyse the energy consumption behaviour of cluster members and cluster heads in the distributed compression case vs. the conventional case we derive the energy balance as follows. For the worst case we assume a cluster member node i in the distributed compression case that may relay only uncompressed (i.e., $c = 1$) packets so that its energy balance is not inequitable improved over the conventional case. Thus, due to

$$
\sum_{j\in D(i)} kc_jn = |D(i)|kn \tag{6}
$$

we can neglect the relay part in our consideration and find

$$
(kn + p)T_x = kE_c + (kc_in+p)T_x. \tag{7}
$$

This leads to the condition

$$c_i \leq 1 - \frac{E_c}{nT_x}, \tag{8}$$

which has to be always fulfilled if a cluster member node i saves energy. Hence, we define the *break-even* point determined by the code rate $c_i = 1 - \frac{E_c}{nT_x}$. Only if the code rates reach the break-even point we automatically switch from the distributed compression scheme to the conventional scheme (i.e., no compression applied).

In case node i is a cluster head, we can ignore the transmission and relay energies in the balance since those are identical in both the distributed compression case and the conventional case. Using

$$|D(i)|R_x(kn + p) = E_t + |D(i)|kE_d + R_x \sum_{j \in D(i)} (kc_j n + p), \tag{9}$$

we find the condition for the cluster head to be

$$\sum_{j \in D(i)} c_j \leq |D(i)|(1 - \frac{E_d}{R_x n}) - \frac{E_t}{R_x kn}. \tag{10}$$

Since $E_d/(R_x n) > 1$ for our energy model and $c_j \geq 0$ is always valid, no energy savings can be achieved at the cluster head. This is not surprising due to the distributed compression principle of shifting the computational complexity from the cluster members to the cluster head. This is the trade-off we face so that the more resource-constrained cluster members, being the majority of the nodes, can conserve significant amounts of energy. For more details the reader is referred to [8]. However, in order to achieve reduced total energy consumption the cluster member level needs to at least compensate the inherent losses on cluster head level. In the following we show that indeed strong total energy savings can be achieved by our proposed approach.

5   Energy-Efficiency Analysis

Applying the presented energy model, see equation (5), we investigate both the impact of distributed compression and the impact of the deployment strategy on the energy-efficiency behaviour of wireless networks.

5.1   Impact of Distributed Compression

For comparison of the compression scheme and the conventional scheme we consider the total energy savings through distributed compression according to different parameters. Figure 1 shows the total energy savings in relation to the correlation distance parameter r_{max}. From the figure we can observe that the topology types behave very similar to each other and that the energy savings are strongly dependent on the correlation properties. From our quantitative results

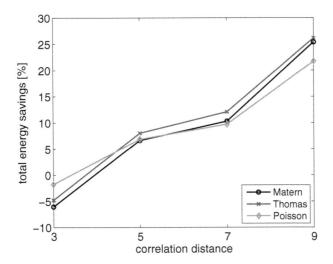

Fig. 1. Total energy savings vs. correlation distance for three topology types; 2000 simulation runs

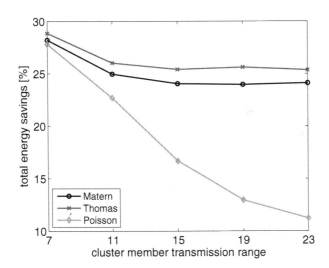

Fig. 2. Total energy savings vs. cluster member transmission range for three topology types; $r_{max} = 9$, 2000 simulation runs

it follows that the savings can differ up to 31 % between phenomena that exhibit weak or strong spatial correlations. Since distributed compression seeks to exploit the correlation in the phenomena data the results confirm the intuition that the stronger the phenomenon is correlated the stronger the energy savings will be. Only for very weak correlations ($r_{max} = 3$) small negative values can be observed. In this case the distributed compression gains on cluster member level cannot compensate for the loss on cluster head level. In addition, for moderate to stronger correlations total energy savings of up to 26 % at $r_{max} = 9$ can be realized by distributed compression. Figure 2 shows the total energy savings according to the transmission range of the cluster members. The transmission range is increased from 7 to 23 units with a constant step size of 4. We can observe that the savings of cluster PP topologies are overall independent on the transmission range. Only at very small transmission ranges the cluster PP topologies exhibit slightly higher energy savings. For the Poisson topology savings significantly increase while decreasing transmission range. The reason for improved savings at reduced transmission ranges in all cases lies in the resulting topologies having increased graph depth. While the node depth is defined as the number of edges that are traversed from the root node to the chosen node, the graph depth is defined as the maximum appearing node depth. Restricting the transmission range leads to cluster members that cannot be directly connected to the respective cluster head. It follows that intermediate nodes are used in order to create a path between such cluster members and the cluster head using the shortest path routing protocol. The intermediate nodes participate in the energy savings since gains can be achieved through multi-hop communication of compressed packets. We see only little improvement in energy savings for cluster PP topologies in contrast to the Poisson topology. The probability that cluster members cannot be directly connected to the cluster head is much lower for the considered cluster PP topologies since nodes are grouped together more closely. It is noteworthy that the transmission range effects the total energy savings of a given topology dependent on the cluster spread parameter of the chosen deployment strategy.

From Figure 3 we can see the relation between total energy savings and the payload size included during packet formation. The number of observations being the payload is increased from 10 to 200. Increasing the payload size leads to less relative header costs per packet and results in improvements independent on the topology type.

Overall we can see from Figure 1 to Figure 3 that independent on the parameter varied the distributed compression gains for cluster PP topologies are superior to those for Poisson PP in all cases. Furthermore, the Thomas PP topology outperforms all other topologies and achieves significant total energy savings through distributed compression of ≈ 26 % in the reference case.

5.2   Impact of Deployment Strategies

For evaluation of different deployment strategies we focus on the total energy consumption of wireless networks as the performance criterion. Because of the significant total energy savings achieved by distributed compression we focus on wireless networks applying this powerful technique.

Figure 4 and Figure 5 compare the deployment strategies considering the parameters correlation distance and number of clusters, respectively. The total en-

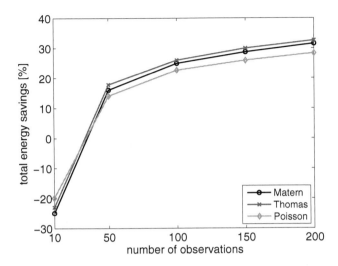

Fig. 3. Total energy savings vs. number of observations per packet payload for three topology types; $r_{\max} = 9$, 2000 simulation runs

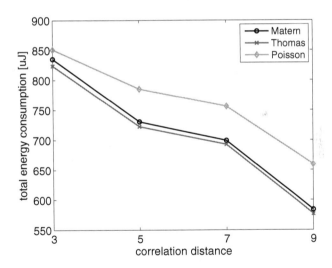

Fig. 4. Total energy consumption vs. correlation distance for three topology types; compression scheme applied; 2000 simulation runs

ergy consumption shows similar behaviour and reaches its minimum for Thomas PP topologies. Taking into account the parameters number of observations and cluster member transmission range confirms this result. Hence, the Thomas deployment is our suggested node deployment strategy since it outperforms the other approaches for all phenomena under study.

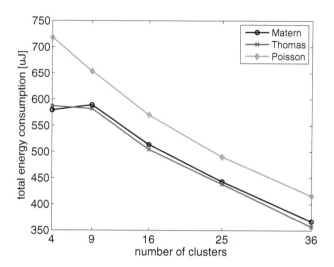

Fig. 5. Total energy consumption vs. number of clusters for three topology types; compression scheme applied; $r_{max} = 9$, 2000 simulation runs

It is noteworthy that the data points at the minimum number of clusters $= 4$ in Figure 5 are not fully reliable. The corresponding node connectivity is decreased by $\approx 20\%$ for cluster topologies and even $\approx 40\%$ for Poisson topologies compared to all other data points. Low number of clusters result in large cluster sizes. This implies inter-node distances exceeding the given transmission range of cluster members thus generating disconnected nodes. Not connected nodes are omitted in the energy consideration which leads to artificially lower values in energy consumption.

We have shown that significant total energy savings can be achiy distribute compression in realistic environments. In addition, optimized deployment strategies lead to strongly reduced total energy consumption of wireless networks. Those candidate approaches thus have high potential to make future wireless networks "green".

6   Network Lifetime Analysis

Operational network lifetime is a major performance criterion for networks also from applications' perspective. Hence, we continue our analysis considering lifetime focusing on cluster members, being the majority of the nodes, since those are typically more resource-constrained than cluster heads. In our studies network lifetime is defined as the number of data gathering cycles elapsed until the first node in the network depletes its energy. After that it is considered to be "dead".

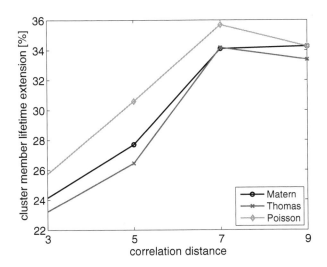

Fig. 6. Lifetime extensions of cluster members vs. the correlation distance for three topology types; 2000 simulation runs

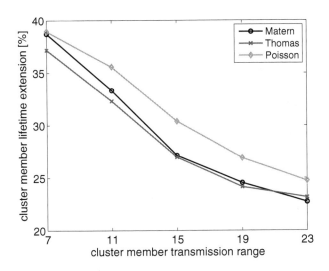

Fig. 7. Lifetime extensions of cluster members vs. the cluster member transmission range for three topology types; $r_{\max} = 9$, 2000 simulation runs

Figure 6 and Figure 7 depict the lifetime extensions on cluster member level in relation to the correlation distance and the cluster member transmission range for three topology types. Overall we can observe from those figures that the Poisson PP topology is superior to all other topology types in terms of cluster member lifetime extension. Other parameters are omitted since corresponding

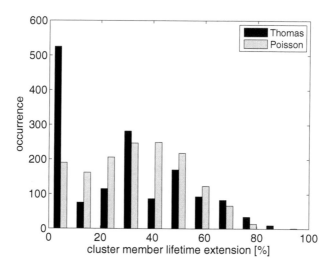

Fig. 8. Histograms of the lifetime extension of cluster members for the Thomas PP and Poisson PP topology; $r_{max} = 9$, 1500 simulation runs

results show similar behaviour. As we have seen this result is contrary to the energy-efficiency analysis. In the following we provide an explanation for this behaviour using the comparison of Thomas PP topology and the Poisson PP topology exemplarily.

Higher cluster member lifetime extensions for the Poisson PP topology compared to the cluster PP topologies are obtained. Reason is that there is on average less reduction in the *maximum* energy consumption of cluster members through distributed compression in the case of the cluster PP topologies. Independent on the topology type some nodes experience high conditional entropy values determined based on the phenomena values observed by the node pairs. Those entropy values can be higher than the break point, thus switching to the conventional scheme for such nodes since no energy savings can be achieved if distributed compression is applied in this particular case. This implies that a certain number of cluster members cannot improve their node lifetime. The overall number of nodes having no lifetime extension is higher for the cluster PP topology than for the Poisson PP topology. Figure 8 compares the histograms of the cluster member lifetime for the Thomas PP topology and the Poisson PP topology. From the figure we observe that the first bin representing no network lifetime extension has ≈ 3 times higher occurrences in the Thomas case than in the Poisson case, while the remaining part of the histograms does not show severe discrepancy.

The strong difference in occurrences of the first bin influences the overall network lifetime defined as the average value over the histogram. The resulting average network lifetime extension is 33.3 % in the Thomas case and 35.6 % in the Poisson case.

The rationale for very different occurrences of the first bin lies in the different probabilities of leaf nodes that are dependent on the topology type. A leaf node is defined as a cluster member that does not have any descendent nodes. The leaf node probability for the cluster PP topology is higher than for the Poisson PP topology. Nodes are located on average closer to the respective cluster head, forming often (albeit not always) direct connections due to the applied shortest path routing protocol. The Poisson PP topology inherently has thus less leaf nodes and more relaying cluster members at the same time. It is noteworthy that this effect is dependent on the cluster member transmission range and the cluster spread parameter since, for example, the Thomas PP topology with extremely large cluster spread can be seen as Poisson PP topology.

In contrast to leaf nodes, relaying cluster members experiencing high conditional entropies can improve their node lifetime. In fact this happens only when relay nodes benefit from their descendent nodes through relaying of compressed packets towards the sink. Required is at least a single descendent node experiencing entropy values below the break-point. Hence, even if relaying nodes face high entropy values their node lifetime can be improved by the help of other nodes.

As a result, considering energy consumption is not sufficient to make reliable statements on lifetime. We have shown that reduced total energy consumption does *not* directly imply extended operational lifetime as indicated in previous works, for example, [13, 22]. However, solutions minimizing total energy consumption can be used as a starting point towards maximizing network lifetime.

7   Conclusions

In this paper we have shown how "green" wireless networks with minimized operational costs can be realized. The two concepts proposed rely on the exploitation of spatial correlations inherent to both the phenomenon under study and the location of the nodes. In particular, we have investigated the distributed compression scheme and optimized node deployment strategies. The application of the candidate solutions show significantly reduced total energy consumption of wireless networks. Furthermore, we provided the analysis of the network lifetime being often a major performance criterion from applications' perspective. As a result, we found that reduced total energy consumption does not always directly imply extended operational lifetime of networks contrary to assumptions made.

Acknowledgment. This work was financially supported by the German Research Foundation (DFG) through the UMIC-research centre at the RWTH Aachen University.

References

1. Hansen, J., Sato, M., Kharecha, P., Russell, G., Lea, D., Siddal, M.: Climate change and Trace gases. Philosophical Transactions of Royal Society 365, 1925–1954 (2007)
2. McKinsey: The Impact of ICT on Global Emissions. Technical report, Note: on behalf of United Nations Environment Management Group (2007)
3. Fehske, A., Richter, F., Fettweis, G.P.: Energy Efficiency Improvements through Micro Sites in Cellular Mobile Radio Networks. In: Proceedings of Int. Workshop on Green Communications, in conjunction with GLOBECOM, Honolulu, USA, pp. 1–5 (2009)
4. Oldewurtel, F., Foks, M., Mähönen, P.: On a Practical Distributed Source Coding Scheme for Wireless Sensor Networks. In: Proceedings of the IEEE Vehicular Technology Conference (VTC spring), Marina Bay, Singapore, pp. 228–232 (2008)
5. Oldewurtel, F., Riihijärvi, J., Mähönen, P.: Efficiency of Distributed Compression and its Dependence on Sensor Node Deployments. In: Proceedings of the IEEE Vehicular Technology Conference (VTC spring), Taipei, Taiwan, pp. 1–5 (2010)
6. Baek, S.J., de Veciana, G., Su, X.: Minimizing Energy Consumption in Large-scale Sensor Networks through Distributed Data Compression and Hierarchical Aggregation. IEEE Journal on Selected Areas in Communications 22(6), 1130–1140 (2004)
7. Cristescu, R., Beferull-Lozano, B., Vetterli, M.: On Network Correlated Data Gathering. In: Proceedings of the INFOCOM, Hong Kong, pp. 2571–2582 (2004)
8. Oldewurtel, F., Mähönen, P.: Efficiency Analysis and Derivation of Enhanced Deployment Models for Sensor Networks. In: International Journal of Ad Hoc and Ubiquitous Computing, IJAHUC (2010) (note: accepted)
9. Oldewurtel, F., Mähönen, P.: Analysis of Enhanced Deployment Models for Sensor Networks. In: Proceedings of the IEEE Vehicular Technology Conference (VTC spring), Taipei, Taiwan, pp. 1–5 (2010)
10. Yang, S., Li, M., Wu, J.: Scan-Based Movement-Assisted Sensor Deployment Methods in Wireless Sensor Networks. IEEE Transactions on Parallel and Distributed Systems 18(8), 1108–1121 (2007)
11. Ganesan, D., Cristescu, R., Beferull-Lozano, B.: Power-efficient Sensor Placement and Transmission Structure for Data Gathering under Distortion Constraints. ACM Transactions on Sensor Networks (TOSN) 2(2), 155–181 (2006)
12. Pattem, S., Krishnamachari, B., Govindan, R.: The Impact of Spatial Correlation on Routing with Compression in Wireless Sensor Networks. ACM Transactions on Sensor Networks (TOSN) 4(4), 1–33 (2008)
13. Chou, J., Petrovic, D., Ramchandran, K.: Tracking and Exploiting Correlations in Dense Sensor Networks. In: Proceedings of the Asilomar Conference on Signals, Systems and Computers, Pacific Grove, CA, USA, pp. 39–43 (2002)
14. Cover, T.M., Thomas, J.A.: Elements of Information Theory. Wiley, USA (2006)
15. Slepian, D., Wolf, J.: Noiseless Coding of Correlated Information Sources. IEEE Transactions on Information Theory 19(4), 471–480 (1973)
16. Xiong, Z., Liveris, A.D., Cheng, S.: Distributed Source Coding for Sensor Networks. IEEE Signal Processing 21(5), 80–94 (2004)
17. Jindal, A., Psounis, K.: Modeling Spatially Correlated Data in Sensor Networks. ACM Transactions on Sensor Networks (TOSN) 2(4), 466–499 (2006)
18. Stoyan, D., Kendall, W.S., Mecke, J.: Stochastic Geometry and its Applications. Wiley, USA (1995)

19. Thomas, M.: A Generalization of Poisson's Binomial Limit for Use in Ecology. Biometrika 36, 18–25 (1949)
20. Gilbert, E.N.: Capacity of a Bursty-Noise Channel. Bell Systems Technical Journal 39(9), 1253–1265 (1960)
21. Ebert, J.-P., Willig, A., Wolisz, A.: A Gilbert-Elliot Bit Error Model and the Efficient Use in Packet Level Simulation. TKN technical report TKN-99-002 (1999)
22. Fasolo, E., Rossi, M., Widmer, J., Zorzi, M.: In-network Aggregation Techniques for Wireless Sensor Networks: a survey. IEEE Wireless Communications 14(2), 70–87 (2007)

Energy-Oriented Models for WDM Networks

Sergio Ricciardi[1], Davide Careglio[1], Francesco Palmieri[2],
Ugo Fiore[3], Germán Santos-Boada[1], and Josep Solé-Pareta[1]

[1] CCABA, Universitat Politécnica de Catalunya, Barcelona, Spain
[2] DII, Seconda Università di Napoli, Aversa (CE), Italy
[3] CSI, Università di Napoli Federico II, Naples, Italy
{sergior,careglio,german,pareta}@ac.upc.edu,
{fpalmier,ufiore}@unina.it

Abstract. A realistic energy-oriented model is necessary to formally characterize the energy consumption and the consequent carbon footprint of actual and future high-capacity WDM networks. The energy model describes the energy consumption of the various network elements (NE) and predicts their energy consumption behavior under different traffic loads and for the diverse traffic types, including all optical and electronic traffic, O/E/O conversions, 3R regenerations, add/drop multiplexing, etc. Besides, it has to be scalable and simple to implement, manage and modify according to the new architecture and technologies advancements. In this paper, we discuss the most relevant energy models present in the literature highlighting possible advantages, drawbacks and utilization scenarios in order to provide the research community with an overview over the different energy characterization frameworks that are currently being employed in WDM networks. We also present a comprehensive energy model which accounts for the foreseen energy-aware architectures and the growth rate predictions which tries to collect the main benefits of the previous models while maintaining low complexity and, thus, high scalability.

Keywords: Energy-oriented models, evolutionary energy-aware WDM networks.

1   Introduction

It is now held as a scientific fact that humans contribute to the global warming of planet Earth through the release of carbon dioxide (CO_2), a Green House Gas (GHG), in the atmosphere. Recently, the carbon footprint of ICT was found to be comparable to that of aviation [1]. It is estimated that 2-3% of the CO_2 produced by human activity comes from ICT [2][3] and a number of studies estimate an energy consumption related to ICT varying from 2% to 10% of the worldwide power consumption [4]. It is worth to mention for example that Telecom Italia and France Telecom are now the second largest consumer of electricity in their country [5][6] and British Telecom is the largest single power consumer in the UK [7].

The reduction and optimization of energy consumption are among the main goals of the European Union (EU). The EU in fact is encouraging the ICT sector to reduce

I. Tomkos et al. (Eds.): BROADNETS 2010, LNICST 66, pp. 534–548, 2012.

its carbon footprint in a drive to drastically reduce Europe's overall carbon emissions by 2020 setting its ambitious 20/20/20 goals: cutting its annual consumption of primary energy by 20% and increase the production of renewable energy to a share of 20% by 2020 [8]. Recent initiatives gathering major IT companies started to explore the energy savings and green energy usage in network infrastructures. For example, Telefonica commits to reducing 30% its network energy consumption by 2015 [9].

In the current telecommunications networks, the vast majority of the energy consumption can be attributed to fixed line access networks. Today, access networks are mainly implemented with copper based technologies such as ADSL and VDSL whose energy consumption is very sensible to increased bitrates. The trend is to replace such technologies with mobile and fiber infrastructure which is expected to increase considerably the energy efficiency in access networks. Such ongoing replacement is moving the problem to the backbone networks where the energy consumption for IP routers is becoming a bottleneck [10][11]. In Japan it is expected that by 2015, IP routers will consume 9% of the nation's electricity [12].

In such a new environment, the development of more accurate cost models which include the energy consumption factor for both the deployment (Capex) and the maintenance (Opex) of network infrastructures is fundamental. In this paper, we discuss the most relevant energy models present in the literature highlighting possible advantages, drawbacks and utilization scenarios in order to provide the research community with an overview over the different energy characterization frameworks that are currently being employed in WDM networks.

This article is structured as follows. Section 2 introduces the energy related problems and the possible energy-efficient and energy-aware solutions. In Section 3, we illustrate the energy-aware architectures on which the energy models are currently based. Section 4 discusses the three main energy models present in the literature. Section 5 illustrates real power consumption models for router architectures with different scaling factors. In Section 6 we present our comprehensive energy model for WDM networks. Finally, Section 7 summarizes the conclusions of this article.

2   Background

Increasing the energy efficiency of the different equipment, operations or processes constituting a network infrastructure is not the ultimate solution, as argued in the Khazzoom-Brookes postulate [13]: "increased energy efficiency paradoxically tends to lead to increased energy consumption" (a phenomenon known as the Jevons Paradox or rebound effect as well). In fact, an improvement of the energy efficiency leads to a reduction of the overall costs, which causes an increase of the demand and consequently of the energy consumption overtaking hence the gained offset.

It is safe to say that a paradigm shift is required in the network in order to sustain the growing traffic rates while limiting and even decreasing the power consumption. In order to overcome the rebound effect, it is necessary to adopt the *carbon neutrality* or, when available, the *zero carbon* approach. In carbon neutrality, GHG emitted by legacy (dirty) energy sources (e.g. fossil-based plants) are compensated – hence, neutrality – by a credit system like the cap and trade or the carbon offset [14]. In the zero carbon approach, renewable (green) energy sources (e.g. sun, wind, tide) are employed and no GHG are emitted at all. Clearly, green energy sources are always preferable with respect to the dirty ones as they limit (or avoid at all) GHG emissions, although renewable sources are variable in nature and their availability may change in time. In order to reduce the energy consumptions and contain the concomitant GHG emissions in the atmosphere, the two following measures have been identified:

- *Energy efficiency:* refers to a technology designed to reduce the equipment energy consumption without affecting the performance, according to the *do more for less* paradigm. It takes into account the environmental impact of the used resources and constraints the computations to be executed taking into account the ecological and potentially the economic impact of the used resources. Such solutions are usually referred to as *eco-friendly solutions.*
- *Energy awareness:* refers to an *intelligent* technology that adapts its behavior or performance based on the current working load and on the quantity and quality of energy that the equipment is expending (*energy-feedback information*). It implies knowledge of the (dirty or green) sources of energy that supply the equipment thus differentiating how it is currently being powered. Energy-aware solutions are usually referred to as *eco-aware solutions.* A direct benefit of energy aware techniques is the removal of the Khazzoom-Brookes postulate.

To become a reality, green Internet must rely on both concepts and a new energy-oriented network architecture is required, i.e. a comprehensive solution encompassing both energy-efficient devices and energy-aware paradigms acting in a systemic approach. The definition of a proper energy model to estimate and characterize the energy consumption of a network infrastructure is hence of primary importance. Nonetheless, due to its distributed character and wide diversity in network equipment types (routers, switches, modems, line cards, etc.), a direct estimation of network equipment power consumption is notoriously difficult. Several energy models have been proposed so far which try to emulate the different network elements (NEs) in an easy and comprehensive manner.

3   Energy-Aware Architectures

Current router architectures are not *energy-aware*, in the sense that their energy consumption does not scale sensibly with the traffic load. In [15] several router architectures have been analyzed and their energy consumptions under different traffic loads have been evaluated. Results show that the energy consumption between an idle and a heavily loaded router (with 75% of offered traffic load) vary only of 3% (about 25 W on 750 W). This happens because the router line cards, which are the most power consuming elements in a router, are always powered on even if they are totally idle. On the contrary, the energy consumption decreases to just 50% if the idle line cards are physically disconnected. Such a scenario suggests that future router architectures will be energy-aware, in the sense that they will be able to automatically switch off or dynamically downclock independent subsystems (e.g. line cards, input/output ports, switching fabrics, buffers, etc.) according to the traffic loads in order to save energy whenever possible. Such energy-aware architectures are advocated both by standardization bodies and governmental programs [16] and have been assumed by various literature sources [15][17][18]. Our study will be therefore focused on such energy-aware architectures that can adapt their behavior, and so, their energy consumption, to the current traffic loads. The energy consumption of such architectures is made up of a fixed part (Φ), needed for the device to be turned on, and a variable part (ε), somehow proportional to the traffic load. It is precisely *how* the variable energy consumption scales with the traffic that differentiates the various energy models. In the following paragraphs, we present them in detail and discuss their major benefits and drawbacks. Note that in each model the power consumption starts from the fixed power consumption value Φ that represents the power necessary for the device to stay up (and idle).

4   Energy Models

Basically, three different types of energy models have been reported in the literature:

1. Analytic energy models
2. Experimental energy models
3. Theoretical energy models.

4.1   Analytic Energy Models

Analytic energy models [18] take into consideration a number of parameters describing the NEs and provide their energy consumption by mean of a mathematical description of the network. The challenge of analytic energy models is to abstract irrelevant details while representing essential aspects in order to obtain a realistic characterization of the network elements energy consumption. Once an analytic model has been set up, it has the ability to describe the energy consumption of NEs in virtually any possible network configuration. Furthermore, as irrelevant hardware, software and configuration details may be totally abstracted or only partially represented, the analytic models have the ability to scale well with the network size. In fact, the abstraction and the generalization are the two key points of this kind of models. Anyway, analytic models have some drawbacks as well. What has to be represented in the model and what should instead kept out is a design choice that has to be carefully planned, as an excessive degree of sophistication may introduce unnecessary complexity and unwanted behaviors. Furthermore, the complexity degree of the modeled devices should resemble the real world devices as far as possible but it is not always possible to know the proprietary internal device architectures and hardware technical specifications.

In [18] the authors propose an analytic energy model in the ILP formulations for energy-efficient planning in WDM networks. They identify three types of traffic: transmitting, receiving and switching traffic, though there is no difference between electronic and optical traffic.

4.2   Experimental Energy Models

Experimental models [19][20][21][22][23] totally rely on energy consumption values of real world devices. They consider the NEs energy consumptions declared by the manufacturers or the experimentally measured values to create a map of well-known off-the-shelf working devices samples. For routers – which are the most studied NEs – the energy consumption is reported against the aggregated throughput and then the mapping is used for interpolating or extrapolating energy consumption data for routers of any size. Anyway, this model has several drawbacks. On the one hand, the declared energy consumptions may not closely resemble the real values especially when the device is working with a specific hardware and/or software configuration. On the other hand, although the experimentally measured energy consumption values may measure the energy consumption under different traffic loads, they only refer to a punctual evaluation under specific assumptions. Furthermore, the interpolation/extrapolation method is not a reliable measure of real devices energy consumption, as the devices energy consumption may vary sensibly with its technology, architecture, features and size (e.g. aggregated throughput, number of line cards, ports, wavelengths, etc.). In fact, in [19] the authors analyze power consumption of core routers based on datasheets found in [20], and conclude that for higher throughputs the routers consume more power. However, smaller routers tend to be located near the edge of the network whereas larger routers are more central in the network where the traffic is more aggregated. Therefore they consider the power consumption per bit rate. This reveals that larger routers consume less energy per bit than smaller ones. When aggregating over the entire network, the power consumption will also be the largest at the edge of the network and smaller in the centre. It is also showed how energy consumption depends on the packets size and on the bitrates of the links. Greater packets need less energy than smaller ones, due to the lower number of headers that have to be processed. In [21] it is showed that circuit-based transport layer reduces energy consumption with respect to packet-switched layer, due to the lower processing required for managing connections and to the higher processing needed for analyzing each packets' headers. Nevertheless, it is often difficult to gather real energy consumption values, so it is not always feasible to create a complete mapping of real world devices, and it is practically impossible to measure energy consumption of future NEs architectures before designing and building them. So, an experimental model, though providing some real energy consumption values, is not enough to cope with the requirements of a comprehensive energy model.

In [22] and [23] the authors propose a mixed energy model. Network nodes energy consumption is modeled by averaging experimental data of a real network scenario, whilst the power consumption of links is analytically modeled by a static contribution due to optical transceivers, and by an additional term which takes into account possible (optical) regenerators.

4.3   Theoretical Energy Models

Theoretical models [24] are instead totally based on the theoretical predictions of the energy consumption as functions of the router size and/or the traffic load (in a way similar for the Moore's law [25] for the central processing units and the Gilder's law for the bandwidth of communication systems [26]). Such models have the benefit of being simple and clear, but the predictions may substantially differ on the long run from the real energy consumption values. Besides, it is often difficult to foreseen the NEs energy consumptions and, as they rely only on empirical data, it is not a based on any rigorous scientific model. Furthermore, both experimental and theoretical energy models do not provide detailed energy consumption of each subsystem or component, but they simply describe at high level the energy consumption at the expense of granularity and accuracy. In [24] the author proposes a simple theoretical model in which the router energy consumption grows with a polynomial function of its capacity. This estimation has been proved to be quite similar to the real energy consumption values [23].

5   Power Consumption Models

Power consumption models express the power consumption (*P*) of routers versus the offered traffic load (*L*). In power consumption models, the current absorbed power, i.e. energy per second, is plotted against the traffic load that the router is currently offering. The power consumption may be expressed through a set of concrete models whose growth behaviors are obtained either from analytical, experimental, theoretical energy models or a combination of them. In the following sections, we analyze four different models: linear, theoretical, combined and statistical power consumption models.

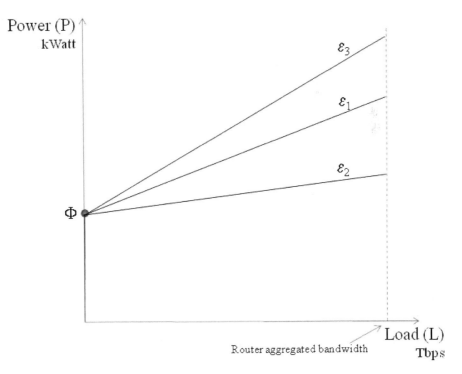

Fig. 1. Power consumption in linear power consumption model

5.1   Linear Power Consumption Models

In linear models, the power consumption scales linearly with the traffic load up to the maximum router capacity (its aggregated bandwidth). Here, routers with diverse technology and/or sizes may scale differently with the traffic: three scale factors (ε_1, ε_2, ε_3) are reported in Fig. 1.

In this model, it holds that:

$$P = \varepsilon_i \cdot L \tag{1}$$

where ε_i is a scaling factor depending on the technology and size of the router i. Alternatively, the diverse slopes (ε_i) may represent different traffic types (see the Section 5.4), as was assumed in [18].

This power consumption model has the benefit of being simple and easy to implement, but it has the drawback that it is not possible to upper bound the power consumption to a desired values (e.g. 2Φ, as the results in [15] suggest).

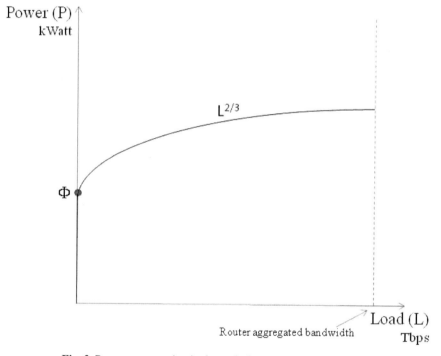

Fig. 2. Power consumption in theoretical power consumption model

5.2   Theoretical Power Consumption Models

In theoretical models, the power consumption is expressed as a function of the load that tries to follow the trend of real devices power consumption. Using a high level formula, theoretical models are usually employed to describe in a simple though effective manner the relation between the power consumption and the current traffic load. The theoretical energy model presented in [24] is the following:

$$P = C^{2/3} \tag{2}$$

which states that the router power consumption grows with a polynomial function of its capacity. Now, if we substitute the router capacity with the load, we obtain a feasible model to represent how the power consumption varies with the traffic load. Such a model has demonstrated to be quite in line with the energy consumption of some real world devices [24], and for this reason has been sometimes used in literature papers [19].

Theoretical power consumption models show an easy-of-use advantage as it suffices to substitute the router aggregate bandwidth or current traffic load to immediately get the power consumption value. No tuning of any parameter is needed (such as ε_i) and the power consumption growth rate is always well predictable. Unfortunately, such models have the same drawbacks as the theoretical energy ones (see the section 4.3).

5.3   Combined Power Consumption Models

Combined models are characterized by different power consumption scaling rates at different traffic loads. They are represented by step functions whose domain is partitioned into different traffic load intervals. Each load interval may be characterized by a different function; for example (see Fig. 3), the power consumption may scale

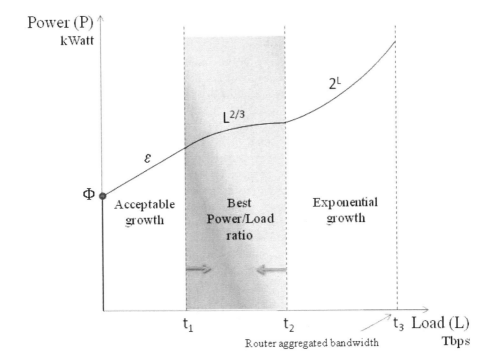

Fig. 3. Power consumption in combined power consumption model

linearly (ε) with low loads (lower than t_1), polynomially ($L^{2/3}$) at medium loads (between t_1 and t_2) and exponentially (2^L) at high loads (greater than t_2). Some or all the sub-functions may be derived from other models, as in the example.

Note that in such a model, it may be convenient to balance the traffic across the network in order to keep the router local traffic inside the acceptable zone where the energy consumption scales polynomially with the traffic load. In fact, it may be worthwhile to keep the traffic above the t_1 threshold, in order to amortize the fixed power consumption Φ, and below the t_2 threshold, to not exceed into the exponential power consumption zone (between t_2 and t_3).

Such power consumption models are pretty complete and may be used to resemble quite complex scenarios in which the network elements have complex architectures and show a known – although not linear – overall power consumption behavior. Note that, thanks to their greater complexity, such models open new perspectives on the traditional network load balancing criteria in order to save energy while achieving low connection rejection ratios. Obviously, such added values come at the expense of computational complexity and scalability.

5.4   Statistical Power Consumption Models

Statistical models consider an additional factor contributing to the energy consumption which is the traffic *type*: all optical or electronic traffic, O/E/O conversions, 3R regenerations, optical amplifications, wavelength conversions, are all examples of different traffic types that affect differently the energy consumption inside a given router. In fact, each type of traffic has in principle different power consumptions when traversing a router (either as an optical lightpath or a packet/circuit-switched electronic path), also depending on the technology and the architectural design that the router adopts. The model is defined as *statistical* because the power consumption depends at each moment on the statistical distribution of the overall traffic in the router. The more traffic of kind i, the more the energy consumption will depend on the scaling factor ε_i. Furthermore, each router may have its different scaling factors depending on its technology, architecture and size. For example, in Fig. 4 three different types of traffic are represented, each with its own scaling factor: electronic traffic (ε_3), optical traffic without wavelength conversion (WC) capability (ε_2), and optical traffic with WC capability (ε_1). The three types of traffic have different impacts on the overall router energy consumption, but all of them grow linearly. Note that the electronic traffic scales worse than the optical traffic, as reported in [27]. Note also that, in the example reported in Fig. 4, the three traffic types scales all linearly, even if with different slopes. Statistical models may assume that the various types of traffic scale at different growth rates, for example the electronic traffic may scale exponentially while the optical traffic with WC may scale polynomially and the optical traffic without WC may scale linearly. Furthermore, each router may have its own statistical energy model depending on its design choices in order to adapt its energy consumption behavior to different technologies and architectures.

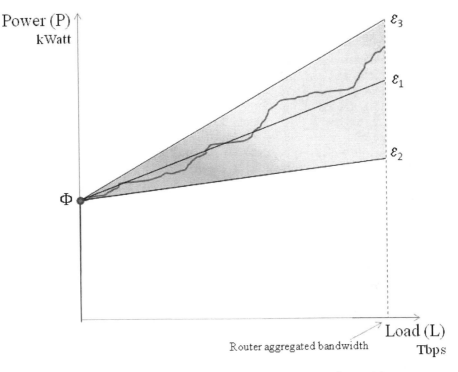

Fig. 4. Power consumption in statistical power consumption model

The statistical model is the most complete one as it allows representing a wide range of devices and power consumption behaviors depending not only on routers technology factors but also on the different traffic types.

6   A Comprehensive Energy Model for WDM Networks

In order to formally characterize the energy consumption of network elements we propose a comprehensive analytic model based on real energy consumption values and in line with the theoretical growth rate predictions encompassing new energy-aware architectures that adapt their behavior with the traffic load in order to minimize the energy consumption.

The energy model comprises three types of traffic of a WDM network:

1. Electronic traffic (with or without add/drop multiplexing, electronic wavelength conversion, 3R regeneration, etc.);
2. Optical traffic with WC;
3. Optical traffic without WC.

These types of traffic are supported by different flavors of optical and electronic network elements (router, switches, transceivers, optical fiber links and amplifiers, 3R regenerators, etc.). Power consumption of real NEs has been obtained by literary sources[15][20][23][27][28] and power consumption equations have been derived from these measurements.

Such an energy model characterizes the different components and sub-systems of the network elements involved in energy consumption. It provides the energy consumptions of network nodes and links of whatever typology and size and under any traffic load. The efforts in the developing of such an energy model have been focused on realistic energy consumption values. For this scope, the energy model has been fed with real values and the energy consumption behavior of NEs has been crafted in order to match with the state-of-the-art architectures and technologies. At this extent, future energy-efficient architectures with enhanced sleep mode features have been considered and implemented in the energy model. The energy model is based on a linear combinations of energy consumption functions derived from both experimental results [15][19][20][23][27][28] and theoretical models [22][23][24]. Besides, following the results reported in [15][16][19][28], the power consumption has been divided into a fixed and a variable part; fixed part is always present and is required just for the device to be on; variable part depends on the current traffic load

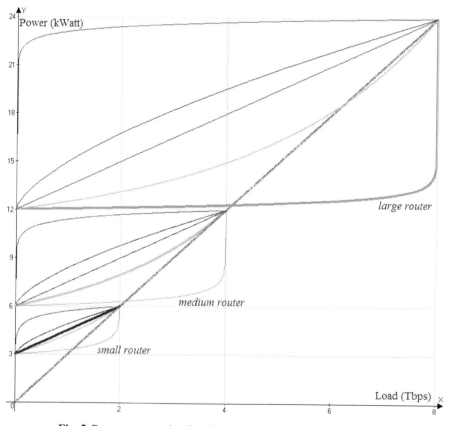

Fig. 5. Power consumption functions for various size electronic routers

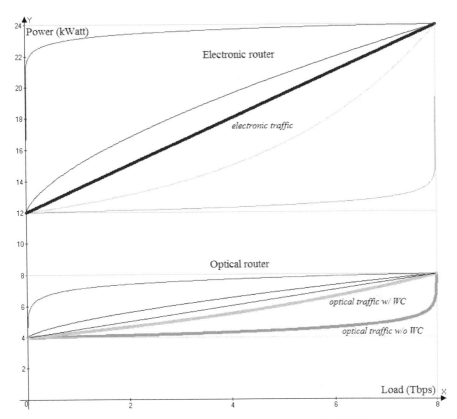

Fig. 6. Power consumption functions for electronic and optical routers

on the device and may vary according to different energy consumption functions. We chose a linear combination of two different functions (logarithmic and line functions) and weighted them with a parameter depending on both the type of traffic and the size of the NE, in order to obtain a complete gamma of values and thus adapting its behavior to the most different scenarios. In particular in our energy model we managed to obtain that larger routers consume less energy per bit than the smaller routers (see Fig. 5), as reported in [19][20], and that electronic traffic consumes more energy per bit that optical traffic (see Fig. 6), as reported in [27][28]. Wavelength conversion and 3R regenerations have a not negligible power consumption which is accounted for in the model. Finally, links have an energy consumption that depends on the length of the fiber strands and thus on the number of optical amplification and regeneration needed by the signal to reach the endpoint with an acceptable optical signal-to-noise ratio (OSNR).

The power consumption functions of three routers of different sizes are reported in Fig. 5. Each router may support different types of traffic, each defined by a different curve. In the example in figure, the thicker lines represent the power required by a given type of traffic (e.g. electronic traffic). We can observe that, according to our model, the larger the router, the larger the *total* energy consumption, as the fixed part notably contributes to (half of) the energy consumption. But if we focus only on the variable power consumptions, we observe that, for example, a traffic load of 2 Tbps, requires as much as 3 kW in the smaller router, about 1.5 kW in the medium one and just 1 kW in the larger router. In this way, we managed to obtain that greater routers consume less energy per bit than smaller ones, as reported in [19][20]. Note also that the overall energy consumption scales linearly with the size of the router and that half of the energy consumption is due to the fixed part and the other half to the variable part, according to literature source [15].

The power consumption functions of an electronic and an optical router are reported in Fig. 6 (optical router values not in scale). Three types of traffic are represented: electronic traffic in the electronic router and optical traffic with and without WC in the optical one. We observe that the electronic traffic grows quickly with respect to the optical traffic and that, among the optical traffic, the WC actually consume a not negligible quantity of energy. As the power consumption functions are obtained by linear combinations of the logarithmic and the line functions, the complete gamma of slopes can be represented by the actual curves.

7   Conclusions

The energy consumption has to be considered as an additional constraint and, given the current ICT energy consumption growth trend, it will likely represent the major constraint in the designing of WDM network infrastructures, even more than the bandwidth capacity. In order to lower the energy consumption and the concomitant GHG emissions of such infrastructures, it is necessary to assess the power consumption of current and future energy-aware architectures through extensive energy models that characterize the behaviors of the network equipment. In this paper we presented and discussed the main energy and power models currently employed in the literature and provided an overview over the different scenarios that are currently being employed in WDM networks. Finally, we presented a comprehensive energy model which accounts for the foreseen energy-aware architectures and the grow rate predictions, including different types of traffic of a WDM networks. The model, based on real energy consumption values, tries to collect the main benefits of the previous models while maintaining low complexity and, thus, high scalability. We believe that such an energy model will help the development of new energy-oriented networks for achieving sustainable society growth and prosperity.

Acknowledgments. This work was supported in part by the COST Action IC0804 on Energy Efficiency in Large Scale Distributed Systems, the Spanish Ministry of Science and Innovation under the DOMINO project (TEC2010-18522), the Catalan Government under the contract SGR 1140 and the DIUE/ESF under the grant FI-201000740.

References

1. Gartner press release (2007)
   http://www.gartner.com/it/page.jsp?id=503867
2. An inefficient Truth by the Global Action Plan,
   http://www.globalactionplan.org.uk/upload/resource/
   Full-report.pdf

3. SMART 2020: Enabling the low carbon economy in the information age, The climate group (2008)
4. Global Action Plan Report, An inefficient truth (2007), http://www.globalactionplan.org.uk/
5. Pileri, S.: Energy and Communication: engine of the human progress. In: INTELEC 2007 keynote, Rome, Italy (September 2007)
6. Souchon Foll, L.: TIC et Énergétique: Techniques d'estimation de consommation sur la hauteur, la structure et l'évolution de l'impact des TIC en France, Ph.D. dissertation, Orange Labs/Institut National des Télécommunications (2009)
7. BT Press, BT announces major wind power plans (October 2007), http://www.btplc.com/News/Articles/Showarticle.cfm? ArticleID=dd615e9c-71ad-4daa-951a-55651baae5bb
8. EU Spring Summit, Brussels (March 2007)
9. Telefónica supplement, The environment and climate change, 2008 special report on corporate responsibility (April 2009)
10. Lange, C.: Energy-related Aspects in Backbone Networks. In: Proc. ECOC 2009, Vienna, Austria (September 2009)
11. Tucker, R.S., Parthiban, R., Baliga, J., Hinton, K., Ayre, R.W.A., Sorin, W.V.: Evolution of WDM Optical IP Networks: A Cost and Energy Perspective. IEEE/OSA Journal of Lightwave Technologies 27(3), 243–252 (2009)
12. Nature Photonics Technology Conference 2007, Tokyo, Japan (October 2007)
13. Saunders, H.D.: The Khazzoom-Brookes postulate and neoclassical growth. The Energy Journal (October 1992)
14. St Arnaud, B.: ICT and Global Warming: Opportunities for Innovation and Economic Growth, http://docs.google.com/Doc?id=dgbgjrct\2767dxpbdvcf
15. Chabarek, J., Sommers, J., Barford, P., Estan, C., Tsiang, D., Wright, S.: Power awareness in network design and routing. In: Proc. IEEE INFOCOM (2008)
16. Energy Star, Small network equipment, http://www.energystar.gov/index.cfm?c=new_specs.small_ network_equip
17. Gupta, M., Singh, S.: Greening of the Internet. In: Proc. ACM SIGCOMM 2003, Karlsruhe, Germany (August 2003)
18. Muhammad, A., Monti, P., Cerutti, I., Wosinska, L., Castoldi, P., Tzanakaki, A.: Energy-Efficient WDM Network Planning with Protection Resources in Sleep Mode. In: IEEE Global Telecommunications Conference (GLOBECOM 2010), December 6-10, pp. 1–5 (2010), doi:10.1109/GLOCOM.2010.5683205
19. Vereecken, W., Van Heddeghem, W., Colle, D., Pickavet, M., Demeester, P.: Overall ICT footprint and green communication technologies. In: Proc. of ISCCSP 2010, Limassol, Cyprus (March 2010)
20. Juniper, http://www.juniper.net
21. Feng, M.Z., Hilton, K., Ayre, R., Tucker, R.: Reducing NGN Energy Consumption with IP/SDH/WDM. In: Proc. 1st International Conference on Energy-Efficient Computing and Networking, Passau, Germany, pp. 187–190 (2010) ISBN:978-1-4503-0042-1
22. Chiaraviglio, L., Mellia, M., Neri, F.: Energy-aware Backbone Networks: a Case Study. In: GreenComm – First International Workshop on Green Communications, Dresden, Germany (June 2009)
23. Van Heddeghem, W., De Groote, M., Vereecken, W., Colle, D., Pickavet, M., Demeester, P.: Energy-Efficiency in Telecommunications Networks: Link-by-Link versus End-to-End Grooming. In: Proc. of ONDM 2010, Kyoto, Japan, February 1-3 (2010)

24. Tucker, R.S.: Modelling Energy Consumption in IP Networks, `http://www.cisco.com/web/about/ac50/ac207/crc_new/events/ assets/cgrs_energy_consumption_ip.pdf` (retrieved)
25. Moore, G.E.: Cramming more components onto integrated circuits. Electronics 38(8), April 19 (1965)
26. Gilder, G.F.: Telecosm: How Infinite Bandwidth Will Revolutionize Our World. The Free Press, NY (2000)
27. BONE project, WP 21 Topical Project Green Optical Networks: Report on year 1 and updated plan for activities, NoE, FP7-ICT-2007-1 216863, BONE project (December 2009)
28. Aleksic, S.: Analysis of Power Consumption in Future High-Capacity Network Nodes. Journal of Optical Communications and Networking 1(3), 245–258 (2009)

Author Index